CHINESE ECONOMIC STATISTICS IN THE MAOIST ERA

1949-1965

T0300183

CHINESE ECONOMIC STATISTICS IN THE MAOIST ERA

1949-1965

EDITED BY

NAI-RUENN CHEN

Routledge
Taylor & Francis Group

LONDON AND NEW YORK

First published 1967 by Transaction Publishers

Published 2017 by Routledge
4 Park Square, Milton Park, Abingdon, Oxon OX14 4RN
605 Third Avenue, New York, NY 10017

Routledge is an imprint of the Taylor & Francis Group, an informa business

Library of Congress Catalog Number: 2008039947

Library of Congress Cataloging-in-Publication Data

Chen, Nai-ruenn, 1926-
  Chinese economic statistics in the Maoist era : 1949-1965 / Nai-Ruenn Chen, editor.
      p. cm.
  Originally published in 1967 under title: Chinese economic statistics
  Includes bibliographical references and index.
  A monograph of the Committee on the Economy of China of the Social Science Research Council.
  ISBN 978-0-202-36281-6
    1. China--Statistics. I. Social Science Research Council (U.S.). Committee on the Economy of China. II. Title.

HA4635.C424 2008
330.951'055--dc22

                                                                    2008039947

  ISBN 13: 978-0-202-36281-6 (pbk)

FOREWORD

The Committee on the Economy of China was appointed by the Social Science Research Council for the purpose of stimulating scholarly analysis of the contemporary economic scene on the Chinese mainland. Support for the Committee's program was provided by the Ford Foundation. This volume is the result of a project commissioned by the Committee, and publication is under its aegis.

The statistical system of any nation harbors many pitfalls for the unwary observer. There are always particular usages, depending upon the nation's economic structure and stage of development. Additional complications arise when one attempts to use the statistics of the communist nations because of fundamental systemic differences that reveal themselves in the way data are assembled. A good example is provided by the communist practice of omitting services not embodied in commodities from the calculation of national product.

All of these difficulties are compounded for most of those who wish to use Chinese statistics. Apart from the factors already mentioned, few non-Chinese are able even to make out table headings and footnotes, let alone read the textual material necessary to clarify the meaning of the data. China is also a relatively underdeveloped country, and a vast one at that, and its statistical system is still at an early stage of evolution to maturity.

For these reasons, the Committee asked Dr. Nai-Ruenn Chen to undertake the arduous task of assembling Chinese statistics from the many sources in which they have appeared and to describe their conceptual basis as far as possible. This has not been an easy task, for, apart from one fairly slender statistical handbook, *Ten Great Years*, published in 1959, the data have appeared in a great variety of books, journals, and newspapers. The guide line for inclusion of data was that they had appeared in a Chinese source or that they could be derived by a simple arithmetic operation. No attempt has been made to synthesize data by inferential methods, nor were non-Chinese estimates used to supplement the original statistical information.

The immediate question that the potential user of this volume will ask is: Can the data be used with confidence? This is a question that can never be answered simply for any set of data, but here the answer is particularly complex. The statistics are distinctly better in some areas than in others, depending upon clarity of concept, method of collection, and degree of statistical manipulation required, among other things. The purpose for which the data are to be used may also determine their value to the user, whether, for example, one is aiming at precision or wants only indicators that provide rough orders of magnitude.

It was decided at the outset not to attempt any evaluation of the data. This is a job beyond the capacity of an individual, requiring the cooperation of specialists in each sector to which the data relate. Given the degree of secrecy in which Chinese data have been shrouded, it is at least questionable whether a satisfactory comprehensive evaluation could be accomplished at this time. Dr. Chen has indicated the major statistical studies in which the Chinese data have thus far been subject to critical review, and it is hoped that more will be appearing in the not distant future.

The Committee believes that, despite its limited objectives, this volume will be of considerable help both to Chinese specialists and to nonspecialists engaged in comparative studies. At a minimum, long, tedious hours of searching for scraps of data can be saved, and the volume helps one to get a good idea of the type of statistical material available. But it cannot be emphasized too strongly that a strict rule of *caveat emptor* applies. The data cannot be accepted at face value but must be used only with a great deal of care.

Unfortunately, everything statistical in China stops after 1959. The regime imposed a statistical blackout unprecedented in modern history. Not even the percentage changes without bases characteristic of the worst of the Stalinist years in the Soviet Union have been published in China. How much longer the Chinese authorities can maintain the veil of secrecy without greatly hampering the operation of their economy remains to be seen. When data once more begin to flow, however, Dr. Chen's volume should be of great value for benchmark orientation.

The Committee on the Economy of China, in sponsoring projects, endeavors to insure that they will be conducted with scholarly objectivity and accuracy. In the final analysis, however, both the ultimate responsibility and the full credit for the finished work must remain with the author.

Walter Galenson
Director of Research

PREFACE

The purpose of this volume is twofold. First, official statistics, both national and provincial, relating to the economy of mainland China since 1949 have been compiled from Communist Chinese sources; and wherever possible, statistics for missing years are computed on the basis of the Communist Chinese definitions. Since 1960 the Peking regime has ceased to publish statistical information, and in consequence the compilation is limited to the period from 1949 to 1959. Second, the concept, coverage, and classification of Communist Chinese statistical data, as well as the procedure involved in their collection, are described as fully as possible.

The volume is divided into eleven sections: (1) area and population; (2) national income; (3) capital formation and related estimates; (4) industry; (5) agriculture; (6) transportation and communication; (7) trade; (8) prices; (9) living standards; (10) public finance, credit, and foreign exchange rates; and (11) employment, labor productivity, and wages. Each section consists of two parts: one containing the explanatory text, and the other, statistical tables grouped largely according to Chinese classifications.

A few words of caution are essential regarding the use of the statistics contained in this volume. The official data collected here are by no means exhaustive, and this is particularly the case for provincial statistics. A complete compilation of provincial data published in Communist China would require an examination of all local newspapers and other publications.

In addition, while technical defects of certain statistical methods employed in Communist China are discussed in the text, no attempt is made to evaluate the reliability or usability of any specific official series. It must be pointed out emphatically, however, that the absence of evaluation should not be taken to mean that Communist Chinese statistics are accurate and reliable. In fact, they must be used with great care. Furthermore, they should not be treated indiscriminately, since the quality of the data differs from field to field. For the purpose of cautioning the reader, the following observation by Professor Choh-Ming Li on the comparative reliability of different types of Communist Chinese statistics is worth quoting:

In early 1955, the director of the State Statistical Bureau gave a relatively objective analysis of comparative reliability as follows: (a) in terms of functional fields, industry was fair; trade, worse; agriculture, worst; (b) in terms of sectors, the state sector was fair; the capitalist sector, worse; and the individual sector (craftsmen and family agriculture), worst; (c) in the state sector, the locally controlled enterprises were worse than those centrally controlled; and non-basic activities (such as industrial statistics of non-industry ministries, trade statistics of non-trade ministries) were much worse than basic activities; and (d) in terms of indicators, physical output and value-product were fair; labor and wages, worse; finance and cost, worst. At the end of 1955, the State Bureau in an editorial commented further on the relative quality of different functional statistics by dividing them into two groups according to the strength of their foundation. The first group, having a fair foundation, included, in a *decreasing* order of strength: industry, transportation and communication, trade, and basic construction. In industry, better than others were the statistics of state enterprises, which, however, were confined to those for value-product, physical output, and labor force; statistics for such indicators as trial-manufacturing, output quota, and utilization of equipment had not been satisfactorily computed, if at all. The second group, having a weak foundation, comprised, in an *increasing* order of weakness, material allocation, culture, education and health, population, finance and cost, labor and wages, and agriculture. In agricultural statistics, the weakest were those on sown area, cultivated acreage, and production, by crops, according to economic classes; on size and production of livestock; and so on. Complete socialization of private enterprises and agriculture in 1956 and 1957 does not affect these conclusions on the relative reliability of different types of statistics.[1]

The reader will find a thorough discussion of the validity of Chinese official statistics from the standpoint of the development of the statistical system in Professor Li's *The Statistical System of Communist China.* Useful discussion of the quality of particular official series is contained in the following scholarly studies:

POPULATION

U.S. Bureau of the Census. *The Size, Composition, and Growth of the Population of Mainland China,* by John S. Aird. International Population Series Report, Series P-90, No. 15, Washington, D.C.: U.S. Government Printing Office, 1961.

NATIONAL INCOME, CAPITAL FORMATION, AND OTHER BASIC ECONOMIC STATISTICS

Alexander Eckstein. *The National Income of Communist China.* New York: Free Press, 1961.

William W. Hollister. *China's Gross National Product and Social Accounts, 1950–1957.* New York: Free Press, 1958.

Choh-Ming Li. *Economic Development of Communist China.* Berkeley: University of California Press, 1959.

Ta-chung Liu and Kung-chia Yeh. *The Economy of the Chinese Mainland: National Income and Economic Development, 1933–1959.* Princeton, N.J.: Princeton University Press, 1965.

INDUSTRY

Kang Chao. *The Rate and Pattern of Industrial Growth in Communist China.* Ann Arbor: University of Michigan Press, 1965.

EMPLOYMENT

U.S. Bureau of the Census. *Nonagricultural Employment in Mainland China; 1949–1958,* by John Philip Emerson. International Population Statistics

[1]Choh-Ming Li, *The Statistical System of Communist China,* Berkeley: University of California Press, 1962, pp. 63–64.

Report, Series P-90, No. 21, Washington, D.C.: U.S. Government Printing Office, 1965.

In preparing this volume, I am indebted to Professors Walter Galenson and Ta-chung Liu, who carefully read through the manuscript, pointed out a number of errors, and offered many valuable suggestions. I am also thankful to Miss Moffett Beall, who not only went through the painful process of typing the manuscript and statistical tables but also helped to improve the general readability of the text. The staff of the Center for Chinese Studies and the East Asiatic Library, both at the Berkeley campus of the University of California, extended to me many courtesies, and I wish to record my deep appreciation.

Of course, I alone am responsible for the errors that may remain.

Nai-Ruenn Chen

Note on Terminologies, References, Signs, and Units of Measurement (Text and Tables)

1. The terms "China", "Mainland China", and "Communist China" are used interchangeably in this volume, and refer to the Chinese mainland under Communist control after 1949.

2. *Op. cit.* and *loc. cit.* refer to publications mentioned in the footnotes of the same section of the text or in notes and sources of the same statistical table.

3. In the statistical tables, the following signs are used:

( ) indicates figures computed according to Chinese definitions.

– – zero or negligible.

n.a. or blank space indicates figures are not available or are not applicable.

4. Conversion rates for Chinese units of measurement are as follows:

1 *mou* (*shih mou*) = 0.0667 hectare
= 0.1647 acre

1 *tan* (*shih tan*) = 0.05 metric ton
= 50 kilograms
= 110.23 pounds

1 *chin* (*shih chin*) = 0.5 kilogram
= 1.1023 pounds

1 *li* (*shih li*) = 0.5 kilometer
= 164.04 feet

1 *chih* (*shih chih*) = $\frac{1}{3}$ meter
= 13.123 inches

TABLE OF CONTENTS

Part II. STATISTICAL DATA AND SOURCES

LIST OF TABLES

3. CAPITAL FORMATION AND RELATED ESTIMATES

4. INDUSTRY

5. AGRICULTURE

6. TRANSPORTATION, POST, AND TELE-COMMUNICATIONS

7. TRADE

9. LIVING STANDARDS

10. PUBLIC FINANCE, CREDIT, AND FOREIGN EXCHANGE RATES

11. EMPLOYMENT, LABOR PRODUCTIVITY AND WAGES

I

Sources, Types, and Uses of Data

1

AREA AND POPULATION

AREA

The aggregate area of a country consists of water area and land area. There has never been an official estimate of the water area for China as a whole. In the 1930's, Buck estimated that water area in China (including Outer Mongolia, but excluding Taiwan) was about 3 per cent of the total area.[1] Since 1949, when the Communists took over the Chinese mainland, a figure of 300 million *mou*, or 200,000 square kilometers, has been mentioned frequently in Chinese publications as the water area of China (excluding Outer Mongolia, but including Taiwan).[2]

The land area of China (excluding Outer Mongolia and Taiwan) was estimated by the Nationalist Government in 1948 to be 9,700,-000 square kilometers.[3] During the first two years of Communist rule, a figure of 9,597,520 square kilometers appeared as the total land area (including Taiwan) in the *1950 and 1951 People's Handbooks*.[4] This figure was originally released by the Liberation Army Headquarters.[5]

Between 1952 and 1957, figures on the land area were missing from the yearly *People's Handbooks,* although different estimates were given in other publications during this period.[6] Among these estimates, one was published in May, 1957, in *A Handbook of Administrative Divisions of the People's Republic of China,* edited by the Ministry of Interior: 9,597,000 square kilometers for the whole area of China including Taiwan, with breakdowns by independent municipalities, provinces and autonomous regions.[7] The estimate thus did not deviate greatly from the figures which first appeared

in the *1950 and 1951 People's Handbooks*. The same estimate for the total area was used in the *1958 and 1959 People's Handbooks,* with some modifications in provincial breakdowns owing to changes in the administrative divisions.[8] This figure was also adopted by the State Statistical Bureau in its *Ten Great Years,* published in September, 1959,[9] and has continued to appear in the annual editions of the *People's Handbooks* since 1960 but with no provincial details. Evidently, the figure of 9,597,000 square kilometers has now been accepted as the official estimate for the land area of China. When the area of Taiwan (36,000 square kilometers) is deducted, the Peking estimate for the land area under Communist control amounts to 9,561,-

[1]John Lossing Buck, *Land Utilization in China,* New York: Council on Economic and Cultural Affairs, Inc., 1956, p. 162.
[2]Hu Ch'ing-Lai, Li Ming, and Ts'ung Ch'un-ch'uan, "The Marine Products Industry in China," *TLCS,* Vol. 7, No. 1 (January, 1956), pp. 6-8.
[3]Directorate General of Budget, Accounts, and Statistics, Republic of China, *Chung-hua-min-kuo t'ung-chi nien-chien (Statistical Yearbook of the Republic of China)* (Nanking: Bureau of Statistics, 1948), p. 3.
[4]*1950 JMST;* Sect. A, p. 1; *1951 JMST* Vol. I, Sect. B, p. 1. In the *1951 JMST,* the figure for the land area was listed as 9,597,500 square kilometers.
[5]An agricultural statistical handbook published in 1956 indicated that the statistical estimate of the land area became the responsibility of the Ministry of Interior. [See Editorial Committee of Statistical Work Handbook, ed., *Nung-yeh tung-chi kung-tso shou-tse (Agricultural Statistical Handbook),* Peking: T'ung-chi ch'u-pan-she, 1956, p. 7.]
[6]For example, in September, 1957, Hu Huan-yung's article on China's population density placed the land area of the whole country (including the area of Taiwan) at 9,650,201 square kilometers. [Hu Huan-yung, "An Index Chart of Area and Population of China by Province and Region," *TLCS,* Vol. 8, No. 9 (September, 1957), pp. 390–91.] Earlier, in the summer of 1956, an Indian delegation to China was given the figure of 9,559,000 square kilometers as the land area of China including Taiwan. (Government of India, Ministry of Food and Agriculture, *Report of the Indian Delegation to China on Agricultural Planning and Techniques,* New Delhi: July–August, 1956, pp. 31–45.)
[7]Ministry of Interior, ed., *A Handbook of the Administrative Divisions of the People's Republic of China (Chung-hua jen-min kung-ho-kuo hsin-cheng chu-hua chien-tse),* Peking: Law Publishing House, May 1957, p. 5.
[8]*1958 JMST,* p. 640; and *1959 JMST,* p. 209.
[9]TGY, p. 8.

3

000 square kilometers. Table 1.1 presents the official estimate of the land area of Communist China by province according to the administrative divisions as of August, 1959.

POPULATION

SOURCES OF DATA

The principal sources of information on Communist China's population are the census of June 30, 1953, the system of population registration, and a number of vital rates surveys.[10]

The 1953 Census

In January, 1953, the Peking Government made known its decision to take a population census for China. On April 6, 1953, "Measures for National Census and Registration of Population," containing eighteen articles, was published.[11] According to the prefatory statement of the census, the purpose was "to prepare for the election of the National People's Congress and the local people's congresses at all levels, to conduct satisfactorily the registration of the electorate, and to acquire accurate census figures for the nation's economic and cultural construction."[12]

A central census office was to be organized by the Ministry of Interior, the Ministry of Public Security, the State Statistical Bureau, and other relevant departments, but placed under the charge of the Ministry of Interior. Similar organizations were to be established at provincial and lower levels.[13] The People's Revolutionary Military Council was in charge of the enumeration of the armed forces. Overseas Chinese, diplomatic personnel stationed abroad, and students studying in other countries were to be estimated, respectively, by the Commission of Overseas Chinese Affairs, the Ministry of Foreign Affairs, and the Ministry of Higher Education.[14]

The census schedule was a simple one. It listed only five questions: (1) relation to the head of household; (2) name and address, (3) sex, (4) age, and (5) nationality (i.e., whether Han race or belonging to a national minority group). Since the traditional Chinese method of

counting age is different from the Western method based on the Gregorian calendar, the census stipulated that age should be calculated in the Western manner.[15]

The members of each household were divided into permanent residents (ch'ang-chu jen-ko) and absentees (wai-ch'u jen-ko), and only permanent residents were counted.[16] For government offices, the army, schools, factories, hospitals, and other institutions, special schedules were issued, on which permanent residents only were to be marked.[17]

The date of the census was fixed as of June 30, 1953; that is, whatever time the enumeration took place, the figures were estimated to be valid for the date of June 30, 1953.[18] Reportedly, 2,579,530 cadres were involved in the census-taking.[19] Most of the cadres were government workers, employees of state enterprises, and staff and students from universities, who were released from their regular duties and transferred to the census offices on a temporary basis.[20]

The original timetable contained in the census instructions required that the census-taking was to be completed before the end of September, 1953, that local returns should reach the provincial and municipal offices by the end of October, and that the reports on provincial totals should be submitted to the Central Census Office by November 15.[21] Actually, the census count lasted about one year. In March, 1954, the Central Census Office issued a circular announcing that, at that late date, 40 percent of the country had not yet completed the census.[22]

---

[10]Detailed discussions of the sources and quality of the Chinese population data were given in U.S. Bureau of the Census, *The Size, Composition, and Growth of the Population of Mainland China*, by John S. Aird, International Population Statistics Reports, Series P–90, No. 15, Washington, D.C.: U.S. Government Printing Office, 1961, 100 pp. See also S. Chandrasekhar, *China's Population, Census and Vital Statistics*, Hong Kong University Press, 1959, 69 pp.

[11]"Measures for National Census and Registration of Population," *1955 JMST*, pp. 25–27.

[12]*Ibid.*, p. 26 (Article 1).

[13]*Ibid.* (Article 2).

[14]*Ibid.* (Article 4).

[15]*Ibid.* (Article 7).

[16]*Ibid.* (Article 8) and Central Office of Population Census and Registration, "How to Distinguish between Permanent Residents and Absentees," *1955 JMST*, pp. 28–29.

[17]"Measures for National Census and Registration of Population," *op. cit.*, pp. 26–27 (Articles 9, 10, and 11).

[18]*Ibid.*, p. 26 (Article 6).

[19]Teng Hsiao-p'ing, "Census and General Election Completed in China: Population of China Over 600 Million," NCNA, Peking, June 19, 1954; reprinted in *1955 JMST*.

[20]S. K. Krotevich, "Vsekitayskaya perepis' naseleniya 1953 g" ("The All-China Population Census of 1953"), *Vestnik statistiki (Statistical Herald)*, No. 5, September, 1955, p. 47.

[21]"Measures for National Census and Registration of Population," *op. cit.*, p. 27 (Article 16).

[22]*JMJP*, March 11, 1954.

The preliminary census results were revealed by Teng Hsiao-p'ing on June 19, 1954, in his report to the Committee of the Central People's Government.[23] Revised and more detailed results were announced in a communiqué by the State Statistical Bureau on November 1, 1954.[24] The census findings were reported as complete and accurate. A sample check of 52,953,400 persons in 343 *hsien* and cities of 23 provinces, 5 municipalities, and one autonomous region (accounting for 9 percent of the enumerated population) indicated that duplications amounted to only 0.139 percent, while omissions were only 0.255 percent.[25]

The System of Population Registration

Since the 1953 census results were published, some other demographic data on mainland China have been made available. These data include total population figures for 1949 to 1957, provincial population figures for 1954 and 1957, population figures for a number of cities in 1957, and some vital statistics for particular cities during the period 1949–57. The major source of these data is the system of population registration.

The Russian expert who served in China as an advisor on the 1953 census reported that a system of population reporting was initiated at the inception of the communist regime.[26] But the formalized system of population registration was begun only in July, 1951, when the Ministry of Public Security promulgated the urban registration regulations.[27] These regulations called for the registration of all urban residents except military forces, security police, and diplomatic personnel. Births were to be reported within one month and deaths within 24 hours. Persons who moved from one city to another were obliged to report to the police station to obtain removal permits before departure, and their permits were to be surrendered to the proper authorities at the place of new residence within three days after arrival. Temporary visitors were required to report their presence to the local police station if they stayed in one place longer than three days. In addition, the regulations required the reporting of changes in the composition of household occasioned by marriage, divorce, separation, adoption, merging of families, and other reasons.

The system of registration was extended to rural areas in June, 1955, when the State Council issued a directive concerning establishment of a permanent system of population registration.[28] The system was to be the responsibility of the Ministry of Interior, but the Ministry of Public Security was to retain full control of urban registration.

The 1955 State Council directive also called for registration of all births, deaths, movements, and changes of family composition as in the 1951 regulations, but the requirements were spelled out in greater detail. The new regulations stipulated that registration statistics were to be compiled once a year. *Hsiang* (village) and *chen* (town) were to submit reports to *hsien* (county) in February, *hsien* to provinces in March, and the province to the Ministry of Interior in April.[29] Six months after the 1955 directive was issued, the State Council vested the Ministry of Public Security with full administrative authority for household registration work in both urban and rural areas.[30]

The system of household registration was revised again in January, 1958, and since then has remained in force, with the Ministry of Public Security continuing to be responsible for the recording and statistical work of the households in the whole country.[31] The 1958 regulations were much the same as before, except that the period for temporary residence was shortened from six to three months.[32] The main feature of the revised system was the strengthening of control over population movements, particularly from rural to urban areas. There is no evidence that efforts have since been made to improve the system as a source of demographic data.

[23]Teng Hsiao-p'ing, *op. cit.*, p. 30.

[24]SSB, "Communiqué on the Results of the Population Census of the Whole Country," *TCKCTH*, No. 8 (November, 1954), pp. 1–2.

[25]*Ibid.*, and Chung Lin and Hsiao Lu, "The 1953 National Census of Population," *TCKTTH*, No. 10 (October 17, 1955), p. 22.

[26]S. K. Krotevich, "Veskitayskaya perepis' naseleniya 1953 g" ("The All-China Population Census of 1953"), *Paslevoyenniye perepisi naseleniya (Postwar Population Census)*, Moscow: Gasstatizdat, 1957, p. 93.

[27]"Ministry of Public Security Promulgates Regulations Governing Urban Population," NCNA, Peking, July 16, 1951.

[28]State Council, "Directive Concerning Establishment of a Permanent System of Population Registration," *1956 JMST*, pp. 329–30.

[29]*Ibid.*, p. 330.

[30]State Council, "Notice on Transferring the Work of Registration and Statistics of Rural Household and the Nationality Work to the Ministry of Public Security," *Collections of Laws of the People's Republic of China (Chung-hua jen-min kung-huo-kuo fa-kuei jui-pien)*, January–June, 1956, pp. 173–175.

[31]"Regulations for Household Registration (Adopted on January 9, 1958, by the Standing Committee of the National People's Congress at Its 91st Meeting)," *1959 JMST*, pp. 288–89.

[32]*Ibid.*

Surveys of Vital Rates

In addition to the 1953 census and the registration system, a number of vital rates surveys reported in Chinese literature supply some further demographic information on mainland China.[33]

Perhaps the most important survey was the one conducted by the Ministry of Interior on the basis of a sample of over 30,180,000 persons. The sample covered the population of 29 large and medium-sized cities, the whole province of Ningsia, and 10 *hsien* of other provinces, as well as 1 *chü* (district), 2 *chen,* 58 *hsiang,* and 7 *ts'un* (hamlets) in 35 *hsien.* The survey results indicated a birth rate of 37, a death rate of 17, and the resulting natural increase rate of 20 per thousand of population.[34] These rates have been accepted officially as the national vital rates for 1953. Since 1954 the national vital rates have been compiled from the household registration data.

TYPES OF DATA

Broadly speaking, the official data available on China's population may be classified into four categories: (1) population totals, (2) breakdowns of totals according to ethnic groups or geographical characteristics, (3) sex and age composition, and (4) vital statistics.

Total Population (Tables 1.2 and 1.3)

During the period between the establishment of the Communist regime in 1949 and the 1953 census, nearly a dozen official estimates of total population of China could be found in print.[35] Very little explanation was given, however, as to the method by which these estimates were obtained, the precise dates to which they pertained, or the definition of the population included. The population data published since the 1953 census, however, are relatively more informative about method, dates, and definitions.

THE 1953 CENSUS TOTALS
(TABLE 1.2)

The population totals of June 30, 1953, given in both the report on preliminary findings by Teng Hsiao-p'ing and the SSB communiqué, consist of two component parts, namely, the

population by direct census registration and the population indirectly surveyed. The latter refers to Taiwan and the overseas population, as well as to the population in "remote border regions where communication facilities were poor and where no local elections took place."[36] The people in the remote border regions were estimated at 8,397,477 persons, or 1.4 percent of the total population on the mainland on June 30, 1953, and reportedly were distributed among the rural areas of Sikang, Sinkiang, Tibet, Western Chinghai, Western Szechuan, and Western Yunnan.[37] The estimate was based on reports of the local authorities in the regions, who submitted the data without completing census schedules and without reference to the census date of June 30, 1953.[38]

[33]The first survey reported in the press was one conduced by the Population Census and Registration Office of Kiangning *Hsien*, Kiangsu Province, during the period from June, 1951 to June, 1953, in the villages of Ailing and Shengi. The results indicated a birth rate of 33.6, a death rate of 19.3, and a natural increase rate of 14.3 per thousand population. The second survey was conducted in 1952–53 by the Ministry of Public Security, the Ministry of Interior, the Militia Department of the People's Revolutionary Military Council, and the Population Registration Office of Kiangning *Hsien*. The sample comprised 29 cities, 5 *hsien*, 2 *hsiang*, and 1 *ts'un*. The findings revealed a birth rate of 38, a death rate of 11, and a natural increase rate of 27. (For both surveys, see "Census and Registration Work Completed in Areas with 60 Percent of Population in China," *JMJP*, March 11, 1954.) A major study of vital rates was reported by Ch'en Ta in his Stockholm paper. The study was based on 16 sample surveys during the period from June, 1951, to February, 1954. The sample was composed of 7 *hsien* in Szechwan, Kwangsi, Honan, and Shensi and 18 *hsiang* in Kiangsu, Chekiang, and Hopei. The areas covered were mainly rural, and the sample population totaled 1,810,107 persons. According to Ch'en, this population had a birth rate of 21.0 and a natural increase rate of 20.06 per thousand. (See Ch'en Ta, *New China's Population Census of 1953 and Its Relation to National Reconstruction and Demographic Research*, Stockholm: International Statistical Institute, August, 1957, p. 25.)
[34]Pai Chien-hua, "600 Million People – A Great Strength for Socialist Construction of Our Country," *TCKTTH*, No. 8 (November, 1954), pp. 9–10, reference on p. 10.
[35]In late 1949, a report from the Liberation Army Headquarters gave 475 million as the size of the Chinese population. (*1950 JMST*, Sec. A, p. 1.) In March, 1950, the Office of Statistics of the Committee of Financial and Economic Affairs of the Government Administrative Council released a figure of 483,687,862, ("Latest Population Figures of China: 483,687,862," *Hsin-wan pao*, Hong Kong, December 7, 1952.) In May, 1950, the Ministry of Interior announced that the total population of China was 483,896,687. /*Chung-hua jen-min kung-ho-kuo feng-sheng ti't'u* (Provincial Atlas of the People's Republic of China), Shanghai: Ti-t'u ch'u-pan she, December, 1953./ On June 16, 1950, Chou En-lai, speaking to the People's Political Consultative Conference, stated that the population under Communist rule totaled 487,-690,000. (NCNA release, June 16, 1950.) On July 1, 1950, the Liberation Army Headquarters reported that the total population was 492,532,000. (*1951 JMST*,Vol. 1, Sect. B, p. 1.) In August, 1952, the *1952 People's Handbook* gave the figure of 486,571,237 for the population of 1950. (*1952 JMST*, p. 153.) At the end of 1951, the population of the mainland (excluding Taiwan) was announced as 556,600,000 by the State Statistical Bureau. At the end of 1952, the Ministry of Interior examined the administrative reports from local areas and found the population, as of the end of 1952, to be 567,700,000, excluding Taiwan. (S. K. Krotevich, "The All-China Population Census of 1953," *Vestnik statistiki*, No. 5, September, 1955, pp. 36–37.) Finally, the 1953 edition of the *Provincial Atlas of the People's Republic of China* gave undated figures for the population on the Chinese mainland as 543,490,000 (*Chung-hua jen-min kung-kuo feng-sheng ti-t'u*, loc. cit.).
[36]SSB, *op. cit.* p. 1.
[37]Krotevich (1955), *op. cit.*, pp. 46–47; Chandrasekhar, *op. cit.*, p. 29.
[38]Krotevich (1955), *loc. cit.*

TOTAL POPULATION, 1949–58 (TABLE 1.3)

In addition to the 1953 census, estimates for total population are available for the years from 1949 to 1958. Figures are given in terms of year-end and average annual numbers. The latter is taken as the mean of current and preceding year-end numbers.[39] The published total population series are not uniform in coverage, due to the inclusion or exclusion of Taiwan and/or overseas populations. According to the State Statistical Bureau, "The estimates for 1949, 1950 and 1951 were derived on the basis of the trends of population growth in the past." The figure of 1952 was calculated from the reported year-end numbers of Peking, Tientsin, Shanghai, Fukien, and Kiangsu, plus the year-end numbers estimated for other provinces from their reports on mid-year population figures. For 1953, the year-end population was estimated from the census results for June 30 of that year. For 1954 and after, the statistics were compiled from annual population reports submitted by the provinces.[40]

Distribution of Total Population by Ethnic Groups and by Geographical Areas (Tables 1.4–1.8)

ETHNIC COMPOSITION (TABLE 1.4)

Detailed statistics on the breakdown of the Chinese population by ethnic groups were released for 1953 in the SSB Census Communiqué. No figures have been published for other years, although approximate magnitudes of some 50 national minorities are given in the *1957, 1958, and 1959 People's Handbooks.*[41]

In the 1953 census, the nationality of persons above 18 years of age was recorded as whatever they chose to give. For those under 18 years, nationality was determined by that of the head of household.[42]

URBAN-RURAL DISTRIBUTION (TABLE 1.5)

The data on urban and rural population were published by the State Statistical Bureau for mid-1953 in the 1953 Census Communiqué

and for 1949–56 in the June, 1957, issue of *Statistical Work (TCKT)*. The statistical tabulation of the urban and rural population during the period covered followed essentially the criteria for demarcation of urban and rural areas outlined in a State Council resolution in 1955.[43] According to the resolution, the criteria for demarcation of urban and rural areas were as follows:

Urban areas (cities and towns) are those where a municipal people's council or a people's council of the *hsien* level or above is located, except for mobile administrative units in the pastoral areas. Urban areas are also those with 2,000 inhabitants or more, of whom at least half are engaged in pursuits other than agriculture. Places of 1,000 to 2,000 population may also be classified as urban, provided that these are industrial, commercial, transport, educational, or research centers, or are residential areas for workers, and provided that at least 75 per cent of the population is non-agricultural. Finally, places with sanitorium facilities in which patients constitute more than half of the local permanent population may also be classified as urban. All other areas are considered rural.[44]

Therefore, the criteria used to distinguish between urban and rural areas are not based on population size alone but on the occupational composition of the population as well. The same criteria apply to the suburbs of a city. While the city is regarded as an urban area, a suburb which falls within the administrative boundaries of the city may be classified as rural if a majority of its population is engaged in agricultural activities.[45] Since the city population consists of the total *de jure* residents under the city administration,[46] it includes rural population in suburbs. Thus, for example, Peking with a total population of 2,768,149 had more than 708,000 persons classified as rural at the time of the 1953 census, and Tientsin's 2,693,831 population included more than 365,000 rural persons.[47]

[39]Tai Shih-kuang, "Population Statistics—Part I," *TCKTTH*, No. 3 (February 14, 1956), p. 23.
[40]Data Office, *TCKT*,"Statistical Data on the Population of Our Country, 1949–1956," *TCKT*, No. 11 (June 14, 1957), p. 24.
[41]*1957 JMST*, pp. 623–24; *1958 JMST*, pp. 650–51; *1959 JMST*, pp. 217–19.
[42]Krotevich (1955), *op. cit.*, p. 46.
[43]State Council, "Resolution on the Criteria for Demarcation of Urban and Rural Areas (adopted on November 7, 1955)," *TCKTTH*, No. 12 (December 17, 1955), p. 4.
[44]*Ibid.*
[45]*Ibid.*; and SSB, "Explanation of Several Major Questions Concerning the Criteria for Demarcation of Urban and Rural Areas," *TCKTTH*, No. 12 (December 17, 1955), p. 6.
[46]I-chu, "Notes on the 'Wall Map of the Population Density of China,'"*TLCS*, Vol. 7, No. 11 (November 14, 1956), pp. 502–4.
[47]SSB, "Explanation of Several Major Questions. . . ," *op. cit.*, p. 6.

NUMBER OF CITIES AND TOWNS BY SIZE (TABLE 1.6)

The 1955 State Council resolution makes the further distinction in urban areas between cities (*ch'eng*) and towns (*chen*). Urban areas with 20,000 inhabitants or more are classed as cities, while all other urban areas are considered to be towns.[48] Chinese economic literature also frequently makes distinctions between large and medium cities and small cities. The former refers to cities with a total population of 50,000 or more.[49] Data are available for 1952 and 1957 on the number of large and medium cities classified by the size of population and for 1953 on the distribution of all cities and towns by size.

POPULATION OF CITIES (TABLE 1.7)

Data on the population of individual cities and towns are usually given in articles or news reports on the development of particular places. Figures gathered from such a variety of sources are often not comparable. The figures themselves are frequently only rough estimates. Usually, no explanation is offered as to how the figures were originally derived, the date to which they refer, and the scope of the population covered. The 1953 census data on city population and the 1957 year-end population figures published for a number of cities appear to be more informative.

Detailed 1953 census reports on city populations are not available, but fragmentary information was assembled in a U.S. Bureau of the Census report from Chinese and Soviet publications.[50] The 1957 figures were registration data. They were given for 34 cities in *Ten Great Years*, and information on an additional six cities was supplied by the State Statistical Bureau to an Indian demographer when he visited China in 1958.[51]

As indicated earlier, a particular city population figure refers to the total *de jure* population under the city administration. Since 1953, a great number of cities in China have undergone changes in their administrative boundaries. During the period from 1953 to 1958, for example, territorial changes of at least 67 cities were reported.[52] Such changes, therefore, should be taken into account in making intertemporal comparisons of city populations.

PROVINCIAL POPULATION (TABLE 1.8)

Data on provincial population are available for 1953, 1954, and 1957. The 1953 figures were census results, while the statistics for the other two years were compiled from annual registration reports. The provincial data for these three years are not strictly comparable, owing to changes in the administrative division.

Age and Sex Compositions (Tables 1.9–1.11)

Data on the age and sex composition of the Chinese population were published only for June, 1953, when the national census took place. Since part of the total population was indirectly estimated in the 1953 census, the age and sex data covered only that part of the population directly surveyed and registered. The data contained in the official census report are very meagre, but additional information can be found in the papers by Ch'en Ta, Tai Shih-kuang, and T'ien Feng-t'iao.

Vital Statistics

NATIONAL VITAL RATES (TABLE 1.12)

Very little information on vital rates has been published by the government agencies in Peking. Chandrasekhar and Pressat were able to obtain the national birth and death rates for 1952–57 from the State Statistical Bureau. These rates are usually expressed in terms of per thousand of population. That is, they refer to the number of births and deaths and the resulting natural increase in relation to the average number of *de jure* population in the country (or within the specified administrative boundaries in the case of provincial and local vital rates) during a calendar year.[53] The national vital rates available for 1952 and 1953 were derived on the basis of the data

[48]State Council, "Resolution on the Criteria for Demarcation of Urban and Rural Areas," *op. cit.*, p. 4; and SSB, "Explanations of Several Major Questions . . . ," *op. cit.*, p. 6.
[49]SSB, *ibid; TGY*, p. 13.
[50]U.S. Bureau of the Census, *Cities of Mainland China: 1953 and 1958*, by Morris B. Ullman, International Population Reports, Series P–95, No. 59, Washington, D.C.; U.S. Government Printing Office, August, 1961, 46 pp.
[51]Chandrasekhar, *op. cit.*, p. 47.
[52]U.S. Bureau of the Census, *Cities of Mainland China: 1953 and 1958, op. cit.*, pp. 42–44.
[53]Tai Shih-kuang, "Population Statistics–Part II," *TCKTTH*, No. 4 (February 29, 1956), p. 30.

obtained from sampling investigations. The figures for 1954 and after were calculated from
population registration data.

LOCAL VITAL RATES
(TABLE 1.13)

Official birth rates and death rates for nine
cities during 1952–56 were also made available
to Pressat. Chandrasekhar was given only the
rates for Peking during 1955–57 and for Shanghai during 1953–57. There are discrepancies
between these two sets of data for Peking, and
such discrepancies cannot be explained with
the information available. Nothing was said by
Pressat concerning possible distortions of the
data because of changes in city boundaries. It is
known that the areas of at least three of the
nine cities were expanded during the period
covered.[54]

INFANT MORTALITY RATES
(TABLE 1.14)

Infant mortality rates in the same nine cities
during 1952–56 were given to Chandrasekhar
by the Ministry of Health in Peking. The infant
mortality rate is the number of infant deaths
below one year of age per 1,000 live births in a
year.[55] This definition implies not only the registration of births and deaths but the age at
death. As indicated earlier, the Chinese traditional method of counting age differs from the
Western method. The Chinese reckon the age
of a newborn infant as one, and the infant becomes two at the New Year. This problem has
been reportedly overcome by assigning age at
death according to the Western method of calculation.[56]

[54]U.S. Bureau of the Census, *Cities of Mainland China: 1953 and 1958, op. cit.*, p. 14.
[55]S. Chandrasekhar, *op. cit.*, p. 52.
[56]*Ibid.*

2

NATIONAL INCOME

CONCEPTS OF
NATIONAL INCOME

National income in Communist China is defined in terms of production, distribution, and final expenditures.[1]

From the standpoint of production, the national income (*kuo-min shou-ju* or *kuo-min shou-yu sheng-ch'an*) denotes "the value added to the country's material wealth from industry, agriculture, construction, restaurants, freight transportation, and that part of communications and trade serving material production."[2] The total of the gross value output of these seven so-called "materially productive" sectors becomes what is known as the *gross social value output*. The national income is the gross social value output net of capital depreciation and other material outlays.[3] Omitted from the national income measurements are not only passenger transportation, private use of communications, and pure service elements of trade but also finance and insurance, government administration, army and police forces, culture, education, public health, and all other professions rendering personal services.[4] These omissions constitute the principal difference between the Chinese and Western concepts of national income.

The national income produced by the materially productive sectors is distributed through two stages, namely, primary distribution and redistribution of national income. The primary distribution of national income (*kuo-min shou-ju chu-tzu fen-pei*) is confined to the personal incomes originating in, and the net revenue of enterprises accuring to, the materially productive sectors. The personal incomes consist

of (1) wages of production personnel, including fringe benefits such as labor insurance funds, union fees, and allowances for medical and other welfare expenses; (2) incomes in cash and kind of agricultural cooperative members distributed among them for work-day units put in; and (3) incomes of individual producers, such as unaffiliated peasants, handicraftsmen, and peddlers. The net revenue of enterprises in the materially productive sectors include (1) profits; (2) taxes, including the turnover tax, business tax, custome duties, salt tax, slaughtering tax, and license fees; and (3) payments in interest, insurance, and labor training.[5]

After the primary distribution, the national income originating in the materially productive sectors is then redistributed throughout the

[1] Discussion of Communist Chinese concepts of national income will be found in Choh-ming Li, *Economic Development of Communist China*, Berkeley: University of California Press, 1959, pp. 75–80; and Ta-chung Liu and Kung-chia Yeh, *Economy of the Chinese Mainland: National Income and Economic Development, 1933–1959*, (Princeton, N.J.: Princeton University Press, 1965), pp. 214–19.

[2] SSB, Research Office, "A Preliminary Analysis of the Production and Distribution of China's National Income," *TCYC*, No. 1 (January 23, 1958), pp. 11–15; quotation on p. 11. See also Po I-po, "On the Correct Handling of the Problem of the Relationship between Accumulation and Consumption," *HHPYK*, No. 20 (October 1956), p. 76, footnote 1; Lu Kuang, "China's National Income," *Peking Review*, Vol. I, No. 6 (April 8, 1958), p. 7, footnote.

[3] SSB, Research Office, *loc. cit.*; Lu Kuang, *loc. cit*, The Chinese concept of national income derives from Marx. Marx distinguishes between newly created value and transferred value, i.e., the value of means of production consumed in the reproduction process. His gross output is composed of both newly created value and transferred value. In *Capital*, Marx writes:

"The value of the annual product in commodities . . . resolves itself into two parts: Part A, which replaces the value of the advanced constant capital, and Part B, which represents itself in the form of wages, profit, and rent." (*Capital*, Chicago: Charles H. Kerr & Co., 1909, Vol. 3, p. 977.)

Since constant capital (or transferred value) includes depreciation or capital consumption (in Western national income terminology) as well as the raw materials consumed, the Marxian concept of gross output is very gross indeed.

[4] Yueh Wei, "The Method of Computing National Income," *CCYC*, No. 3 (June 17, 1956), pp. 48–66, reference on p. 52.

[5] *Ibid.*, pp. 56–59.

economy, including the so-called "nonproductive" sectors. The redistribution of national income *(kuo-min shou-ju tsai fen-pei)* is achieved through fiscal, credit, and price policies, as well as the business activities of the service industries. The redistribution provides the source of revenue for nonproductive activities.[6]

In the Chinese definitions of national income in terms of production and distribution, a closed economy is implicitly assumed. From the standpoint of final disposal, however, the national income should be adjusted in accordance with "the balance in the international account in order to arrive at the amount available for actual domestic use."[7] This *national expenditure (kuo-min shou-ju shih yung)* is then divided into "accumulation" and "consumption."[8]

According to Po I-po, Chairman of the State Economic Commission, accumulation takes the following forms:[9]

1. In the case of centralized state expenditures: investment in capital construction of productive and nonproductive undertakings minus depreciation charges for fixed assets; increases in circulation funds (working capital); increases in state material reserves, etc.

2. In the case of state enterprises: accumulation within each enterprise.

3. In the case of agricultural producer cooperatives, handicraft producer cooperatives, and supply and marketing cooperatives: reserve funds of the cooperatives.

4. In the case of individuals: investments made by industrialists, merchants, individual peasants, and handicraftsmen.

In other words, accumulation is that part of national income used to increase fixed capital assets (productive and nonproductive), working capital, and material reserves.[10]

Consumption refers to the sum of personal, governmental, and communal consumption. Communal consumption includes expenditures of the state and the enterprises in cultural, educational, and public health work and welfare services for workers and employees.[11] It should be noted that depreciation of private housing and minor repairs and depreciation of the fixed assets of government agencies, armed forces, and all other nonproductive enterprises are included in consumption.[12]

METHODS OF ESTIMATION

Theoretically, the various definitions from the viewpoints of production and distribution should lead to the same national income figure; and this figure, when adjusted for the balance in the international account, should equal the national expenditure. These definitions represent three different approaches to estimation of national income.[13] In practice, because of the paucity of many pertinent statistical series and because of the absence of a well-established accounting system, the basic approach employed by the State Statistical Bureau appears to be the production (value-added) method. According to this method, the net-value output of each of the seven materially productive sectors is derived from its gross-value output. The national income figure is then obtained by summing up the net-value outputs of these sectors. The gross- and net-value outputs of each sector are estimated as follows:[14]

1. *Industry.* Industry, by definition, includes manufacturing, mining, electric power generation, and lumbering.[15] The gross industrial value output is computed on the basis of the "factory method"; that is, the gross output of each enterprise is valued at ex-factory prices *(ch'u-ch'an ch'an)*, and the sum total of the gross value outputs of all the enterprises in the industry becomes gross industrial value output. Included in the gross industrial output of each enterprise are finished products, changes in the stocks of semi-finished products, and tools, equipment, and parts manufactured for self use.

[6]*Ibid.*, pp. 59–60.
[7]*Ibid.*, p. 64.
[8]*Ibid.*, pp. 60–64.
[9]Po I-po, *op. cit.*
[10]Fuller discussion on the concept and estimation of accumulation and its components appears in the section on capital formation.
[11]SSB, Research Office, *op. cit.*, pp. 12–13.
[12]Yueh Wei, *op. cit.*, pp. 61–63.
[13]The three approaches are not altogether dissimilar to the value-added, distributive-shares, and final-expenditures methods used in international standard practice, except for the more restrictive scope of the Chinese concept of national income.
[14]Yueh Wei, *op. cit.*, pp. 52–56. See also Yueh Wei, "Problems of Computing National Product," *TCKTTH*, No. 1 (January 1956), pp. 15–17. Unless otherwise indicated, the following summary is based on these two articles.
[15]According to the *Agricultural Statistical Handbook* of 1956, natural fishery products were considered part of industry and should be included in industrial production. At least up to 1960, however, the value of all fishery products had been included in agricultural value output. [*Agricultural Statistical Handbook, op. cit.*, p. 59; State Economic Commission, Bureau of Consolidated Economic Planning, Department of Methodology, "Major Changes in the Tabulation Forms for National Economic Planning for 1958," *CHCC*, No. 8 (August, 1957), pp. 24–27; Huang Chien-t'o, "Major Tasks in the Agricultural Statistical Work Program for 1960," *CHYTC*, No. 2 (February, 1960), pp. 18–21.]

Productive activities of nonindustrial units attached to the industrial enterprises, such as freight transportation outside factory units, basic construction, farms and ranches, and mess halls, are not included in industrial output, but in the output of respective sectors.

The net value output of industry is obtained by deducting material outlays from the gross-value output. These outlays include raw materials, fuel, electricity, depreciation, and miscellaneous expenses. Depreciation charges for "nonproductive" assets, such as mess halls, clubs and workers' housing, and nonusable raw materials are not included in the material outlays.

2. *Agriculture.* Agriculture consists of three principal activities—crop growing, animal raising, and farm subsidiary production.[16] Included in the farm subsidiary production are the collection and hunting of natural products, such as herbs, minerals, wild animals and fish, and the processing of own farm produce, and the handicraft work for own household use as well as for other consumers who supply the raw materials.[17] Double counting frequently takes place in the estimation of agricultural output. For example, food grown on the farm will go into the valuation of crops, and the same food used for animal feed will also enter into the value of animal raising.

The gross agricultural output is valued at the "average of prices at the places of production."[18] The value of the products which are sold to the state is estimated on the basis of government-purchase prices. Valuation of the products consumed on the farm or not sold at the village level is imputed according to "either the average market prices less transport cost or production costs or the prices of similar products."[19]

The material outlays of the agricultural sector include the costs of seed, sprouting grains, fertilizers, insecticides, animal feed, fuel, and electricity; depreciation charges for agricultural machinery and equipment and for draft animals and barns; and expenses of transportation and communication. Net value added by agriculture is derived by deducting the material outlays from the gross agricultural value output.

3. *Construction.* Construction includes (1) the building of productive and nonproductive structures including mines, factories, steel furnaces, and houses; (2) the construction of railways, highways, communication lines, and large

dams; (3) installation of equipment; (4) major repairs; (5) drilling and dredging; and (6) designing and geological prospecting as well as geological surveys connected with construction work.[20] The actual cost of these items is used for estimating the gross value output. The value of machinery and equipment installed is not included in the estimate.

The material outlays include (1) raw materials and fuels; (2) charges for services such as transportation, communications, water supply, and electricity; and (3) depreciation of fixed assets. In principle, the net value output of construction also can be obtained by employing "the production method," that is, by deducting the material outlays from the gross value output. In computing the net value added by construction, however, the State Statistical Bureau adopted "the income approach."[21]

According to this approach, the net value output of construction is made up of two types of incomes: wages and net social revenue. Wages include (1) wage and fringe benefit payments to the production personnel in the building and installation enterprises; (2) payments to draft labor, including soldiers, civilians, and criminals being reformed through labor; and (3) income in cash and in kind received by peasants for engaging in construction activities. Net social revenue includes (1) net profits of the building and installation enterprises; (2) business taxes;[22] (3) miscellaneous payments such as insurance charges, interest, and training expenses.[23]

4. *Freight transportation.* Freight transportation refers to all means of transportation, including railways, coastal and inland shipping, air transport, motor transport, and carts and

[16]Wang Keng-chin, "My Views on Methods of Calculating the Gross Agricultural Value Output," *TCKT*, No. 4 (February 28, 1957), pp. 3–4. According to Wang, agriculture also includes the activities of machine tractor stations. But the gross value output of the machine tractor stations has been negligible. It constituted, for example, less than 0.02 percent of gross agriculutral value output in 1955.

[17]*Ibid.*

[18]Huang Meng-fan, "Agricultural Production Statistics," *TCKTTH*, No. 12 (June, 1956), p. 33.

[19]*Ibid.*

[20]Yueh Wei, "Method of Computing National Income," *op. cit.*, p. 53; SSB, "The Basic Situation of China's Construction Enterprises," *TCKTTH*, No. 24 (December, 1956), pp. 31–33; Lung Hua-yung, Chi Hsi-yung, and Chen Ming-kai, "Several Problems Concerning the Measurement of the Value Output of Construction," *TCKT*, No. 8 (April, 1957), pp. 14–16, reference on p. 14. It may be noted that the building of roads, small dams, dikes, and the like, done by mobilizing mass labor, is not included in construction. (See State Economic Commission, *op. cit.*, p. 25.)

[21]The income approach was used for computing net-value output of construction, at least for 1952–55. (See Lung Hua-yung, Chi Hsi-yung, and Chen Ming-kai, *op. cit.*, p. 16.)

[22]Since 1954 business taxes imposed on state-operated building and installation enterprises have been abolished.

[23]Lung Hua-yung, Chi Hsi-yung, and Chen Ming-kai, *op. cit.*, p. 16.

wheelbarrows operated by animals or men. The gross value output of freight transportation consists of the gross receipts of transportation enterprises from moving freight, including loading and unloading. The value added by freight transport is the gross value output net of all material cost.

5. *Communications.* The gross value output of communication is defined as that part of business receipts of the post and tele-communications enterprises derived from serving material production. The distinction between productive and nonproductive services of the communications enterprises is made on the basis of sample surveys. The net value output is obtained by subtracting material outlays from the gross value output.

6. *Trade.* Trade refers to state purchase and supply, wholesaling, and retailing. Much of the activity associated with trade is considered to be an extension of material production. This includes the storing, packing, and unpacking, sorting, and weighing of goods. Theoretically, only that part of trade serving material production is considered as part of the national income. For practical purposes, however, the State Statistical Bureau has included the entire value added by trade. The gross value output of trade is determined primarily as the difference between total sales and cost of purchases, from which value added is derived by deducting outlays such as loading and unloading, carting and carrying, commodity spoilage, communications charges, office expenses, and depreciation of fixed assets.

7. *Restaurants.* The gross value output of restaurants is the total volume of sales valued at retail prices. The net value excludes cost outlays such as materials, fuel, electricity, ice, and depreciation of equipment.

The net value outputs of the above seven sectors constitute the entire source of the national income,[24] and it is measured in terms of both current and constant prices. For the current price valuation, the net outputs of the productive sectors are measured at market prices,[25] except the net output of agricultural products the bulk of which, as has been pointed out, are sold to the state and valued at government-purchase prices. The national income at constant value was measured in terms of 1952 prices for the years prior to 1957, and since then 1957 prices have been used for the basis of measurement. Except for the agricultural and industrial sectors, in which value output at both current and constant prices is reported directly from the production units, the constant-price valuation of the output of the other sectors is obtained by adjusting each value-output series by appropriate price indices.[26]

NATIONAL INCOME STATISTICS

Beginning in 1954, the State Statistical Bureau attempted to estimate the national income of China. In early 1956, the work on the accounts for 1952 through 1954 was completed.[27] In late 1957 and early 1958, the national income figures for 1952 through 1956 appeared in a number of publications.[28] Later, these estimates seemed to have been revised slightly for 1952–55 but substantially upward for 1956. The revised absolute figures were never made available, but the rates of growth of the national income from 1950 through 1958 were published in *Ten Great Years.*

No data on the absolute amount of accumulation and consumption have ever been published, but a number of series showing accumulation and consumption as percentages of the national expenditures for 1952 through 1956 were found in print. These series conflict with one another, and in a few cases there were no explanations as to whether the estimates were based on constant or current prices.[29] Nevertheless, it appears that the series in current prices as they were released by the State Statistical Bureau and those in 1952 prices given in Hsü Ti-hsin's study are consistent with one another and with the national income figures and the related data. Accordingly, these two series have been used to derive the amount of accumulation and consumption in constant and current prices.

---

[24]Accordingly, the national income actually amounts to what should be called the "net domestic material product." (See Choh-ming Li, *op. cit.* p. 80.)

[25]Or, as Yueh Wei puts it, at current prices prevailing on the consumers' or users' level.

[26]The compilation of these price indices and the conversion ratios between the current and constant price valuation will be explained in the section on "Prices."

[27]Yueh Wei, "Methods of Computing National Income," *op. cit.,* pp. 48–49.

[28]Niu Chung-huang, *Accumulation and Consumption in China's National Income (Wo-kuo kuo-min shou-ju ti chi-jui ho hsiao-fei),* Peking: Chung-kuo chin-nien chu-pan she, November, 1957; SSB, Research Office, *TCYC, op. cit.,* pp. 11–15; Lu Kuang, *op. cit.,* pp. 7–9.

[29]See Table 2.7.

3

CAPITAL FORMATION AND RELATED ESTIMATES

Statistical data on China's capital formation and related estimates may be grouped into four categories: (1) the gross value of fixed assets, (2) industrial and commercial capital, (3) accumulation, and (4) basic construction investment.

FIXED ASSETS

THE CONCEPT OF FIXED ASSETS

In China's bookkeeping practice, fixed capital is conventionally called the "fixed asset" *(ku-ting tzu-ch'ang)*. A fixed asset is defined as one with a working life of at least one year and a cost of over 500 yuan.[1] Therefore, fixed assets do not include objects serviceable for less than a year, no matter what their cost. Nor do they include objects of value of less than 500 yuan per unit. These objects are called "low-value and short-life articles" *(ti-chih yi-hou p'ing)* and are regarded as part of working capital.[2]

In Chinese statistics, two types of fixed assets are frequently distinguished: productive and nonproductive. Productive fixed assets are those which function in the production process,[3] such as factories, mines, blast furnaces, dams and other construction works, power equipment, machinery and various types of equipment used in production, transport equipment, and livestock. Nonproductive fixed assets include residential buildings, government offices, schools, hospitals, recreation centers, nurseries, and other buildings not used in the production process.[4]

One of the characteristics of productive fixed assets, as distinct from working capital

(raw materials, supplementary materials, etc.), is that these assets retain their original form until they wear out completely and transfer their value to the commodities produced, not wholly but little by little. In addition, productive fixed assets are those which have already begun to take part in production. Objects which might be utilized in the production process but have not yet begun to function are not considered fixed assets. Thus, a plant under construction or equipment to be installed is not counted as a fixed asset but included in working capital. New construction projects or new machinery and equipment can be considered as fixed assets only when they have been completed or installed and have been put into operation.[5]

THE METHODS OF EVALUATING FIXED ASSETS

In theory, the value of fixed assets may be assessed in four different ways. First, fixed as-

[1] The minimum-cost standard for a fixed asset was initiated in 1951, when one million old yuan, or 100 yuan, was used as the limit. (See "Provisional Regulations Concerning Liquidation and Evaluation of the Assets of State Enterprises," *JMJP*, August 3, 1951.) The limit was raised to 500 yuan in 1955. (See "Unified Accounting Items and Accounting Reporting Forms of State Enterprises," in Ministry of Finance, ed., *Collections of the Financial Laws and Regulations of the Central Government*, Peking: Ts'ai-cheng ch'u-pan-she, 1955, p. 23.) But the 500-yuan limit has not been universally adopted, since certain enterprises were reportedly using a 200-yuan or 300-yuan standard. (See "Provisional Regulations Concerning the Problems of Classifying Certain Expenditures in the Financial Plans of the State Enterprises in 1956 (promulgated on October 6, 1955)," in Ministry of Finance, ed., *Collections of the Financial Laws and Regulations of the Central Government, 1955,* Peking: Ts'ai-cheng ch'u-pan-she, 1957, pp. 365–70, reference on p. 367; Feng Ta-lin, *Basic Construction in Industry and Transportation during the First Five-Year Plan,* Shanghai: Hsin chih-shih ch'u-pan-she, 1956, p. 2, footnote 1; Yu Tao and Wang Wen-sheng, "Statistics of National Wealth and Fixed Assets," *TCKTTH*, No. 5 (March 14, 1956), pp. 36–40; reference on p. 38; and Department of Planning and Statistics, Hupeh University, *Industrial Statistics,* Wuhan: Jen-min ch'u-pan-she, 1960, p. 241.)

[2] Yu Tao and Wang Wen-sheng, *op. cit.*; and Department of Planning and Statistics, Hupeh University, *op. cit.*

sets may be valued in terms of full original cost. The value of fixed assets existing at a particular moment, determined in this way, is the sum of the full original cost of construction, acquisition, transportation, and installation of these assets. Secondly, the value of existing fixed assets can be estimated at full replacement cost. Full replacement cost is the amount of money which would have been spent at the present time in order to obtain the existing fixed assets in their original form and at current prices. Therefore, replacement cost represents the cost of reproducing the fixed assets under present conditions. Finally, existing fixed assets may be valued at either original or replacement cost on the basis of that part of the fixed assets the value of which has not yet been transferred to the output. In other words, the original or replacement cost is calculated after deducting depreciation.[6]

In practice, revaluation of fixed assets was undertaken at full replacement cost for state enterprises in June, 1951,[7] and for private enterprises in 1952.[8] Since then, fixed assets have been valued at full original cost.[9]

Valuation of fixed assets at full original cost may introduce certain bias into the estimate. Since these estimates are the aggregates of the original expenditures made during different periods, various price levels enter into their valuation. In consequence, price variation will affect the value of the assets: a declining (rising) price trend will yield upward (downward) bias to the estimates. During the period 1949–59, for which data on the gross value of fixed assets were published, prices of producer goods—building materials and industrial supplies in particular—showed a declining trend beginning in 1953 and dropped sharply in 1955 and 1956. Therefore, fixed assets in China, valued at full original cost for 1953 and after, would be larger than would have been the case if valued at full replacement cost.

STATISTICS OF THE GROSS VALUE OF FIXED ASSETS

Gross Value of Total Fixed Assets (Table 3.1)

Official figures on the gross value of total fixed assets have never been published, but they can be derived from percentage data given for 1949, 1952, and 1955 in the January, 1957, issue of *Statistical Work* (*TCKT*). These fig-

ures do not include government administration and individual economic units such as peasants and handicraftsmen.[10]

Except for industry and a part of construction, information on the breakdown of the gross value of total fixed assets by sector is not available. Data for construction were published for 1953, and those for 1954 through 1956 can be computed from available information on the annual rate of increase of fixed assets in construction. These data cover only the construction enterprises under the jurisdiction of various ministries in the central government and, therefore, do not include state construction enterprises of the local governments, construction cooperatives, and individual constructors.

The Gross Value of Industrial Fixed Assets

Compared with those on total fixed assets, data on the gross value of industrial fixed assets are relatively abundant. These include only modern industry (that is, modern factory and handicraft factories) and exclude handicraft cooperatives and individual handicrafts.[11] *Ten Great Years* presents estimates for 1949, 1952, 1957, and 1958. An alternative series can be derived for 1949, 1952, 1955, and 1959 on the basis of the information given in the January, 1957, issue of *Statistical Work* (*TCKT*) and the October, 1959, issue of *Economic Research* (*CCYC*). These two series appear to be consistent with one another. It should be pointed out that the figure for 1959 must be regarded as provisional, since it is an *ex ante*, rather than an *ex post* estimate.

In addition to the gross value of total industrial fixed assets, data on assets are also available for the following breakdowns:

1. By ownership of industrial establishment, 1949–55 (Table 3.2).

[3]The production process refers to the process of transforming raw materials or semi-finished products into finished products.
[4]Yueh Wei, "The Methods of Computing National Income," *CCYC*, No. 3 (June 17, 1956), pp. 48–66, reference on p. 63.
[5]Department of Planning and Statistics, Hupeh University, *op. cit.*
[6]*Ibid.;* and Yu Tao and Wang Wen-sheng, *op. cit.*, p. 39.
[7]"Provisional Regulations . . . . ," *JMJP, op. cit.*
[8]Ch'ien Hua *et al., Changes in Private Industry and Trade in China during the Past Seven Years (1949–1956)*, Shanghai: Ts'ai-cheng ching-chi ch'u-pan-she, 1957, p. 166. No revaluation of fixed assets was taken for the state-private jointly operated enterprises until 1956, when nearly all the private enterprises were incorporated into the joint enterprises.
[9]Department of Planning and Statistics, Hupeh University, *op. cit.*, p. 253.
[10]Data Office, *TCKT*, "A General Survey of Industrial Capital in China," *TCKT*, No. 1 (January 14, 1957), pp. 31–33, reference on p. 31.
[11]*Ibid.*

2. By size of industrial establishment, 1955 (Table 3.3).

3. By inland and coastal areas, 1953 and 1955 (Table 3.4).

4. By producer goods and consumer goods industries, 1949, 1952, and 1955 (Table 3.5).

5. By individual industry, 1952–57 (Table 3.6).

6. For the Inner Mongolia Autonomous Region, 1952–58 (Table 3.7).

The classification of industrial establishments by ownership and the definitions of small, medium, and large-sized establishments, inland and coastal areas, and producer goods (group A) and consumer goods (group B) industries will be explained in the section on industry.

Among the various individual industries, statistics on the gross value of fixed assets were published only for four: iron and steel, metal processing, textiles, and paper manufacturing. Data for these industries, as well as for the Inner Mongolia Autonomous Region, were broken down further according to whether or not the fixed assets are used for industrial production. Fixed assets used for industrial production refer to those serving directly or indirectly in the production process. Included are buildings, structures, machinery and equipment (including power-generating equipment and transmission equipment), and instruments and transport equipment. Nonindustrial fixed assets include those used for housing, public utilities, cultural, health and insurance services, supply and marketing activities, agricultural production, and scientific research.[12]

INDUSTRIAL AND COMMERCIAL CAPITAL

INDUSTRIAL CAPITAL

The Concept and Measurement of Industrial Capital

Industrial capital—or industrial funds (*kung-yeh tzu-ching*), as they are usually called in China—consists of the net value of fixed assets and the amount of working capital.[13] Net

value is derived by estimating existing fixed assets at full original cost after depreciation has been deducted.[14]

Working capital of industrial enterprises refers to the monetary value of production stocks, semi-finished goods, and goods in process (including finished goods not immediately sold). Production stocks consist of raw and basic materials, supplementary materials, fuel, spare parts for equipment, low-value and short-life articles, packages and packing materials, and other materials of value.[15]

The amount of working capital of state, cooperative, and joint industrial enterprises is estimated from its sources. Prior to 1959, there were three major sources of working capital for these enterprises: (1) "normalized liabilities" *(ting-o fu-chai)*, such as liabilities capital, wages payable, auxiliary wages payable,[16] taxes payable, and payables to material suppliers and other; (2) appropriations from the state budget for the formation of minimum necessary production stocks and stocks of unfinished and finished goods; and (3) short-term loans from the People's Bank for meeting seasonal and other needs.[17] Since the beginning of 1959, the state budget does not include grants of working capital to enterprises (with the exception of state farms); and bank loans have thus become the sole source of working capital outside the enterprises.[18]

It is not clear how working capital of the private industrial enterprises was estimated before they became joint enterprises. Since working capital of private enterprises was taken in its usual accounting meaning of the differ-

[12]Department of Planning and Statistics. Hupeh University, *op. cit.*, pp. 242–43.
[13]Data Office, *TCKT, op. cit.*, pp. 31–32.
[14]Department of Planning and Statistics, Hupeh University, *op. cit.*, p. 253. The discussion in the Chinese literature indicates that a straight-line method of determining depreciation has been adopted. See Chang Shen and Wang En-yung, "A Brief Discussion on the Fixed Assets of Industrial Enterprises and Their Depreciation," *CCYC*, No. 5 (October 17, 1956), pp. 69–78; and Chang Wei-ta, "The Methods of Calculating the Depreciation Rate of Fixed Assets Used in Production," *CCYC*, No. 3 (June 17, 1956), pp. 99–112.
[15]Sheng Mu-chieh, *Working Capital of Socialist Industrial Enterprises (She-hui tsu-yi kung-yeh ti liu-tung tzu-ching)*, Shanghai: Jen-min ch'u-pan-she, 1956, pp. 17–23.
[16]For the meaning of auxiliary wages, see the section on employment, labor productivity, and wages.
[17]*Ibid.*, pp. 41–52.
[18]State Council, "Supplementary Regulations Concerning the Transfer of the Unified Control of Working Capital of the State Enterprises to the People's Bank," in Ministry of Finance, ed., *Collections of Financial Laws and Regulations of the Central Government, January–June, 1959*, Peking: Ts'ai-cheng ch'u-pan-she, 1960, pp. 82–85; and Ministry of Finance and the People's Bank, "Joint Notice on Resolution of Current Problems Concerning Working Capital of the State Farms," in *ibid.*, pp. 99–100.

ence between current assets and current liabilities, the estimate was probably made on the basis of the balance sheets of these enterprises.

Data on the amount of capital in the handicraft industry were published only for 1949, 1952, and 1955. It is not known how these figures were estimated. An article by a high-ranking official in the State Statistical Bureau indicated that handicraft capital was estimated for 1953 on the basis of data obtained from model surveys (*tien-hsin tiao-cha*) conducted in a number of *hsien* and that the estimate for 1954, for which model surveys were not undertaken, was obtained by multiplying the gross value of handicraft output in 1954 by the ratio of working capital to gross value of output in the handicraft industry in 1953.[19] It is probable that the data published for the three years 1949, 1952, and 1955, were estimated by one of these two methods.

Statistics of Industrial Capital
(Tables 3.8 – 3.10)

In addition to the data on handicraft capital, figures on the amount of capital in modern industry are available for 1948 and 1949 and for 1952 through 1956, together with breakdowns by ownership of industrial establishments for 1949 – 55 and breakdowns between the net value of fixed assets and the amount of working capital for 1952 and 1955. Some other data are also available: the annual rate of increase of working capital of the central state enterprises during 1953 – 56 and the amount of working capital of the iron and steel enterprises under the Ministry of Metallurgical Industry for 1953 through 1956.

COMMERCIAL CAPITAL

While available data on industrial capital are very meagre, those on commercial capital are even more scarce. Only the following figures for private trade have been found:

1. Total capital of private trade and restaurants, 1950 – 55 (Table 3.12).
2. Total capital of private wholesale trade, with breakdowns by type of trading units, 1955 (Table 3.13).

In theory, the scope of commercial capital

should parallel that of industrial capital. In other words, commercial capital can also be measured on the basis of the net value of fixed assets and working capital, although the latter usually accounts for a much larger proportion of total capital in trade than in industry. In practice, however, such a measurement was not and could not be done for the private commercial sector. In China, the size of private trading units was extremely small, and, in fact, the majority did not employ workers. In 1955, for example, only 2 percent of the private trading units employed one worker, and another 2 percent had two employees or more.[20] This was because prior to the socialization of private trade, business capital and family property could not be easily distinguished. Furthermore, very few private trading units kept financial statements. As a result, the published figures on the amount of capital owned by private trade and restaurants were merely those registered with the government and reportedly varied greatly from actual figures.[21] Data on the capital of private wholesale trade in 1955 seem, however, to be more reliable, since they were based on a census survey undertaken in August of that year.[22]

ACCUMULATION

THE CONCEPT OF ACCUMULATION

The meaning of accumulation was explained in the previous section. To recapitulate, accumulation is composed of three types of investment: (1) net addition to fixed assets, (2) net increase in working capital, and (3) net increase in material reserves.

Net addition to fixed assets is the result of basic construction investment; its concept and measurement will be dealt with later in this section. It may be pointed out here that in the Chinese concept, accumulation does not include depreciation. Maintenance and replace-

[19]Yueh Wei, "Some Understanding from the Use of the Method of Estimation," *TCKTTH*, No. 18 (September 29, 1956), pp. 25 – 27, reference on p. 26.
[20]Ch'ien Hua *et al., op. cit.,* p. 13.
[21]*Ibid.,* p. 9.
[22]*Ibid.,* p. 132.

ment of productive fixed assets are excluded from national income (but included in the gross social value output), while those of nonproductive fixed assets are considered as a part of current consumption.

The second form of investment increases working capital in the productive sectors, such as raw materials, supplementary materials, fuel, spare parts for equipment, short-life and low-value articles, semi-finished and unfinished goods in industry, unfinished projects in basic construction, and young farm animals, seed, animal feed, fertilizers, and afforestation in agriculture.[23] The third and final type of investment serves to increase material reserves, which consist of inventories of the commercial sector and the stockpiles of the state (including military equipment).[24]

The Estimation of Accumulation

Accumulation is estimated from a "balance sheet of the distribution of accumulation" (*kuo-ming shou-ju chi-jui pu-feng ping-heng-piao*), which is prepared each year, containing data on changes in fixed assets, working capital, and material reserves. These data are taken from various annual statistical and accounting reports and survey findings.[25]

Since all the sectors covered by the state plan are required to prepare periodic reports on fixed assets, working capital, and material reserves, no serious difficulties are encountered in estimating accumulation for these sectors. But there are problems in the sectors outside the state plan, particularly agriculture.

Accumulation in agriculture consists of houses, farm implements, agricultural machinery, water conservation, repairs of bridges and roads, land reclamation, soil improvement, livestock, afforestation, and reserves of agricultural products including cash.[26] The First Five-Year Plan envisaged that agricultural accumulation would amount to 10 billion yuan, with 6 billion yuan invested in fixed assets and 4 billion yuan in working capital.[27] It is not known, however, to what extent the plan was fulfilled. The discussion of agricultural accumulation in the Chinese literature has revealed little statistical information at the national level, but it is frequently centered on conceptual and methodological problems. Two of them are most important and are worthy of mention here.

In the first place, there is the problem of valuing livestock. Chinese statistics include livestock of working age as fixed assets in agriculture and those below working age as a part of working capital. Data on the accumulation of certain agricultural producer cooperatives indicate that livestock, and especially cattle, constitute the most important forms cr parts of agricultural capital in China.[28] But livestock may not only be used as draught animals but may also provide a source of meat. Therefore, inclusion of all livestock in agricultural capital raises questions of concept. Furthermore, there exists the problem of measuring livestock as a form of capital. For example, how should the huge population of cattle and other draught animals be valued, particularly in view of the fact that a certain proportion of them have a negative productivity in the sense that they consume more than they add to the value of agricultural output? The discussion in China seems to have found no easy way out of these difficulties.

The second problem has to do with the measurement of the creation, extension, improvement, and upkeep of agricultural fixed assets by labor. Investment by peasants in the form of time and effort has played an important role in the formation of agricultural capital in China, but such investment has been disregarded in Chinese national income measurement. According to the surveys conducted in a number of agricultural producer cooperatives before the commune system came into being, the share of labor in the total cost of a number of projects was found to be as follows: 93 percent in irrigation work, 99 per cent in land reclamation and soil improvement, 73 percent in house building, and nearly 100 percent in afforestation.[29] In practice, only the material costs of these projects are included in the estimation of agricultural accumulation. As a result, statistical omission of labor inputs in the agricultural

[23]Yueh Wei, *op. cit.,* p. 63.

[24]*Ibid.;* and Hsu Ti-hsin, *An Analysis of China's National Economy in the Transition Period,* rev. ed., Peking: K'o-hsueh ch'u-pan-she, 1959, p. 261.

[25]Yueh Wei, *op. cit.*

[26]Wang Shu-pen, "Review of 'Preliminary Analysis of the Accumulation in the Lien-pan Agricultural Producer Cooperative' by Fukien Province," *TCYC,* No. 7 (July 23, 1958), pp. 13–17.

[27]*The First Five-Year Plan for the Development of the National Economy, 1953–1957,* Peking: Jen-min ch'u-pan-she, 1955, p. 26.

[28]Wang Shu-pen, *op. cit.*

[29]Yueh Wei, "On the Principles and Methods of Studying the Problem of Accumulation," *TCYC,* No. 5 (May 23, 1958), pp. 16–21, reference on p. 19.

sector tends to underestimate total accumulation. Such an underestimation is particularly misleading when estimates of accumulation are related to estimates of national income in the form of a ratio such as the so-called "rate of accumulation" (*chi-jui-lü*). The estimates of accumulation exclude labor investments in agriculture, while the national income figures include estimates of the value of the annual returns derived from these excluded investments. The rate of accumulation is, therefore, lower than the facts warrant, and conclusions drawn from these rates will be misleading. This has been recognized in China. In fact, in his 1958 article, Yueh Wei, who was responsible for the measurement work of national income at the State Statistical Bureau, argued for inclusion of labor inputs in the calculation of agricultural accumulation.[30]

ACCUMULATION STATISTICS

Figures on total accumulation have never been released officially, but some of them can be computed from percentage data given in Chinese publications. Generally speaking, available accumulation statistics fall into three groups: (1) total accumulation, (2) breakdowns of the total, and (3) accumulation in the industrial sector.

Total Accumulation at Current and at Constant Prices, 1952–58 (Table 3.14)

Figures on total accumulation at current and at 1952 and 1957 prices were derived in Table 2.7, where explanations are given as to how these figures were computed.

Breakdowns of Total Accumulation

PRODUCTIVE AND NONPRODUCTIVE ACCUMULATION AT 1952 PRICES, 1952–56 (TABLE 3.15)

Figures on productive and nonproductive accumulation at 1952 prices were derived from the data on percentage distribution between these two types of accumulation given by the State Statistical Bureau. Productive accumulation refers to "the material products accumu-

lated for expanded reproduction, such as machinery, equipment, factory buildings, railways, raw materials and fuels,"[31] Nonproductive accumulation includes residential housing, office buildings, clubs, auditoriums, warehouses for consumer goods, and other buildings for private, collective or social uses.[32]

DISTRIBUTION OF ACCUMULATION BETWEEN FIXED AND LIQUID ASSETS, AT 1952 PRICES, 1952–57 (TABLE 3.16)

Chinese statistics also distinguish between accumulation of fixed assets and liquid assets; the latter refer to working capital and material reserves. Figures on these two types of assets at 1952 prices can be computed from the data on their percentage distribution in accumulation, as they were given by the State Statistical Bureau for 1952 through 1957.

DISTRIBUTION OF ACCUMULATION BY TYPE OF OWNERSHIP, 1953 AND 1956 (TABLE 3.17)

Information on percentage distribution of accumulation among six sectors in the economy, as they were classified according to types of ownership (*i.e.,* state, joint, cooperative, individual, capitalist, and resident), was given by Niu Chung-huang for two years: 1953 and 1956. Since Niu did not explain whether these percentages were based on current or 1952 prices, the absolute figures cannot be computed.

Accumulation in the Industrial Sector

Data on the accumulation of various productive sectors are not available, except for industry for which the following information can be found:

1. Accumulation of heavy and light industry as percentages of state budgetary revenue for 1952 through 1955 and accumulation of handicraft cooperatives for 1955 and 1956 (Table 3.18).

2. Accumulation of the state enterprises in the paper industry for 1953 through 1957 (Table 3.19).

[30]*Ibid.*
[31]Research Office, SSB, "A Preliminary Analysis of Production and Distribution of China's National Income," *TCYC,* No. 1 (January, 1958), pp. 11–15, reference on p. 13.
[32]*Ibid.,* pp. 13–14.

BASIC CONSTRUCTION INVESTMENT

THE CONCEPT AND SCOPE OF BASIC CONSTRUCTION INVESTMENT

In China, "basic construction" (*chi-pen chien-she*) refers to the investment which will result in addition to the productive and nonproductive fixed assets.[33] Included in basic construction investment are not only expenditures on construction and installation and on purchases of machinery and equipment but also all such expenditures ancillary to the process of fixed capital formation as geological surveys and exploration, engineering design, scientific testing and research, workers' training, and compensation for moving expenses paid to the original residents on construction sites.[34]

Basic construction investment falls both within and outside the state plan. Included in the state plan are the basic construction activities undertaken by "the state-operated enterprises (central and local, Sino-Soviet jointly-operated enterprises, and other undertakings of various ministries and independent agencies of the State Council and of the People's Councils of all the provinces, autonomous regions and municipalities."[35] The state plan covers the following sectors, which are under the control of the central or local governments: industry, agriculture, forestry, water conservation, meteorological services, transportation, education, health, culture, broadcasting, athletics, urban public utilities, and construction.[36]

Basic construction investment outside the state plan consists primarily of investment by union and cooperative organizations, by state and joint enterprises with their premium funds or workers' welfare funds, and by the state in newly organized joint enterprises. Basic construction work undertaken outside the country by government agencies, such as the Ministry of Foreign Trade and the Ministry of Foreign Affairs, is not considered in the state plan and hence becomes a part of investment outside the state plan.[37]

The investments within and outside the state plan as thus defined constitute the total amount of basic construction investment. Therefore, this concept does not include investment by private enterprises, agricultural collectives, and individual handicraftsmen.

THE VALUATION OF BASIC CONSTRUCTION INVESTMENT

Official data on annual basic construction investment are given at so-called current budgetary prices (*hsien-hsin yü-shüan-chia ko*). These prices are used in setting up the basic construction budget for the year and differ from the actual prices prevailing in the market. For every construction project, there is a corresponding budgetary price. When a construction budget has been planned and designed and is to be included in the budget, its budgetary price is calculated. The price is the value of the amount of labor, materials, and equipment to be consumed for the project, plus a percentage markup to cover indirect costs and a percentage markup for profit.[38] Budgetary appropriations for basic construction are the sum of each of the construction projects planned for the year multiplied by its budgetary price.

When a budget year comes to an end, basic construction investment for the year is determined from the volume of work actually completed by various projects valued at their original budgetary prices. The resulting figure is the completed amount of basic construction investment (*chi-pen chien-she tou-tzu wang-ch'eng-o*) within the state plan for the year.[39] Investment completed outside the state plan, which is only a small portion of the total investment, is valued at actual cost.[40] The sum of the basic construction investment completed within and outside the state plan equals the completed amount of total basic construction investment.

[33]Yun Chung, *Basic Construction in China* (*Wo-kuo ti chi-pen chien-she*), Peking: Kung-jen chu-pan-she, 1956, p. 3.
[34]*First Five-Year Plan for the Development of the National Economy, 1953–1957, op. cit.*, p. 23, footnote.
For convenience, all the expenses ancillary to the process of fixed capital formation will be classified under "ancillary expenses" in the statistical tables. It should be noted that this term is not used in China. It first appeared in Cho-Ming Li's *Economic Development of Communist China* (Berkeley: University of California Press, 1959), pp. 113–14, and later was also used by Ta-chung Liu and Kung-chia Yeh. (*Economy of the Chinese Mainland: National Income and Economic Development, 1933–1959*, Princeton, N.J.: Princeton University Press, 1965), pp. 230–36.
[35]Peng Jung-chuan. "The Tabular Forms for Basic Construction Planning," *CHCC*, No. 5 (May 9, 1957), pp. 29–33, reference on p. 30.
[36]*Ibid.*
[37]*Ibid.*
[38]Lung Hua-yung, Chi Hsi-yung, and Chen Min-kai, "Several Problems Concerning the Measurement of the Value Output of Construction." *TCKT*, No. 8 (April 29, 1957), pp. 14–16, reference on p. 15. Therefore, the procedure of determining budgetary price is similar to the average-cost-plus, or full-cost, pricing method frequently used by businessmen in the West.
[39]"Several Problems Concerning the Methods of Measuring the Completed Amount of Basic Construction Investment," *TCKT*, No. 10 (May 29, 1957), pp. 4–8, reference on pp. 5–6.
[40]Lung Hua-yung, Chi Hsi-yung, and Chen Min-kai, p. 15.

Two major defects of the official pricing method of basic construction investment caused a considerable amount of discussion among statisticians in China during 1957–58.[41] In the first place, the annual completed investment valued at current budgetary prices does not represent the actual amount of money capital invested in basic construction for the year. In other words, official data on annual investment do not measure faithfully the actual value of basic construction completed during the year.[42] Secondly, the fact that investment data are not given in constant prices makes intertemporal comparisons difficult. The use of constant budgetary prices was reportedly under consideration, but there is no indication that this has been done.

BASIC CONSTRUCTION INVESTMENT STATISTICS

There are two groups of official data on basic construction investment: one is given in terms of monetary value and the other in terms of physical volume.

The Value Data

There exist two types of value data on basic construction investment: budgetary appropriations and the amount completed.

BASIC CONSTRUCTION APPROPRIATIONS, 1952–57 (TABLE 3.20)

The appropriation figures were given in current budgetary prices for 1952–56 by Feng Chi-hsi in the December, 1957, issue of *Statistical Work* (*TCKT*), and for 1957 in an official budget report for that year. No figures on breakdown by sector are available except for agriculture, for which statistics appeared in the February, 1958, issue of *Planned Economy* (*CHCC*).

The amount of appropriations and that of completed investment differ in two respects. In the first place, while both are valued at the same budgetary prices, the former represents the volume of work planned and the latter that actually completed. Secondly, they differ in coverage: the former covers only the sectors in the state plan, while the latter includes those outside the state plan as well.[43]

DATA ON THE COMPLETED AMOUNT OF BASIC CONSTRUCTION INVESTMENT

Data on the completed amount of basic construction investment may be presented in three groups: (1) total basic construction investment, (2) basic construction investment within the state plan, and (3) basic construction investment in the industrial sector.

TOTAL COMPLETED AMOUNT
OF BASIC CONSTRUCTION
INVESTMENT AT CURRENT PRICES

Within and Outside the State Plan, 1950–59 (Table 3.21)
Ten Great Years gives figures on the amount of total basic construction investment and on that within the state plan for 1950–58. Investment outside the state plan can thus be derived as a residual. State investment data also appear in the annual communiqués of the State Statistical Bureau for 1952–59, either in absolute amount or in terms of percentage rate of increase. These two series appear to be largely consistent with each other, and the slight discrepancies that exist for a few years are probably due to rounding errors.

National Minority Areas, 1950–58 (Table 3.22)
Statistics on basic construction investment in the national minority areas are shown in *Ten Great Years* for 1950–58. These areas are not defined in the original source but probably refer to Inner Mongolia Autonomous Region, Sinkiang Uihur Autonomous Region, Kwangsi Chuan Autonomous Region, Ningsia Hui Autonomous Region, Tibet and Chamdo area, and all the autonomous *chou* and *hsien* throughout the country.

[41] "Several Problems. . . . ," *TCKT*, No. 10 (May 29, 1957), *op. cit.,* "Several Problems Concerning the Adoption of Constant Budgetary Prices in Basic Construction,"*TCKT*, No. 1 (January, 1957), pp. 10–15; Kuo Keng-Chih, "Some Views on the Selection of Research Topics on Basic Construction Statistics," *TCKT*, No. 4 (February 28, 1957), pp. 9–11; and Yang Pan-chieh, "A Proposal for the Adoption of Constant Prices in the Preparation of Basic Construction Planning and Budget," *CHCC*, No. 2 (February 9, 1958), pp. 30–31.

[42] More on this point will be discussed later in this section.

[43] For a basic construction unit, the difference between the amount of appropriations and that of investment may be shown as follows: Basic construction investment = basic construction appropriations − the value of materials, machinery, and equipment purchased in the current year but to be used in the following year + the value of materials, machinery, and equipment, as well as cash balances, carried over from the preceding year + the value of machinery and equipment received without compensation + the value output of construction done by mobilizing military personnel and civilians + investment funds originating outside the state budget + incomes of the basic construction unit. (See Peng Jung-chuan, *op. cit.,* p. 31.)

By Sectors, 1952–58 (Tables 3.23 and 3.24)

Ten Great Years also gives total basic construction investment figures with breakdowns by thirteen sectors. These sectors are (1) industry; (2) construction; (3) geological survey; (4) agriculture, forestry, and meteorological services; (5) water conservation; (6) railways; (7) other transports and post and tele-communication; (8) trade; (9) culture, education, and scientific research; (10) health and welfare; (11) urban public utilities; (12) general administration; and (13) other, probably including housing, finance, and engineering design. The classification of these sectors is made on a functional rather than on an administrative basis. For example, the construction of a school building by a factory for its workers' children is considered as investment in education. It would be classified as industrial investment if the administrative criterion is used.

Figures on basic construction investment by sector at the provincial level are available for the Inner Mongolia Autonomous Region for 1952 through 1958. The data are also broken down into thirteen major sectors, but the groupings are slightly different from those of the national data. The original source did not indicate whether these groupings were made on a functional or on an administrative basis.

Productive and Nonproductive Investment, 1952–57 (Table 3.25)

Figures on productive and nonproductive basic construction investment can be derived from the data on percentage distribution between these two types of investment given for 1952–55 in *Ten Great Years* and for 1956–57 in the February and April, 1958, issues of *Planned Economy* (*CHCC*). Productive investment refers to the amount completed in the productive sectors, such as industry, agriculture, forestry, water conservation, transportation, and other material sectors, while investment in housing, culture, education, and other nonmaterial sectors is considered nonproductive.[44]

Investment in New Construction, Reconstruction and Rehabilitation (Tables 3.26 and 3.27)

Total investment in new construction and in reconstruction and rehabilitation of existing enterprises can be derived for 1952 and 1955

from the percentage data given in the September, 1956, issue of *Statistical Work Bulletin* (*TCKTTH*). Rehabilitation refers to the construction work for recovering damaged structures to their original scale. Reconstruction means enlarging the scale of existing plants and expanding their productive capacity. New construction includes new engineering projects and the existing plants which have been expanded to such a size that the newly added value of fixed assets is at least three times as large as the full replacement cost of the original fixed assets.[45] It may be pointed out that under Chinese practice major repairs are not included in basic construction investment.[46]

Provincial data are available for Liaoning Province during the period 1952–58. Investment in new construction, reconstruction, and rehabilitation is, however, given only in terms of percentages of total basic construction investment in the province, and no absolute figures are available.

Additions to the Gross Value of Fixed Assets and Ancillary Expenses, 1950–58 (Table 3.28)

It has been pointed out that basic construction investment consists of additions to the gross value of fixed assets and ancillary expenses. The former comprise the cost of construction and installation and the payment for purchases of machinery and equipment, while unfinished construction projects and machinery and equipment to be installed are excluded. Data on the additions to the gross value of fixed assets are given in *Ten Great Years* for 1950 through 1958, and those on the cost of construction and installation can be found for 1953 through 1955 in the December, 1956, issue of *Statistical Work Bulletin* (*TCKTTH*). Figures on the cost of purchases of machinery and equipment can be derived as residuals. Ancillary expenses may be obtained by subtracting additions to the gross value of fixed assets from total basic construction investment during 1950–58. Expenditures on geological surveys and engineering design have been reportedly excluded from basic construction investment since 1955[47] but, as Table 3.21 shows, these

[44]Lu Ko, "Basic Construction Statistics," *TCKTTH*, No. 13 (July 14, 1956), pp. 30–33, reference on p. 31.
[45]Peng Jung-chuan, *op. cit.*, p. 29.
[46]Ko Chih-ta, *China's Budget during the Transition Period (Kuo-tu shih-chi ti chung-kuo yü-shuan)*, Peking: Financial Publishing House, 1957, pp. 81–82.
[47]*Ibid.*, p. 30; and Ko Chih-ta, *op. cit.*, p. 110.

expenditures are still included in the data given in *Ten Great Years.*

Additions to the Gross Value of Productive and Nonproductive Fixed Assets (Tables 3.29 and 3.30)

Statistics of investment in productive and nonproductive fixed assets for the economy as a whole are shown in *Ten Great Years* for 1952 through 1958. Provincial data are available for the Inner Mongolia Autonomous Region for 1953 through 1957. Investment in productive fixed assets includes "factory buildings, machinery and equipment used for production purposes, railways, highways, harbors, wharves and other transport facilities, warehouses for commercial and banking undertakings, etc."[48] Additions to the gross value of non-productive fixed assets refer to investment in "housing, school buildings, hospitals, nurseries, cinemas and theaters, clubs, dining halls and offices for government and people's organizations."[49]

Additions to the Gross Value of Industrial and Nonindustrial Fixed Assets (Tables 3.31 and 3.32)

Figures on the additions to the gross value of industrial fixed assets in the country are given for 1950 through 1958 in *Ten Great Years,* and those of nonindustrial fixed assets can be computed. Provincial data can be found for the Inner Mongolia Autonomous Region for 1953 through 1958. The distinction in classification between industrial and nonindustrial fixed assets is based on the nature of these assets, that is, whether or not they are used for industrial production. On an administrative basis, the additions to the gross value of industrial fixed assets in the economy during the First Five-Year Plan would have been 21.4 billion yuan.[50]

BASIC CONSTRUCTION INVESTMENT
COMPLETED WITHIN THE STATE PLAN

By Sector, at Current Prices (Except for 1955), 1952–57 (Table 3.33)

Information on basic construction investment within the state plan in 10 sectors for 1952 through 1957 can be found in the State Statistical Bureau communiqués for 1955 and 1956, the *1956 People's Handbook,* the Febru-

ary, 1957, issue of *Statistical Work (TCKT),* and Po I-po's report on the 1958 economic plan. The 10 sectors are industry; construction; agriculture; water conservation; railways; other transports and posts and tele-communications; urban public utilities; housing; trade and finance; and education and health. It should be noted that the basis for classifying these sectors is administrative and, therefore, differs from the functional basis used for grouping sectors in Table 3.23.

The data are expressed in terms of current prices except for 1955, for which the figures are given in so-called "prices comparable to previous years."[51] The use of comparable prices was due to an unusually heavy drop in the prices of construction materials and of machinery and equipment in 1955, beginning in June of that year. Thus, investment within the state plan in 1955 amounted to 8,212 million yuan in comparable prices, but to 8,630 million yuan in current prices. The investment at current prices in 1955, as may be recalled, was not valued at current market prices but at current budgetary prices which were primarily determined by the market prices prevailing in 1954, when the 1955 budget was being prepared. Hence, valuation at current budgetary prices would yield inflationary bias to the investment figure for 1955, while the figure priced on a comparable basis would represent the actual costs of basic construction in that year.

Additions to the Gross Value of Fixed Assets and Ancillary Expenses, 1953–57 (Table 3.34)

Additions to the gross value of fixed assets within the state plan during the period 1953–57 were reported to be 41.1 billion yuan in a number of publications, including *Ten Great Years* and the State Statistical Bureau communiqué on the implementation of the First Five-Year Plan. Data on annual additions can be derived for only three years (1954 through 1956) from the information given in the State Statistical Bureau communiqué for 1955 and in the *People's Daily* (June 16, 1956, and August 2, 1957). Ancillary expenses can be derived as residuals from basic construction investment and increases in the gross value of fixed assets.

[48]*TGY,* p. 64.
[49]*Ibid.*
[50]*Ibid.,* p. 66.
[51]SSB, *Communiqué on the Results of Implementation of the 1955 National Economic Plan,* Peking: T'ung-chi ch'u-pan-she, 1956, p. 28.

BASIC CONSTRUCTION INVESTMENT
IN INDUSTRY AT CURRENT PRICES

*Basic Construction Investment in Industry,
1950–58 (Table 3.35)*

Data on basic construction investment in
industry at current prices were given by Chao
I-wen for 1952 through 1956, by the Department of Industrial Statistics of the State Statistical Bureau for 1950 through 1956, and in *Ten
Great Years* for 1952 through 1958. Small discrepancies exist in these series for 1953, 1954,
and 1956, probably because of revisions made
for the *Ten Great Years* series.

*Basic Construction Investment in Industry
Within and Outside the State Plan, 1952–57
(Table 3.36)*

Basic construction investment in industry
within the state plan for 1952 through 1957 was
presented in Table 3.28. Industrial investment
outside the state plan can be computed as a
residual from total industrial investment and the
amount completed within the state plan.

*Industrial Basic Construction Investment in
Coastal and Inland Areas,*[52] *1950–55 (Table
3.37)*

Figures on annual industrial investment in
coastal and inland areas are not available, but
those for the periods 1950–52 and 1953–55
may be computed from percentages given in the
November, 1956, issue of the *Statistical Work
Bulletin (TCKTTH).*

*Additions to the Gross Value of Industrial
Fixed Assets and Ancillary Expenses in Industry, 1950–58 (Table 3.38)*

Information on annual additions to the gross
value of industrial fixed assets for 1950–58 is
contained in *Ten Great Years*. These figures
may be used to derive ancillary expenses of
basic construction in industry.

*Basic Construction Investment in Heavy and
Light Industries and in Producer Goods and
Consumer Goods Industries, 1952–58
(Tables 3.39 and 3.40)*

As will be seen in the section on industry,
Chinese statistics distinguish between heavy
and light industries and between producer and
consumer goods industries. Annual investment
statistics at the national level in heavy and light

industries were published for 1952–58 in *Ten
Great Years*, but with respect to investment in
producer goods and consumer goods industries,
only percentages in total investment can be
found for the First Five-Year Plan Period. Investment data at the provincial level are available for heavy and light industries in the Inner
Mongolia Autonomous Region for 1952–58.

*Basic Construction Investment within the State
Plan in Selected Industries (Table 3.41)*

Fragmentary data on state investment in a
number of industries can be gathered for the
years prior to 1957.

1. *The Iron-and-Steel Industry for
1952–57, with Above-Norm Investment for
1953–57.* The "above-norm" or "below-norm"
investment refers to a standard amount of investment. When basic construction investment
of a certain project is larger than the standard
amount, the project is "above the norm" and
subject to the direct control of the State Economic Commission. If investment is "below the
norm," the project comes under the control of
various ministries, provincial governments, and
governments of autonomous regions and of independent municipalities. The "norm" varies
with different industries; it was 10 million yuan
for the iron-and-steel industry for the First
Five-Year Plan.[53]

2. *The coal industry* for the period
1950–52 and 1953–57 and for the years 1950,
1953, and 1956.

3. *The petroleum industry* for the period
1953–57.

4. *The metal processing industry* for the
periods 1950–52 and 1953–57 and for the
years 1952–56, as well as *the machine-building
industry* for 1952–57.

5. *The building materials industry* for the
period 1950–52 and for the year of 1952.

6. *The textile industry* for 1950–56, together with *the cotton textile industry* for the
same years and *the enterprises for the Ministry
of Textile Industry* for 1952–56.

7. *The state enterprises of the paper industry* for 1950–57 with data on annual additions
to the gross value of fixed assets for 1950–56.

[52]For the definitions of coastal and inland areas, see the section on industry.
[53]*First Five-Year Plan for the Development of the National Econ-omy, 1953–1957, op. cit.,* p. 18.

The Physical Data

Physical data of investment contain information on the volume of basic construction work done in industry, water conservation, transport, building, urban construction, geological survey, and engineering design. These data cover only state investment in basic construction and are given in *Ten Great Years* and the annual communiques issued by the State Statistical Bureau. The data may be grouped as follows:

1. *Industry.* Number of major projects completed or under construction in 10 industries during the period 1953 – 58 (Table 3.42). The term "major projects" is not defined in the original source, but available evidence indicates that these projects refer to the "above-norm" projects. These ten industries and their standard amounts for above-norm projects are as follows:[54]

a. Coal industry – 5 million yuan.
b. Electric power industry – 5 million yuan.
c. Petroleum industry – 5 million yuan.
d. Ferrous metals industry – 10 millian yuan.
e. Chemical industry – 6 million yuan.
f. Building materials industry – 6 million yuan.
g. Metal processing industry – 5 million yuan.
h. Textile industry – 5 million yuan.
i. Paper industry – 4 million yuan.
j. Food industry – 4 million yuan for the sugar industry and 3 million yuan for other food industries.

2. *Water conservation.* Major reservoirs built during the period 1950 – 58 (Table 3.43). Information is given for 23 reservoirs with respect to their location, dates of completion, and storage capacity expressed in cubic meters.

3. *Transport*
a. Length of railway track built and repaired for 1950 through 1958, in kilometers (Table 3.44).
b. Major railways built during the period 1950 – 58, in kilometers (Table 3.45).
c. Major bridges built during the period 1950 – 58, with their location and length in meters (Table 3.46).

d. Length of highways built and repaired for 1950 through 1958, in kilometers (Table 3.47).
e. Major trunk highways built during the period 1952 – 58, with their location and length in kilometers (Table 3.48).
f. Annual increase in railway and highway mileage in the Inner Mongolia Autonomous Region, given in kilometers, for 1949 through 1958 (Table 3.49).

4. *Buildings*
a. New buildings constructed during 1953 through 1957, in square meters of floor space (Table 3.50).
b. New school buildings constructed during 1950 through 1958, with breakdowns into institutes of higher learning, normal middle schools, middle schools, and primary schools, in square meters of floor space (Table 3.51).
c. New buildings in the Inner Mongolia Autonomous Region given in square meters of floor space for 1952 through 1958, with breakdowns by factories, houses, and schools (Table 3.52).

5. *Urban construction.* Construction of urban public utilities for the country as a whole in 1949, 1952, 1957, and 1958 and for the Inner Mongolia Autonomous Region in 1952, 1957, and 1958.

Data are published on water supply, urban transport facilities and number of passengers carried, and road drainage construction (Tables 3.53 and 3.54).

6. *Engineering and geological survey*
a. Data on the volume of work of engineering design are given in terms of designed plant capacity for 1952, 1957, and 1958 for a number of industries, such as coal mining, electric power, iron and steel, machine building, paper, and sugar (Table 3.55).
b. Data on the volume of work of geological prospecting are given in meters drilled or tested, for the country as a whole during 1952 – 58, and for the Inner Mongolia Autonomous Region during 1953 – 58 (Tables 3.56 and 3.57).

[54]*Ibid.*

4

INDUSTRY

CONCEPT AND CLASSIFICATIONS OF INDUSTRY

THE CONCEPT AND SCOPE OF INDUSTRY

By Chinese definition, industry is "the materially productive sector of extracting and collecting natural material wealth in whose creation no human efforts are involved, and of processing such wealth and agricultural products."[1] Therefore, industry comprises three major sectors: (1) extracting, (2) collecting, and (3) processing. Extracting industries refer to the mining of coal, fuel, iron ores, and the like; collecting activities in industry include logging, fishing, and hunting; and processing industries, whose output value accounts for the lion's share of the value of total industrial output, embraces manufacture and the repair of industrial products.[2]

The concept and scope of the various so-called "materially productive" sectors were explained in the section on national income. It is useful to explore further here how industry is distinguished from other productive sectors, according to Chinese usage.

Industry and Agriculture

Agriculture, in principle, is composed of crop-planting and animal-raising.[3] In practice, a substantial amount of industrial activity occurs in rural areas. Such activities, as already pointed out, include collecting wild fruits and herbs, hunting wild animals, and fishing by peasants during off-seasons. They include also the processing, for sale and for peasants' own use,

of agricultural products, such as grinding grains and slaughtering animals, and of industrial products, such as tailoring and making shoes and socks. All these activities are industrial in nature. Prior to agricultural communalization, they were classified in Chinese statistics as a part of agriculture if they were sideline occupations of peasants but as a part of handicraft industry if they were engaged in by independent handicraftsmen in rural areas.[4]

Since the introduction of the commune system in 1958, many industrial establishments have been set up in rural areas. As a result, a new criterion for the demarcation between industry and agriculture was adopted in 1959.[5] Industrial establishments in rural areas are considered as a part of industry if they are directly operated by communes but as subsidiary occupations in agriculture if they are run by basic accounting units of communes.[6]

Industry and Construction

As has been indicated, construction activities include primarily the building of structures and of railways and highways as well as the installation of machinery and equipment. Building materials and machinery and equipment are products of industrial activities. Construction and industry are closely related, particularly because machinery and equipment is frequently installed by its manufacturers and because con-

[1]Department of Statistics and Planning, Hupeh University, *Industrial Statistics*, Wuhan: Hupeh jen-min ch'u-pan-she, 1960, p. 7.
[2]*Ibid.*, pp. 7–8.
[3]*Ibid.*, p. 8. See also the section on national income for the discussion of the concept of agriculture.
[4]*Ibid.*, pp. 9–10.
[5]*Ibid.*, p. 11.
[6]A basic accounting unit of the commune was the "production brigade" prior to 1960 but since then has been changed to the "production team."

struction enterprises sometimes are engaged in the production of building materials on construction sites. In China, the following criteria are used to distinguish between industry and construction: (1) the installation of machinery and equipment is considered as an industrial activity if it is done by manufacturers but as a part of construction if it is carried out by construction enterprises; (2) subsidiary production units on a construction site are regarded as industrial enterprises if they have a separate labor force and an independent balance sheet; otherwise, they are included in construction.[7]

Industry and Freight Transport

In theory, there are two types of transport in connection with industrial production. One type is the so-called "transport within a factory" (*ch'ang-nei yün-shu*), referring to the shipment of materials and unfinished and finished products between warehouses and shops and from one shop to another. Transport within a factory is a part of the production process and, therefore, falls within the sphere of industrial production. The other type is "transport outside a factory" (*ch'ang-wai yün-shu*), which is concerned with moving finished products from the factory to places of consumption and consequently belongs to freight transport. In practice, however, such a distinction between industry and freight transport may not be so clear-cut. In many factories where there is a long distance between warehouses and shops or between shops, the shipment of materials and products within the factory is frequently performed by freight transport enterprises. On the other hand, some factories at times are directly engaged in the transportation of finished products to consumers and other producers for consumption. Under Chinese practice, the following criteria are adopted for the distinction between industry and freight transport: the shipment of materials and products, both inside and outside a factory, belongs to freight transport if performed by a specialized transport enterprise but is a part of industrial production if carried out by the factory itself.[8]

Industry and Trade

The major function of trade is to transfer products from producers to consumers. Thus, trade differs from industry in that the latter is

engaged in the production of commodities, while the former is engaged in their distribution. In actuality, however, trade and industry are not mutually exclusive. Many industrial enterprises also participate in selling activities, while work of an industrial nature may be found frequently in the commercial sector. In order to distinguished trade from industry, the following criteria have been adopted in China:[9]

1. An establishment which is engaged in the production and selling of products is classified as an industrial enterprise.
2. An establishment whose primary function is to sell products produced by others but which also is engaged in the production of some commodities as a subsidiary activity is regarded as a commercial enterprise.
3. An establishment whose primary function is to sell products but which also is engaged in packaging, drying, selecting, or repairing these products is included in trade.
4. An establishment which primarily sells spare parts for machinery and equipment but also is engaged in installation and repairing services is considered a commercial enterprise.

Industry and Restaurants

Restaurant trade, like the foodstuffs industry, is engaged in the production of food by processing industrial and agricultural products. But unlike the foodstuffs industry, restaurants also sell food directly to customers. Included in restaurant trade are restaurants, dining halls, grills, bars, cafés, and tea rooms. The foodstuffs industry is restricted to processing and is not involved in retailing activities.

CLASSIFICATIONS OF INDUSTRY

Chinese sources give several standard groupings of industry. Included are (1) classification by branches (electric power, coal, iron and steel, etc.) and sub-branches; (2) grouping of these branches and sub-branches into heavy and light industry, as well as producer goods and consumer goods industry; (3) division into large- and small-scale industry according to the size of enterprises; (4) breakdown between modern industry and handicrafts; (5) break-

[7]*Ibid.*, p. 12.
[8]*Ibid.*, p. 13.
[9]*Ibid.*, p. 14.

down by ownership of enterprise; (6) division into central and local industry; (7) grouping into industrial enterprises, urban handicraft industry, and communal industry; and (8) classification by area, such as inland and coastal areas, or according to administrative division, such as provinces and equivalents.

Grouping of Industry by Branches

According to the 1957 edition of *Catalogue for Standard Classification of Industrial Departments*, issued by the State Statistical Bureau, industry in China is grouped into 21 major branches with 250 sub-branches. These 21 major branches are shown as follows:[10]

1. Electric power
2. Fuel
3. Ferrous metals
4. Nonferrous metals
5. Metal processing
6. Chemicals
7. Rubber
8. Nonmetallic mining
9. Building materials
10. Glass
11. Ceramics
12. Lumber
13. Matches
14. Paper-making
15. Textiles
16. Tailoring
17. Leather
18. Fats and cosmetics
19. Food
20. Cultural, educational, and art supplies
21. Other

The grouping of industry into the above branches is made principally on the basis of the "economic use of the products produced."[11] This is not, however, the only criterion employed. In some cases, types of raw material used are also taken into account.[12] For example, a factory producing leather footwear and a factory producing rubber footwear do not belong to the same industry, although their products are close substitutes for one another, because these factories use different types of raw material. Leather footwear factories are included in the leather industry, while rubber footwear factories are considered as a part of the rubber industry.

In other cases, classification of industry also depends upon "the nature of the technological process of production."[13] For example, a weaving factory and a knitting factory are not grouped in the same industry, although they produce products substitutable for one another and use the same type of raw materials. This is because weaving and knitting factories are quite different in the degree of mechanization of the production process. Thus, in China weaving factories are included in the textile industry, while knitting factories are in the tailoring industry.

Heavy and Light Industries; Producer Goods and Consumer Goods Industries

In Chinese planning and statistics, the various branches of industry are classified further into two major divisions: heavy and light industry. The former is defined as that producing producer goods and the latter, consumer goods.[14] Heavy industry is composed of electric power, coal-ming, petroleum, iron and steel, nonferrous metals, metal-processing, basic chemicals, building materials, and lumber, while light industry includes paper, textile, food-processing, pharmaceuticals, leather, printing, and other industries manufacturing daily necessities.[15]

Official definitions that identify heavy and light industries as producer goods and consumer goods industries bring forth inconsistencies. A good part of the products of heavy industry are used for consumption purposes and, therefore, in fact, belong to the category of consumer goods, e.g., electricity, coal, and kerosene. On the other hand, the products of light industry cannot be wholly identified as consumer goods, since some of them are used as producer goods, e.g., paper and simple farm tools. Because of such difficulties in definition, discussion about the distinction between heavy and light industry and producer and consumer goods industries has been going on in China since early 1957, and a number of classification methods have

[10]*Ibid.*, p. 442.
[11]*Ibid.*, p. 440.
[12]*Ibid.*
[13]*Ibid.*
[14]State Planning Commission, *Brief Explanations of the Terminologies in the First Five-Year Plan for the Development of the National Economy of the People's Republic of China*; Peking: People's Publishing House, 1955, p. 1.
[15]*Ibid.*, and State Planning Commission. *The First Five-Year Plan for the Development of the National Economy of the People's Republic of China*, Peking: People's Publishing House, 1955, pp. 41–68.

been suggested.[16] Statistical data published in China since 1956 have frequently distinguished heavy and light industries from producer goods and consumer goods industries, although no new official definitions can be found.

Large- and Small-Scale Industrial Enterprises

In Chinese statistics, a distinction is made between large-scale and small-scale industrial enterprises, depending on the number of workers employed and on whether or not motive power is used.[17] According to the State Planning Commission, the criteria for demarcation between large- and small-scale enterprises are as follows:[18]

1. Any establishment with mechanical power is classified as a large-scale enterprise if it has 16 or more workers and employees; otherwise, it is a small-scale enterprise.
2. Any establishment with no mechanical power is regarded large if the number of its workers and employees is 31 or more, otherwise, it is small.
3. All independent electric power plants with a capacity of over 15 kilowatts are considered as large-scale enterprises, regardless of the size of the work force employed.

Large-scale enterprises sometimes are subclassified further according to the size of employment. Standard groupings of the subclassification are (1) 16 or 31 to 99 persons, (2) 100 to 499 persons, (3) 1,000 to 4,999 persons, (4) 5,000 to 9,999 persons, and (5) 10,000 persons and more.[19]

Modern Industry and Individual Handicrafts

Another standard classification of industry in China is the division between modern industry and individual handicraft operators not engaged in agriculture.[20] Modern industry is composed of modern factories and handicraft factories.[21] Modern factories refer to "those industrial establishments with modernized techniques and equipment, whose production processes are carried out by machines."[22] Handicraft factories are "a kind of corporate enterprise *(hsieh-tso)* based on the division of work processes and on the skills of hand labor; their principal processes still use hand labor for production. Handicraft factories do not include individual handicrafts.[23]

Both handicraft factories and individual handicrafts are characterized by the use of hand labor in their principal production processes. The distinction between them lies in the number of workers employed. Individual handicraftsmen are "those engaged in handicraft production with the labor of their own or of their family members without hired workers or apprentices, or with three or less hired workers and apprentices.[24] Any handicraft establishment with four or more hired workers is considered a handicraft factory. A handicraft factory remains a small-scale enterprise as long as the number of its workers does not exceed 30.

Grouping of Industry by Ownership of Enterprises

Ownership of enterprises is one of the most important criteria adopted in China for the classification of industry. According to this

[16]The question of distinguishing heavy and light industries from producer goods and consumer goods industries was first raised in February, 1957. [Tzu Ssu, "Producer Goods and Products of Heavy Industry are Conceptually Different," *HH*, No. 3 (February 3, 1957), p. 23.] Since then, a number of criteria have been suggested for improving the classification of heavy and light industries. The discussion can be found in the following articles:
Li Hui-hung, Sun Chi-jen, and Wang Hua-hsin. "Views on the Problem of Classifying Light and Heavy Industry," *TCKT*, No. 18 (September 29, 1957), pp. 13–15.
Chen Tsen-yu. "On the Methods of Classifying Producer Goods and Consumer Goods," *TCYC*, No. 18 (September 29, 1957), pp. 16–18.
Liu You-chin. "On the Problems of Classifying Light and Heavy Industry," *TCYC*, No. 7 (July 23, 1958), pp. 18–21.
Hsu Ping-wen. "The Relationship between the Classification of the Two Major Divisions of Social Products and the Classification of Agriculture, Light Industry, and Heavy Industry," *TKP*, March 30, 1962.
Chu Chao-chin. "Looking at the Relationships among Agriculture, Light Industry and Heavy Industry from the Relationships between the Two Major Divisions of Social Products," *KMJP*, August 13, 1962.
Wang Hu-sheng, "Some Problems Concerning the Classification of Heavy Industry and Light Industry," *CCYC*, No. 4 (April 17, 1963), pp. 16–26.
[17]Industrial enterprises in light industry sometimes are classified into three groups according to the size of employment: small, medium, and large. Enterprises with 100 workers or less are considered small. Enterprises are of medium size if the number of workers employed is between 101 and 500 persons but are large if the size of employment exceeds 500 persons. (See "Lectures on Fundamentals of Industrial Management," *Chung-kuo ch'ing-kung-yeh (Light Industry in China)*, No. 18 (September 28, 1959), pp. 33–34, reference on p. 33.)
[18]State Planning Commisssion, *Brief Explanations . . . , op. cit.*, p. 2.
[19]Department of Planning and Statistics, Hupeh University, *op. cit.*, pp. 447.
[20]This classification was regarded very important prior to 1956, when a large proportion of individual handicraft operators joined handicraft producer cooperatives.
[21]The classification of modern industry into modern factories and handicraft factories was reportedly to be eliminated in the 1958 economic planning. [See Department of Methodology, Bureau of Comprehensive Planning of National Economy, State Planning Commission, "Explanations of Major Changes in the Tabular Form for the 1958 National Economic Planning," *CHCC*, No. 8 (August 9, 1957), pp. 24–27; reference on p. 24.] But available evidence indicates that such a classification was still effective as of 1960. (See Department of Statistics and Planning, Hupeh University, *op. cit.*, p. 448.)
[22]State Planning Commission, *Brief Explanations . . . , op. cit.*
[23]*Ibid.*
[24]*Ibid.*

criterion, industrial enterprises are classified into four groups: (1) state-operated enterprises, (2) cooperative enterprises, (3) state-private jointly operated enterprises, and (4) private enterprises.

Two types of state-operated enterprises can be distinguished: centrally controlled state enterprises and locally controlled state enterprises. The former are those under the control of various industrial ministries of the central government, while the latter refer to the state enterprises within the jurisdiction of local governments.[25]

Cooperative enterprises include the processing factories of supply and marketing cooperatives and handicraft producer cooperatives.[26]

State-private jointly operated enterprises are those whose capital assets are owned jointly by the state and individual capitalists. State-appointed officials and capitalists are jointly responsible for the management of these enterprises.[27]

Private enterprises, referring to those with privately owned capital assets, are broken down into two groups: capitalist enterprises and residential enterprises (chü-min chi-yeh). Private enterprises with four or more workers are considered capitalist; otherwise, they are residential. Residential enterprises comprise primarily individual handicrafts.

Since by 1958–59 private enterprises had been nearly eliminated in China, and since a great number of industrial enterprises were then operated by the people's communes, the category of private enterprises had been superseded by that of commune-operated enterprises in the classification of industry by form of ownership.[28]

Central and Local Industry

The division between central and local industry is made in accordance with the jurisdiction within which industrial enterprises fall. Central industry includes the enterprises under the control of various central ministries (with the exception of the Ministry of Local Industry and the Third Ministry of Machine Industry) and those directly operated or administered by other agencies of the State Council. Included in central industry are thus the state enterprises and the state-private joint enterprises, which are under central control. On the other hand, local industry includes local state enterprises, commune-operated enterprises, cooperative en-

terprises, private enterprises, and those state-private joint enterprises which are administered by local governments.[29]

Industrial Enterprises, Urban Handicrafts, and Communal Industry

In recent years, a new classification of industry has been adopted in China primarily for the purpose of reporting industrial statistics. According to this classification, industry is grouped into three categories: (1) industrial enterprises, (2) urban handicraft industry, and (3) communal industry.[30]

Industrial enterprises refer to those controlled by the government at the levels of *hsien* or *shih* (city) and above, including enterprises operated by public organizations and schools but excluding state-controlled handicraft establishments.

Urban handicrafts include: (1) state-controlled handicraft establishments; (2) handicraft producer cooperatives, handicraft production teams, and cooperative factories; and (3) individual handicrafts in urban areas.

Communal industry comprises all of the industrial production units operated by rural and suburban people's communes.

Grouping of Industry by Area

Statistical data on Chinese industry are frequently published for various regions and provinces. The following list gives the seven industrial regions with their provincial components:[31]

1. North China
   a. Peking
   b. Hopei
   c. Honan
   d. Shantung
   e. Shansi
   f. Inner Mongolia
2. Northeast China
   a. Liaoning
   b. Kirin
   c. Heilungkiang
3. East China
   a. Shanghai
   b. Kiangsu
   c. Chekiang
   d. Anhwei
4. Central China
   a. Hupeh

[25]*Ibid.,* p. 1.

[26]*Ibid.,* and "Lectures on Fundamentals of Industrial Management," *op. cit.,* p. 33.

[27]Government Administrative Council, "Provisional Regulations Concerning State-Private Jointly Operated Industrial Enterprises (promulgated on September 5, 1956)," in Ministry of Justice and the Editorial Committee of Laws and Regulations, ed. *Selected Collection of the Laws and Regulations of the People's Republic of China,* Peking: Law Publishing House, 1956, pp. 246–52, reference on p. 247.

[28]"Lectures on Fundamentals . . . ," *op. cit.*

[29]*Ibid.,* and State Planning Commission, *Brief Explanations . . . , op. cit.*

[30]Department of Planning and Statistics, Hupeh University, *op. cit.,* pp. 48–49.

[31]*CH,* p. 189

b. Hunan
c. Kiangsi
5. South China
   a. Kwangtung
   b. Kwangsi
   c. Fukien
6. Southwest China
   a. Szechuan
   b. Kweichow
   c. Yunnan

7. Northwest China
   a. Shensi
   b. Kansu
   c. Chinghai
   d. Ningsia
   e. Sinkiang
   f. Tibet

Various provinces are conventionally grouped between inland and coastal areas. The latter refer to Peking, Tientsin, Shanghai, Hopei, Liaoning, Shantung, Kiangsu, Fukien, Kwangtung, and Chekiang, with the rest of the country classified as an inland area.[32]

Industrial data are often published separately for the national minority areas as a whole. As indicated above, included in these areas are the Inner Mongolia Autonomous Region, Sinkiang-Uighur Autonomous Region, Ningsia Hui Autonomous Region, Kwangsi Chuang Autonomous Region, Tibet, and Chamdo and all the autonomous *chou* and *hsien* throughout the country.

SOURCES OF
INDUSTRIAL STATISTICS

The Chinese Communists inherited from the Nationalist government a weak statistical system when they took over the mainland in 1949. Very meager statistical information on Chinese industry existed at that time.[33] Immediately after its establishment, the Peking regime began to institute a system of industrial reporting and to conduct a number of industrial surveys. With the building up of a national statistical system during the First Five-Year Plan Period,[34] a unified system of regular statistical reporting was introduced. This system, supplemented by special surveys, has provided the basic source of statistical data on Chinese industry.

THE SYSTEM OF
REGULAR STATISTICAL SCHEDULES

The Development of the System

1950 - 52

The system of regular statistical schedules (*ting-ch'i pao-piao chih-tu*), which requires

continuous reporting of certain indicators by industrial enterprises on monthly and quarterly bases, was first introduced in the state enterprises of Manchuria in April, 1950. The system was expanded in August of the same year to all the state and joint industrial enterprises throughout the country. At the same time, reporting of annual summary schedules was added. In 1952, private industrial enterprises were also requested to submit annual reports.[35]

The system was revised in June, 1952, at the First National Conference of Industrial Statistics. It was at this conference that the decision was made to adopt the classification of industry between small- and large-scale enterprises. These two groups of enterprises were required to submit different forms of schedules at different time intervals. Small-scale enterprises were to report only a few major indicators on a quarterly basis, while large-scale enterprises were subject to a more detailed and frequent reporting.

The whole system was still in its infancy at the end of 1952, when rehabilitation of the national economy was announced to have been completed. Lack of standardization of definitions, classifications, computing methods, and national indicators led to confusion of statistical schedules and to incomparability of resulting data. It was against this background that the Peking regime attempted to institute a unified system of statistical reporting when the First Five-Year Plan began in 1953.

1953 - 57

The establishment of such a unified system was the central theme of the Second National Statistical Conference, convened in December, 1952. The conference concluded that the state

[32]Data Office, *TCKT*, "A General Survey of Industrial Capital in China," *TCKT*, No. 1 (January, 1957), p. 32.

[33]The earliest publication of Chinese industrial statistics, *Statistical Tables of the Ministry of Agriculture, Industry and Commerce (Nung-kung-shang-pu t'ung-chi)*, appeared in 1908, during the Ch'ing Dynasty. After the establishment of the Republic of China, the Peiyang Military Government published *Agricultural and Commercial Statistics (Nung-shang t'ung-chi)* during 1916–24 and *Labor Statistics of Nation-Wide Industry and Mines (Ch'uan-kuo kung-yeh yu k'uang-shan lao-tung-tse jen-shu t'ung-chi)* during 1912–20. In 1935, the Ministry of Industry and the National Defense Council of the Central Government conducted two surveys: "A Survey of Nation-Wide Industry" and "A Survey of Factories in Various Industries." These surveys covered 6,334 factories in East China, North China, and Central China. In 1935, 1940, and 1948, the Directorate General of Budgets, Accounts, and Statistics published three editions of *Statistical Abstracts of the Republic of China*, in which some industrial data were included.

[34]An excellent survey of the historical development and inner working of the statistical system in China from 1949 to 1959 will be found in Choh-Ming Li, *The Statistical System of Communist China*, Berkeley: University of California Press, 1962.

[35]Department of Planning and Statistics, Hupeh University, *op. cit.*, p. 25.

statistical system, including the system of regular statistical schedules, should be unified under central control. In early 1953, the State Statistical Bureau, which was established in October, 1952, was vested with full authority to control statistical work of local governments for purposes of standardization and coordination.[36] Statistical services of local governments and enterprises were required to comply with all statistical regulations and methods of the State Bureau and to fill out all standardized schedules the State Bureau issued.[37] At the same time, efforts were made by the State Bureau to supervise the organization and operation of statistical services in state and joint enterprises, particularly those centrally controlled.[38]

In 1957, as a result of nearly complete socialization of private industry, almost all industrial enterprises in China were brought into the unified system of regular reporting, and the State Bureau continued to engage itself in supervising the organization of statistical work at the enterprise level. Toward the end of 1957, statistical services had been installed in practically all industrial enterprises.[39] Hsüeh Mu-ch'iao then the Director of the State Statistical Bureau, was so confident that he formulated, at the Sixth National Statistical Conference in September, 1957, a work program for the Second Five-Year Plan Period, with emphasis on the strengthening and improvement of regular reporting services.[40]

1958

When the State Statistical Bureau had gained full control over statistical work of all enterprises and over the standarization of all statistical schedules, including the selection of indicators, definitions of these indicators, methods of computing them, and the format of tables, central ministries and local party and government authorities were not allowed to modify the schedules according to their needs or to issue new schedules without prior approval from the State Bureau. This gave rise to discontent on the part of central ministries and local authorities. The state statistical system under the central control of the State Statistical Bureau was criticized as "detached from politics and from reality."[41] The State Bureau was attacked for putting so much emphasis on the national work program that it failed to take into account local needs and to recognize local

party and government leadership.[42] The standardization of computing methods and statistical methodology was branded a case of "dogmatism" on the ground that the wide diversity of local conditions was ignored.[43] As a result of this criticism, Hsüeh was forced to admit, in February, 1958, that statistical services did deviate from politics and from reality and that statistical methodology was indeed too mechanical and too rigid.[44]

The attack on the state statistical system became stronger with the advent of the Great Leap Forward Movement. The movement called for an endless chain of emulative drives among workers, factories, agricultural cooperatives, production teams, and localities; and major objectives of emulation were local in scope, determined by local leadership. In determining these objectives, local party and government officials required all relevant statistics, such as those showing daily or weekly progress.[45] Local statistics came into direct conflict with basic national statistics in certain fundamental respects, such as selection of indicators, methods of computation, and timing of presentation. The state statistical system was further criticized on the ground that it was too conservative to meet the Great Leap Movement. Attempts were made by local party cadres to control local statistical offices, and it was even suggested that the State Statistical Bureau be abolished.[46]

Faced with these shattering effects on the state statistical system, the State Statistical Bureau in June, 1958, convened a national conference in Paoting, Hopei Province, later known as the Paoting Conference. At the conference,

[36]Government Administrative Council, "Decisions Concerning the Strengthening of Statistical Organizations and Statistical Work (Promulgated on January 8, 1953)," in *A Collection of the Laws of the Central People's Government*, Peking: Law Publishing House, 1955, pp. 69–70.
[37]Government Administrative Council, "A Directive on Clarifying Current Statistical Schedules and Forbidding Improper Issuance of Statistical Schedules (Promulgated on September 5, 1953)," in *ibid.*, pp. 71–76.
[38]SSB, "A Directive Concerning the Strengthening of Industrial Statistical Work," *TCKTTH*, No. 6 (September, 1954), pp. 1–3.
[39]Director Hsüeh Mu-ch'iao's Report at the Sixth National Statistical Conference," *TCKT*, No. 21 (November, 1957), pp. 1–21.
[40]*Ibid.*
[41]T'ao Jan (Deputy Director of the State Statistical Bureau), "Report at the Wuhan Meeting of Statistical Workers," *TCYC*, No. 5 (May 23, 1958), pp. 4–8.
[42]Chia Chi-yun, "Several Problems in the Present Reform Movement of Statistical Services," *TCKT*, No. 15 (August, 1958), pp. 5–10.
[43]Chao I-wen, "My Recognition of Dogmatism in Statistical Services," *TCYC*, No. 5 (May 23, 1958), pp. 9–11; and Ho Wen-ho (Director of Kiangsu Provincial Statistical Bureau), "Oppose Dogmatism and Develop the Spirit of Independent Creation," *TCKT*, No. 12 (July, 1958), pp. 9–12.
[44]Hsüeh Mu-Ch'iao, "How Does Statistical Work Make a Great Leap?" *TCKT*, No. 5 (March, 1958), pp. 1–5.
[45]Known as "progress statistics" (*chin-tu t'ung-chi*).
[46]Chia Chi-yun, *op. cit.*

two major steps were taken as part of the so-called statistical reform movement *(t'ung-chi kai-ko yün-tung)*. In the first place, the national statistical work program was to be integrated with emulative drives sponsored by local leadership, and the state statistical service was to provide local party and government officials with relevant statistical data. The second step was to "let politics take command" *(cheng-chi kua-shuai)* in statistical work. Statistical services were to be operated by "the whole party and all the people,"[47] and mass participation in statistical work under party leadership was regarded as essential in the reform movement. The "masses" were now relied upon to do statistical work, including the assembly of data, the computation of figures, and even the design of forms.[48]

1959 AND AFTER

Developments in 1958 resulted in what Choh-Ming Li has called the "statistical fiasco" in China,[49] which threatened the very existence of the state statistical system in general and the unified system of regular statistical schedules in particular.

During the Great Leap Movement, in many districts statistical units and statistical cadres were reduced heavily, reporting and computation were not carried out carefully, and scientific methods were ignored.[50] As a consequence, the quality of statistical data deteriorated considerably. The Party in early 1959 began to realize that the centralized statistical system should be maintained and that the statistical work should be done by trained statisticians, rather than by party cadres and the "masses."

In an effort to regain full control over statistical operations, the State Statistical Bureau convened in April, 1959, a national conference of the directors of provincial and municipal statistical bureaus. The conference mapped out the statistical work program with emphasis on the following:[51] (1) to enhance the accuracy of the progress statistics of "focal-point programs"[52] and to insure the timely report of these statistics; (2) to submit monthly telegraphic reports on time to superior statistical units; (3) to enforce strictly the system of regular statistical schedules; (4) to expand the use of "model surveys," particularly those combined with the progress statistics of focal-point programs and with the system of regular statistical

schedules; and (5) to extend the statistical network to the people's communes. Further steps were taken by the State Bureau after the April conference to improve the quality of statistical data. Apparently the system of regular statistical schedules survived the 1958 fiasco and continues to supply basic data on Chinese industry. But the State Statistical Bureau no longer has full control over the issuance of statistical schedules, since, as the following paragraphs will show, certain central ministries are allowed to issue schedules to enterprises under their jurisdication.

Types of Statistical Schedules

In addition to the monthly telegraphic reports which have been introduced since 1958 to provide information on a few important national indicators, industrial enterprises in China are required to submit two types of regular schedules: (1) basic schedules *(chi-pen pao-piao)* and 2) special schedules *(chuang-yeh pao-piao)*.[53]

Basic schedules which have indicators common to all industrial enterprises are issued by the State Statistical Bureau. Included in these schedules are the following indicators:

1. Output indicators, including the gross value of output, the value of commodity production,[54] the output of major products in physical units, and new types of products tested and manufactured.

2. Indicators of labor, wages, productivity, and working time, such as the number of workers and employees, the total amount and the composition of wage funds, labor productivity, and the utilization of working time.

3. Indicators of the material-technical supply, such as the supply of products to other producers, the movement of materials, the utilization of materials and fuel, and material balance sheets.

4. Indicators of "technical innovations" *(chi-shu ko-hsin)*, such as mechanization, auto-

[47]Editorial, "The Operation of Statistical Services by the Whole Party and All the People," *JMJP*, August 13, 1958.
[48]Chen Chien-fei, "Blooming, All the Places, Towns and Villages Together Have Carried Out a Great Leap Forward in Statistical Work throughout the Province," *TCKT*, No. 14 (July 29, 1958), pp. 8–12.
[49]Choh-Ming Li, *op. cit.,* pp. 83–108.
[50]Department of Planning and Statistics, Hupeh University, *op. cit.,* p. 31.
[51]*Ibid.,* pp. 32–33.
[52]Focal-point programs" *(chung-hsin kung-tso)* refer to the emulation drives formulated by local party and government leaders.
[53]*Ibid.,* pp. 41–42.
[54]The meaning of "the value of commodity production" is explained later in this chapter.

mation, introduction of new techniques, and modernization of equipment.

5. Technical and economic indicators (*chi-shu ching-chi chih-piao*), such as the utilization of equipment capacity, output of products per unit of input of material and equipment, and input per unit of output.

6. Indicators of cost and financial conditions, such as reduction in cost of production, cost per unit of output, the volume and composition of working capital, and the amount of profits.

Special schedules are prepared by the statistical units of central industrial ministries for the specific use of the enterprises under the respective jurisdictions of these ministries. Power generating plants, for example, are supposed to fill out not only basic schedules prepared by the State Statistical Bureau but also special schedules, such as "the comprehensive monthly report on the output of electric power" and "the comprehensive quarterly report on the consumption of electricity," as they are issued by the Ministry of Water Conservancy and Electric Power.

Reporting Units

To fill out regular statistical schedules is the responsibility of reporting units. Reporting units are those enterprises which receive and answer regular schedules. Not all industrial enterprises are reporting units. As may be recalled, one of the current classifications of industry is the grouping of all industrial production units into three categories: (1) industrial enterprises, (2) urban handicraft establishments, and (3) industrial production units of the people's communes. The criteria for determining reporting units in these categories are not the same.

Two groups of industrial enterprises may be distinguished, depending upon whether or not they have independent economic accounting systems (*ching-chi ho-shuan chih-tu*). Industrial enterprises with independent economic accounting systems are those which possess financial and administrative integrity, i.e., which have their own balance sheets. Only these enterprises are reporting units of regular schedules. Enterprises without independent economic accounting systems, i.e., without their own balance sheets and independent administrative

structure, are not required to prepare regular reports.[55]

Reporting units of the urban handicraft industry are also determined by economic accountability. Urban handicraft establishments with independent economic accounting systems are supposed to submit regular reports. In some cases, a combined economic accounting system is established among a number of handicraft establishments, frequently in the form of an accounting network; then the network becomes a reporting unit.[56]

For communal factories, the people's communes are supposed to fill out regular schedules. In other words, not factories, but the communes which operate these factories are the reporting units.[57]

SPECIAL SURVEYS

Special surveys have provided the second major source of information on Chinese industry since the Communists came to power. Before the establishment of the system of regular statistical schedules, the Peking regime relied wholly on special surveys for collecting statistical data. As early as 1948, model surveys of private industry and commerce were conducted in Harbin, Mukden, and other large cities in Manchuria by the Department of Statistics of the Financial and Economic Commission of the Northeast.[58] In March, 1950, a national census of state and joint industrial enterprises was undertaken by the Department of Statistics of the Financial and Economic Commission of the Government Administrative Council. The results of the census provided the basis for drafting the first state plan of industrial rehabilitation and reconstruction. At the same time, a census of private industry was conducted. During 1951–52, a number of surveys were carried out independently by various governmental departments in different areas.[59]

With the establishment of the system of regular reporting in state and joint industrial enterprises in 1951, special surveys were conducted largely for private industry. The most important were the national surveys in 1954 of individual handicrafts and private industrial

[55]*Ibid.*, pp. 47–48.
[56]*Ibid.*
[57]*Ibid.*
[58]*Ibid.*, p. 23.
[59]*JMJP*, December 29, 1952.

enterprises employing more than ten persons.[60] The survey of individual craftsmen, undertaken in the latter part of 1954 was organized by the State Statistical Bureau and the All-China Federation of Cooperatives. Data from this survey were published for most of the provinces by the Institute of Economic Research of the Chinese National Academy of Sciences.[61] The census of private industrial enterprises employing more than 10 persons was organized by the State Statistical Bureau.

As pointed out above, almost all of the industrial enterprises had been brought into the system of regular reporting by the end of 1956, when private industry was nearly completely socialized. Since then, no large-scale national surveys have been undertaken, and the emphasis has been shifted to model surveys. In other words, surveys have no longer been national in scope but have been limited to selected localities.

TYPES OF INDUSTRIAL DATA[62]

Industrial statistics published in China may be grouped into the following categories: (1) the structure of industry, (2) output, (3) capacity and its utilization, (4) mechanization, (5) input-output relations, (6) production efficiency, (7) the consumption of products, and (8) cost of production and other financial conditions.

THE STRUCTURE OF INDUSTRY

Data on the structure of industry contain information on the number of enterprises and on the classification of these enterprises by size. An industrial enterprise refers to a production unit which possesses an integrated administrative structure and accounts for its profits and losses independently. The following data are available for Chinese industrial structure:

1. The number of industrial enterprises confiscated by the Communist government as of the end of 1949 and the classification of these enterprises by size of employment (Table 4.1).

2. The number of industrial enterprises for the years 1949 through 1957, classified by ownership of enterprise (state, joint, coopera-

tive, and private), and by size of enterprise (large and small) (Table 4.2).

3. The number of state-private joint enterprises in four industries: iron and steel for 1952 through 1956, and machine-building and metal-products manufacturing and paper-making for 1949 through 1955 (Table 4.3).

4. The number of enterprises in the iron-and-steel industry as of the end of 1954, with breakdowns according to size of employment (Table 4.4).

5. The number of individual handicraft operators, handicraft production teams, and handicraft producer cooperatives for 1949 through 1956 (Table 4.5).

6. The number of individual handicraft operators, handicraft producer cooperatives, and those handicraft factories with no more than 10 hired workers at the end of 1954 in various provinces and municipalities. These figures are given together with data on the value of handicraft output in Tables 4.60–4.63. All of these data were the results of the national survey of individual handicrafts conducted in 1954.

INDUSTRIAL OUTPUT

The Concept and Classification of Industrial Output

THE CONCEPT OF INDUSTRIAL OUTPUT

Industrial output in China is defined as "the aggregate of products produced by labor as a direct useful result of industrial production activities of industrial enterprises.[63] According to this definition, there are four requisites of industrial output.[64]

[60]In addition to these two industrial surveys, there were national surveys conducted for other sectors. Included were the national census of private trade and food-and-drink catering establishments as of August 31, 1955, and that of employment in nonprivate sectors as of September 30, 1955.

[61]Handicraft Section of the Institute of Economic Research, Chinese National Academy of Science, *Nationwide Survey Data on Individual Handicrafts in 1954*, Peking: Tu-shu, shen-ho san-lien ch'u-pan-she, 1957.

[62]Under Chinese practice, employment, wages, and labor productivity of industry are also included in industrial statistics. For the purpose of convenience, these will be treated separately in a later section. Industrial labor productivity in physical terms is, however, included in this section under "Input-Output Relations."

[63]Department of Planning and Statistics, Hupeh University, *op. cit.*, p. 69

[64]*Ibid.*, pp. 69–70.

First, the output of an industrial enterprise is a result of *its own* production activities. Hence, raw and supplementary materials in stock which have not been used for processing as yet cannot be regarded as the output of the given enterprise.

Second, the output is a result of *industrial* production activities of the given enterprise. Thus, products of the farms and basic construction units attached to the enterprise are not classified as industrial output.

Third, the output is a *useful* result of the industrial production activities of the given enterprise. Products are useful only when they meet all the requirements originally determined. Rejected articles which do not meet these requirements are useless and, therefore, are supposed to be excluded from the recorded output.

Fourth and finally, the output is a *direct* useful result of the industrial production activities of the given enterprise. Wastes and leavings, which are residues of raw materials left by virtue of their incomplete utilization, are not to be considered as a part of industrial output, since they are useless and are not direct objectives of industrial production activities. By-products and joint products, however, which are supposedly useful and are usually included in the state plan with the so-called basic products, are to be considered as a part of industrial output.

THE CLASSIFICATION OF INDUSTRIAL OUTPUT

Two types of industrial output are distinguished according to Chinese usage: (1) material products and (2) work of an industrial nature *(kung-yeh-hsing tso-yeh)*. The latter refers to repair and the industrial processing of customers' materials and is probably based on the Marxian concept of "services."[65]

Material products, which account for the major share of industrial output, are classified in China in three groups (1) finished output, (2) semi-finished products, and (3) goods in process.[66]

Finished output (wang-cheng-p'in) is composed of the products ready to be delivered by the given enterprise. A finished product is supposed to conform to a prescribed standard or to the technical specifications fixed in the order contracts. A product is considered finished at the moment it is transferred to the enterprise's warehouse for finished output, or, alternatively, shipped out to the customer.

Semi-finished products (pan-cheng-p'in) are those whose processing has been completed in a single shop or several shops in the given enterprise and which are subject to further fabrication in other shops within the same enterprise. The distinction between semi-finished and finished products lies in the degree of vertical integration of the enterprise. Both are required to meet established standards or technical specifications.

Goods in process (tsai-chih-p'in) refer to those whose processing has not been completed as yet in the given shop and which are awaiting further fabrication within the same shop.

Both semi-finished products and goods in process are called *unfinished products (wei-wang-cheng ch'an-p'in)*. In estimating the value of the gross output of an industrial enterprise, semi-finished products are usually included in the computation. Goods in process are included only for those enterprises whose period of production is very long.

Measuring Output in Physical Terms

Since a vast number of commodities are produced and since many of them can be measured in more than one physical unit, a "catalogue of industrial products" *(kung-yeh ch'an-p'in mu-lu)* was published by the State Statistical Bureau to standardize commodity nomenclature, specifications, and units of measure.[67] Only the products listed in the catalogue are to be reported by the enterprise in physical units. Generally, the enterprise reports the output of a product in one standard physical unit as specified in the catalogue, such as cubic meters for lumber or tons for paper. But for a few products, the output is to be given

[65]With regard to the nature of services, Marx states: "When money is exchanged directly for labor without producing capital, and consequently without becoming productive labor, the labor is bought as a service. In sum, this word 'service' is merely an expression for the particular use value furnished by labor as by any commodity whatever, but it is a specific expression. The laborer renders services not as objects but as activity; and in this aspect it does not differ from a machine, from a watch, for example." (See Karl Marx, *A History of Economic Theories*, translated from the French edition by Terence McCarthy, New York: Langland Press, 1952, pp. 321–22.)

[66]Department of Planning and Statistics, Hupeh University, *op. cit.*, pp. 71–72. Chinese definitions and classifications of industrial output are virtually the same as those of the Soviet Union. See Gregory Grossman, *Soviet Statistics of Physical Output of Industrial Commodities*, Princeton, N.J.: Princeton University Press, 1960, pp. 31–32.

[67]State Statistical Bureau, Department of Trade Statistics, "Explanations of Some Problems Concerning the Unified Catalogue of Commodities in Domestic Trade," *TCKTTH*, No. 9 (December, 1954), pp. 38–41.

in two standard units. For example, electric generators and turbines are to be measured both in number and by power (in 1,000 kilowatts), and metal-cutting machines in number and in tons.

But many products are not homogeneous, and the degree of heterogeneity varies for different products. Some of them are so heterogeneous that it is not possible to add them together in physical units, while others, though differentiated, possess some common measurable characteristics. The latter are generally those products which have the same nomenclature but different gradations and technical specifications. In such a case, the output may be measured in terms of so-called "conventional physical units" *(piao-chun shih-wu chih-piao)*, which are usually determined according to either relative "use value" *(shih-yung chia-chih)* or relative "labor consumption" *(lao-tung hsiao-hao-liang)* of products.[68] The conversion method according to relative use value, for example, is used to measure the output of tractors: tractors of different horsepower rating are converted into conventional units of 15 horsepower each. The conversion method on the basis of relative labor consumption is used in the textile industry to measure the output of cotton yarn: the 20-count yarn is adopted as the conventional unit for converting various types of yarn.

There exists still another method of output measurement in China, the converting of the output of all products of a given enterprise into labor units. When this method is used, the output of the enterprise is measured in terms of the so-called "working-time norm" *(ting-o kung-shih)*, i.e., the amount of labor requirements fixed by the state plan but not the amount of labor actually expended.[69] This method is used primarily in machine-building enterprises, in which the working-time norm is fixed for all parts and machines produced in each shop. The output of every worker, team, shop, and sometimes the whole factory is expressed in terms of the working-time norm.[70] The enterprise also reports the output in natural units.

Measuring output in Monetary Terms

The measurement of the output of an enterprise in natural units or in conventional physical units is possible only when its products are homogeneous or have the same nomenclature but different characteristics such as type, brand, size, shape, or power. The measurement of the output in labor units is possible only for those enterprises for which the number of man-hours spent in producing each of the products is fixed by the state plan. For enterprises whose products are so heterogeneous that none of the above methods is applicable, the total output has to be measured in value terms. To measure output in terms of currency is, of course, an international standard practice. All varieties of products can be expressed in monetary units with the help of the prices of these products. In China, in addition to reporting the output in various nonmonetary terms as may be required, each enterprise is supposed to report two major indicators of output measured in yuan: the value of gross output and the value of commodity production. Before we explore the concept and measurement of these indicators, it is necessary to consider first the problem of pricing output.

PRICING PROBLEMS

An immediate question arises as to which of the pricing methods are used in China to value industrial output. Are wholesale prices or retail prices, current or constant, to be used as the unit of measurement? Wholesale prices are composed of "ex-factory prices", the cost of distribution, and a profit mark-up. The ex-factory price of a product is the sum of the cost of production and accumulation (profits and taxes). Retail prices refer to wholesale prices plus the cost of distribution and a profit mark-up at the retail level. In China, the output is valued at ex-factory prices on the ground that the cost and profit elements in the distribution process bear no relation to industrial production.[71]

The system of regular reporting requires each enterprise to report the value of the gross output and the value of commodity production at constant prices in all of the monthly, quarterly, and annual schedules but at current prices only in annual schedules. The current price for a product is the average of its ex-factory prices prevailing within the year. The constant prices used vary for different periods of time. Prior

[68]Department of Planning and Statistics, Hupeh University, *op. cit.*, pp. 77–78.
[69]This method appears to be a direct application of the Marxian theory of labor value. The "working-time norm" seems to approximate the Marxian concept of "socially necessary labor."
[70]*Ibid.*, p. 79.
[71]*Ibid.*, p. 82.

to 1953, the constant prices used were the average prices of 1943 for Manchuria and the prices prevailing in June, 1950, for the rest of China. During the First Five-Year Plan, the average prices during the third quarter of 1952 were adopted as the constant prices. Beginning in 1958, the prices prevailing on January 1, 1957, have been used.

A number of problems arise from the use of constant prices for valuing industrial output. These problems are of great practical importance, and a brief discussion is in order.

In the first place, there is the problem of the "new product effect." Numerous products have been manufactured for the first time each year in China. During the First Five-Year Plan, the price of a new product was based primarily on "test-manufacturing" expenses, which are those incurred during the final stage of successfully developing the product. This practice would exaggerate the gross value of industrial output, since the "test-manufacturing" expenses of new products are generally exceedingly high. For example, in Shanghai, a 6,000-kilowatt engine for steamships was priced at 1,320,000 yuan in 1955 when first manufactured but at only 380,000 yuan the following year.[72] This problem was so serious that the State Statistical Bureau decided beginning in 1958 to change the basis of pricing new products to actual cost of ex-factory prices during the first month, or quarter, of production. But the actual cost or ex-factory price of a new product must still be very high in its first month or quarter of production, declining only as the volume of output increases. Therefore, the current method of pricing new products is not free from the defect of inflating the importance of new products and, thus, the year-to-year increase in Chinese industrial production.

Secondly, there exists the problem of pricing work of an industrial nature. Unlike material products which are valued at ex-factory prices, work of an industrial nature does not have prices of such. According to a provision established by the State Statistical Bureau, the current value of the work is to be determined primarily on the basis of the charges for the processing of customers' materials and for repair services. The work valued at constant prices is then obtained by multiplying its current value by the ratio of finished output at constant prices to that at current prices.[73]

Thirdly, constant prices are not applied universally throughout the country. In principle, the constant price of a product should be the average of the ex-factory prices of the product produced in various parts of the country at a given time. In other words, for each product there can be only one single constant price applicable nationally. In practice, however, a large part of the products do not have a single universal constant price. Currently, for the purpose of preparing the 1957 constant prices, industrial products are grouped into three categories. The first category consists of major industrial products which number more than 7,000 and account for over 70 percent of the gross value of industrial output. The constant prices of these products are compiled by the State Statistical Bureau to be applied nationally. Products in the second category are those of secondary importance, and their constant prices are determined by various central ministries or local statistical bureaus to be applied within each ministry or each area. The third category comprises those products with small value, with wide difference in quality and brands, or with small regional price differentials. The 1957 constant prices of these products are simply their ex-factory prices on January 1, 1957, to be applied only within the same enterprise.[74]

Fourth and finally, there is the problem of determining the constant prices for products with the same nomenclature but different technical specifications such as quality, size, grade, brand, and power. According to the regulations established by the State Statistical Bureau, the average of the prices of these products is taken as the constant price, provided that there are no differences, or very small differences, in their prices. But if prices differ substantially for products of the same commodity label, these products are classified into groups according to prices, and the average price of each group is taken as the constant price for the products in that group.[75] The problem became very serious in 1958, when the people's communes were engaged in the production of a great number of products without technical and quality standardization. There were no constant prices for nearly

[72]Fan Jo-i, "The Pricing Policy for Products of Heavy Industry," CCYC, No. 3 (June, 1957), pp. 54–67, reference on p. 66.
[73]Department of Planning and Statistics, Hupeh University, op. cit.
[74]Ibid., pp. 83–85.
[75]Ibid.

all of these products, and only current prices were used in computing the gross value of output. Beginning in 1959, the State Statistical Bureau has compiled unified constant prices for major products produced by the people's communes. Constant prices of products not covered by the national constant price list are determined locally by provincial or municipal statistical bureaus.[76]

THE GROSS VALUE OF INDUSTRIAL OUTPUT

The gross value of the output of an industrial enterprise is "an output indicator in value terms representing the final results of industrial production activities of that enterprise."[77] The concept was first adopted in 1950 from Soviet usage.[78] Directly stemming from this concept is the so-called "factory method" (*kung-ch'ang-fa*) of computing the gross value of industrial output. According to this method, the output of an industrial enterprise is measured at current ex-factory prices after elimination of the intra-enterprise turnover.[79] Specifically, the gross value output of the given enterprise consists of the following elements:[80]

1. The value of finished output produced during the given period, including raw materials and basic and supplementary materials used in production.
2. The value of semi-finished products sold during the given period.
3. The value of changes in the stock of semi-finished products and goods in process during the given period.
4. The value of the work of an industrial nature completed during the given period, including major repairs to the machinery and equipment of the enterprise done by its own production workers.

The intra-enterprise turnover (*nei-pu chou-chuan-ol*) is excluded from the computation. The major portion of such turnover consists of semi-finished products produced for further fabrication within the enterprise. For example, in a metallurgical plant the amount of steel produced by its open-hearth shop and delivered to the rolling mill for further processing belongs to the intra-enterprise turnover, since the steel used up in the production of rolled steel is not transferred outside the plant but consumed internally within the plant itself. But this rule is not universally applied, since the State Statistical Bureau makes certain exceptions. For some basic and supplementary materials, the intra-enterprise turnover is allowed to be included in the gross value of industrial output. These materials include ore and coke used in metallurgical plants, pulp used in paper plants, and coal, mineral oil, peat, shale, and gas used by enterprises extracting them.[81]

There are a number of technical defects of the "factory method," arising primarily from the "grossness" of the value of industrial output. According to the method, all materials coming from outside the enterprise enter in full value into the gross output of the enterprise. The gross-value output of the industry as a whole is simply the sum total of the gross-value outputs of all industrial enterprises. As a consequence, the factory method gives a disproportionate emphasis to highly fabricated products and will inevitably result in multiple counting in the measurement of the gross value of industrial output. Reportedly, multiple counting accounted for as much as 61.8 percent of the gross value of industrial output in 1954.[82]

Furthermore, the gross total calculated by the factory method is affected by the degree of vertical integration and by the amalgamation and splitting up of enterprises.[83] Therefore, as the height of socialist transformation of private industry was reached in 1956, reduction in multiple counting led to a decrease in the gross value of private industrial output for the year by 1 percent.[84] On the other hand, the decentralization of control over industrial enterprises and the establishment of numerous industrial production units in 1958 must have increased the degree of multiple counting and hence exaggerated the gross value of industrial production for the year.

[76]*Ibid.*

[77]K'o Po, "Industrial Output Statistics," *TCKTTH*, No. 11 (June 14, 1956), pp. 30–33, reference on p. 31.

[78]"Materials on Methods of Computing the Gross Value of Industrial Output," *TCKTTH*, No. 17 (September 14, 1956), pp. 2–5.

[79]Yueh Wei, "Methods of Computing National Income," *CCYC*, No. 3 (August, 1956), pp. 48–66.

[80]Department of Planning and Statistics, Hupeh University, *op, cit.*, pp. 87–91.

[81]*Ibid.*, p. 93.

[82]"Several Problems of Computing the Gross Value of Industrial Output," *TCKTTG*, No. 17 (September 14, 1956), pp. 1–2, reference on p. 4.

[83]Department of Planning and Statistics, Hupeh University, *op. cit.*, p. 99.

[84]"Diverse Opinions on the Methods of Computing the Gross Value of Industrial Output," *TCKTTH*, No. 24 (December 29, 1956), pp. 5–10.

THE VALUE OF INDUSTRIAL COMMODITY PRODUCTION

The value of commodity production (*shang-p'in ch'an-chih*) of an industrial enterprise is the value of finished and semi-finished products turned out and sold or awaiting sale during the given period, plus the value of the work of an industrial nature performed for customers in the same period.[85]

Commodity production refers to only that part of industrial output which enters the sphere of distribution and, therefore, excludes changes in the stock of goods in process and of those semi-finished products not intended for sale. Products manufactured out of raw materials supplied by customers are included in commodity production, not at their full value but only to the extent of the value which is added by manufacture. Similarly, the commodity output of repair shops is measured by the value added by repair and not by the value of the products repaired.[86]

Thus, the value of industrial commodity production differs from the gross value of industrial output mainly in the composition of output. Moreover, certain materials transferred within the enterprise which are allowed to be included in the gross value of industrial output, according to the State Statistical Bureau provision as indicated above, do not enter the computation of commodity production.[87]

The value of industrial commodity production is also computed by the factory method. The major purpose of computing commodity production is to indicate the amount of industrial output available for market supply. For each enterprise, the value of commodity production in a year indicates the maximum amount of the total revenue which the enterprise may receive during the year.[88]

THE NET VALUE OF INDUSTRIAL OUTPUT

The net value of the output of an industrial enterprise is defined as the newly created value resulting from industrial production activities of the enterprise during a given period of time. The net value of the output of the industry as a whole is the sum total of the net-value outputs of all industrial enterprises.

Under current practice, enterprises are not required to report the net value of their output.

The State Statistical Bureau and local statistical bureaus estimate once a year the net value of industrial output at the national and local levels on the basis of the annual returns from enterprises.[89]

As indicated in the section on national income, the production method (that is, the value-added method) is used in China to estimate the net value of industrial output. According to this method, the value added is obtained by subtracting material outlays from the gross value of industrial output. Data on material outlays, which include raw materials, basic and supplementary materials, fuel, electricity, depreciation, and other expenses, can be obtained either directly from the schedules of production expenses submitted by enterprises or estimated indirectly on the basis of model surveys or certain a priori information.[90] The net value of industrial output is measured both at current and at constant prices. For constant-price valuation, data on material outlays have to be deflated by appropriate price indices, and the value added by industry is then the gross value of industrial output at constant prices net of deflated material outlays.

THE INDEX OF INDUSTRIAL PRODUCTION

In China, the index of industrial production for a particular period is derived as the ratio of the gross value of industrial output at constant prices of the given period to that of the base period. Algebraically, the index may be obtained from the following formula:[91]

$$\frac{\Sigma \, q_1 p_0}{\Sigma \, q_0 p_0} \quad \text{or} \quad \frac{\Sigma \, q_1 p_1}{\Sigma \, q_0 p_0} \div \frac{\Sigma \, q_1 p_1}{\Sigma \, q_1 p_0}$$

where q_0 and q_1 represent the number of units of a single product produced during the base period and the reporting period, respectively, and p_0 and p_1 stand for the price of the product during the base period and the reporting period, respectively.

The difference between Chinese and Western methods of preparing the index of industrial

[85]Department of Planning and Statistics, Hupeh University *op. cit.*, p. 101; and K'o Po, *op. cit.*, p. 32.
[86]Department of Planning and Statistics, Hupeh University, *loc. cit.*
[87]*Ibid.*
[88]K'o Po, *op. cit.*
[89]Department of Planning and Statistics, Hupeh University, *op. cit.*, p. 115.
[90]*Ibid.*, p. 114.
[91]*Ibid.*, pp. 128–29.

production lies in the formula used and in the size of the sample: the Chinese formula uses prices instead of value-added as weights,[92] and the data used in China are obtained from regular reports of enterprises, which cover practically all products; whereas in the West data are usually derived from a sample of selected products.

In computation of the index of industrial production, the average prices during the third quarter of 1952 were used as the constant prices for the years prior to 1958, and since then the prices at the beginning of 1957 have been chosen. Thus, the problem arises as to how to combine the indices for different periods into a single time series with the same constant prices. In solving this problem it has been the practice of the State Statistical Bureau to use the link-chain procedure; that is, the link index numbers are chained back to a common base year by a process of multiplication.[93]

Statistical Data on Industrial Output

Statistical data on industrial output in China fall into two broad categories: (1) physical output statistics and (2) value output statistics.

PHYSICAL OUTPUT STATISTICS

Physical output data may be classified into three groups: (1) the output of major industrial products, (2) breakdowns of the output of various individual industries according to standard classifications, and (3) provincial data.

OUTPUT OF MAJOR INDUSTRIAL PRODUCTS (TABLES 4.6 AND 4.7)

Table 4.6 gives data on the output of 57 products of 11 major industries, while data on 18 of these products produced by private enterprises are presented in Table 4.7.

BREAKDOWN OF THE OUTPUT
OF INDIVIDUAL INDUSTRIES

The Electric Power Industry (Tables 4.8–4.10)
Three types of data on the output of electric power are available:
1. The division of the output between hydraulic and thermal electric power for 1949 and for 1952 through 1957 (Table 4.8).
2. The breakdown of the output according

to state, joint and private enterprises for 1949 and for 1952 through 1956 (Table 4.9).
3. The output generated by the electric power plants under the jurisdiction of the Ministry of Electric Power Industry for 1949 through 1952 (Table 4.10).

The Coal Industry (Table 4.11)
Data on the percentage distribution of the output of modern coal mines among state, cooperative, joint, and private establishments were published by the State Statistical Bureau for 1949 through 1956.

The Nonferrous Metals Industry (Table 4.13)
Data on the output of nonferrous metals produced by private industry were given in terms of percentage of national totals for 1953 through 1957 in the March, 1958, issue of *Planned Economy*. Included are tungsten ore, refined tin, mercury, lead, zinc, and gold.

The Iron-and Steel Industry (Table 4.12)
Data are available for the output of pig iron, steel, and rolled steel according to the ownership of establishments for 1952 through 1956.

The Metal-Processing Industry (Table 4.14)
Statistics were published by the State Statistical Bureau for the output of major products of the metal-processing industry produced in inland and coastal areas in 1955. Data on coastal areas were broken down further into Peking, Tientsin, Shanghai, Liaoning, and Shantung.

[92]This is a problem well investigated by students of the Soviet economy. The major deficiency inherent in the Chinese formula, which was adopted from Russian usage, is its tendency to inflate year-to-year increases in industrial production. Such an inflationary bias may be explained partly by the Gerschenkron effect. Relating Laspeyres' and Paasche's formulae of aggregate index number to the process of industrialization, Gerschenkron develops a hypothesis that the Laspeyres index, based on pre-industrialization prices, must yield a higher rate of growth than the Paasche index, which is based on the post-industrialization prices. The hypothesis is based on the observation that declines in prices and increases in physical output tend to be correlated in the course of industrialization. (See Alexander Gerschenkron, *A Dollar Index of Soviet Machinery Output 1927/28 to 1937*, Santa Monica: RAND Corporation, 1951, Chapter 4.) Another factor which may account for the inflationary bias is the Chinese practice of pricing new products at experimental costs or at the prices of these products during their first month (quarter) of production.

[93]Department of Planning and Statistics, Hupeh University, *op. cit.*, pp. 130–31. For instance, the industrial production index for 1958 at 1952 prices may be obtained by calculating first the link index for 1958 with 1957 as base, both in terms of 1957 prices, which is then multiplied by the chain index of 1957 at 1952 prices. The procedure is as follows:

$$\frac{\text{1958 gross value of industrial output at 1952 prices}}{\text{1952 gross value of industrial output at 1952 prices}} = \frac{\text{1958 gross value of industrial output at 1957 prices}}{\text{1957 gross value of industrial output at 1957 prices}} \times \frac{\text{1957 gross value output at 1952 prices}}{\text{1952 gross value of industrial output at 1952 prices}}$$

The Paper Industry (Tables 4.15–4.17)

Data are available for the division of the output of paper between machine and handicraft production for 1949 through 1957. Data on the output of machine-made paper were broken down further into newsprint, cigarette paper, and paperboard. Data can be found also for the total output of machine-made paper pulp for 1949 through 1957, with breakdowns into chemical wood pulp, machine wood pulp, and reed pulp.

The Textile Industry (Tables 4.18–4.21)

Table 4.18 gives figures on the output of 11 major products of the textile industry for 1949 through 1956, and data on 9 of these products are classified by ownership of establishment in Table 4.19. Data on the output of major cotton textile products with breakdown into inland and coastal areas for 1949, 1952, and 1956 and by region for 1956 are given, respectively, in Tables 4.20 and 4.21.

The Sugar Industry (Table 4.22)

Figures on the output of sugar produced by machines for 1952 through 1956 were given in the September, 1957, issue of *Geographical Knowledge*. Since data on the total output of sugar are available, figures on the handicraft production can thus be computed as a residual.

OUTPUT OF MAJOR INDUSTRIAL PRODUCTS
OF VARIOUS PROVINCES (TABLES 4.23–4.36)

Data on the output of major industrial products are assembled for 14 municipalities and provinces. Included are Peking, Shanghai, Inner Mongolia, Kirin, Heilungkiang, Kansu, Ningsia, Chinghai, Sinkiang, Anhwei, Fukien, Kwangtung, Kwangsi, and Szechuan. These data are compiled from either the communiqués issued by provincial statistical bureaus or the reports of provincial government officials.

VALUE OF OUTPUT DATA

Available data on the gross value of industrial output are relatively abundant, but those on the value of industrial commodity production are practically non-existent. Very meager information can be found for the net value of industrial output. Figures relating to the index of industrial production are available in a number

of publications, but they were merely converted from gross-value data, frequently using 1949, 1952, or 1957 as base years.

THE GROSS VALUE OF INDUSTRIAL OUTPUT

Five broad categories of statistics on the gross value of industrial output may be distinguished: (1) gross value of industrial output according to standard classifications, (2) gross value of factory output according to standard classifications, (3) gross value of the output of various individual industries according to standard classifications, (4) gross value of industrial output of various provinces, and (5) structure and the gross-value output of the handicraft industry.

The Gross Value of Industrial Output

1. By *sector* (Table 4.37). Data on the division of the gross value of industrial output between modern industry and individual handicrafts for 1949 through 1957 may be found in *Ten Great Years* and in the State Statistical Bureau's annual communiqués for 1954 through 1956. Data on the gross-value output of modern industry are divided further between modern factory and handicraft factory. *Ten Great Years* also gives data on the gross value of industrial output and the gross value of modern factory output, both at 1957 prices, for 1957 and 1958.

2. By *ownership of establishment* (Table 4.38). Data are available on the gross value of industrial output and the gross value of factory output, both at 1952 prices, according to the ownership of establishments for 1949 through 1956. Data are also available for the gross value of factory output of state and joint enterprises at 1952 prices for 1949 through 1957, and at 1957 prices for 1957 and 1958.

3. By *production use* (Table 4.39). *Ten Great Years* and the annual communiqués of the State Statistical Bureau gives figures on the gross value output of producer and consumer goods at 1952 prices for 1949–57 and at 1957 prices for 1957–59. The data include the output of producer and consumer goods produced by modern industry and by individual handicrafts.

4. By *size of enterprise* (Table 4.40). Data on the gross-value output of large-scale industrial enterprises, at 1952 prices, for 1952–55 were given in the November, 1956, issue of *Statistical Work Bulletin (TCKTTH)*. Since data on the gross value of industrial output are

available, the gross value of small-scale enterprises can be derived as a residual.

5. By *individual industry* (Table 4.41). Figures on the gross-value output at 1952 prices can be found for 19 individual industries. Most of these figures covered the period from 1952 to 1956.

6. By *province* (Table 4.42). Provincial data on the gross value of industrial output can be found from the annual communiqués issued by various provincial statistical bureaus and the work reports of governors or deputy governors of various provinces. Data are assembled in Table 4.42 for 27 provinces, autonomous regions, and independent municipalities with Hupeh and Tibet missing.

Gross Value of Factory Output

In addition to Tables 4.38 and 4.39, in which data on the gross value of factory output by ownership of establishment and by production use were given, data are available also for the following classifications of the gross value of factory output.

1. By *area* (Table 4.43). Estimates of the gross value of factory output in inland and coastal areas can be derived from relative weights given in the November, 1956, issue of *Statistical Work Bulletin* and the August, 1957, issue of *Planned Economy*. These data were given in 1952 prices and cover 1949 and 1952–56.

2. *The gross value of factory output of private industry*. Data on a number of classifications of the gross value of factory output of private industry are available:

   a. By *sector* (Table 4.44). Data on the gross-value output at 1952 prices of modern factory and of handicraft factory in private industry can be found for 1953–55 in Ch'ien Hua, *et al., Changes in Private Industry and Trade in China during the Past Seven Years (1949–57).*[94]

   b. By *production use* (Table 4.45). The same source also gives figures on the gross value of producer and consumer goods produced by private factories. Data are expressed in 1952 prices and are available for only one year—1954.

   c. By *size of establishment* (Table 4.46). Data on the division of the gross value of factory output of private industry between large- and small-scale enterprises can be found also in the above source.

Data are given in 1952 prices and cover 1953–55.

   d. By *individual industry* (Table 4.47). Figures on the gross value of factory output at 1952 prices of 14 branches of private industry are compiled in Table 4.47. Most of these figures cover the period from 1952 to 1954.

Gross Value of Output of Various Branches of Industry

Data are available for the gross-value output of the following industries, at 1952 prices.

1. The *electric power* industry. By state, joint, and private enterprises for 1949–57 (Table 4.48).

2. The *coal* industry. By state, joint, co-operative and private enterprises for 1949–56 (Table 4.49).

3. The *iron-and-steel* industry. By factory and handicraft production for 1949–56. Data on the gross value of factory output are classified further by ownership of enterprise (Table 4.50).

4. The *metal-processing* industry

   a. By *subbranches,* such as machine building, metal-products manufacturing, and repairing. Data on machine-building and metal-products manufacturing industries are classified further by ownership of enterprise (Table 4.51).

   b. Between *inland and coastal areas* for 1952 and 1955 (Table 4.52).

5. The *paper* industry. By factory and handicraft production for 1949–57 and by factory production by ownership of enterprise (Table 4.53).

6. The *textile* industry

   a. By *factory and handicraft production* for 1949–57, and further by factory production by ownership of enterprise and by handicraft production by handicraft cooperatives and individual handicrafts (Table 4.54).

   b. By *producer and consumer goods* for 1952–56 (Table 4.55).

The Gross Value of Industrial Output of Various Provinces

In addition to Table 4.42, data on the gross value of industrial output at constant prices at the provincial level are available for the following groups:

[94]Peking: Finance Publishing House, 1957.

1. Percentage distribution of the gross value of industrial output of various provinces, by major branches of industry (Table 4.56). Data are assembled for 15 provinces and municipalities: Shanghai, Liaoning, Kirin, Heilungkiang, Shantung, Kiangsu, Anhwei, Chekiang, Hupeh, Hunan, Kiangsi, Kwangtung, Kwangsi, Szechuan, and Kweichow.

2. Gross value of the output of producer and consumer goods in the Inner Mongolia Autonomous Region for 1952–56 (Table 4.57).

3. Gross value of the output of various branches of industry in the Inner Mongolia Autonomous Region for 1947, 1949, 1952, 1957, and 1958 (Table 4.58).

The Structure and the Gross-Value Output of The Handicraft Industry

Data on the structure and the gross-value output of the handicraft industry are available for the following groups.

1. Gross value of the output of handicraft cooperatives and of individual handicraft operators for 1949–55 (Table 4.59).

2. Number of establishments, number of gainfully occupied persons, and gross-value output of individual handicrafts, handicraft cooperatives, and handicraft factories employing 10 workers or fewer in various provinces for 1949–54 (Table 4.60). These data are compiled for 21 provinces, autonomous regions, and independent municipalities from the statistics given by the Economic Research Institute of the Chinese National Academy of Sciences.

3. Number of establishments, number of gainfully occupied persons, and gross-value output of individual handicrafts in 20 provinces in 1954, with breakdown between individual handicrafts and subsidiary farm crafts and further breakdown of individual handicrafts into stationary handicrafts, itinerant handicrafts, and joint tool groups (Table 4.61).

4. Number of establishments, number of gainfully occupied persons, and gross-value output of individual handicrafts in urban and rural areas of 12 provinces in 1954 (Table 4.62).

5. Number of establishments, number of gainfully occupied persons, and gross-value output of individual handicrafts engaged in the production of producer and consumer goods in 15 provinces and municipalities in 1954 (Table 4.63).

THE NET VALUE OF
INDUSTRIAL OUTPUT (TABLE 4.64)

As indicated above, available data on the net value of industrial output are very scarce. In addition to the net value of total industrial output, the estimates of which were derived for 1952–56 in Table 2.5, data can be found only for the enterprises of the Ministry of Coal Industry as well as those of the Ministry of Food.

COMPOSITION AND UTILIZATION OF POWER AND PRODUCTION EQUIPMENT

As indicated in the section on capital formation, there are two types of fixed assets in industry: one type is used for industrial production, and the other is not. The most important components of industrial fixed assets used for industrial production are power equipment and production equipment. The following will deal with these two types of equipment with regard to three aspects: (1) the composition of equipment, (2) the measurement of equipment capacity, and (3) indicators of capacity utilization.[95]

Power Equipment

THE COMPOSITION
OF POWER EQUIPMENT

Power equipment includes "the total stock of machines and equipment for converting energy from one form into another or for changing the parameters (potential, temperature, and the like) of a particular kind of energy."[96] Also included are the machinery and equipment which transmit energy over distance or supply it to consumers.

Power equipment may be classified into the following groups:

1. *Power-generating equipment* refers to the machinery and equipment which convert potential energy of natural resources, such as fuel, water, and wind, into thermal, mechanical, or electrical energy. Included in the power generating equipment are boilers, prime movers, electric motors, and power generators.

[95]Unless otherwise indicated, the following summary is based largely on Department of Planning and Statistics, Hupeh University, *op. cit.*, Chapters 5 and 8.
[96]*Ibid.*, p. 244.

2. *Transforming plants* are those used for converting the parameters of a particular kind of energy. For example, transforming stations usually receive electrical energy of high voltage and release it with much lower voltage. Transformers are the most important equipment of these plants.

3. *Transmitting plants* are those used for transmission of energy: power transmission lines, electric and heating networks, and long-distance gas-pipeline networks.

4. *Consuming plants* receive the final form of energy, which is consumed directly for production. To these plants belong receivers of all kinds: electric motors, electric furnaces, electric welding apparatus, and lighting equipment.

MEASUREMENT OF GENERATING CAPACITY

UNITS OF MEASUREMENT

Energy generated by power equipment usually may be measured in terms of kilowatts or horsepower. One horsepower is the energy generated by the weight of 1 kilogram in falling through a height of 1 meter and is equivalent to 75 kilogram-meters per second. A kilowatt is equal to 102 kilogram-meters per second. Currently, kilowatts are adopted as the standard unit of measurement in China. Horsepower is to be converted to kilowatts according to the ratio of 1 to 0.736.

CATEGORIES OF CAPACITY

There are several categories of generating capacity:

1. *Maximum effective capacity (tsui-ta yu-hsiao neng-li).* The effective capacity of a piece of generating equipment refers to the power generated by the equipment, exclusive of mechanical losses caused by the friction of parts. Maximum effective capacity is the largest amount of power generated by a piece of equipment over a period of time without breakdown.

2. *Installed capacity (an-chuan neng-li, or she-pei neng-li).* The installed capacity of a power station is the sum of the maximum effective capacities in kilowatts of all installed electric generators connected to prime movers.

3. *Available capacity (k'o-yung neng-li).* The available capacity of a power station is

determined in the same way as the installed capacity but takes into account the bottlenecks which may exist in the different shops or sections of the station.

4. *Maximum Capacity (ting-tien neng-li).* The maximum capacity, often called the "peak load" or the "peak capacity," of a power station refers to the highest amount of power generated during an interval of half an hour in the course of a year, a month, or a day.

INDICATORS OF CAPACITY UTILIZATION

The most important indicators used in China to signify the degree of the utilization of generating equipment capacity are (1) the average number of utilization hours of the installed capacity and (2) the rate of utilization of the installed capacity.

The average number of utilization hours is the ratio of daily or annual output of electric power to average installed capacity. Algebraically, the indicator may be written as follows:

$$\text{Number of utilization hours of the installed capacity (hours)} = \frac{\text{output of electric power (kilowatt-hours)}}{\text{average installed capacity (kilowatts)}}$$

The rate of utilization of the installed capacity during a given period is the ratio of the average number of utilization hours to the number of calendar hours, or the ratio of the actual output of electric power to the theoretical output (which is the product of the average installed capacity multiplied by the number of calendar hours). In algebraic terms the indicator may be shown as follows:

$$\text{Rate of utilization of installed capacity (\%)} = \frac{\text{average number of utilization hours}}{\text{number of calendar hours}} \times 100$$

$$= \frac{\text{output of electric power (kilowatt-hours)}}{\text{average installed capacity (kilowatts)} \times \text{number of calendar hours}} \times 100$$

Production Equipment

Production equipment consists of machines, machine tools, apparatus, and devices with which workers work on raw materials and unfinished products. Power equipment, factory buildings, and warehouses are not included in production equipment.

In industry, there are a large number of different types of production equipment whose capacity may be measured in terms of output per unit of time. For example, the capacity of an air hammer is indicated by the amount of coal in tons extracted per hour, and the capacity of a rice grinder by the amount of rice in kilograms ground per hour. Secondly, equipment capacity may be expressed by the number of working machines. For example, the number of spindles is used to indicate the capacity of spinning equipment. Thirdly, the working volume or area of a piece of equipment may be used to measure its capacity. For example, the effective volume of a blast furnace in cubic meters and the floor space of an open-hearth furnace in square meters are used to represent the capacity of the blast furnace and of the open-hearth furnace, respectively.

In China, a rough measure is frequently used to indicate the utilization of the capacity of the existing equipment. This measure is called the rate of utilization of existing equipment *(hsien-yu she-pei shih-yung-lü)*, which is the ratio of the amount of equipment in operation to the amount of existing equipment. But for major branches of industry, certain more sophisticated measures are employed. The following will explain the concepts of some of these measures for which statistics are available.

THE COAL INDUSTRY

The basic operation of the coal industry is the extraction of coal. This is done by cutting and hewing primarily with the help of mining equipment, such as coal combines and coal-cutting machines. The degree of capacity utilization is expressed in terms of the so-called "rate of utilization of mining equipment." As an example, the utilization of coal-cutting machines can be measured by the following formula:

$$\text{Rate of utilization of coal-cutting machines (\%)} = \frac{\text{average number of machines in operation}}{\text{average number of machines registered}} \times 100$$

The number of registered machines includes those in reserve as well as those not utilized. In other words, registered machines are those which an enterprise actually has. The average number of registered machines is derived by dividing the sum of the daily number of registered machines during a reporting period by the number of calendar days in the period. The average number of machines in operation is obtained by dividing the sum of the daily number of machines actually employed during a reporting period divided by the number of working days in the period (that is, exclusive of off-days and holidays).

THE IRON-AND-STEEL INDUSTRY

There are three basic operations of the iron-and-steel industry: blast furnace, open-hearth furnace, and rolling mills.[97] Indicators of the utilization of the capacity of these furnaces, as well as that of electric furnaces, are expressed in terms of the so-called "coefficients of utilization."

The capacity of a blast furnace is indicated in terms of the effective volume *(yu-hsiao jung-chih)* in cubic meters. Since a blast furnace operates continuously, a working day of the furnace consists of 24 hours. The coefficient of utilization of a blast furnace is, then, the output of pig iron in tons per cubic meter of the effective volume in 24 hours.

The capacity of an open-hearth furnace is measured by the floor space in square meters. The coefficient of utilization of the open-hearth furnace is the output of steel in tons per square meter of the floor space in 24 hours.

The capacity of a revolving furnace is measured in terms of metric tons or cubic meters of the furnace. The coefficient of utilization of the revolving furnace is the output of steel in tons

---

[97]The purpose of blast-furnace production is to smelt pig iron out of charge materials, such as fuel, ores, and limestone. The open-hearth furnace process is directed towards the production of steel from pig iron. The purpose of rolling is to process steel by rolling it between revolving furnaces of a rolling mill.

per metric ton, or per cubic meter, of the furnace in 24 hours.

The capacity of an electric furnace is measured in million volt-amperes. The coefficient of utilization of the electric furnace is the output of steel in tons per million volt-amperes in 24 hours.

THE METAL-PROCESSING INDUSTRY

There are four basic operations in the metal-processing industry: casting, forging, mechanical processing, and assembly. The major production equipment of the industry consists of various types of metal-cutting machines and forging equipment.

The degree of utilization of equipment capacity in the metal processing industry during a given period is estimated on the basis of the following formula:

$$\text{Rate of utilization (\%)} = \frac{\text{actual number of machine hours}}{\text{possible number of machine hours}} \times 100$$

The actual number of machine hours refers to the sum of the daily number of machine hours of the equipment actually in operation during the reporting period. The possible number of machine hours is estimated by first multiplying the sum of the daily number of machines already installed during regular working days of the reporting period[98] by 15.5 hours and then subtracting from the number of machine hours thus derived the actual number of machine hours used for repairing.

THE CEMENT INDUSTRY

The basic production equipment of the cement industry consists of revolving furnaces for the production of clinkers — the intermediate product for the manufacture of cement, mills for grinding raw materials, cement mills for grinding clinkers, and driers.

The indicator for the utilization of revolving furnaces is represented by the output of clinker in tons per square meter of the furnace in each operating hours.[99] For indicating the utilization

of mills and driers, the measure for the output of cement in tons per hour is used.

THE COTTON TEXTILE INDUSTRY

The major operations of the cotton textile industry are spinning and weaving, and spindles and looms are the basic equipment employed. The degree of capacity utilization of spindles and looms is measured by the following formula:

$$\text{Rate of utilization of spindles (looms) (\%)} = \frac{\text{number of spindle (loom) hours operated}}{\text{number of spindle (loom) hours equipped}} \times 100$$

The number of spindle (loom) hours operated refers to the sum of the spindles (looms) each multiplied, respectively, by the accumulated total of actual operating hours during a month. The number of spindle (loom) hours equipped is obtained by summing up the spindles (looms) already installed during the month, each multiplied, respectively, by the accumulated total of regular working hours. The accumulated total of regular working hours of an installed spindle (loom) is the number of its regular working days multiplied by 22.5 hours.

**Statistics of Capacity
and Capacity Utilization**

CAPACITY OF POWER AND PRODUCTION EQUIPMENT

POWER EQUIPMENT CAPACITY

Three types of data on power equipment capacity are available: (1) the total generating capacity and breakdowns of the total, (2) the length of power transmission lines installed, and (3) the construction of hydroelectric power stations in rural areas.

1. Nation-wide generating capacity for 1949–59 and the generating capacity of the

[98]The number of regular working days during the reporting period refers to the number of calendar days during the period, exclusive of holidays and off-days.
[99]Lou Chi-cheng, "Major Technical-Economic Norms of the Cement Industry," *CHCC*, No. 7 (July 9, 1957), pp. 29–30.

enterprises of the Ministry of Electric Power for 1949–52 (Table 4.65).

In addition, figures are available for the following breakdowns of the total capacity:

    a. Between hydraulic and thermal power for 1952, 1956, and 1957 (Table 4.66).

    b. By capacity of machines for 1949, and 1952–57 (Table 4.67).

    c. By ownership of establishment for 1949 and 1952–56 (Table 4.68).

    d. Between public and industry-owned power stations for 1952 and 1956 (Table 4.69).

    e. By region for 1949 through 1956 (Table 4.70).

    f. For northeast ultra-high-tension network, Peking-Tientsin-Tangshan network, and Shanghai network for 1949–56 (Table 4.71).

    g. For Szechuan, Sinkiang and Inner Mongolia from 1949 to 1959 (Table 4.72).

2. Figures on the length of power transmission lines with 11,000 volts and above are available for 1949 and 1952–56 (Table 4.73).

3. Statistics were published for the construction of hydroelectric power stations in rural areas in the first half of 1958 in various provinces (Table 4.74).

PRODUCTION EQUIPMENT CAPACITY

The following data on the capacity of production equipment of a few major industries were published by the Department of Industrial Statistics of the State Statistical Bureau for the years prior to 1957:

1. The *coal industry.* Annual increases in the equipment and in the output capacity of the enterprises of the Ministry of Coal Industry (Tables 4.75 and 4.76).

2. The *iron-and-steel industry.* Annual increases in the number and the capacity of blast and open-hearth furnaces, as well as in the output capacity of pig iron, steel ingot, and rolled steel (Tables 4.77–4.79).

3. The *metal-processing industry.* The number and geographic distribution of metal-cutting machines used in the metal-processing industry (Tables 4.80 and 4.81).

4. The *paper-making industry.* The number of major machines used in the paper industry and annual increase in the output capacity of state paper-manufacturing enterprises (Tables 4.82 and 4.83).

5. The *textile industry.* The number of major machines used in the textile industry and the distribution of spindles and looms between inland and coastal areas (Tables 4.84 and 4.85).

UTILIZATION OF POWER AND PRODUCTION EQUIPMENT CAPACITY

Data on the rate of utilization of power-generating and production equipment are gathered for 11 industries in Table 4.86. In addition, the following data on capacity utilization are available:

1. Hours of utilization of generating equipment of the electric power industry for 1949–58 (Table 4.87).

2. Rates of utilization of the capacity output of steam boilers, a-c electric motors, and transformers in 1957 (Table 4.88).

3. Coefficients of utilization of blast and open-hearth furnaces of all enterprises in the iron-and-steel industry, the enterprises of the Ministry of Metallurgical industry, as well as the iron-and-steel enterprises in Liaoning Province, including Anshan Iron and Steel Company, for 1949–58 (Tables 4.89 and 4.90).

4. Coefficients of utilization of electric and revolving furnaces of the enterprises of the Ministry of Metallurgical Industry for 1952 through 1956 (Table 4.91).

5. Hours of machine stoppage in the enterprises of the First Ministry of Machine Industry for 1955 and 1956 (Table 4.92).

MECHANIZATION

A number of measures were adopted in China to indicate mechanization of industry. Included are (1) fixed assets per worker, (2) electric power per worker, and (3) percentage share of work performed by manual and mechanical processes.

Fixed Assets per Worker (Table 4.93)

Fixed assets per worker in an industry are obtained by dividing the gross value of fixed assets used for industrial production by the number of production workers in that industry.[100]

---

[100]Data Office, *TCKT*, "The Technological Level of Industrial Production in China," *TCKT*, No. 8 (April 29, 1957), pp. 30-33. For the concepts of fixed assets and production workers, see, respectively, the sections on capital formation and on employment.

Statistics on fixed assets per worker are available for 21 industries. Most of these statistics cover only state and joint enterprises for the period 1953–55.

Electric Power per Worker (Table 4.94)

Electric power per worker in an industry is obtained by dividing the total amount of electricity consumed by the industry by the number of its production workers.

Data on electric power per worker were published by the Department of Industrial Statistics of the State Statistical Bureau for 10 industries for 1953 and 1956 with the exception of the iron-and-steel industry, for which data are also available for 1954–55.

Percentage Shares of Work Performed by Manual and Mechanical Processes (Table 4.95)

In industry, a given type of work may be performed either by labor or by machines, or by both. Percentage shares of the work done by labor and machines are frequently used to indicate the degree of mechanization. Such statistics are available for the coal industry for 1952–56. Data were given for percentage shares of the volume of extraction, loading, and transport performed by labor and by machines.

INPUT-OUTPUT RELATIONS

One type of statistics which is considered of great importance in China in planning industrial production and in checking the performance of enterprises is the so-called "economic-technical indicators." Included are principally measures showing the amount of output per unit of input and the amount of input per unit of output. Such statistics are available for a number of industries and may be grouped into four categories: (1) output per unit of labor, (2) output per unit of capital, (3) consumption of electric power and coal per unit of output, and (4) consumption of raw materials and basic and supplementary materials per unit of output.

Output per Unit of Labor (Tables 4.96–4.97)

Data on labor productivity in value terms will be given in the section on employment,

productivity, and wages, but those in physical terms are presented in Tables 4.96 and 4.97.

Output per Unit of Capital

Coefficients of utilization of various furnaces in the iron-and-steel industry are designed to indicate not only the utilization of these furnaces but also their productivity. Data on coefficients of utilization of blast, open-hearth, revolving, and electric furnaces were given in Tables 4.89–91. In addition, the following statistics on productivity of fixed assets and production equipment are available:

1. Gross-value output at 1952 prices per yuan of the gross fixed assets in state industry for 1953–55, in the enterprises of the First Ministry of Machine Industry for 1952–56, and in the textile industry for 1952–56 (Table 4.98).
2. Physical output per unit of production equipment of the following industries:
    - *a.* The metal-processing industry for 1953 through 1956 (Tables 4.99 and 4.100).
    - *b.* The cement industry for 1952 and 1955 –1958 and the glass industry for 1952 and 1958 (Table 4.101).
    - *c.* State-operated paper-making enterprises for 1952–57 (Table 4.102).
    - *d.* The cotton textile industry for 1949 and 1952–58 (Table 4.103).

Consumption of Electricity and Coal per Unit of Output

The following data are available for the amount of electricity and coal consumed per unit of major product:

1. Amount of electricity consumed per unit of output of nine major products for 1952 through 1956 (Table 4.104).
2. Amount of coal consumed per unit of output of electric power and building materials for the period 1949–58 (Table 4.105).

Consumption of Raw and Other Materials per Unit of Output

Data on the input of raw materials and of basic and supplementary materials can be classified into the following groups according to the type of material consumed:

1. Amount of iron ore, pig iron, coke, and scrap iron consumed per unit of output in the

iron and steel industry for 1952–57 (Table 4.106).

2. Amount of rolled steel consumed per unit of output of major products of the metal-processing industry for 1953–56 (Table 4.107).

3. Amount of explosives, fusecap, and blasting fuse consumed per unit of output of coal, iron ore, and limestone, the amount of mining timber consumed per unit of output of coal, and the amount of processed coal consumed per unit of output of metallurgical coke, for 1953–56 (Table 4.108).

4. Amount of sulfuric acid, nitric acid, caustic soda, and soda ash consumed per unit of output of the products of the chemical, paper, and glass industries (Table 4.109).

5. Amount of rubber consumed per unit of output of tire and rubber footwear, for 1953–56 (Table 4.110).

6. Amount of wood and reep consumed per unit of output of pulp and amount of paper pulp consumed per unit of output of paper for 1952–57 (Table 4.111).

7. Amount of raw cotton consumed per bale of cotton yarn for 1949 and 1952–58 and the amount of cotton yarn consumed per thousand kilometers of cotton cloth for 1952–57 (Table 4.112).

8. Amount of tobacco consumed per case of cigarettes for 1952–57 (Table 4.113).

9. Amount of soybeans, rapeseed, peanuts, cottonseed, and sesame consumed per unit of output of various edible vegetable oils for 1952–56 (Table 4.114).

In addition, data are assembled in Table 4.115 for the rate of output from raw materials of sugar, white wine, and edible vegetable oils. The rate of output of a product from a given material is the ratio of the output of the product to the input of material, given in percentage terms. The rate of output of sugar from sugar cane, for example, may be obtained from the following formula:[101]

$$\text{Rate of output of sugar from sugar cane (\%)} = \frac{\text{output of sugar (in tons)}}{\text{input of sugar cane (in tons)}} \times 100$$

PRODUCTION EFFICIENCY

A number of indicators are employed in China to show the efficiency of production in various industries. Such data are available for

four industries: electric power, coal, metal processing, and paper.

The Electric Power Industry (Tables 4.116 and 4.117)

1. Figures were published for the rate of loss in transmission of the electric power industry for 1952–58 and of the enterprises of the Ministry of Electric Power for 1949–56. The rate of loss of a power plant may be obtained from the following formula:[102]

$$\text{Rate of loss (\%)} = \frac{\text{total losses of electricity (in kilowatt-hours)}}{\text{total supply of electricity (in kilowatt-hours)}} \times 100$$

The total supply of electricity is the amount of electric power generated by the plant, exclusive of the amount used for own production needs. The amount of losses is the difference between the total supply of electricity and the amount actually sold to customers.

2. Data are also available for the number of accidents and the amount of electricity not transmitted due to accidents in the electric power industry for 1951–56.

The Coal Industry (Table 4.118)

Data on the productive efficiency of the coal industry can be found in the form of the recovery rate *(hui-tsai-lü)* or the loss rate *(sun-shih-lü)* for 1949 and 1952–56. The recovery rate is the ratio of the amount of coal extracted in a given area to the amount of coal reserve in that area. The loss rate is the ratio of the amount of coal lost in the recovery area to the amount of coal reserve. Both rates are given in terms of percentages. Since the total coal reserve in a given area is by definition composed of the amount of recovery and that of losses, the sum of the recovery and loss rates is necessarily equal to unity.[103]

The Metal Processing Industry (Tables 4.119 and 4.120)

Two types of data are available for the productive efficiency of the metal-processing in-

[101]Department of Planning and Statistics, Hupeh University, *op. cit.*, p. 385.
[102]*Ibid.*, p. 359.
[103]*Ibid.*, p. 363.

dustry. One type gives the rates of rejection of cast iron, cast steel, and mechanical processing in state enterprises for 1953–56. The rate of rejection of a given product is the ratio of the amount of the products rejected by prescribed standards to the total output.

Another type of data explains in terms of percentage distribution the causes for rejection of the parts produced by the enterprises of the First Ministry of Machine Industry in 1956.

The Paper Industry (Table 4.121)

The efficiency indicator of the paper industry is the rate of the total finished output of paper *(chih-chang tsung-cheng-p'in-lü)*, which is the ratio of the finished output to the sum of the finished output and the amount of paper rejected and lost in the manufacturing process. The finished output of paper refers to the output which has completed the processes of cutting, selecting, and packaging and has met prescribed standards.[104]

Figures on the rate of the total finished output of paper were published for the state paper-making enterprises for 1952–57.

CONSUMPTION OF PRODUCTS

Statistics are available for the total consumption of a few products, with breakdowns according to sectors, areas, and purposes of consumption. The following data give information on the consumption of four products: electricity, paper, cotton cloth, and knitted cotton products.

Electricity

1. The State Statistical Bureau published data on the amount of electricity consumed in the entire economy for 1949 through 1956, with breakdowns into industry, agriculture, and transport (Table 4.122).
2. The information on the amount of electricity consumed by industry was broken down further into nine branches of industry (Table 4.123).
3. The State Bureau also published information on average rates of self-consumption of electricity by power plants for the economy as a whole and for the plants under the Ministry of Electric Power for 1949–56, with breakdowns

into thermal and hydro power plants (Table 4.124).

The rate of self-consumption of electricity by a power plant is obtained by the following formula:

$$\text{Rate of self-consumption (\%)} = \frac{\text{amount of electricity consumed by the plant itself (in kilowatt-hours)}}{\text{amount of electricity generated by the plant (in kilowatt-hours)}} \times 100$$

The amount of self-consumption refers to that used for the purposes of generating electricity, including the use of electricity for electric motors, lighting, heating, and ventilation.[105]

Paper

Data are available for 1952–56 for the following breakdowns of the amount of paper consumed:

1. By industry and by agricultural cooperatives (Table 4.125).
2. By governmental agencies and public organizations and by residents (Table 4.126).
3. For cultural and educational purposes (Table 4.127).

Cotton Cloth and Knitted Cotton Products (Table 4.128)

Statistics were published for the total consumption of cotton cloth and knitted cotton products with breakdowns into urban and rural consumption for 1950–56.

COST OF PRODUCTION

The Concept and Composition of Cost

The cost of industrial products of an enterprise is the sum of expenditures incurred by the enterprise in producing these products.[106] According to the regulation of the State Planning

[104]*Ibid.*, p. 384
[105]*Ibid.*, p. 359.
[106]*Ibid.*, p. 388.

Commission and the Ministry of Finance,[107] these expenditures include the following items:

1. Raw material and basic material.
2. Supplementary material.
3. Fuel.
4. Power.
5. Wages.
6. Auxiliary wages, such as labor insurance fees, union fees, medical and health allowances, and welfare allowances.
7. Shop expenditures (*ch'e-chien ching-fei*), including depreciation charges, repairing and maintenance expenses for factory buildings and for machinery and equipment, and research and testing expenses.
8. Administrative expenditures, such as warehouse expenditures, interest payments, labor training expenses, and allowances for the personnel transferred to rural areas.
9. Losses due to products rejected.
10. Losses due to work stoppage.
11. Sale expenses, including those for packaging and transportation.

There are a number of cost indicators: total cost, average cost, and the rate of cost reduction. The rate of reduction compares the actual cost of given products either with the planned cost for the same products or with the actual cost of comparable products *(k'o-pi ch'ang-p'in)* in the preceding year. A comparable product refers to the same product produced in both the current and the previous years. A product produced for the first time during the current year is a noncomparable product.

Cost Data

Available statistics on the cost of industrial production are very scarce. Only the following data have been found in print:

TOTAL COST (TABLE 4.129)

Data on the cost of the total commodity production and of comparable products of the enterprises of the Ministry of Textile Industry were published by the State Statistical Bureau for 1952–56, with breakdowns into planned and actual costs.

AVERAGE COST (TABLE 4.130)

Data on cost per unit of output can be found for the electric power and the cotton textile industries for 1952–56 and for the coal industry for 1957 and 1958.

THE RATE OF COST REDUCTION OF COMPARABLE PRODUCTS (TABLES 4.131 AND 4.132)

The State Statistical Bureau published figures on the rate of cost reduction of comparable products for all state enterprises during 1952–58 and for state-operated iron and steel, paper, and textile enterprises for 1953 through 1956. In addition, *Ten Great Years* gives the rate of reduction for 1957 over 1952 and the average annual rate of reduction for the period 1953–57 of the cost of 11 major products produced by the enterprises under various central industrial ministries.

WORKING CAPITAL AND PROFITS

Working Capital

Statistical indicators of working capital in industry are the volume of working capital, the volume of normalized working capital, and the rate of turnover of working capital.

The concept of working capital was explained in the section on capital formation. Normalized working capital of an enterprise refers to that amount of working capital which is specified in the state plan to meet minimum production needs of the enterprise. The rate of turnover of working capital is given in terms of days and is obtained by dividing 360 days in a year by the number of turnovers of working capital during the year. The number of turnovers is derived by dividing the total sale proceeds by the average volume of working capital. The total sale proceeds are estimated on the basis of ex-factory prices and therefore exclude taxes.[108]

Data on the annual rate of growth of working capital in central state industrial enterprises for

[107]*Ibid.*, pp. 389–90; and State Planning Commission and the Ministry of Finance, "Regulations Concerning the Agents of Production, Cost Items and the Cost Accounting of State Industrial Enterprises," *Chi-yeh kuai-chi (Enterprise Accounting)*, No. 17 (September 7, 1959), pp. 5–7.

[108]Department of Planning and Statistics, Hupeh University, *op. cit.*, pp. 421–22; and Shen Mu-chieh, *She-hui chu-yi kung-yeh chi-yeh ti liu-tung tzu-ching (Working Capital of Socialist Industrialist Enterprises)*, Shanghai: Jen-min ch'u-pan-she, 1956, pp. 59–91.

1953–56 were given in Table 3.9. In addition, the following data are available:

1. The volume and the rate of turnover of working capital of the iron-and-steel enterprises under the Ministry of Metallurgical Industry for 1953–56 (Table 4.133).

2. The volume of normalized working capital per thousand kilowatts and the rate of turnover of normalized working capital in the electric power industry for 1953–57 (Table 4.134).

Profits

The accumulation of enterprise resulting from the sale of commodities is the difference between the sale proceeds and the cost of producing these commodities. This difference is composed of profits and taxes. The amount of the profits of the enterprise, therefore, may be obtained by subtracting the sum of cost and taxes from the sale proceeds.[109] The state plan requires that a certain amount of the profits are to be remitted to the state.

Figures on industrial profits can be found for private enterprise and state-operated coal, iron-and-steel, and paper enterprises. The amount of profits remitted to the state are available for state-operated electric power and paper enterprises (Table 4.135).

[109]Department of Planning Statistics, Hupeh University, *op. cit.*, p. 423.

5

AGRICULTURE

SOURCES OF AGRICULTURAL DATA[1]

Like industrial statistics in China, agricultural data are compiled mainly from a system of regular schedules, supplemented by special surveys conducted from time to time. Prior to the Great Leap Forward Movement in 1958, there were five major types of regular schedules: (1) consolidated statistical reports on agricultural production, (2) annual statistical reports on agricultural production, (3) rural basic statistical reports, (4) statistical schedules for use in rural areas, and (5) statistical reports of agricultural producer cooperatives.

CONSOLIDATED STATISTICAL REPORTS ON AGRICULTURAL PRODUCTION

Consolidated statistical reports on agricultural production, which were initiated in 1953 by the State Statistical Bureau in nationally standardized form, provided the major source of basic data on agricultural production. These reports were to be submitted periodically by local governments to the State Bureau. During 1953–55, the governments of various provinces, autonomous regions, and centrally controlled municipalities were designated as the primary units for filling out the regular schedules on the basis of data supplied by *hsien* and relevant departments.[2] The system was revised in 1956 to include nine main schedules and eight supplementary schedules relating to agricultural production and the basic conditions of agricultural producer cooperatives. The *hsien* govern-

ments now became the primary reporting units and were required to compile the comprehensive data from the reports submitted by *hsiang* and the villages, as well as from the Rural Basic Statistical Reports.[3] The reports from *hsiang* and villages were based on the following investigations undertaken each year: (1) at least one survey of sown acreage and harvested volume on the basis of actual production conditions of the area, (2) a survey of the production of tea, silkworms, and fruits in key producing areas, and (3) a census of livestock, cultivated acreage and agricultural mutual-aid teams and producer cooperatives.[4] The statistical bureaus and the departments of agriculture and forestry at the provincial level were in turn required to prepare reports on the basis of returns from *hsien* and then to submit them to the State Bureau. Any changes in the form made by local governments were subject to the State Bureau's approval.[5]

ANNUAL STATISTICAL REPORTS ON AGRICULTURAL PRODUCTION

Annual statistical reports on agricultural production, which presented a summary of agricultural production during the year, were

[1] A discussion of sources and quality of agricultural statistics will be found in Choh-ming Li, *The Statistical System of Communist China,* Berkeley: University of California Press, 1962.
[2] Editorial Committee for Statistical Work Handbook, *Handbook for Agricultural Statistical Work,* Peking: Statistical Publishing House, 1956, p. 4. Hereafter the source will be cited as *Handbook for Agricultural Statistical Work.*
[3] *Ibid.*
[4] Huang Chien-t'o, "Sum Up Work Experiences and Make Effort to Improve Agricultural Statistical Work," *TCKT,* No. 8 (April 29, 1957), pp. 5–8, reference on p. 8.
[5] *Handbook for Agricultural Statistical Work, op. cit.,* pp. 4–5.

the most important of all regular schedules.[6] These reports were introduced in 1951 by the Statistical Department of the Planning Bureau of the Financial and Economic Commission under the then Government Administrative Council in Peking. At that time, the governments at the provincial level were designated as the primary reporting units, but the special-district, or *hsien*, governments were, in fact, responsible for preparing the reports.[7]

The procedure was revised in 1953 with the establishment of the State Statistical Bureau. The statistical bureaus and agricultural departments at the provincial level were now called upon to assume joint responsibility for compiling the annual reports on the basis of the returns on the periodic statistical schedules and other relevant forms.[8] The provincial governments were to submit the annual reports to the State Bureau by February 20 of the following year.[9] But these reports were usually several months late. For example, out of 27 provinces, autonomous regions, and centrally controlled municipalities, only 10 submitted the 1955 annual reports on time.[10] As a result, the publication of the annual communiqué on the national economy was delayed. This prompted the State Bureau to issue "simplified and express" annual reports toward the end of 1955. These reports consisted of 13 forms relating to various targets for agriculture, forestry, and irrigation as they were needed in preparing the annual communiqué. The provincial governments were requested to fill out these reports in addition to the regular annual reports. However, such a "simplified and express" version of the annual reports was later considered a duplication of effort. Speaking in October, 1957, at the Sixth National Statistical Conference, Hsüeh Mu-ch'iao, then the Director of the State Statistical Bureau, suggested the use of other measures to expedite the publication of the annual communiqué.[11]

RURAL BASIC STATISTICAL REPORTS

Beginning in 1956, the State Statistical Bureau issued a set of basic statistical schedules for rural areas on an experimental basis. These schedules included 10 major forms and two supplementary forms relating to agricultural production and cooperation, as well as certain major indicators used in national economic

planning. According to the regulations set up by the State Bureau, the provincial governments were permitted to change the number of indicators shown in the schedules according to local needs. But changes could not be made by the governments at the special-district, or *hsien*, level and below.[12] The schedules were to be filled out by the people's councils of *hsiang* and villages on the basis of surveys undertaken by the people's councils and data supplied by agricultural producer cooperatives.[13]

STATISTICAL SCHEDULES FOR USE IN RURAL AREAS

For the purpose of supplementing the rural basic statistical reports, the State Statistical Bureau initiated in 1956 a set of schedules, known as "statistical schedules for use in rural areas" (*nung-tsung pei-yung t'ung-chi pao-kao-piao*). These schedules, designed primarily to meet the needs of local government and party leadership, contained 21 forms dealing with data on a variety of subjects, such as the preparation of cultivation, progress of production, technical measures, natural calamities, and subsidiary products. In obtaining these data, local governments were requested by the State Bureau to rely primarily on "model surveys" or "key-point surveys" and resort less to complete enumeration.[13]

STATISTICAL REPORTS OF AGRI-CULTURAL PRODUCER COOPERATIVES

As a part of the effort made by the State Statistical Bureau to establish a system of regular schedules in the rural areas, a set of statistical schedules was also issued in 1956 to agricultural producer cooperatives. These schedules contained seven major forms and one supplementary form relating to the following subjects: (1) the basic conditions of agricultural producer cooperatives (including indicators on

[6]Hsüeh Mu-ch'iao, "Report at the Sixth National Statistical Conference," *TCKT*, No. 21 (November 14, 1957), pp. 1–21.
[7]*Handbook for Agricultural Statistical Work, op. cit.*, p. 6.
[8]*Ibid.*
[9]Huang Chien t'o, *op. cit.*
[10]*Handbook for Agricultural Statistical Work, op. cit.*
[11]Hsüeh Mu-ch' iao, *op. cit.*
[12]*Handbook for Agricultural Statistical Work, op. cit.*, p. 3.
[13]*Ibid.*
[13] *Ibid.*, p. 5.

the number of households joining the cooperatives, population, labor power, and the utilization and socialization of major producer goods, such as land and draught animals), (2) sown acreage and crops harvested; (3) the output of tea, silkworms, and fruits, (4) afforestation; (5) saplings grown, (6) seed selection, (7) irrigation, and (8) income distribution. Agricultural producer cooperatives were to submit these forms to the people's councils of *hsiang* and villages according to the dates specified by the State Bureau.[14] Since the information to be reported covered a wide variety of areas, this cause a great deal of confusion for the peasants. The problem became so serious that in early 1957 the head of the Agricultural Statistical Department of the State Bureau found it necessary to suggest that these schedules be simplified.[15]

The system of regular schedules in the rural areas was disrupted in 1958 with the advent of the Great Leap Forward and the people's communes. The effects of the Great Leap Forward on the state statistical system were discussed in the section on industry. Suffice it here to summarize a few major developments in agricultural statistical services since 1958.[16]

1. As may be recalled, during the Great Leap Forward Movement, the State Statistical Bureau lost its control over statistical services in the country, and statistical schedules, indicators, computing methods, and reporting dates were all subject to the views of the local party leadership. During this period, statistics were given great local importance, and progress statistics and comparative statistics became the major sources for agricultural data.

2. In 1958, monthly telegraphic reports on major indicators were initiated. After a crop was harvested, the governments at the provincial level were required to submit within one month a telegraphic report giving figures for each *hsien* on sown acreage, harvested acreage, total output, and yield per unit of sown area and harvested area.[17]

3. Beginning in 1959, statistical services were inaugurated in the people's communes.[18] Statistical officers were installed in the communes, and an operational system was introduced. The system was designed to collect primary source data and was composed of original records, permanent files of statistical materials and statistical schedules and figures. Original records were the most basic of all and

covered records of such items as changes in population, cultivated acreage, farm implements, livestock and poultry, cropping, and farm management.

4. Early in 1959, a national movement of farm-output surveys was initiated, and since then these surveys have become part of the foundation for agricultural statistics. Surveys were confined to important farm products — especially food grains, cotton, and oil-bearing crops — and their major production areas. For the purpose of conducting surveys, special committees were organized at every level from province through special district and *hsien* to commune and production brigade, with the local party secretary as the chairman. The method of investigation employed in these surveys was concisely summarized by Professor Li in his *The Statistical System of Communist China:*

The entire investigation was generally broken into four stages, starting with estimating cropped area and output, usually by means of visual observation, during the period of crop growth. These estimates — aside from serving the needs of those engaged in tax collection, state purchasing and preliminary distribution within the communes — furnished the basis for the second stage, namely, dividing the production areas into types in accordance with their estimated productivity and then choosing from each type a small "model area" judged to be representative of it. With harvest came the third stage that centered on sample cutting on each one of the "model areas." As the final stage, total output was computed by applying the results of the cutting surveys to the model areas and then to whole areas.[19]

TYPES OF AGRICULTURAL DATA

Available statistics on Chinese agriculture may be grouped into five categories: (1) agricultural land area and afforested area, (2) agricultural physical output and livestock, (3) value of agricultural output, (4) state farms, meteoro-

[14] *Ibid.*, pp. 3–4.

[15] Huang Chien-t'o, *op. cit.*, p. 7.

[16] The effects of the Great Leap Forward and the people's communes on the system of agricultural statistics in 1958 and its' development during 1959–60 were investigated by Cho-ming Li in his *Statistical System of Communist China (op. cit.*, particularly pp. 83–98 and 123–135).

[17] Huang Chien-t'o, "Agricultural Statistical Work Must Cope with the New Situation Arising from the Universal Establishment of Rural People's Communes," *CHYTC*, No. 2 (January 23, 1959), pp. 15–17. No. 2 (January 23, 1959), pp. 15–17.

[18] "Statistical Services in the Rural People's Communes Are Being Inaugurated," *CHYTC*, No. 2 (January 23, 1959), p. 20.

[19] Choh-ming Li, *op. cit.*, pp. 123–24.

logical services, and agricultural mechanization, and (5) socialization of agriculture.

Included in official agricultural statistics are also those on income distribution of agricultural producer cooperatives and of people's communes and peasant household budgets. For convenience, these statistics will be treated in the section on the standard of living.

AGRICULTURAL LAND AREA AND AFFORESTED AREA

Scope and Classification of Agricultural Land

Agricultural land includes cultivated land, tea gardens, mulberry fields, oak groves, fruit orchards, fish ponds, lotus ponds, oil-yielding tea groves, tung groves, and land grown with reeds. In Chinese practice, when a piece of agricultural land is used for more than one purpose, it is classified according to the major one. For example, a piece of land is classified as cultivated land if it is used primarily for cropping, although some fruit or mulberry trees may also be planted on it.[20]

The statistical estimation of agricultural land was begun in 1956, when the statistical reports on agricultural production were initiated. Prior to that time, only cultivated acreage was estimated. According to the specification in the statistical reports, agricultural land acreage existing on July 1 is to be reported as the acreage for the calendar year, on the ground that usually the land newly reclaimed in the autumn or winter would not be sown in the same year.[21]

CULTIVATED LAND

The most important type of agricultural land is cultivated land. *Cultivated land* refers to "the kind of land which is devoted to the cultivation of various crops and in need of constant ploughing. Included are developed land, newly reclaimed land, land uncultivated for less than three consecutive years, and land currently fallowed."[22] The land which has been developed with labor or machinery but is not sown for the current year is considered cultivated. Excluded from the estimation of cultivated land is the land in the frontier regions and in the minority areas, where the methods of cultivation employed are most primitive.[23]

Cultivated land is divided into two categories: wet fields and dry fields. A *wet field*, sometimes known as a paddy field, refers to "a plot of land around which irrigation channels have been built with water accumulated over it during the course of the growth of the crop, capable of being used for the growing of paddy rice, lotus plants and other plants growing in water."[24] Where, for certain reasons, water is temporarily stored on the land and other crops are planted on it, or where rice and other dry field crops are alternatively planted, the land should still be considered wet field.[25] A *dry field* is "a plot of land on which crops can be raised but which cannot be regularly flooded with water."[26] The growing of crops on dry fields is generally dependent on rain for water supply.

IRRIGATED LAND

Chinese irrigation statistics give information on the total area of irrigated land, the increase in irrigated acreage, and the acreage of improved irrigation. *Irrigated land* refers to the cultivated land that is provided with water through fixed and permanent irrigation facilities, such as channels, reservoirs, ponds and dams, wells, water wheels, and pumps.[27] Irrigated land is made up of both wet fields and watered fields (*shui-chiao-ti*).[28] The latter refers to "that part of dry fields which are supplied with water, according to the needs of the crops, through rivers, fountains, wells, channels, reservoirs, water wheels or other irrigation facilities."[29] The area of irrigation is computed on the basis of cultivated area and not sown area.[30] In Chinese practice, the reporting period for irrigation statistics covers from October 1 of the preceding year to the end of September in the current year.[31]

[20]*Handbook for Agricultural Statistical Work, op. cit.*, pp. 7–8.
[21]*Ibid.*, p. 8; and Liu Te-ling, "Why Are the Statistics of July 1 Taken as the Annual Figures for the Basic Conditions of Agricultural Producer Co-operatives, Cultivated Acreage, and Livestock?" *TCKTTH*, No. 4 (February 29, 1956), pp. 14, 24.
[22]*Handbook for Agricultural Statistical Work, op. cit.*, p. 8.
[23]*Ibid.*
[24]*Ibid.*
[25]*Ibid.*
[26]*Ibid.*
[27]Liao Hsien-hao, "Tabular Forms for Agricultural Production Planning," *CHCC*, No. 4 (May 9, 1957), pp. 30–33; and "Brief Explanations of the Terminologies Used in the Draft of the Second Five-Year Plan," *ibid.*, No. 10 (October 9, 1956).
[28]This definition has been adopted only since 1958. Prior to that year, wet fields not equipped with fixed and permanent irrigation facilities were not considered part of an irrigated area.
[29]*Handbook for Agricultural Statistical Work, op. cit.*, p. 9.
[30]*Ibid.*, p. 34; and Liao Hsien-hao, *op. cit.*, p. 32.
[31]*Handbook for Agricultural Statistical Work, op. cit.*, p. 53.

The increase in *irrigated acreage* is "the actual area of irrigation expanded during the reporting period through various measures, such as the construction of new and the repair of old irrigation facilities, the improvement in management, and the popularization of the scientific method of control over the use of water.[32] Also included is the area which "could be effectively irrigated during the reporting period following the completion of repairs to irrigation facilities but on which, due to certain conditions, such as sufficient rainfall, irrigation was not carried out."[33] The increase in irrigated acreage refers only to the area of dry fields turned into irrigated fields and does not include the fields for single-crop rice turned into those for double-crop rice.[34]

The area of *improved irrigation* is "that part of existing irrigated area which has actually shown a greater resistence to drought and a higher crop yield during the reporting period resulting from various measures, such as constructing or repairing irrigation facilities, strengthening irrigation management, and using extensively the scientific method of control over the use of water."[35]

SOWN ACREAGE

THE CONCEPT AND SCOPE OF SOWN ACREAGE

Sown acreage refers to "the area sown or transplanted with agricultural crops."[36] Sown acreage is not identical with, and is generally larger than, cultivated acreage, for the following reasons:

1. Crops are sometimes sown on agricultural land other than crop land, such as orchards and mulberry fields.

2. There exists multiple cropping, that is, the sowing of another crop following the harvest of the first crop, such as the continued sowing of paddy rice.

3. Acreage sown to perennial crops which do not yield a harvest during the same year of sowing is not considered as sown acreage for the year, but acreage of perennial crops sown the previous year or earlier and presently yielding a harvest is included in the sown acreage of this year. In other words, whatever the time of sowing, the year in which a crop is reaped is taken into account for the computation of sown acreage.[37]

4. Cultivated area lying fallow or left idle is not included in sown acreage.

Besides (3) and (4) mentioned above, the State Statistical Bureau set up the following additional rules for estimating sown acreage, at least up to 1957:

1. Since the sown acreage of a year is not determined by the sowings done within the year, the computation of sown acreage is primarily made on the basis of the area from which harvests were expected at the time of investigation (that is, at the conclusion of a major sowing season). The area lost to calamities before that time is not included in the sown acreage.[38]

2. The area reserved for stubbled rice is not counted as sown acreage, on the ground that stubbled rice is grown from stubbles of the harvested crops without going through the process of sowing and transplanting. The same rule applies to stubbled tobacco and kaoliang.[39]

3. Seed beds devoted to the cultivation of seedling for transplanting are not included in the sown acreage.[40]

4. The area originally used for seed beds but, upon the removal of seedlings for transplanting, subsequently given to the cultivation of crops is considered sown acreage. For this reason, in the case of paddy rice, sweet potatoes, and tobacco crops, which require transplanting, their sown acreage is the acreage after transplanting.[41]

5. Where the seedlings grow in a scattered manner, or where a lack of seedlings lead to a field not being fully filled, the whole area of the field is considered sown acreage.[42]

6. The sides of fields along which crops are sown in a scattered manner are not included in the sown acreage.[43]

MULTIPLE-CROPPING ACREAGE AND INDEX OF MULTIPLE CROPPING

Multiple-cropping acreage serves to indicate the degree of land utilization and is an important

[32] *Ibid.*, pp. 53–54; and Liao Hsien-hao, *op. cit.*
[33] *Handbook for Agricultural Statistical Work, op. cit.*, p. 54.
[34] *Ibid.*
[35] *Ibid.*
[36] *Ibid.*, p. 11. "Transplanting" refers to sowing a crop on every other row or several rows in a field, with one or more other crops sown on the other rows.
[37] One important exception to this rule is sugar cane. The area sown to sugar cane in the current year that yields in the current year through the spring of the following year will still be regarded as part of the sown area of the current year.
[38] *Ibid.*
[39] *Ibid.* This rule was criticized for having the effect of underestimating sown acreage. See Chen Han-chang, "Total Sown Area Should Include Acreage for Stubbled Crops and Secondary Interplanted Crops," *TCKT*, No. 3 (February, 1957), pp. 15–16.
[40] *Handbook for Agricultural Statistical Work, op. cit.*, p. 11.
[41] *Ibid.*
[42] *Ibid.*, p. 12.
[43] *Ibid.*

measure in Chinese agricultural statistics. Within an agricultural (calendar) year, in order to acquire several harvests from one plot of land, several sowings may be carried out, and this is referred to as "multiple cropping." Examples are the double cropping of paddy rice and the sowing of a late crop of corn, millet, or maize after the wheat harvest. The area thus resown is the acreage of multiple cropping.[44] It can be computed by subtracting the cultivated acreage from the total sown acreage for the year.

In order to measure land utilization, the multiple-cropping acreage is usually related to the cultivated acreage in the form of a ratio known as the index of multiple cropping. Since green manure crops generally contribute to the fertility of land and do not yield a harvest, the State Statistical Bureau in 1956 adopted the following formula for computing the index of multiple cropping.[45]

$$\text{Index of multiple cropping} = \frac{\text{total sown acreage} - \text{acreage sown to green manure crops}}{\text{total cultivated acreage}}$$

THE METHODS OF
INVESTIGATING SOWN ACREAGE

The method of investigating sown acreage has undergone several changes since 1949. Before 1954 the methods employed were not standardized, and different areas used different measures, according to local expediency, to carry out investigations. One method was to take *hsien* or *ch'ü* as the unit for investigation, the estimate of sown acreage being made on the basis of the reports and discussions in local production conferences as well as relevant data from other sources. Another method was also to take *hsien* or *ch'ü* as the unit for investigation but to select model *hsiang* and villages for survey, the survey data thus derived being used as the basis for estimation. A third method was for all *hsiang* and villages to conduct surveys and report the results to *hsien*.[46] In 1954 and 1955, with the exception of frontier regions and national minority areas, investigation forms were issued by the *hsien* government to the *hsiang* and villages, where field surveys were conducted by mutual-aid teams, agricultural producer co-operatives, and local cadres.[47] Figures on sown acreage were then compiled by the

hsiang and village governments and submitted to the *hsien* government.

Beginning in 1956, the system of regular schedules was introduced for rural areas. At the request of the State Statistical Bureau, each agricultural producer cooperative was to set up records on sown acreage and to submit reports regularly to the *hsiang* government. As for the sown acreage of individual peasant households and of those members of agricultural producer cooperatives possessing self-retained land, the estimate was made on the basis of surveys to be conducted by *hsiang* government or by agricultural producer co-operatives.[48]

The procedure underwent a significant change in 1959, when the national movement of agricultural-output surveys was introduced. This method of estimating sown area was closely related to that of estimating farm output. This problem was discussed at length earlier in this section and need not be repeated here.

The Meaning of Afforested Area and the Classification of Forests

Afforested area refers to the area of barren land and mountains where forests have been built up by human labor.[49] According to current forestry statistics, there are four types of forests: (1) protective forests, (2) lumber forests, (3) forests for special uses, and (4) other forests. Protective forests are for the purpose of improving natural conditions and of reducing wind and sand storms, floods, droughts, and other natural calamities. Lumber forests are those grown primarily for the purpose of providing lumber materials, including fir, euculyptus, and pine. Forests for special uses include trees which provide products for consumption or raw materials for processing, such as fruits, bark, sap, lacquer, camphor, cork, tung oil, tea oil, and white wax. Other forests refer to those not included in the above three categories, such as forests for landscape purposes. Trees planted on sidewalks or around houses are not included in the statistics on the area of afforestation.[50]

[44]*Ipid.,* p. 14.
[45]*Ibid.;* and Yin Shan-shou and Chu Feng-shu, "Our Views on the Methods of Computing the Annual Output of Food Grains per *Mou*," *TCKTTH,* No. 13 (July 14, 1956), pp. 15–17.
[46]*Handbook for Agricultural Statistical Work, op. cit.,* p. 9.
[47]*Ibid.,* pp. 9–10.
[48]*Ibid.,* p. 10.
[49]*Ibid.,* p. 55.
[50]*Ibid.;* and Liao Hsien-hao, *op. cit.,* p. 31.

Statistical Data on Agricultural Land Area and Afforested Area

Available national statistics on the area of various types of agricultural land and on the afforested areas are shown in Tables 5.1–5.6. Data on total cultivated area, total sown area, increase in irrigated area, improved irrigated area, and afforested area are assembled for 16 provinces and autonomous regions in Tables 5.7–5.23. In addition, provincial data on sown area, by crop, are given in Tables 5.24–5.40. The main sources of the provincial data in these tables are the various monographs on regional economic geography published by the Research Institute of Geography of the Chinese National Academy of Sciences in Peking. Data for Inner Mongolia were taken from a statistical abstract compiled by the Statistical Bureau of the Inner Mongolia Autonomous Region.

Statistical data on land area are generally given in *mou*, the unit of area officially adopted in China. For the convenience of readers, data in both *mou* and hectares are given in the statistical tables. One hectare is equal to 15 *mou*.

CROPS, AQUATIC PRODUCTS, AND LIVESTOCK

Crop Production

THE CLASSIFICATION OF CROPS

The classification of crops usually can be made according to different uses, harvest seasons, or cultivation methods. According to the *Handbook for Agricultural Statistical Work* (pp. 15–16 and 40), published in 1956, the classification adopted in China is as follows:

I. Food grains
   A. Rice
      1. Paddy rice
         a. Single-crop rice
            i. Early rice
            ii. Semi-late rice
            iii. Late rice
         b. Double-crop rice
            i. Early double-crop rice
            ii. Late double-crop rice
            iii. Early alternatively planted rice
            iv. Late alternatively planted rice
            v. Deep-water rice
      2. Upland rice

   B. Wheat
      1. Winter wheat
      2. Spring wheat
   C. Coarse grains
      1. Millet
      2. Corn
      3. Kaoliang
      4. Barley
      5. Buckwheat
      6. Oats
      7. Proso-millet
      8. Small beans
      9. Green beans, small
      10. Broad beans
      11. Peas
      12. Others
   D. Potatoes
      1. Sweet potatoes
      2. Irish potatoes
      3. Other potatoes
II. Soya beans
   A. Yellow soya beans
   B. Green beans
   C. Black beans
III. Technical crops
   A. Cotton
      1. Fine-staple cotton
      2. Coarse-staple cotton
   B. Hemp
      1. Jute
      2. Kenafe
      3. Ramie
      4. Flax
      5. Abutilom hemp
      6. Bowstring hemp
      7. Sisal hemp
   C. Tobacco
      1. Flue-cured tobacco
      2. Native tobacco
   D. Oil-bearing crops
      1. Peanuts
      2. Rapeseed
      3. Sesame
      4. Seed of bowstring hemp
      5. Linseed
      6. Sunflower seed
      7. Perilla seed
      8. Castor seed
      9. Other oil-bearing crops
   E. Sugar-bearing crops
      1. Cane
         a. Sugar cane
         b. Fruit cane
      2. Sugar beets
   F. Medical herbs

G. Other technical crops, including tea, spices, and dyestuff

IV. Other crops
  A. Gardening crops
    1. Vegetables
    2. Fruits
    3. Commercial flowers
  B. Fodder crops
    1. Grazing grass, cultivated or gathered
    2. Green fodder crops
    3. Mulberry trees
  C. Green-manure crops
  D. Others

In the above classification, potatoes do not include yams, cotton does not include kapok, and medical herbs refer only to crops cultivated, not including wild plants.

THE RATE OF HARVEST

The rate of harvest (*sho-ho-lü*) refers to the volume of crops harvested from each unit of area. In China, the *shih mou* is the unit of area, and the rate of harvest is, therefore, also known as the yield per *mou*.[51]

The rate of harvest may be computed according to harvested area, sown area, or cultivated area. The meaning of sown area and cultivated area was explained above. Harvested area refers to the area over which crops have been actually harvested. It is the portion of the total sown area remaining after deducting the area from which crops have been lost in the course of their growth through flood, drought, hailstorm, disease, pests, and other natural calamities.[52] For areas entirely free of natural calamities, the harvested area is identical with the sown area, and hence the rate of harvest according to the former is the same as that according to the latter.

The rate of harvest according to sown area was considered more important than that according to harvested area or cultivated area, since only the former was used for planning purposes.[53] The rate of harvest according to the harvested area was also computed, however, primarily for two purposes. In the first place, the rate of harvest according to sown area was frequently derived from that according to the harvested area. Secondly, the rate according to the harvested area would measure the yield per *mou* for areas entirely free of natural calam-

ities.[54] Beginning in 1956, the rate of harvest according to cultivated area was also computed for food grains for the purpose of indicating the "average annual rate of harvest" of these crops.[55]

THE OUTPUT OF CROPS

The output of a crop in a given locality is the volume of harvests of the crop in a year, equal to the product of the area sown to the crop in the locality multiplied by the rate of harvest according to sown area. It was an established practice in China to measure crop output by biological yield, but since 1960 the basis for crop statistics has been changed to barn yield.[56]

According to the State Statistical Bureau's regulations, crops with moisture content at the time of storage were to be taken as the standard for measurement. In addition, the following regulations were set up by the State Bureau for preparing crop statistics:[57]

1. Except for potatoes, all grains should be measured on the basis of their original weights.
2. Potatoes should be converted into the grain equivalent at the rate of four catties of potatoes to one catty of grain.
3. Beans should be measured after the removal of the pods.
4. Cotton should be measured on the basis of ginned cotton after the removal of seeds.
5. Except for flax, hemp should be measured on the basis of raw hemp bast. (Raw hemp bast refers to that not yet treated, and generally two catties of the raw bast may be converted into one catty of the treated bast.) Flax should be measured on the basis of the stalks.
6. Tobacco should be measured on the basis of dried tobacco.
7. Peanuts should be measured on the basis of dried peanuts with shells.
8. Sugar cane should be measured on the basis of the cane weight.

[51]*Ibid.*, p. 18.
[52]*Ibid.*, p. 12.
[53]Kung Chien-yao, "The Method of Computing the Rate of Harvest," *TCKTTH*, No. 6 (March, 1956), pp. 16–18.
[54]*Handbook for Agricultural Statistical Work, op. cit.*, p. 19.
[55]*Ibid.*; and Wang Kuang-shen, "The Concept of the Indicator 'Annual Average Output of Food Grains per *Mou*,' and A Preliminary Enquiry into the Methods of Computing It," *TCYC*, No. 1 (January 23, 1958), pp. 33–38.
[56]Huang Chien-t'o, "Major Tasks in the Agricultural Statistical Work Program for 1960," *CHYTC*, No. 2 (February, 1960), pp. 18–22. The effects of using biological and barn yields as the bases for measurement on Chinese crop output statistics are discussed by Choh-ming Li (*op. cit.*, Chapter VIII).
[57]*Handbook for Agricultural Statistical Work, op. cit.*, pp. 20–21.

9. Sugar beets should be measured on the basis of the beet weight.

THE METHOD OF ESTIMATING THE HARVEST

With the establishment of the Peking regime in 1949, local governments at different levels began to engage in the estimation of the volume of various harvested crops. After 1952, when the State Statistical Bureau was established, survey committees were set up at the *hsien* level for the purpose of carrying out the statistical study of the volume of harvests. In 1956, the State Bureau formulated a plan stipulating that both the departments of statistics and of agriculture at local levels were to assume the major responsibility for surveys of summer and autumn harvests with grain, finance, commerce, and agricultural procurement departments participating in the survey.[58] In 1959, with the advent of the national movement of farm-output surveys, statistical study of the volume of harvests entered a new stage. As may be recalled, for the purpose of carrying out surveys, special committees were organized at every level from province through special district and *hsien* to commune and production brigade, with the local party secretary as the chairman.

A number of survey methods were used. At the beginning, the methods of "registration by household" and "estimation on the basis of relevant data" were adopted. Later, the first method was seldom used, because "it was not scientific" and "peasants were not capable of telling honestly their actual output figures,"[59] and the second method remained in use only in areas with poor statistical services, because "the figures so estimated were frequently at great variance with actual conditions."[60] The method most widely employed was that of the "model survey." According to this method, a *hsien* or *ch'ü* was divided into a number of classes, each represented by a few model *hsiang* and villages. For each model *hsiang* or village, a few model households or collectives were selected. The volume of agricultural harvests of these model households or collectives was then investigated. The results thus obtained were used as the basis for estimating the volume of harvests for the *hsien* or *ch'ü* as a whole.[61] The model-survey method has become "the most fundamental method for national farm-output surveys."[62]

It is important to point out that according to the Chinese "model survey" method households were selected for investigation primarily at the surveyers' discretion. Therefore, there was no statistical sampling design involved at all.

Aquatic Products

Aquatic products include "natural or cultivated fish, shrimp, crabs, mollusca and crustacea, and seaweed in both fresh water and salt water."[63] Water plants such as water chestnuts, catercaltrops, and lotus roots do not come within the scope of aquatic products. The fishing of natural aquatic products belongs to the scope of industrial activities, and hence the output of natural aquatic products is included in industrial statistics. On the other hand, the culture or rearing of aquatic products is considered part of agriculture.[64] Beginning in 1958, the physical output of cultivated aquatic products was merged with that of natural aquatic products and included in industrial statistics under the heading of "total aquatic products," while the value of cultivated aquatic products continued to be included in the gross value of agricultural output.[65]

Livestock

Livestock statistics cover a variety of subjects, of which the size of livestock population and the output of animal products are most important.

THE NUMBER OF LIVESTOCK

Chinese statistics frequently divide livestock into large and small animals. Included in the category of large animals are cattle, buffalo, horses, asses, mules, and camels, while goats, sheep, and pigs are considered small.[66]

Unlike agricultural output, which is a *flow* concept, livestock is a *stock* concept, referring

[58]*Ibid.*, pp. 17–18; and Huang Chien-t'o, *TCKT, op. cit.*, p. 7.
[59]Kung Chien-yao, "A Discussion of Statistical Methods of Investigating the Volume of Agricultural Harvests." *TCKTTH*, No. 10 (October 17, 1955), pp. 33–36, quotation on p. 33.
[60]*Ibid.*
[61]*Ibid.*, and *Handbook for Agricultural Statistical Work, op. cit.*, p. 18.
[62]Kung Chien-yao, *op. cit.*
[63]*Handbook for Agricultural Statistical Work, op. cit.*, p. 59.
[64]*Ibid.*
[65]State Economic Commission, Bureau of Comprehensive Planning for the National Economy, Department of Methodology, "Explanation of Major Changes in the Tabular Forms for National Economic Planning for 1958," *CHCC*, No. 8 (August 9, 1957), pp. 24–27.
[66]Liao Hsien-hao, *op. cit.*, p. 31.

to the number of domestic animals existing at a given *point* of time. In China, the survey of livestock population is conducted once a year. Except for the animals kept by the armed forces, all livestock in both urban and rural areas are included in the survey.[67] The date of reference used to be July 1,[68] but it was changed to December 31 in 1957.[69]

In the first few years of the Peking regime, the survey of livestock was made by the cadres at the *hsiang* and village levels. Beginning in 1956, the State Statistical Bureau introduced standardized survey forms to be distributed by the statistical departments at the provincial and *hsien* levels to those at lower levels. State farms and ranches were required to report the actual figures on livestock to the *hsien* governments. *Hsiang* and villages were to submit reports on the basis of the statistical reports of agricultural producer cooperatives and the survey or interview data on individual peasant households and all nonfarm units, such as factories and schools. In the urban areas, the number of livestock was to be surveyed by the *shih* (city) governments.[70]

Among the various animals, pigs have been given special attention. Quarterly reports on the number of live pigs were initiated in 1957, and by 1959 these reports also included data on the number of live pigs slaughtered and the number which died, reproduced, and were procured by the state.[71]

ANIMAL PRODUCTS

Animal products may be divided into two categories: (1) products obtained without slaughtering the animals, such as wool, eggs, cow's and sheep's milk, honey, bee's wax, and animal excrement and (2) products obtained through reproduction and feeding, such as offspring of animals and natural-weight increase of animals.

Animal products are included in agricultural output statistics and should be distinguished from the processing of animal products. Such activities as the slaughtering of animals and washing of sheep's wool belong to the scope of industrial activities and, therefore, are included in industrial statistics.[72]

Data on animal products are obtained in the following way: The rates of production for various animals are computed on the basis of the data acquired through sample or model surveys. These rates are then multiplied by the

number of animals in order to derive the quantity of animal products.[73]

Satistical Data on the Physical Output of Agriculture and on Livestock

Table 5.41 presents data on the yield per unit of area of major crops for the country as a whole during 1949–59. Statistics at the local level were compiled for 21 provinces and autonomous regions and are shown in Tables 5.42–5.63. All the figures were computed on the basis of sown area. The official unit of measurement is *chin* per *mou*, but data in kilograms per hectare are also included in the statistical tables. One kilogram is equivalent to 2 *chin*, and 1 hectare, as may be recalled, equals 15 *mou*.

National statistics on agricultural physical output and livestock are shown in Tables 5.64–5.67, while provincial data may be found in Tables 5.68–5.92. Data at the national level were published by the State Statistical Bureau, and provincial statistics were compiled on the basis of the various monographs on regional economic geography published by the Chinese National Academy of Sciences, the communiqués or statistical abstracts issued by provincial statistical bureaus, and the reports of provincial government and party officials.

THE VALUE OF AGRICULTURAL PRODUCTION

The Gross Value of Agricultural Output

The gross value of agricultural output is "the monetary manifestation of total agricultural production."[74] As pointed out in the section on national income, agricultural production by definition consists of three major activities —crop-growing, animal-raising, and subsidiary work of peasants. The components of the first two categories were discussed above in this section, and those of agricultural subsidiary work were explained in the section on national income.

[67]*Handbook for Agricultural Statistical Work, op. cit.,* pp. 22–23.
[68]Huang Meng-fan, "Agricultural Output Statistics," *TCKTTH,* No. 12 (June, 1956), pp. 30–33.
[69]Liao Hsien-hao, *op. cit.*
[70]*Handbook for Agricultural Statistical Work, op. cit.,* p. 23.
[71]Huang Chien-t'o, *CHYTC, op. cit.*
[72]*Handbook for Agricultural Statistical Work, op. cit.,* pp. 22–25.
[73]*Ibid.*
[74]*Ibid.,* p. 39; and Liao Hsien-hao, *op. cit.,* p. 32.

The gross value of agricultural output for the economy as a whole was computed by the State Statistical Bureau. Such computation was not required at the local levels, but it was usually made by provincial and *hsien* governments for their own planning purposes. The gross value of the output of crops and animal products was made on the basis of regular statistical reports, and that of agricultural subsidiary work was estimated primarily from survey data.[75] Since the reliability of the estimate for subsidiary work was admitted to be very low, the State Bureau decided to separate it from the gross value of agricultural output beginning in 1958.[76]

In computing the gross value of agricultural output, both current and constant prices were used. The constant prices adopted were 1952 prices for the years before 1957 and have been 1957 prices since 1958.[77]

The Value of Agricultural Commodity Production

Agricultural commodity production refers to the amount of agricultural products sold or delivered to the state by state farms and ranches, agricultural producer cooperatives (people's communes), and individual peasants and is composed of the following elements:

1. The amount of products delivered to the state by state farms and ranches.
2. The amount of products delivered to the state by collectives and individual peasants for the payment of agricultural taxes.
3. The amount of products procured by the state.
4. The amount of products sold by peasants on the market.
5. The amount of products exchanged between state farms, collectives, and peasants.
6. The amount of products paid to machine tractor stations for their services.
7. The amount of products used to pay loans.

Agricultural commodity production during a year indicates the total amount of agricultural products available in that year for consumption, export, and industrial processing. Such an amount given in monetary terms is referred to as the "value of agricultural commodity production." In practice, the value of agricultural commodity production is computed on the basis of the survey data on peasant household budgets as well as the data on agricultural procurement and taxation.[78]

The Net Value of Agricultural Output

The net value of agricultural output is the total value of agricultural production net of material outlays. Included in material outlays are depreciation charges, seed, fertilizers, insecticides, animal feed, repair of farm tools, drugs for prevention and treatment of veterinary diseases, and other material expenses.[79]

Data from peasant household budget surveys provided the basis for estimating the material outlays in agricultural production. The method of estimating the net value of agricultural output was discussed in the section on national income and need not be repeated here.

Statistics on the Value of Agricultural Production

Table 5.93 presents national data on the gross value of agricultural output at 1952 prices for 1949–57 and at 1957 prices for 1957–59. Provincial data were assembled for 19 provinces and autonomous regions and are presented in Table 5.94.

The State Statistical Bureau never published data on the value of agricultural commodity production and the net value of agricultural output. The latter, however, can be derived from the data on the percentage distribution of national income by sector. These data and the method of derivation were discussed in the section on national income. The estimates of the net value of agricultural output at 1952 prices for 1952–56 are shown in Table 2.2.

STATE FARMS, METEOROLOGICAL SERVICES, AND AGRICULTURAL MECHANIZATION

State Farms and Ranches

State farms and ranches, which operate as part of the hierarchy of the Ministry of State Farms and Reclamation, were also required to fill out various regular statistical schedules. Information on the following items were requested: (1) area cultivated, (2) area reclaimed, (3) num-

[75]*Ibid.*
[76]Hsüeh Mu-ch'iao, "Exert Efforts to Improve Agricultural Statistical Work," *TCKT*, No. 22 (November 29, 1957), pp. 7–11.
[77]For a discussion of 1952 prices for constant-price valuation of agricultural output, see the section on national income.
[78]*Handbook for Agricultural Statistical Work, op. cit.*, pp. 41–42.
[79]*Ibid.*, pp. 42–43.

ber of employees and workers, (4) number of tractors, (5) number of harvesting combines, and (6) number of draft animals. Data on these items were published by the State Statistical Bureau for all of the state farms for 1950–55 (Table 5.95), state mechanized farms for the same period (Table 5.96), and the state farms and ranches under the direct control of the Ministry of State Farms and Reclamation for 1949, 1952, 1957, and 1958 (Table 5.97). Provincial data were compiled for Inner Mongolia and Shantung in Tables 5.98–5.100.

Meteorological and Other Agricultural Services

In 1954, the Central Meteorological Bureau initiated a system of regular reports on meteorological work. Included in the reports were (1) the fulfillment of meteorological plans, covering mainly statistics on the increase in number of meteorological observatories, meteorological stations, and weather forecasting stations at all levels and (2) the meteorological services rendered on the forecasting and warning of calamitous and ordinary climates.[80]

Table 5.101 presents data on the number of meteorological observations, meteorological stations, and weather forecasting stations for 1949–58. The same table also gives information on the number of agricultural technical stations, livestock breeding stations, veterinary stations, and steppe development stations.

Agricultural Mechanization

The most important information on agricultural mechanization deals with the number of tractors used for farming. Table 5.103 shows figures for the country as a whole, as well as for the Inner Mongolia Autonomous Region. These figures were given in standard units of 15 horsepower each.

SOCIALIZATION OF AGRICULTURE

Tables 5.104 and 5.105 contain information on the number of agricultural producer cooperatives and the number of farming households joining these cooperatives from 1950 through 1956. There were two types of agricultural producer cooperatives: elementary and advanced. An elementary agricultural producer cooperative was one that paid its members for use of their land and did not own all the draft animals and main farm implements, while an agricultural producer cooperative of the advanced type made no payment for use of land and owned all the draft animals and farm implements.[81]

Data on the number of the people's communes and the number of farming households joining in the communes in the months of August through December, 1958, were published in *Ten Great Years* and are shown in Table 5.106.

[80]*Ibid.*, p. 51
[81]*Ibid.*, p. 32.

6

TRANSPORTATION, POST, AND TELE-COMMUNICATIONS

TRANSPORTATION

THE CONCEPT AND CLASSIFICATIONS OF TRANSPORTATION

Transportation refers to the activity of moving goods or persons from one place to another.[1] Transportation is closely related to industrial production. It may be recalled that two types of transportation in connection with industrial production are distinguished: (1) transport within a factory and (2) transport outside a factory.[2] In theory, the former falls within the sphere of industrial production and the latter belongs to freight transportation. In practice, however, the shipment of materials and products, both inside and outside the factory, is classified as a part of freight transportation in Chinese statistics if it is performed by specialized transport enterprises.

There are three standard classifications of transportation in Chinese statistics.[3] One classification is made on the basis of the means of transportation and includes railways, highways, inland waterways, coastal shipping, and civil air transport. The second classification distinguishes between modern and traditional means of transportation. The former refers to rail and air transportation, as well as to motor vehicles and steamships, while the latter includes junks and carts and wheelbarrows operated by animals or men. Only modern means of transportation are included in the state plan. The third classification is the division into freight and passenger transportation. In the case of civil air transportation, a third category, mail transport, is added.

SOURCES OF TRANSPORTATION STATISTICS[4]

Like industrial and agricultural statistics, the major source of transportation data is the system of regular statistical schedules. Since various means of transportation have their own peculiar characteristics, different schedules and indicators are required. In general, four types of transportation statistics can be distinguished: railways, highways, water transport, and civil air transport.

In China there are two types of railways. One consists of the special lines built by forestry and industrial enterprises for the purpose of transporting materials and products within the enterprises, and the other consists of public railways. The latter is largely under the control of the Ministry of Railways, which is responsible for compiling data on freight and passenger railway transport and for submitting reports regularly to the State Statistical Bureau. Statistical reports relating to the railways of forestry and industrial enterprises are filled out by the respective central ministries within whose jurisdiction these enterprises fall; they are submitted quarterly to the State Bureau.

Highway and water transport enterprises employing modern means of transportation are under the control of the Ministry of Transportation. These enterprises are supposed to supply,

[1]Editorial Committee for Statistical Work Handbook, *Statistical Work Handbook for Transportation and Post and Tele-Communications*, Peking: Statistical Publishing House, 1956, p. 6. Hereafter referred to as *Statistical Work Handbook for Transportation and Communication*.

[2]For the meaning of these two types of transportation and the distinction between industry and freight transport, see the section on industry.

[3]Ch'en Tieh-cheng, "Tabular Form for Transport Planning," *CHCC*, No. 3 (March 9, 1957), pp. 29–33.

[4]*Statistical Work Handbook for Transportation and Communication, op. cit.*, pp. 2–4.

on a regular basis, statistical data on freight and passenger transportation to the Ministry which, in turn, fills out regular schedules and submits them to the State Statistical Bureau. All enterprises using traditional means of transportation belong to the local governments. Since there is a large variety of traditional means of transportation, local governments are requested to report only a few major indicators to the State Bureau.

Statistics relating to civil air transportation are compiled by the Bureau of Civil Aviation. Major indicators include freight transportation, passenger transportation, mail transportation, and the services rendered to industrial and agricultural production.

TYPES OF TRANSPORTATION DATA

Chinese statistical data on transportation may be grouped into the following categories: (1) length of traffic lines, (2) volume and turnover of freight and passenger transportation, (3) gross and net value output of freight transportation, (4) socialist transformation of transportation, (5) major technical indicators, (6) productivity of freight transport workers and employees, and (7) cost of transportation.

Length of Traffic Lines

The length of railway traffic lines is computed on the basis of three types of railway lines. The most important one is main lines *(cheng-hsien)*, referring to the lines between stations. The second type is station lines *(chan-hsien)*, referring to the lines within the marshaling yards. The third type is special-use lines *(chuang-yung-hsien)*, which are built between a station and regular customers for the purpose of shipping goods.[5] Forestry and industrial railways are not included in the calculation of the length of railway traffic lines.

The length of highway lines for a year is computed on the basis of those open to traffic during the year.[6] The length of inland waterways and of coastal shipping routes between two locations is calculated on the basis of the actual distance.[7] The length of civil air traffic lines is measured on the basis of the distance between airports as determined by the Bureau of Civil Aviation. Under present practice, the figure on

the length of air traffic lines at the end of the year is taken as the estimate for the year.[8]

Statistics on the length of railway, highway, water, and air traffic lines for 1949 through 1959 are given in Table 6.1. These statistics are also shown in Tables 6.5, 6.6, 6.8, and 6.10, which contain information on the development of various types of transportation. Table 6.2 presents figures on the length of railway and highway traffic lines in national minority areas for four years: 1949, 1952, 1957, and 1958. Provincial data are compiled only for Inner Mongolia Autonomous Region in Tables 6.3, 6.7, and 6.9.

Volume and Turnover of Freight and Passenger Transportation

VOLUME OF FREIGHT AND PASSENGER TRANSPORTATION

The volume of freight and passenger transportation refers to the amount of goods and the number of persons carried by a given means of transportation. The volume of freight transportation is measured in terms of tons.[9] Both the volume of freight and passenger transportation may be measured either at their point of departure or upon arrival at their destination. In Chinese practice, the number of passengers is estimated at their departure,[10] but the method of measuring the freight transport volume varies for different types of transportation. It is estimated at the point of departure for railways and inland waterways but upon arrival for highways and coastal shipping.[11]

TURNOVER OF FREIGHT AND PASSENGER TRANSPORTATION

Transport turnover, an indicator of the amount of work performed by transport enterprises, is determined by multiplying the volume of transportation by the distance carried. The freight turnover *(huo-wu chou-chuang-liang)* and the passenger turnover *(lü-ko chou-chuang-liang)* are given in terms of ton-kilometers and passenger-kilometers, respectively. For coastal

[5]*Ibid.*, p. 19.
[6]*Ibid.*, p. 69.
[7]*Ibid.*, p. 46.
[8]*Ibid.*, p. 81.
[9]*Ibid.*, pp. 4–5; and Ch'en Tieh-cheng, *op. cit.*, p. 30–31.
[10]*Ibid.*
[11]*Statistical Work Handbook for Transportation and Communication*, *op. cit.*, p. 5–6.

shipping, ton-nautical miles and passenger-nautical miles are used as the unit of measurement. (One nautical mile is equivalent to 1,853 kilometers.)[12]

The sum of freight and passenger turnover is given in "converted ton-kilometers" (*huan-shuan-tun-kung-li*). In calculating the total turnover, the passenger turnover is converted into ton-kilometers. The rate of conversion is determined by comparing the cost of transporting one passenger with the cost of transporting one ton of goods for the same distance. For railway, the Yangtze River and coastal shipping, one passenger-kilometer is equivalent to one ton-kilometer. There is no uniform ratio of conversion for inland water transportation, but the ratio is generally four to five passenger-kilometers per ton-kilometer. For highway transportation, 10 passenger-kilometers are converted into one ton-kilometer.[13]

Table 6.4 presents data on the volume of goods carried by railways, motor vehicles, and ships and barges and on the freight turnover of railways, motor vehicles, ships and barges, and airplanes. Also included in the same table are data on the number of passengers carried by railways and the passenger turnover of railways and airplanes. These figures can also be found in Tables 6.5, 6.6, 6.8, 6.10, which contain information on the development of various types of transportation. Provincial data on the volume and turnover of freight and passenger transportation are compiled for Inner Mongolia Autonomous Region in Tables 6.3, 6.7, and 6.9.

Gross and Net Value of the Output of Freight-Transportation

As pointed out in the section on national income, according to Chinese practice freight transportation is classified as a productive sector, while passenger transportation is non-productive. Therefore, in estimating national income, only the value created by freight transportation is calculated. Included in the gross value of freight-transportation output are not only the income of freight-transport enterprises but also that part of income of factories, construction enterprises, and farms resulting from the performance of freight-transport activities.[14]

The net value of freight-transportation output is obtained by deducting from the gross value of freight-transportation output the amount of material outlays, such as depreciation of transport equipment, fuel, and lubrication oil.[15]

Data on the gross and net value of transportation output have never been published by the Chinese government. But figures on the gross-value output, the net-value output, and the material outlays of both transportation and communication combined were derived from a variety of sources in Table 2.2. These figures are given in 1952 prices for 1952 through 1956. The concept and the method used in estimating the output of communications will be explored later in this section.

Socialist Transformation of Transportation

Chinese statistics on transport socialization are given in terms of the distribution of freight turnover by ownership of transport enterprise. Like industrial enterprises, four types of transport enterprises can be distinguished according to their ownership: state, cooperative, joint, and private. State transport enterprises refer to those operated by central and local governments.[16] Transport cooperatives are of two types—elementary and advanced. The transport equipment of each individual member is valued when he joins a cooperative, and such value becomes his capital share. The major difference between elementary and advanced transport cooperatives lies in the fact that in the former dividends are paid to members in proportion to their capital shares, while in the latter such payment is not made.[17] Joint transport enterprises are those in which capital is owned by both the state and by capitalists. Moreover, these enterprises are jointly managed by both capitalists and government-appointed officials.[18] Private transport enterprises refer to those the capital of which is owned entirely by individuals.

Table 6.11 presents data on the distribution of the total freight turnover among state, joint, and private transport enterprises for the years

[12]*Ibid.*, pp. 6–7; Ch'en Tieh-cheng, *op. cit.*; and State Planning Commission, *Brief Explanations of the Terminologies of the First Five-Year Plan for the Development of the National Economy*, Peking: People's Press, 1955, p. 35.

[13]*Statistical Work Handbook for Transportation and Communications, op. cit.*

[14]Hsu Ch'ien, Tai Shih-kuang, Yu Tao, et al., *Lectures on Economic Statistics*, Peking: Statistics Publishing House, 1957, p. 138.

[15]*Statistical Work Handbook for Transportation and Communication, op. cit.*, pp. 7–8.

[16]*Ibid.*, pp. 14–15.

[17]*Ibid.*

[18]*Ibid.*

1949–57. Figures in this table include only the freight turnover of modern means of transportation. The freight turnover of wooden junks, animal-drawn cars, wheelbarrows, and other vehicles not mechanically operated is not included. For this reason, data on the freight turnover of transport cooperatives are not shown in the table, since virtually all means of transportation owned by transport cooperatives, at least up to 1954, were not mechanically operated. Table 6.12 presents figures on the distribution of the freight turnover of barges and ships by state, joint, and private transport enterprises and on the distribution of the freight turnover of motor vehicles by local state enterprises, joint enterprises, transport cooperatives, and private enterprises. These figures are available for the years 1952–55, but data on the total freight turnover of barges and ships and that of motor vehicles were published for 1956 as well. Provincial data are compiled for the Inner Mongolia Autonomous Region in Table 6.13, which gives figures on the percentage distribution of the total freight turnover among state enterprises, transport cooperatives, and private enterprises for 1952–57.

Major Technical Indicators of Freight Transportation

Statistics are available for a number of major technical indicators of railway and highway freight transportation. Table 6.14 presents 11 indicators of railway freight transportation:[19]

1. *Average daily run per freight locomotive, 1949, 1952, and 1956–58*, refers to the average distance in kilometers each freight locomotive moves in 24 hours.
2. *Average gross weight hauled per freight locomotive, 1949–1952 and 1956–58*, refers to the average gross weight of goods in tons hauled by each freight locomotive during a year.
3. *Average daily efficiency per freight locomotive, 1949, 1952, 1957, and 1958*, is a comprehensive indicator measuring the degree of capacity utilization of freight locomotives and refers to the average number of ton-kilometers performed by each freight locomotive in 24 hours.
4. *Coal consumption per freight locomotive, 1949, 1952, 1957, and 1958*, refers to the average amount of coal in kilograms consumed by

each freight locomotive per thousand ton-kilometers during a year.
5. *Average turn-around time per freight car, 1949, 1952, 1957, and 1958*, refers to the average time interval between two successive loadings of freight in a freight car and is given in terms of days. The time interval between two successive loadings includes the time spent in loading freight at the point of departure and in unloading freight at the destination and the time spent in carrying the freight car after unloading to the next loading station.
6. *Average turn-around distance per freight car, 1949, 1952, and 1956–58*, refers to the average distance in kilometers each freight car moves between two successive loadings. The indicator includes not only the distance between the point of departure and the destination but also the distance each freight car moves after unloading to the next station for loading.
7. *Average daily run per freight car, 1949, 1952, and 1956–58*, refers to the average number of kilometers each freight car runs in 24 hours.
8. *Average stopping time per freight car, 1952, 1957, and 1958* refers to the average number of hours for which each freight car stops at stations in each run.
9. *Average speed per freight train, 1949, 1952, 1957, and 1958*, refers to the average number of kilometers per hour at which each freight train moves, not including stopping time.
10. *Average load per freight car, 1949, 1950, 1952, and 1956–58*, refers to the average weight of freight in tons carried by each freight car during a year.
11. *Average daily efficiency per freight car, 1949, 1952, and 1956–58*, measures the average number of ton-kilometers a freight car carried in 24 hours. It is a comprehensive indicator measuring the degree of capacity utilization of freight car.

Statistics of four major indicators of highway freight transportation for 1950, 1952, 1957, and 1958 are given in Table 6.15.

1. *Percentage of trucks in serviceable condition* is obtained as a ratio of the number of truck-days in serviceable condition to the number of operating truck-days. One operating

[19]The meaning of these indicators was explained in *Statistical Work Handbook for Transportation and Communication, op. cit.*, pp. 20–45; and Su Yang-nei, ed., *Practical Dictionary of the National Economy*, Shanghai: Chun-min ch'u-pan-she, 1953, pp. 6003–19.

truck-day *(yin-yung ch'e-jih)* refers to a truck under control of a transport unit for 24 hours, including Sundays and holidays. The total number of operating truck-days of the transport unit in a reporting period is the sum of truck-days of all trucks in operation. The total number of operating truck-days consists of three categories: (1) the number of truck-days in use, (2) the number of truck-days in repair and awaiting repair, and (3) the number of truck-days not in use. The number of truck-days in serviceable condition is the number of operating truck-days exclusive of those in repair and awaiting repair.[20]

2. *Percentage of trucks in actual use* is the ratio of the number of truck-days in use to the number of operating truck-days.[21]

3. *Average daily run per truck* refers to the average number of kilometers per truck-day in use.[22]

4. *Average daily efficiency per ton of capacity of trucks* refers to the average converted turnover in ton-kilometers per ton of capacity of trucks. The average converted turnover includes the passenger turnover converted into ton-kilometers according to a given ratio as explained above.[23]

Labor Productivity in Freight Transportation

Labor productivity in freight transportation is calculated on the basis of the freight turnover and the number of registered personnel.[24] Statistics are available only for the index of the productivity of freight transport personnel in railways, inland waterways, and coastal shipping for 1957 and 1958, with 1952 being the base year. These figures were given in *Ten Great Years* and are reproduced in Table 6.16.

Cost of Transportation

Cost of freight (passenger) transportation generally refers to the amount of expenditure incurred in carrying 1 ton-kilometer (passenger-kilometer). Cost of both freight and passenger transportation is the expenditure per converted ton-kilometer and is obtained simply by dividing the total turnover in converted ton-kilometers into the total expenditure.[25] Available cost data cover both freight and passenger transportation. Table 6.17 presents figures on the cost index of state-operated railways and water transportation

for 1957 and 1958, with 1952 being the base, as well as those on unit cost of railways for 1950, 1952, and 1956–58. In addition, data on the cost of railway and Yangtze River transportation are compiled in Table 6.18 for 1956, with breakdowns into wages, fuel and power, material, repair expenses, depreciation charges, and others.

POST AND TELE-COMMUNICATIONS

SOURCES OF COMMUNICATION STATISTICS[26]

The system of regular statistical schedules provides the basic source of statistical information relating to post and tele-communications. These schedules and annual reports are issued by the Ministry of Post and Tele-Communications. Provincial bureaus of communications are supposed to fill out these schedules on the basis of data supplied by the *hsien* or *shih* bureaus and then submit them to the Ministry. The State Statistical Bureau does not issue regular schedules to local bureaus of communications but requires the Ministry to report regularly certain indicators. For enterprises and public organizations having tele-communication facilities but not belonging to the system of the Ministry of Post and Tele-Communications, no regular schedules have been issued; but an independent system has been developed in the railways to record statistical data on tele-communications.

Types of Communication Data

Available communication statistics may be classified into five categories: (1) length of postal routes, (2) length of tele-communication wires, (3) total volume of business, (4) gross and net value of output, and (5) development of post and tele-communications in the rural areas.

[20]*Statistical Work Handbook for Transportation and Communication, op. cit.,* pp. 69–71.
[21]*Ibid.*
[22]*Ibid.*
[23]*Ibid.,* p. 79.
[24]Hsü Ch'ien *et al., op. cit.,* p. 172. For the meaning of registered personnel, see the section on employment, labor productivity and wages.
[25]*Ibid.,* pp. 206–7.
[26]*Statistical Work Handbook for Transport and Communication, op. cit.,* pp. 83–84.

LENGTH OF POSTAL ROUTES

The length of postal routes is an indicator of the area covered by postal services. In China, postal routes are classified according to various means of transportation employed, i.e., railways, airplanes, ships, motor vehicles, animals, and bicycles. The distance of the postal route for each of these means of transportation is estimated separately. Figures on the length of postal routes at the end of the reporting period are taken as the estimates for the period. Postal routes canceled before the end of the period are not included in the estimates.[27]

LENGTH OF TELE-COMMUNICATION WIRES

The length of tele-communication wires, which is estimated on the basis of the distance between poles, is primarily an indicator of the development of telephone services. The total length of tele-communication wires may be borken down into four categories: main lines, intra-province lines, intra-*hsien* lines, and intra-city lines.[28] Main lines refer to those connecting between Peking and the capitals of various provinces and autonomous regions and between one provincial capital and another. Intra-province lines connect the provincial capital and all of the *hsien* within the province and one *hsien* with another. In Chinese statistics, the length of the long-distance telephone lines is the length of both main lines and intra-province lines combined. Intra-*hsien* telephone lines are those connecting the city in which the *hsien* government is located and villages and towns within the *hsien* and running between one village or town and another. Intra-city telephone lines refer to those installed for local use only.

Statistics on the total length of tele-communications wires with breakdowns into long-distance, intra-*hsien,* and intra-city telephones are included in Table 6.19. Provincial data are available for the Inner Mongolia Autonomous Region and are given in Table 6.20.

TOTAL VOLUME OF BUSINESS

There are a variety of business activities in post and tele-communications, and the output of these activities cannot be measured in terms of a common physical unit. The total work volume

of communications can be measured, however, in monetary terms, and the resulting measure is known as the total volume of business (*yeh-wu tsung-liang*), generally valued in constant prices. For example, for the years 1952–57 the total volume of business was obtained by summing up various types of business activities valued, respectively, at their average rate of charges in 1952. The 1952 average rate of charges of a particular type of communication business was derived by dividing the work volume of the given type of business into its total revenue in the same year.[29]

Figures on the total volume of business of post and tele-communications for 1952–58 are given in Table 6.19. Data for Inner Mongolia Autonomous Region are included in Table 6.20.

GROSS AND NET VALUE OF COMMUNICATION OUTPUT

The gross value of communication output refers to "the value of the work performed by independent post and tele-communications enterprises for materially productive sectors."[30] Omitted from the measurement of the gross value of output, therefore, are those services considered nonproductive, such as postal services for individuals. Such omission constitutes the difference between the gross value of output and the total volume of business in the communication sector. To estimate the gross value of communication output, special surveys are sometimes conducted for certain enterprises to obtain a ratio of that part of their revenue resulting from productive services to their total revenue. The gross value of output is then derived by applying this ratio to the total revenue of all communication enterprises.[31] The net value added by all of the communication enterprises is estimated by deducting material outlays from the gross value of communication output.

Data on the gross and net value of communication output are not available. Only estimates of the gross- and net-value output, at 1952 prices, of both transportation and communications combined can be derived for 1952–56, and these figures are included in Table 2.2.

[27]*Ibid.,* p. 85.
[28]*Ibid.*
[29]*Ibid.,* pp. 89–90.
[30]Hsü Chien *et al., op. cit.,* p. 140.
[31]*Ibid.*

DEVELOPMENT
OF COMMUNICATION
IN THE RURAL AREAS

Ten Great Years gives statistics on the development of post and tele-communications in the rural areas. Included are data on postal routes in the rural areas and percentages of towns and townships having postal and telephone services. These data cover the years 1952 – 58 and are reproduced in Table 6.21. The meaning of the rural areas was explained in the section on area and population and need not be repeated here.

7

TRADE

DOMESTIC TRADE

CONCEPT AND
CLASSIFICATIONS OF TRADE

The primary function of trade is to transfer goods from producers to consumers. It includes state purchase and supply, wholesaling, and retailing.

In Chinese statistics, there are two standard classifications of trade organization. One classification is made according to the nature of the organizations:[1] (1) regular commercial enterprises (*chǔn shang-yeh ch'i-yeh*), (2) commercial units attached to industrial and handicraft enterprises, (3) restaurants, (4) service trade, and (5) agricultural procurement enterprises. Trade organizations are also classified into five groups according to their ownership: (1) state trade, (2) cooperative trade, (3) state-private jointly operated trade; (4) private trade, including resident merchants (*tso-shang*), itinerant merchants (*hsin-shang*), and peddlers (*t'ang-fan*), and (5) peasant trade.

SOURCES OF TRADE DATA

Statistical data on Chinese domestic trade are obtained from regular reports, the national census, model surveys, and a number of special surveys.[2]

Data on state and cooperative trade stem primarily from regular statistical reports. State commercial enterprises fall into two categories: one refers to those enterprises belonging to various central ministries, such as the Ministry

of Commerce, the Ministry of Urban Service, the Ministry of Foreign Trade, and the Ministry of Food,[3] and the other includes sales agencies and stores operated by other central ministries, such as salt-sale agencies of the Ministry of Forestry and various bookstores of the Ministry of Culture.[4] All these ministries are required to report periodically certain indicators to the State Statistical Bureau on the basis of the regular schedules submitted by the enterprises under their jurisdication. All the supply and marketing cooperatives are controlled by the All-China Federation of Supply and Marketing Cooperatives. These cooperatives are supposed to fill out regular statistical schedules and submit them to the Federation, which then reports to the State Statistical Bureau.[5]

Data on joint and private trade are obtained mainly from the following sources: (1) information contained in the regular statistical schedules filled out by state commercial enterprises and

[1]Sun Chih-fang, "Tabular Form for Commercial Planning," *CHCC*, No. 2 (February 9, 1957), pp. 27–31, reference on p. 27.
[2]Editorial Committee for Statistical Work Handbook, *Trade Statistical Work Handbook*, Peking: Statistical Publishing House, 1957, pp. 1–2. Hereafter referred to as *Trade Statistical Work Handbook*.
[3]The Ministry of Commerce was first created to control both internal and external trade when the Peking regime was established in 1949. A number of specialized trading companies were organized in the following year by the Ministry to deal in major categories of commodities. In 1952 the Ministry of Commerce was divided into two, with one retaining the original name but administering internal trade only and the other being the Ministry of Foreign Trade. In 1955, a Ministry of Agricultural Purchase was set up to control the purchase of important agricultural products. In May, 1956, a Ministry of Urban Services was established for the purpose of controlling trade in subsidiary foodstuffs and certain other commodities. In February, 1958, a Second Ministry of Commerce was added, with the original Ministry now becoming the First Ministry of Commerce. At the same time, the Ministry of Urban Services was merged with the All-China Federation of Supply and Marketing Cooperatives to form a new body under the Second Ministry of Commerce. In September, 1958, the two Ministries were combined to become a single Ministry of Commerce.
[4]Sun Chih-fang, *op. cit.*
[5]Department of Trade Statistics, State Statistical Bureau, "An Explanation Concerning the Revision of the Statistical System of Supply and Marketing Cooperatives for 1956," *TCKTTH*, No. 12 (December 17, 1955), pp. 19–21.

supply and marketing cooperatives, such as the major commodities sold to joint and private trade agencies;[6] (2) the national census, such as the census of private trade and restaurants in 1955;[7] (3) model surveys and special surveys conducted from time to time;[8] (4) statistical data on tax collections;[9] and (5) regular reports submitted by joint and private enterprises.[10]

Data on peasant trade are estimated on the basis of relevant statistics, such as those obtained from peasant family budget surveys and from model surveys.[11]

TYPES OF TRADE DATA

Available Chinese trade statistics fall into three broad categories: (1) the trade network, (2) the volume of trade, and (3) the value of the output of trade.

The Trade Network

THE CONCEPT AND CLASSIFICATIONS OF THE TRADE NETWORK

The trade network (shang-yeh-wang) consists of a number of agencies (chi-ko) or units (tan-wei), such as agricultural procurement agencies and wholesaling and retailing agencies directly dealing with purchase or sale of commodities. Commercial enterprises which are organized to administer trade and are not directly engaged in buying and selling are not included in the trade network.[12]

There appear to be no rigorous and uniform definitions of an "agency" or a "unit." In some cases, an agency is defined as an enterprise which has been approved by its superior organization with respect to name, location, and organization, regardless of the nature of business, the amount of capital and employment, and the independency of accounting.[13] In others an agency simply refers to an enterprise having an independent place for the purpose of buying and selling commodities.

There are three standard groupings of the trade network.[14] One grouping classifies trading agencies according to their ownership: state, cooperative, joint, and private. Another is the classification by function, e.g., agricultural procurement network, wholesaling network, retailing network, and restaurant network. A

third is the division into urban and rural networks.

MAJOR INDICATORS OF THE TRADE NETWORK

In addition to the trade volume, which will be considered separately later in this section, other major statistical indicators of the trade network include the density of the retail trade network, the amount of capital funds, the number of persons employed, and labor productivity.

The density of the retail trade network (ling-shou shang-yeh-wang mi-tu) measures the distribution of retail outlets among the population. Generally, the density measure is calculated as the average number of residents per retailing agency. Since population is distributed in a scattered manner in the rural areas, two additional measures are sometimes computed to indicate the density of the rural retail network. One gives the average number of retail outlets per square kilometer and the other the average number of villages per retail outlet or alternatively the average number of retail outlets per village.[15]

The amount of capital funds includes both fixed and working capital. For private trade, the amount of capital generally refers to that registered with the government and therefore need not correspond to the amount actually employed.[16]

Employment of trading agencies is given as the number of persons engaged in trade. In state trading agencies, persons engaged in trade are workers and employees in these agencies. In private trading agencies, persons engaged

[6]Ch'en Wu-ying, "The Need of a Unified Commodity Catalogue for Regular Statistical Schedules of Trade," *TCKT*, No. 22 (November 29, 1957), pp. 14–15; and Department of Trade, Provincial Statistical Bureau of Heilungkiang, "Some Understanding from the Processing and Compilation of Trade Statistical Data," *TCKT*, No. 22 (November 29, 1957), pp. 21–23.

[7]*Trade Statistical Work Handbook, op. cit.*

[8]*Ibid.*

[9]Lu Ch'ang-fu, "Several Methods of Estimating the Trade Volume of Subsidiary Food Products in the Free Market," *TCKT*, No. 22, (November 29, 1957), p. 25; and "The National Trade Statistical Work Conference Has Been Satisfactorily Concluded," *TCKT*, No. 23 (December 14, 1957), pp. 33.

[10]*Ibid.*

[11]Department of Trade, Provincial Statistical Bureau of Heilungkiang, *op. cit.*; and Hsieh Ying *et al.*, "How Can It Be Said That Trade Statistics Cannot Reflect Market Changes?" *TCKT*, No. 17 (September 14, 1957), pp. 23–25.

[12]*Trade Statistical Work Handbook, op. cit.*, p. 18.

[13]Wang Pei-hsün, "Several Problems Concerning Present Trade Statistical Work Need to Be Studied and Discussed," *TCKT*, No. 8 (April 29, 1957), pp. 17–19.

[14]*Trade Statistical Work Handbook, op. cit.*, pp. 18–19.

[15]*Ibid.*, pp. 20–21.

[16]Ch'ien Hua *et al.*, *Changes in Private Industry and Trade in China during the Past Seven Years (1949–1956)*, Peking: Financial and Economic Publishing House, 1957, p. 9.

in trade include owners of these agencies and the workers and employees they hire.

Labor productivity is calculated as the average volume of trade per registered personnel. Usually, labor productivity is also measured on the basis of sales personnel.[17]

Trade Volume

THE MEANING AND SCOPE OF TRADE VOLUME

Commodities produced by industry and agriculture reach the consumer through trade. The volume of trade, known as "commodity turnover" *(shang-p'in liu-chuan-o),* is a multitude of sales and purchases of these commodities. Not every transaction is a part of turnover, however. For each transaction, there must be involved the sale of a material object, on the one hand, and the monetary payment for such an object, on the other. Thus, excluded from the volume of trade are the following categories: (1) the sale of services by barber shops, laundries, theaters, doctors, etc.; (2) the transfer of commodities without involving monetary payments, such as taxes in kind, gifts, and relief; (3) barter trade between peasants; and (4) the distribution of goods by the state to state and joint enterprises.[18]

From the viewpoint of the economy as a whole, during a given period of time the volume of trade should be the same as total purchases, which, in turn should equal total sales. But, so far as an individual enterprise is concerned, the amount of purchases may not be equal to the sales volume, the difference being changes in inventory. Therefore, in trade volume statistics, there are three major indicators to be reported by each enterprise: (1) sales, (2) purchases, and (3) inventory changes.[19] Among these indicators, the volume of sales is the most important, since in practice it is used to represent the volume of trade.[20] In fact, trade statistics published thus far in China have not included any detailed information on commodity purchases and inventory changes, with the exception of government purchases of agricultural products. For this reason, only those indicators relating to

sales and agricultural procurement will be treated.

GROSS AND NET SALES

Gross sales are the sum of the sales of all trading enterprises. For an individual enterprise, its gross sales includes an intra-enterprise turnover. For the economy as a whole, gross sales equal the sum of wholesale and retail sales. *Net sales* of an enterprise are its gross sales minus the intra-enterprise turnover, and those of the economy as a whole can be computed as the amount of commodities sold to final consumers and thus are equal to the total volume of retail sales. The ratio of gross sales to net sales is frequently computed in China to indicate the number of intermediate links of commodity circulation. The larger the number of such links are, the slower commodities will circulate, and the greater the overhead expenses will be.[21]

WHOLESALE VOLUME

Wholesale volume refers to the sale of commodities by enterprises and trade agencies to other trade agencies for subsequent resale, and to industrial enterprises for the manufacture of other commodities.[22] But under current practice the amount of producer goods sold to peasants is included in retail sales.[23]

The major part of the wholesale trade is handled by various specialized trading companies organized by the Ministry of Commerce in 1950 for the purpose of controlling commodity supplies. These companies purchase commodities from domestic producers and from import trade agencies and then distribute them to their local retail stores or resell them to other producers. Supply and marketing cooperatives also handle some of the wholesale trade, particularly that of handicraft and agricultural commodities. The wholesale volume of joint and private trade has been negligible since trade was almost completely socialized in 1956.

RETAIL SALES

Retail sales refers to the sale of commodities to industrial consumers and public organizations and enterprises for their consumption.[24]

[17]Hsü Ch'ien, Yu Tao, Tai Shih-kuang, *et al., Lectures on Economic Statistics,* Peking: Statistical Publishing House, 1957, p. 173.
[18]Sun Chih-fang, *op. cit.;* and *Trade Statistical Work Handbook, op. cit.,* pp. 2–3.
[19]*Ibid.,* p. 3.
[20]*Ibid.,* p. 5.
[21]*Ibid.,* pp. 5–6; and Hsü Ch'ien, *et al., op. cit.,* pp. 222–24.
[22]Wang Pei-hsün, *op. cit.; Trade Statistical Work Handbook, op. cit.,* p. 7; and Hsü Ch'ien *et al.,op. cit.,* p. 225.
[23]Wang Pie-hsün, *op. cit.*
[24]*Trade Statistical Work Handbook, op. cit.,* pp. 7–8.

Goods sold to producers for further fabrication are included in wholesale trade. But, as pointed out above, producer goods purchased by peasants are a part of retail sales.

There are four classifications of retail trade: (1) urban and rural retail sales, (2) sales to households and to public organizations and enterprises, (3) sales by trade agencies, restaurants, industrial enterprises, and peasants, and (4) grouping by ownership of trade agency, such as state, cooperative, joint, and private retail sales.

Two most important indicators of retail sales for which statistics are available are the social commodity retail volume and retail sales of major commodities.

The social commodity retail volume (she-hui shang-p'in ling-shou-o) is the monetary value of total retail sales. Not included in the computation, however, is the volume of peasant trade.[25] Reportedly, the social commodity retail volume is calculated in the following way. First, figures on state and cooperative sales are taken directly from regular statistical schedules. Figures on joint and private retail sales are computed from the data on commodity supplies to joint and private trade enterprises from state enterprises and supply and marketing cooperatives. Figures on retail sales in the free market are estimated on the basis of relevant data such as those on output, consumption, and state purchases.[26]

Data on retail sales of major commodities are estimated in the same way.[27] These data are given in physical terms. All state trade enterprises and supply and marketing cooperatives are required to report periodically in natural units the volume of retail sales of certain commodities specified by the State Statistical Bureau. These commodities are usually essentials, such as grains, salt, pork, cotton cloth, rubber shoes, and paper. In 1957, for example, retail sales of 19 such commodities were to be reported by trade enterprises.[28]

STATE PURCHASE

State purchase, which is a form of commodity turnover, refers to an official monopoly of dealing in certain commodities. These com-

modities are mostly agricultural, and their producers are required to fulfill compulsory sales to the state.

State purchase began in 1953 with the introduction of two systems known, respectively, as "planned purchase and planned supply" (chi-hua sho-ko yu chi-hua kung-yin) and "unified purchase" (t'ung-ko).[29]

Commodities subject to planned purchase and planned supply are those considered vital to the national economy, such as food grains and raw cotton. Producers of these commodities are to deliver obligatory quotas to the state at official prices. The surplus over the quota can be sold only through the state trade network at slightly higher prices. At the same time, the supply of these commodities is rationed to consumers.

The system of unified purchase embraces a large number of mainly agricultural products which are not as vital to the national economy as the commodities in the other system but are important raw materials used in industry or essential for consumption and exports. The system differs from the first one chiefly in that producers are allowed to sell the remainder on the open market and that the commodities are not rationed.

The list of commodities included in the two systems was revised from time to time. Since 1959, all commodities produced in nonstate sectors have been classified into three categories. There are 38 commodities falling under the system of planned purchase and planned supply, known as the "first-category" commodities, including food grains, edible vegetable oil, salt, sugar, cured tobacco, raw cotton, cotton yarn, cotton cloth, gasoline, kerosene, diesel oil, lubrication oil, and a number of important Chinese medicinal materials. The second category consists of 293 commodities, all of which are subject to unified purchase. Included are such commodities as ramie, hemp, sugar cane, draft animals, live pigs, eggs, tung oil, tea leaves, fertilizers, insecticides, certain kinds of fruits, and a number of aquatic products.[30] Commodities not included in the first and second categories belong to a third one. Planned or unified purchase is not required for the third-category commodities.

[25]Sun Chin-fang, op. cit.
[26]Ch'en Wu-ying, op. cit; and Department of Trade, Provincial Statistical Bureau of Heilungkiang, op. cit.
[27]Ibid.
[28]Sun Chih-fang, op. cit.

[29]The system of planned purchase and planned supply was first introduced in 1950, when certain metals and ores, such as tungsten, aluminum, and tin ores and ingots were to be purchased, supplied, or exported by state trading companies only.
[30]"Classified Commodity Catalogue," TKP, April 4, 1959; reprinted in 1959 JMST, p. 383.

Statistics on state purchase in physical units are compiled for each *hsien* and for each commodity. Value data are also calculated on the basis of official purchase prices.[31]

COST OF COMMODITY TURNOVER

Another statistical measure which is related to commodity turnover and is considered very important in economic planning is selling expenses, known as the "cost of commodity turnover" *(shang-p'in liu-chuan fei-yung)*. Included in the cost of commodity turnover are wages, interest payments, depreciation expenses, and charges for transportation, loading and unloading, storage, and wrapping. Taxes, fines, and commodity damages due to natural calamities and mismanagement are excluded from the computation.[32] Little information on the cost of commodity turnover has been published. One source indicates that for the enterprises under the Ministry of Commerce transportation charges, interest payments, and wages accounted for, respectively, 32.43 percent, 24.99 percent, and 9.14 percent of the commodity-turnover cost in 1954.[33]

Gross and Net Value of Trade Output

As pointed out above, in theory only that part of trade serving material production is included in national income. In practice, however, the entire value added by trade has been estimated in China. The gross-value output of trade is computed as the difference between the total sales revenue and the cost of purchases. The value added by trade is obtained by deducting material outlays from the gross-value output of trade.

Statistical Data

STATISTICS ON THE TRADE NETWORK (TABLES 7.1–7.9)

Statistical data on the trade network are assembled in Tables 7.1–7.9. Included are figures on the number of agencies, the number of operating personnel, the amount of capital funds, the volume of trade (i.e., the sum of the wholesale and retail trade), the density of the

retail trade network, and labor productivity. These data are classified by ownership of trade agency, by urban and rural areas, or by wholesale and retail trade. No trade network statistics have been published for the years after 1955. Figures for 1955 were compiled from a national census of trade conducted in that year.

STATISTICS ON THE VOLUME OF TRADE (TABLES 7.10–7.28)

Available data on trade volume may be classified in the following categories:

TOTAL TRADE VOLUME

Data on total trade volume are not available, but those on private trade in eight large cities can be found and are shown in Table 7.10. These data were given in index numbers covering the years of 1954 and 1955, with 1953 being the base year. In addition, estimates are available for trade volume in the free market, with breakdowns by type of buyers and by type of products. These estimates are given in Tables 7.11–7.13.

WHOLESALE VOLUME

Data on wholesale volume by ownership of enterprise are given for 1950 through 1955 in Table 7.14. These data cover only the wholesale volume of regular commercial organizations. Figures on the wholesale trade through other channels are not included.

RETAIL VOLUME

1. Table 7.15 presents statistics on the volume of retail rade by ownership of enterprise for the years 1950–59. Figures are given for both the social commodity retail volume and the retail volume of regular commercial organizations.

2. Table 7.16 presents data on the social commodity retail volume in urban and rural areas for 1956–58. There are some discrepancies between these figures and the figures given in *Ten Great Years*, as shown in Table 7.15. Such discrepancies probably result from a revision made for the *TGY* series.

3. Data on the social commodity retail volume and on the retail volume of state stores and supply and marketing cooperatives are

---

[31] Hsü Ch'ien *et al., op. cit.,* pp. 239–41.
[32] *Trade Statistical Work Handbook, op. cit.,* pp. 22–23.
[33] Ch'en Yi, *The Commodity Turnover Planning of State Commercial Enterprises,* Shanghai: People's Press, 1956, p. 254.

compiled for the national minority areas and a number of provinces. These data are shown in Table 7.17.

4. Data on retail sales of major commodities in physical units are compiled for the entire economy in Table 7.18 and for Inner Mongolia Autonomous Region and Kansu Province, respectively, in Tables 7.19 and 7.20.

5. Tables 7.21–7.24 present figures on production and sales of a number of commodities, such as cotton textile products, machine-made paper, and resin.

6. Table 7.25 presents retail sales of salt, sugar, and edible vegetable oils by supply and marketing cooperatives from 1952 to 1955.

7. Data on supply of producer goods to agriculture are assembled for the entire economy and for Inner Mongolia Autonomous Region in Tables 7.26–7.28

STATE PURCHASE OF AGRICULTURAL
PRODUCTS (TABLES 7.29–7.34)

1. Table 7.29 presents data on state purchase of agricultural products and products of agricultural subsidiary occupations. These data, given in yuan, cover the entire economy, the national minority areas, Inner Mongolia Autonomous Region, and Hunan Province.

2. Data on state purchase of major agricultural products in physical units are compiled for the entire economy and Inner Mongolia Autonomous Region in Tables 7.30–7.34.

THE RATIO OF MARKETABLE OUTPUT TO
TOTAL OUTPUT OF MAJOR AGRICULTURAL
PRODUCTS (TABLE 7.35)

Statistics are available on the ratio of marketable output to total output of food grains, cotton, and cured tobacco for 1952–55 and are shown in Table 7.35. The marketable output of an agricultural product refers to that portion of the output of the product actually sold during a given period of time, with the remainder being retained by peasants for consumption or processing.

GROSS AND NET VALUE
OF TRADE OUTPUT

Estimates of the gross and net value of trade output, together with those of material outlays were included in Table 2.2 for 1952 and 1956. These figures were given in 1952 prices.

FOREIGN TRADE

SOURCES, MEASUREMENT, AND
CLASSIFICATIONS OF
FOREIGN TRADE DATA

The major source of Chinese foreign trade statistics is the system of regular statistical schedules. The Ministry of Foreign Trade is required to submit regular reports to the State Statistical Bureau. In addition, the Bureau of Customs compiles and publishes its own customs statistics on the basis of various primary records.[34] In the early 1950's it was also engaged in computing foreign trade indices.[35]

Import and export statistics are recorded in both physical and value terms. Units of measurement for various commodities are based on the *Unified Commodity Catalogue for Foreign Trade* compiled by the Ministry of Foreign Trade.[36] Commodities are measured according to net weight, i.e., natural weight exclusive of external wrappings.[37] Values of imports are based on prices F.O.B., and exports are valued C.I.F.[38] The volume of trade with the Soviet Union and East European countries is valued in both yuan and rubles, but only yuan is used for measuring the volume of trade with Asian communist countries. For trade with non-communist countries, both yuan and the U.S. dollar are used as units of measurement.[39]

In foreign trade statistics, a number of classifications are made according to the following characteristics: (1) country, (2) commodity group, (3) customs house, and (4) ownership of trading enterprise. Commodities exported are also grouped into three classes: (1) industrial and mining products, (2) processed products of agriculture and subsidiary occupations, and (3) products of agriculture and subsidiary occupations. In addition, commodities imported from foreign countries are divided into producer and consumer goods. As noted in the section on industry, it is difficult to make a clear-cut distinction between producer and consumer goods. For example, coal cannot be totally identified as a producer good, since it is also

[34]Ch'en Chi-shih and Liu Po-wu, *Foreign Trade Statistics*, Peking: Finance and Economics Press, 1958, pp. 129–32.
[35]*Ibid.*, pp. 167–79.
[36]*Ibid.*, pp. 134, 152.
[37]*Ibid.*, p. 134.
[38]*Ibid.*, p. 135; and *Trade Statistical Work Handbook, op. cit.*, pp. 33–34.
[39]Ch'en Chi-shih and Liu Po-wu, *op. cit.*, pp. 135–36.

used by households for heating purposes, and sugar may not be used entirely by consumers, since it can be used to produce candies. In China the major use of an imported commodity is adopted as the criterion for the demarcation between producer and consumer goods. In foreign trade statistics, therefore, coal is classified as a producer good and sugar as a consumer good.[40]

FOREIGN TRADE STATISTICS (TABLES 7.36 – 7.42)

Official statistical information on Chinese foreign trade is very scanty. *Ten Great Years* gives figures on the total combined volume of import and export trade in yuan for 1950 through 1958 without detailed breakdowns. In 1956, in the Chinese Export-Commodity Fair held at Canton, there was an exhibit of some figures on import and export trade indices and on the percentage distribution of imports and exports in the total volume of Chinese foreign trade for 1950 through 1955. These figures were published in a Japanese periodical in 1957[41] and have become the chief source used for estimating the volume of import and export trade for those years. Tables 7.36 and 7.37 present official data and derived estimates on import and export trade volume.

There are some other official data on foreign trade which can be found in print. Included are:

1. Figures on the percentage distribution of exports among industrial and mining products, processed products of agriculture and subsidiary occupations, and products of agriculture and subsidiary occupations for 1950–58 (Table 7.38).

2. Figures on the percentage distribution of imports between producer and consumer goods for 1950–58 (Table 7.39).

3. Figures on the percentage distribution of imports and exports by customs house for 1952–54 (Table 7.40).

4. Figures on the export of food grains and soybeans in tons for 1953–57 (Table 7.41).

5. Figures on the import of cotton in tons for 1949–56 (Table 7.42).

[40]*Ibid.*, pp. 154–59.
[41]*Asia Keizai Jump* (Tokyo), No. 316 (March, 1957), pp. 6–13, reference on p. 6.

8

PRICES

CATEGORIES OF PRICES

In China only prices of commodities of minor importance are determined through supply-demand relationships. Included are the commodities sold on the open market, such as the so-called "third-category" commodities, which do not fall within the government procurement scheme. Prices of the majority of commodities are fixed or approved by the state. The following are several principal categories of these prices.

1. *Ex-factory prices* (*ch'u-ch'ang chia-ko*) are the transfer prices at which an industrial enterprise disposes of its products to other enterprises or to wholesalers. The ex-factory price of a product is composed of costs, profits, and taxes.[1] Costs include wages and salaries, basic and supplementary materials, including fuel and power, depreciation charges, and various administrative expenses, such as those for business trips and postage. Rent and capital charges are excluded from costs.[2]

2. *Agricultural purchase prices* are the prices which peasants receive from the state for delivering obligatory quotas. The purchase price of an agricultural product is said to cover costs, including a "reasonable compensation" for labor but excluding land rent, and to provide for accumulation (i.e., investment in fixed and working capital) of the people's communes.[3]

3. *Wholesale prices* are the prices at which wholesalers sell their commodities to state industrial enterprises, state retailers, supply and marketing cooperatives, and the commercial agencies of the people's communes. Industrial (or agricultural) wholesale prices include, in addition to ex-factory prices (or agricultural purchase prices), the commodity-turnover

cost of wholesalers and a profit margin. No taxes are levied at the wholesale level.[4]

4. *Retail prices*, being the prices charged to final consumers, are composed of the following elements: (1) wholesale prices, (2) taxes, (3) the commodity-turnover cost at the retail level, and (4) a profit margin for retailers.[5]

DETERMINATION OF PRICES

EX-FACTORY PRICES

In principle, Chinese price-setting rules are based on average-cost-plus methods.[6] The ex-factory price of a product is composed of the average cost of production of all enterprises producing the product in question, a profit margin calculated in relation to cost, and a specific amount of tax proportionate to sales. In practice, however, a variety of methods had been used in China to determine ex-factory prices. The one most commonly adopted is the so-called "model cost method."[7] According to

[1]Department of Planning and Statistics, Hupeh University, *Industrial Statistics*, Wuhan: Hupeh People's Press, 1960, pp. 388–90: and Ch'en Hsi-jun, "Price Planning," *CHCC*, No. 6 (January 23, 1956), pp. 30–33.

[2]State Planning Commission and Ministry of Finance, "Regulations Concerning Agents of Production Expenses, Items of the Cost of Products and the Checking and Computation of the Cost of State Industrial Enterprises," *Ch'i-yeh k'uai-chi (Enterprise Accounting)*, No. 17 (September 7, 1959), pp. 5–9.

[3]Chang Wen and Chao Li-kuang, "An Analysis of Factors Forming Commodity Prices under Socialism," *HCS*, No. 12 (December 20, 1963), pp. 28–35.

[4]*Ibid.*

[5]*Ibid.*

[6]Chinese concepts of average cost differ from Western usage; the difference lies primarily in the omission of capital charges and rent in Chinese cost accounting.

[7]Lo Ken-mo, *Problems of Commodity and Value under Socialism* Peking: Science Press, September, 1957, pp. 162–65.

this method, model firms, which are supposed to be representative of all firms producing the same product, are selected; and the average cost of production of these model firms is computed as the basis for pricing. Profits per unit of product are calculated as a percentage of cost or capital.[8] Another method used is to deduct distribution costs and trade profits from retail prices in order to arrive at ex-factory prices.[9] A third method which has frequently been employed in China for adjusting prices is to use "historical price data" as a basis for adjustment.[10] Such data usually refer to those prevailing during 1930–36, since the relationships among prices during that period are considered to be relatively normal.

Ex-factory prices are determined by various administrative levels, depending upon the importance of the products in question. For products which are vital to the national economy and are controlled directly by the central government, ex-factory prices are determined by the State Council. For products controlled by central industrial ministries, ex-factory prices are determined by these ministries. For products which are produced and sold locally, the determination of their ex-factory prices is primarily the responsibility of provincial governments. In the case of products sold directly by producing enterprises, ex-factory prices are sometimes reached through negotiations between these enterprises.[11] Ex-factory prices of new products, as noted in the section on industry, are determined primarily at experimental cost levels.

AGRICULTURAL PURCHASE PRICES

In theory, agricultural purchase prices are supposed to be based on the average cost of production of farms on an average grade of land, with average efficiency and under normal weather conditions, plus a mark-up for communal accumulation. Like exfactory prices, however, agricultural purchase prices are not actually set by any uniform rules.

As may be recalled, agricultural procurement policy began in 1953, when the systems of planned purchase and planned supply and of unified purchase were introduced. During the first few years, state purchase prices for agricultural products were determined primarily by deducting an estimated amount of distribu-

tion costs and trade profits from retail prices prevailing in the market.[12] Since 1957 the average cost of production has been used as the basis for setting agricultural purchase prices.[13]

Prior to 1959, the Ministry of Food collected cost data on food grains by employing interview and model-survey methods, and these cost estimates served as the basis for pricing food grains. State purchase prices for industrial crops were related to those for food grains according to certain ratios determined largely by historical price relationships between these two types of crops during the period 1930–36.[14]

In recent years, "survey and accounting networks of agricultural costs" have been established in various provinces to undertake the measurement of the cost of production in the communes. Such networks were first instituted by Kwangtung Province in 1958 and by other provinces in the following years. Available evidence indicates that rent and interest on fixed capital do not enter into the cost measurement, while interest payments on agricultural loans are treated as costs.[15] Cost data on various types of crops obtained through these networks are used as the basis for determining agricultural purchase prices.

In addition to cost, some other factors reportedly have been taken into account in setting agricultural purchase prices. Included are (1) historical relationships between agricultural and industrial prices, (2) regional differences (in fertility, transportation, etc.), (3) supply-demand relationships, and (4) government policy objectives, such as using prices to influence the allocation of resources to certain crops in preference to others.[16]

[8]Niu Chung-huang, *Accumulation and Consumption in China's National Income*, Peking: Chinese Youth Press, 1957, pp. 94–97; Yang Hung-tao, "Several Problems Concerning Profits in the Formation of Industrial Prices," *CCYC*, No. 8 (August 17, 1963), pp. 43–49, 66; and Chang Wen and Chao Li-kuang, *op. cit.*

[9]Chao Li-kuang and Hsiang Ching-chuan, "Objective Criteria for Commodity Price Differentials and Bases for Determining these Differentials under Socialism," *CCYC*, No. 2 (February 17, 1964), pp. 52–61.

[10]Lo Ken-mo, *op. cit.*

[11]Ch'en Hsi-jun, *op. cit.*

[12]Chao Li-kuang and Hsiang Ching-chuan, *op. cit.*

[13]*Ibid.*

[14]Fan Jo-yi, "A Brief Discussion of Agricultural Price Policy," *CCYC*, No. 2 (February 17, 1959), pp. 26–30; and Ho Wei, "The Significance and Methods of Comparing Current Agricultural Prices with Pre-War Levels," *HH*, No. 7 (April 18, 1957), pp. 15-17, 21.

[15]Price Department, Bureau of Commerce, Kwangtung Province, "The Method of Estimating Agricultural Costs in the People's Communes," *CYHTTH*, No. 2 (February 11, 1959), pp. 20–21; and Wu Yuan-hung, "How to Establish Survey and Accounting Networks of Agricultural Costs in the People's Communes," *CCYC*, No.8 (August 17, 1959), pp. 63–64.

[16]Yao Yi-lin, "Commerce in the Past Ten Years," in *Ten Glorious Years*, Peking: People's Daily Press, 1959, pp. 359–76; Chao Li-kuang and Hsiang Ching-chuan, *op. cit.*; and Fan Jo-yi, *op. cit.*

Purchase prices for the first-category products must be approved by the State Council, but various related central ministries and provincial governments are vested with the authority to determine the purchase prices for the second-category products.[17]

WHOLESALE AND RETAIL PRICES

As pointed out above, wholesale and retail prices are determined on the basis of ex-factory or agricultural purchase prices, plus certain mark-ups such as distribution costs, taxes, and profits. There is, however, an important function which retail prices are called upon to perform: they are supposedly set at the level which would equate planned supply and expected demand both for an individual commodity and in aggregate terms.

Wholesale and retail prices charged by state and joint enterprises, as well as by supply and marketing cooperatives, are controlled by the Ministry of Commerce and its branch organizations. For all important commodities, wholesale and retail prices are determined either directly by the Ministry itself or by various state trading companies under the Ministry. For commodities of lesser importance, prices are set by commercial departments or trading companies at local levels.[18]

PRICE INDICES

SOURCES OF DATA

There are two major problems involved in the preparation of price statistics: (1) collecting price data and (2) selecting the methods used for computing price indices.

For commodities controlled by state and joint trade enterprises, as well as by supply and marketing cooperatives, information on price changes is taken from regular reports. As may be recalled, these enterprises and cooperatives are supposed to submit regular statistical schedules, in which data on various trade indicators, including price changes, are reported. For commodities sold on the open market, price data are based on sample surveys or registration records. For example, in 1957 retail prices of certain commodities prevailing at major markets were registered on the 5th, 15th and 25th of each month.[19]

METHODS OF COMPUTING PRICE INDICES

For the purpose of showing price trends, price data are usually summarized and presented in the form of index numbers. The price index of an individual commodity can be obtained simply as the ratio of the average price of the commodity during the current period to that of the base period. For a group of commodities, however, the computation of the price index is complicated by the problem of weighting. The Chinese literature indicates that, in principle, current-period quantities of commodities are used as weights for aggregative price indices.[20] The weighted aggregative price index with current-period quantities as weights is called the composite index (ts'ung-ho chih-shu) and is given by the following formula:

$$\text{Composite index} = \frac{\Sigma \, p_1 q_1}{\Sigma \, p_0 q_1} \times 100$$

where p_1 and q_1 represent, respectively, the price and the sales quantity of a single commodity during the current period and p_0 represents the price of the commodity during the base period. Therefore, the composite index is the same as what is commonly known as the "Paasche index."

In the above formula, the numerator ($\Sigma \, p_1 q_1$) is the commodity turnover during the current period, and the denominator ($\Sigma \, p_0 q_1$) is the commodity turnover during the current period valued at base period prices. The application of this formula thus involves three types of data: the current value of total commodity turnover, the sales quantities of individual commodities during the current period, and base-period prices of these commodities. Chinese sources indicate that data on the current value of the total commodity turnover are frequently

---

[17]For the meaning of the first- and second-category products see the section on trade.

[18]Hsü Ch'ien, Tai Shih-kuang, Yu Tao, et al., *Lectures on Economic Statistics*, Peking: Statistics Publishing House, 1957, pp. 243–44.

[19]*Ibid.*

[20]*Ibid.*, p. 249; and Editorial Committee for Statistical Work Handbook, *Trade Statistical Work Handbook*, Peking: Statistics Publishing House, 1957, pp. 29–30. Hereafter cited as *Trade Statistical Work Handbook*.

incomplete at the time when aggregate price indices are computed.[21] Moreover, in the regular statistical schedules filled out by commercial enterprises and cooperatives, sales of individual commodities are reported in value terms,[22] and data in natural units are given only for certain major commodities.[23] As a result, the composite index formula is not generally applicable. In practice, two other formulas have been more frequently adopted.

One formula gives the weighted harmonic mean index *(chia-ch'üan t'iao-ho p'ing-chün chih-shu)* and the other the weighted arithmatic mean index *(chia-ch'üan suan-shu p'ing-chün chih-shu)*. These formulas can be shown, respectively, as follows:

$$\text{Weighted harmonic mean index} = \frac{\Sigma p_1 q_1}{\Sigma (1/K) p_1 q_1} \times 100$$

$$\text{Weighted arithmatic mean index} = \frac{\Sigma K p_0 q_1}{\Sigma p_0 q_1} \times 100$$

where p_0, p_1, and q_1 are defined as before and K represents the price index of an individual commodity (i.e., p_1/p_0).[24] Theoretically, these two formulas will yield the same result as the composite index formula.[25] But different sets of data are employed in the computation. In addition, owing to lack of data, as well as to computational convenience, commodities are classified into a number of groups; and data on the price indices and sale volume of these commodity groups, instead of individual commodities, are used to estimate aggregative price indices.

TYPES OF PRICE INDICES

In China, five major types of price index are computed: (1) wholesale price index, (2) retail price index, (3) the index of cost of living of workers and employees, (4) agricultural purchase price index, and (5) the index of relative prices between industrial and agricultural products.

Wholesale Price Index

Chinese sources indicate that wholesale price indices are constructed either from the weighted-harmonic-mean formula or from the constant-weighted arithmetic-mean formula.[26] The latter is a special form of the weighted-

arithmetic-mean formula and can be shown as follows:

$$\text{Constant-weighted arithmetic-mean index} = \frac{\Sigma (p_1/p_0) W}{\Sigma W}$$

where p_1/p_0 is the price index of an individual commodity (i.e., the same as K defined in the above formulas) and $W/\Sigma W$ represents a fixed weight. It is not clear, however, how these fixed weights are determined.

Wholesale price indices at the national level are computed for all commodities as a whole as well as for certain commodity groups. For the purpose of computing wholesale price indices, commodities are classified in several ways. One is the division into industrial and agricultural products, and another is into producer and consumer goods.[27] A third grouping is to classify commodities into eight categories: (1) food, (2) subsidiary food, (3) textile products (including cotton yarn), (4) fuel, (5) building material, (6) industrial supplies, (7) miscellaneous, and (8) special indigenous products.[28] Finally, wholesale price indices are calculated for major individual commodities. In addition, wholesale price indices are prepared for all commodities

[21] *Trade Statistical Work Handbook*, p. 30.
[22] Hsü Ch'ien *et al., op. cit.*, p. 250.
[23] *Ibid.*
[24] *Ibid.*, pp. 250–52; and *Trade Statistical Work Handbook, op. cit.*
[25] This can be proved from the following operations:

$$\text{Composite price index} = \frac{\Sigma p_1 q_1}{\Sigma p_0 q_1} \times 100$$

$$= \frac{\Sigma p_1 q_1}{\Sigma (p_1/p_1) p_0 q_1} \times 100$$

$$= \frac{\Sigma p_1 q_1}{\Sigma (p_0/p_1) p_1 q_1} \times 100$$

$$= \frac{\Sigma p_1 q_1}{\Sigma (1/K) p_1 q_1} \times 100 = \text{weighted harmonic mean price index}$$

$$\text{Composite price index} = \frac{\Sigma p_1 q_1}{\Sigma p_0 q_1} \times 100$$

$$= \frac{\Sigma (p_0/p_0) p_1 q_1}{\Sigma p_0 q_1} \times 100$$

$$= \frac{\Sigma (p_1/p_0) p_0 q_1}{\Sigma p_0 q_1} \times 100$$

$$= \frac{\Sigma K p_0 q_1}{\Sigma p_0 q_1} \times 100 = \text{weighted arithmetic mean price index}$$

[26] For example, the wholesale price index of state trading enterprises in 1956 was computed on the basis of the weighted-harmonic-mean formula, and the arithmetic mean with fixed weights was used in computing the wholesale price index of Shanghai for the period 1949–57. (See Hsü Ch'ien *et al., op. cit.*, p. 251; and Shanghai Economic Research Institute of the Chinese National Academy of Sciences and Economic Research Institute of the Shanghai Academy of Social Sciences, *A Collection of Shanghai Price Data Before and After the Liberation (1921–1957)*, Shanghai: Shanghai People's Press, 1958, pp. 448–59.

[27] *Trade Statistical Work Handbook, op. cit.*, p. 31.

[28] Shanghai Economic Research Institute of the Chinese National Academy of Sciences *et al., op. cit.*

and for various commodity groups at local levels.

Retail Price Index

In preparing retail price indices, commodities are grouped into two major categories: food and nonfood products. For large and medium-size cities, the food category is subclassified into four groups: (1) food, (2) subsidiary food, (3) tobacco, liquor, and tea, and (4) other food products. The nonfood category contains six groups: (1) clothing, (2) fuel, (3) daily necessities, (4) drugs, (5) household utensils, and (6) cultural and educational supplies. For *hsien* (including *hsiang* and villages), the classification is the same, except that the group of "other food products" is replaced by "agricultural producer goods."[29] For each group certain commodities considered to be representative of the group are selected. The selection of the commodities is based on the volume of retail sales and the importance of these commodities. The retail price index of each group is computed on the basis of the representative commodities within the group. Retail price indices of the 10 commodity groups thus obtained serve as the basis for measuring an aggregate retail price index.[30]

According to the *Statistical Reporting System of Nation-wide Prices*, issued by the State Statistical Bureau, the weighted-arithmetic-mean formula is used for computing retail price indices. In principle, weights are determined on the basis of the retail volume in the fourth quarter of the preceding year and in the third quarter of the current year. But the State Bureau stipulates further that weights thus determined should be appropriately adjusted in the light of anticipated developments in the fourth quarter of the current year and in the following year as well as in the light of certain relevant data such as those on residents' purchasing power.[31]

Retail price indices are calculated at both national and local levels as well as for urban and rural areas. For the purpose of showing price differentials between industrial and agricultural products, the retail price index of industrial products sold in rural areas is also computed.

The Index of the Cost of Living of Workers and Employees

The index of the cost of living of workers and employees is computed for indicating changes in the level of prices of goods and services consumed by the urban population and for measuring real wages.[32] The difference between the method of computation of the cost-of-living index and that of the retail price index lies in the number of commodities covered and the weighting system employed.

In the cost-of-living index, commodities are classified into three major categories: food, nonfood, and services.[33] The food and nonfood categories are classified further into 10 groups in the same way as in the case of the retail price index for large and medium cities. Service expenditures are divided into two groups: (1) rents, water, and electricity and (2) other services. Service expenditures are not included in the computation of the retail price index.

Available evidence indicates that the constant-weighted-arithmetic-mean formula is also used in computing the cost-of-living index.[34] But fixed weights are determined differently from those employed in preparing the retail price index. In principle, the proportion of the expenditure on a given group of commodities or services in the total consumption expenditure of an average family is used as a weight for that group. Such a weight is estimated from survey findings on family budgets and other relevant model survey data.[35]

The Index of Agricultural Purchase Prices

The index of agricultural purchase prices is used in China to indicate changes in the level of agricultural prices as well as the level of peasant income. It is calculated at both national and provincial levels. It is also calculated for urban and rural areas and for the national minority areas.

Agricultural commodities subject to state purchase are classified into four categories: (1) food grains, (2) technical crops, (3) animal products, and (4) special indigenous products.[36]

[29] *Trade Statistical Work Handbook, op. cit.*; and Chung Chi-sheng, "Several Problems Concerning the Compilation of Retail Price Indices at the Present Time," *Amoy University Journal*, social science edition, No. 2, December, 1957, pp. 95–110.

[30] Chung Chi-sheng, *ibid.*

[31] *Ibid.* For the meaning of residents' purchasing power, see the section on living standards.

[32] Yang Po, "A Discussion of the Problems Concerning the Compilation of the Index of the Cost of Living of Workers and Employers," *TCKTTH*, No. 11 (June 14, 1956), pp. 4–5, 25.

[33] Shanghai Economic Research Institute of the Chinese National Academy of Sciences *et. al., op. cit.*, p. 463.

[34] *Ibid.*, and *Trade Statistical Work Handbook, op. cit.*, p. 32.

[35] *Ibid.*

[36] *Ibid.*, pp. 32–33; Data Office, *TCKT*, "A Survey of Changes in the Price Differentials between Industrial and Agricultural Products since Liberation," *TCKT*, No. 17 (September 14, 1957), pp. 4–7.

Indices of the purchase prices of these four categories are computed, and the results are used to obtain an aggregate index of agricultural purchase prices.

It is not clear which method has been used to compute the agricultural purchase price index. One source implied that the composite formula was employed.[37]

The Index of Relative Prices between Industrial and Agricultural Products

The index of relative prices between industrial and agricultural products is calculated to indicate changes in the terms of trade between industry and agriculture. In China, the relative price index takes the form of a ratio of the retail price index of industrial products in rural areas to the agricultural purchase price index.[38] Therefore, the smaller the value of the relative price index becomes, the better the terms of trade will be from the point of view of the peasants.

In addition to the relative price index, the exchange ratio in physical terms between an industrial product and an agricultural product is frequently used to indicate the terms of trade between industry and agriculture. For example, the State Statistical Bureau computed the number of *shih-chih* of white fine cloth in exchange for 100 *chin* of wheat for seven provinces for the years of 1950, 1952, and 1956.[39]

STATISTICAL DATA ON PRICES

WHOLESALE PRICES

The following data on wholesale prices have been found in Chinese publications:

1. There are three series of nationwide wholesale price indices. One covers the period 1951–56, with 1950 being the base year. Another series was published for the same period, but the average prices during March, 1950, were used as the base. A third one covers the period 1950–58 with average prices during 1952 equal to 100. These three series are included in Table 8.1.

2. Table 8.2 presents data on the wholesale price index of coal from 1954 to 1958 with the price prevailing on December 31, 1953, equal to 100. These data were compiled from

officially announced wholesale prices (*p'i-fa p'ai-chia*) in 31 large and medium cities. Included in Table 8.4 are data on the wholesale price indices of eight commodity groups for 1956, with 1955 as the base year.

3. Both Table 8.5 and Table 8.6 present data on the monthly wholesale price index covering a number of major cities. Data in Table 8.5 cover the period 1950–56, with December of the preceding year as the base period, while those in Table 8.6 include only five years (i.e., 1950–54) with March, 1950, equal to 100.

4. Data on the December, 1956, wholesale price indices for Tientsin, Shanghai, Wuhan, Canton, Chungking, Sian, and Shenyang with December, 1955, as the base period are included in Table 8.3.

5. Data on the monthly wholesale price indices in Shanghai for 1949–57 are shown in Table 8.7. Included are not only data on the aggregate wholesale price index but also those on the wholesale price indices of eight major commodity groups.

6. Table 8.8 contains information on wholesale prices of 47 major commodities in Shanghai for 1949–57. Figures in this table are given in yuan.

RETAIL PRICES

Fragmentary data on retail price indices are assembled in the following tables:

1. Included in Table 8.1 are the following data on retail price indices:

   a. A nation-wide retail price index for 1953–58, with 1952 as the base period.

   b. Several series of retail price indices compiled for eight big cities with different base periods.

   c. The retail price index in rural areas for 1953–57, with 1952 as the base year.

   d. Three series of the retail price index of industrial products sold in rural areas with 1930–36, 1950, and 1952, respectively, being the base periods.

2. Table 8.2 includes data on retail price indices of individual commodities: ammonium sulfate, insecticides, insecticide sprayers, medium-sized double-wheel plows, and drugs.

---

[37]*Trade Statistical Work Handbook, op. cit.*
[38]*Ibid.,* p. 33.
[39]Data Office, *TCKT, op. cit.* One *shih-chih* is equivalent to 0.333 meter, and one *chin* to 0.5 kilogram.

3. Data on the retail price indices of 10 commodity groups for 1956, with 1955 as the base year, are shown in Table 8.9.

4. Table 8.10 presents figures on the quarterly retail price index in urban and rural areas for 1957.

5. Table 8.11 presents figures on the retail price index of industrial products in Inner Mongolia Autonomous Region for 1950–58.

6. Table 8.12 contains information on the retail price index of 15 major cities during the first quarter of 1957, with the first quarter of 1956 as the base period, and data on the 1956 retail price indices of 8 major cities, with 1955 as the base period, are included in Table 8.3.

7. Data on the retail price indices of major commodity groups in 8 big cities are shown in Table 8.13 for 1953–56, with 1952 as the base year.

8. Data on the retail price indices of major commodity groups in main cities during the first quarter of 1957 are shown in Table 8.14, with the first quarter of 1956 as the base quarter.

9. Table 8.15 presents statistics on the retail price index in Shanghai for 1953–57, with 1952 being the base year. Data are given for the aggregate retail price index, as well as for the retail price indices of 10 commodity groups and their subgroups.

COST OF LIVING

The State Statistical Bureau published data on the cost-of-living index for workers and employees in 12 cities for 1953–57, with 1952 being the base year. These data are included in Table 8.1. Data are also available for 8 major cities for 1956, with 1955 as the base year, and are included in Table 8.3. In addition, data with detail breakdowns are shown for Shanghai in Tables 8.16 and 8.17.

AGRICULTURAL PURCHASE PRICES

Available data on agricultural purchase price indices are very scanty. Data on three series of the agricultural purchase price index are included in Table 8.1, and their base periods are 1930–36, 1950, and 1952, respectively. In addition, the State Statistical Bureau published figures for 1956, with the same three base periods; and figures for 1958 were given in the

April, 1959, issue of the *Central Co-operative Bulletin*, with 1957 as the base year. These figures, shown in Table 8.18, cover all of the commodities purchased, as well as four main commodity groups: food grains, technical crops, animal products, and special indigenous products.

Figures on the purchase-price ratio between technical crops and food grains are shown in Table 8.19. These figures were derived by dividing the purchase price index for technical crops by that for food grains.

RELATIVE PRICES BETWEEN INDUSTRIAL AND AGRICULTURAL PRODUCTS

Data on relative prices between industrial and agricultural products are available primarily in the form of the ratios between retail price indices for industrial products in rural areas and purchase price indices for agricultural products. In addition, some figures on the exchange ratio in physical units between certain industrial and agricultural products can be found in Chinese publications.

Table 8.20 presents data on the ratio between industrial and agricultural price indices for 1950–58. There are four different series in this table, with 1936, 1930–36, 1950, and 1952 being, respectively, the base periods. The same type of data can be found in Tables 8.21 and 8.22. These data cover the national average, coastal areas, inland areas, national minority areas, *Han* nationality areas, and seven provinces for the year of 1956, with 1930–36, 1950, and 1952 as the base periods. In addition, data for national minority areas are given in Table 8.23 for 1952 and 1957, with 1930–36 and 1950 as the base periods.

Table 8.24 contains data on the ratio of the price index for food to that for cloth. These data cover the national average from 1951 through 1956 and seven provinces for 1956, with 1950 as the base year. The original source did not indicate whether wholesale or retail price indices were employed in the computation. Neither was there any explanation with regard to what kinds of food and cloth were used in the comparison.

Table 8.25 presents information on the exchange rate in physical units between wheat and white fine cloth in seven provinces during 1950, 1952, and 1956. Figures are shown in terms of the number of feet of white fine cloth per 100 *chin* of wheat. One *chin* is equivalent to 1/2 kilogram and 1 foot to 0.333 meter. In addition, data on the physical exchange rate between certain industrial and agricultural products are assembled for Inner Mongolia Autonomous Region and Kansu Province in Tables 8.26 and 8.27.

9

LIVING STANDARDS

TYPES AND SOURCES OF DATA ON LIVING STANDARDS

In Chinese statistics, there are several types of data related to living standards. Included are retail sales, retail price and cost-of-living indices, wages, social purchasing power, and income and consumption per household and per capita. Since the first three categories are dealt with in separate sections, only the last two are discussed here.

SOCIAL PURCHASING POWER

The Concept and the Scope of Social Purchasing Power

"Social purchasing power" *(she-hui ko-mai-li)* is "the capacity of urban and rural residents and collective units to purchase retail commodities, and is expressed in monetary terms."[1] "Urban and rural residents" means the population as a whole, and collective units include government agencies, public organizations, schools, and economic enterprises. Social purchasing power is employed in China to measure the total effective monetary demand for consumption goods and serves as a basis for estimating the social commodity retail volume.[2]

In the early years of the Peking regime, the commercial departments of certain local governments were engaged in collecting data on the purchasing power of residents. But a nationwide, unified investigation began only in 1953.[3] In July, 1957, the State Economic Commission and the State Statistical Bureau jointly promulgated a new scheme for compiling data on social purchasing power, in which the scope and methods of estimation underwent substantial

changes. Problems relating to the statistical computation of social purchasing power are summarized in the following points:[4]

1. The social purchasing power of collective units refers to their monetary expenditure on consumption goods, such as office supplies and cultural and recreational facilities. Prior to 1957, the total consumption expenditures of the armed forces and foreigners (including embassy personnel, experts, and visitors) were included in the computation, but since then only expenditures on those goods which are consumed collectively have been considered as a part of the social purchasing power of collective units. In other words, personal consumption expenditures of the armed forces and foreigners are now included in the social purchasing power of residents.

2. Expeditures on producer goods consumed by industrial, construction, and transportation enterprises are not included in the social purchasing power, on the ground that these goods are primarily distributed by the state in a planned way. But outlays on producer goods purchased by peasants are considered a part of their purchasing power, since virtually all these goods are obtained through market channels. In the first few years, only peasant expenditures on seed, fertilizers, insecticides, and farm implements were calculated. But the 1957 scheme

[1]Ch'en Yi, *The Commodity Turnover Plan of the State Commercial Enterprises,* Shanghai: Shanghai People's Press, 1956, p. 35.
[2]*Ibid.*
[3]Editorial Committee for Statistical Work Handbook, *Agricultural Statistical Work Handbook,* Peking: Statistics Publishing House, 1956, p. 49; hereafter referred to as *Agricultural Statistical Work Handbook.*
[4]Department of Trade Statistics, State Statistical Bureau, "Carefully Set Up the Balance Sheet for Monetary Income and Outlay of Residents, and Compile the Social Purchasing Power," *TCKT,* No. 17 (September 14, 1957), pp. 30–33; Wu Ting-ch'eng, "Explanation of Certain Problems Concerning the Proposal for Computing Social Purchasing Power," *CHCC,* No. 9 (September 9, 1957), pp. 27–29; and Chang Tsi-sheng and Yang Teh-jun, "Several Views on the Method of Computing Social Purchasing Power," *CYHTTH,* No. 2 (February 11, 1959), pp. 16–18.

called for an inclusion of additional commodities, such as cotton, cotton yarn, hemp, coal, lumber, and bamboo.

3. Before 1957, the purchasing power of residents was computed for both urban and rural areas. The major constituents of the urban residents' purchasing power were the total amount of wages received from the collective units and the cash payments between residents for professional services. The rural residents' purchasing power was chiefly made up of the income received from the sale of agricultural products to the collective units and to urban residents, and the barter trade among the peasants was not taken into account. The division between urban and rural residents was abolished in the 1957 scheme, but since then the purchasing power has been computed separately for peasants and for workers and employees.

4. The rural residents' purchasing power calculated for the years prior to 1957 included the money income of rural households and that of the agricultural producer cooperatives. But, according to the 1957 regulations, the money income of these cooperatives and their bank deposits were deducted from the computation. Available evidence indicates that this practice has continued with the introduction of the commune system in 1958.[5]

The Measurement of Social Purchasing Power

The purchasing power of residents is derived by deducting service expenditures, which are known in China as noncommodity expenditures (*fei-shang-p'in chih-ch'u*), and savings from their money income. It is equal to the residents' commodity expenditures (*chü-min shang-p'in chih ch'u*).[6]

The money income of the residents is estimated from its sources, such as the total wages of workers and employees, the incomes of capitalists and individual handicraftsmen and traders, and the peasant income from the sale of agricultural products. Data on wages and the sale of agricultural products by peasants are taken from those contained in the state plan, and data on the incomes of capitalists and individual handicraftsmen and traders are based on model surveys or estimated from relevant statistics.[7]

The residents' noncommodity expenditures include rents, educational expenses, insurance payments, union fees, and donations, as well as expenses for transportation, postage, and telephones, culture and recreation, purchases of government bonds, hospital care, and other services, such as haircuts.[8] Data on these expenditures are either taken from the information contained in the state plan or estimated on the basis of model surveys of actual expenditures during the preceding year.[9] Annual savings are computed from data given in the credit and cash plans of state banks.[10]

The purchasing power of collective units is estimated according to their expenditures on commodities. For governmental agencies, public organizations, schools, and state and joint industrial, construction, and transportation enterprises, estimates are made on the basis of budgetary and related data. For state and cooperative trade, data on distribution costs serve as the basis for estimation. The purchasing power of private enterprises is calculated from model survey data.[11]

PERSONAL INCOME AND CONSUMPTION

The major sources of data on income and consumption per household and per capita are the family budget surveys of peasants and of workers and employees.

Family Budget Surveys of Peasants

Family budget surveys of peasants are known in China as "income and expenditure surveys of peasant households" (*nung-chia shou-chih t'iao-cha*). Actually, these surveys are not designed merely for collecting data relating to the living standards of the peasants. The purpose of these surveys is said to be

to gather information on the property and total income and expenditure, both in cash and in kind, of each peasant household and take it as a basis on which to calculate the income and expenditure of the peasant household and to ascertain their level of material welfare, the principal farm produce and marketable grain they have on hand, and their cash and purchasing power.[12]

[5]Chang Tsi-sheng and Yang Teh-jung, *op. cit.*
[6]Ch'en Yi, *op. cit.*, p. 36.
[7]*Ibid.*
[8]It may be noted that purchases of government bonds are included in noncommodity expenditures rather than in savings.
[9]*Ibid.*, pp. 36–37.
[10]*Ibid.*
[11]*Ibid.*
[12]*Agricultural Statistical Work Handbook, op. cit.*, p. 43; and Ho Kan, "An Introduction of the Program for the Income and Expenditure Survey of Peasant Households for 1955," *TCKTTH*, No. 6 (March 29, 1956), pp. 19–21.

Where individual economy is predominant, survey data can also be used "for computing the gross value of agricultural output and for studying the changes in class status that take place among the peasants."[13]

In the first few years of the communist regime, family budget surveys were sometimes conducted in rural areas by the departments of finance and commerce of local governments according to their needs.[14] But a unified, national survey began only in February, 1955, when a survey for 1954 of 16,000 households was undertaken.[15] The survey was repeated for 1955 in early 1956 and again for 1956 at the end of that year. By 1957 a system of regular recording of income and expenditure of peasant households was installed. The system covered over 18,000 households selected from more than 1,250 agricultural producer cooperatives scattered in about 770 *hsien* of 25 provinces and autonomous regions.[16] The system has continued to operate since the people's communes were established.[17]

The selection of households was said to be based on scientific sampling methods. Sampling was carried out in two steps: (1) a number of villages in each province or autonomous region were selected according to the principle of systematic sampling, and (2) in each village in the sample certain households were then selected according to both the methods of systematic sampling and of proportional stratified sampling.[18] But there was evidence that these sampling rules were not strictly followed in practice.[19]

Before the commune system came into being, the survey program called for collection of the following data:[20]

1. The number of persons in each peasant household and their age, sex, and cultural level, the labor hired in and out of the household, the amount of grain consumed by the whole peasant household.

2. The property owned by each peasant household, including house, land, livestock, and tools. In order to study the changes that took place in the course of agricultural cooperation, the portion of the property which was privately owned but used by the cooperative and the portion of the property sold to the cooperative were listed separately. In the survey conducted for 1954, the property owned by each peasant household at the time of land reform was in-

vestigated for the purpose of ascertaining the changes in class status of the peasants.

3. The source and composition of income, both in kind and in cash, of each peasant household with the following breakdowns:

   a. Income from private productive activities, such as growing crops, raising animals and fowls, preliminary processing of farm products, and various types of handicraft work.

   b. Cash income from products and properties sold to the state, cooperative, and others.

   c. Income in cash and in kind received by each member household from the cooperative's distribution of dividends.

   d. Other incomes in cash and in kind, including wages, rent, and interest.

4. Types and composition of expenditures, both in cash and in kind, of each peasant household. Included are

   a. Cash paid for purchases of commodities and properties;

   b. Expenses for production, consumption, taxes, and others. Consumption expenditures were itemized according to commodity groups such as staple food, subsidiary food, clothing, fuel, and other. In addition, peasant households were required to report the consumption of major commodities in physical units.[21]

   c. Other expenses paid in cash or in kind, including wages, rent, and interest payments.

During the period 1958–60 a new system of distribution was adopted in the people's com-

[13]*Ibid.*

[14]Department of Agricultural Statistics, SSB, "Several Views on the Statistics Concerning the Living Conditions of Rural Residents," *CYHTTH*, No. 3 (March 11, 1959), pp. 16–18.

[15]Department of Agricultural Statistics, SSB, "Basic Experience from the Income and Expenditure Survey of Peasant Households for 1954," *TCKTTH*, No. 10 (May 29, 1956), pp. 25–27, 20.

[16]Huang Chien-t'o, "Carefully Improve the Work of Income and Expenditure Surveys of Peasant Households in Our Country," *TCYC*, No. 2 (February 23, 1958), pp. 4–11.

[17]Department of Agricultural Statistics, SSB, *CYHTTH, op. cit.*

[18]*Agricultural Statistical Work Handbook, op. cit.*, pp. 44–45; Department of Agricultural Statistics, SSB, *TCKTTH, op. cit.*; and Ho Kan, "My Views on the Tendency of a Single Survey of Income and Expenditure of Peasant Households to Deviate from Reality," *TCKTTH*, No. 18 (September 29, 1956), pp. 28–30.

[19]Sun Yeh-fan (Deputy Director of State Statistical Bureau), "Several Problems Concerning the Income and Expenditure Survey of Peasant Households," *TCKT*, No. 6 (March 29, 1957), pp. 11–17.

[20]*Agricultural Statistical Work Handbook, op. cit.*, pp. 45–46; Ho Kan, *TCKTTH, op. cit.*; and Huang Chien-t'o, *op. cit.*

[21]For example, in the 1958 survey peasant households were required to report the amount of 31 commodities consumed by them. (See Department of Agricultural Statistics, *CYHTTH, op. cit.*)

munes. Commune members were paid partly in cash and partly in kind, and at one point, the "in-kind" portion reached as high as 80 to 90 percent of distribution. At the same time, private plots were taken away from the peasants and the rural free markets abolished. As a result, the State Statistical Bureau pointed out in 1959 that the significance of rural family budget surveys had declined and much of the data could be obtained directly from the income and expenditure accounts of the communes.[22] Toward the end of 1960, the part-"in-kind"–part-money-wage distribution system was discarded. In addition, private plots were returned to the peasants, and the rural free markets reappeared. The fragmentary data published in China seem to indicate that rural family budget surveys have regained their significance, and the types of data collected are largely the same as those listed above.

**Family Budget Surveys
of Workers and Employees**

Family budget surveys of workers and employees (*chih-kung chia-t'ing shou-chih t'iao-cha*) provide the basic source of data on living standards of the urban population. In addition, survey data can also be used to study wage differentials, compute the social purchasing power of urban residents, and determine the manpower reserve.[23]

In the early 1950s, family budget surveys of workers and employees or of urban residents were conducted in many localities and branches of industry. But the quality of these survey data was said to be very poor, owing to "a small number of families investigated, unscientific methods, inadequate representation, and moreover, non-unified indicators."[24] In 1956, a national, unified family budget survey of workers and employees began to operate on a regular recording basis. A number of families were requested to record their income and expenditure, and these families were to be visited regularly by official interviewers.[25]

The families selected in the 1956 sample were those workers, engineering and technical personnel, and employees in state and state-private joint enterprises of ten branches of industry in 27 cities. The sample was enlarged in 1957 to include operating personnel in state and joint commercial enterprises, teachers of elementary and middle schools, and administra-

tive personnel of government agencies and public organizations.[26]

The methods employed in 1956 for selecting families were those of proportional stratified sampling, with systematic sampling inside the strata. Sampling was carried out in three states. First the number of families to be selected in 10 branches of industry was determined in proportion to the number of workers and employees in these branches. Second, in each branch of industry enterprises were selected according to systematic sampling. Finally, for each enterprise, selected families of workers and employees were chosen again on the basis of systematic sampling. The procedure was intended to insure the representation of the sample for the families of workers and employees in the country as a whole. But the proportion of the workers and employees in the 10 industrial branches varied greatly for the 27 cities. Data obtained according to this sampling procedure were by no means representative of the city population and thus were of little value to city officials. Therefore, the sample size in each city was frequently increased by its officials in order to meet their needs. As a result, more than 12,000 families were interviewed in 1956, as compared with 6,000 families called for in the original plan.[27]

Because of these defects in the 1956 plan, a new sampling procedure was adopted in 1957. The choice of a sample for each city was now left to the discretion of its officials on the basis of the composition of the labor force, the degree of wage differentials, the distribution of enterprises and their scale of production in the city in question. The methods adopted by various cities were either systematic sampling or the so-called "model selection."[28]

The program of family budget surveys required the collection of the following data:[29]

1. The number of persons in each family and their age, sex, cultural level, employment status, and living conditions.

[22]*Ibid.*
[23]Editorial Committee for Statistical Work Handbook, *Labor Statistical Work Handbook*, Peking: Statistics Publishing House, 1958, pp. 75–77. Hereafter cited as *Labor Statistical Work Handbook*.
[24]Yang Pen-chuang, "The Family Budget Survey of Workers and Employees," *TCKTTH*, No. 10 (October 17, 1955), pp. 46–47.
[25]*Labor Statistical Work Handbook, op. cit.*, p. 78.
[26]*Ibid.*, p. 77.
[27]Fang Pin-chu, "Views on Improving the Sampling Methods Used in the Family Budget Survey of Workers and Employees," *TCKT*, No. 4 (February 28, 1957), pp. 11–14.
[28]*Labor Statistical Work Handbook, op. cit.*
[29]*Ibid.*, pp. 74–75.

2. The source and composition of income, both in cash and in kind, of each family, with the following breakdowns:

   a. Wage income of the family and of the interviewee.
   b. Nonwage income of the family, including pensions, bonus, fringe benefits, and other receipts.

3. Categories of expenditure, including

   a. Commodity expenditure, which is classified into

      i. Expenditure on food itemized by products such as food grains, coarse grains, potatoes, flour, meat, poultry, fish, and vegetables.
      ii. Expenditures on nonfood products, such as clothes, fuel, daily necessities, furniture, drugs, and cultural and recreational supplies.

   b. Noncommodity expenditure consisting of four broad groups:

      i. Rents, water, and electricity.
      ii. Service payments.
      iii. Cultural and recreational outlays.
      iv. Other outlays.

In addition, the consumption of certain major commodities is also recorded in natural units.

STATISTICAL DATA ON LIVING STANDARDS

In addition to data on retail sales, retail price, and cost-of-living indices and wages, other available statistics relating to living standards may be grouped into three categories: (1) figures on social purchasing power, (2) value data on income and consumption expenditure, and (3) physical data on the consumption of major commodities.

SOCIAL PURCHASING POWER

Data on social purchasing power are available primarily in the form of index numbers. Table 9.1 presents five series of the social purchasing power index which have appeared in various books or articles. There are certain discrepancies among these series, and the one

given by Hsü Ti-hsin was probably the most authoritative and credible in view of his official status in the Chinese government,[30] as well as the fact that Hsü's series was published later than the others. Data in absolute terms can be found only for 1952 and 1955–57. In addition, data on the purchasing power of rural residents are available for 1950, 1956, and 1958 and those of urban residents for 1956. All these figures are included in Table 9.1.

PERSONAL INCOME AND CONSUMPTION EXPENDITURES

Tables 9.2–9.6 present data on per capita income and consumption expenditure of peasants and of workers and employees. These data, given for the national average and selected provinces, were obtained in part through family budget surveys.

Table 9.7 indicates net increase in peasant income due to changes in industrial and agricultural prices for 1953–57.

Tables 9.8–9.11 show data on the level and the composition of the consumption expenditure of peasants and of workers and employees for selected years.

CONSUMPTION OF MAJOR COMMODITIES

Data on the consumption of major commodities are given in physical units. These data were collected primarily through family budget surveys.

Table 9.12 presents figures on the per capita consumption of cotton cloth, rubber footwear, and paper for 1949–58, and Table 9.13 contains information on the total and per capita consumption of food grains in urban and rural areas for 1953–57. Data on the per capita consumption of pork and vegetables are compiled in Table 9.14 for Peking for the years 1949–58.

Tables 9.15–9.17 present national data on the per capita consumption of major commodities by peasants and by workers and employees for 1952, 1955, and 1956. Provincial data are compiled in Tables 9.18–9.21.

[30]Hsü Ti-hsin has been Director of the Central Administration of Industry and Commerce of the State Council since it was established in November, 1954.

10

PUBLIC FINANCE, CREDIT, AND FOREIGN EXCHANGE RATES

PUBLIC FINANCE

THE BUDGETARY SYSTEM

The state budget (*kuo-chia yü-shuan*) of China comprises the revenues and expenditures of both the central government and all levels of local government. In 1957, for example, the state budget contained the revenues and expenditures of 89 departments in the central government and of 28 governments at the provincial level.[1] Like the state budget, a provincial budget consists of the revenues and expenditures of both the provincial government and all levels of local government within the province.[2]

The development of the Chinese budgetary system and its institutional aspects have been treated elsewhere and need not be discussed here.[3] The present section deals only with the following problems: (1) the structure and classification of budgetary revenues and expenditures and (2) the financial relationship between the central and local governments. A discussion of these problems will help to clarify the concept and coverage of Chinese budgetary data.

The Structure and Classification of Budgetary Revenues[4]

Chinese budgetary revenues have been classified according to two different bases: (1) by source of revenue and (2) by ownership of economic units, such as state enterprises, cooperative enterprises, state-private joint enterprises, private enterprises, agricultural producer cooperatives (communes), and individual peasants.[5] In official budget messages at both the central and provincial levels, however, revenue data have been given primarily by source, while the classification by ownership of economic units was sometimes used only as supplementary information.

According to Chinese usage, the sources of budgetary revenue are classified into four broad categories: (1) taxes, (2) receipts from state enterprises and undertakings, (3) state credit and insurance receipts, and (4) miscellaneous receipts.

TAX REVENUE

INDUSTRIAL AND COMMERCIAL TAXES

In China taxes levied on industrial and commercial activity are grouped under the heading of "industrial and commercial taxes." Prior to 1958, included in industrial and commercial taxes were the commodity tax, the business tax, the business income tax, the stamp tax, and the commodity circulation tax. Since then these taxes have been merged into a consolidated industrial and commercial tax. In addition, other industrial and commercial taxes adopted by the Peking regime include the cus-

---

[1]Including 22 provinces, three centrally-controlled municipalities, two autonomous regions, and the Tibet area.
[2]Ko Chih-ta, *Kuo-tu shih-chi ti chung-kuo yü-shuan (China's Budget during the Transition Period)*, Peking: Finance Press, 1957, pp. 36–38.
[3]See Ching-wen Kwang, "The Budgetary System of the People's Republic of China: A Preliminary Survey," *Public Finance*, Vol. XVIII, No. 304, 1963, pp. 253–86.
[4]A discussion of the Chinese budgetary revenue will be found in George N. Ecklund, *Financing the Government Budget of China*, Chicago: Aldine Publishing Company, 1966.
[5]Ko Chih-ta, *op. cit.*, pp. 50–57.

toms duties, the salt tax, the interest income tax, the slaughter tax, the urban real estate tax, the special consumption tax, and miscellaneous license taxes and fees.

The Commodity Tax

The commodity tax *(huo-wu-shui)* was first adopted in January, 1950, when the then Government Administrative Council promulgated the "Provisional Regulations on the Commodity Tax."[6] According to these regulations, taxes on 358 specified commodities were paid by manufacturers or buyers at rates ranging from 3 to 120 percent of the wholesale price or the official announced price *(pai-chia)* of these commodities.[7] For commodities manufactured or processed domestically, taxes were collected in one of the following three ways: (1) they were collected at the factory by the tax collector stationed there; (2) in the case of small factories where no tax collectors were stationed, taxes were paid on the basis of the output determined by officials; or (3) when taxes were not paid according to either of these two methods, they could be collected at the time commodities were delivered to buyers.[8] For commodities imported from abroad, taxes were collected together with the customs duties at the customs houses.[9]

In January, 1953, rates of the commodity tax were revised, and the number of commodities subject to the commodity tax was reduced to 173.[10]

The Business Tax and the
Business Income Tax

In January, 1950, "Provisional Regulations on Taxes on Industry and Commerce" were promulgated, stipulating that all industrial and commercial enterprises operating for profit, with specified exceptions, were subject to two kinds of taxation: the business tax *(ying-yeh-shui)* and the income tax *(shuo-te-shui)*.[11] The former was a tax based on the volume of business *(ying-yeh-o)*, i.e., gross business receipts, while the latter was based on net business income.[12] State enterprises were exempt from the income tax but were required to pay the business tax.[13] Exempt from both taxes were state-monopolized enterprises, poor handicraftsmen, subsidiary occupations, and all other businesses approved by the Ministry of Finance.[14]

The rates of the business tax varied from 1 to

3 percent for industry, from 1.5 to 3 percent for trade, from 1.5 to 2 percent for public utilities and transportation, and from 2 to 15 percent for service trade.[15] The rates of the income tax were progressive, with a minimum rate of 5 percent for an income level of less than 300 yuan and a maximum rate of 30 percent at 10,000 yuan.[16]

For the purpose of encouraging private investment in certain activities considered important to economic development, a series of tax reductions, stated as percentages of the income tax payable, varying from 10 to 40 percent, were provided.[17] These reductions were abolished in April, 1957, on the ground that virtually all the private enterprises had been socialized.[18]

The Stamp Tax

"Provisional Regulations on the Stamp Tax," which were promulgated by the then Government Administrative Council in December, 1950, stipulated that all documents used in commercial transactions and in the transfer of property were subject to a stamp tax.[19] Exempt from the tax, however, were land deeds issued after the agrarian land reform and various transportation tickets.[20] Documents representing a transaction value of less than 1.5 yuan were also tax exempt, except for various amusement tickets.[21] The stamp tax was imposed on a document either as a specific amount ranging from 0.02 to 0.5 yuan or as a percentage of the

[6]Government Administrative Council "Provisional Regulations on the Commodity Tax (Approved on January 27, 1950, at the Seventeenth Meeting of the Government Administrative Council, and Promulgated on January 30, 1950)," in *A Collection of Laws and Regulations Concerning the Tax Affairs of the Central Government*, Peking: Central Bureau of Tax Affairs of the Ministry of Finance of the Central People's Government, October, 1952, pp. 23–31.

[7]*Ibid.* (Articles 2 and 5).

[8]*Ibid.* (Article 8).

[9]*Ibid.* (Article 9).

[10]Ko Chih-ta, *op. cit.*, pp. 65–66.

[11]Government Administrative Council, "Provisional Regulations on Taxes on Industry and Commerce (Approved on January 27, 1950, at the Seventeenth Meeting of the Government Administrative Council and Promulgated on January 30, 1950)," in *Collection of Laws and Regulations Concerning the Tax Affairs of the Central Government, op. cit.*, pp. 115–31. See particularly Articles 1 and 3.

[12]*Ibid.* (Article 5).

[13]*Ibid.* (Article 6).

[14]*Ibid.* (Article 8).

[15]*Ibid.* (Appendix A to Article 9).

[16]*Ibid.* (Appendix B to Article 9).

[17]*Ibid.* (Appendix C to Article 9).

[18]Ko Chih-ta, *op. cit.*, p. 67.

[19]Government Administrative Council, "Provisional Regulations on the Stamp Tax (Approved at the 63rd Meeting of the Government Administrative Council on December 15, 1950, and Promulgated on December 19, 1950), in *Collection of Laws and Regulations Concerning the Tax Affairs of the Central Government, op. cit.*, pp. 239–47. See particularly Articles 1 and 2.

[20]*Ibid.* (Article 4).

[21]*Ibid.* (Article 6).

value of the transaction shown in the document ranging from 0.01 to 0.3 percent.[22]

The Commodity Circulation Tax

A commodity circulation tax (*shang-p'in liu-t'ung-shui*), introduced in January, 1953, was imposed on 22 commodities totally or largely controlled by state enterprises, including pig iron, cotton yarn, cigarettes, cured tobacco leaves, liquor, matches, and flour.[23] The tax replaced all other taxes previously imposed on these commodities, such as the commodity tax, the business tax, business surtaxes, the stamp tax, and the unified sale tax on cotton yarn. As a consequence, only one sales tax was levied on these commodities from production to consumption,[24] while the income tax was still payable by nonstate enterprises.[25]

The Consolidated Industrial and Commercial Tax

Extensive changes in the Chinese tax structure were made in September, 1958, when a consolidated industrial and commercial tax (*kung-shang t'ung-i-shui*) was initiated to replace the commodity tax, the business tax, the stamp tax, and the commodity circulation tax, all of which were abolished at the same time.[26] The new tax has since then become the most important source of tax revenue in China.

All enterprises and individuals engaged in industrial production, agricultural procurement, import, retail trade, transportation, and service trade are required to pay the consolidated industrial and commercial tax.[27] The amount of tax levied on industrial products is based on the sales proceeds calculated according to actual selling price, and intermediate products produced for inclusion in finished products are not taxed.[28] Agricultural procurement and import trade enterprises are required to pay the consolidated tax according to the value of the commodities purchased. The tax paid by retailers and by enterprises and by persons engaged in transporation and service trade is based on sales proceeds.[29] Business receipts of state banks and insurance agencies, agricultural machine tractor stations, and hospitals and other health organizations and income received by scientific research institutions for experimental work are all tax-exempt.[30]

Rates for the consolidated industrial and commercial tax vary from 69 percent for Class A cigarettes to 1.5 percent for unbleached

cotton cloth. In addition to retail trade and various types of transportation and service trade, some 264 commodities are subject to the consolidated tax. Table 1 presents tax rates for selected commodity categories, retail trade, transportation, and service trade.

Customs Duties

In May, 1951, "Regulations on the Customs Duties" were promulgated. The regulations stipulate that all imports are subject to import duties at a lower rate for countries having signed a reciprocal trade treaty or agreement with China and at a general rate for other countries.[31] The import duties are imposed on C.I.F. value. In cases where an adequate C.I.F. value is not available, the dutiable value of a commodity is determined according to an adjusted domestic wholesale price by the following formula:

$$\text{Dutiable value} = \frac{\text{domestic wholesale price} \times 100}{100 + \text{lower rate of import duties} + 20}$$

If the domestic wholesale price is not known, the dutiable value is to be estimated by customs authorities.[32]

Tax rates and commodity nomenclature have been revised from time to time since the regulations were promulgated. As of September 30, 1961, import duties were applicable to 939 commodity items classified under 17 main categories and 89 subcategories. Rates of the

[22]*Ibid.* (Article 5).

[23]Economic and Financial Commission of Government Administrative Council, "A Notice Concerning Certain Revisions of the Tax System (Dated December 31, 1952)." *1953 JMST*, pp. 290–91.

[24]Ko Chih-ta, *op. cit.*, p. 65.

[25]Beginning in 1958, joint enterprises under the so-called "fixed-interest system" were no longer required to pay an income tax but had to remit part of their profits to the state. See Ministry of Finance, "A Notice Concerning the Abolition of the Income Tax on the Joint Enterprises under the Fixed-Interest System," *Jen-min shui-wu (People's Tax Affairs)*, No. 14 (July 19, 1958).

[26]"Regulations on the Consolidated Industrial and Commercial Tax (Draft), Approved at the 101st Meeting of the Standing Committee of the National People's Congress on September 11, 1958, and Promulgated by the State Council on September 13, 1958," *Jen-min sui-wu (People's Tax Affairs)*, No. 18 (September 19, 1958), pp. 3–7.

[27]*Ibid.* (Article 2).

[28]*Ibid.* (Article 4); "Detailed Explanations Regarding the Enforcement of the Regulations on the Consolidated Industrial and Commercial Tax (Draft), Issued by the Ministry of Finance on September 13, 1958," *Jen-min shui-wu (People's Tax Affairs)*, No. 18 (September 19, 1958), pp. 8–10; see particularly Articles 5 and 6.

[29]"Regulations on the Consolidated Industrial and Commercial Tax (draft) . . . ," *op. cit.* (Articles 5–8).

[30]*Ibid.* (Article 10).

[31]"Provisional Regulations for Enforcing the Law of Customs Duties of the People's Republic of China, Approved at the 83rd Meeting of the Government Administrative Council on May 14, 1951," in Bureau of Customs of the Ministry of Foreign Trade, ed., *Regulations on the Customs Duties of the People's Republic of China*, Peking: Law Publishing House, 1961, pp. 114–18.

[32]*Ibid.* (Articles 5 and 6).

TABLE 1. *Rates of the Consolidated Industrial and Commercial Tax for Selected Commodity Categories, Retail Trade, Transportation, and Service Trade*

Item	Tax rate (percent)
I. Industrial and agricultural products:	
1. Tobacco	40–69
2. Wine and alcohol	20–60
3. Sugar	27–44
4. Tea	40
5. Food grains	4
6. Edible vegetable oil	12.5
7. Aquatic products	5–35
8. Fruit juice and soda drink	25
9. Milk	2.5–10
10. Canned food	10
11. Textile products	1.5–35
12. Leather, hair, and feathers	10–40
13. Paper and pulp	3–20
14. Pens and pencils	6–22
15. Matches	23
16. Thermos bottles	14–19
17. Glass and porcelain products	11–15
18. Bicycles and parts	13
19. Watches, cameras, and films	25–35
20. Radios, televisions, recorders, and records	13–15
21. Cosmetics	6–51
22. Electrical products	11–25
23. Paints, dyes, rubber, and rubber products	10–18
24. Chemical acids and alkalies	6–12
25. Building materials	5–20
26. Coal and petroleum products	2–20
27. Metal ores and metallurgical products	5–15
28. Water and electric power	2–5
29. Nonmetal and mining products	7
30. Machinery and equipment	4.5–5
31. Books and magazines	2.5
32. Firecrackers and other religious products	35–55
II. Retail trade	3
III. Transportation and post and tele-communications	2.5
IV. Service trade	3–7

Source: "A List of Tax Items and Tax Rates for the Consolidated Industrial and Commercial Tax," *Jen-min shui-wu (Peoples' Tax Affairs)*, No. 18 (September 19, 1958), pp. 4–7.

import duties for the 17 main categories are shown in Table 2.

The export duties are based on F.O.B. value according to the following formula:

$$\text{Dutiable value} = \frac{\text{F.O.B. price} \times 100}{100 + \text{rate of export duties}}$$

In cases where the F.O.B. value of a commodity

TABLE 2. *Rates of the Import Duties for 17 Main Commodity Groups in China, September 30, 1961*

Commodity group	Rate of import duties (percent)	
	General rate	Lower rate
1. Food grains, fruits, vegetables, meat, eggs, milk, vegetable oils, and other food products	20–250	17.5–150
2. Sugar, tea, tobacco, wine, and drink	30–200	40–400
3. Aquatic products	7.5–250	5–150
4. Medical herbs, seeds and nuts, tanning materials, resins, rubber, and other plant products	0–180	0–120
5. Timber, bamboo, palm, rattan, straw, and manufacturing thereof	7.5–150	5–100
6. Animals and animal products	0–200	0–150
7. Skins, leather, and their products	17.5–180	15–120
8. Mining products, glass, and ceramic products	0–200	0–150
9. Oil, fats, wax, and their products	10–250	7.5–150
10. Chemical products, drugs, fertilizer, plastics, dyes, paints, cosmetics, and explosives	0–180	0–120
11. Textile materials and products	0–400	0–200
12. Pulp, paper, paper products, and prints	0–250	0–150
13. Metals and metal products	0–200	0–150
14. Machinery, equipment, tools, and electrical materials	10–250	7.5–150
15. Scientific and precision measures, watches and clocks, and musical instruments	0–150	0–100
16. Transportation equipment	0–120	0–80
17. Miscellaneous products	0–250	0–150

Source: Bureau of Customs, Ministry of Foreign Trade, ed., *Regulations on the Customs Duties of the People's Republic of China*, Peking: Law Publishing House, 1961, pp. 3–11.

is not available, its dutiable value is determined by customs authorities.[33]

When the regulations on the customs duties were published in 1951, export duties were levied on six commodities: peanut oil taxed at 10 percent, peanuts (both with and without shells) at 15 percent, hog bristles at 30 percent, tung oil at 10 percent; and peppermint oil and menthol, both at 55 percent. But the export duties on tung oil and hog bristles were abolished on November 10, 1952, and September 1, 1953, respectively. In addition, the rate of export duties on peppermint oil and menthol were both reduced to 20 percent beginning from January 12, 1953.[34]

The Interest-Income Tax

"Provisional Regulations on the Interest-Income Tax" were promulgated in December, 1950. According to these regulations, a tax was levied on income from interest received on bank deposits, government bonds, corporate bonds, and other securities and loans to employers.[35] Exempt from the tax were the interest received by educational, cultural, welfare, and relief organizations, by individuals for their investment in enterprises, and by workers and peasants for credit among themselves, as well as interest receipts amounting to less than 5 yuan.[36] A flat rate of 5 percent was applied to the taxable income from interest.[37]

The regulations were later modified to exempt the interest on government bonds from taxation.[38] In January, 1959, the interest-income tax was abolished.[39]

[33]*Ibid.* (Article 8).

[34]*Ibid.*, pp. 7, 17, 29, 42, 43.

[35]"Provisional Regulations on the Interest-Income Tax, Approved at the 63rd Meeting of the Government Administrative Council on December 15, 1950 and Promulgated on December 29, 1950," in *Collection of Laws and Regulations Concerning the Tax Affairs of the Central Government, op. cit.*, pp. 233–35 (Article 1).

[36]*Ibid.* (Article 4).

[37]*Ibid.* (Article 2).

[38]Ministry of Finance, "Notice Concerning the Exemption of the Income Tax on Interest from the First People's Victory Bonds, January 27, 1951," *ibid.*, p. 235.

[39]"State Council's Approval on the Abolition of the Income Tax on Interest from Bank Deposits Beginning in 1959 (January 6, 1959)"

The Slaughter Tax

The "Provisional Regulations on the Slaughter Tax," promulgated in December, 1950, requires that a tax be imposed on the slaughtering of livestock, including hogs, lambs, and cattle.[40] Slaughtering for home consumption, however, is not subject to taxation.[41] The tax is proportional to the actual weight of the animal valued at state retail prices. The rate was 10 percent until March, 1957, when it was reduced to 8 percent.[42]

The Urban Real Estate Tax

The urban real estate tax is a municipal tax on land and houses. According to the "Provisional Regulations on the Urban Real Estate Tax" promulgated in August, 1951, the tax is payable by property owners or by property renters or users.[43] Municipal governments had to secure permission from the Ministry of Finance for levying the urban real estate tax until January, 1952, when the authority was transferred to the Commission on Military and Political Affairs in various administrative retions.[44] Properties owned and used by government agencies, the armed forces, public organizations, schools, parks, Muslim and Lama temples, and certain Christian churches are not subject to the real estate tax.[45]

The annual tax rates are 1 percent for houses and 1.5 percent for land according to their "standard value." The standard value of houses in an area is determined by their general price level and construction costs currently prevailing in the area, and that of land is based on location, transportation, economic conditions and the general price level of land in the area, and other relevant factors.[46]

The Special Consumption Behavior Tax

The special consumption behavior tax (t'e-chung hsiao-fei hsin-wei-shiu), introduced in January, 1951, is a local tax on "special kinds of consumption," such as theatres, circuses, musical and other amusements, restaurants, coffee shops and hotels. The tax is borne by consumers but paid by business agents. The tax base is gross receipts, and the rates are 10 to 30 percent for theatres, circuses and other amusements, 50 percent for dancing halls, 10 to 20 percent for restaurants and coffee shops, and 5 to 20 percent for hotels.[47]

Miscellaneous License Taxes and Fees

There are a number of license taxes and fees collected by local governments for their needs. The most important one is probably the license tax on vehicles and vessels.[48] Others include survey and construction license fees and various types of registration and inspection fees.

AGRICULTURAL TAXES

The Agricultural Tax System, 1950–57

The Chinese have had a relatively long experience in collecting agricultural taxes as compared with industrial and commercial taxes. During the eight years of the Sino-Japanese war, the agricultural tax—known as kung-liang, or public grains—yielded around 80 percent of the total revenue in the area of the Communist-controlled Border Region Government.[49]

After the Communists took over the mainland, "Provisional Regulations on the Agricultural Tax in Newly Liberated Areas" were promulgated, requiring all peasants to pay a tax on their output. The tax was levied not on the actual farm yield but on the "normal annual yield (ch'ang-nien ch'an-liang)," jointly determined, according to legal provisions, by the

in Ministry of Finance, ed., Collection of Financial Laws and Regulations of the Central Government, January–June, 1959, Peking: Finance Publishing House, October, 1959, p. 115.

[40]"Provisional Regulations on the Slaughter Tax, Approved at the 63rd Meeting of the Government Administrative Council on December 15, 1950, and Promulgated on December 19, 1950," in Collection of Laws and Regulations Concerning the Tax Affairs of the Central Government, op. cit., pp. 263–65, Article 1.

[41]Ibid. (Article 2).

[42]Ibid. (Article 4); and Ministry of Finance, "Notice on the Adjustment of the Rate of the Slaughter Tax and Other Problems, January 15, 1957," in Ministry of Finance, ed., Collection of Financial Laws and Regulations of the Central Government, January–June, 1957, Peking: Finance Publishing House, December, 1957, p. 93.

[43]"Provisional Regulations on the Urban Real Estate Tax, Promulgated by the Government Administrative Council on August 8, 1951," in Collection of the Laws and Regulations Concerning the Tax Affairs of the Central Government, op. cit., pp. 271–74; Article 3.

[44]Ministry of Finance, "Directive on Authorizing the Departments of Finance of Various Administrative Regions to Determine Cities Levying the Urban Real Estate Tax Beginning in 1952, Issued on January 31, 1952," in ibid., p. 275.

[45]"Provisional Regulations on the Urban Real Estate Tax," in ibid., (Article 4); and Ministry of Finance, "A Notice Concerning Supplementary Regulations on the Exemption of Church Properties from the Urban Real Estate Tax, Issued on February 16, 1952," in ibid., p. 278.

[46]"Provisional Regulations on the Urban Real Estate Tax," in ibid., Articles 6 and 7.

[47]"Provisional Regulations on Special Consumption Behavior Tax, Promulgated by the Government Administrative Council on January 16, 1951," in ibid., pp. 281–83.

[48]"Provisional Regulations on the Operation of Vehicles and Vessels, Approved and Promulgated by the Government Administrative Council on September 13, 1951," in ibid., pp. 291–95.

[49]Li Ch'eng-jui, "The Agricultural Tax System and the Peasants' Burdens in Several People's Revolutionary Bases during the Anti-Japanese War," CCYC, No. 2 (April 17, 1956), pp. 100–15.

tax collector, the local villagers' representative body, and the owner of the land. The normal annual yield was estimated according to the natural conditions of cultivation — with reference to the quality of the soil, weather, irrigation, manpower, animal power, number of harvests, and so forth — for a normal season of the land in question in a particular locality.[50] It was provided in the regulations that no extra tax would be imposed on income in excess of the normal annual yield, obtained through more intensive cultivation or other improvements.[51] Tax reductions would be allowed for a loss of yield due to natural calamities but not due to the tiller's negligence or laxity.[52]

Prior to the 1958 tax reform, either progressive or proportional tax rates were applied to the normal annual yield. These rates varied from province to province and may be summarized as follows: (1) progressive rates from 7 percent for a per capita income of 165–220 pounds of grain to 30 percent for a per capita income of 2,145 pounds or more of grain in 13 provinces in East China (except Shantung province), Central South China, and Southwest China; (2) progressive rates from 5 percent for a per capita income of 165–209 pounds of grain to 30 percent for a per capita income of 1,859 pounds or more of grain in the newly liberated areas of Shensi, Kansu, and Chinghai provinces;[53] (3) a proportional rate of 23 percent of the normal annual yield for Kirin and Heilungkiang provinces, 21 percent for Liaoning Province, 22 percent for Hopei and Shansi provinces, and 18–20 percent for the former Shensi-Kansu-Ninghsia border region; and (4) a proportional rate of an unknown magnitude for Shantung Province and Inner Mongolia Autonomous Region.[54]

The agricultural tax was paid in the form of public grain calculated in terms of the principal crop of the region, such as rice in areas south of the Yangtze River, millet in North China, kaoliang in Northeast China, and wheat in Northwest China.[55] Sometimes the tax was payable in cash or other agricultural crops. In practice, however, the bulk of the agricultural tax was collected in the form of food grains and cotton.[56]

The Agricultural Tax System since 1958

The agricultural tax structure was revised in June, 1958, when the "Regulations on the

Agricultural Tax" was approved by the Standing Committee of the National People's Congress.[57] The regulations have since remained in effect.

It is stipulated in the new regulations that the agricultural tax is levied on the output of the following crops: (1) food grains and potatoes, (2) cotton, hemp, and jute, tobacco leaves, oil-bearing crops, sugar crops, and other technical crops, and (3) garden crops; and that the tax is payable by organizations and individuals engaged in agricultural production, including agricultural producer cooperatives (communes), members of the cooperatives (communes) with private plots of land, individual peasants, state farms, and state-private joint farms, and certain public organizations with agricultural income, such as enterprises, government agencies, the armed forces, schools, temples, and churches.[58] Output of the crops grown by agricultural scientific research institutions and agricultural schools and planted in a scattered way in residential areas is tax-exempt.[59] Agricultural producer cooperatives were designated as taxpaying units[60] until the latter part of 1958, when these cooperatives were merged into the communes, which became the taxpayers. The taxpaying units were then changed to the production brigades of the communes in 1959 and to the production teams in 1961.

The normal annual yield remains as the tax base. Once the normal annual yield for a locality has been determined, it will not be changed for

[50]Government Administrative Council, "Provisional Regulations on the Agricultural Tax in Newly Liberated Areas, Approved at the 9th meeting of the Committee of the Central People's Government on September 5, 1950," in Commission on Financial and Economic Affairs of the Government Administrative Council, ed., *Collection of Fiscal and Economic Policy Statements, Laws, and Regulations of the Central Government*, Vol. II, Peking, June, 1951, pp. 301–11. See particularly Articles 6 and 17.
[51]*Ibid.* (Articles 7 and 8).
[52]*Ibid.* (Articles 4, 7, and 24).
[53]Referring to the areas taken over by the communists after 1949.
[54]Li Hsien-nien, "Report on the 1955 Final Accounts and the 1956 State Budget," *HHPYK*, No. 14 (July 21, 1956), pp. 1–9; and Government Administrative Council, "Directive on the Agricultural Tax Work in 1951," *JMJP*, June 23, 1951. See also Chao Kuo-chün, *Agrarian Policies of Mainland China: A Documentary Study (1949–1956)*, Cambridge, Mass.: Harvard University Press, 1957, p. 152.
[55]Ministry of Finance, "Regulations on the Standards of Determining Land Area and Normal Annual Yield for Agricultural Taxation," *Collection of Policy Statements . . . , op. cit.*, pp. 314–15.
[56]In 1955, for example, approximately 85 percent of the agricultural tax was paid in food grains and 8 percent in cotton. See Chao Kuo-chün, *op. cit.*, p. 154.
[57]"Regulations on the Agricultural Tax of the People's Republic of China, Approved at the 96th Meeting of the Standing Committee of the National People's Congress on June 3, 1958," *HHPYK*, No. 12 (June 25, 1958), pp. 82–83.
[58]*Ibid.* (Articles 3 and 4).
[59]*Ibid.* (Article 17).
[60]*Ibid.* (Articles 6–9).

five years. A proportional tax rate is adopted.[61] The average rate for the country as a whole is set at 15.5 percent of the normal annual yield.[62]

The Pastoral Tax and Agricultural Surtaxes

The pastoral tax was levied on the livestock holdings of each household, primarily in north and northwest China. Progressive tax rates were adopted until 1959, when most of the pastoral households had joined the communes. Since then a proportional rate has been applied to the livestock hold by the communes.

In 1950, local governments were authorized to levy surtaxes at rates not exceeding 15 percent of the regular agricultural tax. These taxes were entirely at the disposal of local governments and hence were not included in the state budgetary revenue. Agricultural surtaxes were abolished in 1952[63] but were restored in 1956 with a ceiling of 22 percent of the regular tax.

RECEIPTS FROM STATE ENTERPRISES AND UNDERTAKINGS

Receipts from state enterprises and undertakings consist of (1) profits of state enterprises, (2) depreciation reserves for amortization of fixed assets of state enterprises, (3) income from selling fixed assets and return of surplus working capital of state enterprises, and (4) receipts from certain undertakings.[64]

PROFITS OF STATE ENTERPRISES

Profits of state enterprises have become increasingly important as a source of state budgetary revenue. In China, profits refer to "the revenue from sales proceeds obtained at official prices net of the cost of production and tax payments."[65] According to an official decree issued in April, 1951, all planned profits of a state enterprise should be delivered to the state treasury, while 30 percent of the profits in excess of the plan were allowed to be retained by the enterprise as a premium fund. This regulation was revised in January, 1952, permitting all enterprises to retain part of their profits as a premium fund, rather than limiting the fund to those overfulfilling their profit targets. In 1957, it was further provided that 40 to 60 percent of the profits in excess of the plan were to be given to government units in charge of industrial enterprises to be used as reserve funds for production and basic construction.[66] In 1958,

both the premium fund and the departmental fund were merged into a single enterprise fund, and enterprises were to share in their profits according to a ration defined by the central authority.

According to Chinese practice, monthly quotas of planned profits were set up for each industrial enterprise. Sixty to 80 percent of the monthly quota was remitted to the state treasury not later than the 25th of the given month, either by the enterprise concerned or through the government agency administering the enterprise, with the remainder to be submitted by the 8th of the following month. Reportedly, about 5 percent of the actual annual profits were usually forwarded to the state treasury only in the following year. For state trade enterprises, profits were collected on the basis of their actual amount; that is, the actual profits for the given month were delivered to the treasury on the 15th of the following month.[67]

DEPRECIATION RESERVES OF STATE ENTERPRISES

There are two types of depreciation reserve in China: (1) the "basic depreciation funds (*chi-pen tse-chiu chi-chin*)" used for amortization purposes and (2) the "major repair funds (*ta-hsiu-li chi-chin*)" used for overhaul of machinery and equipment. The latter are handled by the enterprise itself in a special bank account, while only the former go to the state treasury.[68]

Amortization schedules for industry were issued in December, 1950, by the Ministry of Finance.[69] These schedules were based on a straight-line method.[70] Monthly amortization funds are remitted to the state treasury either directly by the enterprise concerned or through

[61]*Ibid.* (Article 2). Tibet was an exception. In 1959, a progressive tax on the actual farm yield was imposed in Tibet.
[62]"Regulations on the Agricultural Tax . . . ," *op. cit.*, Article 10.
[63]Government Administrative Council, "Directive on the Agricultural Tax Work in 1951," *op. cit.*
[64]Ko Chih-ta, *op. cit.*, pp. 73–83.
[65]*Ibid.*, p. 74.
[66]Ministry of Finance, "Several Problems Concerning the Regulations on the Sharing and Utilization of the Profits in Excess of the Plan—An Answer to the Bureau of Finance of Kansu Province, January 7, 1957," in *Collection of Financial Laws and Regulations of the Central Government, January–June, 1957, op. cit.*, pp. 51–52.
[67]Ko Chih-ta, *op. cit.*, pp. 79–81.
[68]*Ibid.*, pp. 81–82.
[69]*Collection of Fiscal and Economic Policy Statements. . . , op. cit.*, pp. 379–83.
[70]Ch'ang Sun and Wang En-yung, "A Brief Discussion on the Fixed Assets of Industrial Enterprises and Their Depreciation," *CCYC*, No. 5 (October 17, 1956), pp. 69–78.

the government department administering the enterprise on the 15th of the following month.

INCOME FROM THE SALE OF FIXED ASSETS AND RETURN OF SURPLUS WORKING CAPITAL

Income from the sale of fixed assets refers to the monetary revenue of state enterprises obtained from disposing fully depreciated fixed assets and other fixed assets which have been approved by the state for sale.[71] Such income is remitted to the treasury together with the basic depreciation fund.

As may be recalled, prior to 1959 working capital was granted to state enterprises by the state through the state budget. Surplus working capital was returned by each enterprise to its superior department, which, in turn, distributed the surplus to meet the deficits in working capital of other enterprises within its jurisdiction. Only after this distribution had taken place was any net surplus returned to the state treasury.[72]

RECEIPTS FROM CERTAIN UNDERTAKINGS

Receipts from undertakings refer to those obtained through business activities of governmental departments. Included are the income received for rendering cultural, educational, broadcasting, news, survey, and design services and sales proceeds from experimental products of reserach institutions. All the receipts from these undertakings are submitted to the treasury and cannot be shared by the departments concerned.[73]

STATE CREDIT AND INSURANCE RECEIPTS

State credit and insurance receipts are obtained through three major forms: (1) government bonds, (2) foreign loans, and (3) insurance operations.

GOVERNMENT BONDS

Government bonds first appeared in China when the Production Development Bond for the Northeast was issued in 1949 and again in 1950.[74] Although these two issues were local in nature, they were serviced by the state budget. The first national bond issued was the 1950

People's Victory Bond, which was scheduled to mature in five years, carrying an annual rate of interest of 5 percent.[75] From 1954 through 1957, National Economic Construction Bonds were issued each year carrying an eight-year maturity for the 1954 series and a ten-year maturity for other series. The state was to pay interest on these bonds all at a rate of 4 percent annually.[76]

National bonds were discontinued in 1958 when provincial governments were permitted to issue "local economic construction bonds." These bonds were to mature within five years and could not bear an annual rate of interest of more than 2 percent.[77]

FOREIGN LOANS

According to the Sino-Soviet Amity Alliance and Mutual Assistance Treaty signed on February 14, 1950, the Soviet Union was to grant a loan of 300 million U.S. dollars to Communist China at an annual interest rate of 1 percent. This loan was to be used over a five-year period beginning in January, 1950. The credit was extended in the form of machinery and equipment.[78]

In October, 1954, an agreement was reached for another Soviet loan to China, amounting to 520 million (pre-1960) rubles. The second loan was again used primarily for the purchase of capital goods from the Soviet Union.[79]

These two loans, used for the purpose of economic construction, were widely reported in the Chinese literature. Chinese budgetary data suggest that apparently some foreign credits other than these two Soviet loans had been made available to China during the period 1950–57.[80] These other credits were presumably also extended by the Soviet Union, but the terms and the purpose of these credits are not known.[81]

[71]Ko Chih-ta, *op. cit.*, pp. 82–83.
[72]*Ibid.*, p. 83.
[73]*Ibid.*
[74]*1951 JMST*, p. 15.
[75]*1955 JMST*, pp. 435–37.
[76]Ko Chih-ta, *op. cit.*
[77]"Regulations on Local Economic Construction Bonds (Approved at the 97th Meeting of the Standing Committee of the National People's Congress on June 5, 1958)," *HHPYK*, No. 12 (June 25, 1958), p.91.
[78]Ko Chih-ta, *op. cit.*, pp. 87–88.
[79]*Ibid.*
[80]See the statistical tables on state revenue.
[81]According to Premier Chou En-lai, the total Soviet loans and interest charged amounted to 1,406 million (post-1960)rubles and were paid back by the end of 1964. See "Government Work Report of Premier Chou-En-lai to the First Session of the Third National People's Congress," *Hung-ch'i*, No. 1 (January 6, 1965), pp. 4–19.

INSURANCE FUNDS

In February, 1951, the then Government Administrative Council issued a directive to enforce compulsory insurance of the properties of government agencies, state enterprises, and cooperatives as well as the passengers of trains, steamships, and airplanes.[82] The People's Insurance Corporation of China was organized to administer insurance activities. Insurance premiums paid by government agencies, state enterprises, and cooperatives were included either in the budgetary expenditures or in the cost of production, and passengers' insurance fees were paid by railway, steamship, and air transport enterprises.[83] In April, 1951, a series of detailed regulations were issued by the Commission on Financial and Economic Affairs of the Government Administrative Council on compulsory insurance of properties, vessels, railway cars, and passengers.[84] At the same time, efforts were made to expand insurance activities to rural areas on a voluntary basis, such as insurance on crop harvests and livestock.[85]

All insurance premiums formed a national insurance fund (*kuo-chia pao-hsien chi-chin*), the functions of which were to idemnify loss, to finance projects preventing accidents or loss, and to contribute to loanable funds of state banks.[86] It is not clear how income from insurance operations was estimated and which portion of the income was included in the state budgetary revenue.

MISCELLANEOUS RECEIPTS

Receipts which do not fall within any one of the above three main categories are classified under "Miscellaneous Receipts" in Chinese budgetary accounts. These receipts are of minor importance and include supplementary income from various public projects, fines, and administrative and service fees.

The Structure and Classification of Budgetary Expenditures

There are several classifications of Chinese budgetary expenditures. One of these is the division between productive and nonproductive expenditures. The former comprise basic construction appropriations, appropriations for cultural, educational, and health enterprises, such as plants manufacturing scientific instruments, medicines, and medical apparatus, and general reserve (*tsung yü-pei-fei*), for subsidizing damage due to accidents and natural calamities. Included in nonproductive expenditures are those for social services, culture, education, government administration, and national defense.[87]

Budgetary expenditures are also classified into five groups according to their use: (1) basic construction, (2) working capital, (3) personnel expenditures, such as wage and fringe payments, (4) office expenditures (*kung-yung chin-fei*), such as those for business trips, books and magazines, and telephones and telegrams, and (5) business expenditures (*yeh-wu-fei*), referring to certain specific expenditures, such as those for purchasing library materials and laboratory instruments by schools and for entertaining foreign visitors by the Ministry of Foreign Affairs. The first two categories belong to productive expenditures, and the rest are considered nonproductive.[88]

A third classification is made according to organizational units, such as ministries and bureaus in the central government and departments at the local level.

Statistical data on budgetary expenditures according to the above three classifications are generally not published. Data on budgetary expenditures given in the budget messages of the central and the local governments are usually classified into several main functional groups, with subfunctions shown for some of the main groups. These main functions and subfunctions are summarized as follows.

[82]Government Administrative Council, "A Decision on Enforcing Compulsory Insurance on the Properties of Government Agencies, State Enterprises and Cooperatives and on Passengers, issued on February 3, 1951," in Commission on Financial and Economic Affairs of the Government Administrative Council, ed., *Collection of Financial and Economic Policy Statements, Laws, and Regulations of the Central Government*, Vol. III, Peking, March, 1952, pp. 285–86.
[83]*Ibid.*
[84]"Regulations on Compulsory Insurance of Properties," "Regulations on Compulsory Insurance of Vessels," "Regulations on Compulsory Insurance of Railway Cars," "Regulations on Compulsory Insurance of Steamship Passengers against Casualties," "Regulations on Compulsory Insurance of Railway Passengers against Casualties," and "Regulations on Compulsory Insurance of Airplane Passengers against Casualties," all issued by the Commission on Financial and Economic Affairs of the Government Administrative Council on April 24, 1951 (*ibid.*, pp. 290–318).
[85]The People's Insurance Corporation of China, "A Directive on Conducting a Large-Scale Experiment for Insurance on Cotton Harvests This Year, Issued on January 9, 1951," and "Directive on the Decision of Promoting Extensive Livestock Insurance This Year, Issued on January 23, 1951," *ibid.*, pp. 319–20.
[86]Ko Chih-ta, *op. cit.*
[87]*Ibid.*, pp. 93–95.
[88]*Ibid.*

ECONOMIC CONSTRUCTION

Expenditures on economic construction refer to those used for investment in basic construction and in working capital. The concepts of basic construction and working capital were explored in the section on capital formation, and need not be repeated here.

Economic construction expenditures are subclassified further according to branches of productive activities. Included are industry, agriculture, forestry, water conservation, meteorological services, transportation, post and tele-communications, trade, banking, and urban public utilities. Discussions on the meaning and the coverage of these branches may be found in the respective sections on industry, agriculture, transportation and communication, and trade.

SOCIAL SERVICES, CULTURE, AND EDUCATION

The second main category of Chinese budgetary expenditures is known as "social services, culture, and education," and is composed of the following 10 subcategories.[89]

Culture. Cultural expenditures include (1) investment in motion picture and publishing enterprises, printing plants, and bookstores, (2) outlays of theatrical groups, cultural stations, and libraries, and (3) expenses on art and on cultural exchange programs.

Higher Education. Expenditures on higher education refer to those on higher educational institutions, such as colleges and higher normal schools and the outlays for sending students abroad.

Education. Educational expenditures include the outlays of kindergartens, elementary and middle schools, and technical schools, as well as the outlays used for eliminating illiteracy and other educational purposes.

Labor Training. Labor training expenditures refer to the outlays on educational programs for cadres *(kan-pu)*.

Athletics. Expenditures on athletics include those used for carrying out athletic games, for building and administering stadiums, and for athletic training.

Science. Scientific expenditures include the outlays of the National Academy of Sciences and other scientific research institutions and the research expenses of various economic and educational departments.

Communication and Broadcasting. Expenditures on communications and broadcasting include investment in communication and broadcasting enterprises, such as radio and television stations, and administrative expenses of these enterprises.

Public Health. Public health expenditures include investment in hospitals and their administrative outlays.

Pensions. Pensions are for the families of soldiers and government employees who died or became disabled in the performance of official duties.

Social Relief and Welfare. Social relief and welfare expenditures are used for relieving the population from hardship due to natural calamities and for subsidizing returned overseas Chinese.

ADMINISTRATION

Administrative expenditures are used for maintaining government and party organizations. Wage and fringe payments constitute the bulk of these expenditures.

Five major categories of administrative expenditures are classified: (1) government management expenditures (used by the executive branches of the government), (2) political affairs expenditure (presumably for the Chinese Communist Party), (3) diplomatic activities expenditures, (4) expenditures for subsidizing political parties (other than the Chinese Communist Party) and people's organizations, and (5) public security, judiciary, and procuratorial expenditures.

NATIONAL DEFENSE

National defense expenditures are used for maintaining the armed forces and for financing defense construction. It may be noted that an increase in military stockpiles is considered as a part of accumulation and hence is excluded from defense expenditures.[90]

CREDIT PAYMENTS

This category includes the payment of foreign and domestic loans borrowed by the

[89]*Ibid.,* pp. 118–25.
[90]Hsü Ti-hsin, *An Analysis of the National Economy of China during*

Chinese government and their interest charges. Included in credit payments are also Chinese loans to foreign governments.[91]

GENERAL RESERVE

The general reserve is budgeted as a kind of contingency fund to defray unexpected expenditures, such as the damages of enterprises caused by accidents or natural calamities and increases in certain outlays resulting from plan errors.

MISCELLANEOUS EXPENDITURES

Expenditures not included in the above categories fall within this grouping. Included are the expenditure on veterans' administration and the subsidy to national minority areas.

Financial Relationship between the Central and the Local Governments

In March, 1950, the then Government Administrative Council issued "A Decision on Unifying the State Financial and Economic Work," in which it was stipulated that certain major revenues, such as public grains, taxes, the sale of warehouse goods, and part of the profits and depreciation reserves, were placed under the control of the central government.[92] In addition, certain criteria were established for government expenditures. The decree was the first important one on fiscal administration issued by the Peking regime. A year later, "A Decision on the Classification of the Fiscal Revenue and Expenditure System for 1951" was promulgated.[93] A system of centralized fiscal control was adopted, together with the so-called "three-level management," which referred to the fact that the state budget comprised the budgets of the central, the regional, and the provincial governments. While in theory the regional and the provincial governments were responsible for preparing their budgets, local revenues and expenditures were largely determined in advance by the central authority. Beginning in June, 1954, when the administrative regions were abolished, the fiscal administration was reduced to a two-level system, and the state budget was now composed of the revenues and expenditures of both the central and the provincial governments. The central government continued to control nearly all of the provincial revenues and expenditures until

January, 1958, when a reform was made for granting greater fiscal authority to local governments.[94]

THE DISTRIBUTION OF BUDGETARY REVENUE BETWEEN THE CENTRAL AND THE LOCAL GOVERNMENTS

The distribution of budgetary revenue between the central and the local governments was said to be based on three criteria: (1) to insure the fulfillment of the national economic plan by both the central and the local governments, (2) to provide both the central and local governments with regular stable revenues, and (3) to provide incentives for the local governments in carrying out the state revenue plan.[95]

According to these criteria, budgetary revenues may be grouped into three categories: (1) fixed revenues (ku-ting sho-ju) of the central government, (2) fixed revenues of the local governments, and (3) revenues to be distributed proportionally between the central and the local governments.[96]

Fixed revenues of the central government refer to the types of budgetary revenue belonging exclusively to the central government. Included are the custom duties, the salt tax, income of central state and joint enterprises, foreign loans, insurance receipts, sales proceeds from material reserves, administrative and judicial fees of the central government, and receipts from various undertakings of the central government.

Fixed revenues of the local governments are entirely disposed of at local levels. Prior to 1958, included in local fixed revenues were the stamp tax, the interest-income tax, the slaughter tax, the livestock trade tax, the urban real estate tax, the cultural and recreational tax, the license tax on vehicles and vessels, the tax on

the Transition Period, revised edition, Peking: Science Press, 1959, p. 261.
[91]But in the published budgetary accounts, "aid to foreign countries" was listed as a separate category for some years and was included in "miscellaneous" for others.
[92]Government Administrative Council, "A Decision on Unifying the State Financial and Economic Work, Approved at the 22nd Meeting of the Government Administrative Council on March 3, 1950," in Commission on Financial and Economic Affairs of the Government Administrative Council, ed., A Collection of Fiscal and Economic Policy Statements, Laws, and Regulations of the Central Government, Vol. I, Peking, August, 1950, pp. 26–31.
[93]Government Administrative Council, "A Decision on the Classification of the Fiscal Revenue and Expenditure System for 1951," promulgated on March 29, 1951," A Collection of Fiscal and Economic Policy Statements . . . ," op. cit., Vol. III, pp. 121–24.
[94]"The State Council's Decision on Improving the System of Fiscal Administration," 1958 JMST, p. 568.
[95]Ko Chih-ta, op. cit., pp. 43–44.
[96]Ibid.

land deeds, the pastoral tax, income of local state enterprises, income from public properties, administrative and judicial fees of the local governments, and receipts from various undertakings of the local governments.[97] In 1958, the stamp tax was merged into the consolidated industrial and commercial tax, and the tax revenue has been shared by the central government. As may be recalled, the interest-income tax was abolished in 1959.

Revenues distributed proportionally between the central and the local governments included the agricultural tax, the business income tax, the consolidated industrial and commercial tax (or the commodity tax, the commodity circulation tax, and the business tax for the years prior to 1958), and income from the sale of government bonds.[98] As pointed out above, the central government has ceased to issue government bonds since 1959, when local governments were allowed to issue short-term bonds according to their needs. As a consequence, income from the sale of government bonds is now a revenue belonging entirely to the local governments.

THE DISTRIBUTION OF BUDGETARY EXPENDITURES BETWEEN THE CENTRAL AND THE LOCAL GOVERNMENTS

The distribution of budgetary expenditures between the central and the local governments is made primarily according to their administrative duties. Generally speaking, the division of the various categories of budgetary expenditures between the central and the local levels may be summarized as follows.[99]

Economic Construction. Economic construction expenditures of the central government include the investment and operating expenses for the following groups of productive activities: heavy industry, large-scale light industry, post and tele-communications, foreign trade, state procurement, banking insurance, state-private joint enterprises, state material reserves, and nationwide development programs for agriculture, forestry, water conservation, and transportation. Included in local budgetary expenditures on economic construction are the investment and operating expenses for certain groups of productive activities undertaken by the local governments, such as local state industry, agriculture, pasturing, fisheries, forestry,

water conservation, transportation, trade, local state-private joint enterprises, public utilities, and urban construction.

Social Services, Culture, and Education. Budgetary expenditures of the central government on social services, culture, and education comprise (1) the expenditures of all of the scientific research and educational institutions under the central governments, (2) the expenditure for sending students abroad, (3) appropriations for national athletic programs and for cultural enterprises and undertakings, (4) subsidies to health organizations, (5) outlays on foreign cultural exchange programs, (6) subsidies to news and publications undertakings, (7) allowances for veterans and retired workers and employees of the central government, and (8) outlays for social relief and welfare services. Included in local expenditures are (1) the operating expenses for schools, athletic programs, and cultural activities all at the local level, (2) subsidies for local news and publications undertakings, (3) operating expenses of local health organizations, (4) allowances for retired workers and employees of the local governments, and (5) outlays for social relief.

National Defense. Since the armed forces and all defense construction activities are under the control of the central government, the category of "national defense expenditure" does not appear in the local budgets.

Administration. Administrative expenditures of the central government are composed of (1) the outlays of the various branches of government at the central level, (2) the expenses budgeted for diplomatic activities and for nationality and overseas Chinese affairs, (3) financial expenditures *(tsai-wu-fei)*, presumably used for supporting the Chinese Communist Party, and (4) subsidies for political parties (other than the Chinese Communist Party) and public organizations. Administrative expenditures of the local governments are primarily the outlays of the governmental departments at local levels.

Credit Payments. Foreign loans and aid to foreign countries belong to the expenditures of the central government. Principal and interest on national bonds are paid by both the central

[97]*Ibid.;* and State Council, "A Decision on Improving the System of Tax Management (Approved at the 75th Meeting of the State Council on April 11, 1958 and Promulgated on June 9, 1958)," *HHPYK,* No.12 (June 25, 1958), pp. 88–89.

[98]*Ibid.*

[99]Ko Chih-ta, *op. cit.,* pp. 44–48.

and the local governments, but those on local bonds are classified as the expenditure of the local governments.

BUDGETARY DATA

Available budgetary data may be classified into three groups: (1) state revenue, (2) state expenditure, and (3) provincial budgets. Unless otherwise indicated, all the data shown in the statistical tables are based on the final accounts.

State Revenue

Table 10.1 presents data on state revenue for 1950 through 1959. Revenue data are broken down into four major categories: tax revenue, revenue from state enterprises, revenue from credit and insurance operations, and other revenue. Data on tax revenue are classified further into industrial and commercial taxes, the agricultural tax, the salt tax, and the custom duties. Data on industrial and commercial taxes are shown by ownership of taxpaying units, such as private business, cooperatives, state-private joint enterprises, and state enterprises. The revenue from state enterprises, as may be recalled, is composed of profits, depreciation reserve, and other income, but official data are available only for the aggregate magnitude.[100] Data on revenue from credit and insurance operations are grouped into three categories: domestic bonds, foreign loans, and insurance operations.

Table 10.2 presents data on state revenue for 1950–56 and 1958, classified into six categories according to ownership of establishment: (1) state enterprises, (2) cooperatives, (3) state-private joint enterprises, (4) peasants, (5) private enterprises, and (6) others.

Table 10.3 contains information on the agricultural tax as a percentage of the agricultural output, and Table 10.4 shows figures on the state revenue obtained from three groups of state enterprises: (1) industry, (2) transportation and post and tele-communications, and (3) trade, food, and foreign trade.

Tables 10.5 and 10.6 indicate sales and terms of domestic bonds issued in China and the sales of these bonds to workers and employees, peasants, and private enterprises.

State Expenditure

Official data on state expenditure for 1950 through 1959 are shown in Table 10.7. These data are grouped into the following categories: economic construction, social services, culture and education, national defense, administration, repayment of loans, aid to foreign countries, credit funds to state banks, and others. Data on economic construction are shown for (1) industry, (2) agriculture, forestry, water conservation, and meteorological services, (3) transportation and post and tele-communications, (4) food supply, domestic and foreign trade, and banking, (5) urban public utilities, and (6) others. Data on social services, culture, and education are broken down into culture and broadcasting, education and training, science, public health, pensions and awards, and social relief and welfare.

Table 10.8 presents data on the distribution of the state expenditure between the central and the local governments for 1951–56.

Table 10.9 shows data on state expenditures on culture, education, public health, and social relief with detailed breakdowns for 1951–56.

Provincial Budgets

Data on local revenues and expenditures are compiled in Tables 10.10–10.27 for 18 provinces, autonomous regions, and centrally controlled municipalities. These data are grouped according to standard classifications. Revenue data are classified into four main categories: (1) taxes, (2) income from local state enterprises and undertakings, (3) government bonds, and (4) miscellaneous incomes. There are also four main categories for expenditure data: (1) economic construction, (2) social service, culture, and education, (3) administration, and (4) miscellaneous expenditures. Except for Inner Mongolia Autonomous Region, data are compiled from provincial budget messages given mostly by deputy governors or directors of the finance bureau and published in local newspapers. Data for Inner Mongolia Autonomous Region are taken from a statistical abstract prepared by the statistical bureau of that region.

---

[100]Estimates on (1) profits from state enterprises and (2) depreciation reserve and other income from state enterprises were made by Ecklund, *op. cit,* for 1950–59.

CREDIT AND FOREIGN EXCHANGE RATES

Chinese statistical data on money and banking are extremely scarce. Data can be found only for the following five categories: (1) bank deposits of the public, (2) agricultural loans issued by state banks, (3) development of rural credit cooperatives, (4) monthly rate of interest charged by state banks on various loans, and (5) foreign exchange rates.

BANK DEPOSITS

The People's Bank of China compiles statistics on the bank deposits of the public, which are composed of individual savings in both time and demand deposit accounts. Such data can be found in print only for the period 1949–59. An article published in February, 1965, indicated that the total bank deposits rose substantially during 1963 and reached a record high at the end of 1964, but there were no absolute data.[101]

There are two series of data on the bank deposits of the public. One was published in the *Impartial Daily (TKP)* for 1949 through 1957, and the other was given later by the People's Bank of China in its official publication *China's Finance (Chung-kuo chin-jung)* for five years: 1949, 1950, 1952, 1957, and 1959. There are discrepancies between these two series for 1952 and 1957, probably because of revisions made in the second series. In addition, data are available on the bank deposits in all cities for 1953 and 1954 and in rural areas for 1952 and 1956. All these data are shown in Table 10.28. Table 10.29 presents data on the index of bank deposits of urban residents in Inner Mongolia Autonomous Region for 1950 through 1958.

AGRICULTURAL LOANS

Agricultural loans were issued by state banks to the peasants and agricultural producer cooperatives (or the communes) for production purposes. Three types of data relating to agricultural loans are available: (1) the amount issued during the year, (2) the year-end balance, and (3) the balance at the end of each June.

Statistics on the amount of agricultural loans issued annually by state banks were published by the People's Bank of China for 1950–58 in *China's Finance* (September 25, 1959) and for 1950–56 in *Agricultural Finance (Nung-ts'un chin-jung*, October, 1957). These two series are not consistent with one another, and the first series perhaps was a revised one. Statistics on the year-end balance of agricultural loans for 1950–56 also appeared in the October, 1957, issue of *Agricultural Finance*. These figures varied greatly with those given in an article by Tsen Lin in the April, 1956, issue of *Economic Research*. Tsen's article also presented data on the balance of agricultural loans at the end of June for 1951–55. All these data are included in Table 10.30.

RURAL CREDIT COOPERATIVES

Prior to 1958, rural credit cooperatives constituted an important part in the cooperativization of rural areas. These cooperatives were organized "by peasant masses for mutal help and mutual benefit" and acted as "an aid supplementing any inadequacies of the state banks, and as a bridge between state banks and farmers"[102] Through various business contracts, the rural credit cooperatives were consigned various banking operations, such as loans and savings. In addition, the cooperatives "would educate and organize peasants in accordance with the state's banking policies."[103] In 1958, the cooperatives were merged into local branches of the People's Bank of China to form the credit department of the communes.[104]

Table 10.31 presents statistics on the development of rural credit cooperatives for 1953–58 as they were published by the People's Bank of China. These statistics cover the number of the cooperatives, their capital funds, and deposit and loan balances, all at the end of each year.

[101]Liu Hung-ju and Tai Ch'ien-tin, "The Stability of the People's Currency Is an Indication of the Supreme Superiority of the New Chinese Socialism," *Kuang-ming jih-pao*, February 8, 1965, p. 4.
[102]Chang Yuan-yuang, "An Urgent Need for Developing Rural Credit Cooperatives," *Ching-chi chou-pao (Economic Weekly)* Shanghai, No. 8 (February 28, 1952), pp. 149–51.
[103]*Ibid.*
[104]Department of Agricultural Finance of the People's Bank of China, "Great Achievements in the Work on Agricultural Finance since 1939," *Chung-kuo chin-jung (China's Finance)*, September 25, 1959, p. 2.

INTEREST RATES

In China rates of interest on savings and loans are determined by the state. The first official decree on interest rates appeared in May, 1949, when differential rates were applied to agricultural loans in kind and in cash. Monthly rates ranging from 0.5 to 1.5 percent were charged on loans in kind and those from 7.5 to 15 percent on loans in cash. The use of such wide differential rates was due primarily to continuing inflation at that time.[105] These differential rates were abolished in 1950, when all agricultural loans were charged at a monthly rate of 2 per cent.[106] Beginning in August, 1953, new monthly rates of interest on various types of loans (such as agricultural, industrial, handicraft, and commercial loans) were put into effect. These rates varied from 0.45 percent for state industrial enterprises to 1.95 percent for private trade. Starting from October, 1955, the monthly interest rates were generally made lower, ranging from 0.4 percent for poor peasant cooperative funds to 1.35 percent for private trade.[107] These rates were lowered again in January, 1958.[108] Beginning in January, 1959, a single monthly rate of 0.6 percent was adopted for all types of loans.[109] This rate has remained effective for industrial, handicraft, and commercial loans, but the rate of interest on agricultural loans has been reduced to 0.48 percent monthly since May, 1961.[110] Table 10.32 presents monthly rates of interest charged by state banks on various types of loans from August, 1953, to May, 1961.

FOREIGN EXCHANGE RATES

The exchange rates between Chinese people's currency (*jen-min-pi*) and currencies of other countries are fixed by the state and announced by the People's Bank of China.

There are two sets of exchange rates between Chinese people's currency and cur-rencies of other communist countries, one being used for settlement of trade accounts and the other for nontrade purposes. The nontrade rates are applicable to the operating costs of embassies, expense incurred by delegations, students, and other individuals sent to the countries concerned, overseas remittances, and other expenses. As of February, 1965, the exchange rates of people's currency for trading purposes were fixed only with the Soviet ruble (222.22 yuan per 100 rubles) and the Roumanian lei (33.33 yuan per 100 lei), while the nontrade rates were fixed with 11 other communist countries. Data on the nontrade rates are shown in Table 10.33. It may be noted that the table does not include Cuba, since the exchange rate between the people's currency and the Cuban peso has not been fixed. Settlement of accounts between China and Cuba is calculated on the basis of pounds sterling.[111]

With respect to noncommunist countries, the People's Bank of China quotes different rates for the buying and selling of currencies of these countries. Table 10.34 presents data on the rates of exchange between people's currency and currencies of some 20 noncommunist countries as of February, 1965. Not included in the table is the exchange rate with United States dollars. In the December, 1957, issue of *Planned Economy (CHCC)*, the conversion ratio between the people's currency and the U.S. dollar was given as 2.617 yuan per U.S. dollar. The ratio was "computed on the basis of relevant materials and meant for general reference only."[112]

[105]*Ibid.*
[106]*Ibid.*
[107]People's Bank of China, ed., *A Collection of Financial Laws and Regulations, 1955*, Peking: Finance Publishing House, 1956, p. 40.
[108]People's Bank of China, ed., *A Collection of Financial Laws and Regulations, 1957*, Peking: Finance Publishing House, 1958, p. 57.
[109]*TKP*, December 31, 1958.
[110]*TKP*, April 30, 1961.
[111]Administrative Bureau for Business with Foreign Countries, People's Bank of China, "Conversion Rates of People's Currency against Foreign Currencies." *Shih-shih shou-ts'e (Handbook of Current Events)*, No. 3 (February, 1965), pp. 37–38.
[112]Conversion Rates between People's Currency and Certain Foreign Currencies," *CHCC*, No. 12 (December 9, 1957), p. 29.

11

EMPLOYMENT, LABOR PRODUCTIVITY, AND WAGES

TYPES AND SOURCES OF LABOR STATISTICS

Chinese labor statistics cover 10 areas: (1) the size and composition of the labor force, (2) the utilization of labor time, (3) labor training, (4) labor productivity, (5) wages, (6) family budget surveys, (7) labor unions, (8) industrial accidents, (9) "cadres" *(kan-pu)* and specialists, and (10) the balance sheet for the labor force *(lao-tung-li p'ing-heng-piao)*.[1] Statistics were published only for four categories: the size and composition of nonfarm employment, nonfarm labor productivity, wages, and family budgets. Since survey findings on family budgets were included in the section on living standards, the present section will deal only with employment, productivity, and wages.

The basic source of labor statistics is the regular statistical reporting system. The statistical schedules filled out regularly by state and joint enterprises contain data on labor indicators. These data provide the State Statistical Bureau and the Ministry of Labor with the basis for preparing labor statistics.[2] In addition, national surveys are sometimes conducted according to special needs. For example, three special surveys were undertaken by the State Statistical Bureau in the mid-1950s. One was the national manpower census for 1955. The purpose of the census was to study the size and composition of the nonfarm labor force as of September 30, 1955.[3] Workers and employees were classified by 32 branches of the national economy, and they were subclassified by sex, age, education, and rank. A second survey was conducted in 1956 for the purpose of investigating the wage standards, the level and composition of wages, and the number of workers and employees classified by wage grade. The third

survey, undertaken in early 1957, was to determine, as of February 28, 1957, the sex, age, skill, cultural level, and political inclination of workers and employees in industry, basic construction, and transportation.[4]

WORKERS AND EMPLOYEES

The labor force in China is composed of peasants, handicraftsmen, and workers and employees.[5] Prior to 1957 when socialization of private trade was largely completed, individual wholesalers and retailers also consituted a significant portion of the total employment.

Peasants account for the majority of the Chinese labor force. No time-series data on the agricultural labor force was available, although some rough estimates were made for the mid-1950s. A frequently quoted estimate was the figure of 262 million persons for 1955, of which 143 million were male and 119 million were female.[6] The estimate was made from data on the total number of peasant households and the average number of males and females per household, which were obtained through a sample survey of agricultural producer cooperatives conducted in 1955.[7] The estimate thus derived

[1]Editorial Committee for Statistical Work Handbook, ed., *Labor Statistical Work Handbook*, Peking: Statistical Publishing House, 1958, pp. 1–2. Hereafter referred to as *Labor Statistical Work Handbook*.

[2]*Ibid*.

[3]Data Office, *TCKTTH*, "A General Survey of the Size, Composition and Distribution of Workers and Employees in 1955," *TCKTTH*, No. 23 (December 14, 1956), pp. 28-30, 33.

[4]*Labor Statistical Work Handbook, op. cit.*

[5]*Ibid.*; and Ch'en Chih-ho, "Problems Concerning the Subject of the Statistical Enumeration of the Labor Force," *CHYTC*, No. 11 (August 23, 1959), pp. 27–30.

[6]Chu Yuan-ch'ien, "The Problem of Agricultural Surplus Labor in China at Present," *Chiao-hsüch yü yen-chiu (Teaching and Research)*, No. 2 (February 4, 1957), pp. 17–20; and Wang Kuang-wei, "Views on Allocating Agricultural Labor Force," *CHCC*, No. 8 (August 9, 1957), pp. 6–9.

[7]*Ibid.*

is at best an approximation and therefore should be used with great caution.

Data on the handicraft labor force are also very scanty. Figures were published, however, on the number of individual handicraftsmen and handicraft cooperative members for 1949–57. In addition, a national survey on handicraft industry was undertaken for 1954, yielding some data on handicraft employment in various provinces.

Available statistics on workers and employees are relatively abundant. This is largely because workers and employees are included in the state plan, and data on their size and composition are readily available from regular statistical reports submitted by enterprises and government agencies. As is evident from the statistical tables, with the exception of some figures on handicraftsmen and merchants, employment data in China deal primarily with workers and employees.

THE CONCEPT AND SCOPE OF THE TERMS "WORKERS AND EMPLOYEES"

Definitions of Workers and Employees

Up to 1958, "workers and employees' (chih-kung) were defined in China as "the laborers, without possessing any means of production, relying on wages as the primary source of income."[8] According to this definition, included among workers and employees were persons employed in state, cooperative, joint, and private enterprises and in government agencies. The definition was modified in 1958, when the economy had undergone drastic changes during the Great Leap Forward Movement, particularly because wages were then used as a distribution method in the communes and handicraft cooperatives. The term of "workers and employees" was now used to denote "persons working for the enterprises owned by all of the people and for government agencies and receiving wages from the state."[9] Included in the "enterprises owned by all of the people" were central and local state enterprises, those state-private joint enterprises subject to "fixed-share and fixed dividend" (ting-ku ting-hsi) regulations,[10] and enterprises operated jointly by hsien and the communes. Persons working for cooperative and private enterprises and for those joint enterprises not covered by the "fixed

share and fixed dividend" regulations were no longer considered as workers and employees. Owing to the small amount of employment in cooperative enterprises and in those joint enterprises not regulated by the fixed-dividend rules and owing to the nearly complete socialization of private enterprises (except in certain minority areas), it was suggested in the Chinese literature that the definitional modification made in 1959 did not cause any drastic change in the scope of workers and employees in Chinese labor statistics.[11]

Actual and Average Number of Workers and Employees

REGISTERED AND NONREGISTERED PERSONNEL

Until 1957 the number of workers and employees of an enterprise or government agency was calculated on the basis of the so-called "registered personnel" (tasi-ts'e jen-yǔan), referring to the regular, temporary, and seasonal personnel whose names were entered in the employment rolls (chih-kung ming-ts'e) of the enterprise or government agency.[12] Temporary and seasonal personnel were to be included in the employment rolls only if they were engaged in essential work at least one full day or in non-essential work not less than five days in a year. The criteria used to distinguish essential from non-essential work varied for different branches of the economy, and in many cases the distinction was not clearly made. All the temporary and seasonal workers not included in the employment rolls were classified as nonregistered personnel.

In practice, the above rules were not strictly followed in some cases. In the so-called "nonproductive" branches, such as government agencies and cultural, educational, and health organizations, only persons regularly employed were classified as registered personnel. In 1957, temporary workers in trade and construction were considered as registered personnel only

[8]Cheng Kang-lin and Hsia Wu, "Tabular Forms for Labor and Wage Planning," CHCC, No. 10 (October 9, 1957), pp. 29–33.
[9]Ch'en Chih-ho, op. cit.; and Department of Planning and Statistics, Hupeh University, Industrial Statistics, Wuhan: Hupeh People's Press, 1960, pp. 145–146.
[10]According to "fixed-share and fixed-dividend" regulations, dividends on private capital shares in certain state-private joint enterprises are paid not proportional to the amount of profits made but according to a fixed rate.
[11]Ch'en Chih-ho, op. cit.
[12]Labor Statistical Work Handbook, op. cit., pp. 4–8.

when they performed basic production activities, such as procurement, sales, selecting, storing, processing, wrapping, and shipping in trade and building and installation in construction.

In determining the scope of workers and employees, the State Statistical Bureau set up the following additional rules:[13]

1. Workers and employees absent from an enterprise or government agency would remain as registered personnel only if their absence was due to proper reasons, such as (*a*) vacation, holidays, and maternity leave, (*b*) sick leave not exceeding six months, (*c*) receiving training elsewhere but being paid by the given enterprise or agency, (*d*) performing duties for the state but still being included in the payrolls of the given enterprise or agency, and (*e*) on leave for an official mission.

2. Part-time personnel and soldiers, peasants, and criminals mobilized to participate in production were not included in the computation of workers and employees.

The distinction between registered and nonregistered personnel was dropped in 1958, but the rules used for computing the number of workers and employees remained largely the same.[14]

YEAR-END AND AVERAGE ANNUAL ESTIMATES

Two types of data on the magnitude of employment are given in Chinese statistics: the year-end and average annual number of workers and employees.

The year-end number of workers and employees of a reporting unit is the actual number counted from its employment rolls on December 31 of the year. The average annual number is generally computed in two different ways, depending on the rate of employment turnover of the reporting unit. If the rate of turnover is high, the average annual number is computed as the mean of the monthly average of daily counts of all personnel on the employment rolls. If the rate is low, the mean of the monthly averages of the monthly first and last day counts is taken as the average number for the year. Data on the average annual number of workers and employees are used as a basis for calculating labor productivity and the total and average wages.[15]

CLASSIFICATIONS OF WORKERS AND EMPLOYEES

Within and Outside the State Plan

It was in the communiqué of the State Statistical Bureau and the report of Po I-po, Chairman of the State Economic Commission, on the fulfillment of the national economic plan for 1956 that the scope of workers and employees within the state plan was for the first time explicitly defined.[16] According to these documents, only workers and employees in state, cooperative, and joint enterprises, government agencies, public organizations, and cultural, educational, and health establishments were included in the state plan. Excluded from the plan were the workers and employees hired in private enterprises, handicraft establishments, and agricultural producer cooperatives.[17]

Data on workers and employees within the state plan were submitted by various central ministries and provincial governments through the regular statistical reporting system, except for those of government agencies and public organizations for which figures were compiled by the State Economic Commission from the state budget and the government employment rolls. The number of workers and employees outside the state plan was estimated on the basis of survey data for private enterprises and handicraft cooperatives. Estimates on the number of workers employed in agricultural producer cooperatives were never made, owing to lack of information.[18]

As noted above, the concept of workers and employees was revised in 1958 to exclude persons working for private enterprises and cooperatives. As a result, the category of "workers and employees outside the state plan" was eliminated, and the number of workers and employees within the state plan and the national total became identical.

[13]*Ibid.*
[14]Department of Industrial Statistics, SSB, "Attention Should be Paid to Several Problems Concerning the 1957 Annual Report on Industry," *TCKT*, No. 23 (December 14, 1957), p. 16; Cheng Kang-lin and Hsia Wu, *op. cit.*; and Ch'en Chih-ho, "Several Views on Improving Labor and Wage Statistical Work," *TCYC*, No. 5 (May 23, 1958), pp. 12–15.
[15]*Labor Statistical Work Handbook, op. cit.*; and Cheng Kang-lin and Hsia Wu, *op. cit.*
[16]SSB, *Communiqué on the Results of the Implementation of the National Economic Plan for 1956*, Peking: Statistics Publishing House, 1957, pp. 11–12; and Po I-po, "Report on the Results of the Implementation of the National Economic Plan for 1956 and a Draft of the National Economic Plan for 1957," *HHPYK*, No. 14 (July, 1957), p. 30.
[17]Cheng Kang-lin and Hsia Wu, *op. cit.*
[18]*Ibid.*

Grouping by Branch

In Chinese labor statistics, workers and employees are usually grouped into nine branches of the national economy: (1) industry, (2) agriculture, forestry, and water conservation, (3) basic construction, (4) transportation and post and tele-communications, (5) trade and restaurants, (6) public utilities; (7) culture, education, and health, (8) banking and insurance, and (9) government agencies, political parties, and public organizations.[19] For national surveys and annual reports, more detailed breakdowns are frequently made.[20]

The classification of workers and employees by branch is made according to the administrative units to which workers and employees belong, rather than according to the nature of work performed.[21] Included among the workers and employees of industry and basic construction, for example, were not only those performing basic production activities, such as industrial production, building, and installation, but also those working on the farms and in transportation units, schools, and health and welfare units attached to industry and basic construction. Accordingly, a person teaching in an elementary school run by an industrial enterprise is treated as an industrial worker in Chinese statistics rather than as a teacher who is included in educational employment statistics. But for certain enterprises which are engaged in an activity substantially different from that of their superior departments and employing a large number of workers and employees, the classification is made according to the nature of the business activity. For example, for the Salt Company of the Ministry of Food Industry, the Lumber Company of the Ministry of Timber Industry, the Transport and Sale Company of the Ministry of Aquatic Products, the Drugs Company of the Ministry of Health, the New China Book Store and the International Book Store of the Ministry of Culture, the supply stores for workers and employees of the Ministry of Railways, all of which are basically engaged in commercial activities and have a large volume of employment, their workers and employees are included in trade employment statistics.[22]

Grouping by Ownership of Enterprise

For industry, basic construction, transportation, and trade, employment statistics published for the years prior to 1958 were usually classified by ownership of enterprise. The primary division was between the socialist and the private sectors. The socialist sector included state, cooperative, and state-private joint enterprises. For each branch, workers and employees of the socialist enterprises were included in the state plan. As noted above, beginning in 1958 employment in the private sector has been excluded from the statistics on workers and employees. The total employment has become the same as the employment in the socialist sector.

Grouping by Function

Workers and employees in each branch are classified further according to the function performed. The classification varies for different branches of the economy.

Until 1957, workers and employees in industry were classified into three mutually exclusive categories based on their relevance to the production activity. The most important category was known as "industrial-production personnel" *(kung-yeh sheng-ch'an jen-yüan)*, referring to those workers and employees who were more or less directly concerning with extraction or fabrication. The second category was called "other business personnel" *(ch'i-ta yeh-wu jen-yüan)*, whose function was of a peripheral or service nature. Included were workers and employees engaged in building repair, transportation outside the factory, auxiliary production, housing and welfare services, and culture, education, and health. Finally, there was the category of political-work personnel *(cheng-chih kung-tso jen-yüan)*, who were completely detached from the production activity but were engaged in political work and were paid by industrial enterprises.[23]

Workers and employees in building and installation enterprises and in basic construction

---

[19]*Ibid.*; and *Labor Statistical Work Handbook, op. cit.*, pp. 27–28.

[20]For example, in the 1955 manpower census workers and employees were classified into 32 branches: (1) industry, (2) agriculture, (3) forestry, (4) water conservancy, (5) basic construction, (6) geological survey, (7) survey and architectural planning, (8) railways, (9) water transport, (10) highways, (11) civil aviation, (12) post and tele-communications, (13) trade, (14) restaurants, (15) material supply, (16) banking and insurance, (17) scientific research, (18) meteorological services, (19) culture, (20) broadcasting, (21) higher education, (22) technical schools, (23) middle and elementary schools, (24) training classes, schools for technicians, and other schools, (25) kindergartens, (26) public health, (27) nurseries (28) athletics, (29) public utilities, (30) economic administration, (31) government administration, and (32) miscellaneous.

[21]Cheng Kang-lin and Hsia Wu, *op. cit.*

[22]*Ibid.*

[23]*Labor Statistical Work Handbook, op. cit.*, pp. 15–18.

units[24] were classified into five categories: (1) building and installation personnel, (2) auxiliary production personnel, (3) transportation personnel, (4) political-work personnel, and (5) other personnel.[25] Building and installation personnel were those taking part directly in the building and installation work or in organizing, guiding, and administering the work. Auxiliary production personnel were the workers and employees working in the production units operated by construction enterprises for the purpose of manufacturing building materials. Transportation personnel referred to those engaged in transportation work outside the construction site and included the employment rolls of the construction enterprise. Political-work personnel were defined in the same way as those in industry. Included in other personnel were those working in the cultural, educational, health, and welfare units.

In state farms and machine tractor stations, the primary division was between agricultural production and other personnel.

In railways, the classification was made according to administrative function, such as various departments under a railway bureau. In highways, workers and employees were grouped into motor-vehicle transport personnel, animal-driven-vehicle transport personnel, loading and unloading workers, and nonproductive personnel.

In trade, there were two employment categories: the commercial work personnel, referring to those directly concerning with buying and selling, and other personnel, such as those working in cultural, educational, health and welfare units of commerical enterprises.

In the so-called "nonproductive" branches, the method of classification varied greatly. For example, the educational employment statistics included instructors, assistant instructors, administrative personnel, minor-service personnel, and other personnel. In public health there were four major employment categories: physicians, pharmacists, nurses, and midwives. In banking and finance and government administration, there were no uniform classifications.

In industry, industrial production personnel, in turn, were classified further into the following six employment categories: (1) production workers (*sheng ch'an kung-jen*), (2) apprentices (*hsüeh-tu*), (3) engineering-technical personnel (*kung-ch'eng chi-shu jen-yüan*), (4) office employees (*chih-yüan*), (5) minor service personnel (*ch'in-tsa jen-yüan*), and (6) security-fire personnel (*ching-wei hsiao-fang jen-yüan*).[26]

Production workers refer to those performing any one of the following types of work: (1) directly controlling simple tools or machines in the process of production, (2) overseeing automatic machines in operation, (3) repairing tools and machines, (4) cleaning production lots, (5) moving raw materials and products, and (6) delivering products to customers.

Apprentices refer to those receiving training under the guidance of skilled workers and participating in production activities.

Engineering and technical personnel are persons with engineering and technical qualifications who organize and direct technical work in the process of production. A person without formal education but competent for assuming engineering and technical duties is qualified to be an engineer or technician.

Office employees are those who perform administrative and auxiliary duties, including accounting personnel.

Minor-service personnel are those not serving production directly, including watchmen, janitors, and office attendants.

Security-fire personnel include guards and firemen.

The above classification was revised in late 1957.[27] As of 1960, industrial workers and employees were grouped into five categories: (1) production workers, (2) apprentices, (3) managerial personnel, (4) service personnel, and (5) others.[28] Production workers and apprentices were defined in the same way as before. Managerial personnel (*kuan-li jen-yüan*) referred to those who participated in organizing, guiding, and administering production. Included were engineering-technical personnel, office employees, and political-work personnel. Service personnel (*fu-wu jen-yüan*) were those "serving production only in an indirect way," such as minor-service and security-fire personnel as defined above, and persons working in cultural, educational, medical, and housing-service units. Included in other personnel were those on sick leave or receiving training elsewhere for over six months.

Reportedly, the six-category classification used in industry prior to 1957 was also applied

[24]For the meaning of basic construction units, see the explanation given in the section on capital formation.

[25]*Ibid.*

[26]*Ibid.*

[27]Ch'en Chih-ho, *TCYC, op. cit.*

[28]Department of Statistics and Planning, Hupeh University, *op. cit.*, pp. 147–48.

to those workers and employees engaged in basic production activities in construction, transportation, agriculture, forestry, and water conservation (such as building and installation personnel in construction).[29] But no explanation was given in Chinese sources as to how employment was classified in these branches after 1957. Probably the classification was also revised to the five-category system as it was adopted in industry.

Grouping by Tenure

Another classification in Chinese employment statistics is the division into regular and temporary personnel. Regular *(ku-ting)* or permanent *(ch'ang-chi)* personnel refer to those whose job is of a regular nature and whose period of employment is not specified. In addition, the appointment of a regular worker or employee in an enterprise must be approved by its superior departments. Temporary *(lin-shih)* or contracted *(ho-t'ung)* personnel are hired according to a contract in which a period of employment is specifically defined. Seasonal workers are included among temporary personnel.[30]

STATISTICAL DATA ON THE SIZE, COMPOSITION, AND DISTRIBUTION OF WORKERS AND EMPLOYEES

There are three categories of employment statistics available in China: (1) year-end data, (2) average annual data, and (3) the census data as of September 30, 1955.

Year-End Data

1. Table 11.1 presents data on the year-end number of workers and employees for 1949 through 1960 with the following breakdowns: (*a*) classification by sex, (*b*) division into productive and non-productive branches, (*c*) grouping into production workers, engineering and technical personnel, and other employees, (*d*) employment within the state plan, (*e*) coverage by labor insurance, and (*f*) coverage by free medical care.

2. Included in Table 11.2 are data on the year-end number of workers and employees by branch of the economy for 1949 through 1958

with breakdowns according to form of ownership.

3. Data are available on year-end employment by type of work for industry, basic construction, transportation and communication, and public health. These data are shown in Table 11.3.

4. Year-end employment data are compiled in Table 11.4 for four industries: metal-processing, building materials, food-processing, and textiles. The 1957 figure for the textile industry was published in December of that year and therefore is necessarily an anticipated estimate.

Average Annual Data

Statistics on the average number of workers and employees have been published only on a yearly basis. Table 11.5 presents average annual data on total employment for 1952–58 and on employment within the state plan for 1955–58. In addition, the same type of data are assembled in Table 11.6 for eight industries: iron and steel, coal, electric power, metal-processing, chemicals, building materials, textiles, and paper. These data are classified further by type of work, and those for the textile industry are also broken down according to ownership of enterprise.

The 1955 Survey Data

As pointed out above, a manpower census was conducted by the State Statistical Bureau on September 30, 1955. Some of the census findings were released in the December, 1956, issue of *Statistical Work Bulletin*. Included were the following four types of data: (1) total employment with breakdown by sex, (2) the percentage distribution between male and female employment in industry, basic construction, banking and insurance, and culture, education, and health, (3) the geographic distribution of employment in industry, trade, transportation and communication, and education, (4) the percentage distribution of employment in industry and basic construction by age group, and (5) the number of specialists, such as engineers, technicians, scientists, teachers, medical personnel, and cultural and art personnel. These data are shown in Tables 11.7–11.10.

[29]*Labor Statistical Work Handbook, op. cit.*
[30]Department of Statistics and Planning, Hupeh University, *op. cit.*, p. 148

LABOR PRODUCTIVITY

LABOR PRODUCTIVITY IN INDUSTRY

In China labor productivity is calculated for industry, basic construction, transportation, and trade, but data were published mainly for industry.

Labor productivity indicates the amount of output produced by one unit of labor per unit of time.[31] Output can be expressed in physical or value terms. But labor productivity in physical terms is meaningful only when the products produced are homogeneous. For workers producing heterogeneous products, productivity can be measured only in terms of the value of these products.

Chinese value data on labor productivity are presented in two forms: the absolute amount and the index.

The official formula for computing the absolute level of labor productivity in industry has been the ratio of gross value of industrial output at constant prices to the number of production workers.[32] Algebraically, the formula may be shown as follows:

$$\text{Absolute level of labor productivity during current period} = \frac{\Sigma\, q_1 p_c}{\Sigma\, m_1}$$

where $\Sigma\, q_1 p_c$ represents gross value of output at constant prices and $\Sigma\, m_1$ the number of production workers of all industry in the current period.

This formulation was critized by a number of economists and statisticians in China.[33] The burden of the charges was levied against the use of both gross value of industrial output as the numerator and the number of production workers as the denominator in the formula. With regard to the numerator, critics of the formula opposed using gross value of industrial output on several grounds. In the first place, the use of gross value of industrial output, as it was computed in China according to the so-called "factory method," would tend to exaggerate labor productivity because of multiple counting.[34] Second, labor productivity statistics would be distorted by the amalgamation or splitting up of enterprises, again because of the factory method of computing industrial production. Finally, labor productivity calculated according to the official formula would not be an appro-

priate measure for evaluating enterprise performance, for it would encourage enterprises to use expensive materials in order to inflate the gross value of their output and hence the productivity of their workers. Therefore, net value of industrial output was proposed to replace the gross value in the official formulation.[35]

With regard to the denominator, opponents of the official formula suggest that labor productivity be calculated on the basis of the number of workers and employees, instead of production workers alone.[36] They justify their proposal by pointing out that workers and employees other than production workers, such as engineers, technicians, office employees, and minor-service personnel, also contribute to production and that labor productivity based solely on production workers would not provide an incentive for enterprises to enhance the efficiency of other employees. Moreover, the proportion of production workers in total employment tends to decline as technological automation advances, and hence labor productivity calculated according to production workers would become higher than the fact warranted.

The official index of labor productivity has been the percentage relationship between the average gross value of output at constant prices per production worker for the current period and the analogous measure for the base period.[37] This may be represented symbolically as follows:

$$\text{Index of labor productivity during current period} = \frac{\Sigma\, q_1 p_c\, /\, \Sigma\, m_1}{\Sigma\, q_0 p_c\, /\, \Sigma\, m_0}$$

where $\Sigma\, q_1 p_c$ and $\Sigma\, m_1$ are defined as before and $\Sigma\, q_0 p_c$ and $\Sigma\, m_0$ represent, respectively, gross value of output at constant prices and the number of production workers of all industry in the base period.

The index constructed according to the official formula is affected not only by changes in the level of labor productivity but also by

[31]*Labor Statistical Work Handbook, op. cit.*, p. 42.
[32]*Ibid.*
[33]*Ibid.*, pp. 42–45; Wang Nai-pu, "Our Views on Computing Labor Productivity According to All Personnel," *TCKTTH*, No. 18 (September 29, 1956), pp. 19–20: and Hsü Kang, "Several Views on the Methods of Computing Labor Productivity," *TCKT*, No. 2 (February 29, 1957), p. 12.
[34]For a discussion of the defects of the factory method, see the section on industry.
[35]Hsü Kang, *op. cit.*
[36]Wang Nai-pu, *op. cit.*
[37]Department of Industrial Statistics, SSB, *Notes on Industrial Statistics*, Peking: Statistics Publishing House, September, 1956, p. 103.

changes in the structure of enterprise employment, i.e., the number of production workers in an enterprise in relation to the industry total.[38] Therefore, the official index would give a distorted picture of productivity change. For this reason, the State Statistical Bureau suggested that two additional indices be calculated by various industries in order to separate the effects of changes in labor productivity upon the level of output from those of changes in employment structure. These two indices are calculated as an arithmetic mean of indices computed separately for each enterprise as a ratio of current to base period value of output per production worker, weighted, respectively, by the number of production workers and the gross value of output of the industry in question during the current period.[39] Algebraically, these two indices may be shown as follows:

Formula I (with current employment as weights)
$$= \frac{\Sigma \, (q_1 p_c / m_1 \, : \, q_0 p_c / m_0) \, m_1}{\Sigma \, m_1}$$

Formula II (with current output as weights)
$$= \frac{\Sigma \, (q_1 p_c / m_1 \, : \, q_0 p_c / m_0) \, q_1 p_c}{\Sigma \, q_1 p_c}$$

where q_0 and q_1 represent, respectively, total output of each enterprise for the base and current periods, m_0 and m_1 the corresponding numbers of production workers, and p_c the constant unit prices.[40] An index constructed according to Formula I would show actual changes in the level of labor productivity with a constant level of employment, while Formula II would yield an index attributing changes in the volume of output to changes in the structure of employment with a constant level of labor productivity.[41] The calculation of these two indices are not mandatory, and all data published on labor productivity index were based on the official formula.

LABOR PRODUCTIVITY IN BASIC CONSTRUCTION, TRANSPORTATION, AND TRADE

Labor productivity in basic construction is calculated primarily in value terms to indicate the volume of building and installation work at constant prices per worker. Like labor productivity in industry, both the absolute level and

the index of productivity are calculated for building and installation workers.[42]

In transportation, labor productivity is measured largely in terms of so-called "converted ton-miles." For railways and water transportation, the number of transportation workers and employees is used as the basis for measurement. For motor-vehicle transportation, the productivity measure is given as converted ton-miles per driver.[43]

Labor productivity in trade is measured both for total employment and for sales personnel. The volume of transactions at constant prices is used for the computation.[44]

STATISTICAL DATA ON LABOR PRODUCTIVITY

Data on the level of labor productivity, computed on the basis of gross value of output,

[38]Cheng Kang-lin and Hsia Wu, *op. cit.* An Example from Cheng Kang-lin and Hsia Wu may help to clarify this point:

	Gross value of output (thousands of 1957 yuan)		Number of production workers (persons)	
Enterprise	1957	1958	1957	1958
All	10,000	12,600	3,000	3,727
Enterprise A	6,000	6,600	1,000	1,000
Enterprise B	4,000	6,000	2,000	2,727

	Average output per worker (yuan)		Percentage change in productivity 1957 to 1958
All	3,330	3,380	1.5
Enterprise A	6,000	6,600	10.0
Enterprise B	2,000	2,200	10.0

In this example, the employment of Enterprise A, which had a relatively high value of output per worker, declined as a percentage of the total employment, while the employment of Enterprise B, characterized by a higher labor productivity, showed a relative increase. As a result, the increase in labor productivity computed according to the official formula would be less than the separate increase of each of the two enterprises. Likewise, it can be shown that a relative increase in the employment of Enterprise A as a percentage of the total employment would result in an increase in aggregate labor productivity more than the separate increase of each individual enterprise.

[39]Department of Statistics, SSB, *op. cit.*; Department of Planning and Statistics, Hupeh University, *op. cit.*, pp. 197–99; and *Labor Statistical Work Handbook*, *op. cit.*, p. 49.

[40]Formula I is identical with the one proposed by Soviet economist S. G. Strumilin. See Walter Galenson, *Labor Productivity in Soviet and American Industry*, New York: Columbia University Press, 1955, p. 11.

[41]It may be noted that the product of these two indices is equal to the official index. This can be seen from the ollowing equation:

$$\frac{\Sigma p_1 p_c / \Sigma m_1}{\Sigma q_0 p_c / \Sigma m_0} = \frac{\Sigma (q_1 p_c / m_1 \, : \, q_0 p_c / m_0) \, m_1}{\Sigma \, m_1} \times \frac{\Sigma (q_1 p_0 / m_1 \, : \, q_0 p_c / m_0) q_1 p_c}{\Sigma \, q_1 p_c}$$

[42]*Labor Statistical Work Handbook*, *op. cit.*, pp. 46–47; and Hsü ch'ien, Tai Shih-kuang, Yu Tao et al., *Ching-chi t'ung-chi-hsüeh chianghua* (*Lectures on Economic Statistics*), Peking: Statistical Publishing House, 1957.

[43]*Ibid.*

[44]*Ibid.*

are available only for industry and handicrafts and for certain branches of industry, and these data are shown in Tables 11.11 and 11.12. Included in Table 11.11 are also data on gross value of social output per worker for 1952 and 1956, but the measure covers only four branches of the economy: industry, construction, transportation and communication, and trade. In addition, data on net value of output per worker in these branches can be found for 1953, 1955, and 1956 and are assembled in Table 11.13. Finally fragmentary data on the index of labor productivity in industry, construction, transportation and communication, and 10 branches of industry are gathered in Tables 11.14 and 11.15.

WAGES

Chinese wage statistics consist of three types of data: (1) the total amounts of wages, (2) average wages per worker, and (3) wage indices.

THE TOTAL AMOUNT OF WAGES

The total amount of wages (*kung-tzu tsung-o*) or wage funds (*kung-tzu chi-chin*) refers to the incomes both in cash and in kind received by workers and employees and by temporary personnel not classified as workers or employees as compensation for their labor.[45] The composition of the total amount of wages was first defined in a 1951 official decree,[46] and was then revised in May, 1955. According to the 1955 regulations, the total amount of wages is composed of the following 26 items:[47] (1) time-rate wages, (2) piece-rate wages, (3) extra payments for pieceworkers for unfavorable working conditions (such as inadequate material supplies, complicated production process, and poor tools and equipment), (4) extra payments for pieceworkers assigned to jobs paying less than the average of their permanent positions, (5) wages of contract workers (*pao-kung*), (6) wages paid according to certain percentage of gross business income, (7) various monetary awards (such as fulfillment and overfulfillment of state plans, economy in use of materials, fuel and power, superior product quality, and high safety levels), (8) allowances for overtime work, (9) allowances for night work, (10) wages

for workers producing defective products not due to workers' fault, (11) wages for workers during work stoppage, (12) allowances for difficult or hazardous working conditions, (13) allowances for holiday work, (14) allowances for performing technical jobs, (15) extra payments for workers performing additional administrative duties, (16) recompense for workers instructing apprentices, (17) payments for writing articles, giving lectures, and other specialized work, (18) allowances for regional differences in cost of living, (19) payments for female workers feeding their babies during working hours, (20) wages for workers performing duties for the state, (21) extra payments as a preferential treatment for minor workers, (22) payments for workers transferred between jobs, (23) payments for vacations, (24) wages for workers receiving training elsewhere but still being included in the employment rolls of a given enterprise, (25) meal, housing, and utility allowances, and (26) dismissal payment.[48]

Excluded from the total amount of wages are the following elements: (1) monetary awards for inventions, innovations, rationalization proposals (i.e., cost-saving suggestions), labor emulation, and the like, (2) supplementary expenses to wages (such as union fees, labor insurance payments, and similar fringe benefits), and welfare expenditures of state agencies and public organizations, (3) various expenditures on labor protection, such as those on purchasing work clothing, respirators, gloves, ventilation facilities, and various types of safety equipment, (4) expenses on business trips, (5) traveling allowances for workers transferred to another job, and (6) allowances for students in training.[49]

AVERAGE WAGES PER WORKER

The average amount of wages per worker during a given period is dervied by dividing the

[45]Cheng Kang-lin and Hsia Wu, *op. cit.*, p. 33.

[46]Regulations on the Composition of the Total Amount of Wages, Promulgated on March 7, 1951," in Commission on Financial and Economic Affairs, Government Administrative Council, ed., *Collection of Fiscal and Economic Policy Statements, Regulations, and Laws of the Central Government*, Vol. III; Peking: March, 1952, pp. 1060–62.

[47]SSB, "Provisional Regulations on the Composition of the Total Amount of Wages (Approved by the State Council on May 21, 1955)," *TCKTTH*, No. 1 (January 14, 1956), pp. 7–8.

[48]In the 1951 decree, a distinction was made between basic wages (*chi-pen kung-tzu*) and auxiliary wages (*fu-chu kung-tzu*). Included in basic wages were items (1), (2), and (6) listed in the 1955 regulations, while (7), (8), (9), (11), (12), (13), (14), and (25) were considered auxiliary wages, and the dismissal payment (item 26) was excluded from the total amount of wages. The remaining items did not appear in the 1951

total amount of wages by the average number of workers and employees. The measure is said to be "the most important indicator of the material living standards of the working class.[50]

The average wages per worker may be calculated on an hourly, daily, monthly, quarterly, or yearly basis. Average hourly wages are measured on the basis of the actual number of working hours during a day. Excluded from the measure are, therefore, wages received not in connection with the work done, such as may be the case during work stoppage and feeding babies by women workers. For average daily, monthly, quarterly, and yearly wages, however, the total amount of wages is used in the computation. [51]

In practice, hourly and daily average wages are not calculated in China.[52] While figures on monthly, quarterly, and yearly bases have been prepared, only yearly statistics can be found in print.

Two methodological problems concerning computation of average wages may be noted. First, the total amount of wages consist of the amount received by both workers and employees and by temporary personnel not classified as workers or employees. In other words, total wages includes those of "nonregistered personnel," the term used in China for pre-1958 years. To divide the total amount of wages by the average number of workers and employees, i.e., the average number of registered personnel, would yield a value higher than actual average wages. Second, according to Chinese practice, the average number of workers and employees for a given month includes those on sick leave and those newly employed or discharged within the month. These persons are counted as full-month workers and employees but are paid for part of the month. In consequence, using the total amount of wages and the average number of workers and employees for the month without appropriate adjustments in the computation, as was the case in China, would tend to understate the monthly average wages per worker.[53]

WAGE INDICES

The official wage index is calculated as the percentage relationship between average wages per worker in the current period and the analogous measure in the base period.[54] In an algebraic form, the index may be represented as follows:

$$\text{Average wage index} = \frac{\Sigma\, w_1 m_1 / \Sigma\, m_1}{\Sigma\, w_0 m_0 / \Sigma\, m_0}$$

where $\Sigma\, w_1 m_1$ and $\Sigma\, w_0 m_0$ represent the total amount of wages in the current and base periods, measured at prices prevailing during the respective periods, and $\Sigma\, m_1$ and $\Sigma\, m_0$ represent the corresponding number of workers and employees in the current and base periods.

Like the official index of labor productivity, the wage index calculated according to the above formula would be distorted by changes in the size of enterprise employment in relation to total employment. In addition, the formula does not take price changes into account, and hence the resulting index would not indicate changes in the level of real wages. In consequence, the State Statistical Bureau has suggested that three additional indices be calculated. The first two indices parallel the indices suggested by the State Statistical Bureau in connection with the calculation of the labor productivity index, for separating the effects of actual productivity changes from those of changes in employment structure on the level of output. These two indices may be constructed as an arithmetic mean of indices computed for each enterprise as a ratio of current to base period average wage per worker, weighted respectively by the number of workers and employees and by the total amount of wages in the current period.[55] Available evidence, however, does not indicate that these indices have been prepared in practice. A third index is the average wage index adjusted by the cost of living index. This is known as the "real average wage index" and can be computed from the following formula:[56]

$$\frac{\text{Real average}}{\text{wage index}} = \frac{\text{average (money) wage index}}{\text{cost of living index}}$$

decree, and it is not clear how these items were classified as basic or auxiliary wages, since such a distinction was not shown in the 1955 regulations.

[49]Ibid.

[50]Department of Planning and Statistics, Hupeh University, op. cit., pp. 221–22.

[51]Hsü Ch'ien et al., op. cit., p. 180; and Labor Statistical Work Handbook, op. cit., pp. 64–65.

[52]Hsü Ch'ien et al., op. cit., p. 177.

[53]Hsü Kang. "Several Problems Concerning the Contents of the National Wage Survey for Workers and Employees," TCKTTH, No. 16 (August 29, 1956), pp. 13–14.

[54]Labor Statistical Work Handbook, op. cit., p. 64.

[55]Ibid., p. 68; and Hsü Ch'ien et al., op. cit., pp. 222–23.

[56]Hsü Ch'ien et al., ibid., p. 227–29.

The index was calculated by the State Statistical Bureau for a number of years, and some data were released.

WAGE STATISTICS

Table 11.16 presents data on the total amount of wages of (1) all workers and employees, (2) workers and employees within the state plan, and (3) workers and employees in government administration and state enterprises. Also included are data on the index of the total amount of wages paid by state and joint industrial enterprises.

Data on average annual wages of workers and employees in various branches of the economy are compiled in Table 11.17. The same type of data are assembled in Table 11.18 for eight industries.

Data on the index of average wages are shown in Table 11.19 for the national average, as well as for industry, construction, railway transportation, and government administration. Table 11.20 contains statistics on the index of average real wages for the national average, industry, and construction.

II

Statistical Data and Sources

TABLE 1.1 Land Area, by Province or Equivalent, Square Kilometers

Province or equivalent	Area	Province or equivalent	Area
Peking	17, 100	Anhwei	139, 900
Shanghai	5, 800	Chekiang	101, 800
Hopei	202, 700	Fukien	123, 100
Shansi	157, 100	Honan	167, 000
Inner Mongolia Autonomous Region	1, 177, 500	Hupeh	187, 500
Liaoning	151, 000	Hunan	210, 500
Kirin	187, 000	Kiangsi	164, 800
Heilungkiang	463, 000	Kwangtung	231, 400
Shensi	195, 800	Kwangsi Chuang Autonomous Region	220, 400
Kansu	366, 500	Szechuan	569, 000
Ningsia Hui Autonomous Region	66, 400	Kweichow	174, 000
Chinghai	721, 000	Yunnan	436, 200
Sinkiang Uighur Autonomous Region	1, 646, 800	Tibet and Changtu area	1, 221, 600
Shantung	153, 300		
Kiangsu	102, 200	Total	9, 561, 000

Note: Figures are shown according to the administrative division of the area under
   Communist rule as of Aguust, 1959. The area of Taiwan (36,000 square kilometers)
   is not included.
Source: *1959 JMST*, p. 209.

TABLE 1.2 Total Population, June 30, 1953, Individuals

Area	SSB Communique,[1] November 1, 1954	Teng Hsiao-p'ing's report[2] June 19, 1954
	(1)	(2)
Total population	601,938,035	601,912,371
By direct census registration	574,205,940	573,876,670
Estimate for border regions where no census took place[a]	8,397,477	8,708,169
Taiwan[b]	7,591,298	19,327,532
Overseas Chinese and students abroad[c]	11,743,320	

[a] Estimates were made on the basis of the administrative reports of local
   authorities in these regions.
[b] According to the figures published by the Nationalist Government in 1951.
[c] The overseas Chinese population was estimated by the Commission of Overseas
   Chinese Affairs, diplomatic personnel stationed abroad by the Ministry of
   Foreign Affairs and students studying in other countries by the Ministry
   of Higher Education.

[1] SSB, "Communique on the Results of the Population Census of the Whole
   Country," *TCKTTH*, No. 8 (November, 1954), p. 1.
[2] Teng Hsiao-p'ing, "Census and General Election Completed in China:
   Population of China Over 600 Million," NCNA, Peking, June 19, 1954; reprinted in *1955 JMST*, p. 30.

TABLE 1.3 Total Population, 1949-58, Individuals

Year	SSB communique[a] (1)	Teng Hsiao-p'ing's report[a] (2)	June 30		December 31	
			$TCKT^{a,1}$ thousands (3)	$TCKT^{b,1}$ thousands (4)	Ministry of Health release,[b,2] millions (5)	Ministry of Health release,[c,2] millions (6)
1949			562,520	541,670	542	549
1950			573,180	551,960		
1951			584,330	563,000		
1952			596,150	574,820	575	582
1953	601,938,035[3]	601,912,371[4]	609,290	587,960		
1954			624,480	601,720		
1955			638,630	614,650		
1956			652,300[d]	627,800[d]		
1957					647	657
1958						

Year	December 31					Annual average	
	$TGY^{c,5}$ thousands (7)	Hu Huang-yung[b] (8)	Hu Huang-yung[c] (9)	Hsü Kang,[e] millions (10)	DuBois,[e] millions (11)	$TCKT^{a,1}$ thousands (12)	$TCKT^{b,1}$ thousands (13)
1949	548,770					557,010	536,360
1950						567,850	546,820
1951						578,760	557,480
1952						590,240	568,910
1953	595,550					602,720	581,390
1954		604,666,212[6]	613,283,212[6]			616,890	594,840
1955						631,560	608,180
1956	656,630					645,470[d]	621,230[d]
1957				670[7]			
1958					680[8]		

TABLE 1.3 (Continued)

a Including the population in Taiwan, overseas Chinese, and students abroad.

b Excluding the population in Taiwan, overseas Chinese, and students abroad.

c Excluding overseas Chinese and students abroad, but including the population in Taiwan.

d Preliminary estimates (see text).

e Coverage unspecified.

1 Data Office, *TCKT*, "Statistical Data on China's Population," *TCKT*, No. 11 (January 14, 1957), pp. 24-25.

2 U.S. Bureau of the Census, *The Size, Composition, and Growth of the Population of Mainland China*, by John S. Aird, International Population Statistics Reports, Series P-90, No. 15, Washington, D.C.: U.S. Government Printing Office, 1961, pp. 45-46. The original source of the figures was a release from the Ministry of Health in Peking without any title or issuing agency designation. Its contents were never formally published in any Chinese source.

3 SSB, "Communique on the Results of the Population Census of the Whole Country (released on November 1, 1954)," *TCKTH*, No. 8 (November, 1954), pp. 1-2.

4 Teng Hsiao-p'ing, "Census and General Election Completed in China: Population of China Over 600 Million," NCNA, Peking, June 19, 1954; reprinted in *1955 JMST*, p. 30.

5 *TGY*, p. 8.

6 Hu Huan-yung, "An Index Chart of Area and Population of China by Province and Region," *TLCS*, Vol. 8, No. 9 (September, 1957), pp. 390-91. It may be noted that there is a discrepancy between the 1954 year-end total population, excluding Taiwan and overseas population, given by Hu and that given in the June, 1957, issue of *TCKT* (in column 4). Aird thinks the discrepancy is probably "due to revisions of the official figures made after the June 1957 release." (U.S. Bureau of the Census, *op. cit.*, p. 41).

7 Hsu Kang, "Make a Success of Wage Statistical Work in 1959," *CHYTC*, No. 4 (February 23, 1959).

8 DuBois, "Excerpts of DuBois Speech," NCNA, Peking, February 24, 1959. Also, "I Sing to China," *China Reconstructs*, Vol. 8, No. 6 (June, 1959), p. 24.

TABLE 1.4 Population by Ethnic Groups, June 30, 1953[a]

Ethnic group	Major geographic distribution[1]	Number[2]
Total		582,603,417
Han	All provinces, municipalities, and regions of China.	547,283,057
Mongolian	Inner Mongolian Autonomus Region, Liaoning, and other provinces	1,462,956
Hui	Ningsia Hui Autonomous Region, Kansu, and other provinces	3,559,350
Tibetan	Tibet, Szechuan, Chinghai, and other provinces.	2,775,622
Uighur	Sinkiang Uighur Autonomous Region	3,640,125
Miao	Kweichow, Yunnan, Hunan, and other provinces	2,511,339
Yi	Szechuan, Yunnan, and other provinces.	3,254,269
Chuang	Kwangsi Chunag Autonomous Region, Yunnan, and other provinces	6,611,455
Puyi	Kweichow	1,247,883
Korean	Kirin and other provinces	1,120,405
Manchu	Liaoning, Kirin, Heilungkiang, and other provinces.	2,418,931
Others		6,718,025
Tung	Kweichow and other provinces	
Yao, Molao, Maonan	Kwangsi Chuang Autonomous Region	
Pai, Hani, Tai, Lisu, Kawa, Masi, Lahu, Chingpo, Pulang, Achang, Nu, Penglung, Tulung	Yunnan	
Tuchia	Hunan and Hupeh	
Li, Ching	Kwangtung	
Yu	Fukien and Chekiang	
Kaoshan	Taiwan	
Tunghsiang, Paoan, Yuku	Kansu	
Khalkha, Russian, Sibo, Tadjik, Uzbek, Tartar	Sinkiang Uighur Autonomous Region	
Tu, Sala	Chinghai	
Tahur, Owenke, Olunchun	Inner Mongolian Autonomous Region and Heilungkiang	
Hoche	Heilungkiang	
Chiang	Szechuan	

[a] Approximate numbers of some 50 national minorities in China are given in the *1957, 1958, and 1959 People's Handbooks*. It is not known to which date these figures pertain. (*1957 JMST*, pp. 623-24; *1958 JMST*, pp. 650-51; and *1959 JMST*, pp. 217-19.

[1] *TGY*, pp. 9-10.
[2] SSB, "Communique on the Results of the Population Census of the Whole Country," *TCKTTH*, No. 8 (November, 1955), p. 2.

TABLE 1.5 Urban and Rural Population, 1949-56[a]

Year	June 30 Total (1)	June 30 Urban (2)	June 30 Rural (3)	Year-end number, thousands Total[1] (4)	Year-end number, thousands Urban[b,1] (5)	Year-end number, thousands Rural[1] (6)	Average annual, thousands Total[1] (7)	Average annual, thousands Urban[1] (8)	Average annual, thousands Rural[1] (9)
1949				541,670	57,650	484,020	536,360	55,640	480,720
1950				551,960	61,690	490,270	546,820	59,670	487,150
1951				563,000	66,320	496,680	557,480	64,010	493,470
1952				574,820	71,630	503,190	568,910	68,980	499,930
1953	582,603,417	77,257,283[c,2]	505,346,135[2]	587,960	77,670	510,290	581,390	74,560[c]	506,740
1954				601,720	81,550	520,170	594,840	79,610	515,230
1955				614,650	82,850[d]	531,800	608,180	82,200[d]	525,980
1956				627,800	89,150[e]	538,650	621,123	86,000[e]	535,230

[a] Excluding the population in Taiwan, overseas Chinese, and students abroad.

[b] Including those living in towns in the suburbs of cities but excluding those living in villages in such suburbs.

[c] The annual average urban population for 1956 is 2.6 million persons fewer than the reported census total for June 30, 1953. The difference cannot be explained with the available information.

[d] The relatively slow increase in urban population in 1955 was due to the transfer of part of the urban population to rural areas to engage in agricultural production. In Shanghai and Tientsin alone, 700,000 persons left in that year, and a large part of them went to rural areas.

[e] The figure of urban population for 1956 was a preliminary estimate based on an assumed 7.6 percent increase over that in 1955. (The 1956 annual population reports from 14 provinces and 3 independent municipalities showed that the urban population in these areas increased by 7.66 percent as compared with that in 1955).

[1] Data Office, TCKT, "Statistical Data on the Population Census of Our Country," TCKT, No. 11 (June 14, 1957), pp. 24-25.

[2] SSB, "Communique on the Results of the Population Census of the Whole Country, November 1, 1954," TCKTTH, No. 8 (November, 1954), pp. 1-2.

TABLE 1.6 Number of Cities and Towns by Size of Population, 1952, 1953, ans 1957[a]

Size of population	Number of cities with 50,000 persons or more		Number of cities and towns in June, 1952			Urban population in June 1953, thousands		
	December, 1952[1]	December, 1957[1]	Total	Number[b] of cities	Number of towns	Total	Cities	Towns
	(1)	(2)	(3)	(4)	(5)	(6)	(7)	(8)
Total	159	176	5,568	422[2]	5,148	77,257[3]	51,320	(25,937)[4]
5,000,000 or more	1	1	1	1[5]				
3,000,000 to 4,999,999		2						
1,000,000 to 2,999,999	8	11	8	8[5]				
500,000 to 999,999	15	20	16	16[5]			51,320[2]	
100,000 to 499,999	81	90	78	78[5]				
50,000 to 99,999	54	52	(319)	(319)[6]				
20,000 to 49,999								
2,000 to 19,999			4,226	4,226[2]				24,699[2]
1,000 to 1,999			727	727[2]				(1,101)[7]
Fewer than 1,000			193	193[2]				137[2]

[a] Urban areas with a total population of 20,000 or more are classifed as cities, and all other urban areas are regarded as towns.

[b] Different figures were given by I I-chu in his "Notes on 'The Wall Map of China's Population Density,'' in *TLCS*, Vol. 7, (November, 1956), pp. 502-4. According to I I-chu, the number of cities with breakdown by size in June, 1953, were as follows:

Size of population	Number of cities
Total	488
1,000,000 or more	9
500,000 to 999,999	15
200,000 to 499,999	34
100,000 to 199,999	51
50,000 to 99,999	72
20,000 to 49,999	307

[1] *TGY*, p. 13.

[2] SSB, "Explanation of Several Major Questions Concerning the Criteria for Remarcation of Urban and Rural Areas," *TCKTTH*, No. 12 (December 17, 1955), pp. 5-6.

[3] Table 1.5.

[4] The residual of the total urban population, as given in column 6, minus the urban population in the cities, as given in column 7.

[5] Table 1.7.

[6] Derived from Table 1.7 and figures cited in source 2.

[7] The residual of the urban population in all the towns, minus the urban population in those towns with a total population of between 2,000 and 19,999 and less than 1,000.

TABLE 1.7 Population of Selected Cities by Province or Equivalent, 1953 and 1957[a]

Province and city	June 30, 1953, Individuals (1)	Dec. 31, 1957, thousands (2)	Province and city	June 30, 1953, Individuals (1)	Dec. 31, 1957, thousands (2)
Centrally-controlled municipalities:			Heilungkiang:		
Peking	2,768,149[1]	4,010[2]	Harbin	1,163,000[1]	1,552[2]
Shanghai	6,204,417[1]	6,900[2]	Ch'i-ch'i-ha-erh	344,700[1]	668
Hopei:			Mu-tan-chiang	151,400[1]	
Tientsin	2,693,831[1]	3,220[2]	Chia-mu-ssu	146,000[1]	
T'ang-shan	693,300[1]	800[2]	Ho-kang	90,000[7]	
Shih-chia-chuang	373,400[1]	598[2]	Pei-an	70,000[8]	
Chang-chia-kou (Kalgan)	229,300[1]		Shensi:		
Pao-ting	197,000[1]	265[3]	Sian	787,300[1]	1,310[2]
Ch'in-huang-tao	186,800[1]		Pao-chi	130,100[1]	
Hsuan-hua	114,100[1]		Han-chung	70,000[8]	
Ch'eng-te	92,900[1]		Hsien-yang	70,000[8]	
Han-tan	90,000[4]		Kansu:		
Shansi:			Lan-chou	397,400[1]	699[2]
T'ai-yuan	720,700[1]	1,020[2]	Yin-ch'uan[c]	84,000[9]	
Ta-t'ung	228,500[1]		T'ien-shui	63,000[5]	
Yang-ch'uan	177,400[5]		P'ing-liang	60,000[10]	
Ch'ang-chih	97,800[5]		Chinghai:		
Yu-tz'u	60,000[5]		Hsi-ning	93,700[1]	300[3]
Fen-yang	25,000[5]		Sinkiang Uighur Autonomous Region:		
Inner Mongolia Autonomous Region:			Urumchi	140,700[1]	275[3]
Pao-t'ou	149,000[1]		I-ning	108,200[1]	
Huehehot	148,400[1]	314[3]	Kashgar	91,000[9]	
Ulanhot	51,400[5]		So-ch'e	80,000[9]	
Hailar	43,200[5]		Shantung:		
Man-chou-li	30,000[6]		Tsingtao	916,800[1]	1,121[2]
Liaoning:			Tsinan	680,100[1]	862[2]
Shengyang (Mukden)	2,299,900[1]	2,411[2]	Chefoo	116,000[1]	806[2]
Lu-ta (Port Arthur-Dairen)[b]	892,400[1]	1,508[2]	Tzu-pu	184,200[1]	
Fu-shun	678,600[1]	985[2]	Wei-fang	148,900[1]	
An-shan	548,900[1]	805[2]	Chi-ning	86,200[5]	
Pen-chi	449,000[1]		Kiangsu:		
An-tung	360,000[1]		Nanking	1,091,600[1]	1,419[2]
Chin-chou	352,200[5]		Wu-hsi	581,500[1]	613[2]
Fou-hsin	188,600[5]		Soochow	474,000[1]	633[2]
Ying-kou	131,400[1]		Hsuchow	373,200[1]	676[2]
Ch'ao-yang	126,000[1]		Ch'ang-chou	296,500[1]	
Kirin:			Nan-t'ung	260,400[1]	
Ch'ang-ch'un	855,200[1]	975[2]		230,000[5]	
Kirin	435,200[1]	565[2]	Hsin-hai-lien:	207,600[1]	
T'ung-hua	129,100[1]		Chen-chiang	201,400[1]	
Ssu-p'ing	125,900[1]		Yang-chou	180,200[1]	
Liao-yuan	120,100[1]		T'ai-chou	159,800[1]	
Yen-chi	70,000[5]		Ch'ang-shu	101,400[1]	
			Ch'ing-chiang	77,000[5]	
			Yen-cheng	50,000[5]	

TABLE 1.7 (Continued, 1)

Province and city	June 30, 1953, Individuals (1)	Dec. 31, 1957, thousands (2)	Province and city	June 30, 1953, Individuals (1)	Dec. 31, 1957, thousands (2)
Anhwei:			Kwangtung:		
Huai-nan	286,900[1]		Canton	1,598,900[1]	1,840[2]
Pang-fou	253,000[1]		Swatow	280,400[1]	
Wu-hu	242,100[1]		Chan-chiang	166,000[1]	
Ho-fei	183,600[1]	304[3]	Hai-k'ou	135,300[1]	
An-ch'ing	105,300[1]		Fo-shan	122,500[1]	
Chekiang:			Ch'ao-chou	101,300[1]	
Hangchow	696,600[1]	784[2]	Shih-ch'i	93,000[11]	
Ningpo	237,500[1]		Chiang-men	85,000[5]	
Wenchow	201,600[1]		Shao-kuan	81,700[5]	
Shao-hsing	130,600[1]		Pei-hai	80,000[11]	
Chia-hsing	78,300[5]		Kwangsi:		
Hu-chou	63,000[11]		Nan-ning	194,600[1]	264[3]
Chin-hua	46,200[5]		Liu-chou	158,800[1]	
Fukien:			Kuei-lin	145,100[1]	
Foochow	553,000[1]	616[2]	Wu-chou	110,800[1]	
Amoy	224,300[1]		Szechuan:		
Ch'uan-chou	107,700[1]		Chungking	1,772,500[1]	2,121[2]
Chang-chou	81,200[5]		Ch'eng-tu	856,700[1]	1,107[2]
Honan:			Tzu-kung	291,300[1]	
Cheng-chou	594,700[1]	766[2]	Lu-chou	289,000[1]	
K'ai-feng	299,100[1]		Wu-t'ung-ch'iao	199,100[1]	
Lo-yang	171,200[1]		Nei-chiang	190,200[1]	
Hsin-hsiang	170,500[1]			160,000[5]	
	143,000[5]		I-pin	177,500[1]	
Shang-ch'iu	134,400[1]		Nan-ch'ung	164,700[1]	
An-yang	124,900[1]		Ya-an	55,200[1]	
Chou-k'ou	85,500[5]		Kweichow:		
Hsu-ch'ang	58,000[5]		Kuei-yang	270,900[1]	504[2]
Hupeh:			Tsun-i	97,500[5]	
Wuhan	1,427,300[1]	2.146[2]	Yunnan:		
Huang-shih	110,500[1]		K'un-ming	698,900[1]	880[2]
Sha-shih	85,800[5]		Ko-chiu	159,700[1]	
Hsiang-fan	73,300[5]		Chao-t'ung	50,000[5]	
Hunan:			Hsia-kuan	26,200[5]	
Ch'ang-sha	650,600[1]	703[2]	Tibet:		
Heng-yang	235,000[1]		Lhasa	70,000[10]	
Hsiang-t'an	183,600[1]		Shigatse	26,000[10]	
Chu-chou	127,300[1]				
Shao-yang	117,700[1]				
Ch'ang-te	94,800[5]				
Kiangsi:					
Nan-ch'ang	398,200[1]	508[2]			
Kan-chou	98,600[5]				
Ching-te-chen	92,000[5]				
Chiu-chiang	64,600[5]				
Chi-an	52,800[5]				
Feng-ch'eng	30,000[5]				

TABLE 1.7 (Continued, 2)

[a] The cities included in this table are those whose population data have become available The 1953 figures are census data, and the 1957 figures are registration data.

[b] The reported population in 1953 was 126,000 for Port Arthur and 766,400 for Dairen.

[c] Yin-ch'uan is now in Ningsia Hui Autonomous Region, which was established in October, 1958.

[1] A.G. Shiger, *Administrativno-territorial 'noye deleniye zarubezhnykh stran (Administrative-Territorial Division of Foreign Countries)*, 2nd ed., Moscow, 1957, pp. 142-4. Population figures for Chinese cities in this and the following Soviet sources are based on the data from the 1953 census. The figures from Soviet sources shown in this table were assembled primarily by Morris B. Ullman. See U.S. Bureau of the Census, *Cities of Mainland China: 1953 and 1958*, by Morris B. Ullman, International Population Reports, Series P-95, No. 59, Washington, D.C.: U.S. Government Printing Office, August, 1961.

[2] *TGY*, p. 12.

[3] S. Chandrasekhar, *China's Population, Census and Vital Statistics*, Hong Kong University Press, 1959, p. 47.

[4] Institute of Geography, Academia Sinica, *Hua-pei ching-chi ti-li (Economic Geography of North China)*, Peking, July, 1957.

[5] *Bol'shaya Sovetskaya entsiklopediya (Great Soviet Encyclopedia)*, 2nd ed., Moscow.

[6] Sun Ching-chih, Teng Ching-chung, *et al.*, *Nei-meng-Ku tzu-chih ch'u ching-chi ti-li (Economic Geography of Inner Mongolia Autonomous Region)*, Peking: K'o-hsueh ch'u-pan she, March, 1956, p. 49.

[7] *China Pictorial*, Peking, July, 1954, p. 7.

[8] *Chung-kuo fen-sheng ti-t'u shuo-ming (An Explanation of Provincial Atlas of China)*, 3rd ed., Shanghai: Ti-t'u ch'u-pan she, 1957.

[9] V.G. Kalmykova and I. Kh. Ovdiyenko, *Severo-zapadnyy Kitay (Northwest China)*, Moscow, 1957, p. 175.

[10] *Chung hua jen-min kung-ho-kuo fen-sheng ching-t'u (Detailed Provincial Atlas of the Chinese People's Republic)*, Shanghai: Ti-t'u ch'u-pan she, 1955.

[11] Liang Jen-ts'ai, *Kwang-tung ching-chi ti-li (Economic Geography of Kwangtun)*, Peking, November, 1956.

TABLE 1.8 Population by Province or Equivalent, 1953, 1954, and 1957, Individuals

Province or equivalent	June 30, 1953 [a,1]	December 31, 1954 [b,2]	December 31, 1957, [c,3] thousands
	(1)	(2)	(3)
Total	601,938,035	613,283,212	656,630
Peking	2,768,149		4,010
Tientsin	2,693,831		
Shanghai	6,204,417		6,900
Hopei	35,984,644	44,433,926 [d]	44,720 [e]
Shansi	14,314,485	14,785,716	15,960
Inner Mongolia Autonomous Region	6,100,104	8,800,000	9,200
Liaoning	18,545,147	21,517,859	24,090
Kirin	11,290,073	11,767,059	12,550
Heilungkiang	11,897,309	12,760,694	14,86)
Jehol [f]	5,160,822		
Shensi	15,881,281	16,663,882	18,130
Kansu [g]	12,928,102	11,594,477	12,800
Ningsia Hui Autonomous Region		1,728,000	1,810
Chinghai	1,676,534	1,768,155	2,050
Sinkiang Uighur Autonomous Region	4,873,608	5,144,700	5,640
Shantung	48,876,548	50,517,020	54,030
Kiangsu	41,252,192	49,228,742 [h]	45,230
Anhwei	30,343,637	31,426,023	33,560
Chekiang	22,865,747	23,589,903	25,280
Fukien	13,142,721	13,682,540	14,650
Honan	44,214,594	46,026,234	48,670
Hupeh	27,789,693	28,653,885	30,790
Hunan	33,226,954	34,296,029	36,220
Kiangsi	16,772,865	17,297,442	18,610
Kwangtung	34,770,059	35,899,744	37,960
Kwangsi Chuang Autonomous Region	19,560,822	20,180,046	19,390
Szechuan	62,303,999	68,043,102	72,160
Kweichow	15,037,310	15,570,491	16,890
Yunnan	17,472,737	18,017,543	19,100
Sikang [i]	3,381,064		
Tibet and Changtu area	1,273,969	1,273,000	1,270
Taiwan	7,591,298	8,617,000	10,100
Overseas Chinese, students abroad, etc.	11,743,320		

[a] 1953 census figures.

[b] The 1954 figures are registration data. The figures were taken according to the administrative divisions as of 1957.

[c] The 1957 figures are registrative data. Figures for Hopei, Kansu, and Ningsia Hui Autonomous Region were taken according to the administrative divisions as of the end of 1958. The rest were taken according to the administrative divisions as of the end of 1957.

[d] Including Peking and Tientsin.

[e] Including Tientsin.

[f] Jehol Province was abolished in 1955 with its area incorporated into Hopei and Liaoning Provinces and the Inner Mongolia Autonomous Region.

[g] In August, 1958, Kansu Province was reduced in size by the establishment of the Ningsia Hui Autonomous Region.

[h] Including Shanghai.

[i] Sikang Province was abolished in 1955 and its area merged into Szechwan Province.

[1] SSB, "Communique of the Results of the Population Census of the Whole Country," *TCKTTH*, No. 8 (November, 1955), p. 2.

[2] Hu Huang-yung, "An Index Chart of Area and Population of China by Province and Region," *TLCS*, Vol. 8, No. 9 (September, 1957), pp. 390-391.

[3] *TGY*, pp. 11-12.

TABLE 1.9 Male and Female Population, 1949, 1952, 1953, and 1957

Year	June 30, 1953						Year-end number					
	SSB Census Communique[a,1] thousands			SSB Census Communique[b,2] thousands			TGY[c,3] thousands			Ministry of Health Release,[c,4] millions		
	Total	Male	Female	Total	Male	Female	Total	Male	Female	Total	Male	Female
	(1)	(2)	(3)	(4)	(5)	(6)	(7)	(8)	(9)	(10)	(11)	(12)
1949												
1952							548,770	285,140	263,630			
1953	574,205,940	297,553,518	276,652,422	582,603	302,101	280,502	595,550	308,850	286,700	582	302	280
1957							656,630	340,140	316,490			

[a] By direct census registration only.

[b] Excluding the population in Taiwan, overseas Chinese, and students abroad.

[c] Including the population in Taiwan but excluding overseas Chinese and students abroad.

1 SSB, "Communique on the Results of the Population Census of the Whole Country," TCKTTH, No. 8 (November, 1954), pp. 1-2.

2 Tien Feng-t'ap, "The Problem of Planned Birth and Population Growth in Our Country," Jen-min pao-chien (People's Health) Vol. 1, No. 5 (May, 1959), p. 463.

3 TGY, p. 8.

4 The original source of the figure was a release from the Ministry of Health in Peking, without any title or issuing agency designation. See note 2 to Table 1.3

TABLE 1.10 Distribution of the Population of Mainland China by Age, [a] June 30, 1953

Ch'en Ta's data[1]		T'ien Feng-t'iao's data[2]		SSB Communique[3]	
Age groups	Percentage distribution	Age groups	Percentage distribution	Age groups	Number
All ages	100.0	All ages	99.9	All ages	574,205,940
Under 1 year	3.3	0 - 6 years	20.44	Under 18 years	235,866,048
1 - 4 years	12.3	7 - 19 years	24.58	18 years and above of	
5 - 14 years	20.3	20 - 29 years	16.00	which:	
15 - 24 years	17.3	30 - 39 years	13.29		
25 - 34 years	14.6	40 - 49 years	10.57		
35 - 44 years	12.0	50 - 59 years	7.85	80 -99 years	1,851,312
45 - 54 years	9.3	60 years and over	7.26	100 years and above	3,384
55 - 64 years	6.5				
65 - 74 years	3.4				
74 years and over	1.0				

[a] By direct census registration

[1] Ch'en Ta, *New China's Population Census of 1953 and Its Relations to National Reconstruction and Demographic Research,* Stockholm: International Statistical Institute, August, 1957, Table 4, p.23.

[2] T'ien Feng-t'iao, "The Problem of Planned Birth and Population Increase in Our Country," *Jen-min pao-chien,* Vol. 1, No. 5 (May, 1959), p. 462

[3] SSB, "Communique on the Results of the Population Census of the Whole Country," *TCKTTH,* No. 8 (November, 1954), p. 2.

TABLE 1.11   Distribution of the Population of Mainland China by Age and Sex,
             June 30, 1953

Tai Shih-kuang's data[1]		T'ien Feng-t'iao's data[2]			
Age groups	Males per 1,000 females	Age groups	Number, thousands		
			Both sexes	Male	Female
All ages	107.7	All ages	582,603	302,101	280,502
Under 1 year	104.9	0 - 4 years	90,871	46,796	44,075
1 and 2 years	106.2	5 - 9 years	63,720	33,760	29,960
3 - 6 years	110.0	10 - 14 years	54,738	29,553	25,185
7 - 13 years	115.8	15 - 19 years	52,971	27,995	24,976
14 - 17 years	113.7	20 - 24 years	48,106	25,001	23,105
18 - 35 years	111.5	25 - 29 years	45,116	24,034	21,082
36 - 55 years	106.8	30 - 34 years	40,146	21,379	18,767
56 years and		35 - 39 years	37,288	19,412	17,876
over	86.7	40 - 44 years	32,337	16,688	15,649
		45 - 49 years	29,261	14,948	14,313
		50 - 54 years	24,798	12,675	12,123
		55 - 59 years	20,936	10,598	10,338
		60 - 64 years	16,897	8,221	8,676
		65 - 69 years	11,909	5,532	6,377
		70 - 74 years	7,960	3,361	4,599
		75 - 79 years	3,695	1,499	2,169
		80 - 84 years	1,225	453	772
		85 years and over	629	196	433

[1] Tai Shih-kuang, *1953 Population Census of China*, Calcutta: Indian Statistical Institute, December 1956, p. 21.

[2] The dates were derived by John S. Aird from an age-sex pyramid given in T'ien Feng-t'iao, "The Planned Birth and Population Increase in Our Country," *Jen-min pao-chien*, Vol. 1, No. 5 (May, 1959), p. 463, with extrapolation for ages 80 years and over. See U.S. Bureau of the Census, *The Size, Composition, and Growth of the Population of Mainland China*, by John S. Aird, International Population Statistics Reports, Series P-90, No. 15, Washington, D.C.: U.S. Government Printing Office, 1961, p. 67.

TABLE 1.12 Crude Birth and Death Rates per 1,000 Population

Year	Birth rate	Death rate	Natural increase
1952	37	18	19
1953	37	17	20
1954	38	13	24
1955	35	12.4	22.6
1956	32	11.4	20.6
1957	34	11	23

Sources: S. Chandrasekhar, *China's Population Census and Vital Statistics,* Hong Kong University Press, 1959, p. 50. The rates in the above table were given to Chandrasekhar when he visited China in December, 1958, by the official agency concerned with vital statistics. In August of the same year, Roland Pressat obtained the figures in Table 1.12A from the State Statistical Bureau.

TABLE 1.12A

Rate	1952	1954	1957
Number, thousands			
Births	21,510	21,560	21,660
Deaths	9,880	7,790	6,890
Natural increase	11,630	13,770	14,770
Rate, per thousand			
Births	37	37	34
Deaths	17	13	11
Natural increase	20	24	23

Source: Roland Pressat, "La population de la Chine et son economie," *Population*, Vol. 13, No. 4, October- December, 1958, p. 570.

TABLE 1.13 Crude Birth and Death Rates in Nine Chinese Cities, 1952-57 per 1,000 Population

City	Birth rates						Death rates					
	1952	1953	1954	1955	1956	1957	1952	1953	1954	1955	1956	1957
Peking[a]	35.0[1]	39.6[1]	43.1[1]	43.2[1]	39.3[1]		9.3[1]	9.3[1]	7.7[1]	8.1[1]	6.7[1]	
				40.6[2]	39.2[2]	42.0[2]				9.6[2]	7.6[2]	7.1[2]
Tientsin	27.1[1]	39.5[1]	44.9[1]	43.9[1]	40.2[1]		6.0[1]	8.6[1]	7.6[1]	8.4[1]	6.6[1]	
Shanghai	38.0[1]	40.4[1]	52.6[1]	41.4[1]	40.3[1]		12.4[1]	9.9[1]	7.6[1]	8.1[1]	6.7[1]	
		40.4[2]	52.6[2]	41.4[2]	40.2[2]	45.7[2]		9.9[2]	7.6[2]	8.1[2]	6.7[2]	5.9[2]
Harbin	47.0[1]	48.1[1]	53.1[1]	47.3[1]	41.3[1]		14.8[1]	15.9[1]	9.7[1]	10.6[1]	8.5[1]	
Sian	33.3[1]	41.2[1]	49.9[1]	45.3[1]	47.7[1]		9.5[1]	7.4[1]	6.9[1]	7.4[1]	7.4[1]	
Hangchow	40.1[1]	40.6[1]	45.4[1]	39.6[1]	36.8[1]		12.4[1]	9.7[1]	9.0[1]	9.6[1]	8.5[1]	
Canton	36.7[1]	41.8[1]	43.7[1]	39.5[1]	39.0[1]		9.2[1]	7.9[1]	7.2[1]	7.0[1]	6.8[1]	
Changchun					45.5[1]						7.2[1]	
Hofei					32.4[1]						6.0[1]	

[a] An article in *JMJP* gives some statistics on the number of births, deaths and natural increase from 1950 to 1956 for Peiping. The figures are given in Table 1.13A.

[1] Roland Pressat, "La population de la Chine et son economie," *Population*, Vo. 13, No. 4, October-December, 1958, pp. 572-573.

[2] S. Chandrasekar, *China's Population, Census and Vital Statistics,* Hong Kong University Press, p. 51.

TABLE 1.13A

Year	Births	Deaths	Natural increase
1950	71,712	29,190	43,522
1951	78,801	32,578	46,223
1952	79,917	25,274	54,643
1953	83,456	21,823	61,633
1954	121,057	27,722	93,335
1955	128,275	30,302	97,973
1956	131,232	25,034	106,198

Source: Sun Kuang, "Urban Population Must be Controlled,"
JMJP, November 27, 1957.

TABLE 1.14 Infant Mortality Rates in Rural and Urban Areas and in Nine Cities, 1949-57
(Deaths below One Year of Age per 1,000 Births)

Area	1949	1952	1953	1954	1955	1956	1957
Rural and urban:							
Rural				138.52	109.66		
Urban				47	42	35	32
Cities:							
Peking	117.6	65.7	59.3	46.1	44.5	35.1	35.4
Tientsin		46.8	51.1	45.3	40.9	29.9	
Shanghai		81.2	51.3	35.1	43.4	31.1	
Harbin		86.6	85.0	45.1	50.1	40.0	
Sian		44.3	45.8	43.3	35.1	33.3	
Hangchow		64.0	51.6	44.6	42.1	42.4	
Canton		47.7	37.0	35.2	31.8	25.1	
Changchun				50.7	30.2	43.8	
Hofei				39.9	40.9	40.6	

Sources: S. Chandrasekhar, *China's Population, Census and Vital Statistics*, Hong Kong
University Press, 1959, pp. 53-54. The data were supplied to Chandrasekhar by the
Ministry of Health in Peking. The same figures for the nine cities from 1952 to
1956 were given to Pressat by the State Statistical Bureau. (See Roland Pressat,
"La population de la Chine et son economie,"*Population*, Vol. 13, No, 4, October-
December, 1958, pp. 572-73.)

137

TABLE 2.1 Gross Social-Value Output at 1952 Prices by Materially Productive Sectors, 1952-56, in Million Yuan

Year	Total	Agriculture[1]	Industry[1]	Construction[2]	Transportation[3] and communications	Trade (including restaurants)[3]
	(1)	(2)	(3)	(4)	(5)	(6)
1952	(102,839)[4]	48,390	34,330	4,560	(3,410)	(12,149)
1953	122,290[5]	49,910	44,700	n.a.	n.a.	n.a.
1954	132,860[5]	51,570	51,970	n.a.	n.a.	n.a.
1955	n.a.	55,540	54,870	n.a.	n.a.	n.a.
1956	(167,425)[4]	58,290	70,360	14,400	(6,197)	(18,196)

[1] *TGY*, pp. 16-17.

[2] Yang Po, "An Understanding of the Proportion between Consumption and Accumulation in the National Expenditure of China," *HH*, No. 20 (October 18, 1957), p. 24

[3] Table 2.2

[4] The sum total of the gross value outputs of the materially productive sectors in that year.

[5] Niu Chung-huang, *Accumulation and Consumption in China's National Income*, Peking: Chung-kuo chin-nien ch'u-pan-she, 1957, p. 16.

TABLE 2.2 Gross-Value Output, Material Outlays and Net-Value Output of Various Materially
Productive Sectors, at 1952 Prices, 1952-56, in Million Yuan

Indicator	1952	1953	1954	1955	1956
Agriculture:					
Gross-value output[1]	48,390	49,910	51,570	55,540	58,290
Material outlays[2]	(12,201)	n.a.	n.a.	(14,285)	(15,601)
Net-value output[3]	(36,189)	n.a.	n.a.	(41,255)	(42,689)
Industry:					
Gross-value output[1]	34,330	44,700	51,970	54,870	70,360
Material outlays[2]	(23,327)	(29,992)	(34,682)	(36,273)	(46,930)
Net-value output[3]	(11,003)	(14,708)	(17,288)	(18,597)	(23,430)
Construction:					
Gross-value output[1]	4,560	n.a.	n.a.	n.a.	14,400
Material outlays[2]	(2,726)	n.a.	n.a.	n.a.	(9,430)
Net-value output[3]	(1,834)	(2,662)	(3,029)	(3,388)	(4,970)
Transportation and communications:					
Gross-value output[1]	(3,410)	n.a.	n.a.	n.a.	(6,179)
Material outlays[2]	(965)	n.a.	n.a.	n.a.	(2,274)
Net-value output[3]	(2,445)	(2,942)	(3,325)	(3,467)	(3,905)
Trade (including restaurants):					
Gross-value output[1]	(12,149)	n.a.	n.a.	n.a.	(18,196)
Material outlays[2]	(2,490)	n.a.	n.a.	n.a.	(4,528)
Net-value output[3]	(9,659)	n.a.	n.a.	(12,293)	(13,668)

[1] *TGY*, pp. 16-17.

[2] The material outlays are derived as residuals, subtracting from the gross-value output
the net-value output of the respective productive sectors.

[3] Table 2.5.

[4] Yang Po, "An Understanding of the Proportion between Consumption and Accumulation in
the National Expenditure of China," *HH*, No. 20 (October 18, 1957), p. 24.

[5] The changes in the proportion of the material outlays in the gross value output of
various productive sectors from 1952 to 1956 were given by Niu Chung-huang in his
Accumulation and Consumption of China's National Income (p. 26). The proportion increased from 28.3 percent to 36.8 percent in transportation and communications, and
from 20.2 percent to 24.4 percent in trade. Since the net value outputs of these
two sectors are already known, their respective gross value output can be derived
from the formula

$$\text{Gross-value output} = \frac{\text{net-value output}}{1 - \text{material outlays/gross-value output}}$$

TABLE 2.3 Gross Social-Value Output, Total Material
Outlays, and National Income, at 1952 Prices.
1952-57, in Million Yuan

Year	Gross social-value output	Total material outlays[1]	National income[2]
	(1)	(2)	(3)
1952	(102,839)[3]	(41,709)	61,130
1953	122,290[4]	(52,250)	70,040
1954	132,860[4]	(58,980)	73,880
1955	n. a.	n. a.	78,800
1956	(167,425)[3]	(78,675)	88,750
1957	177,800[5]	(84,150)[6]	(93,650)[7]

[1] The total material outlays are the residuals of
the gross social-value output minus national
income. They are also equal to the sum totals
of the material outlays of various productive
sectors given in Table 2.2.

[2] SSB, Rearch Office, "A Preliminary Analysis of
the Production and Distribution of China's
National Income," *TCYC*, No. 1 (January 23,
1958), p. 11. The figure for 1956 is a preliminary estimate.

[3] Table 2.1.

[4] Niu Chung-huang, *Accumulation and Consumption
in China's National Income,* Peking: Chung-
kuo chin-nien chu-pan-she, 1957, p. 16.

[5] Data Office, *TCYC,* " The Great Achievements
of China's National Economic Construction
in the Past Nine Years," *TCYC,* No. 9
(September, 1958), p. 2.

[6] According to the source cited in note 5, the
national income for 1957 was given as 96.5
billion yuan. But this figure appeared to
to be inconsistent with either the preliminary data or the series revised later (see
Table 2.4). Had the figure been accepted
here, the total material outlays for 1957
would have been 81.3 billion yuan.

[7] Table 2.4.

TABLE 2.4 National Income, 1949-59

Indicator	1950	1951	1952	1953	1954	1955	1956	1957	1958	1959
Index:[a]										
1949=100:[1]	118.6	138.8	169.7	193.4	204.4	217.8	248.3	259.7	348.0[b]	
1952=100:										
TGY[1]			100.0	114.0	120.4	128.3	146.3	153.0	205.0	
Hsu Ti-hsin[2]			100.0	114.6	120.9	128.9	145.2[b]	153.2		
Preceding year=100:										
TGY[1]	118.6	117.0	122.3	114.0	105.7	106.5	114.0	104.6	134.0	(121.5)[3]
Wang Sheng-ming[4]	118.6	117.0	122.3	114.6	105.5	106.7	112.6[b]	105.5		
Amount, millions of yuan:										
At current prices			61,130[5]	(74,049)[6]	(77,358)[6]	(82,047)[6]	(93,180)[7]	(95,000)[8]		
At 1952 prices			61,130[5]	70,040[5]	73,880[5]	78,800[5]	88,750[5],[b]	93,650[5],[9]		
At 1957 prices								(95,000)[8]	(127,300)[8]	(154,720)[3]

[a] The indices are based on data at 1952 prices for the years 1949-57 and at 1957 prices for 1958 and 1959.

[b] Preliminary estimates.

[1] *TGY*, p. 20.

[2] Hsu Ti-hsin, *Analysis of China's National Economy in the Transition Period*, Peking: K'o-hsueh ch'u-pan she, re. ed., 1959, p. 249.

[3] SSB, *Communique on the Growth of China's National Economy in 1959*, Peking: Jen-min jih-pao she, January, 1960, p. 3. The national income increased by 62.8 percent in 1959 as compared with 1957.

[4] Wang Sheng-ming, "On Fluctutions in the Growth of a Socialist Economy," *CCYC*, No. 1 (January, 1960), p. 5.

[5] SSB, Research Office, "A Preliminary Analysis of the Production and Distribution of China's National Income," *TCYC*, No. 1 (January 23, 1958), p. 11. Also, Lu Kuang, "China's National Income," *Peking Review*, Vol. 1, No. 6 (April 8, 1958), p. 7.

[6] In the article by the Research Office of the State Statistical Bureau cited above, the percentages of basic construction appropriations in national income for 1953, 1954 and 1955 were given as 11, 12.4, and 11.6 percent, respectively. Basic construction appropriations were 8,145.4 million yuan in 1953, 9,592.38 million yuan in 1954, and 9,517.48 million yuan in 1955 (see Table 3.20). The national income at current prices for 1953 through 1955 were derived on the basis of these two sets of data.

[7] Based on the per capita national income at current prices in 1956 (which was 150 yuan), given on p. 12 of the SSB article cited above, and the average total population in 1956 (which was 621,230,000), given in Table 1.3.

[8] Li Fu-chun, "On the Big Leap Forward in China's Socialist Construction," *Hung-ch'i*, No. 19 (October, 1959), p. 37. According to Li Fu-chun, "as compared to 1957, the national income in 1958 increased by 32.3 billion yuan, representing a rate of growth of 34 per cent."

[9] Derived from multiplication of the national income in 1952 by 153.2 percent.

TABLE 2.5 National Income at 1952 Prices, by Materially Productive Sectors, 1952-56

Indicator	1952	1953	1954	1955	1956
Percentage distribution:					
National income	100.0	100.0	100.0	100.0	100.0
Agriculture[1]	59.2	n.a.	n.a.	n.a.	48.1
Industry[2]	18.0	21.0	23.4	23.6	26.4
Construction[2]	3.0	3.8	4.1	4.3	5.6
Transportation and communications[2]	4.0	4.2	4.5	4.4	4.4
Trade[1]	15.8	n.a.	n.a.	n.a.	15.5
Amount, million of yuan:					
National income[3]	61,130	70,040	73,880	78,800[5]	88,750
Agriculture	(36,189)[4]	n.a.	n.a.	(41,255)[5]	(42,689)[4]
Industry[4]	(11,003)	(14,708)	(17,288)	(18,597)	(23,430)
Construction[4]	(1,834)	(2,662)	(3,029)	(3,388)	(4,970)
Transportation and communications[4]	(2,445)	(2,942)	(3,325)	(3,467)	(3,905)
Trade	(9,659)[4]	n.a.	n.a.	(12,248)[5]	(13,756)[4]

[1] SSB, Research Office, "A Preliminary Analysis of Production and Distribution of China's National Income," *TCYC*, No. 1 (January, 1958), p.11.

[2] "Socialist Educational Materials for the Workers," *Chinese Workers (Chung-kuo kung-jen)*, No. 4 (Febuary 27, 1958), p. 7.

[3] Table 2.4.

[4] Derived from applying the percentages to the national income figures.

[5] Data Office, *TCKTTH*, "The Basic Situation of China's Construction Enterprise," *TCKTTH*, no. 24 (December 29, 1956), pp. 31-33. According to this article, the net value outputs of agriculture and trade increased by 14 and 26.8 percent, respectivly, during the period from 1952 to 1955. It may be noted that the sum total of the net value outputs of all material sectors in 1955 derived in this table amounts to 78,955 million yuan, which is large than the corresponding national income figure given in the table by an amount of 155 million yuan.

TABLE 2.6 National Income at 1952 Prices by Ownership of Enterprise, 1952-57

Indicator	1952	1953	1954	1955	1956	1957
Percentage distribution: [1]						
National income	100.0	100.0	100.0	100.0	100.0	100.0
State	19.1	23.9	26.8	28.0	32.2	33.2
Cooperative	1.5	2.5	4.8	14.1	53.4	56.4
Joint	0.7	0.9	2.1	2.8	7.3	7.6
Capitalist	6.9	7.9	5.3	3.5	--	--
Individual	71.8	64.8	61.0	51.6	7.1	2.8
Amount, millions of yuan:						
National income [2]	61,130	70,040	73,880	78,800	88,750	93,650
State [3]	(11,676)	(16,740)	(19,800)	(22,064)	(28,578)	(31,092)
Cooperative [3]	(917)	(1,751)	(3,546)	(11,111)	(47,393)	(52,819)
Joint [3]	(427)	(630)	(1,551)	(2,206)	(6,479)	(7,117)
Capitalist [3]	(4,218)	(5,533)	(3,916)	(2,758)	--	--
Individual [3]	(43,891)	(45,386)	(45,067)	(40,661)	(6,301)	(2,622)

[1] TGY, in a chart shown on an unnumbered page. Slightly different figures were published for 1952 and 1956 in a number of publications which appeared in late 1957 and early 1958. (Niu Chung-huang, *Accumulation and Consumption in China's National Income*, Peking, November, 1957, p. 22; Yang Po, "On the Distribution of China's National Income," CCYC, No. 6 (December, 1957), pp. 2-3; SSB, Research Office, "A Preliminary Analysis of Production and Distribution of China's National Income," TCYC, No. 1 (January, 1958), p. 11; and Lu Kuang, "China's National Income," Vo. 1, No. 6 (April 8, 1958), p. 7.). These figures were given as follows:

But the TGY series are consistent with the data given in the following publications, which appeared in late 1959 and early 1960: Hsu Ti-hsin, *An Analysis of China's National Economy in the Transition Period*, Peking, 1959, p. 248, and Yang Chien-pai, "On the Great Significance of the Production, Distribution and Expenditure of the National Income in a Socialist Economy," HCS, No. 3, 1960, p. 14.

[2] Table 2.4.

[3] Derived from applying the corresponding percentages to the national income figures.

Year	State	Cooperative	Joint	Capitalist	Individual
1952	19.3	1.6	0.7	7.0	71.4
1956	32.1	53.3	7.4	0.1	7.1

143

TABLE 2.7 Distribution between Accumulation and Consumption in National Expenditure, 1952-58

Indicator	1952	1953	1954	1955	1956	1957	1958
Percentage distribution:							
At current prices:[1]							
National expenditure	100.0	100.0	100.0	100.0	100.0		
Accumulation	18.2	21.4	22.3	20.9	22.5		
Consumption	81.8	78.6	77.7	79.1	77.5		
At 1952 prices:							
Hsu Ti-hsin's data:[2]							
National expenditure	100.0	100.0	100.0	100.0	100.0	100.0	
Accumulation	18.2	22.4	23.5	22.9	26.1	24.0	
Consumption	81.8	77.6	76.5	77.1	73.9	76.0	
Niu Chung-huang's data:[3]							
National expenditure	100.0	100.0	100.0	100.0	100.0		
Accumulation	16.1	17.4	21.9	20.4	22.8		
Consumption	83.9	82.6	78.1	79.6	77.2		
Po I-po's data:[4]							
National expenditure	100.0	100.0	100.0	100.0	100.0		
Accumulation	15.7	18.3	21.6	20.5	22.8		
Consumption	84.3	81.7	78.4	79.5	77.2		
Price basis unspecified:							
Yen I-Shen's data:[5]							
National expenditure	100.0	100.0	100.0	100.0	100.0	100.0	
Accumulation	19.7	22.4	22.7	21.6	24.4	23.7	
Consumption	80.3	77.6	77.3	78.4	75.6	76.3	
Li Lin-ku's data:[6]							
National expenditure	100.0	n.a.	n.a.	n.a.	n.a.	100.0	
Accumulation	19.8	n.a.	n.a.	n.a.	n.a.	24.3	
Consumption	80.2	n.a.	n.a.	n.a.	n.a.	75.7	
Amount, millions of yuan:							
At current prices:							
National income[7]	61,130	(74,049)	(77,358)	(82,047)	(93,180)	(95,000)	
National expenditure[8]	(62,880)	(75,099)	(77,728)	(83,207)	(92,910)	(94,470)	
Accumulation[9]	(11,440)	(16,071)	(17,333)	(17,390)	(20,905)	(19,839)	
Consumption[9]	(51,440)	(59,028)	(60,395)	(65,637)	(72,005)	(74,631)	

TABLE 2.7 (Continued)

Indicator	1952	1953	1954	1955	1956	1957	1958
At 1952 prices:							
National income[7]	61,130	70,040	73,880	78,800	88,750	(93,650)	
National expenditure	(62,880)[8]	(71,489)[10]	(73,936)[10]	(79,376)[10]	(88,180)[1]	(92,540)[11]	
Accumulation	(11,440)[12]	(16,037)[13]	(17,375)[13]	(18,177)[13]	(23,010)[12]	(22,171)[14]	
Consumption	(51,440)[12]	(55,452)[15]	(56,561)[15]	(61,199)[15]	(65,170)[12]	(70,370)[14]	
At 1957 prices:							
National income						(95,000)[7]	(127,300)[7]
National expenditure						(94,470)[8]	
Accumulation						(19,839)[9]	(39,083)[16]
Consumption						(74,631)[9]	

1   SSB, Research Office, "A Preliminary Analysis of Pro-
    duction and Distribution of China's National Income,"
    TCYC, No. 1 (January, 1958), p. 12   Niu Chung-huang,
    *Accumulation and Consumption of China's National In-
    come*, Peking, 1957, p. 51; and Yang Po, "On the Dis-
    tribution of China's National Income," *CCYC*, No. 6
    (December, 1957), p. 5.

2   Hsu Ti-hsin, *An Analysis of China's National Economy in
    the Transition Period*, Peking: K'o-huseh ch'u-pan-she,
    1959,0. 262.

3   Niu Chung-huang, *op. cit.*

4   Po I-po, 'On the Correct Handling of the Problem of the
    Relationship between Accumulation and Consumption,"
    HHPYK, No. 20 (October, 1956), p. 74.

5   Yen I-shen, "Some Views on the Production of Means of
    Production and Materials for Consumption in Relation
    to Government Revenue and Expenditure," *CCYC*, No. 7
    July, 1959), p. 8.

6   Li Lin-ku, "The Structure of Socialism and the Popula-
    tion Problems," *HCS*, No. 4 (April, 1960), p. 51.

7   Table 2.4.

8   Derived from the national income figures at current
    prices, which are adjusted for balance in inter-
    national account.

9   Derived from appling the percentages to the corre-
    sponding figures on national expenditure.

10 Quotients of the figures on consumption divided by the
    ratios of consumption to national expenditure given by
    Hsu Ti-hsin.

11 The sum of components.

12 Derived from appling the precentages for 1952 and 1956
    to the corresponding national expenditure figures.

13 Derived as residuals.

14 Derived from the data on the percentage increase of
    accumulation and consumption during the First Five-
    Year Plan, given in Yang Chien-pai, "On the Great
    Significance of Production, Distribution, and Ex-
    penditure of the National Income in a Socialist
    Economy," *HCS*, No. 3 (March, 1960), p. 17.
    Accumulation and consumumtion at 1952 prices in-
    creased by 97 and 38 percent respectively, in 1957 as
    compared with 1952.

15 Derived from the data on the annual rates of growth of
    the total consumption expenditures at 1952 prices
    given in Niu Chung-huang, *op. cit.*, p. 71. These
    rates were 7.8, 2, 8.2, and 6.5 percent for 1953, 1954,
    1955, and 1956, respectively.

16 Accumulation in 1958 increased by 97 percent over the
    year. (Yang Chien-pai, *op. cit.*)

145

TABLE 3.1 Gross Value of Fixed Assets at Original Cost in the Entire
Economy and in Industry and Construction, 1949-59, [a]
Millions of Yuan

Year	Economy as a whole [b]	Industry		Construction [c]	
		TGY^1	$TCKT$	Total	Of which: Machinery and transportation equipment
	(1)	(2)	(3)	(4)	(5)
1949	(24,410) [2]	12,800	(12,840) [3]		
1950	n.a.	n.a.	n.a.		
1951	n.a.	n.a.	n.a.		
1952	(29,680) [2]	15,800	(15,850) [3]		
1953	n.a.	n.a.	n.a.	480 [4]	220 [5]
1954	n.a.	n.a.	n.a.	(806) [4]	(398) [5]
1955 [d]	(46,220) [2]	n.a.	(26,300) [3]	(1,078) [4]	(526) [5]
1956		n.a.	n.a.	(1,600) [6]	
1957		35,200	n.a.		
1958		47,400	n.a.		
1959			(57,840) [7]		

[a] Year-end estimates.

[b] Excluding government administration and individual economic units such as
peasants and handicraftsmen.

[c] Consisting only of the building and installation enterprises under the
jurisdiction of the central ministries.

[d] At the end of 1955 the percentage distribution of the gross fixed assets by
sectors was reported as 56 percent for industry, 33 percent for transportation, 6 percent for trade, and 5 percent for construction and service
industries. These figures appear to be very rough estimates and, therefore,
have not been used to derive the gross value of fixed assets of individual
sectors. (See Data Office, TCKT, "A General Survey of Industrial Capital in
China," TCKT, No. 1 (January 14, 1957), pp. 31-33, reference on p.31.)

[1] TGY, p. 93. Of the gross value of industrial fixed assets, 13,300 million
yuan in 1952, 29,300 million yuan in 1957, and 40,400 million yuan in 1958
were used for industrial production.

[2] The gross value of industrial fixed assets in 1949 was 52.6 percent of total
fixed assets, in 1952 53.4 percent of the total fixed assets, and in 1955
56.9 percent of total fixed assets. These figures are given in Chao I-wen,
"Socialist Transformation of the Capitalist Industry in China," TCKTTH,
No. 22 (November 29, 1956), pp. 25-33. Since the gross value of industrial
fixed assets in 1949, 1952 and 1955 has been given in column 3, the gross
value of total fixed assets in these three years can be readily derived.

[3] Table 3.2.

[4] Data Office, TCKTTH, "The Basic Situation of the Construction Industry in
China," TCKTTH, No. 24 (December 29, 1956), pp. 31-33, reference on p. 31.

[5] Ibid, pp. 32-33.

[6] Data Office, TCKT, "The Great Achievement of Basic Construction in China in
the Past Seven Years," TCKT, No. 17 (September 14, 1957), pp. 1-3,
reference on p. 3.

[7] The total increase in the gross value of industrial fixed assets during
1949-59 was expected to reach 45,000 million yuan. (See Cheng Chin-ching,
"The Great Achievements of Socialist Construction in China during the
Past Ten Years," CCYC, No. 10 (October 17, 1959), pp. 1-10; reference on
p. 6). The figure should be regarded as a preliminary estimate.

TABLE 3.2 Gross Value of Fixed Assets in Industry at Original Cost, by Type of Ownership, 1949-55,[a] Millions of Yuan

Year	Total	State	Cooperative	Joint	Private
	(1)	(2)	(3)	(4)	(5)
1949	(12,840)[1]	(10,330)[2]	(30)[2]	(190)[2]	(2,290)[2]
1952	(15,850)[1]	(12,790)[2]	(70)[2]	(640)[2]	(2,350)[2]
1953	n.a.	(15,020)[3]		n.a.	n.a.
1954	n.a.	(19,410)[3]		n.a.	n.a.
1955	(26,300)[1]	22,300[2]	(130)[2]	(2,800)[2]	(1,070)[2]

[a] Year-end figures.

[1] Data Office, *TCKT*, "A General Survey of Industrial Capital in China," *TCKT*, No. 1 (January 14, 1957), pp. 31-33. It was reported in this article that the gross value of total fixed assets in industry increased by 3,100 million yuan during 1949-52, and by 10,450 million yuan during 1953-55, representing an increase of 39.8 percent over the 1953 level.

[2] Data Office, *TCKTTH*, "A General Survey of Socialist Industrialization in China," *TCKTTH*, No. 22 (November 29, 1956), pp. 25-33. This article gave the following data on percentage distribution of the gross value of industrial fixed assets by type of ownership:

	Total	State and cooperative	Joint	Private
1949	100.0	80.7	1.5	17.8
1952	100.0	81.1	4.1	14.8
1955	100.0	85.3	10.7	4.0

In addition, it was reported that the gross value of fixed assets of the state industrial enterprises increased by 2,460 million yuan during 1949-52 and by 9,520 million yuan during 1953-55, and was 22,300 million yuan at the end of 1955. (Data Office, *TCKT, op. cit.*)

[3] Data Office, *TCKTTH, op. cit.* As compared with 1952, the gross value of the fixed assets of state and cooperative industrial enterprises increased by 16.8 percent in 1953 and 50.9 percent in 1954.

TABLE 3.3   Gross Value of Industrial Fixed Assets at Original Cost, by Size of Establishment, December 31, 1955[a]

Size of establishment	Percentage distribution[1]	Amount, millions of yuan
	(1)	(2)
Total	100.0	(26,300)[2]
500 employees or more	81.6	(21,460)[3]
Fewer than 500 employees, of which:	18.4	(4,840)[3]
Small-sized enterprises[b]	0.9	(240)[3]

[a] Excluding handicrafts.

[b] Comprising establishments employing fewer than 15 persons and using motive power and those employing fewer than 30 persons and not using motive power.

[1] Data Office, TCKT, "A General Survey of Industrial Capital in China," TCKT, No. 1 (January 14, 1957), p. 31.

[2] Ibid. See also Table 3.2.

[3] Derived by multiplying the gross value of industrial fixed assets in 1955 by the percentages given in column 1.

TABLE 3.4   Gross Value of Industrial Fixed Assets at Original Cost in Inland and Costal Areas, 1953 and 1955[a]

Area	Percentage distribution		Amount, millions of yuan, December 31, 1955
	December 31, 1953[1]	December 31, 1955[1]	
	(1)	(2)	(3)
Total	100.0	100.0	(26,300)[2]
Inland areas[b]	52.0	57.0	(15,000)[3,c]
Coastal areas[b]	48.0	43.0	(11,300)[3,d]

[a] Excluding handicrafts.

[b] Coastal areas consist of Peking, Tientsin, Shanghai, Hopei, Liaoning, Shantung, Kiangsu, Fukien, Kwangtung, and Chekiang. The rest of the country belongs to inland areas.

[c] During the period 1953-55, the gross value of industrial fixed assets was more than doubled in Sinkiang, Kansu, Inner Mongolia, Kiangsi, and Honan, increased by over 50 percent in Shansi, Kirin, Heilungkiang, Shensi, Chinghai, Anhwei, Hunan, Szechuan, Kweichow, and Yunnan, and increased by less than 50 percent in Kwangsi.

[d] During the period 1953-55 the lowest rate of growth of the gross value of industrial fixed assets was 9 percent for Shanghai, followed by 17 percent for Kiangsu and Tientsin.

[1] Data Office, TCKT, "A General Survey of Industrial Capital in China," TCKT, No. 1 (January 14, 1957), p. 32.

[2] Table 3.2.

[3] Derived from multiplying the gross value of industrial fixed assets in 1955 by the percentages given in column 2.

TABLE 3.5 Gross Value of Fixed Assets at Original Cost in Producer Goods and Consumer Goods Industries, 1949, 1952, and 1955, Millions of Yuan

Year	Total	Producer goods industries	Consumer goods industrial
	(1)	(2)	(3)
1949	(12,840) [1]	(8,265) [2]	(4,575) [2]
1952	(15,850) [3]	(10,683) [4]	(5,167) [4]
1955	(26,300) [3]	(18,805) [4]	(7,495) [4]

Note: During the period 1952-55 the gross value of fixed assets in state-operated industry increased by 9.52 billion yuan, of which 7.64 billion yuan went to the producer goods enterprises and 1.88 billion yuan to the consumer goods enterprises. See Data Office, TCKT, "A General Survey of Industrial Capital in China," TCKT, No. 1 (January, 1957), pp. 31-33, reference on p.32.

[1] The sum of the items in columns 2 and 3.

[2] As of the end of 1955, 56 percent of the gross value of the existing fixed assets in the producer goods industries and 39 percent of that in the consumer goods industry were added during the period 1949-55. (*ibid.,* p. 31).

[3] Table 3.2.

[4] Derived from the following data on percentage distribution of gross fixed assets between producer goods and consumer goods industries:

Year	Gross value of fixed assets	
	Producer goods industries	Consumer goods industries
1952	67.4	32.6
1955	71.5	28.5

Source: Data Office, TCKT, *op. cit.,* p. 32.

TABLE 3.6 Gross Value of Fixed Assets at Original Cost in Selected Industries, 1952-57, Thousands of Yuan

Industry	1952	1953	1954	1955	1956	1957
Iron and steel[1]	(1,585,000)				(2,893,000)	
Used for industrial production[2]	(1,243,000)	(1,419,000)	(2,068,000)	(2,469,000)	(2,673,000)	
Iron and maganese mining[2]	(31,000)	(32,000)	(71,000)	(70,000)	(52,000)	
Iron and steel smelting[2]	(1,212,000)	(1,387,000)	(1,997,000)	(2,399,000)	(2,621,000)	
Not used for industrial production[3]	(342,000)	n.a.	n.a.	n.a.	(220,000)	
Metal processing[4]	2,116,923	2,530,444	2,962,067	(3,461,732)	4,719,162	
Used for industrial production[4]	1,684,785	1,939,316	2,300,383	(2,756,711)	3,748,554	
Not used for industrial production[5]	(432,138)	(591,128)	(661,684)	(705,021)	(970,608)	
Enterprises of the First Ministry of Machine Building,[6,b]	620,000	820,000	990,000	1,190,000	1,880,000	2,080,000
Textile[7]	2,522,340	2,853,300	3,283,390	3,680,090	3,862,150	
Used for industrial production[7]	2,249,640	2,541,800	2,849,710	3,124,190	3,215,230	
Not used for industrial production[8]	(272,700)	(311,500)	(433,680)	(555,900)	(646,920)	
By ownership[9]						
State enterprises	1,451,720	1,671,830	1,917,550	2,168,840	n.a.	
Cooperative enterprises	17,840	25,280	31,240	39,090	n.a.	
Joint enterprises	295,630	396,020	924,920	1,258,640	n.a.	
Private enterprises	757,150	760,170	409,690	213,530	n.a.	

TABLE 3.6 (Continued)

Industry	1952	1953	1954	1955	1956	1957
Paper[10]						
Used for industrial production[10]	352,874	426,468	482,612	520,758	521,134	
Not used for industrial production[11]	314,084	369,927	410,668	439,192	439,165	
	(38,790)	(56,541)	(71,944)	81,566	81,969	

[a] Year-end estimates.

[b] Excluding the enterprises of the Bureau of Electrical Engineering.

[1] The gross value of fixed assets of the iron-and-steel industry was 10 percent of that of total industrial fixed assets in 1952 and 11 percent in 1955. See Data Office, TCKT, "A General Survey of Industrial Capital in China," TCKT, No. 1 (January, 1957), pp. 31-33, reference on p. 32. The figures on the gross value of industrial fixed assets were derived in Table 3.2 as 15.85 billion yuan for 1952 and 26.3 billion yuan for 1955.

[2] Derived from the data on the number of production workers and the gross value per worker of the fixed assets used for industrial production in the iron and steel industry, as they were given in CH, pp. 18 and 32.

[3] Derived by subtracting iron and steel fixed assets used for industrial production from total iron and steel fixed assets.

[4] CH, p. 119.

[5] Derived by subtracting metal-processing fixed assets used for industrial production from total metal processing fixed assets.

[6] Chang Ching-eng, "The Utilization of Productive Potentials," CHCC, No. 4.

[7] CH, p. 161.

[8] Derived by subtracting textiles fixed assets used for industrial production from total textile fixed assets.

[9] CH, p. 176.

[10] Ibid., p. 206.

[11] Derived by subtracting fixed assets used for industrial production of the paper industry from total fixed assets of the same industry.

TABLE 3.7 Gross Value of Industrial Fixed Assets at Original Cost in the Inner Mongolia Autonomous Region, 1952-58, Thousands of Yuan

Year	Total[1]	Used for industrial production[1]	Not used for industrial production[2]
	(1)	(2)	(3)
1952	47,470	38,110	(9,360)
1953	84,060	64,840	(19,220)
1954	117,550	91,170	(26,380)
1955	203,660	163,310	(40,350)
1956	289,900	225,380	(64,520)
1957	357,550	313,170	(44,380)
1958	645,480	512,240	(133,240)

[1] *NMKTC*, p. 115.
[2] Derived by subtracting items in column 2 from items in column 1.

TABLE 3.8 Industrial Capital, 1948-56, Millions of Yuan

Year	Grand total	Modern Factory					Handi-crafts
		Total	State	Cooperative	Joint	Private	
	(1)	(2)	(3)	(4)	(5)	(6)	(7)
1948		9,820[1]					
1949	9,430[2]	9,100[2]	6,890[2]		200[2]	2,010[2,3]	330[2]
1950					(307)[4]	2,111[3]	
1951						2,834[3]	
1952	14,770[2]	14,320[2]	10,840[2]	50[2]	830[2]	2,600[3]	450[2]
1953		14,476[5]			(1,092)[4]	2,941[3]	
1954		21,750				1,965[3]	
1955	24,480[2]	23,869[2,5]	19,730[2]	130[2]	2,720[2]	1,290[3]	610[2]
1956		27,325[5]					

Note: Industrial capital consists of the net value of fixed assets and the amount of working capital in industry. The figures given in this table are year-end estimates.

[1] Data Office, *TCKT*, "A general Survey of industrial Capital in China," *TCKT*, No. 1 (January, 1957), pp. 31-33, reference on p. 31.
[2] *Ibid.*, p. 32.
[3] Ch'ien Hua *et al.*, *Changes of Private Industry and Commerce in China during the Past Seven Years (1949-1956)*, Peking: Tsai-cheng chin-chi chu-pan she, 1957, p. 8.
[4] Chao I-wen, *Industry in New China*, Peking: Tung-chi chu-pan she, 1957, p. 78. According to Chao, the amount of industrial capital of the joint and private industrial enterprises increased from 2,418 million yuan in 1950 to 4,033 million yuan in 1953.
[5] *Ibid.*, p. 24

TABLE 3.9   Net Value of Fixed Assets and Working Capital in Industry(Excluding Handicrafts), 1952 and 1955,[a] Millions of Yuan

Year	Total	Net value of fixed assets	Working capital
	(1)	(2)	(3)
1952	14,320[1]	10,140[2]	(4,180)[3]
1955	23,870[4]	18,140[4]	5,730[4]

Note: The original source did not indicate the method and the price basis used to estimate the net fixed assets and the working capital in industry.

[1] Data Office, *TCKT,* "A General Survey of Industrial Capital in China," *TCKT,* No. 1 (January, 1957), pp. 31-33, reference on p. 32.
[2] NCNA, October 1, 1957.
[3] Derived as a residual.
[4] Data Office, *TCKT, op. cit.,* p. 31.

TABLE 3.10   Annual Percentage Rate of Increase of Working Capital, at Current Prices of the Centrally Controlled State-Operated Industrial Enterprises, 1953-56

Year	Increase over preceding year
1953	35.5
1954	11.0
1955	6.4
1956	17.4

Source: Jung Tzu-ho, 'The Question of Balance for State Budget, for State Credit Plan and for Supply and Demand of Commodities," *Ts'ai-cheng,* No. 6 (June 5, 1957), pp. 1-4, reference on pp. 1-2.

TABLE 3.11   Working Capital of the Iron and Steel Enterprises under the Jurisdiction of the Ministry of Metallurgical industry, 1953-56, Millions of Yuan

Year	Total	Anshan Steel Company	Bureau of Iron and Steel
	(1)	(2)	(3)
1953	427	164	263
1954	448	180	268
1955	505	212	293
1956	532	249	283

Source: *CH,* p. 28.

TABLE 3.12 Total Capital of Private Trade and Restaurants, 1950-55, Millions of Yuan

Year	Total[1]	Resident merchants	Itinerant merchants	Small traders and peddlers	Restaurants[2]
	(1)	(2)	(3)	(4)	(5)
1950	1,990	1,850[3]	50[3]	90[3]	90
1951	2,200	2,030[3]	70[3]	80[3]	100
1952	2,020	1,860[4]	80[4]	80[4]	100
1953	1,920	1,750[4]	70[4]	100[4]	
1954	1,420	1,300[4]	40[4]	80[4]	
1955	1,010	880[4]	20[4]	110[4]	

Note: Total capital of private trade and restaurants refers to the amount of capital registered with the government, which does not necessarily coincide with the amount of capital actually employed.

[1] Ch'ien Hua *et al., Changes in Private Industry and Trade in China during the Past Seven Years (1949-1956),* Peking: Tsai-cheng ch'u-pan she, 1957, p. 9.
[2] *Ibid.,* p. 52.
[3] *Ibid.,* p. 53.
[4] *Ibid.,* p. 123.

TABLE 3.13 Amount of Capital in Private Wholesale Trade, August, 1955

Private wholesale trade	Number of trading units, thousands	Total capital, millions of yuan	Average capital per trading unit, yuan
	(1)	(2)	(3)
Total	125	180	1,400
Resident merchants	42	150	3,577
Itinerant merchants	66	20	356
Small traders and peddlers	17	10	191

Source: Ch'ien Hua *et al., Changes in Private Industry and Trade in China during the Past Seven Years (1949-1956),* Peking: Ts'ai-cheng ch'u-pan she, 1957, p. 132. The data were based on a survey of private wholesalers conducted at the end of August, 1955.

TABLE 3.14 Total Accumulation, 1952-58, Millions of Yuan

Year	At current prices	At 1952 prices	At 1957 prices
	(1)	(2)	(3)
1952	(11,440)	(11,440)	
1953	(16,071)	(16,037)	
1954	(17,333)	(17,375)	
1955	(17,390)	(18,177)	
1956	(20,905)	(23,010)	
1957	(19,839)	(22,171)	(19,839)
1958			(39,083)

Source: Table 2.7.

154

TABLE 3.15 Productive and Nonproductive Accumulation at 1952 Prices, 1952-56

| Year | Percentage distribution[1] | | | Amount, millions of yuan | | |
	Total	Productive accumulation	Nonproductive accumulation	Total[2]	Productive accumulation[3]	Nonproductive accumulation[4]
	(1)	(2)	(3)	(4)	(5)	(6)
1952	100.0	67.9	32.1	(11,440)	(7,768)	(3,672)
1953	100.0	69.6	30.4	(16,037)	(11,162)	(4,875)
1954	100.0	61.1	38.9	(17,375)	(10,616)	(6,759)
1955	100.0	63.3	36.7	(18,177)	(11,506)	(6,671)
1956	100.0	78.7	21.3	(23,010)	(18,109)	(4,901)

[1] SSB, Research Office, "A Preliminary Analysis of the Production and Distribution of China's National Income," *rcyc*, No. 1 (January 23, 1958) p. 14.
[2] Table 2.7.
[3] Derived by multiplying items in column 4 by items in column 2.
[4] Derived by multiplying items in column 4 by items in column 3.

TABLE 3.16 Distribution of Accumulation between Fixed and Liquid Assets at 1952 Prices, 1952-57

| Year | Percentage distribution[1] | | | Amount, millions of yuan | | |
	Total	Fixed assets	Liquid assets	Total[2]	Fixed assets[3]	Liquid assets[4]
	(1)	(2)	(3)	(4)	(5)	(6)
1952	100.0	39.6	60.4	(11,440)	(4,530)	(6,910)
1953	100.0	54.6	45.4	(16,037)	(8,756)	(7,281)
1954	100.0	55.9	44.1	(17,375)	(9,713)	(7,662)
1955	100.0	62.4	37.6	(18,177)	(11,342)	(6,835)
1956	100.0	90.9	9.1	(23,010)	(20,916)	(2,094)
1957[a]	100.0	73.0	27.0	(22,171)	(16,185)	(5,986)

[a] Preliminary estimates.

[1] SSB, Research Office, "A Preliminary Analysis of Production and Distribution of China's National Income," *rcyc*, No. 1 (January 23, 1958), p. 14.
[2] Table 2.7.
[3] Derived by multiplying items in column 4 by items in column 2.
[4] Derived by multiplying items in column 4 by items in column 3.

TABLE 3.17 Sources of Accumulation by Type of Ownership, 1953 and 1956,
Percent

Source	1953	1956
	(1)	(2)
Total	100.0	100.0
Government administration and state economy	80.0	75.5
Public-private joint economy	1.6	6.0
Cooperative economy	4.8	14.3
Of which: Agricultural producers' cooperatives	0.05	12.1
Individual economy	9.1	1.1
Capitalist economy	2.5	0.1
Inhabitants	2.0	3.2

Source: Niu Chung-huang, *Accumulation and Consumption in China's National
Income*, Peking: Chung-kuo chin-nien ch'u-pan she, 1957, pp. 61-62. No explanation was given as to whether the percentages were based on the data at
current or at 1952 prices.

TABLE 3.18 Accumulation of Heavy and Light Industry and of Handicraft Cooperatives, 1952-56

Year	Accumulation as percentage of state budgetary revenue[1]		Accumulation of handicraft cooperatives, millions of yuan[2]
	Heavy industry	Light industry	
	(1)	(2)	(3)
1952-55	10.1	14.4	
1952	6.2	13.3	
1953	8.5	13.0	
1954	10.7	15.3	
1955	13.4	15.5	1,200
1956			4,300

[1] Data Office, *TCKTTH*, "Several Problems Concerning Socialist Industrialization in China," *TCKTTH*, No. 21 (November, 1956), reprinted in *HHPYK*, No. 1
(January, 10, 1057), pp. 67-71, reference on p. 69. This source does not explain whether the state budgetary revenue is gross or net of foreign loan
proceeds. Thus, two different estimates of accumulation of heavy and light
industries may be made from the date in Table 3.18A, depending on whether
such proceeds are included in the state revenue or not. Available information is not sufficient to determine which estimate is correct.

TABLE 3.18A State Revenue and Accumulation of Heavy and Light Industry

Year	State revenue including foreign loan proceeds, millions of yuan	Accumulation, millions of yuan		State revenue excluding foreign loan proceeds, millions of yuan	Accumulation, millions of yuan	
		Heavy industry	Light industry		Heavy industry	Light industry
1952	17,560	(1,089)	(2,335)	17,367	(1,077)	(2,310)
1953	21,762	(1,850)	(2,829)	21,270	(1,808)	(2,765)
1954	26,237	(2,807)	(4,013)	24,443	(2,615)	(3,740)
1955	27,203	(3,645)	(4,216)	24,842	(3,329)	(3,850)

Source: Data on state revenue are taken from "Statistics on State Budgetary Revenue and Expenditures during the First Five-Year Plan Period," *Ts'ai-cheng*, No. 8 (August 5, 1957), pp. 32~33.

[2] Teng Chieh, *Preliminary Results of the Socialist Transformation of the Handicraft Industry in China*, Peking: Jen-min ch'u-pan she, 1958, p. 23.

TABLE 3.19 Accumulation of the State-Operated Enterprises of the Paper Industry, at Current Prices, 1953-57, Thousands of Yuan

Year	Accumulation	Profits		Taxes
		Total	Of which: remitted to the state	
	(1)	(2)	(3)	(4)
1953-57	659,432	517,284	499,643	142,148
1953	77,347	56,531	54,996	20,816
1954	88,796	65,281	63,729	23,515
1955	119,663	93,702	92,360	25,962
1956	170,216	137,916	136,402	32,300
1957	203,410	163,854	152,156	39,556

Source: *CH*, p. 213.

TABLE 3.20 State Budgetary Appropriations for Basic Construction at Current Prices, 1952-57, Millions of Yuan

Year	All sectors	Agriculture[1]
	(1)	(2)
1952	5,013.5[2]	
1953	8,145.4[2]	588
1954	9,592.4[2]	475
1955	9,517.5[2]	556
1956	14,874.3[2]	1,262
1957	(13,008.0)[3]	983

[1] Han Po, "On the Economization of Agricultural Operating Expenses," CHCC, No. 2 (February 9, 1958), pp. 17-21, reference on p. 17.

[2] Feng Chi-hsi, "The Growth of China's National Economy as Viewed from the State Budget," TCKT, No. 12 (June 29, 1957), pp. 28-33, reference on p. 32.

[3] NCNA, February 12, 1958. Total budgetary expenditures for economic construction and social, cultural, and educational expenditures in 1957 were reported to be 19.6 billion yuan, of which 5.552 billion yuan were working capital and 1.04 billion yuan were operating expenses. Basic construction appropriations in 1957 can then be derived as a residual from the total budgetary expenditures and the sum of working capital and operating expenses.

TABLE 3.21 Total Basic Construction Investment at Current Prices Completed Within and Outside the State Plan, 1950-59, Millions of Yuan

Year	Total[1]	Within the state plan		Outside the state plan[3]
		TGY[2]	SSB Communiques	
	(1)	(2)	(3)	(4)
1950	1,130	1,040		(90)
1951	2,350	1,880		(470)
1952	4,360	3,710	3,711[4]	(650)
1953	8,000	6,510	6,506[4]	(1,490)
1954	9,070	7,500	7,498[4]	(1,570)
1955	9,300	8,630	8,630[4]	(670)
1956	14,800	13,990	(13,986)[5]	(810)
1957	13,830	12,640	(12,680)[6]	'(1,190)
1958	26,700	21,440	(21,400)[7]	(5,260)
1959			(26,700)[8]	

[1] TGY, p. 55.

[2] Ibid., p. 56.

[3] Derived by subtracting items in column 2 from items in column 1.

[4] SSB, Communiqué on the Results of the Imprementation of the 1955 National Economic Plan, Peking: T'ung-chi ch'u-pan-she, June 1956, p. 28.

[5] The amount of basic construction investment completed within the state plan during the period 1953-56 is given as 36.62 billion yuan in Data Office, TCKT, "The Great Achievement of Basic Construction in China in the Past Seven Years," TCKT, No. 17 (September 14, 1957), p. 1.

[6] The amount of basic construction investment completed within the state plan during the First Five-Year Plan was reported to be 49.3 billion yuan in SSB, Communiqué on the Results of the Imprementation of the First Five-Year National Economic Plan (1953-1957), Peking: T'ung-chi ch'u-pan-she, April, 1959, p. 3.

[7] SSB, Communiqué on the Development of the National Economy in 1958, Peking: T'ung-chi ch'u-pan-she, April, 1959, p. 18.

[8] Communiqué on the Development of the National Economy in 1959, Peking: Jen-min ch'u-pan-she, January, 1960, p. 2.

TABLE 3.22 Basic Construction Investment at Current Prices in National
Minority Areas, 1950-58, Millions of Yuan

Year	Total[1]	Inner Mongolia Autonomous Region[2]
	(1)	(2)
1950-52	560	
1953	390	90.2
1954	570	202.0
1955	660	184.5
1956	1,160	323.1
1957	1,150	339.2
1958	2,670	925.6

[1] *TGY*, p. 63.
[2] *NMKTC*, p. 62.

TABLE 3.23 Total Basic Construction Investment at Current Prices by Sectors,
1952-58, Millions of Yuan

Sector	1952	1953	1954	1955	1956	1957	1958
Industry	1,690	2,840	3,830	4,300	6,820	7,240	17,300
Construction	90	360	360	320	650	460	270
Geological survey	70	190	290	250	400	300	470
Agriculture, forestry, and meteorology	190	290	200	210	480	460	670
Water conservation	410	480	220	410	710	730	1,960
Railways	510	650	950	1,220	1,760	1,340	2,030
Other transportation and posts and tele-communications	250	420	550	540	850	720	1,370
Trade	120	270	390	350	760	370	570
Culture, education, and scientific research	280	620	680	590	1,000	920	600
Health and welfare	60	150	150	110	110	130	110
Urban public utilities	170	250	240	220	350	380	580
Government administration	20	280	210	140	160	180	190
Others	500	1,200	1,000	640	750	590	580
Total	4,360	8,000	9,070	9,300	14,800	13,830	26,700

Note: The classification of sectors in this table is made on a functional,
rather than an administrative basis. On an administrative basis, the percentage distribution of total basic construction investment completed
during the First Five-Year Plan would be as follows: industry (including
construction and geological prospecting), 56 percent; agriculture,
forestry, meteorology, and water conservation, 8.2 percent; transport,
post and telecommunications, 18.7 percent.

Source: *TGY*, pp. 57-58.

TABLE 3.24 Total Basic Construction Investment at Current Prices in the Inner
Montolia Autonomous Region, by Sectors, 1952-58, Thousands of Yuan

Sector	1952	1953	1954	1955	1956	1957	1958
Industry	6,753	21,483	64,153	68,501	75,824	130,970	671,230
Construction	634	4,171	4,760	10,608	53,840	30,121	16,230
Geological exploration	870	3,340	43,520	122	707	2,025	4,070
Survey and planning			629	142	1,639	1,872	546
Agriculture, grazing, forestry, water conservation, and meteorology	3,533	5,927	7,039	8,243	25,709	13,218	40,766
Grazing	9	1,090	633	3,565	6,913	3,188	5,447
Water conservation	3,049	1,369	1,658	808	4,759	3,163	15,690
Transportation	1,915	19,809	86,065	63,288	68,323	94,196	118,487
Railways		17,264	78,860	60,040	58,585	83,728	103,295
Post communications	820	3,410	2,105	3,208	6,352	3,655	15,218
Trade	1,944	7,171	8,268	7,895	24,467	17,396	18,208
Culture and scientific research	3,001	7,045	6,013	6,323	23,895	19,988	16,366
Health and welfare	520	8,737	2,222	1,030	3,338	5,474	4,197
Urban public utilities	1,618	1,882	4,961	6,069	18,307	12,197	7,991
Government administration	3,462	7,491	10,697	8,206	12,533	7,904	10,096
Others	205	2,768	772	832	8,152	226	2,201
Total	24,492	90,228	202,036	184,467	323,086	339,242	925,606

Source: NMKTC, pp. 62-66.

TABLE 3.25 Productive and Nonproductive Basic Construction Investment at
Current Prices, 1952-56

Year	Percentage distribution[1]			Amount, millions of yuan		
	Total	Productive investment	Nonproductive investment	Total[2]	Productive investment[3]	Nonproductive investment[4]
	(1)	(2)	(3)	(4)	(5)	(6)
1952	100.0	66.4	33.6	4,360	(2,895)	(1,465)
1953	100.0	58.6	41.4	8,000	(4,688)	(3,312)
1954	100.0	66.1	33.9	9,070	(5,995)	(3,075)
1955	100.0	75.8	24.2	9,300	(7,049)	(2,251)
1956	100.0[5]	77.6[5]	22.4[5]	14,800	(11,485)	(3,315)

[1] For the period 1952-55, data on the percentage distribution between productive and nonproductive basic construction investment are given in Niu Chung-huang, *The Relationship between Production and Consumption in China during the First Five-Year Plan Period*, Peking: Ts'ai-cheng chin-chi ch'u pan-she, February, 1959, p. 44.

[2] TGY, p. 55.

[3] Derived by multiplying items in column 4 by items in column 2.

[4] Derived by multiplying items in column 4 by items in column 3.

[5] CHCC editorial, "Important Problems in the Implementation of the 1958 Basic Construction Plan," CHCC, No. 2 (February 9, 1958), pp. 4-6, reference on p. 4.

TABLE 3. 26 Total Investment at Current Prices in New Construction and in
Reconstruction and Rehabilitation of Existing Enterprises,
1952 and 1955, Millions of Yuan

Year	Total[1]	New construction[2]	Reconstruction and rehabilitation [2]	Others[2]
	(1)	(2)	(3)	(4)
1952	4, 360	(1, 430)	(2, 860)	(70)
1955	9, 300	(5, 340)	(3, 380)	(580)

[1] TGY, p. 55.

[2] In 1952, 65.7 percent of basic construction investment was for reconstruction and rehabilitation of existing enterprises, while 32.7 percent was
for construction of new ones; the corresponding percentages for 1955 were
36. 6 and 57.4 percent. See Data Office, TCKTTH, "The Scope and Development
of Basic Construction in China," TCKTTH, No. 18 (September 29, 1956), pp.
4-6, reference on p. 4.

TABLE 3. 27 Percentage Distribution of Total Investment at Current Prices in
New Construction, Reconstruction, and Rehabilitation of Existing
Enterprises in Liaoning Province, 1952-58

Year	Total	New construction	Reconstruction	Rehabilitation
	(1)	(2)	(3)	(4)
1952	100.0	13.6	82.3	4. 1
1953	100.0	16.7	81.1	2. 2
1954	100.0	22.0	76. 6	1. 4
1955	100.0	27.5	69. 1	3. 4
1956	100.0	29.8	68. 6	1. 6
1957	100.0	35.0	64. 1	0. 9
1958	100.0	36.1	63. 2	0. 7

Source: Hu I-min, ' 'Liaoning's Rapid Industrial Growth Is the Victory of the
Party General Line,'' Liao-ning Shih-nien, published by Liao-ning Jen-min
ch'u-pan she, Shenyang, June, 1960; translated as Liao-ning Province during
the Past Decade in JPRS No. 17; 18 2, January 17, 1963, p. 57.

TABLE 3.28 Composition of Total Basic Construction Investment at Current Prices, 1950-58, Millions of Yuan

Year	Grand total[1]	Gross additions to value of fixed assets					Ancillary expenses[b,8]
		Total[2]	Building and installation[a]			Purchases of machinery and equipment	
			Total	Performed by building and installation enterprises[3]	Performed by construction units[c,4]		
	(1)	(2)	(3)	(4)	(5)	(6)	(7)
1950	1,130	1,010					(120)
1951	2,350	1,780					(570)
1952	4,360	3,110	(2,007)[5]			(1,103)[6]	(1,250)
1953	8,000	6,560	5,350[3]	3,280	(2,070)	(1,210)[7]	(1,440)
1954	9,070	7,370	5,620[3]	3,650	(1,970)	(1,750)[7]	(1,700)
1955	9,300	8,020	5,550[3]	3,630	(1,920)	(2,470)[7]	(1,280)
1956	14,800	11,160	8,550[3]	5,430	(3,120)	(2,610)[7]	(3,640)
1957	13,830	12,920					(910)
1958	26,700	19,960					(6,740)

[a] Not including major repairs.

[b] Including expenditures ancillary to the process of fixed capital formation, such as geological survey and exploration, engineering design and planning, scientific research and testing, labor training, and compensation for moving expenses to the original residents of the construction sites.

[c] Construction units are those engineering projects which have their own designing and building budgets. A construction unit may be that of a building, a factory, a mine, a farm, a machine tractor station, a railway, a school, or a hospital. The building and installation work of a construction unit may be performed by workers of the building and installation enterprises or by the labor force organized by the construction unit. (See *Simplified Explanation of the Terminologies in the First Five-Year Plan for Developing the National Economy*, ed. by the State Planning Commission, Peking: Jen-min ch'u-pan-she, 1955, p. 42.

[1] *TGY*, p. 55.

[2] *Ibid.*, p. 66.

[3] Data Office, *TCKTTH*, "The Basic Situation of the Construction Industry in China," *TCKTTH*, No. 24 (December 29, 1956), pp. 31-33, reference on p. 31; and Data Office, *TCKT*, "The Basic Situation of the Production Activities of the Construction Industry in China in the Past Four Years," *TCKT*, No. 18 (September 29, 1957), pp. 31-32, reference on p. 31.

[4] Derived by subtracting items in column 4 from items in column 3.

[5] Derived as a residual of gross additions to the value of fixed assets minus the cost of machinery and equipment purchased in 1952.

[6] 25.3 percent of the basic construction investment in 1952 was for machinery and equipment. See Data Office, *TCKTTH*, "The Scope and Development of Basic Construction Investment in China," *TCKTTH*, No. 18 (September 29, 1956), pp. 4-6, reference on p. 4.

[7] Derived by subtracting items in column 3 from items in column 2.

[8] Derived by subtracting items in column 2 from items in column 1.

TABLE 3.29 Gross Additions to the Value of Productive and Nonproductive Fixed Assets at Current Prices, 1952-58, Millions of Yuan

Year	Gross additions		
	To total fixed assets	To productive fixed assets	To nonproductive fixed assets
	(1)	(2)	(3)
1952	3,110	1,950	1,160
1953	6,560	3,750	2,810
1954	7,370	4,610	2,760
1955	8,020	5,780	2,240
1956	11,160	8,240	2,920
1957	12,920	9,680	3,240
1958	19,960	17,160	2,800

Note: See text for the concepts of productive and nonproductive fixed assets.

Source: TGY, p. 64.

TABLE 3.30 Gross Additions to the Value of Productive and Nonproductive Fixed Assets at Current Prices in the Inner Mongolia Autonomous Region, 1952-58, Thousands of Yuan

Year	Gross additions		
	To total fixed assets	To productive fixed assets	To nonproductive fixed assets
	(1)	(2)	(3)
1952	25,378		
1953	85,748	51,925	33,823
1954	108,801	72,269	36,532
1955	270,673	213,995	56,678
1956	243,588	156,288	87,300
1957	218,883	130,538	88,345
1958	806,095		

Source: NMKTC, p. 72.

163

TABLE 3.31 Gross Additions to the Value of Industrial and Nonindustrial Fixed Assets at Current Prices, 1950-58,[a] Millions of Yuan

| Year | Gross additions | | |
	To total fixed assets[1]	To industrial fixed assets[1]	To nonindustrial fixed assets[2]
	(1)	(2)	(3)
1950	1,010	300	(710)
1951	1,780	500	(1,280)
1952	3,110	1,130	(1,980)
1953	6,560	2,340	(4,220)
1954	7,370	2,820	(4,550)
1955	8,020	3,530	(4,490)
1956	11,160	4,900	(6,260)
1957	12,920	6,470	(5,450)
1958	19,960	12,370	(7,590)

[a] The classifications in this table are based on the nature of investment in fixed assets. On an administrative basis, during the period 1953-57 the gross value of industrial fixed assets increased by 21.4 billion yuan, while that of nonindustrial fixed assets increased by 24.63 billion yuan.

[1] *TGY*, p. 66.
[2] Derived by subtracting items in column 2 from items in column 1.

TABLE 3.32 Gross Additions to the Value of Industrial and Nonindustrial Fixed Assets at Current Prices in the Inner Mongolia Autonomous Region, 1953-58, Thousands of Yuan

| Year | Gross additions | | |
	To total fixed assets[1]	To industrial fixed assets[2]	To nonindustrial fixed assets[2]
	(1)	(2)	(3)
1953	85,748	18,051	(67,697)
1954	108,801	32,223	(76,578)
1955	270,673	79,027	(191,646)
1956	243,588	55,605	(187,983)
1957	218,883	87,594	(131,289)
1958	806,095	500,150	(305,945)

[1] *NMKTC*, p. 77.
[2] Derived by subtracting items in column 2 from items in column 1.

TABLE 3.33 Basic Construction Investment within the State Plan at Current Prices, Except for 1955, by Sector, 1952-57, Millions of Yuan

Year	Total[1]	Industry[1]	Construction[1]	Agriculture[1]	Water conservation[1]	Railways[1]	Other transports[1]	Municipal construction[1]	Housing[1]	Education and health[1]	Trade and finance[1]
	(1)	(2)	(3)	(4)	(5)	(6)	(7)	(8)	(9)	(10)	(11)
1952	3,711	1,549	92	186	331	502	229	171	286[2]	320	
1953	6,506	2,756	345	276	376	642	354	250	n.a.	767	
1954	7,498	3,634	355	144	219	917	445	232	733[3]	771	
1955[a]	8,212	4,204	290	199	402	1,202	452	218	574[3]	689	(207)[4]
1956	13,986	6,483	629	410	702	1,738	690	338	857[3]	1,091	(433)[4]
1957	12,640[5]	6,550[6]									

[a] Except for housing and for trade and finance, basic construction investment in 1955 is given at "prices comparable to previous years." The basic construction investment within the state plan, measured in terms of current prices, was 8.63 million yuan in 1955.

1 SSB, *Communique on the Fulfillment of the National Economic Plan for 1956*, Peking: T'ung-chi ch'u-pan-she, 1957, p. 36.

2 Jui Mu, "The Development of Civil Legislation since 1949," in 1956 *JMST*, pp. 334-39, reference on p. 337.

3 Chai Mou-chou, "Our Method of Predicting the Results of an Investment Plan," *TCKT*, No. 4 (February 28, 1957), pp. 15-16, reference on p. 16.

4 *Ibid.* State investment in trade and finance was given as 2.4 percent of total state basic construction investment in 1955 and 3.1 percent in 1956.

5 *TGY*, p. 56.

6 Po I-po, "Report on the Draft 1958 National Economic Plan," *HHPYK*, No. 5 (March, 1958), pp. 12-13, reference on p. 12.

TABLE 3.34 Composition of Basic Construction Investment within the State Plan
at Current Prices, 1953-57, Millions of Yuan

Year	Total[1]	Gross addition to fixed assets	Ancillary expenses[a]
	(1)	(2)	(3)
Total (1953-57)	49,270	41,100[2]	(8,170)[5]
1953	6,510	n.a.	n.a.
1954	7,500	(6,400)[3]	(1,100)[5]
1955	8,630	(7,420)[4]	(1,210)[5]
1956	13,990	(10,490)[6]	(3,500)[5]
1957	12,640		

[a] For the meaning of ancillary expenses, see text or note *b* to Table 3.28.

[1] *TGY*, p. 56.

[2] *Ibid.*, p. 64.

[3] According to Li Hsien-nien, the Minister of Finance, fixed assets had increased in 1955 by 16 percent (at current prices) over 1954 as a result of basic construction investment. See *JMJP*, June 16, 1956.

[4] 86 percent of state basic construction investment in 1955 resulted in fixed assets. See SSB, *Communique on the Results of the Implementation of the 1955 National Economic Plan*, Peking: T'ung-chi ch'u-pan-she, June, 1956, 57 pp., reference on p. 7.

[5] Derived by subtraction items in column 2 from items in column 1.

[6] 75 percent of state basic construction investment in 1956 was turned into fixed assets. See *JMJP*, August 2, 1957.

TABLE 3.35 Basic Construction Investment in Industry, at Current Prices,
1950-1958, Millions of Yuan

Year	*TGY*[1]	*CH*	Chao I-wen[2]
	(1)	(2)	(3)
1950		429[3]	
1951		712[3]	
1952	1,690	1,689[3]	1,689
1953	2,840	2,830[4]	2,834
1954	3,830	3,840[4]	3,808
1955	4,300	4,300[4]	4,293
1956	6,820	6,820[4]	6,806
1957	7,240		
1958	17,300		

[1] *TGY*, p. 61.

[2] Chao I-wen, *Industry in New China*, Peking: T'ung-chi ch'u-pan-she, 1957, p. 23.

[3] *CH*, p. 9.

[4] *Ibid.*, p. 166.

TABLE 3.36 Basic Construction Investment in Industry within and outside the State Plan, at Current Prices, 1952-57, Millions of Yuan

Year	Total[1]	Within the state plan	Outside the state plan[2]
	(1)	(2)	(3)
1952	1,690	1,549[3]	(141)
1953	2,840	2,756[3]	(24)
1954	3,830	3,634[3]	(196)
1955	4,300	4,204[3]	(96)
1956	6,829	6,483[3]	(337)
1957	7,240	6,550[4]	(690)

[1] TGY, p. 61.

[2] Derived by subtracting items in column 2 from items in column 1.

[3] SSB, *Communique on the Fulfillment of the National Economic Plan for 1956*, Peking: T'ung-chi ch'u-pan-she, 1957, p. 36.

[4] Po I-po, "Report on the Draft 1958 Economic Plan," HHPYK, No. 5 (March, 1958), pp. 12-13, reference on p. 12.

TABLE 3.37 Distribution of Basic Construction Investment in Industry at Current Prices between Coastal and Inland Areas[a] during 1950-55

Year	Percentage distribution [1]			Amount, millions of yuan		
	Total	Coastal areas	Inland areas	Total[2]	Coastal areas[3]	Inland areas[4]
	(1)	(2)	(3)	(4)	(5)	(6)
1950-52	100.0	49.8	50.2	2,830	(1,409)	(1,421)
1953-55	100.0	44.8	55.2	11,080	(4,964)	(6,116)
1950-55	100.0	45.8	54.2	13,910	(6,373)	(7,537)

[a] Coastal areas consist of Peking, Tientsin, Shanghai, Hopei, Liaoning, Shantung, Kiangsu, Fukien, Kwangtung, and Chekiang. The rest of the country belongs to inland areas.

[1] Data Office, TCKTTH, "Several Problems Concerning Socialist Industrializtion in China," TCKTTH, No. 21 (November, 1956); reprinted in HHPYK, No. 1 (January 10, 1957), pp. 67-71, reference on p. 71.

[2] CH, p. 9.

[3] Derived by multiplying items in column 4 by items in column 2.

[4] Derived by multiplying items in column 4 by items in column 3.

TABLE 3.38 Composition of Basic Construction Investment in Industry, at
Current Prices, 1950-58, Millions of Yuan

Year	Total basic construction investment in industry	Gross additions to the value of industrial fixed assets[1]	Ancillary expenses[a,2]
	(1)	(2)	(3)
1950	429[3]	300	(129)[b]
1951	712[3]	500	(212)
1952	1,690[4]	1,130	(560)
1953	2,840[4]	2,340	(500)
1954	3,830[4]	2,820	(1,010)
1955	4,300[4]	3,530	(770)
1956	6,820[4]	4,900	(1,920)
1957	7,240[4]	6,470	(770)
1958	17,300[4]	12,370	(4,930)

[a] For the meaning of ancillary expenses, see note b to Table 3.28.

[b] The amount of the ancillary expenses of basic construction investment in industry in 1952, as derived here, is larger than the total ancillary expenses in the same year shown in Table 3.8. The inconsistency is probably due to the rounding of the figure of the increase in the groos value of industrial fixed assets in 1952.

[1] *TGY*, p. 66.

[2] Derived by subtracting items in column 2 from items in column 1.

[3] *CH*, p. 9.

[4] *TGY*, p. 61.

TABLE 3.39 Basic Construction Investment at Current Prices in Heavy and Light
Industries and in Producer Goods and Consumer Goods Industries,
1952-58, Millions of Yuan

Investment	1952	1953	1954	1955	1956	1957	1958
Heavy industry[1]	1,280	2,340	3,160	3,770	5,880	6,140	15,120
Light industry[1]	410	500	670	530	940	1,100	2,180
Total[1]	1,690	2,840	3,830	4,300	6,820	7,240	17,300
Producer goods[2]				(21,426)			
Consumer goods[2]				(3,604			
Total[1]				(25,030)			

[1] *TGY*, p. 61. According to the same source, the percentage distribution of
state basic construction investment in industry during the First Five-
Year Plan Period was 87.4 percent for heavy industry and 12.6 percent
for light industry.

[2] During the First Five-Year Plan Period, 85.6 percent of total industrial
basic construction investment went to the producer goods industry, and
14.4 percent to the consumer goods industry. See Niu Chung-huang, *The
Relation between Production and Consumption in China during the First
Five-Year Plan Period*, Peking: Ts'ai-cheng chin-chi ch'u-pan she, February, 1959, p. 45.

According to another source, 80 percent of the state basic construction investment in industry during the rehabilitation period (1950-52)
was turned to the producer goods industry. See Data Office, *TCKTTH*, "A
General Survey of Socialist Industrialization in China," *TCKTTH*, No. 22
(November, 1956); reprinted in *HHPYK*, No. 2 (January 15, 1957), pp.
54-62, reference on p. 55.

TABLE 3.40 Basic Construction Investment at Current Prices in Heavy and
Light Industries in the Inner Mongolia Autonomous Region,
1952-58, Thousands of Yuan

Year	Total	Heavy industry	Light industry
	(1)	(2)	(3)
1952	6,753	5,869	884
1953	21,483	17,801	3,682
1954	64,153	41,658	22,495
1955	68,501	48,964	19,537
1956	75,824	60,419	15,405
1957	130,970	118,134	12,836
1958	671,230	631,618	39,612

Source: *NMKTC*, p. 73.

TABLE 3.41 State Basic Construction Investment at Current Prices in Industries, 1950-57, Thousands of Yuan

Industry	1950-52	1950	1951	1952	1953-57	1953	1954	1955	1956	1957
Iron and steel[1]	329,234	86,750	52,800	189,684	2,928,890[a]	300,300[a]	282,200[a]	630,140[a]	832,780[a]	883,470[a]
Of which: above norm[2]	196,000[3]				2,415,320[a]	183,090[a]	195,880[a]	474,120[a]	751,690[a]	810,540[a]
Electric power	361,000[5]	n.a.	n.a.	n.a.	2,714,700[4]	262,000[4]	392,000[4]	535,000[4]	724,000[4]	801,700[4]
Coal		(88,335)[6]		n.a.	2,970,000[7]	180,000[7]			480,000[7]	
New construction						(66,420)[8]			(26,256)[8]	
Reconstruction						(76,320)[8]			(13,824)[8]	
Rehabilitation						(5,040)[8]			(5,616)[8]	
Production						(32,220)[8]			(2,304)[8]	
Petroleum	262,310[10]				1,900,000[9]					
Metal-processing		n.a.		250,000[11]	3,413,000[a,12]	460,000[11]	660,000[11]	720,000[11]	950,000[11]	
Of which: machine building				190,000[11]	n.a.	320,000[11]	460,000[11]	570,000[11]	730,000[11]	
Building materials	93,000[13]	n.a.	n.a.	380,000[a,13]						
Textile		36,450[14]	99,280[14]	253,630[15]		273,980[15]	424,140[15]	219,890[15]	333,910[15]	
Cotton		21,330[14]	54,420[14]	151,160[15]		232,440[15]	380,780[15]	201,540[15]	287,770[15]	
Ministry of textile industry				181,250[15]		219,630[15]	347,680[15]	196,820[15]	291,010[15]	
Paper (state-operated)	42,488[16]	8,834[16]	11,941[16]	21,713[16]	379,921[17]	40,944[17]	38,753[17]	36,625[17]	122,258[17]	141,341[17]
Gross additions to fixed assets	34,898[18]	5,878[18]	10,333[18]	18,687[18]		n.a.	29,537[19]	24,665[19]	63,713[19]	
Central							21,975[19]	19,924[19]	48,078[19]	
Local							7,742[19]	4,741[19]	15,635[19]	
Ancillary expenses[20]	(7,590)	(2,956)	(1,608)	(3,026)		n.a.	n.a.	(9,216)	(11,660)	(58,545)

170

[a] Planned target.

[1] *CH*, pp. 9 and 14.

[2] *Ibid.*, p. 15.

[3] Chao I-wen, *Industry in New China*, Peking: T'ung-chi ch'u-pan-she, 1957, p. 44.

[4] *CH*, p. 54.

[5] Chao I-wen, *op. cit.*, p. 47.

[6] State basic construction investment in the coal industry in 1950 was 20.6 percent of total industrial investment. See *CH*, p. 88.

[7] *CH*, p. 92.

[8] Derived from the following data on the percentage distribution of state basic construction investment in the coal industry among new construction, reconstruction, and rehabilitation of the coal mines and production:

Year	Total	New construction	Reconstruction	Rehabilitation	Production
1953	100.0	36.9	42.4	2.8	17.9
1954	100.0	55.8	30.5	7.7	6.0
1955	100.0	48.7	32.9	12.6	5.8
1956	100.0	54.7	28.8	11.7	4.7

Source: *CH*, p. 92.

[9] *1958 JMST*, p. 473.

[10] *CH*, p. 111.

[11] *Ibid.*, p. 116

[12] Chao I-wen, *op. cit.*, p. 42.

[13] *Ibid.*, p. 52.

[14] *CH*, p. 154.

[15] *Ibid.*, p. 159. The figures include that part of the state investment by other ministries directly related to textile manufacturing, such as the Ministry of Machine Building.

[16] *Ibid.*, p. 202.

[17] *Ibid.*, p. 205.

[18] *Ibid.*, p. 202.

[19] *Ibid.*, p. 207.

[20] Derived by subtracting gross additions to fixed assets in state paper industry from state basic construction investment in paper industry.

TABLE 3.42 Number of Major Factory and Mining Projects Completed or under Construction during the Period 1953-58

Industry	Number of projects completed or under construction	Of which: number of projects wholly or partially in operation
	(1)	(2)
Total	2,056	1,037
Coal industry	376	179
Electric power industry	268	154
Petroleum industry	28	17
Ferrous metals industry	117	68
Chemical industry	116	54
Building materials industry	103	37
Metal processing industry	489	215
Textile industry	120	74
Paper industry	47	21
Food industry	103	49

Note: A project on which construction continues for several years and which goes into operation by stages is counted only once in this table

Source: *TGY*, p. 67.

TABLE 3.43 Major Reservoirs Built during the Period 1950-58

Reservoir	Location	Date completed	Storage capacity, millions of cubic meters
Kuanting	Peking	May, 1954	2,270
Futseling	Juoshan, Anhwei	October, 1954	582
Poshan	Chuehshan, Honan	December, 1954	292
Nanwan	Hsinyang, Honan	December, 1955	932
Meishan	Chinchai, Anhwei	April, 1956	2,275
Touho	Tangshan, Hopei	December, 1956	134
Paisha	Yuhsien, Honan	August, 1957	274
Panchiao	Miyang, Honan	August, 1957	418
Shihmen	Chunghsiang, Hupeh	July, 1957	123
Huaijou	Peking	July, 1958	90
Tahofong	Fushun, Liaoning	September, 1958	1,970
Taihangti	Tsaohsien, Shantung	August, 1958	1,230
Tungpinghu	Liaocheng, Liangshan, Shantung	October, 1958	4,000
Tungchang	Fuching, Fukien	December, 1958	186
Mokuhu	Manass, Sinkiang	December, 1958	158
Hsianghungtien	Chinchai, Anhwei	December, 1958	2,650
Motsetan	Huoshan, Anhwei	December, 1958	336
Ming Tombs	Peking	July, 1958	82
Mo-li-miao	T'ung-liao Shih, Inner Mongolia	n.a.	156
T'a-la-kan	K'ai-lu Hsien, Inner Mongolia	n.a.	132
Meng-chia-tuan	Nai-man Banner, Inner Mongolia	n.a.	120
Ka-t'u-hao	Nai-man Banner, Inner Mongolia	n.a.	109
Pai-yin-hu-t'ao	K'o-yu Middle Banner, Inner Mongolia	n.a.	100

Sources: For reservoirs in Inner Mongolia Autonomous Region: *NMKTC*, p. 81.
For reservoirs in other areas: *TGY*, p. 68.

TABLE 3.44 Length of Railway Track Laid during 1950-58, Kilometers

Year	Grand total	Public lines					Special-purpose lines
		Total	New lines	Restored lines	New double-track lines	Restored double-track lines	
	(1)	(2)	(3)	(4)	(5)	(6)	(7)
1950	980	808	97	427	- -	284	172
1951	1,206	1,021	743	138	- -	140	185
1952	1,469	1,233	480	605	- -	148	236
1953	1,200	706	587	- -	14	105	494
1954	1,415	1,132	831	- -	49	252	283
1955	1,864	1,406	1,222	39	87	58	458
1956	3,108	2,242	1,747	285	206	4	866
1957	1,735	1,166	474	150	538	4	569
1958	3,564	2,376	1,332	105	939	- -	1,188

Note: Special-purpose lines refer to the railways used specifically by enter-prises. See SSB, *Communique on the National Economic Development in 1958*, Peking: T'ung-chi ch'u-pan-she, 1959, p. 21. During the period 1950-58, 4,400 kilometers of narrow-gauge track for forest railways were also built.

Source: *TGY*, p. 69.

TABLE 3.45 Major Railways Built during 1950-58

Railway	Length of track laid, kilometers	Date opened to traffic
Laipin-Munankuan (Kwangsi)	419	October, 1951
Chengtu-Chungking (Szechuan)	505	July, 1952
Tienshui-Lanchow (Kansu)	354	October, 1952
Litang (Kwangsi)-Chankiang (Kwangtung)	315	July, 1955
Fengtai (Peking)-Shacheng (Hopei)	101	July, 1955
Chining-Erhlien (Inner Mongolia)	337	December, 1955
Hsiaoshan-Chuanshan (Chekiang)	140	April, 1956
Paochi (Shensi)-Chengtu (Szechuan)	669	July, 1956
Yingtan (Kiangsi)-Amoy (Fukien)	733	April, 1957
Paotow (Inner Mongolia)-Lanchow (Kansu)	991	August, 1958
Nanping-Foochow (Fukien)	167	December, 1958
Tuyun-Kweiyang (Kweichow)	146	December, 1958
The Great Khingan Mountains Forest Railway	258	1957 (Huder-Kenho and Etulgol-Gangol sections)
The Lesser Khingan Mountains Forest Railway	115	1957 (Yichun-Hsinching section)
Huaijou (Peking)-Chengteh (Hopei)	106	1958 (Shangpancheng-Yingshouyingtse and Huaijou-Miyun sections)
Lanchow (Kansu)-Sinkiang Friendship Line	1,151	October, 1958 (up to Kizil Ulson)
Neikiang (Szechuan)-Kunming (Yunnan)	116	October, 1958 (Neikiang-Ipin section)

Source: *TGY*, p. 70.

TABLE 3.46   Major Bridges Built during 1950-58

Bridge	Province	Length, meters
Wuhan Yangtse River Bridge	Hupeh	1,670
Tungkuan Yellow River Bridge (temporary structure)	Shensi	1,070
Hunan-Kweichow Railway Hsiangkiang Bridge	Hunan	844
Shenyang-Shanhaikuan Railway Talingho Bridge	Liaoning	830
Fengtai-Shacheng Railway Yungtingho No. 1 Bridge	Hopei	722
Lunghai Railway Hsinyiho Bridge	Kiangsu	700
Paotow-Lanchow Railway Sanshengkung Yellow River Bridge	Inner Mongolia	683
Peking-Paotow Railway Kueishiu Bridge	Hopei	663
Hunan-Kwangsi Railway Liukiang Bridge	Kwangsi	616
Pekin-Canton Railway Changho Bridge	Hopei	569
Fengtai-Shacheng Railway Yungtingho No. 8 Bridge	Hopei	526

Note: It was reported that the length of the railway bridges built during the period 1949-59 amounted to 200,000 meters (NCNA, December 18, 1959).

Source: *TGY*, p. 71.

TABLE 3.47   Length of Highways Constructed and Repaired, 1950-58, Kilometers

Year	Total	Of which: New highways
	(1)	(2)
1950	15,463	540
1951	19,545	1,366
1952	11,168	1,940
1953	9,654	2,598
1954	7,164	3,824
1955	8,138	3,579
1956	89,717	55,930
1957	38,168	17,472
1958	210,000	150,000

Note: Figures for 1956 and after include lower grade highways.

Source: *TGY*, p. 72.

TABLE 3.48 Major Trunk Highways Built during 1952-58

Highway	Year completed	Length, kilometers
New highways		
Golmo-Sorhal (Chinghai)	1952	544
Yangchieh-Yinmin (Yunnan)	1953	243
Taotangho-Yushu (Chinghai)	1953	723
Sikang-Tibet (from Chinchikuan in Yaan, Szechuan to Lhasa, Tibet	1954	2,271
Chinghai-Tibet (from Sining, Chinghai, to Lhasa, Tibet)	1954	2,100
Haikow-Yulin (Hainan Island, Kwangtung)	1954	297
Taliyuan-Menghai (Yunnan)	1954	675
Chengtu-Ahpa (Szechuan)	1954	506
Yangpachan-Shigatze (Tibet)	1954	247
Shigatze-Pharhi (Tibet)	1954	253
Tunhuang (Kansu)-Golmo (Chinghai)	1954	588
Nata-Paso (Hainan Island, Kwangtung)	1954	126
Hsinyi-Loting section of Canton-Hainan Line (Kwangtung)	1954	124
Pengkow-Chuehwei (Fukien)	1955	274
Menghai-Lantsang (Yunnan)	1955	119
Kaiping-Chuangho (Liaoning)	1955	150
Foochow (Fukien)-Wenchow (Chekiang)	1956	446
Haipachuang-Mengting (Yunnan)	1956	574
Yanglin-Huitse (Yunnan)	1956	280
Tungyuanpao-Chuangho (Liaoning)	1956	198
Eh-odot-Mangyai (Chinghai)	1956	371
Lenghu-Chalengkou (Chinghai)	1956	130
Odo-Shaliangtse (Chinghai)	1956	150
Moho-Huangkualiang (Chinghai)	1956	757
Tseli-Tajung (Hunan)	1956	111
Mae Tag-Khoshtologai (Sinkiang)	1956	288
Charklik-Cherchen (Sinkiang)	1956	353
Hsinshihchen-Hsichang (Szechuan)	1956	336
Lhasa-Chetang (Tibet)	1956	184
Sinkiang-Tibet (Karghalik, Sinkiang-Gartok, Tibet	1957	1,210
Tangin-Mangyai (Chinghai)	1957	363
Weifang-Jungcheng (Shantung)	1958	332
Tungngolo-Patang (Szechuan)	1958	406
Taiho (or Santu)-Chinkangshan (Kiangsi)	1958	95
Hungliuyuan-Tunhuang (Kansu)	1958	127
Rebuilt highways		
Shangyao (Kiangsi)-Foochow (Fukien)	1952	488
Kiangshan (Chikiang)-Chienou (Fukien)	1954	280
Nanping-Pengkow (Fukien)	1955	266
Urumchi-Korla-Kashgar (Sinkiang)	1958	1,513

Source: *TGY*, pp. 73-74.

TABLE 3.49 Newly Constructed Railway and Highway Transport Mileage in the Inner Mongolia Autonomous Region, 1949-58, Kilometers

Year	Additions to railway mileage[1]			Additions to highway mileage[2]
	Total	Trunk and branch railway lines	Industrial spurs	
	(1)	(2)	(3)	(4)
1949				547
1950				865
1951				778
1952	17	17		784
1953	71	71		674
1954	388	388		758
1955	62	62		2,072
1956	194	194		2,711
1957	563	415	148	1,984
1958	374	240	134	5,000

Note: Data on newly constructed railway mileage do not include narrow-gauge tracks for forest railways.

[1] NMKTC, p. 78.

[2] Ibid., p. 80

TABLE 3.50 New Buildings, 1953-57, Thousand Square Meters of Floor Space

Year	Total	Residential buildings	School buildings[1]
	(1)	(2)	(3)
1953	30,000[2]	12,000[2]	4,220
1954	47,000[3]	13,000[3]	4,500
1955		14,000[4]	3,710
1956		25,000[5]	5,040
1957		(30,540)[6]	5,430

Note: Buildings include factories, warehouses, offices, houses, schools, hospitals, and military camps.

[1] TGY, p. 75.

[2] SSB, Communique on the National Economic Development and on the Results of the Implementation of the State Plan for 1953, Peking: Ts'ai-cheng ching-chi ch'u-pan-she, 1954, p. 8.

[3] SSB, Communique on the National Economic Development and on the Results of the Implementation of the State Plan for 1954, Peking: T'ung-chi ch'u-pan-she, 1955, p. 10.

[4] SSB, Communique on the Results of the Implementation of the National Economic Plan for 1955, Peking: T'ung-chi ch'u-pan-she, pp. 7-8.

[5] SSB, Communique on the Results of the Implementation of the National Economic Plan for 1956, Peking: T'ung-chi ch'u-pan-she, 1957; reprinted in 1958 JMST, pp. 456-59, reference on p. 458.

[6] SSB, Communique on the Results of the Implementation of the First Five-Year Plan for National Economic Development (1953-1957), Peking: T'ung-chi ch'u-pan-she, 1959, p. 12. It was reported that state housing investment during the First Five-Year Plan resulted in an increase of 94.54 million square meters of floor space.

TABLE 3.51 New School Buildings, 1950-58, Thousand Square Meters of Floor Space

Year	Total	Institutes of higher learning	Normal middle schools	Middle schools	Primary schools
	(1)	(2)	(3)	(4)	(5)
1950	540	190	90	150	110
1951	1,280	520	120	510	130
1952	2,820	1,020	300	1,270	230
1953	4,220	1,510	480	2,010	220
1954	4,500	1,530	210	2,300	460
1955	3,710	1,330	150	1,460	770
1956	5,040	2,050	300	2,200	490
1957	5,430	1,920	270	2,540	700
1958	6,050	1,650	150	3,210	1,040

Note: The data given in this table do not include new buildings for technical middle schools.

Source: TGY, p. 75.

TABLE 3.52 New Buildings in the Inner Mongolia Autonomous Region, 1952-58, Hundred Square Meters of Floor Space

Year	Total[1]	Factories[1]	Houses[1]	Schools[1]	Others[2]
	(1)	(2)	(3)	(4)	(5)
1952	917	63	138	384	(332)
1953	4,865	364	1,863	435	(2,203)
1954	8,615	613	3,181	327	(4,494)
1955	9,822	688	4,263	552	(4,319)
1956	22,675	688	10,343	1,446	(10,198)
1957	19,609	1,405	9,828	1,583	(6,793)
1958	33,956	9,262	12,017	2,088	(10,589)

[1] NMKTC, p. 83.
[2] Derived as residuals.

TABLE 3.53   Construction of Urban Public Utilities, 1949, 1952, 1957, and 1958

Utility	1949	1952	1957	1958
Water supplies				
Length of pipes, kilometers	6,480	8,099	12,570	14,617
Volume of water supplied, million cubic meters	n.a.	460	950	1,260
Of which: for household use, million cubic meters	n.a.	250	550	640
Buses				
Number of buses	1,264	2,220	4,445	5,830
Number of passengers carried, million rides	n.a.	450	1,930	2,220
Street-cars				
Number of cars	866	1,049	1,224	1,245
Number of passengers carried, million rides	n.a.	550	940	890
Trolley busses				
Number of busses	166	244	493	688
Number of passengers carried, million rides	n.a.	110	320	390
Length of roads paved, kilometers	11,084	12,223	17,730	18,698
Length of drainage pipes, kilometers	6,568	7,070	10,122	11,074

Source: *TGY*, p. 78.

TABLE 3.54   Construction of Urban Public Utilities in the Inner Mongolia
Autonomous Region, 1952, 1957, and 1958

Utility	1952	1957	1958
Water supplies			
Length of pipes, kilometers	4.4	82.1	88.2
Volume of water supplied, thousand cubic meters	360	3,384	7,773
Of which: for household use, thousand cubic meters	197	2,030	4,858
Buses			
Number of buses	3	33	55
Number of passengers carried, thousand rides	396	6,234	7,733
Length of roads paved, kilometers	64.5	258.9	262.7
Length of water reservoirs, kilometers	30.1	152.3	156.2

Source: *NMKTC*, p. 85.

TABLE 3.55   Volume of Work of Engineering Design, 1952, 1957, and 1958,
(Designed Plant Capacity)

Industry	1952	1957	1958
Coal mining, thousands of tons per year	n. a.	2, 400	3, 000
Hydroelectric power stations, thousands of kilowatts	12	1, 000	1, 000
Thermal power stations, thousands of kilowatts	10	650	650
Iron-and-steel integrated works, thousands of tons per year	n. a.	1, 500	3, 600
Heavy machine-building works thousands of tons per year	n. a.	74	120
Paper mill, tons per day	n. a.	120	300
Sugar mill			
Sugar beet, tons processed per day	800	1, 000	1, 000
Sugar cane, tons processed per day	1, 000	2, 000	2, 000

Source: *TGY*, p. 76.

TABLE 3.56   Volume of Work of Geological Prospecting, 1952-58, Thousands of
Meters

Year	Drilling		Pit testing
	Total	Of which; Mechanical core drilling	
	(1)	(2)	(3)
1950-52	496	409	52
1952	355	286	50
1953	922	744	151
1954	1, 479	1, 157	222
1955	2, 095	1, 599	251
1956	4, 141	3, 270	401
1957	4, 261	3, 603	433
1958	8, 700	7, 400	660

Source: *TGY*, p. 77.

TABLE 3.57   Volume of Work of Geological Prospecting in the Inner Mongolia
Autonomous Region, 1953-58

| Year | Number of meters drilled | |
	Total	Mechanical drilling
	(1)	(2)
1953	39,096	39,096
1954	34,034	33,165
1955	33,818	33,621
1956	25,026	24,973
1957	81,292	81,110
1958	316,731	298,111

Source: *NMKTC*, p. 85.

TABLE 4.1 Number of Industrial Enterprises Confiscated, as of the End of 1949, by Size of Employment

Size of employment	Number of industrial enterprises	Number of production workers, thousands
	(1)	(2)
Total	2,677	753
Below 100 persons	1,687	57
100 to 500 persons	686	151
500 to 1,000 persons	145	104
1,000 to 5,000 persons	130	252
Over 5,000 persons	14	189
Unknown	15	n.a.

Source: Chao I-wen, *Hsin-chung-kuo ti kung-yeh (New Industry in China)*, Peking: T'ung-chi ch'u-pan-she, 1957, p. 35.

TABLE 4.2 Number of Industrial Establishments, by Size and by Ownership of Enterprise, 1949-56

Establishment	1949	1950	1951	1952	1953	1954	1955	1956
Grand total				167,403	176,405	167,626	125,474	
Large				27,527	31,379	31,187		
Small				139,876	145,026	136,439		
State:								
Central and local government				10,671	12,295	13,666	15,190	
Large				8,609	9,351	10,273		
Small				2,062	2,944	3,393		
Central				2,409	2,722	3,392	4,077	
Large				2,035	2,338	2,658		
Small				374	384	734		
Local				8,262	9,573	10,274	11,113	
Large				6,547	7,013	7,615		
Small				1,688	2,560	2,659		
Cooperative				6,164	12,799	17,938	18,282	
Large				1,025	1,988	2,173		
Small				5,139	10,811	15,765		
Joint:								
Central and local state-private joint	193	294	706	997	1,036	1,744	3,193	32,166
Large				820	878	1,603		
Small				177	158	141		
Central state-private joint				88	101	130	147	
Large				88	101	129		
Small				0	0	1		
Local state-private joint				909	935	1,614	3,046	
Large				732	777	1,474		
Small				177	158	140		

TABLE 4.2 (Continued)

Establishment	1949	1950	1951	1952	1953	1954	1955	1956
Private	123.165	133.018	147.650	149,571	150,275	134,278	88,809	
Large				17,073	19,162	17,138		
Small				132,498	131,113	117,140		

Sources: Data in this table are given in SSB, *Communique on the Results of the Implementation of the National Economic Plan for 1955*, Peking: T'ung-chi ch'u-pan-she, 1956, p. 23, except for the total number of joint and of private industrial enterprises. Figures on the total number of joint enterprises are taken from Chao I-wen, *Industry in New China*, Peking: T'ung-chi ch'u-pan-she, 1957, p. 75; and data on the total number of private industrial enterprises appear in Ch'ien Hua *et al.*, *Changes in Private Industry and Trade in China during the Past Seven Years (1949-56)*, Peking: Ts'ai-cheng ch'u-pan-she, 1957, p. 8.

TABLE 4.3 Number of State-Private Jointly Operated Enterprises in
Selected Industries, 1949-56

Year	Iron-and-steel industry[1]	Machine-building industry[2]	Metal products manufacturing industry[3]	Paper industry[3]
	(1)	(2)	(3)	(4)
1949		9	2	5
1950		1	8	7
1951		24	39	19
1952	19	42	50	26
1953	27	41	56	37
1954	45	141	138	49
1955	58	283	268	98
1956	178			

[1] CH, p. 29.   [2] Ibid., p. 130.   [3] Ibid., p. 214.

TABLE 4.4 Number of Enterprises in the Iron-and-Steel
Industry, by Size of Employment, 1954

Size of employment	Number of enterprises
Total	1,071
100 persons and below	966
101 to 500 persons	69
501 to 1,000 persons	9
1,001 to 3,000	16
3,001 to 5,000 persons	6
5,001 to 10,000 persons	2
10,000 persons and above	3

Source: CH, p. 18.

Table 4.5 Number of Gainfully Occupied Persons in the Handicraft Industry,
1952-56, Thousands

Year	Total	Individual handicraftsmen	Members of handicraft cooperatives[a]
	(1)	(2)	(3)
1952	7,364	7,136	288
1953	7,789	7,488	301
1954	8,910	7,697	1,213
1955[b]	8,202	5,996	2,206
1956[b]	6,583	544	6,039[c]

[a] There are unexplained gaps between TGY data and Chao I-wen's data on the
   number of persons joining handicraft cooperatives. Chao's data, which also
   give breakdowns into producer cooperatives, supply and marketing cooperatives and production teams are shown in TABLE 4.5 A.
[b] In 1955 and 1956 the number of handicraftsmen decreased because, in the
   course of forming cooperatives, some of the handicraftsmen in the cities
   were absorbed by industrial enterprises, while in the countryside some of
   the handicraftsmen joined agricultural producer cooperatives.
[c] The figure for cooperative members in 1956 covers more than one million
   handicraftsmen belonging to fishing and salt cooperatives.
Sources: TGY, p. 36.

TABLE 4.5A Number of Persons Joining Handicraft Cooperatives, 1949–56

	1949	1950	1951	1952	1953	1954	1955	1956
Number of cooperatives and teams	311	1,321	1,066	3,658	5,778	41,619	64,591	99,322
Number of persons joining handicraft cooperatives	88,941	260,000	139,613	227,786	301,487	1,139,009	1,874,590	5,095,186
Producer cooperatives				218,018	271,297	521,209	.849,485	3,697,834
Supply and marketing cooperatives				4,288	15,851	227,216	507,343	674,578
Production teams				5,480	14,339	390,584	517,762	332,774

Source: Chao I-wen, *Industry in New China*, Peking: T'ung-chi ch'u-pan-she, 1957, pp. 109, 111.

TABLE 4.6 (1A) Output of Major Industrial Products, 1949-60

Product	1949	1950	1951	1952	1953
Iron and steel, tons:					
Iron ore[1]	588,558	2,349,842	2,703,172	4,286,807	5,821,122
Manganese ore[1]	673	87,812	112,231	190,591	195,043
Pig iron (including native iron)	251,991[1]	977,794[1]	1,147,940[1]	1,928,585[1]	2,234,098[1]
Steel	158,378[1]	605,796[1]	895,982[1]	1,348,509[1]	1,773,954[1]
Rolled steel	141,104[1]	463,921[1]	807,798[1]	1,311,897[1]	1,754,161[1]
Non-ferrous metals, tons:					
Primary refined lead[5]					
Primary tin		(6,000)[6]	(7,300)[7]		
Aluminum ingots					
Electric power and fuel:					
Electric power, million kw-hr	4,310[2]	4,550[2]	5,750[2]	7,260[2]	9,200[2]
Coal, thousand tons	32,430[2]	42,920[2]	53,090[2]	66,490[2]	69,680[2]
Crude petroleum, thousand tons	121[2]	200[2]	305[2]	436[2]	622[2]
Natural	70[8]	n.a.	n.a.	195[9]	n.a.
Synthetic	51[8]	n.a.	n.a.	240[9]	n.a.
Gasoline[12]					
Kerosene[12]					
Diesel oil[12]					
Metal-processing:					
Metal-cutting machines,[c] units	1,582[2]	3,212[2]	5,853[2]	13,734[2]	20,502[2]
Steam boilers, units[12]	209	479	782	1,000	n.a.
Steam turbines, units[13]				11	n.a.
Hydraulic turbines, units[14]					
Diesel engines, hp				27,261[14]	n.a.
Power machinery, thousand hp[2]	10	11	26	35	144
Electric motors, thousand kw[2]	61	199	225	639	918
Electric generators, kw	10,181[13]	22,798[13]	31,731[13]	29,678[13]	(58,760)[16]
Power-generating equipment, thousand kw					
Transformers, units[19]				16,185	n.a.
Double-wheeled plows, thousand units				5[19]	n.a.
Tractors, units[2]					
Locomotives, units[2]				20	10
Freight cars, units	3,155[13]	696[13]	2,882[13]	5,792[13]	4,500[21]
Trucks, units					
Merchant vessels, thousand dwt tons				16	35
Bicycles, thousand units	14	21	44	80	165
Building materials:					
Cement, thousand tons	660[2]	1,410[2]	2,490[2]	2,860[2]	3,880[2]
Plate glass, thousand cu m				(21,320)[22]	(24,300)[16]
Timber, thousand cu m	5,670[2]	6,640[2]	7,640[2]	11,200[2]	17,530[2]
Chemicals:					
Sulfuric acid, thousand tons[2]	40	49	149	190	260
Soda ash, thousand tons[2]	88	160	185	192	223
Caustic soda, thousand tons[2]	15	23	48	79	88
Chemical fertilizer,[d] thousand tons	27[2]	70[2]	129[2]	181[2]	226[2]

TABLE 4.6 (1B)

1954	1955	1956	1957	1958	1959	1960
7,228,667	9,596,998	15,483,904				
172,201	276,544	524,070				
3,113,703[1]	3,872,421[1]	4,826,249[1]	5,936,000[2]	13,690,000[a,2]	20,500,000[3]	
2,224,595[1]	2,853,105[1]	4,465,422[1]	5,350,000[1]	8,000,000[b,1]	13,350,000[3]	
1,965,337[1]	2,504,817[1]	3,920,975[1]				18,450,000[4]
		17,000				
					70,400[3]	
11,000[2]	12,280[2]	16,590[2]	19,340[2]	27,530[2]	41,500[3]	
83,660[2]	98,300[2]	110,360[2]	130,000[2]	270,000[2]	347,800[3]	
789[2]	966[2]	1,163[2]	1,458[2]	2,264[2]	3,700[3]	
n.a.	n.a.	589[9]	850[10]	(1,472)[11]		
n.a.	n.a.	574[9]	608[10]	(792)[11]		
		417[9]				
		193[9]				
		323[9]				
15,901[2]	13,708[2]	25,928[2]	28,000[2]	50,000[2]	70,000[3]	
n.a.	n.a.	1,035				
		23				
n.a.	n.a.	57				
n.a.	n.a.	540,761[14]	609,000[5]			
172	247	657	690	2,000		
957	607	1,069	1,455	6,052		
(55,000)[17]	108,000[17]	288,263[18]				
			198[2]	800[2]	2,150[3]	
n.a.	n.a.	110,514				
60[21]	523[21]	1,793[19]				
	3	22	124	545		
52	98	184	167	350		
5,446[21]	9,258	7,122	7,300	11,000		
		1,654	7,500	16,000		
62	120	104	54	90		
298	335	640	806	1,174		
4,600[2]	4,500[2]	6,390[2]	6,860[2]	9,300[2]	12,270[3]	
(31,350)[21]	n.a.	30,750				
22,210[2]	20,930[2]	20,840[2]	27,870[2]	35,000[2]	41,200[3]	
344	375	517	632	740		
309	405	476	506	640		
115	137	156	198	270		
298[2]	332[2]	523[2]	631[2]	811[2]	1,333[3]	

TABLE 4.6 (2A)

Product	1949	1950	1951	1952	1953
Pharmaceutical products:					
Penicillin, kilograms[23]				46	593
Antibiotics, tons[24]					
Rubber products:					
Tires, units[25]	26,020	n.a.	n.a.	417,184	488,067
Rubber footwear, thousand pairs[2]	28,900	45,670	65,060	61,690	76,360
Paper,[e] thousand tons	228[2]	380[2]	492[2]	539[2]	667[2]
Textiles:					
Cotton yarn, thousand bales	1,803[26]	2,408[26]	2,683[26]	3,618[26]	4,104[26]
Cotton cloth, million meters	1,889[26]	2,522[26]	3,058[26]	3,829[26]	4,685[26]
Printed cloth, million meters[27]				1,924	2,743
Gunny sacks, thousand units[28]	9,730	15,331	39,033	67,353	59,077
Woolen fabrics, thousand meters[28]	5,435	4,880	4,025	4,233	6,227
Woolen yarn, tons[28]	1,760	1,246	801	1,980	3,718
Wool rugs, thousand units[28]	222	485	1,083	717	393
Food:					
Cigarettes, thousand crates[f,2]	1,600	1,848	2,002	2,650	3,552
Edible vegetable oils, thousand tons	444[2]	607[2]	731[2]	983[2]	1,009[2]
Sugar, thousand tons	199[2]	242[2]	300[2]	451[2]	638[2]
Salt, thousand tons	2,985[2]	2,464[2]	4,346[2]	4,945[2]	3,569[2]
Flour,[g] thousand tons	1,279[29]	n.a.	n.a.	2,995[30]	3,390[30]
Aquatic products, thousand tons[2]	448	912	1,332	1,666	1,900

[a] Of the 13,690,000 tons, 4,160,000 tons were produced by indigenous methods.

[b] Not including 3,080,000 tons produced by indigenous methods.

[c] Not including simple indigenous machine tools.

[d] Not including ammonium nitrate.

[e] Including paper board.

[f] One crate contains 50,000 cigarettes.

[g] Not including handicraft production.

[1] CH, pp. 11, 19.

[2] TGY, pp. 95-100..

[3] JMJP, January 23, 1960.

[4] PO I-pp. "Struggle for the New Victory of Industrial Production and Construction in China, "Hung-ch'i, Nos. 3-4 (February 1, 1961), pp. 19-25, reference on p. 19.

[5] Yeh-chin-pao, January 14, 1957.

[6] Production amounted to 38 per cent of the peak output of 15,865 metric tons before World War II. See JMJP, October 5, 1951, and Hsin-chien she, 1950.

[7] Production amounted to 46 per cent of the peak pre-war output. See JMJP, October 5, 1951.

[8] Netrusov, A.A. "Petroleum Industry in China," Bulletin tekniko-ekonomicheskoi informatsu, No. 10, 1958, pp. 80-82, translated in Library Lending Unit Translation Bulletin, London, March, 1959, pp. 9-13.

[10] Shih-yu lien-chih (Petroleum Refining), April, 1958, translated in JPRS: 818-D, p. 44.

[11] Wang Chih-chun, "The Petroleum Industry in the People's Era," China News Service, September 12, 1959. The ratio of natural to synthetic petroleum output in 1958 was given by Wang as 65 to 35.

Table 4.6 (2B)

1954	1955	1956	1957	1958	1959	1960
2,189	7,829	14,037	18,266	76,607		
			35	145		
701,259	593,241					
85,840	97,450	103,480	128,850	182,360		
842[2]	839[2]	998[2]	1,221[2]	1,630[2]	1,700[3]	
4,598[26]	3,968[26]	5,246[26]	4,650[2]	6,100[2]	8,250[3]	
5,230[26]	4,361[26]	5,803[26]	5,050[2]	5,700[2]	7,500[3]	
3,134	2,753	3,273				
59,064	52,605	78,683				
7,823	10,271	14,267				
3,273	3,743	5,658				
712	784	920				
3,728	3,567	3,907	4,456	4,750		
1,066[2]	1,165[2]	1,076[2]	1,100[2]	1,250[2]	1,460[3]	
693[2]	717[2]	807[2]	864[2]	900[2]	1,130[3]	
4,886[2]	7,535[2]	4,940[2]	8,277[2]	10,400[2]	11,040[3]	
3,724[30]	4,530[30]	4,519[29]				
2,293	2,518	2,648	3,120	4,000		

[12] *CH*, pp. 113, 122.

[13] *CH*, p. 113.

[14] *CH*, pp. 122-123.

[15] SSB, *Communique on the Results of the Implementation of the First Five-Year Plan for National Economic Development*, Peking: T'ung-chi ch'u-pan-she, 1959, p. 7.

[16] SSB, *Communique on the National Economic Development and the Implementation of the State Plan for 1953*, Peking: Ts'ai-cheng ching chi chu-pan-she, 1954, p.4. The output of electric generators in 1953 was 198 percent of the 1952 level.

[17] *Communique on the Implementation of the National Economic Plan for 1955*, Peking: T'ung-chi ch'u-pan-she, 1956, p. 3.

[18] *CH*, p. 122.

[19] *CH*, p. 123.

[20] 1955-58: *TGY*, p.

[21] SSB, *Communique on the results of the Implementation of the National Economic Plan for 1954*, Peking: T'ung-chi ch'u-pan-she, 1955, p. 4; and SSB, *1955 Communique*, *op. cit.*,

[22] Chao, I-wen, *op. cit.*, p. 52.

[23] *TGY*, pp.

[24] SSB, *1958 Communique*, p. 17.

[25] SSB, *1955 Communique*, p. 25, p. 26.

[26] *CH*, pp. 155, 166.

[27] *CH*, p. 166.

[28] *CH*, pp. 155, 166.

[29] Chao I-wen, *op. cit.*, p. 57.

[30] Data Office, *TCKTTH*, "A General Survey of Socialist Industrialization in China," *TCKTTH*, No. 22 (November, 1956), reprinted in *HHPYK*, No. 2 (January 25, 1957), pp. 54-62, reference on p. 58.

TABLE 4.7 Output of Major Products of Private Industry, 1949-56

Product	1949	1950	1951	1952	1953	1954	1955	1956
Pig iron (including native iron), tons[1]				53,941	65,410	46,852	27,873	662
Steel, tons[1]				4,699	10,112	499	2,382	n.a.
Rolled steel, tons[1]				128,567	217,880	144,140	155,712	n.a.
Copper, tons[2]		2,079		n.a.	12,134			n.a.
Coal, thousand tons[3]	(9,178)	(13,305)	(16,246)	(7,779)	(5,783)	(4,685)	(4,325)	(331)
Electric power, million kw-hr[4]	1,570	n.a.	n.a.	440	300	70	10	n.a.
Metal-cutting machines, units	n.a.	969[2]	n.a.	n.a.	10,678[2]	n.a.	n.a.	n.a.
Electric motors, kw	n.a.	72,666[2]	n.a.	(134,190)	155,738[2]	n.a.	(42,490)[5]	n.a.
Cement, tons	(171,600)[5]	383,855[2]	n.a.	(772,200)[5]	1,049,916[2]	n.a.	n.a.	n.a.
Caustic soda, tons	(8,850)[5]	11,711[2]	n.a.	(26,070)[5]	27,473[2]	n.a.	(24,660)[5]	n.a.
Rubber footwear, thousand pairs	(20,230)[5]	33,510[2]	n.a.	(32,696)[5]	50,943[2]	n.a.	(24,363)[5]	n.a.
Paper, tons	n.a.	56,715[5]	n.a.	n.a.	121,393[5]	n.a.	(24,363)	n.a.
Cotton yarn, bales	(847,410)[6]	900,837[2]	n.a.	1,319,330[7]	1,282,157	531,118[7]	22,929[7]	n.a.
Cotton cloth, thousand meters	(755,600)[6]	n.a.	n.a.	1,486,250[7]	1,720,950[7]	1,327,240[7]	867,240[7]	430[7]
Printed cloth, thousand meters	n.a.	n.a.	n.a.	1,243,460[7]	1,693,520[7]	1,126,940[7]	732,300[7]	610[7]
Flour, tons	(1,010,410)[6]	730,414[2]	n.a.	(1,377,770)[6]	1,214,197[2]	n.a.	(317,100)[6]	n.a.
Edible vegetable oils, tons[6]	n.a.	n.a.	n.a.	(471,840)	n.a.	n.a.	(198,050)	n.a.
Cigarettes, crates[6]	(1,280,000)	n.a.	n.a.	(768,500)	n.a.	n.a.	(178,350)	n.a.

TABLE 4.7 (Continued)

1 *CH*, pp. 30-31.

2 Ch'ien Hua *et al.*, *Changes in Private Industry and Trade in China during the Past Seven Years (1949-1956)*, Peking: Tsai-cheng ch'u-pan-she, 1957, p. 89.

3 Derived from annual data on total output of coal and percentage share of private production in total output, as given in *CH*, pp. 95 and 99.

4 *CH*, p. 70.

5 Derived from the data on total output of these products and the percentage shares of these products produced by private industry in total output, as given, respectively, in *TGY*, pp. 95-100, and SSB, "The Great Changes in the Production of Private Industry during the Past Several Years," *TCKTTH*, No. 7 (April 14, 1956), p. 3.

6 Derived from the data on the total output of these products given in *TGY*, pp. 95-100, and on the percentage share of private production in the total output, given in *TCKTTH*, *op. cit.*

7 *CH*, p. 177.

TABLE 4.8 Output of Electricity Generated by Hydraulic and Thermal Power,
1949 and 1952-57, Millions of Kilowatt-Hours

Output of electricity	1949[1]	1952[1]	1953[1]	1954[1]	1955[1]	1956[1]	1957
Total	4,310	7,260	9,200	11,000	12,280	16,590	19,340[a,2]
Generated by hydraulic power	710	1,260	1,540	2,180	2,360	3,460	3,500[3]
Generated by thermal power	(3,600)	(6,000)	(7,660)	(8,820)	(9,920)	(13,130)	15,500[3]

[a] The components do not add up to the total because of rounding.

[1] *CH*, p. 64. The figures for thermal electric power are derived as residuals.

[2] *TGY*, pp. 95-100.

[3] "Data on the Electric Power Industry of Certain Countries in Early 1958,"
*Shui-li shui-tien chien-she (Water Conservation and Hydro-electric
Construction)*, No. 9, 1959, pp. 58-59. This source gives the total
output of electric power in 1957 as 19 billion kw-hr.

TABLE 4.9 Output of Electric Power by Ownership of Establishment.
1949 and 1952-56, Millions of Kilowatt-Hours

Ownership	1949	1952	1953	1954	1955	1956
Total output	4,310	7,260	9,200	11,000	12,280	16,590
State	2,480	6,410	8,100	9,740	11,160	15,490
Central	2,090	6,230	7,820	9,420	10,790	14,960
Local	390	180	280	320	370	530
Joint	260	410	800	1,190	1,110	1,100
Central	n. a.	200	470	600	570	470
Local	n. a.	210	330	590	540	630
Private	1,570	440	300	70	10	

Source: *CH*, p. 70.

TABLE 4.10 Output of Electric Power of Enterprises
of the Ministry of Electric Power Industry, 1949-52, Millions Kilowatt-Hours

Enterprise	1949	1950	1951	1952
National total	4,310	4,550	5,750	7,260
Ministry of Electric Power Industry	1,690	2,450	3,300	4,280

Source: *CH*, pp. 46-47.

TABLE 4.11 Percentage Distribution of Coal Output, Excluding Handicraft Production, by Ownership of Establishment, 1949-56

Ownership	1949	1950	1951	1952	1953	1954	1955	1956
Total	100.0	100.0	100.0	100.0	100.0	100.0	100.0	100.0
State	68.2	67.0	66.1	84.5	88.3	90.3	91.2	92.3
Cooperative	--	--	--	0.1	0.1	0.1	0.2	0.2
Joint	3.5	2.0	3.3	3.7	3.3	4.0	4.2	7.2
Private	28.3	31.0	30.6	11.7	8.3	5.6	4.4	0.3

Source: *CH*, p. 99.

TABLE 4.12 Output of Major Products of the Iron-and-Steel Industry, by Ownership of Establishment, 1952-56, Tons

Products and ownership of establishments	1952	1953	1954	1955	1956
Pig iron (including native iron)	1,928,585	2,234,098	3,113,703	3,872,421	4,826,249
State	1,811,813	2,098,310	2,939,789	3,687,975	4,674,469
Cooperative	--	--			
Joint	12,701	10,867	5,844	17,624	11,548
Private	53,941	65,410	42,162	61,156	90,718
Handicrafts	50,130	59,511	46,852	27,873	662
Steel	1,348,509	1,773,954	79,056	77,793	48,852
State	1,274,579	1,617,631	2,224,595	2,853,105	4,465,422
Cooperative	--	--	1,978,518	2,485,567	3,973,643
Joint	69,231	146,211	--	--	--
Private	4,699	10,112	245,578	365,156	491,779
Rolled steel	1,311,897	1,754,161	499	2,382	--
State	1,089,924	1,401,027	1,965,337	2,504,817	3,920,975
Cooperative	--	--	1,535,793	1,891,091	2,979,685
Joint	93,406	135,254	--	--	--
Private	128,567	217,880	285,434	458,014	941,290
			144,140	155,712	--

Source: *CH*, pp. 30-31.

TABLE 4.13 Output of Nonferrous Metals by Local Industry as Percentages of Total Output, 1953-57

Product	1953	1954	1955	1956	1957
Tungsten ore	70.5	52.8	43.6	37.9	37.9
Refined tin	12.8	49.8	44.8	37.8	38.4
Mercury	33.2	44.1	56.8	56.3	59.5
Lead	25.1	41.4	31.4	35.6	29.6
Zinc	31.3	40.2	23.2	17.5	21.2
Gold	35.9	35.8	36.0	30.8	42.4

Source: Ku T'ieh-liu, "Energetically Develop Local Nonferrous Metals Industry," *CHCC*, No. 3 (March 9, 1958), pp. 10-13, reference on p. 11.

TABLE 4.14 Geographic Distribution of Output of Major Products of Metal-Processing Industry in 1955

Area	Steam boilers		Lathes,	Pumps,	A-C electric generators		A-C electric motors		Transformers	
	Units	Tons of steam output	Units	Units	Units	Kw	Units	Kw	Units	KVA
Total	1,274	2,059	13,708	37,397	2,517	107,595	107,387	606,890	55,660	1,925,989
Inland areas	115	101	1,578	3,574	53	34,031	16,750	329,155	5,545	73,993
Coastal areas	1,159	1,958	12,130	33,823	2,464	73,564	90,637	277,735	50,115	1,851,996
Peking	99	123	608	1,818	--	--	4	3	3,495	22,037
Tientsin	163	142	511	1,552	2	3	6,053	14,932	3,077	35,273
Shanghai	385	1,284	4,174	17,858	2,428	73,291	42,950	183,758	28,568	472,122
Liaoning	545	376	3,242	7,536	--	--	21,265	46,900	10,647	1,300,290
Shantung	17	13	630	246	--	--	20,064	31,372	1,630	4,041

Source: *CH*, p. 139.

TABLE 4.15 Output of Paper by Machines and by
Handicrafts, 1949-57, Tons

| Year | Total | | Machine-made[3] | Handicraft[4] |
	TGY[1]	(3)+(4)[2]		
	(1)	(2)	(3)	(4)
1949	228,000	228,138	108,138	120,000
1950	380,000	379,664	140,664	239,000
1951	492,000	492,052	240,878	251,174
1952	539,000	603,507	371,760	231,747
1953	667,000	666,871	427,138	239,733
1954	842,000	852,018	518,273	333,745
1955	839,000	839,048	574,621	264,427
1956	998,000	997,965	729,319	268,646
1957	1,221,000	1,221,409	912,989	308,420

[1] *TGY*, pp. 95-100.

[2] The sum of items in columns 3 and 4. The discrepancies between this series and the *TGY* series for 1952 and 1954 cannot be explained with the available information.

[3] *CH*, pp. 204, 209.

[4] "A Brief Summary of the Development of Handicraft Production of Paper in 1958," *Tsao-chi kung-yeh (Paper Industry)*, No. 2 (February 7, 1959), p. 47.

TABLE 4.16 Output of Major Machine-Made Products of the Paper Industry, 1949-57, Tons

Product	1949	1950	1951	1952	1953	1954	1955	1956	1957
Total	108,138	140,664	240,878	371,760	427,138	518,273	574,621	729,319	912,989
Newsprint	14,571	29,013	53,433	60,907	88,411	85,302	88,768	102,584	121,926
Cigarette paper				5,028	6,338	10,487	6,973	9,574	8,803
Paperboard				16,965	26,303	84,764	136,551	158,273	195,158

Source: *CH*, pp. 204, 209.

TABLE 4.17 Output of Machine-Made Paper Pulp, 1949-57, Tons

Product	1949	1950	1951	1952	1953	1954	1955	1956	1957
Total	35,000	84,398	120,439	242,991	326,082	451,957	520,266	628,279	800,688
Chemical wood pulp	13,358	30,598	41,337	64,107	72,910	82,105	94,913	111,754	157,642
Machine wood pulp	5,193	9,046	16,100	26,972	22,974	41,757	56,357	75,134	102,464
Reed pulp				84,217	108,257	128,857	138,575	182,031	210,194

Source: *CH*, pp. 204, 210.

TABLE 4.18 Output of Major Products of Textile Industry, 1949–56

Product	1949[1]	1950[1]	1951[1]	1952[1]	1953[2]	1954[2]	1955[2]	1956[2]
Cotton yarn, thousand bales	1,803	2,408	2,683	3,618	4,104	4,598	3,968	5,246
Cotton cloth, thousand meters	1,888,730	2,522,420	3,058,190	3,828,910	4,685,400	5,230,180	4,361,290	5,803,190
Native cloth, thousand meters	262,410	273,460	284,980	329,160	316,500	310,630	149,490	74,470
Printed cloth, thousand meters				1,924,380	2,743,360	3,133,600	2,753,320	3,273,460
Gunny sacks, thousand units	9,730	15,331	39,033	67,353	59,077	59,064	52,605	78,683
Woolen fabrics, thousand meters	5,435	4,880	4,025	4,233	6,227	7,823	10,271	14,267
Woolen yarn, tons	1,760	1,246	801	1,980	3,718	3,273	3,743	5,658
Woolen rugs, thousand units	222	485	1,083	717	393	712	784	920
Domestic silk, tons	479	2,002	2,932	3,548	4,319	4,607	5,377	6,191
Tussah silk, tons	61	241	444	504	707	546	587	1,337
Silk fabrics, thousand meters	51,120	63,300	64,760	73,800	78,250	93,970	118,610	

Note: The figures cover factory output only, except for cotton cloth, printed cloth, and silk fabrics,
for which handicraft output is also included.

[1] CH, p. 155.
[2] Ibid., p. 166.

TABLE 4.19 Factory Output of Major Products of Textile Industry, by Ownership of Establishment, 1952-56

Products and ownership of establishment	1952	1953	1954	1955	1956
Cotton yarn, bales	3,618,080	4,104,281	4,597,730	3,967,501	5,246,558
State	1,772,128	2,205,253	2,304,354	2,028,891	2,715,283
Cooperative	--	--	--	--	--
Joint	526,622	616,871	1,762,258	1,915,681	2,531,275
Private	1,319,330	1,282,157	531,118	22,929	—
Cotton cloth, thousand meters	3,071,530	3,605,650	4,098,180	3,489,750	4,607,300
State	1,380,360	1,601,240	1,884,440	1,630,530	2,247,550
Cooperative	12,690	12,630	15,510	12,500	9,470
Joint	192,230	270,830	870,990	979,480	2,349,850
Private	1,486,250	1,720,950	1,327,240	867,240	430
Printed cloth, thousand meters	1,875,380	2,694,280	3,085,140	2,709,330	3,188,230
State	506,390	660,300	928,010	859,210	1,002,270
Cooperative	9,030	19,710	32,360	16,890	13,150
Joint	116,500	320,750	997,830	1,100,930	2,172,200
Private	1,243,460	1,693,520	1,126,940	732,300	610
Gunny sacks, thousand units	67,353	59,077	59,064	52,605	78,683
State	53,817	46,653	45,495	39,613	53,840
Cooperative	--	--	--	--	--
Joint	348	414	10,518	12,921	24,843
Private	13,188	12,010	3,051	71	--
Woolen fabrics, thousand meters	4,233	6,227	7,823	10,271	14,267
State	2,180	2,956	4,016	5,848	7,154
Cooperative	--	--	--	--	--
Joint	338	354	1,589	4,170	7,113
Private	1,715	2,917	2,218	253	
Wool yarn, tons	1,979	3,718	3,273	3,743	5,506
State	700	1,402	1,279	1,644	1,602
Cooperative	--	--	--	--	--
Joint	37	97	506	1,756	3,904
Private	1,242	2,219	1,488	343	--
Woolen rugs, units	716,713	393,495	712,102	783,735	920,376
State	676,365	283,577	540,173	576,229	687,376
Cooperative	--	--	--	--	33
Joint	13,304	37,003	142,440	205,218	232,967
Private	27,044	72,915	29,489	2,288	--
Domestic silk, tons	3,548	4,319	4,607	5,377	6,191
State	1,035	1,206	1,483	1,778	2,167
Cooperative	--	--	--	--	6
Joint	917	1,317	2,094	3,413	4,018
Private	1,596	1,796	1,030	186	---
Tussah silk, tons	504	707	546	587	1,333
State	504	707	546	587	1,333

Source: CH, pp. 177-79.

TABLE 4. 20   Distribution of Output of Cotton Yarn and Cotton
Cloth between Inland and Coastal Areas,
1949, 1952, and 1956

Product	1949	1952	1956
Cotton yarn, thousand bales	1,803	3,618	5,246
Inland areas	246	644	1,483
Coastal areas	1,557	2,974	3,763
Cotton cloth, thousand meters[a]		3,071,500	4,645,100
Inland areas		372,500	951,000
Coastal		2,699,000	3,694,100

[a] Not including handicraft production.
Source: CH, p. 188.

TABLE 4.21   Regional Distribution of Output of Major Cotton Textile Products in 1956

Area	Cotton yarn, thousand bales	Cotton cloth, thousand meters	Printed cloth, thousand meters
	(1)	(2)	(3)
Total	5,246	5,803,200	3,188,200
By inland and coastal areas:			
Inland	1,483	1,456,800	431,700
Coastal	3,763	4,346,400	2,756,500
By region:			
Northeast China	365	389,900	231,700
North China	1,437	1,713,000	885,600
East China	2,331	2,495,700	1,693,800
Shanghai	1,622	1,411,800	1,487,200
Central China	491	355,600	91,900
South China	28	172,300	61,000
Southwest China	254	340.400	104,000
Northwest China	340	336,400	120,200

Source: CH, p. 190.

TABLE 4. 22   Output of Sugar by Machines and by Handicrafts,
1952-56, Thousand Tons

Year	Total[1]	Machine-made[2]	Handicraft[3]
	(1)	(2)	(3)
1952	451	249	(202)
1953	638	298	(304)
1954	693	347	(346)
1955	717	410	(307)
1956	807	518	(289)

[1] TGY, pp. 95-100.
[2] Hsiang Ou and Li Lai, "Sugar Manufacturing Industry in
China," TLCS, September, 1957, pp. 392-96, reference
on p. 393.
[3] Derived by subtracting items in column 2 from items in
column 1.

TABLE 4.23 Output of Major Industrial Products in Peking,
1949, 1957, and 1958

Product	1949	1957	1958
Pig iron, thousand tons	26	430	520
Steel, thousand tons	n. a.	28	160[a]
Rolled steel, thousand tons	n. a.	14	58.4
Electric power, million kw-hr	150	700	1,050
Coal, thousnad tons	1,110	2,570	4,600
Metal-cutting machines, units	n. a.	1,900	4,770
Cotton yarn, thousand bales	n. a.	109	180

[a] Including 40,000 tons of steel produced by indigenous
methods.

Source: "Deputy Mayor Wan Li's Report to the Second
Session of the Third People's Congress of Peking,"
JMJP, September 11, 1959.

TABLE 4.24 Output of Major Industrial Products in Shanghai, 1949, 1957, and 1958

Product	1949	1957	1958
Steel, tons	5,250	590,000	1,220,000
Metal-cutting machines, units	690	4,390	12,700
Heavy machines, tons	n. a.	16,260	112,000
Steam turbines, kw	n. a.	127,070	521,000
Power machinery, hp	n. a.	203,630	460,000
AC electric motors, kw	n. a.	349,940	1,630,000
Transformers, KVA	n. a.	774,940	3,030,000
Tires, units	5,160	160,000	n. a.
Rubber footwear, thousand pairs	23,090	66,270	n. a.
Cotton yarn, thousand bales	714	1,414	1,982
Cotton cloth, thousand meters	n. a.	1,118	1,490

Sources: Tsao Ti-ch'iu (Deputy Mayor of Shanghai), "Work Report of Shanghai's
Municipal People's Council," Wen-hui-pao, Shanghai, June 14, 1959; and Pan
Hsueh-ming, "Industrial Development in Shanghai," TLCS, No. 7 (July 6, 1957),
pp. 302-5.

TABLE 4.25 Output of Major Industrial Products in the Inner Mongolia Autonomous Region, 1947–58

Product	1947	1948	1949	1950	1951	1952	1953	1954	1955	1956	1957	1958
Steel, thousand tons												13
Iron, thousand tons												88
Coal, thousand tons	352	422	460	520	657	746	848	1,084	1,397	1,719	2,165	5,874
Electric power, thousand kw	13,168	13,412	11,868	13,317	14,721	15,225	29,052	37,756	48,513	73,172	91,855	199,198
Lumber, thousand cubic meters	65	159	175	358	422	427	952	1,269	1,452	1,706	1,867	3,201
Coke, thousand tons					50	4,753	8,492	32,201	21,437	14,518	24,355	221,512
Fire brick, tons				415	224	860	2,102	4,705	3,367	8,967	11,253	49,457
Paper, tons	238	233	229	224	220	228	339	220	681	570	4,353	6,712
Soap, tons	660	482	361	260	193	148	257	321	304	397	664	1,979
Natural soda, tons	15,000	2,500	3,000	3,550	4,210	30,000	25,879	38,260	42,857	60,058	1,279	106,372
Soda, tons					11	52	206	1,922	2,667	3,327	4,243	5,112
Mica, tons				10	75	106	140	193	174	230	192	428
Asbestos, tons					33	53	454	569	662	820	792	967
Bricks, thousand pieces	66,984	59,278	52,459	46,769	69,806	67,167	114,431	184,229	259,368	495,823	524,771	766,545
Tiles, thousand pieces					3,369	1,750	4,836	9,440	8,932	16,023	21,102	97,135
Woolens, thousand square meters						2	3	4	16	14	16	94
Carpets, pieces						8,702	40,519	62,518	55,868	40,346	29,892	45,114
Heavy Leather, tons	201	168	109	129	165	196	214	429	441	800	840	1,161
Light leather, square meters	63,570	66,420	82,610	32,168	66,876	53,036	36,770	137,572	159,540	317,380	285,528	205,011
Leather shoes, thousand pairs							64	72	73	165	239	425
Milk products, thousand tons				59	137	471	858	1,163	1,662	1,815	2,286	3,860
Sugar, tons									8,241	26,105	18,357	8,941
Edible vegetable oil, tons	698	942	652	1,158	1,604	2,587	3,515	7,048	9,708	8,629	10,868	12,699
Wine, tons			1,182	2,702	5,104	4,439	8,765	10,273	10,169	10,439	11,127	15,122
Salt, tons	68,360	69,228	65,076	51,608	106,301	119,058	76,495	112,198	302,184	217,770	438,930	653,377

Source: NMKTC, pp. 117–212.

201

TABLE 4.26 Output of Major Industrial Products in Kirin Province, 1957-58

Product	1957	1958
Electric power, thousand kw-hr	3,008,110	3,369,080
Coal, tons	679,214	10,011,614
Coke, tons	88,832	497,459
Crude petroleum, tons	37,435	44,398
Metal-cutting machines[a], units	38	3,919
Power machinery, hp	400	361,163
Electric generators, units	10	129
kw	150	1,452
A C electric motors, units		2,392
kw		52,443
Transformers, units	129	1,742
KVA	17,567	107,508
Mining equipment, tons	1,892	3,274
Water pumps, units	1,003	3,799
Automobiles, units	7,513	14,988
Cement, tons		16,411
Fire bricks, tons	7,882	115,860
Lumber shipped out, cubic meters	2,176,693	2,895,002
Sulfuric acid, tons		22,615
Rubber footwear, thousand pairs	9,080	11,386
Machine-made paper (including cardboard), tons	152,164	164,946
Cigarettes, cases	108,346	116,255
Sugar, tons	30,529	32,758
Alcohol products, tons	17,733	23,142

[a] Including native machine tools.

Source: Kirin Provincial Statistical Bureau, "Communique on the Fulfillment of the Economic Plan for 1958 in Kirin Province," *Kirin JP*, Ch'ang-chun, March 18, 1959, pp. 1-2.

TABLE 4.27 Output of Major Products of Lumber and Food Industries in Heilungkiang Province, 1949-58

Product	1949	1950	1951	1952	1953	1954	1955	1956	1957	1958
Lumber, thousand cu m:										
Amount of cutting,	n.a.	350	368	650	852	885	479	503	931	1,047
Amount shipped out	n.a.	298	218	425	646	894	773	631	732	804
Food:										
Cigarettes, cases	8,106	n.a.	n.a.	78,335	n.a.	n.a.	n.a.	n.a.	78,642	n.a.
Sugar, tons	7,631	n.a.	n.a.	23,318	n.a.	n.a.	n.a.	n.a.	105,179	n.a.
Flour, tons	82,824	n.a.	n.a.	71,590	n.a.	n.a.	n.a.	n.a.	299,338	n.a.
Edible vegetable oils, tons	22,334	n.a.	n.a.	58,006	n.a.	n.a.	n.a.	n.a.	53,792	n.a.
Powdered milk, tons						n.a.	n.a.	n.a.	1,035	n.a.
Wine, tons	10,231	n.a.	n.a.	25,053	n.a.	n.a.	n.a.	n.a.	32,772	n.a.
Alcohol, tons	1,219	n.a.	n.a.	5,171	n.a.	n.a.	n.a.	n.a.	11,140	n.a.

Source: Wu Ch'uan-chun *et al.*, *Tung-pei ti-ch'u ching-chi ti-li (Economic Geography of Northeast China)*, Peking: K'o-hsueh ch'u-pan-she, 1959, 211 pp.; translated in JPRS: 15,388, September 21, 1962, reference on p. 376.

TABLE 4.28   Output of Major Industrial Products in Kansu Province,
            1952, 1956, and 1957

	1952	1956	1957
Electric power, thousand kw-hr	10,222	61,477	96,833
Coal, tons	363,623	853,070	1,225,265
Crude petroleum, tons	142,649	533,235	755,381
Gasoline, tons	48,962	124,853	128,761
Cement, tons	107	2,731	8,962
Fire bricks, tons	549	7,331	9,139
Bricks, thousand pieces	41,417	433,410	537,168
Tiles, thousand pieces	12,765	28,179	48,786
Lumber (amount of cutting), cubic meters	5,829	116,429	86,786
Lumber (amount shipped out), cubic meters	53,976	67,938	76,165
Machine-made paper, tons	63	621	651
Woolen fabrics, thousand meters	53	122	207
Cigarettes, cases	6,566	8,035	8,238
Edible vegetable oils, tons	1,483	4,297	5,874
Flour, tons	37,080	150,859	189,343

Source: Kansu Provincial Statistical Bureau, "Communique on the Results of
   the Implementation of the National Economic Plan for 1957 in Kansu Province,"
   Kansu JP, Lanchow, June 12, 1958, p. 2.

TABLE 4.29   Output of Major Ind-
            ustrial Products in
            Ningsia Hui Auto-
            nomous Region, 1958

Product	Output thousand tons
Pig iron[a]	31
Steel[a]	36
Coal	1,200

[a] Produced by indigenous methods.
Source: Ma Hsin, "Building
Industry of Ningsia Hui Autonomous
Region around Coal Production."
JMJP, August 16, 1959.

TABLE 4.30   Output of Major Industrial Products
            in Chinghai Province, 1952 and 1957

Product	1952	1957
Electric power, kw-hr	840	9,881
Coal, tons	96,410	482,070
Brick, thousand pieces	4,482	121,002
Tiles, thousand pieces	108	46,178
Flour, tons	1,070	17,022
Edible vegetable oils, tons	1	1,599

Source: Chinghai Provincial Statistical Bureau,
   "Communique on the Results of the Implemen-
   tation of the First Five-Year Plan for the
   Development of the National Economy in
   Chinghai Province, 1953-1957," *Chinghai JP*,
   Hsi-ning, September 30, 1958, p. 2

TABLE 4.31 Output of Major Industrial Products in Sinkiang-Uighur Autonomous Region, 1949, 1952, 1957, and 1958

	1949	1952	1957	1958
Electric power, thousand kw-hr[1]	(960)	(4,470)	79,280	114,021
Coal, thousand tons[2]			860	3,600
Crude petrolem, thousand tons[2]			94	350

[1] Bureau of Electric Power Industry of Sinkiang-Uighur Autonomous Region, "The Ten Years of the Electric Power Industry in Sinkiang-Uighur Autonomous Region" *Shui-li yu tien-li (Water Conservancy and Electric Power)*, No. 18 (September 2p, 1959), pp. 31-33. Figures in parenthesis are derived estimates.

[2] Sai Fu-ting, "Report to the First Session of the Second People's Congress of the Sinkiang-Uighur Autonomous Region on January 22, 1959," *Sinkiang JP*, Urumchi, January 30, 1959, pp. 2-3.

TABLE 4.32 Output of Major Industrial Products in Anhwei Province, 1956-57

Product	1956[1]	1957[2]
Pig iron, tons	177,423	290,759
Steel, tons	1,694	2,314
Electric power, thousand kw-hr	151,366	197,685
Coal, tons	3,717,766	5,024,107
Belt conveyor, meters	3,825	2,995
Hopper hoist, units	118	383
Screw conveyor, meters	68	235
Grain-seeding machines, units	3	n. a.
Double wheeled plows, units	93,667	n. a
Water carts, units	42,004	n. a.
Water pumps, units	17	n. a.
Phosphorous powder, tons	12,330	n. a.
Fire bricks, tons	1,110	2,211
Machine-made paper, tons	2,984	4,290
Cotton yarn, bales	33,033	46,046
Cotton cloth, thousand meters		108,717
Printed cloth, bolts	360,896	n. a.
Jute bags, units	180,000	n. a.
Gold pens, units	20,000	22,000
Thermos bottles, thousand units	1,034	1,587
Matches, cases	338,000	375,000
Edible vegetable oils, tons	23,393	36,872
Flour, tons	124,600	180,490
Cigarettes, cases	147,045	225,081
Wine, tons	14,797	21,394
Soap, tons	5,348	4,794

[1] Anhwei Provincial Statistical Bureau, "Communique on the Results of the Implementation of the National Economic Plan for 1956 in Anhwei Province," *Anhwei JP*, Ho-fei, September 25, 1957, p. 2.

[2] Anhwei Provincial Statistical Bureau, "Communique on the Results of the Implementation of the National Economic Plan for 1957 in Anhwei Province," *Anhwei HP*, Ho-fei, April 30, 1958.

TABLE 4.33 Output of Major Industrial Products in
Fukien Province, 1957 and 1958

Product	1957	1958
Coal, tons	86,250	690,000
Metal-cutting machines, units	334	1,336
Power machinery, hp	25,211	36,808
Cement, tons	52,630	80,000
Machine-made paper, tons	7,500	21,000
Sugar, tons·	93,700	104,000

Source: Liang Ling-Kuang (Governor of Fukien),
"Fukien Provincial Plan for 1959,"
Fukien JP, February 11, 1959, pp. 1-2.

TABLE 4.34 Output of Major Industrial Products in Kwangtung Province, 1952, .1957,
and 1958

Product	1952	1957	1958
Pig iron, tons		8,500[1]	190,000[a,1]
Steel, tons		2,500[1]	42,000[b,1]
Tungsten ore, tons	3,974[2]	8,000[c,2]	
Refined tin, tons	1,374[2]	4,484[c,2]	
Electric power, thousand kw-hr	10,430[2]	25,180[c,2]	
Coal, tons	56,701[d,2]	968,570[1]	3,390,000[1]
Machine-made paper, tons	1,707[2]	4,907[c,2]	
Rubber footwear, thousand pairs	3,820[2]	4,710[c,2]	
Cotton yarn, bales	21,019[2]	28,006[c,2]	
Cotton cloth, thousand bolts	2,000[d,2]	2,970[c,d,2]	
Factory-made silk, tons	385[2]	538[c,2]	
Gunny sacks, units	1,144,447[2]	5,890,000[c,2]	
Cigarettes, cases	79,684[2]	153,000[c,2]	
Sugar, tons	226,000[3]	400,000[3]	
Edible vegetable oils, tons	44,312[2]	86,827[c,2]	
Salt, tons	293,628[2]	478,000[4]	

[a] In addition, 430,000 tons of pig iron were produced by indigenous methods.
[b] In addition, 200,000 tons of steel were produced by indigenous methods.
[c] Planned targets.
[d] Not including handicraft production.
[1] Kwangtung Provincial Statistical Bureau, "Communique on the Development of the
National Economy in Kwangtung Province in 1958 and the First Half of 1959,"
Wen-hui Pao, Hong Kong, October 5, 1959.
[2] Liang Jen-tsai, *Kuang-tung ching-chi ti-li (Economic Geography of Kwangtung),*
Peking: K'o-hsueh ch'u-pan-she, November, 1956, p. 96.
[3] Sun Ching-chih, ed. *Hua-nan ti-ch'u ching-chi ti-li (Economic Geography of
South China(,* Peking: K'o-hsueh ch'u-pan-she, 1959, 147 pp.; translated in
JPRS: 14,954, August 24, 1962, p. 90.
[4] *Ibid.,* p. 95.

TABLE 4.35 Output of Major Industrial Products in Kwangsi Chuan Autonomous Region, 1949 and 1958

Product	1949	1958
Electric power, thousand kw-hr	21,220	174,010
Coal, thousand tons	n.a.	2,470
Machine-made sugar, tons	44	24,221

Source: Wei Kuo-ching (Governor of Kwangsi), "Reviewing the Achievements in the Past Ten Years and Marching Bravely Forward," *Min-tzu tuan-chieh (Unity of Nationalities)*, No. 10 (October 6, 1959), pp. 9-12, reference on p. 11.

TABLE 4.36 Output of Major Industrial Products in Szechuan Province 1949, 1952, and 1957-59

Product	1949	1952	1957	1958	1959
Pig iron, tons			284,100	838,800	
Steel, tons			353,600	702,900	
Electric power, million kw-hr	147	249	676	1,070	1,802
Coal, thousand tons		3,370	7,730	20,280	33,000
Chemical fertilizer, tons		1,700	126,000		
Paper (including paper board), tons			93,150	132,000	
Cotton yarn, bales			165,260	274,000	

Sources: Li Pin (Deputy Governor of Szechuan), "Draft of 1959 Economic Plan for Szechuan Province," *Szechuan JP*, Chengtu, June 25, 1959, p. 2.
Ye A. Afanas'yeskiy, *Szechuan*, published by Publishing House of Oriental Literature, Moscow, 1961, 267 pp.; translated in JPRS: 15,306, September 17, 1962, pp. 125, 143, 171.

TABLE 4.37 Gross Value of Industrial Output at Constant Prices by Sector, 1949-58, Millions of Yuan

Industry	At 1952 Prices									At 1957 Prices	
	1949	1950	1951	1952	1953	1954	1955	1956	1957	1957	1958
	(1)	(2)	(3)	(4)	(5)	(6)	(7)	(8)	(9)	(10)	(11)
Total	14,018[1]	19,120[2]	26,350[2]	34,326[1]	44,696[1]	51,975[1]	54,871[1]	70,360[1]	78,390[2]	70,400[2]	117,000[2]
Modern industry	10,781[1]	(14,058)[3]	(20,209)[3]	27,014[1]	35,577[1]	41,513[1]	44,748[1]	(58,660)[3]	(65,020)[3]	n.a.	n.a.
Modern factory	7,913[1]	10,890[4]	15,910[4]	22,049[1]	28,809[1]	33,986[1]	37,082[1]	50,340[4]	55,630[4]	49,670[4]	87,270[4]
Handicraft factory	2,868[1]	(3,167)[5]	(4,299)[5]	4,965[1]	6,768[1]	7,527[1]	7,666[1]	(8,320)[5]	(9,390)[5]	n.a.	n.a.
Handicrafts[a]	3,237[1,6]	5,062[6]	6,141[6]	7,312[1,6]	9,119[1,6]	10,462[1,6]	10,128[1,6]	11,700[7]	13,370[7]	n.a.	n.a.

[a] Including handicraft cooperatives and indivdual handicrafts.

[1] SSB, *Communique on the Results of the Implementation of the National Economic Plan for 1955*, Peking: T'ung-chi ch'u-pan-she, June, 1956, p. 20.

[2] *TGY*, p. 87.

[3] Derived as residuals from the gross-value output of the industry as a whole and that of handicrafts.

[4] *TGY*, p. 91.

[5] Derived as residuals from the gross-value output of modern industry and that of modern factories.

[6] Chao I-wen, *Industry in New China*, Peking: T'ung-chi ch'u-pan-she, 1957, p. 104.

[7] *TGY*, p. 94.

TABLE 4.38 Gross Value of Industrial Output at Constant Prices, by Ownership of Establishment, 1949-59, Millions of Yuan

	At 1952 prices				
	1949	1950	1951	1952	1953
	(1)	(2)	(3)	(4)	(5)
Gross value of industrial output	14,018[1,2]	19,120[2]	26,350[2]	34,326[1,2]	44,696[1,2]
State	3,683[1]	(6,256)[4]	(9,074)[4]	14,258[1]	19,239[1]
Cooperatives	65[1]	(150)[6]	(345)[6]	1,109[1]	1,702[1]
Factory[a]	50[1]	(110)[8]	(211)[1]	863[1]	1,216[1]
Handicraft[b]	15[1,7]	40[7]	134[7]	246[1,7]	486[1,7]
Joint	220[1,10]	414[10]	806[10]	1,367[1,10]	2,013[1,10]
Private	6,828[1,11]	7,278[11]	10,118[11]	10,526[1,11]	13,109[1,11]
Individual handicrafts[c]	3,222[1,12]	5,022[12]	6,007[12]	7,066[1,12]	8,633[1,12]
Gross value of factory output	10,781[1]	(14,058)[4]	(20,209)[4]	27.014[1]	35,577[1]
State	3,683[1]	6,256[4]	(9,074)[4]	14,258[1]	19,239[1]
Cooperative	50[1]	(110)[8]	(211)[8]	863[1]	1,216[1]
Joint	220[1,10]	414[1,10]	806[1,10]	1,367[1,10]	2,013[1,10]
Private	6,828[1,11]	7,278[11]	10,118[11]	10,526[1,11]	13,109[1,11]
Gross value of factory output of state and joint enterprises	3,730[14]	6,360[14]	9,290[14]	15,120[14]	20,450[14]

[a] Including processing factories of supply and marketing cooperatives, and consumers' cooperatives.

[b] For 1949-55, the output of handicraft cooperatives consisted only that of handicraft producers' cooperatives. In 1956, the output of handicraft supply and marketing cooperatives and of handicraft production teams were also included.

[c] The output of handicraft supply and marketing cooperatives and of handicraft production teams were included in the output of individual handicrafts for 1949-1955, but were excluded for 1956.

[1] SSB, *Communique on the Results of the Implementation of the National Economic Plan for 1955*, Peking: T'ung-chi ch'u-pan-she, June, 1956, pp. 22 and 24.

[2] *TGY*, p. 87.

[3] *JMJP*, January 23, 1960.

[4] Chao I-wen, *Industry in New China*, Peking: T'ung-chi ch'u-pan-she, 1957, p. 66. According to Chao, the proportions of the gross value output of the state and the private industrial enterprises in the total gross value of factory output in 1950 were 44.5 percent and 51.8 per-

TABLE 4.38 (Continued)

At 1952 prices				At 1957 prices		
1954	1955	1956	1957	1957	1958	1959
(6)	(7)	(8)	(9)	(10)	(11)	(12)
51,975[1,2]						
24,488[1]	54,871[1]	70,360[2]	78,390[2]	70,400[2]	117,000[2]	163,000[3]
2,454[7]	28,142[1]	38,383[1]	n. a.	n. a.	n. a.	n. a.
1,598[1,7]	3,453[1]	(12,000)[8]	n. a.	n. a.	n. a.	n. a.
856[1,10]	1,301[1,10]	(10,860)[9]	n. a.	n. a.	n. a.	n. a.
5,986[1,10]	7,188[1,10]	19,108[5]	n. a.	n. a.	n. a.	n. a.
10,341[1,12]	7,266[1,11]	29[5]	n. a.	n. a.	n. a.	n. a.
9,606[1,12]	8,822[1,12]	840[5]	n. a.	n. a.	n. a.	n. a.
41,513[1]	44,748[1]	(58,660)[13]	(65,020)[13]	n. a.	n. a.	n. a.
24,488[1]	28,142[1]	38,383[5]	n. a.	n. a	n. a.	n. a
1,598[1,10]	2,152[1,10]	(1,140)[8]	n. a.	n. a.	n. a.	n. a.
5,086[1,11]	7,188[1,11]	19,108[5]	n. a.	n. a	n. a	n. a.
10,341	7,266[1,11]	29[5]	n. a.	n. a.	n. a.	n. a.
26,090[14]	30,290[14]	39,520[14]	44,350[14]	39,470[14]	81,290[14]	n. a.

cent, respectively. The corresponding proportions for 1951 were 44.9 percent and 50.1 percent.

[5] SSB, *Communique on the Results of the Implementation of the National Economic Plan in 1956*, Peking: T'ung-chi ch'u-pan-she, 1957.

[6] Derived as a sum total from its two components.

[7] Chao I-wen, *op. cit.*, pp. 109 and 111.

[8] Derived as a residual by subtracting the gross-value output of state, joint, and private enterprises from the total gross-value of factory output.

[9] Derived by subtracting the gross-value output of individual handicrafts (840 million yuan) from the gross-value output of handicrafts (11,700 million yuan).

[10] Ch'ien Hua *et al., Changes in Private Industry and Trade in China in the Past Seven Years (1949-1956)*, Peking: Ts'ai-cheng chin-chi ch'u-pan-she, 1957, p. 112.

[11] *Ibid.*, p. 8.

[12] Chao I-wen, *op. cit.*, pp. 104, 190, and 111.

[13] Derived by subtracting the gross-value output of the handicrafts from the gross industrial value outputs.

[14] *TGY*, p. 37.

TABLE 4.39 Gross-Value of Industrial Output at Constant Prices: Producer and Consumer Goods, 1949-59. Millions of Yuan

	Gross value of industrial output			Gross value of factory output			Gross value of output of individual handicrafts (including cooperatives)		
	Total[a] (1)[1]	Producer goods (2)[1]	Consumer goods (3)[1]	Total[a] (4)[2]	Producer goods (5)[3]	Consumer goods (6)[3]	Total (7)[4]	Producer goods (8)[5]	Consumer goods (9)[6]
At 1952 prices:									
1949	14,020	3,730	10,290	10,781	3,100	7,681	3,237	(630)	(2,609)
1950	19,120	5,650	13,470	(14,058)	n.a.	n.a.	5,062	n.a.	n.a.
1951	26,350	8,500	17,850	(20,209)	n.a.	n.a.	6,141	n.a.	n.a.
1952	34,330	12,220	22,110	27,014	10,730	16,284	7,312	(1,490)	(5,826)
1953	44,700	16,680	28,020	35,577	14,670	20,907	9,119	(2,010)	(7,113)
1954	51,970	19,990	31,980	41,513	17,578	23,935	10,462	(2,412)	(8,045)
1955	54,870	22,890	31,980	44,748	20,578	24,170	10,123	(2,312)	(7,810)
1956	70,360	32,040	38,320	(58,660)	(29,241)	(29,419)	11,700	(2,799)	(8,901)
1957	78,390	37,940	40,450	(65,020)	n.a.	n.a.	13,370	n.a.	n.a.
At 1957 prices:									
1957	70,400	33,000	27,400						
1958	117,000	67,000	50,000						
1959	163,000	96,000	67,000						

[a] Components may not add up to the totals shown because of rounding.

[1] Data are taken from *TGY*, p. 87, except for 1959, for which figures are given in *JMJP*, January 23, 1960.

[2] For 1949 and 1952-55, figures are given in SSB, *Communique on the Results of the Implementation of the National Economic Plan for 1955*, Peking; T'ung-chi ch'u-pan-she, 1956, p. 24. For 1950-51 and 1956-57, figures are derived as residuals from corresponding items in columns 1 and 7.

[3] For 1949 and 1952-55: SSB, *op. cit.* For 1956: Derived from the index numbers given in Chi Ts'ung-wei, "On the Balanced Growth of Industry in China," *CHCC*, No. 7 (July 9, 1957), pp. 4-8.

[4] *TGY*, p. 94.

[5] Derived by substracting items in column 5 from items in column 2.

[6] Derived by substracting items in column 6 from items in column 3.

TABLE 4.40 Gross-Value of Industrial Output at 1952 Prices, by Size of Enterprise, 1952-55, Millions of Yuan

Output	1952	1953	1954	1955
Gross value of industrial output[1]	34,326	44,696	52,100	54,876
Large-scale enterprises[1]	23,387	30,806	37,309	40,877
Small-scale enterprises[2]	(10,939)	(13,890)	(14,791)	(13,999)

[1] Data Office, *TCKTTH*, "A General Survey of Socialist Industrialzation in China," *TCKTTH*, No. 22 (November, 1956); reprinted in *HHPYK*, No. 2 (January 25, 1957), pp. 54-62, reference on p. 58.

[a] Derived as residuals from the total gross industrial value output and the gross-value output of large-scale industrial enterprises.

TABLE 4.41 Gross-Value Output of Selected Industries, at 1952 Prices, 1949-57, Thousands of Yuan

Industry	1949	1950	1951
Electric power industry	263,400[1]	277,000[2]	351,000[2]
Coal industry[3]	370,000	n.a.	n.a.
Enterprises of the Ministry of Coal Industry[4]			
Petroleum industry[5]	(30,000)		
Iron-and-steel industry[6]	191,798	609,521	911,784
Modern factory	191,296	607,842	909,422
Handicrafts	502	1,679	2,362
Metal-processing industry (modern factory)[7]	(734,986)	(1,181,123)	(2,098,385)
Machine-building industry (modern factory)	(290,696)	(523,543)	(974,994)
Chemical industry (modern factory)[8]	(162,700)		
Building materials industry[9]	170,000	n.a.	n.a.
Modern factory[8]	(118,600)	n.a.	n.a.
Lumber industry (modern factory)[8]	(743,890)	n.a.	n.a.
Paper industry[10]			
Modern factory	136,600	251,600	459,800
Handicrafts			
Food industry[11]			
Modern factory[8]	(2,544,300)	n.a.	n.a.
Handicrafts[12]			
Enterprises of the Ministry of Food[13]			
Textile industry[14]			
Modern factory[15]	3,973,290	4,642,000	5,956,000
Handicrafts[14]			
Rubber goods industry (consumer goods only)[16]			
Ceramics and earth products industry (consumer goods only)[16]			
Leather and furs industry[16]			
Glass and mirror industry[16]			
Match industry[16]			
Furniture and other bamboo and wooden products industry[16]			
Educational supplies industry[16]			
Soap, perfumes, and cosmetics industry[16]			

[a] The gross value of factory output of the building materials industry for 1952 and 1956, as derived from the data given in TGY and Chi Ts'ung-wei's article appeared to be larger than the gross-value output of the building materials industry given for these two years by Chao I-wen. Such inconsistencies cannot be explained with available information.

[1] CH, p. 71.

[2] CH, p. 48.

[3] CH, p. 95.

[4] SSB, Department of Comprehensive Statistics, "On the Gross and the Net Value Output," TCYC, No. 2 (February 23, 1958), pp. 27-30, reference on p. 28.

TABLE 4.41   (Continued)

1952	1953	1954	1955	1956	1957
430,800 [1]	512,800 [1]	616,000 [1]	699,100 [1]	927,800 [1]	
830,000	890,000	1,080,000	1,280,000	1,510,000	
				1,300,000	
				650,000	
1,369,594	1,871,333	2,327,556	2,896,611	4,124,915	
1,365,920	1,865,303	2,319,081	2,883,004	4,113,151	
3,674	6,030	8,475	13,607	11,764	
2,852,481	(4,407,083)	(5,350,200)	5,749,255	9,354,038	
1,423,248	(2,190,379)	(2,683,214)	3,034,695	5,670,000	
(864,448)					(4,291,320)
(615,100) [a]	n.a.	n.a.		1,475,000 [a]	
(621,322) [a]	(919,557)	(994,961)	(1,009,885)	(1,491,160) [a]	(1,625,500)
(1,215,630)	(1,552,360)	(1,833,340)	(1,562,000)	(1,807,200)	(1,950,600)
(764,442)	(838,787)	(968,804)	(1,121,990)	(1,439,719)	
655,240	711,104	844,135	982,791	1,318,053	1,663,005
109,202	127,683	124,669	139,199	121,666	
(7,667,000)	n.a.	n.a.	n.a.	13,395,000	
(6,105,160)	n.a.	n.a.	n.a.	n.a.	(13,264,000)
(1,561,840)					
9,425,260	11,500,295	12,669,297	12,166,277	14,694,856	
8,015,510	9,885,155	11,134,748	10,754,398	13,048,571	
1,409,750	1,615,140	1,534,549	1,411,879	1,646,285	
254,000	334,000	382,084	397,156	464,000	
94,147	126,067	156,373	168,122	220,876	
444,859	516,302	495,638	501,100	743,291	
57,315	88,787	123,445	119,840	167,612	
108,490	102,726	131,189	151,366	146,000	
820,311	1,010,812	1,147,923	1,049,871	1,250,616	
230,162	366,003	375,400	406,206	519,385	
235,759	260,461	267,761	292,092	298,600	

1958), pp. 27-30, reference on p. 28.

[5] Chao I-wen, *The Industry of New China*, Peking: T'ung-chi ch'u-pan-she, 1957, p. 50.

[6] *CH*, pp. 10-11 and 30-31.

[7] *CH*, pp. 113, 120, and 140. Figures in parentheses are derived estimates.

[8] *TGY*, p. 92 and Table 4.37.

[9] Chao I-wen, *op. cit.*, p. 52.

[10] *CH*, pp. 203-4, 209, and 214-15.

[11] Chao I-wen, *op. cit.*, p. 57.

[12] Derived as a residual.

[13] SSB, Department of Comprehensive Statistics, *op. cit.*

[14] *CH*, p. 180.

[15] *CH*, pp. 155 and 176.

[16] Chao I-wen, *op. cit.*, p. 59.

TABLE 4.42 Gross Value of Industrial Output at Constant Prices,* by Province or Equivalent, 1949–59, Millions of Yuan

Province or equivalent	1949	1950	1951	1952	1953	1954	1955	1956	1957	1958	1959
Peking[1]	170	n.a.	n.a.	n.a.	n.a.	(1,316)	n.a.	n.a.	2,100	4,600	n.a.
Shanghai[2]	3,100	n.a.	n.a.	(6,000)	n.a.	n.a.	n.a.	n.a.	11,400	17,130	24,540
Tientsin[3]						(2,836)					
Hopei[4]						(1,673)					
Shansi[5]						(926)					
Inner Mongolia Autonomous Region[6]	68	111	136	160	243	358	421	570	631	1,157	n.a.
Liaoning[7]						(7,459)	n.a.	n.a.			
Kirin[8]						(1,495)	n.a.	n.a.	(2,168)	3,230	(4,270)
Heilungkiang[9]						2,461	n.a.	n.a.	4,146	6,840	
Shensi[10]						(785)					
Kansu[11]						(302)					
Ningsia Hui Autonomous Region[12]										18	
Chinghai[13]				32	n.a.	n.a.	n.a.	n.a.	104	399	
Sinkiang-Uihur Autonomous Region[14]				169	n.a.	n.a.	n.a.	n.a.	446	740	
Shantung[15]							1,341	1,634	n.a.	7,000	
Kiangsu[16]									(4,130)	7,540	
Anhwei[17]				631	n.a.	(782)	911	1,158	1,501	4,000	
Chekiang[18]				1,137	1,501	1,613		2,000	2,274		
Fukien[19]						(728)	n.a.	n.a.	(747)		
Honan[20]						1,227	n.a.	n.a.	n.a.		
Hunan[21]				(766)	n.a.		n.a.	n.a.	1,363	1,330	
Kiangsi[22]				(355)	n.a.		n.a.	n.a.	(780)	(1,412)	
Kwangtung[23]									(3,571)	(5,800)	
Kwangsi Chuang Autonomous Region[24]							n.a.			1,238	
Szechuan[25]						(2,774)			(4,283)	6,668	
Kweichow[26]						(336)					
Yunnan[27]						630					

TABLE 4.42 (Continued, 1)

Note: Data are given in 1952 prices for 1949-57 and in 1957 prices for 1958 and 1959.

[1] 1949, 1957, and 1958: "Deputy Mayor Wan Li's Report to the Second Session of the Third Peking People's Congress," *JMJP*, September 11, 1959.
1954: Chinese Academy of Sciences, Economic Research Institue, Handicraft Section, ed., *Nationwide Survey Data on Individual Handicrafts in 1954*, Peking: Sheng-huo, tu-shu, hsin-san-lien shu-tien, 1957, page 1.

[2] 1949, 1952, 1957, and 1958: NCNA, Shanghai, June 8, 1959. 1959: Ts'ao Ti-chin (Depty Major of Shanghai), "Shanghai 1960 Economic Plan," *CFJP*, May 18, 1960, pp. 2-3.

[3] Chinese Academy of Sciences, *op. cit.*, p. 30.

[4] 1954: *Ibid.*, p. 89. the 1954 figure was an anticipated estimate.

[5] 1954: *Ibid.*, p. 94.

[6] 1949-58: *NMKTC*, p. 99.

[7] 1954: Chinese Academy of Sciences, *op. cit.*, p. 47.

[8] 1954: *Ibid.*, p. 47. 1957 and 1958: Kirin Provincial Statistical Bureau," Communique on the Fulfillment of Kirin Economic Plan for 1958," *Kirin JP*, March 18, 1959, pp. 1-2.
1959: Li Yu-wen (Governor of Kirin), "Work Report to the Third Session of the Second Kirin Provincial People's Congress, on May 23, 1960," *Kirin JP*, Chang-ch'un, May 25, 1960, pp. 2-3.

[9] 1954: Chinese Academy of Sciences, *op. cit.*, p. 52. 1957: Wu Ch'uan-chun et. al., *Economic Geography of Northeast China (Tung-pei ti-ch'u ching-chi ti-li)*, Peking: K'o-hsueh ch'u-pan-she, 1959, 211 pp; translated in JPRS: 15,388, September 21, 1962,

p. 364. 1958: Ou-yang Ch'in, "Heilungkiang 1958 Work Report," *Heilungkiang JP*, Harbin, January 25, 1959, pp. 1-3.

[10] 1954: Chinese Academy of Sciences, *op. cit.*, p. 227.

[11] 1954: *Ibid.*, p. 240.

[12] 1954: Liu Ke-p'ing, "Great Leap Forward in Production, Great Unites of Nationalities," *JMJP*, April 10, 1959.

[13] 1952 and 1957: Chinghai Provincial Statistical Bureau, "Communique on the Development of the Economy of Chinghai Province and the Results of the Implementation of the First Five-Year Plan, 1953-1957," *Chinghai JP*, Hsi-ning, September 30, 1958, p. 2.
1958: Yuan Jen-yuan (Governor of Chinghai), "Chinghai 1958 Work Report and 1959 Work Plans," *Chinghai JP*, Hsi-ning, May 21, 1959, pp. 1-3.

[14] 1952, 1957, and 1958: Sai Fu-ting, "Work Report of the People's Council of the Sinkiang-- Uighur Autonomous Region," *Sinkiang JP*, Urumchi, January 30, 1959, pp. 2-3.

[15] 1955-56: Wang Che-ju (Deputy Governor of Shantung), "Report on the 1957 Economic Plan and the Implementation of the 1956 Economic Plan for Shantung," *Ta-chung JP*, Tsinan, August 17, 1957, p. 2.
1958: Pai Ju-ping (Deputy Governor of Shantung), "Report on the Draft Plan for the Economic Development of Shantung in 1959," *Tsingtao JP*, May 25, 1959, p. 2.

[16] 1957-58: Liu Sun-yuan, "Work Report to the Third Session of the Third Kiangsu Provincial Congress of the Chinese Communist Party," *HHPYK*, No. 7 (April 10, 1959), pp. 15-22.

TABLE 4.42 (Continued, 2)

[17] 1952 and 1957: Anhwei Provincial Statistical Bureau, "Communique on the Results of the Implementation of the National Economic Plan for 1957 in Anhwei Province," *Anhwei JP*, Ho-fei, April 30, 1958. 1954: Chinese Academy of Sciences, *op. cit.*, p. 118. 1955-56: Chang K'ai-fan (Deputy Governor of Anhwei), "Government Work Report at the Fouth Session of the First Provincial People Congress of Anhwei on September 21, 1957," *Anhwei JP*, Ho-jei, September 23, 1957, pp. 2-3. 1958: Tseng Hsi-sheng (Governor of Anhwei), "Continue to Advance under the Banner of the General Line--1958 Work Report of Anhwei Province," *Anhwei JP*, Ho-fei, February 12, 1959, pp. 1-3.

[18] 1952-54: Chinese Academy of Sciences, *op. cit.*, p. 106. 1956-57: Wu Hsien, "Report on the Implementation of Chekiang's Economic Plan for 1957," *Chekiang kung-jen pao*, Hangchow, January 25, 1958.

[19] 1954: Chinese Academy of Sciences, *op. cit.*, p. 130.

[20] 1954: Chinese Academy of Sciences, *op. cit., p. 158.* 1958: Yang Wei-p'ing, "Work Report to the Third Session of the First Honan Provincial Congress of the Chinese Communist Party on December 24, 1958," *Honan JP*, Cheng-chou, January 16, 1959, pp. 1-3.

[21] 1952 and 1957: Hunan Provincial Statistical Bureau, "Achievements of Hunan Province in Economic Work in 1957," *Hsin Hunan Pao*, May 4, 1958.

[22] 1952 and 1957: Huang Hsien (Deputy Governor of Kiangsi), "Report on Draft Summary of the Second Five-Year Plan for the Development of the National Economy in Kiangsi Province," *Kiangsi JP*, Nanch'ang, July 3, 1958, p. 2.

[23] 1957-58: Kwangtung Provincial Statistical Bureau, "Communique on the Development of the National Economy in Kwangtung Province in 1958 and the First Half of 1959," *Wen-hui-pao*, Hong Kong, October 5, 1959.

[24] Wei Kuo-ching, "Reviewing the Achievements in the Past Ten Years and marching Bravely Forward," *Min-tzu tuan-chieh (Unity of Nationalities)*, No. 10 (October 6, 1959), pp. 1-12, reference on p. 11.

[25] 1954: Chinese Academy of Sciences, *op. cit.*, p. 205. 1957-58: Li Pin (Deputy Governor), "Draft of 1959 Economic Plan for Szechuan," *Szechuan JP*, Chengtu, June 25, 1959, p. 2.

[26] 1954: Chinese Academy of Sciences, *op. cit.*, p. 222.

[27] 1954: *Ibid.*, p. 215.

TABLE 4.43 Distribution of the Gross Value of Factory Output at 1952 Prices between Inland and Coastal Areas, 1949-56, Millions of Yuan

Area	1949	1952	1953	1954	1955	1956
Total gross value of factory output	10,781[1]	27,014[1]	35,577[1]	41,513[1]	44,748[1]	58,660[1]
Inland areas	(2,480)[2]	(7,267)[3]	(9,868)[4]	(12,500)[4]	(14,319)[2]	(18,830)[3]
Coastal areas	(8,301)[2]	(19,747)[3]	(25,710)[4]	(29,130)[4]	(30,429)[2]	(39,830)[3]

[1] SSB, *Communique on the Results of the Implementation of the National Economic Plan for 1955*, Peking: T'ung-chi ch'u-pan-she, June, 1956, p. 20. See also Table 4.37, for the 1956 figure.

[2] Computed from relative weights given in Data Office, *TCKTTH*, "Several Problems of Socialist Industrialization in China," *TCKTTH*, No. 21 (November, 1956), reprinted printed in *HHPYK*, No. 1 (January 10, 1957), pp. 67-71.

[3] Computed from relative weights given in Yang Ch'ing-wen, 'Two Problems of Industrial Location," *CHCC*, No. 8, (August 9, 1957), pp. 13-15.

[4] Computed from index numbers given in Data Office, *TCKTTH*, *op. cit*. The figures for 1953 and 1954 do not add up to the total gross value of factory output because of apparent inaccuracy in the index numbers for those two years.

217

TABLE 4.44   Gross Value of Factory Output of Private
Industry at 1952 Prices, by Sector,
1953-55, Millions of Yuan

Sector	1953	1954	1955
Total	13,109	10,341	7,266
Modern factory	9,570	7,385	4,965
Handicraft factory	3,539	2,956	2,301

Source: Ch'ien Hua *et al., Changes in Private Industry
and Trade in China during the Past Seven Years
(1949-1956)*, Peking: Ts'ai-cheng ch'u-pan-she,
1957, p. 88.

TABLE 4.45   Gross Value of Factory Output of Private
Industry at 1952 Prices, by Production
Use, 1954

Use	Number of enterprises[a]	Gross value of factory output, thousands of Yuan
Total	133,962	10,341,267
Producer goods	50,734	2,544,999
Consumer goods	83,228	7,796,268

[a] As of the end of 1954.

Source: Ch'ien Hua *et al., Changes in Private Industry and Trade in China during the Past Seven
Years (1949-1956)*, Peking: Ts'ai-cheng ch'u-
pan-she, 1957, p. 10.

TABLE 4.46   Gross Value of Factory Output
of Private Industry at 1952
Prices, by Size of Enter-
prise, 1953-55, Millions
of Yuan

Size	1953	1954	1955
Total	13,109	10,341	7,266
Large-scale enterprises	8,959	6,952	4,669
Small-scale enterprises	4,150	3,389	2,597

Source: Ch'ien Hua *et al., Changes in
Private Industry and Trade in China
during the Past Seven Years (1949-1956)*,
Peking: Ts'ai-cheng ch'u-pan-she,
1957, p. 88.

TABLE 4.47 Gross Value of Factory Output of Private Industry at 1952 Prices, by Branch, 1949-56, Thousands of Yuan

Industry	1949	1950	1951	1952	1953	1954	1955	1956
Electric power[1]	120,300	n.a.	n.a.	33,400	7,600	7,600	6,200	
Coal[2]	(93,000)	n.a.	n.a.	(67,000)	(50,700)	(42,000)	(46,000)	
Iron and steel[3]	27,323	67,778	114,269	131,629	207,327	152,924	115,046	
Smelting[4]				131,141	206,678			
Mining[5]				(488)	(649)			
Nonferrous metals[4]				132,941	227,851			
Metal processing[6]	(293,994)	(176,126)	(428,983)	(1,086,795)				
Machine building[7]	(94,034)			467,630	707,592	574,774	(1,115,355)	
Metal products[4]				519,191	898,141	894,816	(373,409)	
Electric wires[4]				65,289	113,588			
Chemicals[4]				317,533	562,139	293,100		
Chemicals products for production use								
Chemical drugs								
Paper[8]	58,000	70,000	138,000	167,000	124,000	162,210	26,474	
Food[9]						60,000		
Textiles[10]	2,502,130	2,794,000	3,534,860	4,108,350	4,977,150	2,300,931		
Cotton textiles[4]						3,644,510	2,317,930	3,900
Spinning[4]						2,941,229		
Weaving[11]						483,148		
Printing[12]				979,026	1,312,161	1,170,168		
Knitted goods[11]						1,151,292		
Tailoring[14]				287,691	348,072	291,265		
Leather[4]				188,141	319,759			
Rubber goods[13]				26,666	44,568			
Cigarettes[14]				210,274	330,186	217,942		
Educational supplies[13]						143,482		

1 *CH*, p. 71.
2 Derived from the data given in *CH*, pp. 95 and 99 and Table 4.37.
3 *CH*, pp. 10-11 and 30-31.
4 Ch'ien Hua *et al.*, *Changes in Private Industry and Trade in China during the Past Seven Years (1949-1956)*, Peking: T'sai-cheng ch'u-pan-she, 1957, p. 89.
5 Derived by subtracting "smelting" from total iron and steel.
6 Derived from the data given in *CH*, pp. 122 and 140 and Table 4.37.
7 Ch'ien Hua *et al.*, *op. cit.*, pp. 10 and 89; and *CH, p. 130* and Table 4.37.
8 *CH*, pp. 203-4 and p. 214.
9 Ch'ien Hua *et al.*, *op. cit.*, p. 10.
10 *CH*, pp. 158 and 176.
11 Chien Hua *et al.*, *op. cit.*, pp. 10 and 89.
12 *Ibid.*, p. 10.
13 *Ibid.*, p. 10.
14 *Ibid.*, p. 89.

219

TABLE 4.48   Gross Value of the Output of the Electric Power Industry at 1952 Prices, 1949-57, Thousands of Yuan

Enterprise	1949	1950	1951	1952	1953	1954	1955	1956	1957
Grand total:									
TGY[1]	(258,740)	n.a.	n.a.	(432,220)	n.a.	n.a.	n.a.	n.a.	(997,220)
CH:	263,400[2]	277,000[3]	351,000[3]	430,800[2]	512,800[2]	616,000[2]	699,100[2]	927,800[2]	
State enterprises:[2]									
Central	107,800	n.a.	n.a.	345,100	421,800	517,000	598,900	827,900	
Local	22,900	n.a.	n.a.	25,400	35,800	38,900	40,600	51,300	
Total	130,700	n.a.	n.a.	370,500	457,600	555,900	639,500	879,200	
Joint enterprises:[2]									
Central	5,200	n.a.	n.a.	15,700	27,600	26,900	24,600	13,100	
Local	7,200	n.a.	n.a.	11,200	20,000	25,600	28,600	35,500	
Total	12,400	n.a.	n.a.	26,900	47,600	52,500	53,200	48,600	
Private enterprises:[2]	120,300	n.a.	n.a.	33,400	7,600	7,600	6,200		

[1] TGY, p. 92. The gross-value output of the electric power industry accounted for 2.4 percent of the gross value of factory output of the industry as a whole in 1949, 1.6 percent in 1952, and 1.7 percent in 1957.

[2] CH, p. 71.

[3] CH, p. 48.

TABLE 4.49 Distribution of the Gross-Value Output of the Coal Industry at 1952 Prices, by Ownership of Establishment, 1949-56

Indicator	1949	1950	1951	1952	1953	1954	1955	1956
Percentage distribution:[1]								
State	70.8	69.3	68.8	88.1	91.0	92.1	92.1	
Cooperative	--	--	--	0.06	0.1	0.1	0.2	
Joint	4.0	2.7	3.8	3.8	3.2	3.9	4.1	
Private	25.2	28.0	27.4	8.04	5.7	3.9	3.6	
Total	100.0	100.0	100.0	100.0	100.0	100.0	100.0	
Amount, millions of yuan:								
State[2]	(262)	n.a.	n.a.	(731)	(810)	(995)	(1,179)	
Coop[2]	--	--	--	(0.5)	(0.9)	(1.1)	(1.6)	
Joint[2]	(15.0)	n.a.	n.a.	(31.5)	(28.4)	(42.0)	(52.4)	
Private[2]	(93.0)	n.a.	n.a.	(67.0)	(50.7)	(42.0)	(46.0)	
Total[3]	370	n.a.	n.a.	830	890	1,080	1,280	1,510

[1] CH, p. 99.
[2] Derived from multiplying total amount in yuan by the appropriate items given in percentages.
[3] CH, p. 95

TABLE 4.50 Gross-Value Output of the Iron-and-Steel Industry, at 1952 Prices, 1949-56, Thousands of Yuan

Year	Grand total	Total[1]	Gross value of factory output by ownership of establishment				
			State	Cooperative	Joint	Private	Handicrafts
	(1)	(2)	(3)	(4)	(5)	(6)	(7)
1949[2]	191,798	(191,296)	158,231	--	5,742	27,323	502
1950[2]	609,521	(607,842)	519,962	--	20,102	67,778	1,679
1951[2]	911,784	(909,422)	754,633	--	40,520	114,269	2,362
1952[2]	1,369,594	(1,365,920)	1,157,250	--	77,041	131,629	3,674
1953[3]	1,871,333	(1,865,303)	1,529,368	--	128,608	207,327	6,030
1954[3]	2,327,556	(2,319,081)	1,909,717	3,236	253,204	152,924	8,475
1955[3]	2,896,611	(2,883,004)	2,373,899	4,352	389,707	115,046	13,607
1956[3]	4,124,915	(4,113,151)	3,371,464	4,428	737,259	--	11,764

[1] Column 2 is derived by subtracting items in column 7 from items in column 1.
[2] CH, pp. 10-11.
[3] CH, pp. 30-31.

221

TABLE 4.51 Gross Value of the Output of the Metal-Processing Industry, at 1952 Prices, 1949-57, Thousands of Yuan

Industry	1949	1950	1951
Metal-processing:			
State, cooperative and joint[1]	(440,992)	n.a.	n.a.
Private[1]	(293,994)	n.a.	n.a.
Total:			
TGY[2]	(733,108)	n.a.	n.a.
CH	(734,986)[3]	(1,181,123)[3]	(2,908,385)[3]
Machine-building:			
State and cooperative	(193,669)[6]	(333,240)[6]	(514,914)[6]
Joint	2,993[7]	14,177[7]	31,097[7]
Private	(94,034)[8]	(176,126)[8]	(428,983)[8]
Total:			
TGY	(291,087)[11]	n.a.	n.a.
Annual communiques	188,000[12]	n.a.	n.a.
CH	(290,696)[14]	(523,543)[14]	(974,994)[14]
Metal products manufacturing:			
State and cooperative			
Joint	1,101[7]	1,675[7]	6,842[7]
Private			
Total			
Electric wires			
Total	(212,411)[18]	(356,700)[18]	(719,746)[18]
Repair services	(208,000)[19]	(274,020)[19]	(348,332)[19]

[1] Derived from the data on the percentage share of the gross-value output of these enterprises in the total gross-value output of the metal-processing industry, given in CH, p. 122.

[2] TGY, p. 92. The gross-value output of the metal-processing industry, excluding handicrafts, constituted 6.8 percent of the gross value of the factory output of the industry as a whole in 1949, 10.6 percent in 1952, and 16.2 percent in 1957.

[3] Derived from the data on the index of the gross-value output of the metal-processing industry for 1949-52, given in CH, p. 113.

[4] CH, p. 140.

[5] Derived from the data on the annual rate of growth of the gross-value output of the metal-processing industry, for 1952-56, given in CH, p. 120.

[6] Derived as residuals.

[7] CH, p. 130.

[8] Derived from the data on the index of the gross-value output of the private machine-building industry for 1949-55, given in CH, p. 130.

[9] Ch'ien Hsia *et al., Changes in Private Industry and Trade in China during the Past Seven Years (1949-1956)*, Peking: T'sai-cheng chin-chi ch'u-pan-she, 1957, p. 89.

[10] *Ibid.*, p. 10.

[11] TGY, p. 92. The gross-value output of the machine-building industry,

222

TABLE 4.51 (Continued)

1952	1953	1954	1955	1956	1957
(1,765,686)	n.a.	n.a.	(4,633,900)	(9,354,038)	
(1,086,795)	n.a.	n.a.	(1,115,355)		
(2,863,484)	n.a.	n.a.	n.a.	n.a.	(10,533,240)
2,852,481[4]	(4,407,083)[5]	(5,350,200)[5]	5,749,255[4]	(9,354,038)[5]	
(896,656)[6]	(1,402,295)[6]	(1,883,612)[6]	(2,295,274)[6]		
58,962[7]	80,492[7]	224,828[7]	366,012[7]		
467,630[9]	707,592[9]	574,774[10]	(373,409)[8]		
(1,404,728)[11]	n.a.	n.a.	n.a.	n.a.	(6,176,900)[11]
1,401,000[12]	2,157,000[12]	2,643,000[12]	3,030,000[12]	5,760,000[13]	
1,423,248[4]	(2,190,379)[15]	(2,683,214)[15]	3,034,695[4]	5,760,000[16]	
(385,656)[17]					
45,029[7]	18,865[7]	120,942[7]	254,927[7]		
519,191[9]	898,141[9]	894,816[10]			
65,289[9]	113,588[9]				
(949,876)[18]					
(419,315)[19]					

excluding handicrafts, constituted 2.7 percent of the gross-value output of the industry as a whole in 1949, 5.2 percent in 1952, and 9.5 percent in 1957.

[12] SSB, *Communique on the Results of the Implementation of the National Economic Plan for 1955*, Peking: T'ung-chi ch'u-pan-she, 1956, p. 24.

[13] SSB, *Communique on the Results of the Implementation of the National Economic Plan for 1956*, Peking: T'ung-chi ch'u-pan-she, 1957; reprinted in *1958 JMST*, pp. 456-95.

[14] Derived from the data on the index of the gross-value output of the machine-building industry for 1949-52, given in *CH*, p. 113.

[15] Derived from the data on the annual rate of growth of the gross-value output of the machine-building industry for 1952-56, given in *CH*, p. 120.

[16] *CH*, p. 121.

[17] Derived as a residual.

[18] Derived from the data on the percentage share of metal products manufacturing in the gross-value output of the metal-processing industry for 1949-52, given in *CH*, p. 112.

[19] Derived from the data on the percentage share of repair services in the gross-value output of the metal processing industry for 1949-52, given in *CH*, p. 112.

TABLE 4.52 Geographic Distribution of the Gross Value of Factory Output of the
Metal-Processing Industry, at 1952 Prices, 1952 and 1955,
Thousands of Yuan

Location	Metal-processing industry		Of which: machine-building industry	
	1952	1955	1952	1955
Total[1]	2,852,481	5,749,255	1,423,248	3,034,695
Inland areas[1]	566,649	1,420,471	256,246	733,882
Coastal areas[1]	2,285,832	4,328,784	1,167,002	2,300,813
Peking[2]		(229,970)		(97,110)
Tientsin[2]		(488,687)		(218,498)
Shanghai[2]		(1,552,300)		(770,813)
Liaoning[2]		(1,253,338)		(831,506)
Shantung[2]		(247,218)		(166,908)

[1] CH, p. 140.

[2] Derived from the data in Table 4.52A on the percentage shares of the gross
value of factory output of the metal-processing industry by the five
localities in 1955.

TABLE 4.52A Gross Value of Factory Output in
Coastal Areas, percentage

Location	Metal-processing industry	Machine-building industry
Total	100.0	100.0
Peking	4.0	3.2
Tientsin	8.5	7.2
Shanghai	27.0	25.4
Liaoning	21.8	27.4
Shantung	4.3	5.5

Source: CH, p. 138.

TABLE 4.53 Gross Value of the Output of the Paper Industry, at 1952 Prices, Thousands of Yuan

Year	Grand Total			Gross value of factory output by ownership of establishment						
	Chao I-wen[2]	CH[3]	TGY[4]	CH	State	Cooperative	Joint	Private		
								Total	Of which: Large-sized enterprises[1]	Handicrafts[1]
	(1)	(2)	(3)	(4)	(5)	(6)	(7)	(8)	(9)	(10)
1949[5]			(140,153)	136,600	76,600	--	2,000	58,000		
1950[5]			n.a.	251,600	176,600	--	5,000	70,000		
1951[5]			n.a.	459,800	296,800	--	25,000	138,000		
1952	764,489	(764,442)	(648,336)	655,240[6]	437,050[7]	2,190[7]	49,000[7]	167,000[7]	157,590	109,202
1953	838,749	(838,787)	n.a.	711,104[6]	504,065[7]	3,090[7]	79,949[7]	124,000[7]	n.a.	127,683
1954	968,804	(968,804)	n.a.	844,135[6]	613,790[7]	4,341[7]	166,004[7]	60,000[7]	n.a.	124,669
1955	1,121,990	(1,121,990)	n.a.	982,791[6]	693,598[7]	6,515[7]	256,204[7]	26,474[7]	14,771	139,199
1956	1,432,652	(1,439,719)	n.a.	1,318,053[6]						121,666
1957			(1,690,520)	1,663,005[6]						

[1] CH, p. 215.
[2] Chao I-wen, *Industry in New China*, Peking: T'ung-chi ch'u-pan she, 1957, p. 59.
[3] Derived as the sum of items in column 4 and items in column 10.
[4] TGY, p. 92. The gross value of the output of the paper industry, excluding handicrafts, constituted 1.3 percent of the gross value of the factory output of the industry as a whole in 1949, 2.4 percent in 1952, and 2.6 percent in 1957.

[5] CH, pp. 203-4.
[6] CH, p. 209.
[7] CH, p. 214.

225

TABLE 4.54 Gross Value of the Output of the Textile Industry, at 1952 Prices, 1949-57, Thousands of Yuan

Year	Grand total[3]	Factory Output						Handicrafts		
		TGV[1]	CH	State[2]	Cooperative[2]	Joint	Private	Total[3]	Cooperatives[4]	Individual[5]
	(1)	(2)	(3)	(4)	(5)	(6)	(7)	(8)	(9)	(10)
1949		(3,978,189)	3,973,290[6]			122,600[7]	2,502,130[7]			
1950		n.a.	4,642,000[6]			214,070[7]	2,794,000[7]			
1951		n.a.	5,956,000[6]			385,190[7]	3,534,860[7]			
1952	9,425,260	(8,023,158)	8,015,510[2]	2,807,550	350,080	749,530[2]	4,108,350[2]	1,409,750	113,711	(1,296,039)
1953	11,500,295	n.a.	9,885,155[2]	3,422,110	493,070	992,830[2]	4,977,150[2]	1,615,140	208,925	(1,406,215)
1954	12,669,297	n.a.	11,134,748[2]	4,027,640	691,360	2,771,240[2]	3,644,510[2]	1,534,549	341,551	(1,192,998)
1955	12,116,277	n.a.	10,754,398[2]	3,830,760	1,200,160	3,405,550[2]	2,317,930[2]	1,411,879	466,694	(945,185)
1956	14,694,856	n.a.	13,048,571[2]	5,592,950	304,250	7,147,380[2]	3,990[2]	1,646,285	1,573,769	(72,516)
1957		(12,418,820)								

[1] TGV, p. 92. The gross value of the output of the textile industry excluding handicrafts, accounted for 36.9 percent of the gross value of factory output of the industry as a whole in 1949; 29.7 percent in 1952; and 19.1 percent in 1957.

[2] CH, p. 176.

[3] CH, p. 180.

[4] CH, p. 181.

[5] Derived by subtracting items in column 9 from items in column 8.

[6] CH, p. 155.

[7] CH, p. 158.

TABLE 4.55 Gross Value of Factory Output of Producer Goods and Consumer Goods in the Textile Industry, at 1952 Prices, 1952-56, Thousands of Yuan

Product	1952	1953	1954	1955	1956
Total	8,015,510	9,885,155	11,134,748	10,754,398	13,048,571
Producer goods	1,123,668	1,166,902	1,274,896	1,903,559	1,894,674
Primary processing of fiber materials and silk spinning	898,437	919,893	994,653	1,611,155	1,466,608
Cotton fabrics for industrial use	65,150	89,581	116,545	112,085	158,744
Woolen fabrics for industrial use	3,465	3,532	4,411	14,879	19,978
Flax fabrics and hemp for jute products for industrial use	156,005	153,916	159,287	165,440	249,344
Consumer goods	6,891,842	8,718,253	9,859,952	8,850,839	11,153,897
Cotton fabrics	6,326,918	7,857,493	8,823,546	7,673,059	9,670,472
Woolen fabrics	144,330	214,732	270,716	289,260	377,076
Flax fabrics	1,820	3,485	4,345	4,824	5,405
Silk fabrics	140,005	214,250	245,828	288,298	415,998
Knitted products	272,573	420,339	505,701	586,856	664,948
Felt products	6,196	7,954	9,716	8,542	19,998

Source: *CH*, pp. 164-65.

TABLE 4.56 Percentage Distribution of Gross Value of Industrial Output at Constant Prices of Various Provinces and Equivalents, by Branches, 1949-58

Province and industry	1949	1950	1952	1957	1958
Shanghai: [1]					
Electric power and fuel					1.9
Ferrous metals					5.9
Metal-processing					28.2
Machine building					18.0
Chemical					7.3
Textile					32.6
Food					5.8
Other					18.3
Liaoning: [2]					
Electric power				9.4	
Ferrous metals				23.3	
Nonferrous metals				3.6	
Machine building				20.4	
Chemical				6.6	
Paper manufacturing				2.2	
Textile				7.3	
Food				6.3	
Other				20.9	
Kirin: [3]					
Electric power			8.3	8.1	
Fuel			6.8	4.5	
Metal-processing			5.7	20.3	
Machine building			2.3	16.0	
Chemical			1.2	4.5	
Building materials			2.4	2.2	
Lumber			20.9	9.8	
Paper products			2.2	1.7	
Paper manufacturing			14.3	14.5	
Textile			3.3	2.4	
Leather			0.6	0.6	
Food			25.0	16.9	
Sugar			1.7	1.7	
Other			9.3	14.5	
Heilungkiang: [4]					
Electric power	2.2	n.a.	1.9	1.7	
Fuel	10.1	n.a.	5.3	6.4	
Ferrous metals		n.a.		1.1	
Metal processing	10.4	n.a.	13.5	21.5	
Machine building	6.9	n.a.	6.2	11.6	
Chemical	0.3	n.a.	0.8	2.3	
Rubber	2.6	n.a.	4.8	4.1	
Building materials	1.2	n.a.	2.4	3.2	
Lumber	34.9	n.a.	29.5	18.4	
Logging	24.6	n.a.	18.3	10.2	
Paper manufacturing	0.3	n.a.	1.2	2.8	
Textile	8.5	n.a.	7.7	5.5	
Food	22.8	n.a.	24.5	18.5	
Other	6.7	n.a.	8.4	14.5	

228

TABLE 4.56 (Continued, 1)

Province and industry	1949	1950	1952	1957	1958
Shantung: [5]					
Coal	4.0	n. a.	2.9		
Metal processing	4.6	n. a.	7.2		
Rubber goods	2.4	n. a.	3.2		
Textiles	61.3	n. a.	49.9		
Food	13.6	n. a.	24.2		
Other	14.1	n. a.	12.6		
Kiangsu: [1]					
Electric power and fuel					1.6
Ferrous metals					1.4
Metal processing					19.8
Machine building					13.9
Chemical					6.2
Textile					32.0
Food					19.6
Other					19.4
Anhwei: [6]					
Electric power		0.4	n. a.	0.7	0.7
Fuel		4.7	n. a.	4.5	5.3
Ferrous metals		1.2	n. a.	2.9	7.6
Nonferrous metals			n. a.	4.1	2.7
Metal processing		4.5	n. a.	9.9	13.6
Machine building		0.1	n. a.	4.3	5.7
Chemical		0.3	n. a.	1.4	9.5
Building materials		1.9	n. a.	4.0	5.9
Textile		12.8	n. a.	13.8	6.7
Food		50.8	n. a.	34.8	29.8
Other		23.4	n. a.	23.9	18.2
Chekiang: [7]					
Electric power	0.9	n. a.	1.0	1.1	
Ferrous metals		n. a.		0.5	
Machine building	2.0	n. a.	2.9	5.4	
Chemical	0.3	n. a.	1.3	4.7	
Building materials	1.8	n. a.	2.5	2.3	
Paper	5.1	n. a.	7.2	4.7	
Textile	29.2	n. a.	30.8	27.6	
Food	51.3	n. a.	45.4	47.2	
Other	9.4	n. a.	8.9	6.5	
Hupeh: [8]					
Iron and steel smelting and refining		2.4	n. a.	6.1	
Metal processing		12.2	n. a.	13.4	
Machine building		2.2	n. a.	7.2	
Building materials		3.2	n. a.	4.9	
Lumber processing		4.2	n. a.	4.3	
Textile		27.3	n. a.	21.2	
Food		38.0	n. a.	31.0	
Other		12.7	n. a.	19.1	

TABLE 4.56 (Continued, 2)

Province and industry	1949	1950	1952	1957	1958
Hunan: [9]					
Nonferrous metals		10.1	n.a.	9.6	
Metal processing		8.7	n.a.	15.4	
Machine building		3.9	n.a.	10.3	
Chemical		0.6	n.a.	8.9	
Textile		17.1	n.a.	11.2	
Food		39.6	n.a.	27.7	
Other		23.9	n.a.	27.2	
Kiangsi: [10]					
Electric power				0.9	
Coal				2.8	
Nonferrous metals				16.5	
Metal processing				5.6	
Ceramics				3.8	
Paper				3.7	
Textile				17.0	
Food				30.9	
Other				18.8	
Kwangtung: [11]					
Fuel	2.6	n.a.	3.4	5.45	
Metal processing	9.6	n.a.	6.5	11.43	
Chemical	4.8	n.a.	4.6	6.37	
Building materials	2.5	n.a.	2.7	2.47	
Lumber	3.5	n.a.	3.5	2.66	
Paper	0.06	n.a.	1.4	3.96	
Textile	23.2	n.a.	13.9	13.00	
Food	41.0	n.a.	52.3	44.50	
Other	12.74	n.a.	11.7	10.16	
Kwangsi: [12]					
Electric power		2.2	n.a.	1.5	
Nonferrous metals		42.4	n.a.	17.4	
Metal processing		7.0	n.a.	9.4	
Chemical		0.3	n.a.	5.5	
Textile		3.2	n.a.	2.4	
Food		28.3	n.a.	44.6	
Other		16.6	n.a.	19.2	
Szechuan: [13]					
Electric power	1.2	n.a.	0.9	1.1	
Fuel	3.2	n.a.	2.5	2.4	
Ferrous metals	2.2	n.a.	6.8	7.7	
Nonferrous metals	0.3	n.a.	0.6	0.5	
Metal processing	3.2	n.a.	7.8	12.2	
Chemical	0.8	n.a.	2.0	6.0	
Nonmetallic		n.a.	0.2	0.6	
Building materials	0.7	n.a.	1.8	1.5	
Textile	31.8	n.a.	21.6	9.8	
Food	30.5	n.a.	33.5	39.3	
Other	26.1	n.a.	22.3	18.9	

TABLE 4.56 (Continued, 3)

Province and industry	1949	1950	1952	1957	1958
Kweichow: [14]					
Electric power			0.4	0.7	
Fuel			2.5	2.3	
Ferrous metals			2.4	2.6	
Nonferrous metals			4.5	7.1	
Metal processing			3.0	10.1	
Chemical			0.3	3.4	
Lumber			7.4	4.6	
Paper			1.9	2.1	
Textile			25.3	10.1	
Food			25.1	33.7	
Other			27.2	23.3	

[1] Sun Ching-chih et al., ed., *Hua-tung ti-ch'u ching-chi ti-li (Economic Geography of East China)*, Peking: K'o-hsueh ch'u-pan-she, 1959, 153 pp.; translated in JPRS: 11,438, December 7, 1961, p. 34.

[2] Wu Ch'uan-chun et al., ed., *Tung-pei ti-ch'u ching-chi ti-li (Economic Geography of Northeast China)*, Peking: K'o-hsueh ch'u-pan-she, 1959, 211 pp.; translated in JPRS: 15,388, September 21, 1962, p. 69.

[3] *Ibid.*, p. 184.

[4] *Ibid.*, p. 363.

[5] Institute of Geography of the Chinese Academy of Sciences, ed., *Hua-pei ching-chi ti-li (Economic Geography of North China)*, Peking, July, 1957; translated in JPRS: 144-D, May 23, 1958, p. 142.

[6] Sun Ching-chih et al., op. cit., p. 155.

[7] *Ibid.*, p. 231.

[8] Sun Ching-chih, ed., *Hua-chung ti-ch'u ching-chi ti-li (Economic Geography of Central China)*, Peking: K'o-hsueh ch'u-pan-she, December, 1958, 156 pp.; translated in JPRS: 2227-N, February 10, 1960, p. 106.

[9] *Ibid.*, p. 236.

[10] *Ibid.*, p. 437.

[11] Sun Ching-chih, ed., *Hua-nan ti-ch'u ching-chi ti-li (Economic Geography of South China)*, Peking: K'o-hsueh ch'u-pan-she, 1959, 147 pp; translated in JPRS: 14,954, August 24, 1962, p. 88.

[12] *Ibid.*, p. 273.

[13] Sun Ching-chih, ed., *Hsi-nan ti-ch'u ching-chi ti-li (Economic Geography of Southwest China)*, Peking: K'o-hsueh ch'u-pan-she, 1960, 218 pp.; translated in JPRS: 15,069, August 31, 1962, p. 170.

[14] *Ibid.*, p. 395.

TABLE 4.57 Gross-Value Output of Producer Goods and Consumer Goods Industries in the Inner Mongolia Autonomous Region, 1947-58, Thousands of Yuan

Year	Total	Producer goods industry	Consumer goods industry
	(1)	(2)	(3)
1947	52,960	9,770	43,190
1948	61,250	14,730	46,520
1949	68,390	20,910	47,480
1950	110,860	42,360	68,500
1951	135,700	42,400	93,300
1952	160,300	59,170	101,130
1953	243,190	104,280	138,910
1954	358,080	166,950	191,130
1955	421,410	189,060	232,350
1956	569,900	267,950	301,950
1957	631,340	297,100	334,240
1958	1,156,490	653,650	502,840

Source: NMKTC, p. 99.

TABLE 4.58 Gross-Value Output of Various Industries in the Inner Mongolia Autonomous Region, 1947, 1949, 1952, 1957, and 1958, Thousands of Yuan

Industry	1947	1949	1952	1957	1958
Electric power	910	820	1,090	6,470	13,480
Petroleum	1,310	2,400	5,430	21,080	75,480
Ferrous metals					15,270
Nonferrous metals		120	270	130	10,730
Metal processing	670	880	4,240	29,690	129,230
Machine-building			1,150	4,550	74,490
Chemical	670	140	4,150	16,970	33,060
Building materials	440	530	2,190	43,440	61,390
Lumber	4,640	14,900	38,210	137,100	232,190
Logging	3,820	13,960	35,450	98,920	177,530
Tailoring	1,990	2,140	3,120	6,630	30,560
Leather	2,160	2,050	5,060	20,710	33,390
Textiles	1,010	1,010	2,350	8,080	39,420
Woolen textiles	320	20	310	3,680	35,090
Food	11,860	12,910	32,570	207,160	232,730
Rice and flour milling	2,120	2,220	10,920	75,070	68,810
Meat products				44,040	45,700
Edible fats		670	3,140	10,560	20,960
Sugar				14,960	8,600
Milk products			380	9,310	17,100
Distilling	460	790	2,940	9,580	12,100
Table salt	1,520	1,410	4,290	15,140	21,750
Educational materials	200	250	1,590	7,060	10,550

Source: NMKTC, pp. 107-10

TABLE 4.59 Gross-Value Output of Handicraft Cooperatives and Individual Handicrafts, at 1952 Prices, 1949-55

Year	Grand total, millions of yuan		Handicraft cooperatives, thousands of yuan				Individual handicrafts, thousands of yuan[5]
	TGY[1]	Chao I-wen[2]	Total[3]	Producers' cooperatives[4]	Supply and marketing cooperatives[4]	Production teams[4]	
	(1)	(2)	(3)	(4)	(5)	(6)	(7)
1949	3,240	3,237	15,000	15,000			(3,222,000)
1950	5,060	5,062	40,000	40,000			(5,022,000)
1951	6,140	6,141	134,360	134,360			(6,006,640)
1952	7,310	7,312	255,140	246,405	7,406	1,329	(7,056,860)
1953	9,120	9,119	506,364	486,070	12,280	8,014	(8,612,636)
1954	10,460	10,462	1,169,389	855,703	91,209	222,477	(9,292,611)
1955	10,120	10,128	2,015,737	1,301,651	187,528	526,558	(8,112,263)

[1] TGY, p. 94.
[2] Chao I-wen, *Industry in New China*, Peking: T'ung-chi ch'u-pan-she, 1957, p. 104.
[3] *Ibid.*, p. 109.
[4] *Ibid.*, p. 111.
[5] Derived by subtracting items in column 3 from items in column 2.

TABLE 4.60 Structure and Gross-Value Output, Thousands of Yuan, of the Handicraft Industry by Organizational Form and by Province or Equivalent, 1949-54[a]

Province or equivalent	1949	1950	1951	1952	1953	1954
Peking:						
Individual operators:						
Number of establishments						32,714
Number of persons	(48,511)	(49,651)	(63,874)	(65,863)	(76,841)	90,275
Gross-value output	(34,440)	(57,470)	(75,390)	(91,310)	(131,590)	169,090
Producer cooperatives:.						
Number of establishments						332
Number of persons		(1,099)	(692)	(1,020)	(26,419)	24,729
Gross-value output		(2,400)	(2,808)	(11,616)	(34,080)	66,320
Factory, percentage (1949=100):						
Number of persons	100	104	136	108	178	136
Gross-value output	100	98	234	229	320	233
Tientsin:						
Individual operators:						
Number of establishments	13,147	n.a.	22,391	n.a.	n.a.	27,603
Number of persons	27,479	n.a.	52,626	(52,353)	n.a.	69,603
Gross-value output	38,580	n.a.	115,270	(94,530)	n.a.	116,540
Producer cooperatives:						
Number of establishments	9	n.a.	n.a.	25	n.a.	173
Number of persons	690	n.a.	n.a.	3,164	n.a.	16,033
Factory:						
Number of establishments	2,937	n.a.	5,413	(5,071)	n.a.	n.a.
Number of persons	31,146	n.a.	60,925	(55,783)	n.a.	n.a.
Gross-value output	143,900	n.a.	271,130	(224,360)	(338,650)	(278,340)
Shanghai: [b]						
Individual operators:						
Number of establishments				32,756	40,831	58,463
Number of persons				82,545	103,857	128,929
Gross-value output		70,330	172,950			
Producer cooperatives:						
Number of establishments						100
Number of persons						7,900
Gross-value output						45,000
Factory:						
Number of establishments						14,107
Number of persons						70,767
Gross-value output						300,890
Hopei:						
Individual operators:						
Number of establishments						89,811
Number of persons						252,575
Gross-value output						(248,029)
Producer cooperatives:						
Number of persons						84,750
Factory:						
Number of establishments						3,741
Number of persons						31,868
Gross-value output						(53,748)
Shansi:						
Individual operators:						
Number of persons						129,564
Gross-value output						123,096
Producer cooperatives:						
Number of persons						88,152
Gross-value output						68,113

TABLE 4.60 (Continued, 1)

Province or equivalent	1949	1950	1951	1952	1953	1954
Factory:						
Number of persons						9,092
Gross-value output						2,088
Inner Mongolia Autonomous Region:						
Individual operators:						
Number of establishments		21,864	26,973	26,582	24,373	23,855
Number of persons		47,939	50,360	48,426	45,505	44,542
Gross-value output		38,289	47,455	51,780	54,183	58,343
Producer cooperatives:						
Number of establishments		4	9	32	73	277
Number of persons		576	587	917	1,926	7,209
Gross-value output		378	546	487	2,934	12,001
Factory:						
Number of establishments		762	966	952	894	873
Number of persons		7,146	9,061	8,927	8,388	8,190
Gross-value output		15,288	17,264	12,454	19,276	21,691
Liaoning:						
Individual operators:						
Number of establishments	(88,197)	(10,054)	(10,945)	(11,078)	(12,189)	117,479
Number of persons	(132,384)	(160,449)	(185,205)	(192,619)	(218,036)	208,373
Gross-value output	(218,191)	(277,975)	(284,521)	(317,686)	(388,816)	402,780
Kirin:						
Individual operators:						
Number of persons						75,442
Gross-value output						(122,848)
Producer cooperatives:						
Number of establishments						379
Number of persons						10,841
Gross-value output						30,168
Factory:						
Number of establishments						1,393
Number of persons						7,358
Gross-value output						27,600
Heilungkiang:						
Individual operators:						
Number of establishments	56,930	61,071	64,276	63,025	66,342	60,311
Number of persons	99,799	98,990	115,447	112,377	118,392	107,529
Gross-value output	73,693	111,543	156,740	170,691	234,392	183,635
Producer cooperatives:						
Number of establishments	9	12	21	118	189	305
Number of persons	2,131	2,711	2,994	8,527	9,653	15,732
Gross-value output	21	778	3,304	14,125	34,064	45,457
Shensi:						
Individual operators:						
Number of establishments						72,418
Number of persons						139,247
Gross-value output						214,437
Producer cooperatives:						
Number of establishments		(20)	(16)	(12)	(29)	1,483
Number of persons		(1,240)	(1,309)	(1,330)	(1,649)	21,696
Gross-value output		(2,340)	(2,256)	(2,882)	(4,284)	18,892
Factory:						
Number of persons						22,168
Gross-value output						35,731

TABLE 4.60 (Continued, 2)

Province or equivalent	1949	1950	1951	1952	1953	1954
Kansu:						
Individual operators:						
Number of establishments	29,952	n.a.	n.a.	n.a.	38,001	52,606
Number of persons	52,239	n.a.	n.a.	n.a.	66,257	92,289
Gross-value output	92,055	n.a.	n.a.	n.a.	122,897	136,315
Producer cooperatives:						
Number of establishments			31	32	39	1,015
Number of persons					5,540	15,818
Gross-value output					3,347	9,622
Factory:						
Number of establishments	(1,111)	(1,212)	(1,471)	(1,489)	1,316	1,902
Number of persons					13,034	13,688
Gross-value output	(20,694)	(23,395)	(31,502)	(30,499)	28,903	23,092
Chinghai:						
Individual operators:						
Number of establishments						5,464
Number of persons						15,370
Gross-value output						22,698
Sinkiang-Uighur Autonomous Region:						
Individual operators:						
Number of establishments						61,666
Number of persons						93,028
Gross-value output						229,827
Producer cooperatives:						
Number of establishments						235
Number of persons						3,548
Factory:						
Number of establishments						444
Number of persons						2,938
Anhwei						
Individual operators:						
Number of establishments	(159,940)	(171,824)	(191,272)	(204,563)	(196,070)	181,708
Number of persons	(354,737)	(377,440)	(415,858)	(425,223)	(403,655)	383,293
Gross-value output	(457,600)	(511,826)	(578,498)	(548,525)	(520,703)	220,737
Individual cooperatives:						
Number of establishments				(57)	(649)	1,353
Number of persons				(272)	(10,445)	(27,096)
Gross-value output				(210)	(10,603)	(21,585)
Factory:						
Number of establishments						1,935
Number of persons						3,049
Gross-value output						17,444
Chekiang:						
Individual operators:						
Number of establishments				350,935	352,569	310,069
Number of persons				678,894	682,461	641,038
Gross-value output				309,390	392,125	361,880
Producer cooperatives:						
Number of persons				14,706	23,397	148,006
Gross-value output				3,651	11,976	34,430
Factory:						
Gross-value output				(138,208)	(168,083)	(147,908)
Fukien:						
Individual operators:						
Number of establishments						107,105
Number of persons						260,038
Gross-value output						270,020

TABLE 4.60   (Continued, 3)

Province or equivalent	1949	1950	1951	1952	1953	1954
Producer cooperatives:						
Number of establishments				46	113	985
Number of persons				2,401	3,905	19,233
Gross-value output				1,570	4,020	15,390
Honan:						
Individual operators:						
Number of establishments						119,899
Number of persons						367,724
Gross-value output						316,387
Kiangsi:						
Individual operators:						
Number of establishments						132,579
Number of persons						250,155
Gross-value output						150,682
Szechuan:						
Individual operators:						
Number of establishments						313,176
Number of persons				633,864	646,000	627,868
Gross-value output				635,010	707,060	700,510
Producer cooperatives:						
Number of establishments				191	234	3,298
Number of persons				7,465	8,074	54,326
Gross-value output				4,130	10,780	33,820
Factory:						
Number of establishments						7,415
Number of persons						43,465
Gross-value output						83,760
Kweichow:						
Individual operators:						
Number of establishments						90,999
Number of persons						152,095
Gross-value output						154,970
Producer cooperatives:						
Number of establishments						993
Number of persons						15,501
Yunnan:						
Individual operators:						
Number of establishments						71,385
Number of persons						152,370
Gross-value output						227,772
Producer cooperatives:						
Number of persons						21,869
Gross-value output						13,966

[a] The gross-value output is given in 1952 prices, except for Liaoning, Heilunkiang, and Honan, for which the gross output is valued at current prices. Except for Peking, Liaoning, and Szechwan, figures on the gross-value output do not include subsidiary farm crafts. Handicraft producer cooperatives include handicraft marketing and production cooperatives and handicraft production teams. Handicraft factory refers to privately operated handicraft workshops hiring 10 persons or fewer.

[b] Excluding itinerant handicraftsmen.

Source: Compiled from Chinese Academy of Sciences, Economic Research Institute, Handicraft Section, ed., *Nation-wide Survey Data on Individual Handicrafts in 1954*, Peking: Sheng-huo, tu-shu, hsin-san-lien shu-tien, 1957, 252 pp. Figures in parentheses are derived estimates.

TABLE 4.61 Number of Establishments, Number of Gainfully Occupied Persons, and Gross-Value Output of Individual Handicrafts, by Type of Handi-craftsmen and by Province or Equivalent, 1954, Thousands of Yuan

Province or equivalent	Grand total (1)	Individual handicrafts				Subsidiary farm crafts (6)
		Total (2)	Stationary (3)	Itinerant (4)	Joint tool groups (5)	
Peking:						
Number of establishments	n.a.	32,714	(23,727)	(6,145)	(2,372)	n.a.
Number of persons	n.a.	90,275	(66,045)	(8,531)	(15,699)	n.a.
Gross-value output	169,090	167,100	(131,670)	(12,770)	(22,660)	1,990
Shanghai:						
Number of establishments	n.a.	n.a.	58,463			n.a.
Number of persons	179,141	166,141	128,929			13,000
Gross-value output	n.a.	280,020	265,660	14,360		n.a.
Hopei:						
Number of establishments	709,795	89,811	n.a.	n.a.	n.a.	619,984
Number of persons	1,579,696	252,575	n.a.	n.a.	n.a.	1,327,121
Gross-value output	(563,884)	(248,029)	n.a.	n.a.	n.a.	(315,855)
Shansi:						
Number of persons	193,416	129,564	n.a.	n.a.	n.a.	83,645
Gross-value output	147,396	123,096	n.a.	n.a.	n.a.	24,300
Inner Mongolia:						
Number of establishments	n.a.	23,855	n.a.	n.a.	1,750	n.a.
Number of persons	n.a.	44,542	n.a.	n.a.	8,733	n.a.
Gross-value output	n.a.	58,343	n.a.	n.a.	11,475	n.a.
Liaoning:						
Number of establishments	n.a.	117,479	(57,800)	(45,229)	(14,450)	n.a.
Number of persons	n.a.	208,373	(115,647)	(46,467)	(46,259)	n.a.
Gross-value output	402,780	(361,293)	(241,668)	(14,097)	(105,528)	(41,486)
Kirin:						
Number of establishments	n.a.	n.a.	n.a.	n.a.	3,640	n.a.
Number of persons	n.a.	75,442	45,653	12,759	17,030	n.a.
Gross-value output	n.a.	(122,848)	(74,962)	(19,561)	28,325	n.a.

TABLE 4.61 (Continued, 1)

	(1)	(2)	(3)	(4)	(5)	(6)
Heilungkiang:						
Number of establishments	n.a.	60,311	n.a.	n.a.	5,749	n.a.
Number of persons	n.a.	107,629	n.a.	n.a.	21,693	n.a.
Gross-value output	198,935	183,635	n.a.	n.a.	39,126	15,500
Shensi:						
Number of establishments	n.a.	72,418	n.a.	n.a.	n.a.	n.a.
Number of persons	n.a.	139,247	n.a.	n.a.	n.a.	n.a.
Gross-value output	n.a.	214,437	n.a.	n.a.	n.a.	n.a.
Kansu:						
Number of establishments	naa.	52,626	n.a.	n.a.	1,307	n.a.
Number of persons	n.a.	92,289	n.a.	n.a.	7,605	n.a.
Gross-value output	174,943	136,315	n.a.	n.a.	6,674	38,628
Chinghai:						
Number of persons	n.a.	12,970	n.a.	n.a.	n.a.	n.a.
Gross-value output	n.a.	22,698	n.a.	n.a.	n.a.	n.a.
Sinkiang:						
Number of establishments	n.a.	61,666	54,793	5,491	1,382	n.a.
Number of persons	n.a.	93,028	82,206	6,342	4,480	n.a.
Gross-value output	n.a.	229,827	n.a.	n.a.	n.a.	n.a.
Anhwei:						
Number of establishments	n.a.	181,708	(140,824)	(36,160)	(4,724)	n.a.
Number of persons	n.a.	383,293	(283,254)	(52,511)	(47,528)	n.a.
Gross-value output	282,151	220,737	(174,967)	(13,010)	(32,760)	61,414
Chekiang:						
Number of establishments	1,182,601	310,069	n.a.	n.a.	n.a.	872,532
Number of persons	2,026,201	641,038	n.a.	n.a.	n.a.	1,385,163
Gross-value output	443,393	361,880	n.a.	n.a.	n.a.	81,513
Fukien:						
Number of establishments	n.a.	107,105	78,544	12,746	15,815	n.a.
Number of persons	n.a.	260,038	186,162	18,105	55,771	n.a.
Gross-value output	393,320	270,020	218,870	7,570	43,580	123,300

239

TABLE 4.61 (Continued, 2)

Province or equivalent	Grand total (1)	Individual handicrafts				Subsidiary farm crafts (6)
		Total (2)	Stationary (3)	Itinerant (4)	Joint tool groups (5)	
Honan:						
Number of establishments	n.a.	119,899	87,263	13,861	18,775	n.a.
Number of persons	n.a.	367,724	233,779	36,857	97,088	n.a.
Gross-value output	516,241	316,387	223,421	9,511	83,455	199,854
Kiangsi:						
Number of establishments	n.a.	132,579	77,869	50,490	4,220	n.a.
Number of persons	n.a.	250,155	141,664	86,964	21,527	n.a.
Gross-value output	178,524	150,682	106,583	23,324	20,775	27,842
Szechuan:						
Number of establishments	n.a.	313,176	n.a.	n.a.	n.a.	n.a.
Number of persons	n.a.	627,868	n.a.	n.a.	n.a.	n.a.
Gross-value output	700,510	557,300	n.a.	n.a.	n.a.	143,210
Kweichow:						
Number of establishments	n.a.	90,999	75,471	n.a.	1,570	246,538
Number of persons	453,024	152,095	122,355	13,953	15,782	300,929
Gross-value output	n.a.	154,970	n.a.	n.a.	n.a.	n.a.
Yunnan:						
Number of establishments	n.a.	71,385	n.a.	n.a.	n.a.	n.a.
Number of persons	665,370	152,370	n.a.	n.a.	n.a.	513,000
Gross-value output	n.a.	227,772	n.a.	n.a.	n.a.	n.a.

Note: Figures on the gross value output are given in current prices for Liaoning, Heilungkiang, and Honan and in 1952 prices for the rest of the provinces and municipalities.

Source: The figures in this table were compiled from Chinese Academy of Sciences, Economic Research Institute, Handicraft Section, ed., *Nation-wide Survey Data on Individual Handicrafts in 1954*. Peking: Sheng-huo tu-shu hsin-san-lien shu-tien, 1957, 252 pp. Figures in parentheses are derived estimates.

TABLE 4.62 Number of Establishments, Number of Gainfully Occupied Persons, and Gross-Value Output of Individual Handicrafts in Rural and Urban Areas of Various Provinces or Equivalents, 1954

Province or equivalent	Number of establishments			Number of persons			Gross-value output, thousands of yuan[a,b]		
	Total	Urban areas	Rural areas	Total	Urban areas	Rural areas	Total	Urban areas	Rural areas
	(1)	(2)	(3)	(4)	(5)	(6)	(7)	(8)	(9)
Peking	32,714	31,134	1,580	90,275	83,166	7,109	169,090	158,020	11,070
Inner Mongolia	22,105	(10,783)	(11,322)	35,809	(18,757)	(17,052)	46,867	(36,561)	(10,306)
Liaoning	117,479	(55,568)	(61,911)	208,373	(103,165)	(105,208)	402,780	(285,974)	(116,806)
Heilunkiang	60,311	(40,463)	(19,848)	107,629	(74,081)	(33,548)	199,135	(153,573)	(45,562)
Chinghai[c]	5,464	2,398	3,066	15,370	5,468	9,902	27,623	11,927	15,696
Sinkiang	61,666	24,474	37,192	93,028	40,722	52,306	229,827	n.a.	n.a.
Anhwei	181,708	(54,149)	(127,559)	383,293	(120,737)	(262,556)	220,737	(109,927)	(110,810)
Fukien	107,105	(35,556)	(71,549)	260,038	(80,872)	(179,116)	393,320	(122,323)	(270,997)
Honan	119,899	49,575	70,324	385,724	102,890	264,834	316,390	130,510	185,880
Kiangsi	132,579	n.a.	n.a.	250,155	n.a.	n.a.	150,681	76,534	74,147
Kweichow	90,999	42,534	(48,465)	152,095	72,704	(79,391)	154,970	n.a.	n.a.
Yunnan	71,385	n.a.	n.a.	152,370	(73,226)	79,144	227,772	(107,919)	119,853

[a] Figures on the gross-value output are given in current prices for Liaoning, Heilunkiang and Honan and in 1952 prices for the rest.

[b] Except for Peking, Liaoning, Heilunkiang, and Fukien, figures on the gross-value output do not include subsidiary farm crafts.

[c] Referring to the whole handicraft industry.

Source: Compiled from the Chinese Academy of Sciences, Economic Research Institute, Handicraft Section, *Nation-wide Survey Data on Individual Handicrafts in 1954*, Peking: Sheng-huo tu-shu hsin-san-lien shu-tsin, 1957, 252 pp. Figures in parentheses are derived estimates.

241

TABLE 4.63 Number of Establishments, Number of Gainfully Occupied Persons, and Gross-Value Output, in Thousands of Yuan, of Individual Handicrafts by Production Use and by Province or Equivalent, 1954,[a,b]

Province or equivalent	Grand total	Producer goods				Consumer goods		
		Total	For industrial use	For agricultural use	For other uses	Total	For daily use	Others
	(1)	(2)	(3)	(4)	(5)	(6)	(7)	(8)
Shanghai:								
Number of establishments	58,463	8,105	4,364	190	3,551	50,358	27,560	12,798
Number of persons	166,141	22,066	12,442	498	9,126	144,075	79,956	64,119
Gross-value output	280,020	66,800	39,200	560	27,040	213,220	158,810	54,410
Tientsin:								
Number of establishments	27,603	4,192	1,999	484	1,709	23,411	16,145	7,266
Number of persons	69,603	12,352	6,090	1,391	4,871	57,251	42,484	14,767
Gross-value output	172,810	42,200	23,970	2,170	16,060	130,610	107,200	23,410
Liaoning:								
Number of establishments	117,479	(24,083)	(4,817)	(11,395)	(7,871)	(93,396)	(79,181)	(14,215)
Number of persons	208,373	(48,134)	(12,919)	(22,088)	(13,127)	(160,239)	(140,860)	(19,379)
Gross-value output	402,780	(84,584)	(44,306)	(24,167)	(16,111)	(318,196)	(290,404)	(27,792)
Shensi:								
Gross-value output	214,437	(59,013)	(24,909)	(22,360)	(11,744)	(155,424)	(131,582)	(23,842)
Kansu:								
Number of establishments	52,606	(14,624)	(2,788)	(9,837)	(1,999)	(37,982)	n.a.	n.a.
Number of persons	92,289	(26,302)	(6,553)	(16,427)	(3,322)	(65,987)	n.a.	n.a.
Gross-value output	136,315	(15,812)	(4,771)	(8,724)	(2,317)	(120,775)	n.a.	n.a.
Chinghai:								
Gross-value output	22,698	(2,383)	(308)	n.a.	n.a.	(20,315)	n.a.	n.a.
Sinkiang:								
Number of establishments	61,666	11,588	5,425	5,045	1,118	50,078	48,550	1,528
Anhwei:								
Number of establishments	181,708	(47,426)	n.a.	n.a.	n.a.	(134,282)	n.a.	n.a.
Number of persons	383,293	(106,172)	n.a.	n.a.	n.a.	(277,121)	n.a.	n.a.
Gross-value output	220,737	(36,422)	n.a.	(21,525)	n.a.	(184,315)	n.a.	n.a.

TABLE 4.63 (Continued)

Province or equivalent	Grand total (1)	Producer goods				Consumer goods		
		Total (2)	For industrial use (3)	For agricultural use (4)	For other uses (5)	Total (6)	For daily use (7)	Others (8)
Chekiang:								
Gross-value output	443,393	(101,094)	(54,626)	(27,269)	(19,199)	(339,196)	(297,384)	(41,812)
Fukien:								
Number of establishments	107,105	(14,138)	(3,213)	(6,855)	(4,070)	(92,967)	(82,792)	(10,175)
Number of persons	260,038	(39,265)	(9,621)	(15,602)	(14,042)	(220,772)	(198,669)	(22,103)
Gross-value output	393,320	(74,337)	(53,885)	(8,653)	(11,800)	(318,982)	(301,283)	(17,699)
Honan:								
Number of persons	367,724	n.a.	(34,934)	(55,526)	n.a.	n.a.	(202,579)	n.a.
Kiangsi:								
Number of establishments	132,579	40,242	5,040	28,190	7,012	92,337	82,501	9,836
Number of persons	250,155	82,172	12,650	53,801	15,721	167,983	149,206	18,777
Gross-value output	178,524	33,890	8,230	16,074	9,586	144,633	131,293	13,340
Szechuan:								
Number of persons	627,868	181,776	75,189	75,536	31,051	446,092	396,906	49,186
Gross-value output	700,510	107,120	45,260	41,790	20,070	593,390	556,200	37,190
Kweichow:								
Number of establishments	90,999	20,508	8,216	8,479	3,813	70,491	56,143	14,348
Number of persons	152,095	40,397	17,517	14,599	8,281	111,698	93,170	18,528
Yunnan:								
Gross-value output	227,773	52,764	24,523	18,758	9,483	175,009	173,717	1,292

[a] The gross-value output is given in current prices for Tientsin and Liaoning and in 1952 prices for the rest of the provinces and municipalities.

[b] Except for Liaoning, Chekiang, Fukien, Kiangsi, and Szechuan, figures on the gross-value output do not include subsidiary farm crafts.

Source: Compiled from Chinese Academy of Sciences, Economic Research Institute, Handicraft Section, ed., *Nation-wide Survey Data on Individual Handicrafts in 1954*, Peking: Sheng-huo tu-shu hsin-san-lien shu-tien, 1957, 252 pp. Figures in parentheses are derived estimates.

TABLE 4.64 Net Value of Industrial Output at 1952 Prices,
1952-56, Millions of Yuan

Year	Industry total[1] (1)	Enterprises of the Ministry of Coal Industry[2] (2)	Enterprises of the Ministry of Food[2] (3)
1952	(11,003)		
1953	(14,708)		
1954	(17,288)		
1955	(18,597)		
1956	(23,430)	680	160

[1] Table 2.5.
[2] SSB, Department of Comprehensive Statistics, "On the Gross and Net Value of Output," *TCYC*, No. 2 (February 23, 1958), pp. 27-30, reference on p. 28.

TABLE 4.65 Generating-Equipment Capacity of the Electric Power Industry, 1949-59, Thousands of Kilowatts

Industry	1949	1950	1951	1952	1953	1954	1955	1956	1957	1958	1959
Nationwide	1,849[1]	1,866[1]	1,883[1]	1,964[1]	2,350[1]	2,597[1]	2,997[1]	3,611[1]	4,640[2]	(6,440)[3]	(9,640)[3]
Enterprises of the Ministry of Electric Power Industry[4]	735	941	1,032	1,066							

Note: Figures are year-end estimates. Plants with generating capacity of less than 500 kw are not included.

[1] *CH*, pp. 51, 64-65.
[2] *Jen-min t'ien-yeh (People's Electric Power Industry)*, No. 18 (September 20, 1958), p. 8.
[3] The generating capacity increased by 1.8 million kw in 1958 and by 3.2 million kw in 1959. See *JMJP*, April 15, 1960, p. 12.
[4] *CH*, p. 46.

TABLE 4.66 Hydraulic and Thermal Power-Generating Equipment Capacity of the Electric Power Industry, 1952, 1956, and 1957, Thousands of Kilowatts

Type of power	1952[1]	1956[2]	1957
Total	1,964	3,611	4,640[2]
Hydraulic power-generating equipment capacity	188	627	970[3]
Thermal power-generating equipment capacity	1,776	2,984	(3,670)[4]
Heat-supply and electricity-generating equipment capacity of central heat and electric power stations	13	360	n. a.

Note: Figures in this table are year-end estimates.

[1] CH, p. 60.

[2] Jen-min tien-yeh (People's Electric Power Industry) No. 18 (September 20, 1958), p. 8.

[3] Feng Hua, "Let Medium and Small-Sized Industrial Enterprises Grow in All the Places," CHCC, No. 4 (April 9, 1958), pp. 29-31, reference on p. 31.

[4] Derived as a residual from the total generating equipment capacity in 1957 and the hydraulic power-generating equipment capacity in the same year.

TABLE 4.67 Distribution of Generating Equipment Capacity of Electric Power Industry, by Capacity of Single Machines, 1949, 1952-56, Thousand Kilowatts

Capacity of single machines	1949	1952	1953	1954	1955	1956
Total	1,849	1,964	2,350	2,597	2,997	3,611
50,000 to 100,000	130	130	325	448	570	743
25,000 to 50,000	100	125	125	175	275	400
25,000 and less	1,619	1,709	1,900	1,974	2,152	2,468

Note: Figures in this table are year-end estimates.

Source: CH, p. 66.

TABLE 4.68 Distribution of Generating-Equipment Capacity of Electric Power
Industry by Ownership of Establishment, 1949, 1952-56, [a]
Thousand Kilowatts

Establishments	1949	1952	1953	1954	1955	1956
Total	1,849	1,964	2,350	2,597	2,997	3,611
State	1,337	1,730	1,988	2,258	2,672[b]	3,331
Central	1,214	1,629	1,836	2,091	2,482	3,114
Local	123	101	152	167	190[b]	217
Joint	88	90	206	289	311	280
Central	n. a.	n. a.	93	118	125	107
Local	n. a.	n. a.	113	171	186	173
Private	424	144	156	50	14	--

[a] Figures in this table are year-end estimates.
[b] Including 3,000 kw of the generating capacity of cooperative establishments.

Source: CH, p. 70.

TABLE 4.69 Distribution of Generating-Equipment Capacity between Public Power
Stations and Industry-Owned Power Stations, 1952 and 1956, [a]
Thousand Kilowatts

Type of station	1952	1956
Total	1,964	3,611
Public power stations	1,504	2,971
Central	1,065[b]	2,674
Local and others	439	297
Industry-owned power stations	46	64

[a] Figures in this table are year-end estimates.
[b] Enterprises under the jurisdiction of the Ministry of Electric Power
Industry.

Source: CH, p. 56.

TABLE 4.70 Distribution of Generating-Equipment Capacity of Electric Power
Industry, by Region, 1949-56, Thousand Kilowatts

Region	1949	1950	1951	1952	1953	1954	1955	1956
Total	1,849	1,866	1,883	1,964	2,350	2,597	2,997	3,611
Northeast China	680	688	695	705	922	1,028	1,235	1,520
North China	326	331	329	340	343	392	468	567
East China	586	575	573	605	674	678	715	768
Central-South China	157	167	171	184	249	287	311	395
Southwest China	69	72	79	88	106	128	157	203
Northwest China	14	16	19	23	37	64	84	117
Inner Mongolia	17	17	17	19	19	20	27	41

Note: Figures in this table are year-end estimates.

Source: CH, p. 71.

TABLE 4.71 Generating-Equipment Capacity of Electric Power Networks of the Ministry of Electric Power Industry System, 1949, 1952-56

Network	1949	1952	1953	1954	1955	1956
Northeast ultra high-tension network						
Generating equipment capacity, thousand kw	367	419	615	731	844	1,067
Length of power transmission lines for 154,000-220,000 volts, km.	1,600	1,700	2,130	2,580	2,590	2,640
Peking-Tientsin-Tangshan network						
Generating equipment capacity, thousand kw	140	140	140	165	184	235
Length of power transmission lines for 110,000 volts, km.				150	260	410
Shanghai network						
Generating equipment capacity, thousand kw		243	243	253	289	320

Note: Figures are year-end estimates.

Source: *CH*, p. 57.

TABLE 4.72 Generating-Equipment Capacity of the Electric Power Plants in Szechuan, Sinkiang-Uighur Autonomous Region, and Inner Mongolia Autonomous Region, 1949-59, Thousand Kilowatts

Year	Szechuan Province[1]	Sinkiang-Uighur Auto. Reg. [2]	Inner Mongolia Auto. Reg. [3]
1949	44	(1)	17
1950	n. a.	n. a.	17
1951	n. a.	n. a.	17
1952	60	(5)	19
1953	n. a.	n. a.	19
1954	n. a.	n. a.	20
1955	n. a.	n. a.	27
1956	n. a.	n. a.	41
1957	185	(39)	n. a.
1958	323	(56)	n. a.
1959	380	n. a.	n. a.

[1] Ye A. Afanas'yeskiy, *Szechuan*, published by Publishing House of Oriental Literature, Moskow, 1961, 267 pp.; translated in JPRS: 15,306, September 17, 1962, p. 143.

[2] Computed from the information given in Bureau of Electric Power Industry of Sinkiang-Uighur Autonomous Region, "The Ten Years of the Electric Power Industry in Sinkiang-Uighur Autonomous Region," *Shui-li yu tien-li* (*Water Conservancy and Electric Power*), No. 18 (September 20, 1959), pp. 31-33.

[3] *CH*, p. 71.

TABLE 4.73 Length of Power Transmission Lines, 1949, 1952-56, Kilometers

Type of line	1949	1952	1953	1954	1955	1956
Length of power transmission lines for 11,000 volts and above	11,410	14,100	15,570	16,280	18,310	20,540
Length of power transmission lines for 110,000-154,000 volts	n.a.	1,135	n.a.	n.a.	n.a.	2,544
Length of power transmission lines	n.a.	902	n.a.	n.a.	n.a.	1,431

Source: *CH*. pp. 57, 64, 65.

TABLE 4.74 Number and Capacity Output of Newly Constructed Hydroelectric Power Stations in Rural Areas in First Half of 1958, by Province

Province	Already completed		Under construction	
	Number, units	Capacity, kilowatts	Number, units	Capacity, kilowatts
	(1)	(2)	(3)	(4)
Total	1,684	25,602	5,763	71,355
Hopei	89	2,338	640	8,163
Shansi	46	3,400		
Inner Mongolia	4	100	2	52
Liaoning	34	1,096	66	6,026
Kirin	331	3,926	57	2,311
Shensi	20	836		
Kansu	51	420		
Chinghai	5	103	6	299
Sinkiang	4	120	10	160
Shantung	4	36	38	1,387
Kiangsu	29	366		
Anhwei	156	2,361	1,330	8,929
Fukien	302	2,092	1,870	17,417
Honan	17	825	354	
Hupeh	47	820	134	2,421
Hunan	14	279	75	1,589
Kwangtung	100	1,593	342	5,986
Szechuan	404	4,014	730	8,693
Kweichow	10	241	91	4,731
Yunnan	17	646	18	3,191

Source: *Shui-li hua-tien (Hydropower Electric Generation)*, No. 17 (September 11, 1958), p. 40.

TABLE 4.75   Annual Increase in the Equipment of the Coal Mines of the Ministry of Coal Industry 1952, 1953, and 1956, Number of Units and Capacity in Kilowatts

Equipment	1952 Units	1952 Capacity	1953 Units	1953 Capacity	1956 Units	1956 Capacity
Extraction:						
Combines	4	299	18	1,242	88	6,195
Cutters	191	8,107	238	10,344	380	17,357
Electric shovels	44	752	65	5,342	92	18,766
Pneumatic drills	2,959		3,938		7,930	
Electric drills	1,661		2,423		5,449	
Air hammers	3,036		3,658		7,985	
Conveyance:						
Electric motors	207		229		673	
Simple conveyors	357		673		3,448	
Chain conveyors	1,052		1,373		1,706	
Leather belt conveyors	149		225		326	
Iron carts	37,687		39,805		65,984	
Wooden carts	24,986		26,506		36,181	
Auxiliary:						
Hoists	437	76,985	448	79,008	651	112,900
Fans	1,877	32,262	2,242	39,329	4,464	83,879
Water pumps	2,827	165,882	3,216	212,190	5,689	333,692
Compressors	594	42,408	678	47,629	1,191	83,983

Source: CH, pp. 95-96.

TABLE 4.76   Annual Addition to Capacity Output of Coal Mines of the Ministry of Coal Industry, 1953-56, Number of Mines and Capacity in Ten Thousand Tons

Addition	1953	1954	1955	1956
Total:				
Number of mines	47	63	60	44
Capacity	1,773	1,762	1,438	2,032
New construction:				
Number of mines	--	29	28	29
Capacity	--	1,059	1,006	1,380
Rehabilitation:				
Number of mines	7	14	10	5
Capacity	370	320	275	99
Reconstruction:				
Number of mines	40	20	22	10
Capacity	1,403	383	157	553

Source: CH, p. 93.

TABLE 4.77   Annual Increase in Number and Effective Volume of Blast Furnaces
in Iron-and-Steel Industry, 1952-56, Number of Units and
Cubic Meters

Size	1952	1953	1954	1955	1956
Total:					
Number	34	50	64	70	79
Volume	5,179	7,739	8,987	9,996	12,077
100 cubic meters and below:					
Number	24	38	51	56	63
Volume	1,051	1,783	2,112	2,197	2,414
101-200 cubic meters:					
Number	2	2	2	2	2
Volume	278	278	285	285	285
201-300 cubic meters:					
Number	1	--	--	--	--
Volume	291	--	--	--	--
301-400 cubic meters:					
Number	2	3	3	3	3
Volume	668	966	958	958	958
401-500 cubic meters:					
Number	1	1	1	1	1
Volume	406	406	406	413	413
501-600 cubic meters:					
Number	2	3	3	3	3
Volume	1,097	1,693	1,697	1,697	1,697
601-700 cubic meters:					
Number	1	--	--	--	--
Volume	602	--	--	--	--
701-800 cubic meters:					
Number	1	1	1	1	1
Volume	786	786	786	786	786
801-900 cubic meters:					
Number	--	2	3	4	6
Volume	--	1,827	2,743	3,660	5,524
901-1,000 cubic meters:					
Number	--	--	--	--	--
Volume	--	--	--	--	--

Source: *CH*, pp. 16-17.

TABLE 4.78 Annual Increase in Number and Area of Floor of Open-Hearth Furnaces in Iron-and-Steel Industry, 1952-56, Number of Units and Square Meters

Size	1952	1953	1954	1955	1956
Total:					
Number	26	27	29	31	42
Area	726.1	808.9	886.2	1,024.3	1,668.6
20 square meters and below:					
Number	11	11	11	11	11
Area	133.1	135.9	146.2	146.7	153.2
21-30 square meters:					
Number	7	7	9	9	9
Area	173.0	173.0	240.0	240.0	240.0
31-40 square meters:					
Number	--	--	--	--	--
Area	--	--	--	--	--
41-50 square meters:					
Number	6	4	4	4	4
Area	300.0	200.0	200.0	200.0	200.0
51-60 square meters:					
Number	2	5	5	3	3
Area	120.0	300.0	300.0	180.0	180.0
60 square meters and above:					
Number	--	--	--	4	12
Area	--	--	--	257.6	782.4

Source: CH, p. 17.

TABLE 4.79 Annual Additions to Capacity Output of Major Projects of Iron-and-Steel Industry, 1949-56, Tons

Year	Pig iron	Steel ingot	Roller steel
	(1)	(2)	(3)
1949-52	764,035	557,792	336,338
1953	810,007	220,615	587,437
1954	330,160	206,000	56,000
1955	358,155	438,167	12,984
1956	893,745	1,424,462	53,200

Source: CH, p. 16.

TABLE 4.80 Number of Metal-Cutting Machines Used in Metal-Processing Industry, 1952-56, Units

Year	Number
1952	80,439
1953	93,517
1954	109,521
1955	124,503
1956	157,158

Source: CH, p. 120.

TABLE 4.81 Geographic Distribution of Number of Metal-Cutting Machines
Used in Metal-Processing Industry at End of 1955

Area	Percentage distribution		Number of units used in the metal-processing industry[2]
	Metal-processing industry[1]	Machine-building industry[1]	
	(1)	(2)	(3)
Total	100.0	100.0	124,503
Inland areas	27.7	23.4	(34,487)
Coastal areas	72.3	76.6	(900,156)
Peking	3.6	3.3	(4,482)
Tientsin	7.6	8.5	(9,462)
Shanghai	29.5	33.9	(36,728)
Liaoning	17.5	18.4	(21,788)
Shantung	4.9	4.9	(6,100)

[1] CH, p. 138.
[2] Derived by multiplying the total number of lathes used in 1955, which is
given in CH, p. 120, by the percentages given in Column 1.

TABLE 4.82 Amount of Major Production Equipment in Paper-Making Industry,
1952-56, Units

	1952	1953	1954	1955	1956
Paper-making machinery	331	354	369	370	401
Long-mesh machinery	51	56	59	63	77
Damping apparatus[a]	324	357	376	380	363

[a] Figures on damping apparatus for 1952-55 include those not yet installed;
the 1956 figure is units already installed.

Source: CH, p. 207.

TABLE 4.83 Annual Increase in Productive Capacity of State Enterprises
of Paper Industry, 1950-57, Tons

	1950	1951	1952	1953	1954	1955	1956	1957
Paper	31,922	22,757	34,451	19,782	29,196	14,814	88,192	97,001
Central state enterprises				9,900	15,261	8,230	45,211	77,190
Local state enterprises				9,882	13,935	6,584	42,981	19,811
Paper pulp	17,190	28,026	20,862					

Source: CH, pp. 202, 206.

TABLE 4.84 Major Production Equipment Purchased and Installed Annually by Textile Industry, 1949-56

Equipment	1949[1]	1950[1]	1951[1]	1952[2]	1953[2]	1954[2]	1955[2]	1956[2]
Cotton spindles, thousands							6,763	6,858
Already installed	4,996	5,128	5,284	5,610	5,891	6,306	6,671	6,820
Power looms, thousands							174	181
Already installed	127	n.a.	n.a.	142	151	164	169	175
Looms in all-purpose mills, thousands							105	108
Already installed	64	65	68	74	81	92	102	106
Wool spindles, thousands				194	188	184	185	183
Already installed	129	119	127	123	124	124	135	134
Wool looms, units				2,505	2,479	2,389	2,394	2,409
Already installed	1,950	1,923	1,829	1,909	1,865	1,874	1,679	1,710
Jute spindles, units				31,926	37,388	37,644	37,912	42,136
Already installed	22,858	22,258	23,594	30,722	35,354	35,266	31,438	33,468
Jute looms, units				1,424	1,662	1,670	1,675	1,916
Already installed	966	872	932	1,212	1,484	1,459	1,340	1,408
Silk-spinning machines, units				25,729	25,441	25,120	24,577	26,858
Already installed	15,238	25,523	24,325	24,692	24,882	24,507	23,379	25,672
Silk spindles, units				28,884	37,384	44,484	45,084	44,673
Already installed, units				27,384	34,984	43,884	44,484	44,659
Silk looms,[a] units								
Already installed	40,728	41,555	43,185	44,189	45,026	45,310	44,788	42,777

[a] Including the amount of equipment in the handicraft industry.

[1] *CH*, p. 154.

[2] *Ibid.*, p. 162.

TABLE 4.85 Major Equipment Installed in Cotton Textile Industry, by Areas, 1949, 1952, and 1956, Thousand Units

Equipment and area	1949	1952	1956
Number of spindles at end of year	4,996	5,610	6,820
Inland areas	638	1,019	1,798
Coastal areas	4,358	4,591	5,022
Of which: Shanghai, Tientsin, and Tsingtao	(3,118)	(3,181)	(3,219)
Number of looms installed in the spinning and weaving mills at end of year	63.9	73.9	105.8
Inland areas	5.1	7.3	27.3
Coastal areas	58.8	66.6	78.5
Of which: Shanghai, Tientsin and Tsingtao	(50.0)	(48.1)	(49.2)

Sources: The figures are taken from *CH*, p. 188, except for Shanghai, Tientsin and Tsingtao, for which figures are derived from the percentage data given on p. 187 of the same source.

TABLE 4.86 Rate of Utilization of Power and Production Equipment in Selected Industries, 1949 and 1952-58, Percent

Industry	1949	1952	1953	1954	1955	1956	1957	1958
Electric power:								
Generating equipment	26.3[3]	42.0[1]			56.4[1]			
Iron-and-steel:								
Iron-smelting equipment	31.6[1]	84.4[1,2]			95.4[1,2]	116.0[2]		
Steel-smelting equipment		58.6[1,2]			83.9[1,2]	87.7[2]		
Metal-processing:								
Nationwide								
Metal-cutting machines		48.9[2]	58.8[3]		58.8[2]		64.8[3]	82.9[3]
Enterprises of the First Ministry of Machine Industry								
Metal-cutting machines			61.0[4]	58.0[4]	59.0[4]	75.0[4]	65.0[4]	
Lathes			68.0[4]	67.0[4]	65.0[4]			
Boring machines			71.0[4]	61.0[4]	{44.6[4]			
Drill presses			41.0[4]	36.0[4]				
Planers			66.0[4]	65.0[4]	{62.5[4]			
Slotting machines			52.0[4]	47.0[4]				
Milling machines			49.0[4]	48.0[4]	53.4[4]			
Broaching machines			19.0[4]	16.0[4]				
Gear-processing machines			46.0[4]	42.0[4]	47.0[4]			
Grinders			51.0[4]	47.0[4]	44.8[4]			
Machine hacksaws			37.0[4]	34.0[4]	42.7[4]			
Other metal-cutting machines			64.0[4]	45.0[4]	27.5[4]			
Rate of utilization of production equipment			60.1[4,5]	56.2[4,5]	56.7[4,5]	68.5[5]		
Cotton textile:								
Cotton-spinning equipment		89.15[6]	92.42[6]	93.79[6]	78.03[6]	94.27[6]		
Cotton-weaving equipment		89.37[6]	94.36[6]	92.93[6]	74.54[6]	94.40[6]		
Production capacity of cotton yarn		83.23[6]	87.90[6]	90.26[6]	76.64[6]	94.00[6]		
Production capacity of cotton cloth		86.68[6]	91.78[6]	89.78[6]	71.68[6]	89.36[6]		
Spindles, per hour	58.2[1]	94.2[1]			79.4[1]			
Looms, per hour	58.0[1]	95.6[1]			75.9[1]			

TABLE 4.86 (Continued)

Industry	1949	1952	1953	1954	1955	1956	1957	1958
Paper:								
Paper-making equipment, per hour		79.2[1]			89.3[1]			
Cigarette:								
Cigarette-manufacturing equipment, per hour		18.7[1]			31.2[1]			
Production equipment							52.0[a,7]	
Canned food:								
Production equipment							53.0[8]	
Sugar:								
Production equipment							66.0[a,7]	
Edible vegetable oils:								
Production equipment							75.0[a,7]	
Flour:								
Production equipment							68.0[a,7]	
Leather:								
Production equipment							69.0[a,7]	

[a] Anticipated figures.

[1] Data Office, *TCKTTH*, "A General Survey of Socialist Industrialization in China," *TCKTTH*, No. 22 (November, 1956); reprinted in *HHPYK*, No. 2 (January 25, 1957), pp. 54-62.

[2] Chi Ts'un-wei, "On the Balanced Growth of Industry in China," *CHCC*, No. 7 (July 9, 1957), pp. 4-8, reference on p. 6.

[3] *TGY*, pp. 108-9.

[4] *CH*, p. 135.

[5] Chang Ching-eng, "On the Utilization of Production Potentials," *CHCC*, No. (April 9, 1958), p. 25.

[6] *CH*, p. 169.

[7] Yang Po, "An Understanding of the Proportions of Consumption and Accumulation in China's National Income," *HH*, No. 20 (October 18, 1957), pp. 24-26, reference p. 25.

[8] Ch'eng Po, "Raising Quality and Lowering Price Are the Keys to the Development of the Canned Food Industry," *CHCC*, No. 7 (July 9, 1958), pp. 17-19, reference on p. 17.

255

TABLE 4.87 Hours of Utilization of Generating Equipment and Utilization of Generating-Equipment Capacity, 1949-58

Utilization	1949	1950	1951	1952	1953	1954	1955	1956	1957	1958
Hours of utilization of generating equipment	2,330[1]	2,450[1]	3,080[1]	3,800[1]	4,400[1]	4,530[1]	4,510[1]	4,760[1]	4,800[2]	5,518[2]
Rate of utilization of generating equipment capacity, percent[3]	26.3	n.a.	n.a.	42.0	n.a.	n.a.	56.4			

[1] CH, pp. 49, 68.

[2] Fu Tso-yi (Minister of Water Conservancy and Electric Power), "The Great Leap Forward of Water Conservancy and Electric Power Construction," in *Ten Glorious Years*, Peking: Jer-min jih-pao ch'u-pan-she, December 1959, pp. 157-71, reference on p. 164.

[3] Data Office, *TCKTTH*, "A General Survey of Socialist Industrialization in China," *TCKTTH*, No. 22 (November, 1956); reprinted in *HHPYK*, No. 2 (January 25, 1957), pp. 54-62, reference on pp. 55 and 59.

TABLE 4.88 Rate of Utilization of Capacity of Major Electrical Machineries in 1957, Percent

Type of machine	Nationwide	Central state enterprises	Local state enterprises
	(1)	(2)	(3)
Steam boilers	77.9	82.8	66.1
A-C electric motors	75.9	79.1	64.7
Transformers	80.4	83.5	66.3

Source: *CH*, p. 137.

TABLE 4.89 Coefficients of Utilization of Effective Volume of Blast Furnaces, 1949-58. Tons per Cubic Meter in 24 Hours

Area	1949	1950	1951	1952	1953	1954	1955	1956	1957	1958
Nationwide:										
All blast furnaces										
TGY[1]	0.62	n.a.	n.a.	1.02	n.a.	n.a.	n.a.	n.a.	1.32	1.49
CH[2]	0.617	0.758	0.858	1.024	1.034	1.080	1.166	1.305		
Large- and medium sized blast furnaces			1.068[3]	1.023[4]	n.a.	n.a.	n.a.	n.a.	1.321[4]	1.437[3]
Ministry of Metallurgical Industry:[5]										
All blast furnaces									1.321	
Large-sized blast furnaces									1.368	
Medium-sized blast furnaces									1.274	
Small-sized blast furnaces									1.144	
Liaoning Province, all blast furnaces[6]				1.175	n.a.	n.a.	n.a.	n.a.	n.a.	1.538
Anshan Iron and Steel Company[7]					1.100	1.076	1.183	1.357	1.389	

Note: Prior to 1959, the coefficient of the effective volume of a blast furnace was defined as the ratio of the effective volume of the blast furnace in cubic meters to the daily average production of pig iron in tons. Since then, the coefficient has been changed to mean the daily average output of pig iron in tons per cubic meter of the effective volume of the blast furnace. In other words, the coefficient currently adopted is the reciprocal of the one used previously. All figures in this table are given in terms of the current definition.

[1] TGY, p. 108.

[2] CH, pp. 10, 25.

[3] Li Hsiung, "The Development of Metallurgical Science and Technology in China during the Past Ten Years," *Ching-shu hsueh-pao (Metallurgical Journal)*, Vol. 4, No. 3 (September, 1959), pp. 1-8, reference on p. 3.

[4] Wang Ho-shou (Minister of Metallurgical Industry), "Rapid Development of the Iron and Steel Industry in China," in *Ten Glorious Years*, Peking: Jen-min jih-pao ch'u-pan-she, December, 1959, pp. 113-27, reference on p. 123.

[5] Hsieh Tseng-hung, "Average Coefficients of Utilization of Blast Furnaces of the Ministry of Metallurgical Industry," *CHCC*, No. 4 (April 9, 1958), p. 23.

[6] Hu I-min, "Liao-ning's Rapid Industrial Growth Is the Victory of the General Line of the Party," in *Liao-ning shi-nien*, published by Liao-ning Jen-min ch'u-pan-she, Shenyang, June, 1960, 172 pp.; translated as *Liaoning Province during the Past Decade*, in JPRS: 17,182, January 17, 1963, 334 pp.; reference on p. 64.

[7] Yen Chen-chung, "Dynamic Equilibrium? Or Static Equilibrium?" *CHCC*, No. 4 (April 9, 1958), p. 22.

TABLE 4.90 Coefficients of Utilization of Open-Hearth Furnaces, 1949–59, Tons per Cubic Meter in 24 Hours

Area	1949	1950	1951	1952	1953	1954	1955	1956	1957	1958	1959
Nationwide:											
TGY[1]	2.42	n.a.	n.a.	4.78	n.a.	n.a.	n.a.	n.a.	7.21	7.78	
CH[2]	2.423	3.306	3.840	4.782	4.910	5.160	6.070	6.670			
Ministry of Metallurgical Industry[3]									7.15		
Liaoning Province[4]				5.81				n.a.	n.a.	7.89	8.26[a]
Anshan Iron and Steel Company[5]					5.17	5.69	6.47	6.58	6.76		

[a] As of the second quarter of 1959.

[1] TGY, pp. 108-9.

[2] CH, pp. 10, 25.

[3] Hsieh Tseng-hung, "Coefficients of Utilization of Open-Hearth Furnaces of the Ministry of Metallurgical Industry," CHCC, No. 4 (April 9, 1958), p. 23.

[4] Hu I-min, "Liaoning's Rapid Industrial Growth Is the Victory of the General Line of the Party," in Liao-ning shih-nien, published by Liao-ning Jen-min ch'u-pan-she, Shenyang, June, 1960, 172 pp., translated as Liaoning Province during the Past Decade, in JPRS: 17,182, January 17, 1963, p. 64.

[5] Yen Chen-chung, "Dynamic Equilibrium? Or Static Equilibrium?" CHCC, No. 4 (April 9, 1958), p. 22.

TABLE 4.91 Coefficients of Utilization of Electric Furnaces and Revolving Furnaces of Enterprises under the Ministry of Metallurgical Industry, 1952-56

Coefficient of utilization	1952	1953	1954	1955	1956
Electric furnaces, output of steel in tons per million volt-amperes in 24 hours	7.40	10.20	13.12	15.00	18.12
Revolving furnaces, output of steel in tons per metric ton in 24 hours	13.11	21.80	30.38	32.97	40.40

Source: *CH*, p. 25.

TABLE 4.92 Hours of Machine Stoppage in Enterprises under the First Ministry of Machine Industry, by Causes for Stoppage, 1955 and 1956, Machine-Hours

Causes for stoppage	1955		1956	
	All production equipment	Of which: metal-cutting machine tools	All production equipment	Of which: metal-cutting machine tools
	(1)	(2)	(3)	(4)
Total machine-hours stoppage	22,508,506	15,797,853	18,365,208	10,703,828
Breakdown repairs	1,106,099	896,846	988,408	713,008
Worker shortage	1,669,191	1,575,199	2,790,321	1,960,340
Power shortage	196,402	142,373	229,926	163,304
No work	14,735,694	10,109,278	11,195,665	5,773,511
Shortage of materials and parts	546,847	430,949	538,713	366,728
Shortage of tools and blueprints	328,113	282,200	243,484	194,169

Source: *CH*, p. 136.

4.93 Fixed Assets for Industrial Production per Production Worker in Various Industries, 1952-56, Yuan

Industry	All enterprises					State and joint enterprises				
	1952	1953	1954	1955	1956	1952	1953	1954	1955	1956
Overall average per worker						5,656	5,273	6,072	6,835	
Electric power							51,197	58,828	58,196	
Mining of fuels							5,021	5,574	6,020	
Coal mining						5,029	n.a.	n.a.	5,417	
Crude oil						24,945	n.a.	n.a.	27,785	
Iron and steel						9,251	9,241	11,662	13,302	12,781
Iron and manganese mining						1,203	1,887	4,407	4,057	3,775
Iron-and-steel smelting						11,166	10,151	12,385	14,244	13,420
Mining and smeling of nonferrous metals						3,192	3,362	5,684	6,480	
Mining of chemicals							828	939	949	
Other nonmetallic mining							952	1,128	3,599	
Logging					3,416		497	1,443	2,931	
Processing of fuels							18,307	18,643	16,248	
Metal processing	2,996	3,139	3,538	4,357	5,037	4,750	5,029	5,528	6,035	
Chemical						8,120	9,066	9,867	11,114	
Building materials						2,431	2,291	2,531	3,641	
Glass							4,273	3,431	3,502	
Ceramics							2,456	1,925	1,482	
Rubber goods						4,725	4,714	4,372	10,688	
Lumber processing							1,210	1,480	1,945	
Matches							466	440	449	
Paper	(5,837)	(6,048)	(6,605)	(7,653)	(7,713)	9,528	8,923	9,856	10,307	
Textiles	2,856	2,899	3,213	3,452	3,143	4,806	4,943	5,125	5,107	
Tailoring							943	1,124	1,292	
Leather and furs							1,750	2,080	2,471	

TABLE 4.93 (Continued)

Industry	All enterprises					State and joint enterprises				
	1952	1953	1954	1955	1956	1952	1953	1954	1955	1956
Oils and fats, soap, spices, and cosmetics							6,000	6,090	6,107	
Food							3,373	3,312	3,566	
Salt							3,653	3,431	3,307	
Printing					2,293		3,072	3,240	3,256	
Educational supplies							1,558	1,755	6,292	
Water supply							49,129	54,743	59,557	
Other industries							4,530	7,087	8,973	

Sources:

All enterprises:

Logging: Su Hsin, "Comment on an Erroneous Point of View Concerning Distribution According to Labor," *HH*, No. 7 (April 3, 1958), pp. 25-26, reference on p. 26.

Metal processing: *CH*, p. 119.

Paper: Derived by dividing the total fixed assets used for industrial production in the paper industry by the year-end number of production workers, given in *CH*, pp. 206 and 211.

Textiles: *CH*, p. 161.

Printing: Su Hsin, *op. cit.*

State and joint enterprises:

Except for the iron-and-steel industry, for which data are taken from *CH*, p. 18, the sources of the data for various industries are as follows:

For 1952: Data Office, *TCKT*, "The Technological Level of Industrial Production in China," *TCKT*, No. 8 (April 29, 1957), pp. 30-33.

For 1953-55: Ma Yin-chu, "A New Theory of Population," *JMJP*, July 5, 1957. The data were computed for Ma by the State Economic Commission.

261

TABLE 4.94 Electricity Consumed per Production Worker in Selected Industries, 1952-56, Kilowatt-Hours

Industry	1952	1953	1954	1955	1956
Industry as a whole	1.430[1]				2,453[1]
Coal industry	2,577[1]			(3,948)[2]	3,747[1]
Petroleum industry	7,847[1]				9,617[1]
Nonferrous metals industry	4,174[1]				7,968
Iron-and-steel industry	5,400[3]	4,800[3]	5,900[3]	6,358[3]	8,025[3]
Mining	760[3]	870[3]	1,535[3]	2,340[3]	2,440[3]
Smelting	6,127[3]	5,857[3]	6,314[3]	6,780[3]	8,453[3]
Ferrous metals industry	2,753[1]				9,268[1]
Chemical industry	5,665[1]				7,649[1]
Building materials industry	1,113[1]				1,582[1]
Metal-processing industry	751[1]			(1,448)[4]	1,296[1]
Textile industry	1,681[1]			(1,951)[5]	2,299[1]
Paper industry	6,188[1]			(9,724)[6]	11,428[1]
Food industry	839[1]				1,135[1]

[1] *CH*, p. 73.

[2] Derived by dividing the amount of electricity consumed by the coal industry, given in Table 4.123, by the number of production workers in that industry, given in *CH*, p. 99.

[3] *CH*, p. 18.

[4] Derived by dividing the amount of electricity consumed by the metal-processing industry, given in Table 4.123, by the number of production workers in that industry, given in Table 4.123.

[5] Derived by dividing the amount of electricity consumed by the textile industry, given in Table 4.123, by the number of production workers in that industry, given in *CH*, p. 174.

[6] Derived by dividing the amount of electricity consumed by the paper industry, given in Table 4.123, by the number of production workers in that industry, given in *CH*, p. 211.

TABLE 4.95 Indicators of Mechanization of Mines of the Ministry of Coal Industry, 1952-56, Percent

Indicator	1952	1953	1954	1955	1956
Exclusively mechanized extraction	17.90	30.62	33.97	39.58	38.03
Mechanized loading		7.93	7.96	11.14	12.93
Mechanized transport	69.62	82.94	86.20	89.54	92.32
Manual extraction	22.36	16.48	9.43	7.99	6.23
Manual loading		92.07	92.04	88.86	87.07
Manual transport	30.38	17.06	13.80	10.46	7.68

Source: *CH*, p. 97.

TABLE 4.96 Physical Labor Productivity in Selected Industries, 1949-58, Output per Worker

Industry	1949	1950	1951	1952	1953	1954	1955	1956	1957	1958
Iron-and-steel (production workers),[1]										
Blast furnace shops, pig iron in tons				261.4	273.0	335.9	446.4	625.7		
Anshan Iron and Steel Company				870.6	1,044.6	1,249.8	1,616.9	2,678.1		
Open-hearth furnace shops, steel in tons				236.1	242.0	285.7	353.6	470.9		
Anshan Iron and Steel Company				416.6	476.5	654.5	743.8	956.4		
Coal,										
All personnel, tons:	0.424[2]	0.513[2]	0.653[2]	0.661[3]	0.736[3]	0.789[3]	0.850[3]	0.943[3]	0.978[4]	1.450[5]
Production workers	0.566[2]	0.698[2]	0.908[2]	0.792[3]	0.913[3]	1.005[3]	1.047[3]	1.162[3]	1.160[4]	
Underground workers	1.121[2]	1.449[2]	1.807[2]	1.081[3]	1.240[3]	1.308[3]	1.357[3]	1.549[3]		
Recovery workers				2.341[3]	2.916[3]	3.133[3]	3.129[3]	3.693[3]		
Enterprises of the Ministry of Textile Industry (production workers):										
Cotton yarn, bales	23.6[6]	n.a.	n.a.	37.52[7]	38.00[7]	40.33[7]	39.94[7]	47.26[7]		
Cotton cloth, bolts	492.4[6]	n.a.	n.a.	864.49[7]	882.27[7]	935.65[7]	776.73[7]	904.15[7]		

[1] CH, p. 20.
[2] Ibid., p. 91.
[3] Ibid., p. 98.
[4] Chang Lin-chih (Minister of Coal Industry), "Struggle for the Rapid Development of the Coal Industry," in Ten Glorious Years, Peking: Jen-min jih-pao ch'u-pan-she, December, 1959, pp. 128-38, reference on p. 131.
[5] SSB, Communique on the Development of the National Economy in 1958, Peking: T'ung-chi ch'u-pan-she, 1959, p. 18.
[6] Ibid., p. 157.
[7] Ibid., p. 170.

TABLE 4.97   Rate of Growth of Physical Output per Unit of Labor in Selected
Industries for 1952-57 and 1949-58, Percent

Increase in average output	1957 (1952=100)	1958 (1949=100)
Daily per coal miner	145.8	341.7
Annual per iron worker	238.5	1,698.5
Annual per steel worker	192.9	857.7
Annual per cement worker	174.3	
Annual of cotton per spinner	108.0	

Note: Figures in this table cover only the enterprises under
central industrial ministries.

Source: *TGY*, p. 110.

TABLE 4.98   Gross Industrial Value Output per Yuan of Fixed Assets, 1952-57,
1952 Yuan

Type of enterprise	1952	1953	1954	1955	1956	1957
State industrial enterprises[1]						
Large-scale (central state)		1.07	1.01	0.99		
Small-scale (local state)		14.63	13.10	13.41		
Enterprises of the First Ministry of Machinery Industry[a,2]	0.9	1.08	1.12	1.19	1.21	1.15
Industrial production in the textile industry[3]	3.563	3.889	3.907	3.442	4.058	

[a] Not including the enterprises of the Bureau of Electrical Engineering

[1] Fan Jo-i, "On the Rate of Profit of Capital Funds and the Policy of Construction," *CHCC*, No. 8 (August 9, 1958), pp. 21-23, reference on p. 22.

[2] Cheng Cin-eng, "On Production Potentials," *CHCC*, No. 4 (April 9, 1958), p. 25.

[3] *CH*, p. 169.

TABLE 4.99   Annual Output of Operating Metal-Cutting Machine Tool in Metal-
Processing Industry, 1953-56

Annual output	1953	1954	1955	1956
Tons per unit of operating metal-cutting machine tool	12.6	21.5	22.8	26.6

Source: *CH*, p. 137.

TABLE 4.100 Output of Metal-Cutting Machine Tools per Area of Shop Space of Major Shops of Enterprises under the First Ministry of Machine Industry, 1953-56, Tons per Square Meter

Type of shop	1953	1954	1955	1956
Iron casting and alloy	0.88	0.89	0.73	0.91
Forging	0.49	0.74	0.92	0.87
Machine-processing	0.45	0.60	0.62	0.73
Assembly	1.51	1.87	2.26	2.47

Source: *CH*, p. 136.

TABLE 4.101 Output per Unit of Production Equipment in Building Materials Industry, 1952, 1955-58

Industry	1952	1955	1956	1957	1958
Cement:					
Hourly output of clinker per square meter of the revolving furnace, kilograms	19.36[1]	23.29[1]	n.a.	22.69[2]	23.34[2]
Hourly output of cement per cement grinder, in tons[1]					
Nationwide	483.24	766.83			
Enterprises of the Ministry of Construction Engineering		747.90	828.45		
Glass:					
Daily (24 hours) output of molten glass-mass per square meter of the glass melting furnace, tons[3]	0.9	n.a.	n.a.	n.a.	1.3

[1] Lou Chi-cheng, "Major Technical and Economic Norms of the Cement Industry," *CHCC*, No. 7 (July 9, 1957), pp. 29-30, reference on p. 29.

[2] *TGY*, pp. 108-109.

[3] Ting Yuan (Director, Bureau of Glass and Ceramics Industry of the Construction Engineering), "Ten Years of Rapid Development of the Glass Industry," *Ch'ien-chu ts'ai-liao kung-yeh (Building Materials Industry)*, No. 19 September 22, 1959), pp. 16-17, reference on p. 16.

TABLE 4.102 Output per Unit of Production Equipment in Paper-Manufacturing Factories under the Ministry of Light Industry, 1952-57, Kilograms

Hourly output	1952	1953	1954	1955	1956	1957
Paper per cubic meter of effective area of drying oven	8.59	9.32	9.67	9.78	11.46	11.41
Raw pulp per cubic meter of damping apparatus:						
Wood pulp	8.72	9.39	9.54	9.70	10.72	11.56
Reed pulp	10.73	13.67	14.88	15.51	19.19	21.97

Source: *CH*, p. 208.

TABLE 4.103 Output per Unit of Cotton Textile Equipment, 1949 and 1952-58

Hourly output	1949	1952	1953	1954	1955	1956	1957	1958
Cotton yarn per thousand spindles, kilograms:								
Nationwide:								
CH		22.49	24.37	25.63	25.53	26.69		
TGY	16.60	19.64					20.67	23.48
Enterprises of the Ministry of Textile Industry (CH)	20.74	25.17	26.48	27.08	26.71	26.79		
Cotton cloth per loom, meters:								
Nationwide:								
CH		4.040	4.258	4.331	4.316	4.393		
TGY	3.516	3.988					4.075	4.160
Enterprises of the Ministry of Textile Industry (CH)	3.372	4.146	4.335	4.471	4.334	4.403		

Sources: TGY series cover all enterprises, but CH series include only large-scale enterprises. CH, pp. 157, 170, and TGY, p. 109.

TABLE 4.104 Electricity Consumed per Unit of Output of Selected Industries, 1952-56, Kilowatt-Hours

Product	1952	1953	1954	1955	1956
Coal, per ton[1]		13.4	14.4	15.5	13.7
Crude petroleum, per ton: [1]					
Natural		140	136	130	109
Synthetic		644	484	356	
Carbide, per ton[1]		2,763	2,704	2,705	3,526
Sulfuric acid, per ton[1]		59	57	56.7	67.5
Caustic soda, per ton[1]		2,075	1,999	2,114	3,296
Electric-furnace steel, per ton[1]		822	798	824	757
Cotton yarn, per bale: [2]					
Nationwide	233.94	246.66	249.22	230.84	218.19
Enterprises of the Ministry of Textile Industry	236.46	248.48	253.81	237.38	223.66
Cotton cloth, per thousand km:					
Nationwide	108.32	110.99	113.45	107.75	107.43
Enterprises of the Ministry of Textile Industry	107.00	107.66	111.03	107.95	106.44

[1] Data Office, TCKT, "Statistical Data on the Actual Amount of Several Major Materials Consumed Per Unit of Output in China during 1953-1956," TCKT, No. 18 (September 29, 1957), p. 18.

[2] CH, p. 170.

TABLE 4.105 Coal Consumed per Unit of Output of Electric Power and Building Materials, 1949-58, Kilograms

Product	1949	1950	1951	1952	1953	1954	1955	1956	1957	1958
Electric power, per thousand kw-hr:										
Nationwide:										
TCKT[1]					685	637	626	590	604	559
CH[2]					653	639	621	594	601	559
TGY[3]				685						
Fu Tso-yi[4]	1,020			727						
Enterprises of the Ministry of Electric Power[5]	925	848	763	659						
Public utility power plants[6]	961			685	629	616	601	576	573	537
Cement, per ton[1]					212	204	185	191.9		
Refractory bricks, per ton[1]					633	569	567	509		
Black bricks, per thousand pieces[1]					248	265	168	295.5		
Red bricks, per thousand pieces[1]					147	123	117	132.9		

[1] Data Office, *TCKT*, "Statistical Data on the Amount of Several Major Materials Actually Consumed per Unit of Output in China during 1953-56," *TCKT*, No. 18 (September 29, 1957), p. 18.

[2] *CH*, p. 69.

[3] *TGY*, p. 108.

[4] Fu Tso-yi (Minister of Water Conservancy and Electric Power), "The Great Leap Forward of Water Conservancy and Electric Power Construction," in *Ten Glorious Years*, Peking: Jen-min jih-pao ch'u-pan-she, December, 1959, pp. 157-71, reference on p. 164.

[5] *CH*, pp. 51, 69.

[6] *TGY*, p. 108.

TABLE 4.106 Iron Ore, Pig Iron, Coke, and Rejected Steel Consumed per Unit of Output in Iron-and-Steel Industry, 1952-57, Kilograms of Raw Materials per Ton of Product

Raw material	Product	1952	1953	1954	1955	1956	1957
Iron ore (containing 55 percent iron)	Pig iron[1]	1,641	1,760	1,735	1,743	1,725	
	Pig iron for smelting steel[2]		1,763	1,735	1,754	1,736	
	Pig iron for casting[2]		1,768	1,755	1,756	1,707	
Pig iron[2]	Open-hearth furnace steel		769	784	763	783	
	Revolving furnace steel		1,148	1,124	1,105	1,117	
	Electric furnace steel		169	183	174	148	
	Cast-iron pipe		784	789	742	911	
Metallurgical coke	Pig iron (Ministry of Metallurgical industry only)[3]					803	779
	Pig iron for smelting steel[2]		941	893	804	791	
	Pig iron for casting[2]		1,086	1,035	960	876	
	Revolving furnace steel[2]		150	159	143	144	
	Cast-iron pipe[2]		166	136	124	115	
Rejected steel[4]	Steel		354	305.5	305	264[a]	

[a] For the first three quarters of 1956.

[1] *CH*, p. 25.

[2] Data Office, *TCKT*, "Statistical Data on the Actual Amount of Several Major Materials Consumed per Unit of Output of Products in China during 1953-1956," *TCKT*, No. 18 (September 29, 1957), p. 33.

[3] Liu Kai-mo, "The Work of the Norm for Material Consumption Should Be Strengthened in the Midst of the Anti-Waste Movement," *CHCC*, No. 3 (March 9, 1958), pp. 24-25.

[4] Chang Shu-shan, "Attention Should Be Given to the Coordinated Development of the Production of the Iron and Steel Industry," *CHCC*, No. 4 (April 9, 1957), pp. 14-15.

TABLE 4.107 Rolled Steel Consumed per Unit of Output of Major Products of Metal-Processing Industry, 1953-56, Kilograms per Unit

Product	1953	1954	1955	1956
Metal-cutting machine tools[a]	539	669	501	629
Cranes	17,656	11,136	14,232	21,510
Pumps	34	18	33	75
Blowers	231	319	221	468
Bicycles	25	25	24	22
Steam locomotives	50,675	61,462	80,473	73,455

[a] Metal-cutting machine tools include lathes, boring machines, milling machines, planers, drill presses, slotting machines, broaching machines, gear-processing machines, grinders, saws, and other machine tools.

Source: Data Office, *TCKT*, "Statistical Data on the Actual Amount of Several Major Materials Consumed per Unit of Output in China during 1953-1956," *TCKT*, No. 18 (September 29, 1957), p. 18. The data were compiled by the State Statistical Bureau, primarily on the basis of information supplied by the First Ministry of Machine Industry and by various provinces.

TABLE 4.108 Explosive, Fuse Caps, Blasting Fuses, Mining Timber, and Processed Coal Consumed per Ton of Output of Selected Products, 1953-56

Raw material	Product	1953	1954	1955	1956
Explosive	Raw coal, kilograms	0.139	0.162	0.169	0.200
	Iron ore, kilograms	0.207	0.289	0.240	0.231
	Limestone, kilograms	0.100	0.070	0.085	0.056
Fuse caps	Raw coal, units	0.378	0.412	0.425	0.413
	Iron ore, units	0.504	0.519	0.480	0.335
	Limestone, units	0.103	0.123	0.134	0.110
Blasting fuses	Raw coal, meters	0.110	0.080	0.050	0.079
	Iron ore, meters	0.770	0.990	0.890	0.699
	Limestone, meters	0.180	0.079	0.036	0.024
Mining timber	Raw coal, cubic meters	241	236	246	236
Processed coal	Metallurgical coke, kilograms	1,408	1,368	1,410	1,376

Source: Data Office, *TCKT*, "Statistical Data on the Actual Amount of Several Major Materials Consumed per Unit of Output in China during 1953-1956," *TCKT*, No. 18 September 29, 1957), p. 33.

TABLE 4.109 Sulfuric Acid, Nitric Acid, Caustic Soda, and Soda Ash Consumed per Unit of Output of Selected Products, 1953-56

Raw material	Product	1953	1954	1955	1956
Sulfuric acid	Ammonium sulfate, kilograms/ton	756	755	784	745
	Light kerosene, kilograms/ton	71.7	69.7	69.6	n.a.
	Nitric acid, kilograms/ton	3,942	3,318	3,410	3,819
	Aniline, kilograms/ton	1,926	1,806	1,583	1,445
Nitric acid	Ammonium nitric acid, kilograms/ton	816	797	795	794
	Dinitrochlorbenzene (DNCB), kilograms/ton	654	658	643	662
	Aniline, kilograms/ton	959	904	827	785
Caustic soda	Carbon dioxide, kilograms/ton	1,683	1,330	1,496	1,507
	Sulfur dyestuffs, kilograms/ton	108	113	113	153
	Soap, kilograms/ton	82	84	74	76
	Paper, kilograms/ton	16.7	23.5	27.1	37.5
Soda ash	Caustic, kilograms/ton	1,438	1,363	1,459	1,369
	Plate glass, kilograms/standard case	9.95	10.56	10.20	9.97

Source: Data Office, *TCKT*, "Statistical Data on the Actual Amount of Several Major Materials Consumed per Unit of Output in China during 1953-56," *TCKT*, No. 18 (September 29, 1957), p. 18.

TABLE 4.110   Rubber Consumed per Tire and per Thousand Pairs of Rubber
Footwear, 1953-56, Kilograms

Product	1953	1954	1955	1956
Tires for automobiles, per unit:				
Tubes	1.37	1.86	2.01	1.94
Tires	16.47	15.79	13.004	17.60
Tires for transportation equipment moved by human and animal power, per unit:				
Tubes	0.21	0.20	0.20	0.19
Tires	0.67	0.63	0.61	0.72
Rubber footwear, per thousand pieces	202.12	168.56	153.88	149.00

Source: Data Office, TCKT, "Statistical Data on the Actual Amount of
Several Major Materials Consumed Per Unit of Output in China during
1953-1956," TCKT, No. 18 (September 29, 1957), p. 18.

TABLE 4.111   Raw Materials Consumed per Ton of Output in Paper Industry, 1952-57

Raw material	Product	1952	1953	1954	1955	1956	1957[a]
Paper pulp	Paper, kilograms:						
	Nationwide[1]	1,083.8	1,074.2	1,061.6	1,020.6	999.3	939.4
	Newsprint[2]	946	n.a.	n.a.	1,031		
	Rubber mat printing paper[2]	893	n.a.	n.a.	956		
	Paperboard[2]				1,042		
	Enterprises of the Ministry of Light Industry,[1]	1,068.9	1,074.7	1,074.3	1,024.6	1,022.1	1,007.9
	Newsprint[1]	1,087.2	1,082.7	1,068.2	1,063.0	1,057.2	1,039.1
	No. 4 rubber mat printing paper[1]	1,023.0	1,029.0	1,041.0	1,011.0	1,004.0	967.4
	M.G. cap paper[1]	1,059.0	1,089.0	1,074.0	1,013.0	1,002.0	968.4
	Cigarette paper[1]	922.0	898.0	889.0	863.0	870.0	861.9
	Typing paper[1]	1,088.0	1,084.0	1,069.0	1,018.0	1,066.0	1,067.3
Wood	Wood pulp, cubic meters[1]		5.00	4.63	4.58	4.34	4.19
	Chemical pulp[1]		5.61	5.59	5.46	5.47	5.28
	Bleach[1]		5.94	5.91	5.71	5.80	5.75
	Natural-color pulp[1]		5.57	5.52	5.39	5.18	4.96
	Sulfate[1]		5.10	5.10	5.24	5.32	4.97
	Mechanical pulp[1]		2.63	2.62	2.37	2.42	2.34
Reed	Reed pulp, kilograms[1]		2,136	2,080	1,999	1,953	1,971

[a] Figures for 1957 cover only the first six months.

[1] Data Office, TCYC, "A Survey of the Implementation of the Norms for the Consumption of Raw
Materials in Major Products of Light Industry during the Past Several Years," TCYC, No. 2
(February 23, 1958), pp. 16-20.

[2] Tsiang Ting-yuen, "Amount of Pulp Consumed per Unit of Paper Output and Hourly Output of
Raw Pulp per Cubic Meter of Steam Boilers," CHCC, No. 10 (October 23, 1956), pp. 32-33,
reference on p. 32.

TABLE 4.112 Raw Cotton and Cotton Yarn Consumed per Unit of Output of Cotton Textile Products, 1949, 1952–58, Kilograms

Raw material	Product	1949	1952	1953	1954	1955	1956	1957	1958
Raw cotton	Cotton yarn, per bale: Nationwide: TCYC and Tsiang Kuang-nai TGY[3]	210.00[1] 205.85	198.97[2] 198.97	196.50[2] n.a.	195.36[2] n.a.	192.62[2] n.a.	194.84[2] n.a.	193.00[1] 193.56	192.85
	Enterprises of the Ministry of Textile Industry	202.83[4]	198.14[3]	195.50[3]	195.49[3]	192.60[3]	194.18[3]	192.95[a,3]	
Cotton yarn	Cotton cloth, per thousand km: Nationwide:[2]		137.31	134.53	136.28	133.70	134.58	131.69[a]	
	Enterprises of the Ministry of Textile Industry[2]		134.78	134.89	136.07	134.66	133.61	131.31[a]	

[a] Figures for 1957 cover only the first six months.

[1] Tsiang Kuang-nai (Ministry of Textile Industry), "Ten Glorious Years of the Textile Industry," in *Ten Glorious Years*, Peking; Jen-min ch'u-pan-she, December, 1959, pp. 236-44, reference on p. 243.

[2] Data Office, *TCYC*, "A Survey of the Implementation of the Norms for the Consumption of Raw Materials in Major Products of Light Industry in the Past Several Years," *TCYC*, No. 2 (February 23, 1958) pp. 16-20.

[3] *TGY*, p. 109.

[4] *CH*, p. 157.

TABLE 4.113 Tobacco Consumed per Case of Cigarettes, 1952-57, Kilograms[a]

Averages	1952	1953	1954	1955	1956	1957
National average	62.10	62.60	60.90	56.70	55.61	57.92
Enterprises of provincial and municipal governments	63.60	62.50	59.90	55.80	54.93	58.17
Enterprises of the Ministry of Food Industry	60.89	62.56	61.58	57.29	56.06	57.75
Grade A cigarettes			64.72	62.84	63.13	62.73
Grade B cigarettes			61.92	59.31	59.91	61.56
Grade C cigarettes			61.11	55.79	53.28	55.93
Grade D cigarettes			61.78	56.28	53.90	54.81

[a] One case contains 50,000 cigarettes
[b] Figures for 1957 cover only the first six months.

Source: Data Office, *rcyc*, "A Survey of Implementation of the Norms for the Consumption of Raw Materials in Major Products of Light Industry in the Past Several Years," *rcyc*, No. 2 (February 23, 1958), pp. 16-20.

TABLE 4.114 Raw Materials Consumed per Unit of Output of Edible Vegetable Oils, 1952-56, Kilograms per Ton

Raw materials	Product	1952	1953	1954	1955	1956
Soybean	Bean oil:					
	National average	8,491.0	7,959.0	7,954.0	7,248.0	7,364.0
	Enterprises of the Ministry of Food Industry	8,904.0	8,998.0	7,095.0	7,466.0	7,932.5
Rapeseed	Rapeseed oil:					
	National average	2,767.5	2,815.2	2,877.5	2,687.9	2,806.5
	Enterprises of the Ministry of Food Industry	2,921.9	2,805.4	2,804.8	2,688.9	2,668.0
Peanuts	Peanut oil:					
	National average	2,515.6	2,527.3	2,406.0	2,431.3	2,461.7
	Enterprises of the Ministry of Food Industry	2,508.1	2,330.8	2,254.1	2,445.9	2,307.9
Cotton seed	Cottonseed oil:					
	National average	8,013.0	7,206.0	7,242.0	6,858.0	7,048.1
	Enterprises of the Ministry of Food Industry	7,650.9	6,914.6	7,739.1	6,675.1	6,991.0
Sesame	Sesame oil:					
	National average	2,326.4	2,144.0	2,036.1	2,017.0	2,001.6
	Enterprises of the Ministry of Food Industry	--	2,092.2	2,053.0	2,037.0	--

Source: Data Office, *rcyc*, "A Survey of the Implementation of the Norms for the Consumption of Raw Materials in Major Products of Light Industry in the Past Several Years," *rcyc*, No. 2 (February 23, 1958), pp. 16-20.

TABLE 4.115 Rate of Output of Sugar, White Wine, and Edible Vegetable Oils from Various Raw Materials, 1952-57, Percent

Product	Raw material	1952	1953	1954	1955	1956	1957
Sugar (Ministry of Food Industry)	Sugar cane					17.77	12.42
	Sugar beets	12.8					14.6
White wine	Starch	51.5					60.5
Bean oil:	Soybean						
National average		11.78	12.56	12.57	13.80	13.58	
Enterprises of the Ministry of Food Industry		11.23	11.11	14.09	13.39	12.61	
Rapeseed oil:	Rapeseed						
National average		36.13	35.52	34.75	37.20	35.63	
Enterprises of the Ministry of Food Industry		34.22	35.65	35.65	37.19	37.48	
Peanut oil:	Peanuts						
National average		39.75	39.57	41.56	41.13	40.62	
Enterprises of the Ministry of Food Industry		39.87	42.90	44.36	40.88	43.33	
Cottonseed oil:	Cottonseed						
National average		12.48	13.88	13.81	14.58	14.19	
Enterprises of the Ministry of Food Industry		13.07	14.67	12.92	14.98	14.30	
Sesame oil:	Sesame						
National average		42.98	46.64	49.11	49.58	49.96	
Enterprises of the Ministry of Food Industry		--	47.80	48.71	49.09	--	

Sources: For sugar and wine— (1) Li Chu-chen, (Minister of Light Industry), "The Leap Forward of Light Industry," *Chung-kuo ching-kung-yeh (Chinese Light Industry)* No. 18 (September 28, 1959), pp. 3-7. (2) Data Office, *TCYC*, "A Survey of Production Increase and Cost Reduction of Light Industry in China," *TCYC*, No. 2 (February 23, 1958), pp. 12-15

For edible vegetable oils—Data Office, *TCYC*, "A Survey of the Implementation of the Norms for the Raw Materials Consumed in Major Products of Light Industry in the Past Several Years," *TCYC*, No. 2 (February 23, 1958), pp. 16-20.

TABLE 4.116   Rate of Loss in Transmission of Electric Power Industry,
1949-58, Percent

Averages	1949[1]	1950[1]	1951[1]	1952[1]	1953[1]	1954[1]	1955[1]	1956[1]	1957[2]	1958[2]
National average				12.44	11.33	10.55	9.49	9.53	9.01	7.57
Average for the enterprises of the Ministry of Electric Power	24.84	16.04	15.55	12.56	11.43	10.53	9.45	9.54		

[1] *CH*, pp. 51, 69.

[2] Fu Tso-yi (Minister of Water Conservancy and Electric Power), "The Great Leap Forward of Water Conservancy and Electric Power Construction," in *Ten Glorious Years*, Peking: Jen-min jih-pao ch'u-pan-she, December, 1959, pp. 157-71, reference on p. 164.

TABLE 4.117   Number of Accidents and Amount of Electricity Not Transmitted Because of Accidents in Electric Power Industry, 1951-56

Accidents	1951	1952	1953	1954	1955	1956
Number of accidents:						
Total	4,776	6,747	6,849	6,295	5,012	3,739
When generating	916	996	954	907	758	434
When transmitting	3,860	5,751	5,895	5,388	4,254	3,305
Amount of electricity not transmitted due to accidents, thousand kw-hr:						
Total	6,907	9,945	9,116	18,191	6,443	4,871
When generating	3,280	4,404	3,049	2,027	1,968	1,150
When transmitting	3,627	5,541	6.067	16,164	4,475	3,721
Average based on capacity at end of year:						
Number of accidents, times per 10,000 kw	46.3	49.45	43.3	34.1	23.0	14.0
Amount of electricity not transmitted due to accidents, kw-hr per kw	6.69	7.29	5.77	9.84	2.95	1.82
Average based on volume of electricity generated:						
Number of accidents, times per million kw-hr	1.45	1.20	0.97	0.73	0.51	0.28
Amount of electricity not transmitted due to accidents, kw-hr per thousand kw-hr	2.09	1.77	1.29	2.11	0.65	0.37

Source: *CH*, p. 69.

TABLE 4.118   Recovery Rate and Loss Rate of Mines of the Ministry of Coal Industry, 1949, 1952-56, Percent

Rate	1949[1]	1952[2]	1953[2]	1954[2]	1955[2]	1956[2]	1957[3]	1958[3]
Recovery rate	63.1	75.3	76.4	79.7	83.2	82.2	81.9	82.7
Loss rate	36.9	24.7	23.6	20.3	16.8	17.8	18.1	17.3

[1] Data Office, *TCKT*, "Technological Level of Industrial Production in China," *TCKT*, No. 8 (April 29. 1957), pp. 30-33, reference on p. 31.
[2] *CH*, p. 98.
[3] *TGY*, p. 108.

TABLE 4.119   Rate of Rejection of Parts in Metal-Processing Industry, 1953-56, Percent

Parts	1953	1954	1955	1956
Cast iron	13.6	14.1	10.9	--
Enterprises of the First Ministry of Machine Industry and of the Ministry of Electrical Machinery	13.5	14.3	10.9	8.0
Enterprises of local governments	14.0	13.3	10.9	--
Cast steel	7.5	9.7	7.4	--
Enterprises of the First Ministry of Machine Industry and of the Ministry of Electrical Machinery	7.5	9.7	7.4	5.3
Machine-processed	2.4	4.8	3.2	--
Enterprises of the First Ministry of Machine Industry and of the Ministry of Electrical Machinery	--	5.2	3.6	2.5
Enterprises of local governments	3.0	2.8	1.8	--

Source: *CH*, p. 134.

TABLE 4.120   Percentage Distribution of Total Rejects of Parts in Enterprises under the First Ministry of Machine Industry, by Cause for Rejection, in 1956

Cause for rejection	Cast-iron	Cast-steel	Machine-processed
Inferiority of material and semi-finished products	2.8	--	5.9
Workers' carelessness	58.7	56.0	45.9
Violations of technical specifications	6.5	5.3	1.5
Inaccuracies of blue-prints or other technical documents	0.4	--	1.8
Faulty or careless inspection	0.3	--	1.5
Others	31.3	38.7	43.4
Total	100.0	100.0	100.0

Source: *CH*, p. 134.

TABLE 4.121   Rate of Finished Output and Rate of Loss of Paper-Pulp Fiber of Paper-Making Enterprises of the Ministry of Light Industry, 1952-57, percent

Rate	1952	1953	1954	1955	1956	1957
Finished output[1]	85.40	84.90	90.90	90.50	89.54	91.93
Loss of paper-pulp[2]				3.74	4.79	4.50[a]

[a] Covering only the first six months of 1957.

[1] *CH*, p. 208.
[2] Data Office, *TCYC*, "A Survey of the Implementation of the Norms for Raw Materials Consumed in Major Products of Light Industry during the Past Several Years," *TCYC*, No. 2 (February 23, 1958), pp. 16-20, reference on p. 18.

TABLE 4.122   Total Consumption of Electricity, by Sectors, 1949-56, Million Kilowatt-Hours

Sector	1949	1950	1951	1952	1953	1954	1955	1956
Total amount of electricity consumed	3,460	4,420	5,540	6,230	7,770	9,620	10,650	13,980
By industry (including nonproductive use)	2,260	3,260	4,120	5,100	6,480	8,220	9,300	11,590[a]
By agriculture				43	40	44	50	77
By transportation				100	108	127	120	131

[a] Including only the amount of electricity consumed for production purposes

Source: *CH*, pp. 48, 72.

TABLE 4.123   Electricity Consumed by Selected Industries, 1949-56, Millions of Kilowatt-Hours

Industry	1949[1]	1950[1]	1951[1]	1952[2]	1953[2]	1954[2]	1955[2]	1956[b,2]
Industry as a whole[a]	2,260	3,260	4,120	5,101	6,480	8,220	9,305	11,596
Coal				820			1,512	1,530
Petroleum				104			213	221
Iron-and-steel (smelting only)	(93)	(278)	(366)	528			1,194	1,630
Metal-processing	(121)	(194)	(255)	383			916	964
Chemical	(187)	(243)	(338)	411			841	899
Building materials				307			434	604
Paper				333			558	650
Textile				1,307			1,691	2,165
Food				393			524	625

[a] Including the amount of electricity consumed for industrial production, basic construction, and other uses.

[b] Including only the amount of electricity used for industrial production.

[1] *CH*, pp. 48-49. Figures in parentheses are derived from data on the percentage share of total amount of electricity consumed by individual industries.

[2] *Ibid*, p. 72.

TABLE 4.124 Rate of Self-Consumption of Electricity by Power Plants, 1949-56, Percentage

Enterprise	1949	1950	1951	1952	1953	1954	1955	1956
National average:								
Total				5.93	5.77	5.44	5.66	5.96
Thermal power plants				7.42	7.15	7.07	7.24	7.11
Hydropower plants				0.22	0.23	0.17	0.16	0.18
Enterprises of the Ministry of Electric Power:								
Total	7.73	6.85	6.32	5.76	5.62	5.30	5.55	5.86
Thermal power plants	12.17	9.83	8.58	7.31	7.06	6.99	7.19	7.05
Hydropower plants	0.86	0.38	0.28	0.22	0.23	0.17	0.15	0.16

Source: *CH*, pp. 51, 69.

TABLE 4.125 Paper Consumed by Industry and by Agricultural Cooperatives, 1952-56, Tons

Enterprise	1952	1953	1954	1955	1956
By industry	120,000	146,000	170,000	200,000	250,000
By agricultural cooperatives		1,000	7,000	14,000	43,490

Note: Figures for agricultural cooperatives are estimated from model-survey data.

Source: *CH*, p. 218.

TABLE 4.126 Paper Consumed by Governmental Agencies and Public Organizations and by Residents, 1952-56, Tons

Use	1952	1953	1954	1955	1956
By governmental agencies and public organizations	55,000	68,000	78,000	90,000	110,000
By residents	85,607	103,198	135,307	166,893	228,536

Source: *CH*, p. 218.

TABLE 4.127 Paper Consumed for Cultural and Educational Purposes, 1952-56

Consumption	1952	1953	1954	1955	1956
Total consumption of paper for newspapers, magazines, and books, 10,000 printed pages	331,383	391,358	444,145	513,455	755,898
Newspapers[a]	133,267	146,684	149,070	171,272	243,942
Magazines	28,042	30,677	42,778	61,581	76,343
Books	170,074	213,997	252,297	280,602	435,613
Amount of paper consumed by students[b] tons	28,986	29,785	30,242	31,474	38,353
Amount of paper used for the purpose of eliminating illiteracy, tons	5,811	4,099	5,693	12,406	19,586

[a] Including only those published by special districts and above.
[b] Not including books, magazines, and newspapers used by students.

Source: CH, p. 217.

TABLE 4.128 Cotton Cloth and Knitted Cotton Products Consumed in Urban and Rural Areas, 1950-56

Area	Unit	1950	1951	1952	1953	1954	1955	1956
Cotton cloth	Million km	1,668	2,256	2,813	3,899	3,791	3,849	5,101
	Thousand bolts	52,680	71,230	86,990	119.370	117,240	117,830	156,170
Urban	Million km	475	598	731	1,014	985	898	1,169
	Thousand bolts	15,010	18,880	22,620	31,040	30,450	27,490	35,780
Rural	Million km	1,193	1,658	2,082	2,885	2,806	2,951	3,932
Knitted cotton products	Hundred units	--	--	3,714	4,253	4,902	4,913	6,639
Urban	Hundred units	--	--	1,300	1,480	1,716	1,720	2,273
Rural	Hundred units	--	--	2,414	2,773	3,186	3,193	4,366

Source: CH, p. 185.

TABLE 4.129 Planned and Actual Cost of Production of Enterprises of the Ministry of Textile Industry, 1952-56, Thousands of Yuan

Cost	1952	1953	1954	1955	1956
Total output of commodity production:					
Planned cost	1,352,260	1,507,700	1,270,870	1,533,660	1,964,610
Actual cost	1,286,180	1,503,950	1,703,540	1,507,250	1,953,230
Of which: output of comparable products:					
Cost estimated on basis of average actual cost during preceding year	1,025,940	1,156,650	1,343,410	1,095,570	1,464,450
Planned cost	1,038,760	1,075,690	1,332,620	1,073,390	1,456,450
Actual cost	991,540	1,080,720	1,331,580	1,063,290	1,454,650

Source: CH, p. 172.

TABLE 4.130 Average Cost of Production of Electric Power, Coal, and Textile Industries, 1949-58

Industry	1952	1953	1954	1955	1956	1957	1958
Electric power:							
National average index of average cost of the amount of electricity sold (1952=100), percent[1]	100.0	99.8	89.1	85.7	81.6	75.5	73.1
Enterprises of the Ministry of Electric Power, yuan per thousand kw-hr[2]							
Average cost of electricity generated by thermal power	39.8	32.3	30.6	27.5	26.3		
Average cost of electricity generated by hydraulic power	3.6	4.5	3.6	3.9	5.2		
Average cost of amount of electricity sold	45.8	44.9	38.9	33.9	32.4		
Average price charged for amount of electricity sold	--	68.5	67.2	65.5	64.5		
Coal, yuan per ton[3]						10.9	9.17
Cotton textiles:[4]							
20-count yarn, yuan per bale	501.69	471.26	468.39	523.73			
32-count yarn, yuan per bale	572.37	531.79	536.21	521.54	529.49		
Wu-fu shih cloth, yuan per bolt	15.53	14.44	15.18	14.72	14.07		
404 worker-peasant blue cloth, yuan per bolt	31.35	29.62	29.15	29.12			

[1] Department of Financial Affairs, Ministry of Water Conservancy and Electric Power, "A Review of the Financial Accounting Work of the Electric Power Industry During the Past Ten Years," *Chi-yeh kuai-chi* (Enterprise Accounting), No. 18, (September 22, 1959), p. 13. Editorial, "March Bravely Forward to Develop Rapidly the Electric Power Industry," *Shiu-li yu tien-li* (Water Conservancy and Electric Power), No. 18 (September 20, 1959), pp. 6-9.

[2] *CH*, p. 73.

[3] Liu Hsiang-san (Vice-Minister of Coal Industry), "Strengthen Business Management Work and March Bravely Forward to Increase Accumulation," *Mei-t'an kung-yeh* (Coal Industry) No. 9 (May 4, 1959), pp. 5-6, reference p. 5.

[4] *CH*, p 173.

TABLE 4.131   Rate of Reduction of Cost of Comparable Products, by Branch of Industry, Percentage Decrease over Preceding Year

Enterprise	1952	1953-57	1953	1954	1955	1956	1958
State industrial enterprises		29.0[1]			8.0[2]		12.5[3]
Iron-and-steel enterprises of the Ministry of Metallurgical Industry[4]			3.61	6.05	8.71	14.11	
Ashan Iron and Steel Company			11.01	9.87	7.02	13.34	
Bureau of Iron and Steel			-1.05	4.07	4.76	14.58	
State and joint paper enterprises[5]				9.19	12.44	11.80	
Enterprises of the Ministry of Textile Industry[6]	3.35		6.56	0.88	2.95	0.67	

[1] SSB, *Communique on the Results of the Implementation of the First Five-Year Plan for the Development of the National Economy (1953-1957),* Peking: T'ung-chi ch'u-pan-she, 1959, p. 8.

[2] SSB, *Communique on the Results of the Implementation of the National Economic Plan for 1955,* Peking: T'ung-chi ch'u-pan-she, 1956, p. 4.

[3] SSB, *Communique on the Development of the National Economy in 1958,* Peking: T'ung-chi ch'u-pan-she, 1959, p. 18.

[4] *CH,* 28.

[5] *Ibid.,* p. 213.

[6] *Ibid.,* p. 172.

TABLE 4.132   Rate of Reduction of Cost of Comparable Products, by Product, 1952-57, Percent

Product	Percentage reductions in 1957 over 1952	Average annual rate of reduction, 1953-57
Total cost of comparable products of enterprises of central industrial ministries	29.0	6.5
Cost per unit of output:		
of major industrial products		
Electric power, thousand kw-hrs	24.5	5.5
No. 56 motor petrol, ton	1.3	0.3
Pig iron, ton	2.6	0.5
Medium-sized rolled steel, ton	28.1	6.4
Welded steel tube, ton	47.5	12.1
Oil of vitriol (98%), ton	18.7	4.1
Caustic soda (95-98%), ton	31.6	7.3
Ammonium nitrate, above 90%, ton	42.5	10.5
32-count cotton yarn, bale	4.2	0.9
23x21 cotton cloth, bolt	4.6	0.9
No. 1 newsprint, ton	33.0	7.7

Source: *TGY,* p. 111.

TABLE 4.133   Amount and Period of Turnover of Working Capital of Iron-and-Steel Enterprises of the Ministry of Metallurgical Industry, 1053-56

Enterprise	Amount, millions of yuan				Period of turnover, days			
	1953	1954	1955	1956	1953	1954	1955	1956
Iron-and-steel enterprise of the Ministry of Metallurgical Industry	427	448	505	532	116	103	93	85
Anshan Iron and Steel Company	164	180	212	249	109	105	88	90
Bureau of Iron and Steel	263	268	293	283	121	101	96	82

Source: *CH*, p. 28.

TABLE 4.134   Amount and Period of Turnover of Normalized Working Capital in Electric Power Industry, 1953-57

Turnover	1953	1954	1955	1956	1957
Amount of normalized working capital per thousand kw, yuan	53.4	51.2	34.5	26.4	29.1
Rate of turnover of normalized working capital, days	56.05	51.16	37.71	24.95	29.3

Source: Department of Financial Affairs, Ministry of Water Conservancy and Electric Power, "A Review of the Financial Accounting Work of the Electric Power Industry During the Past Ten Years," *Chi-yeh kuai-chi (Enterprise Accounting)*, No. 18 (September 22, 1959) p. 13.

TABLE 4.135 Industrial Profits at Current Prices, 1950-58, Millions of Yuan,

Profits	1950	1951	1952	1953	1954	1955	1956	1957	1958
Total:									
Private industrial enterprises	348[1]	817[1]	-(371)[2]	913[1]	{ 658[2]				
Enterprises of Ministry of Coal Industry									800[4]
Iron-and-steel enterprises of the Ministry of Metallurgical Industry			386[5]	522[5]	622[5]	806[5]	801[5]		
Anshan Steel Company			206[5]	294[5]	333[5]	456[5]	518[5]		
Enterprises under Bureau of Iron and Steel			180[5]	228[5]	289[5]	350[5]	283[5]		
Paper-making enterprises of the Ministry of Light Industry				56.5[6]	65.3[6]	93.7[6]	137.9[6]	163.9[6]	
Amount remitted to state:									
Enterprises of the Ministry of Electric Power Industry			60[7]	110[7]	200[7]	270[7]	350[7]		
Paper-making enterprises of the Ministry of Light Industry				55[6]	63.7[6]	92.4[6]	136.4[6]	152.2[6]	

1 Ch'ien Hua *et al*, *Changes in Private Industry and Trade in China during the Past Seven Years (1949-1956)*, Peking: Ts'ai-cheng ching-chi ch'u-pan-she, 1957, p. 90.

2 The profits of private industry increased by 146 percent in 1953 as compared with the 1952 level. Se Chao I-wen, *New Industry in China*, Peking: T'ung-chi ch'u-pan-she, 1957, p. 67.

3 The total profits of private industry during the period 1950-55 amounted to 3,107 million yuan. (*Ibid.*, p. 80.)

4 Liu Hsian-san (Vice Minister of Coal Industry), "Strengthening Business Management Work and Marching Bravely Forward for the Increase of Accumulation," *Mei-t'an kung-yeh* (Coal Industry) No. 9 (May 4, 1959), pp. 5-6, reference on p. 5.

5 *CH*, p. 28.

6 *CH*, p. 213.

7 *CH*, p. 33.

TABLE 5.1   Cultivated Areas, Sown Area, and Index of Multiple Cropping, 1949-58

Area	Unit, thousands	1949	1950	1951	1952
Cultivated area area	Mou	1,468,220[1]	1,505,340[1]	1,555,070[1]	1,618,780[1]
	Hectares	97,881	100,356	103,671	107,919
Wet field[2]	Mou	342,270	n.a.	n.a.	387,800
	Hectares	22,818	n.a.	n.a.	25,853
Dry field[2]	Mou	1,125,950	n.a.	n.a.	1,230,980
	Hectares	75,063	n.a.	n.a.	82,066
Non-irrigated field	Mou	1,077,510	n.a.	n.a.	1,157,640
	Hectares	71,834	n.a.	n.a.	77,176
Watered field	Mou	48,440	n.a.	n.a.	73,340
	Hectares	3,229	n.a.	n.a.	4,890
Sown area[1]	Mou				2,118,840
	Hectares				141,256
Index of multiple cropping[1]	Percent				130.9

Note: Index of multiple cropping is the percentage of sown area to the cultivated area. An area may be sown more than once in a year, and each sowing is
counted separately. Therefore, the sown area can be much larger than the
cultivated area. For the concepts of cultivated area and sown area and the
method of computing the index of multiple cropping, see the text.

TABLE 5.1   (Continued)

1953	1954	1955	1956	1957	1958
1,627,930 [1]	1,640,320 [1]	1,652,350 [1]	1,677,370 [1]	1,677,450 [1]	1,616,800 [1]
108,529	109,355	110,157	111,825	111,830	107,787
389,320	394,020	398,100			
25,955	26,268	26,540			
1,238,610	1,246,300	1,254,240			
82,574	83,087	83,616			
1,163,320	1,166,450	1,171,500			
77,555	77,763	78,100			
75,290	79,850	82,740			
5,019	5,324	5,516			
2,160,530	2,218,880	2,266,220	2,387,590	2,358,660	2,344,020
144,035	147,925	151,081	159,173	157,244	156,935
132.7	135.3	137.2	142.3	140.6	145.0

[1] *TGY*, p. 128.

[2] SSB, *Communique on the Results of the Implementation of the National Economic Plan for 1955* (with Economic Statistical Abstract), Peking: T'ing-chi chu-pan-she, 1956, p. 29.

TABLE 5.2 Sown Area for Various Crops, 1949-58

Crop	Unit, thousands	1949	1950	1951	1952
All crops	Mou				2,118,840
	Hectares				141,256
Food grains	Mou	1,524,597	1,572,050	1,604,520	1,684,491
	Hectares	101,640	104,803	106,968	112,300
Rice	Mou	385,628	392,240	404,000	425,734
	Hectares	25,708	26,149	26,933	28,382
Wheat	Mou	322,734	342,000	345,820	371,698
	Hectares	21,516	22,800	23,055	24,780
Coarse grains	Mou	711,076	722,370	730,410	756,743
	Hectares	47,405	48,158	48,694	50,450
Corn	Mou				188,435
	Hectares				12,562
Potatoes	Mou	105,159	115,440	124,290	130,316
	Hectares	7,011	7,696	8,286	8,688
Sweet potatoes	Mou				97,640
	Hectares				6,509
Irish potatoes	Mou				26,598
	Hectares				1,773
Soybeans	Mou	124,782			175,191
	Hectares	8,319			11,679
Industrial crops					
Cotton	Mou	41,550	56,790	82,270	83,636
	Hectares	2,770	3,786	5,485	5,576
Jute	Mou	342			1,244
	Hectares	23			83
Flax	Mou				427
	Hectares				28
Tobacco	Mou				6,405
	Hectares				427
Cured Tobacco	Mou	915			2,790
	Hectares	61			186
Peanuts	Mou	18,816			27,064
	Hectares	1,254			1,804
Rapeseed	Mou	22,725			27,946
	Hectares	1,515			1,863
Sesame	Mou	12,402			15,848
	Hectares	827			1,057
Sugar cane	Mou	1,623			2,737
	Hectares	108			182
Sugar beets	Mou	239			526
	Hectares	16			35

Sources: For all crops: *TGY*, p. 128.
For food grains, soybeans, and industrial crops: 1949 and 1952-57: Bureau of Planning, Ministry of Agriculture, *A Collection of Statistical Data on Agricultural Production*

TABLE 5.2 (Continued)

1953	1954	1955	1956	1957	1958
2,160,530	2,218,880	2,266,220	2,387,590	2,358,660	2,344,020
144,035	147,926	151,082	159,172	157,244	156,934
1,714,120	1,745,118	1,775,961	1,864,395	1,813,273	1,819,490
114,275	116,341	118,397	124,293	120,885	121,299
424,817	430,827	437,601¹	499,677	483,617	491,170
28,321	28,722	29.173	33,312	32,241	32,745
384,540	404,514	401,085	409,079	413,126	399,350
25,636	26,967	26,739	27,272	27,542	26,623
769,526	763,063	786,467	790,762	759,109	684,780
51,302	50,871	52,431	52,717	50,607	45,652
197,008	197,558	219,584	264,937	224,148	
13,134	13,170	14,639	17,662	14,943	
135,237	146,714	150,808	164,877	157,421	244,190
9,016	9,781	10,054	10,992	10,495	16,279
102,475	112,446	116,430	124,197	118,910	
6,832	7,496	7,762	8,280	7,927	
25,913	26,988	27,850	31,857	30,962	
1,728	1.799	1,857	2,124	2,064	
185,430	189,806	171,626	180,699	191,223	
12,362	12,654	11,442	12,047	12,748	
77,700	81,930	86,591	93,834	86,629	85,840
5,180	5,462	5,773	6,256	5,775	5,723
902	976	1,663	1,959	2,049	
60	65	111	131	137	
565	736	875	599	522	
38	49	58	40	35	
5,905	6,090	6,840	8,690	8,130	
394	406	456	579	542	
2,865	3,270	3,780			
191	218	252			
26,628	31,449	34,025	38,725	38,124	
1,775	2,097	2,268	2,582	2,542	
25,007	25,596	35,070	32,477	34,619	
1,667	1,706	2,338	2,165	2,308	
16,334	15,661	17,199	14,269	14,130	
1,089	1,044	1,057	1,089	1,044	
2,885	3,281	3,063	3,316	3,999	
192	219	204	221	267	
730	1,095	1,723	2,241	2,390	
49	73	115	149	159	

of China and Other Major Countiees, Peking: Agricultural Publishing House, 1959. pp. 7, 11, 14, 17, 20, 23, 26, 29, 32, 41, 44, 47, 50, 53, 56; 1950, 1951, and 1958: *TGY*, p. 129.

TABLE 5.3 Area Sown to Improved Seeds of Staple Crops, 1952-58

Crop	1952	1953	1954	1955	1956	1957	1958
Percent of area sown to improved seeds of staple crops, (total area sown to a crop equals 100%):[1]							
Food grains	4.7	7.4	14.9	20.6	36.4	55.2	77.5
Rice	5.4	7.9	12.0	19.0	41.3	62.9	81.0
Wheat	5.1	7.4	23.5	32.7	58.7	68.7	86.1
Coarse grains	5.0	8.0	12.9	16.5	21.4	42.5	67.9
Potatoes	0.4	2.2	9.9	13.8	38.3	56.5	81.5
Cotton	50.2	61.4	67.7	70.5	89.5	93.9	97.0
Oil-bearing crops	1.9	2.4	2.9	4.0	31.5	47.7	61.6
Area sown to improved seeds of staple crops, thousand hectares:[2]							
Food grains	(5,278)	(8,456)	(17,335)	(24,390)	(42,243)	(66,729)	(94,007)
Rice	(1,533)	(2,096)	(3,447)	(5,543)	(13,758)	(17,797)	(26,818)
Wheat	(1,264)	(1,897)	(6,337)	(8,744)	(16,009)	(18,921)	(22,922)
Coarse grains	(2,523)	(4,104)	(6,562)	(8,651)	(11,281)	(21,508)	(30,998)
Potatoes	(35)	(198)	(968)	(1,387)	(4,210)	(5,930)	(13,267)
Cotton	(2,799)	(3,180)	(3,698)	(4,070)	(5,600)	(5,423)	(5,551)

[1] TGY, p. 131.
[2] Derived from the percentages given above and the data on sown area for various crops given in Table 5.2.

288

TABLE 5.4 Area of Irrigation and of Water and Soil Conservation, 1949-59

Area	Unit	1949[1]	1950[1]	1951[1]	1952[2]	1953[1]	1954[1]	1955[1]	1956[1]	1957[1]	1958[1]	1959[2]
Area of irrigations:												
Existing total	Thousand *Mou*	240,000	250,000	280,000	320,000	330,000	350,000	370,000	480,000	520,000	1,000,000	1,070,000
	Thousand Hectares	16,000	16,667	18,667	21,333	22,000	23,333	24,667	32,000	34,667	66,667	71,333
Annual increase	Thousand *Mou*		12,040	27,960	40,180	18,020	16,020	22,260	118,700	43,090	480,430	70,000
	Thousand Hectares		803	1,864	2,679	1,201	1,068	1,484	7,913	2,873	32,209	4,667
Area of transformed water-logged, low-lying land	Thousand *Mou*						58,090		84,640	51,730	206,830	
	Thousand Hectares						3,873		5,643	3,449		
Area under preliminary water and soil conservation	Square Kilometers						78,310		73,650	51,543	318,720	
							5,221		4,910	3,436	21,248	

1 *TGY*, p. 130.
2 SSB, *Communique on the Development of the National Economy in 1959*, Peking: Jen-min jih-pao ch'u-pan-she, January, 1960, p. 9.

TABLE 5.5 Flood Areas, 1949-57

Location	Unit, thousands	1949	1959	1951	1952	1953	1954	1955	1956	1957
National total	*Mou*	127,870	70,650	22,140	27,660	47,970	169,580	46,090	164,870	85,020
	Hectares	8,524	4,710	1,476	1,844	3,198	11,305	3,073	10,991	5,668
Five provinces (Hopei, Shantung, Honan, Anhwei and Kiangsu)	*Mou*	94,300	64,920	11,640	25,000	36,450	124,460	33,830	126,700	62,700
	Hectares	6,287	4,328	776	1,667	2,430	8,297	2,255	8,446	4,180

Source: "Give Priority to the Elimination of Floods in Agricultural Construction," *CHCC*, No. 1 (January 9, 1958), pp. 15-19.

TABLE 5.6 Afforested Area, 1950-59

	Unit, thousands	1950[1]	1951[1]	1952[1]	1953[1]	1954[1]	1955[1]	1956[1]	1957[1]	1958[1]	1959[2]
Afforested area	Mou	1,900	6,760	16,280	16,690	17,490	25,660	85,850	65,330	261,900	280,000
	Hectares	127	451	1,085	1,113	1,166	1,711	5,723	4,355	17,460	18,667
Shelter Belts	Mou	1,010	3,790	8,540	6,250	5,080	5,900	20,270	14,920	50,020	
	Hectares	67	253	569	417	339	393	1,351	995	3,335	
Timber	Mou	210	1,150	3,310	6,710	9,540	14,210	36,810	26,020	90,230	
	Hectares	14	77	221	447	636	947	2,454	1,735	6,015	
Area devoted to seedlings	Mou	30	70	180	210	150	250	1,150	1,060	4,620	
	Hectares	2	5	12	14	10	17	77	71	308	
Area devoted to saplings	Mou	--	--	1,230	1,840	3,730	10,230	29,880	31,730	105,000	
	Hectares	--	--	82	123	249	682	1,992	2,115	7,000	

[1] TGY, p. 133.
[2] SSB, Communique on the Development of the National Economy in 1959, Peking: Jen-min jih-pao ch'u-pan-she, January, 1960, p. 8.

TABLE 5.7   Areas of Various Types of Agricultural Land and Afforested Area in Inner Mongolia Autonomous Region, 1949-58

Type of land	Unit, thousands	1949	1950	1951	1952	1953	1954	1955	1956	1957	1958
Cultivated area	Mou	63,668			75,300					83,146	80,766
	Hectares	4,245			5,020					5,543	5,384
Sown area	Mou	57,187			72,095					76,761	73,691
	Hectares	3,812			4,806					5,117	4,913
Existing irri-gated area	Mou	4,270	4,470	5,260	6,300	6,970	7,700	8,780	10,940	12,057	20,700
	Hectares	285	298	351	420	465	513	585	729	804	1,380
Increase in irrigated area	Mou	--	200	790	1,040	670	730	1,080	2,160	1,117	8,643
	Hectares	--	13	53	69	45	49	72	144	74	576
Swamp lands improved	Mou								294	681	987
	Hectares								20	45	66
Water and soil conservation area	Sq. km								1.4	3.5	15.8
Afforested area	Mou		80.4	249.4	659.2	537.9	584.3	556.2	1,913.4	1,225.6	10,311.1
	Hectares		5.4	16.6	43.9	35.9	39.0	37.1	127.6	81.7	687.4
Shelter belts	Mou		80.4	249.4	620.2	520.6	565.7	378.8	1,451.6	764.0	6,023.3
	Hectares		5.4	16.6	41.3	34.7	37.7	25.3	96.8	50.9	401.6
Lumbering	Mou				39.0	16.9	15.7	19.3	295.6	381.7	3,290.1
	Hectares				2.6	1.1	1.0	1.3	19.7	25.4	219.3
Tree nursery	Mou		2.9	5.4	34.2	35.0	12.6	15.8	43.7	30.3	148.5
	Hectares		0.2	0.4	2.3	2.3	0.8	1.1	2.9	2.0	9.9

Source: *NMKTC*, pp. 144, 156, and 160.

TABLE 5.8   Development of Conservancy Construction in the Grazing Area of
            Inner Mongolia Autonomous Region, 1954-58

Improvement	1954	1955	1956	1957	1958
Newly added wells	78	2,100	3,197	667	5,463
Newly added reservoirs	--	--	--	15	15
Water-short areas newly developed, sq km	780	3,000	4,800	1,100	9,115
Newly added fodder areas irrigated, thousand *mou*	--	--	30	262	292

Source: *NMK TC,* p. 186.

TABLE 5.9   Increase in Irrigated Area and Afforested Area in Kirin Province,
            1949, 1955, 1956, and 1958.

Type of land	Unit, thousands	1949	1955	1956	1958
Total afforested area	*Mou*				687
	Hectares				10,310[1]
Increase in irrigated area	*Mou*	1,275	1,980	3,960	8,630[1]
	Hectares	85[2]	132[2]	264[2]	358

[1] Kirin Provincial Statistical Bureau, "Communique on the Fulfillment of
the Economic Plan for 1958 in Kirin Province," *Kirin JP,* March 18,
1959, pp. 1-2.

[2] Wu Ch'uan-chun *et al.,* comp., *Economic Geography of Northeast China,*
(Tung-pei ti-ch'u ching-chi ti-li) Peking; K'o-hsueh ch'u-pan-she,
1959, 211 pp.; translated in JPRS: 15,388, September 21, 1962, p. 212.

TABLE 5.10   Reclaimed Area and Increase in Irrigated Area in
Heilungkiang Province, 1952-57, Thousand Hectares

Type of land	1952	1953	1954	1955	1956	1957
Reclaimed area[1]	135.4	139.5	165.5	186.9	303.8	329.4
Increase in irrigated area[2]				71	120	

[1] Wu Ch'uan-chun et al., comp., Tung-pei ti-ch'u ching-chi ti-li, Economic Geography of Northeast China), Peking: K'o-hsueh ch'u-pan-she, 1959, 211 pp.; translated in JPRS: 15,388, September 21, 1962, p. 392.

[2] Yang I-chen, "Report at the First Session of the Second Heihungkiang Provincial People's Congress on August 28, 1958," Heilungkiang JP, Harbin, September 19, 1958.

TABLE 5.11   Area of Various Types of Agricultural Land
and Afforested Area in Kansu Province,
1956 and 1957

Type of land	Unit, thousands	1956	1957
Cultivated area	Mou	56,196	59,388
	Hectares	3,746	3,959
Sown area	Mou		81,750
	Hectares		5,450
For food grains	Mou		72,512
	Hectares		4,834
For cotton	Mou		531
	Hectares		35
Increase in irrigated area	Mou		1,130
	Hectares		75
Afforested area	Mou		3,200
	Hectares		213

Source: Kansu Provincial Statistical Bureau, "Communique on the Results of the Implementation of the National Economic Plan for 1957 in Kansu Province," Kansu JP, Lanchow, June 12, 1958, p. 2.

TABLE 5.12   Area of Various Types of Agricultural Land
and Afforested Area in Chinghai Province,
1949, 1952, 1957, and 1958.

Type of land	Unit, thousands	1949	1952	1957	1958
Total arable land[1]	*Mou*		68,239	75,950	
	Hectares		4,549	5,063	
Total irrigated area[1]	*Mou*	747	962	1,717	
	Hectares	50	64	114	
Increase in irrigated area[2]	*Mou*				3,870
	Hectares				258
Improved irrigated area[2]	*Mou*				750
	Hectares				50
Afforested area[2]	*Mou*				2,030
	Hectares				135

[1] Chinghai Provincial Statistical Bureau, "Communique on the Development of the National Economy of Chinghai Province and the Results of the Implementation of the First Five-Year Play, 1953-1957," *Chinghai JP*, Hsi-ning, September 30, 1958, p. 2.

[2] Yuan Jen-yuan (Governor of Chinghai), "Work Report of the Chinghai Provincial People's Council for 1958," *Chinghai JP*, Hsi-ning, May 21, 1959, pp. 1, 3.

TABLE 5.13   Area of Various Types of Agricultural Land and Afforested
Area in Sinkiang-Uighur Autonomous Region,
1949, 1957, and 1958

Type of land	Unit, thousands	1949	1957	1958
Cultivated area	*Mou*	18,110[1]	25,730[2]	36,170[1]
	Hectares	1,207	1,715	2,411
Sown area	*Mou*	16,760[1]		28,730[1]
	Hectares	1,117		1,915
Increase in irrigated area	*Mou*			6,610[3]
	Hectares			441
Afforested area	*Mou*			3,800[3]
	Hectares			253

[1] Sai Fu-ting (First Secretary of the Sinkiang-Uighur Autonomous Region Committee of the Chinese Communist Party), "Great Achievements in Agriculture of Sinkiang in the Past Ten Years," *Chung-kuo nung-pao (Chinese Agricultural Bulletin)*, No. 19, 1959, 19-23, reference on p. 21.

[2] *Documents of the Fifth Session of the First National People's Congress*, Peking: People's Publishing House, 1958, pp. 602-6.

[3] Sai Fu-ting, "Work Report to the First Session of the Second People's Congress of Sinkiang-Uighur Autonomous Region on January 22, 1959," *Sinkiang JP*, January 30, 1959, pp. 2-3

TABLE 5.14   Area of Various Types of Agricultural Land
and Afforested Area in Shantung Province,
1955 and 1956

Type of land	Unit, thousands	1955	1956
Cultivated area[1]	Mou		139,440
	Hectares		9,296
Sown area[1]	Mou		203,420
	Hectares		13,561
Increase in irrigated area[2]	Mou		17,930
	Hectares		1,195
Afforested area[1]	Mou	1,500	2,900
	Hectares	100	193

[1] Shantung Provincial Statistical Bureau, "Communique
on the Results of the Implementation of the Nation-
al Economic Plan for 1956 in Shantung Province,"
Ta-chung JP, August 9, 1957, p. 3.
[2] Wang Che-ju, "Report on the Draft of the 1957 Economic
Plan and the Implementation of the 1956 Economic
Plan for Shantung Province," Ta-chung JP, Tsinan,
August 17, 1957, p. 2.

TABLE 5.15   Areas of Various Types of Agricultural Land
and Afforested Area in Kiangsu Province,
1953-58

Type of land	Unit, thousands	1953-57	1958
Total land area	Mou		160,500
	Hectares		10,700
Cultivated area	Mou		84,470
	Hectares		5,965
Increase in irrigated area	Mou	7,330	16,610
	Hectares	489	1,107
Improvements of irrigated area	Mou	14,730	20,160
	Hectares	982	1,344
Afforested area	Mou		1,764
	Hectares		118

Note: Figures for 1958 include the seven hsien which
were merged into the municipal administration of
Shanghai. When these seven hsien were excluded, the
cultivated area in Kiangsu in 1958 amounted to
83,040,000 mou.
Source: Chin Chi-min, "Rapid Development of Agriculture
in Kiangsu," TLCS, No. 6, (June, 1959), pp. 244-47.

TABLE 5.16   Area of Various Types of Agricultural Land and Afforested Area in Anhwei Province, 1955-58

Type of land	Unit, thousands	1955	1956	1957	1958
Cultivated area	Mou			88,000[1]	87,330[2]
	Hectares			5,867	5,822
Sown area					
Grain crops	Mou			119,380[3]	
	Hectares			7,959	
Economic crops	Mou			10,450[4]	
	Hectares			697	
Afforested area					
Existing total	Mou			32,000[5]	
	Hectares			2,133	
Annual increase	Mou	803[6]	1,940[6]	2,440[5]	
	Hectares	54	129	163	
Irrigated area					
Existing total	Mou			34,000[7]	55,000[7]
	Hectares			2,267	3,667
Annual increase	Mou		7,270[5,6]		
	Hectares		485		
Improved	Mou		13,080[5,6]		
	Hectares		912		

[1] Sun Ching-chih, ed., Hua-tung ti-ch'u ching-chi ti-li (Economic Geography of East China), Peking: Institute of Geography of the Chinese National Academy of Sciences, November, 1959, 153 pp.; translated in JPRS: 11,438, December 7, 1961, p. 137.

[2] Bureau of Agriculture, Anhwei Province, "Anhwei-The Province produces 1,000 chin of Early Rice Per Mou," Chung-kuo nung-pao (Chinese Agricultural Bulletin), No. 22, 1958, pp. 8-13, reference on p. 8.

[3] Sun ching-chih, ed., op. cit.

[4] Ibid., p. 145.

[5] Anhwei Provincial Statistical Bureau, "Communique on the Results of the Implementation of the National Economic Plan for 1957 in Anhwei Province," Anhwei JP, April 30, 1958.

[6] Chang K'ai-fan (Deputy Governor of Anhwei), "Government Work Report at the 4th Session of the First Provincial People's Congress of Anhwei, on September 21, 1957," Anhwei JP, September 23, 1957, pp. 2-3.

[7] Sun Ching-chih, ec., op. cit., p. 140.

TABLE 5.17 Irrigated Area and Afforested Area in
Fukien Province, 1957 and 1958

Type of land	Unit, thousands	1957	1958
Total irrigated	Mou	14,800[1]	
	Hectares	986	
Increase in irrigated area	Mou		4,140[2]
	Hectares		276
Afforested area	Mou		6,590[2]
	Hectares		439

[1] Sun Ching-chih, ed., *Hua-nan ti-ch'u ching-chi ti-li*
   (*Economic Geography of South China*) Peking: K'o-hsueh
   ch'u-pan-she, 1959, 147 pp.; translated in JPRS:
   14,954, August 24, 1962, p. 376.

[2] Liang Ling-kuang (Governor of Fukien Provincial Plan
   for 1959,'' *Fukien JP*, Foochow, February 11, 1959,
   pp. 1-2.

TABLE 5.18 Land Area and Water Area in Kiangsu Province, 1957

Type of land	In thousand *Mou*	In thousand Hectares
Total area	252,870	16,858
Cultivated area	42,190	2,813
Reclaimed area	17,500	1,167
Forest area	50,200	3,347
Afforested area	69,800	4,653
Rivers and lakes	25,000	1,667
Others	48,180	3,212

Source: Sun Ching-chih, ec., *Hua-chung ti-ch'u ching-chi ti-li*
(*Economic Geography of Central China*), Peking: K'o-hsueh ch'u
-pan-she, December, 1958, 156 pp.; translated in JPRS: 2227-N,
February 10, 1960, 514 pp.

TABLE 5.19 Sown Area, Irrigated Area, and Afforested Area in Kwangtung Province, 1949, 1952, 1957, and 1958

Type of land	Unit, thousands	1949	1952	1957	1958
Sown area	*Mou*	90,750[1]	98,320[1]	114,630[2]	
	Hectares	6,050	6,555	7,642	
Increase in irrigated area	*Mou*				12,900[2]
	Hectares				860
Improvement of irrigated area	*Mou*				14,580[2]
	Hectares				972
Total forest area	*Mou*				150,000[3]
	Hectares				10,000
Afforested area	*Mou*				31,910[2,3]
	Hectares				2,127

[1] Sun Ching-chih, ed., *Hua-nan ti-ch'u ching-chi ti-li* (*Economic Geography of South China*) Peking: K'o-hsueh ch'u-pan-she, 1959, 147 pp.; translated in JPRS: 14,954, August 24, 1962, p. 63.

[2] Kwangtung Provincial Statistical Bureau, "Communique on the Development of the National Economy in Kwangtung Province in 1958 and the First Half of 1959," *Wen-hui-pao*, Hong Kong, October 5, 1959.

[3] Ch'en Yu, "Report Delivered to the Second Session of the Second Kwangtung Provincial People's Congress," *NFJP*, October 12, 1959.

TABLE 5.20 Cultivated Area, Irrigated Area, and Total Forest Area in Kwangsi Chuan Autonomous Region, 1957 and 1958

Type of land	Unit, thousands	1957[1]	1958[2]
Cultivated area	*Mou*	37,960	
	Hectares	2,531	
Paddy field	*Mou*	24,290	
	Hectares	1,619	
Dry field	*Mou*	13,670	
	Hectares	911	
Total forest area	*Mou*	24,000	
	Hectares	1,600	
Addition to and improvement of existing irrigated area	*Mou*		17,000
	Hectares		1,133

[1] Sun Ching-chih, ed., *Hua-nan ti-ch'u ching-chi ti-li* (*Economic Geography of South China*) Peking: K'o-hsueh ch'u-pan-she, 1959, 174 pp.; translated in JPRS: 14,954, August 24, 1962, p. 247.

[2] Wei Kuo-ch'ing (Governor of Kwangsi) "Review the Achievements in the Past Ten Years and March Bravely Forward," *Min-tzu tu'an-chieh* (*Unity of Nationalities*), No. 10 (October 6, 1959), pp. 9-12, reference on p. 11.

TABLE 5.21   Area of Various Types of Agricultural Land and Afforested Area in Szechuan Province, 1949, 1950-53, and 1957-58.

Type of land	Unit, thousands	1949	1950	1952	1953	1957	1958
Cultivated area[1]	*Mou*		105,370	112,020			
	Hectares		7,024	7,468			
Paddy field	*Mou*		53,390	55,850			
	Hectares		3,559	3,723			
Dry field	*Mou*		51,980	56,170			
	Hectares		3,465	3,745			
Sown area[2]	*Mou*			161,655		195,880	
	Hectares			10,777		13,058	
Total irrigated area	*Mou*				51,750	55,350	57,900
	Hectares				3,450[3]	3,690[3]	3,860[4]
Afforested area	*Mou*	200[5]		490[3]		1,930[5]	
	Hectares	13		33		129	

[1] Sun Ching-chih, ed., *Hsi-nan ti-ch'u ching-chi ti-li (Economic Geography of Southwest China)*, Peking: K'o-hsueh ch'u-pan-she, 1960, 218 pp.; translated in JPRS: 15,069, August 31, 1962, p. 82.

[2] Table 5.38.

[3] Ye A. Afanas'yeskiy, *Szechwan*, Moscow: Publishing House of Oriental Literature, 1960, 267 pp.; translated in JPRS: 15,036, September 17, 1962, p. 221.

[4] *Ibid*, p. 224.

[5] Sun Ching-chi, ed., *op. cit.*, p. 76.

TABLE 5.22   Sown Area, Irrigated Area, and Afforested Area in Kweichow Province, 1949-58

Type of land	Unit, thousands	1949	1950	1952	1957	1958
Sown area	*Mou*	26,970		28,270		31,360
	Hectares	1,798		1,885		2,091
Irrigated area	*Mou*	2,850				
	Hectares	190				
Afforested	*Mou*		10	50	2,000	
	Hectares		0.7	3.3	133	

Sources: Sun Ching-chih, *Hsi-nan ti-ch'u ching-chi ti-li (Economic Geography of Southwest China)* Peking: K'o-hsueh ch'u-pan-she, 1960, 218 pp.; translated in JPRS: 15,069, August 31, 1962, pp. 348, 351, and 352.

TABLE 5.23 Cultivated Area and Afforested Area in Yunnan
Province, 1949-58

Type of land	1949	1952	1957	1958
Cultivated area:				
Thousand *Mou*	33,800			41,100
Thousand Hectares	2,253			2,740
Afforested area:				
Thousand *Mou*	420	1,060	3,020	
Thousand Hectares	28	71	201	

Sources: Sun Ching-chih, ed., *Hsi-nan ti-ch'ü ching-chi ti-li*
(*Economic Geography of Southwest China*) Peking: K'o-hsüeh
ch'u-pan-she, 1960, 218 pp.; translated in JPRS: 15,069,
August 31, 1962, pp. 509 and 513.

TABLE 5.24 Sown Area for Various Crops in Inner Mongolia Autonomous Region,
1947-58

Crop	Unit, thousands	1947	1949	1952	1957	1958
All crops	*Mou*	50,929	57,187	72,095	76,761	73,691
	Hectares	3,395	3,812	4,806	5,117	4,913
Food grains	*Mou*	44,487	49,296	61,341	63,441	61,990
	Hectares	2,966	3,286	4,089	4,229	4,133
Rice	*Mou*	116	206	221	601	1,335
	Hectares	8	14	15	40	89
Wheat	*Mou*	3,268	3,878	6,148	8,869	8,286
	Hectares	218	259	410	591	552
Coarse grains	*Mou*	38,920	42,807	51,850	50,818	46,865
	Hectares	2,595	2,854	3,457	3,388	3,124
Potatoes	*Mou*	2,183	2,405	3,122	3,153	5,504
	Hectares	146	160	208	210	367
Soybeans	*Mou*	2,198	2,476	2,362	4,012	3,177
	Hectares	147	165	157	267	212
Industrial and other crops	*Mou*	4,244	5,415	8,392	9,308	8,524
	Hectares	283	361	559	621	568

Source: *NMKTC*, pp. 144-45.

TABLE 5.25   Sown Area for Various Crops in Liaoning
Province, 1957 and 1958

Crop	Unit, thousands	1957	1958
Food grains[1]	Mou	53,949	52,080
	Hectares	3,597	3,472
Rice	Mou	4,203	5,560
	Hectares	280	371
Wheat	Mou	1,005	600
	Hectares	67	40
Millet	Mou	9,500	7,845
	Hectares	633	523
Corn	Mou	10,459	23,160
	Hectares	697	1,544
Kaoliang	Mou	19,004	6,660
	Hectares	1,267	444
Potatoes	Mou	2,625	3,600
	Hectares	175	240
Others	Mou	15,233	4,655
	Hectares	1,016	310
Industrial crops[2]	Mou	6,285	6,930
	Hectares	419	462
Cotton[a]	Mou	2,925	3,090
	Hectares	195	206
Tobacco	Mou	285	270
	Hectares	19	18
Peanuts	Mou	2,235	2,550
	Hectares	149	170
Others	Mou	734	1,020
	Hectares	49	68

[a] The area sown to cotton amounted to 6.6 million *mou*
   in 1951 and 3 million *mou* in 1956.

[1] Wu Ch'uan-chun *et al.*, comp., *Economic Geography of
   Northeast China (Tung-pei ti-ch'u ching-chi ti-li)*,
   Peking: K'o-hsueh ch'u-pan-she, 1959: translated in
   JPRS: 15,388, September 21, 1962, p. 90.

[2] *Ibid.*, p. 96.

TABLE 5.26 Sown Area for Various Crops in Kirin Province, 1949-50 and 1952-58

Crop	Unit, thousands	1949	1950	1952	1953	1954	1955	1956	1957	1958
Total sown area	Mou								69,137[1]	
	Hectares								4,609	
Food grains	Mou			51,179[1]					50,811[1]	
	Hectares			3,412					3,387	
Rice	Mou	1,284[2]		1,697[1]					4,252[1]	5,195[2]
	Hectares	86		113					283	346
Wheat	Mou			1,757[1]	(1,235)[3]	(1,751)[3]	(968)[3]	(741)[3]		
	Hectares			117	(117)	(117)	(65)	(49)		
Millet	Mou			13,113[1]					12,652[1]	
	Hectares			874					843	
Corn	Mou			12,454[1]					13,615[1]	
	Hectares			830					908	
Kaoliang	Mou			13,536[1]					10,696[1]	9,608[4]
	Hectares			902					713	641
Potatoes	Mou			1,666[1]					1,609[1]	
	Hectares			111					107	
Others	Mou			6,956[1]					7,256[1]	
	Hectares			464					484	
Soybeans	Mou								13,609[1]	
	Hectares								907	
Industrial crops	Mou			1,881[5]					2,262[1]	
	Hectares			125					151	
Flax	Mou			114[5]					107[5]	
	Hectares			8					7	
Ambari hemp	Mou			104[5]					155[5]	
	Hectares			7					10	

TABLE 5.26 (Continued)

Crop	Unit, thousands	1949	1950	1952	1953	1954	1955	1956	1957	1958
Ramie	Mou			144[5]					305[5]	
	Hectares			10					20	
Tobacco	Mou			156[5]					140[5]	
	Hectares			10					9	
Sesame	Mou			199[5]					118[5]	
	Hectares			13					8	
Sunflower	Mou			158[5]					421[5]	
	Hectares			11					28	
Castor beans	Mou			426[5]					263[5]	
	Hectares			28					18	
Beets	Mou		74[6]	163[5]			26.19[6]		503[5]	803[6]
	Hectares		5	11					34	54
Others	Mou		417[5]						250[5]	
	Hectares		28						17	
Other crops	Mou								2,457[1]	
	Hectares								164	

[1] Wu Ch'uan-chun et al., comp., *Economic Geography of Northeast China*, Peking: K'o-hsueh ch'u-pan-she, 1959, 211 pp., translated in JPRS: 15,388, September 21, 1962, p. 216.

[2] *Ibid.*, p. 217.

[3] Computed from indices given in Shen Yu-ch'ing, "My Views on the Geographic Distribution of Wheat and the Prospect for Its Development in China," *TLCS*, No. 8 (August, 1957), pp. 339-45; reference on p. 344.

[4] Wu Ch'uan-chun et al., *op. cit.*, p. 218.

[5] *Ibid.*, p. 221

[6] *Ibid.*, p. 220.

303

TABLE 5.27 Percentage Distribution of the Areas Sown to Various Crops in Heilungkiang Province, 1943, 1949, and 1952-57

Crop	1943[1]	1949[1]	1952[1]	1956[2]	1957[1]	1953-57 average[1]
Food grains	73.3	75.0	72.4	70.31	69.5	73.7
Rice	1.6	2.0	1.9	4.16	3.6	3.1
Wheat	6.0	8.7	16.7	8.45	12.7	12.8
Millet	20.0	18.2	15.5	15.33	16.0	16.3
Corn	19.1	26.5	18.9	23.71	17.8	20.7
Koaliang	12.9	11.0	10.4	9.65	8.3	10.4
Potatoes	2.5	2.5	3.1	3.26	3.2	3.5
Others	11.6	6.1	5.9	5.75	7.9	6.9
Soybeans	19.3	20.3	21.6	21.71	21.2	2.9
Industrial crops and others	7.0	4.7	6.0	7.98	9.3	3.4
Flax	0.7	0.2	0.3	} 3.33	0.4	0.6
Sugar beets	0.3	0.2	0.4		1.6	1.2
Others	6.0	4.3	5.3	4.65	7.3	1.6

[1] Wu Ch'uan-chun *et al.*, comp., *Tung-pei ti-ch'u ching-chi ti-li (Economic Geography of Northeast China)*, Peking: K'o-hsueh ch'u-pan-she, 1959, 211 pp.; translated in JPRS: 15,388, September 21, 1962, p. 398.

[2] Li Shu-yen, "A General Survey of the Agricultural Geography of Heilungkiang Province," *TLCS*, No. 11 (November, 1957), pp. 497-99, reference on p. 497.

TABLE 5.28 Sown Area for Various Crops in Kiangsu and Shanghai, 1957

Crops	In thousand *Mou*	In thousand Hectares
Grain crops	118,740	7,916
Rice	32,690	2,179
Wheat	31,640	2,109
Barley	11,020	735
Oats	11,790	786
Maize	9,380	625
Sorghum	3,290	219
Sweet potatoes	5,320	355
Others	10,010	667
Industrial crops	16,250	1,083
Cotton	10,840	723
Jute, bast fibers, etc.	450	30
Oil-bearing crops	4,790	319
Peanuts	2,510	167
Rapeseed	2,100	140
Others	170	11

Source: Sun Ching-chih, ed., *Hua-tung ti-ch'ü ching-chi ti-li (Economic Geography of East China)* Peking: Research Institute of Geography of the Chinese National Academy of Sciences, November, 1959, 153 pp.; translated in JPRS: 11,438, December 7, 1961, p. 57.

TABLE 5.29 Sown Area for Various Crops in Kiangsu Province, 1950-51 and 1956-58

Crops	Unit, thousands	1950	1951	1955	1956	1957	1958
Food grains	Mou						105,030[1]
	Hectares						7,002
Rice	Mou		30,900[1]	32,380[2]		35,770[1]	34,380[1]
	Hectares		2,060	2,159		2,385	2,292
Wheat	Mou		28,790[1]	34,000[3]		31,230[1]	27,120
	Hectares		1,919	2,267		2,082	1,808
Soybeans	Mou		14,050[1]			13,060[1]	8,180[1]
	Hectares		937			871	545
Industrial crops							
Cotton	Mou		8,220[1]		12,000[4]	10,070[1]	8,740[1]
	Hectares		548		800	671	583
Oil-bearing crops	Mou						3,700[b]
	Hectares						247
Peanuts	Mou		1,550[1]			2,510[1]	1,810[1]
	Hectares		103			167	121
Tobacco	Mou						19[5]
	Hectares						1.3
Sugar beets	Mou						47[5]
	Hectares						3.1
Other crops							
Tea	Mou						50[6]
	Hectares						3.3
Mulberries	Mou	460[7]			550[8]	810[7]	
	Hectares	31			37	54	

[1] Chin Chi-min, "The Rapid Development of Agriculture in Kiangsu Province," *TLCS*, No. 6 (June, 1959), pp. 244-7; reference on p. 245.
[2] Wang Wei-p'ing, *Kiangsu, The Waterland*, Shanghai: Hsin-chi-shih ch'u-pan-she, December, 1956, p. 59.
[3] *Ibid.*, p. 61.
[4] *Ibid.*, p. 63.
[5] Chin Chi-min, *op. cit.*, p. 246.
[6] *Ibid.*, p. 247.
[7] *Ibid.*, p. 244.
[8] Wang Wei-p'ing, *op. cit.*, p. 65.

305

TABLE 5.30   Sown Area for Various Crops in Anhwei Province, 1949 and 1957

Crop	1949		1957	
	In thousand *Mou*	In thousand Hectares	In thousand *Mou*	In thousand Hectares
Food grains			119,380	7,959
Rice			33,720	2,248
Wheat			40,210	2,681
Coarse grains			34,130	2,753
Potatoes			11,320	755
Industrial crops			10,450	697
Cotton			3,008	201
Cured tobacco	60	4	409	27
Hemp-type fibers			513	34
Oil-bearing crops			6,446	430
Others			74	5

Source: Sun Ching-chih, ed., *Hua-tung ti-ch'u ching-chi ti-li (Economic Geography of East China)*, Peking: Institute of Geography of the Chinese National Academy of Sciences, November, 1959, 153 pp.; translated in JPRS: 11,438, December 7, 1961, pp. 141, 145, and 147.

TABLE 5.31   Sown Area for Various Crops in Chekiang Province, 1957

Crop	In thousand *Mou*	In Thousand Hectares
Food grains	40,890	2,726
Rice	24,430	1,629
Wheat	4,680	312
Barley	3,040	203
Maize	2,390	159
Horse beans	1,650	110
Sweet potatoes	2,660	177
Others	2,040	136
Industrial crops	5,232	349
Cotton	1,129	75
Jute	770	51
Rapeseed	2,456	164
Peanuts	250	17
Sugar cane	129	9
Others	498	33

Source: Sun Ching-chih, ed., *Hua-tung ti-ch'ü ching-chi ti-li (Economic Geography of East China)*, Peking: Institute of Geography of the Chinese National Academy of Sciences, November, 1959, 153 pp.; translated in JPRS: 11,438, December 7, 1961, pp. 215-16, 218.

TABLE 5.32 Sown Area for Various Crops in Fukien Province, 1952-58

Crops	Unit, thousands	1952[1]	1955[1]	1957[1]	1958[2]
Food grains	Mou	27,899		30,952	
	Hectares	1,860		2,063	
Rice	Mou	21,466	20,380	22,117	
	Hectares	1,431	1,359	1,474	
Wheat	Mou	1,564		2,466	
	Hectares	104		164	
Potatoes	Mou	4,051		4,519	
	Hectares	270		301	
Coarse grains	Mou	818		1,850	
	Hectares	55		123	
Industrial crops	Mou			2,174	
	Hectares			145	
Sugar cane	Mou			372	
	Hectares			25	
Jute	Mou			84	
	Hectares			6	
Ramie	Mou			13	
	Hectares			1	
Cured tobacco	Mou			23	
	Hectares			2	
Dried tobacco	Mou			73	
	Hectares			5	
Peanuts	Mou			1,107	
	Hectares			74	
Rapeseed	Mou			449	
	Hectares			30	
Sesame	Mou			43	
	Hectares			3	
Others	Mou			5	
	Hectares			0.3	
Other crops: Fruits	Mou			383	510
	Hectares			26	34
Tea oil trees	Mou		500		
	Hectares		33		

[1] Sun Ching-chih, ed., *Hua-nan ti-ch'u ching-chi ti-li (Economic Geography of South China)*, Peking: K'o-hsueh ch'u-pan-she, 1959, 147 pp.; translated in JPRS: 14,954, August 24, 1962, pp. 378, 379, 385, 392, 394.
[2] Liang Ling-kuang (Governor of Fukien), "Fukien Provincial Plan for 1959," *Fukien JP*, Foochow, February 11, 1949, pp. 1-2.

TABLE 5.33 Sown Area for Various Crops in Hupeh Province, 1949, 1952, and 1956-58
1956-58

Crop	Unit, thousands	1949[1]	1952[1]	1956[1]	1957[1]	1958[2]
All crops	Mou				10,986	
	Hectares				732	
Food grains	Mou				8,031	
	Hectares				535	
Rice	Mou				3,253	
	Hectares				217	
Wheat	Mou				1,734	
	Hectares				116	
Barley	Mou				873	
	Hectares				58	
Corn	Mou				692	
	Hectares				46	
Millet	Mou				160	
	Hectares				11	
Buckwheat	Mou				146	
	Hectares				10	
Sweet potato	Mou				285	
	Hectares				19	
Horsebeans	Mou				206	
	Hectares				14	
Garden peas	Mou				174	
	Hectares				12	
Others	Mou				507	
	Hectares				34	
Soybeans	Mou				527	
	Hectares				35	
Industrial crops	Mou				1,629	
	Hectares				109	
Cotton	Mou		840	890	875	
	Hectares		56	59	58	
Ramie	Mou				33	345
	Hectares				2.2	23
Sesame	Mou				309	
	Hectares				21	
Peanuts	Mou	360			111	
	Hectares	24			7	
Rapeseed	Mou				264	
	Hectares				18	
Others	Mou				37	
	Hectares				2.4	
Other crops[a]	Mou				800	
	Hectares				53	

[a] Including green fertilizer, vegetables, and melons.
[1] Sun Ching-chih, ed., *Hua-chung ti-ch'ü ching-chi ti-li (Economic Geography of Central China)*, Peking: K'o-hsüeh ch'u-pan-she, December, 1958, 156 pp.; translated in JPRS: 2227-N, February 10, 1960, pp. 77, 78, 89, and 98.
[2] *NCNA*, Wuhan, February 27, 1959.

TABLE 5.34   Sown Area for Various Crops in Hunan Province,
            1952 and 1957

Crops	Unit, thousands	1952	1957
All crops[1]	Mou	80,210	102,620
	Hectares	5,347	6,841
Food grains[1]	Mou	63,254	81,214
	Hectares	4,217	5,414
Rice[2]	Mou		56,690
	Hectares		3,779
Wheat[2]	Mou		5,000
	Hectares		333
Barley[2]	Mou		2,210
	Hectares		147
Corn[2]	Mou		2,490
	Hectares		166
Kaoliang[2]	Mou		500
	Hectares		33
Millet[2]	Mou		280
	Hectares		19
Buckwheat[2]	Mou		3,980
	Hectares		265
Horse beans[2]	Mou		920
	Hectares		61
Garden peas[2]	Mou		840
	Hectares		56
Sweet potatoes[2]	Mou		6,210
	Hectares		414
Potatoes[2]	Mou		400
	Hectares		27
Others[2]	Mou		1,690
	Hectares		113
Soybeans	Mou	(1,840)[3]	2,540[4]
	Hectares	(123)	169

Table 5.34 (Continued)

Crops	Unit, thousands	1952	1957
Industrial crops[5]	*Mou*		5,700
	Hectares		380
Cotton	*Mou*		1,210
	Hectares		81
Flax	*Mou*		250
	Hectares		17
Peanuts	*Mou*		500
	Hectares		33
Rapeseed	*Mou*		2,940
	Hectares		196
Sesame	*Mou*		220
	Hectares		15
Tobacco	*Mou*		160
	Hectares		11
Others	*Mou*		420
	Hectares		28
Other crops[6]	*Mou*		(13,166)
	Hectares		(878)

[1] Hunan Provincial Statistical Bureau, "Achievements of Hunan Province in 1957 National Economic Work," *Hsin Hunan Pao*, Ch'ang-sha, May 4, 1958.

[2] Sun Ching-chih, ed., *Hua-chung ti-ch'u ching-chi ti-li (Economic Geography of Central China)*, Peking: K'o-hsueh ch'u-pan-she, December, 1958, 156 pp.; translated in JPRS: 2227-N, February 10, 1960, pp. 264-65.

[3] The sown acreage for soybeans increased by 700,000 *mou* during 1952-57. See Hunan Provincial Statistical Bureau, *op. cit.*

[4] Sun Ching-chih, *op. cit.*, p. 278.

[5] *Ibid.*, p. 279.

[6] Derived as residual.

TABLE 5.35 Sown Area for Various Crops in Kiangsi Province, 1957

Crops	Thousand *Mou*	Thousand Hectares
All crops	81,580	5,439
Food grains	54,840	3,656
Rice	44,140	2,943
Wheat	2,260	151
Barley	1,060	71
Buckwheat	2,270	151
Millet	710	47
Corn	260	17
Horse beans	360	24
Garden peas	450	30
Potatoes	2,960	197
Others	370	25
Soybeans	4,560	304
Industrial crops	8,720	581
Cotton	1,090	73
Jute	220	15
Ramie	70	5
Peanuts	680	45
Sesame	1,350	90
Rapeseed	5,150	343
Sugar cane	80	5
Others	80	5
Other crops	13,730	915

Source: Sun Ching-chih, ed., *Hua-chung ti-ch'u ching-chi ti-li (Economic Geography of Central China)* Peking: K'o-hsueh ch'u-pan-she, December, 1958, 156 pp., translated in JPRS: 2227-N, Febuary 10, 1960, pp. 406, 417, and 421.

TABLE 5.36 Sown Areas for Various Crops in Kwangtung Province, 1949-58

Crop	Unit, thousands	1949	1952	1954	1955	1957	1958
Total[1]	Mou	90,750	98,320			114,630	
	Hectares	6,050	6,555			7,642	
Food grains	Mou	83,771[2]	88,620[1]	91,000[3]		100,403[2]	97,500[4]
	Hectares	5,585	5,908	6,067		6,693	6,500
Rice	Mou	70,301[2]				72,707[2]	68,000[4]
	Hectares	4,687				4,847	4,533
Wheat[2]	Mou	1,100				3,591	
	Hectares	73				239	
Potatoes	Mou	10,853[2]				18,630[2]	18,600[4]
	Hectares	724				1,242	1,240
Others[2]	Mou	1,516				5,565	
	Hectares	101				364	
Soybeans[1]	Mou	1,480	1,540			1,660	
	Hectares	99	103			111	
Industrial crops	Mou	2,000[1]	4,100[1]		7,000[5]	7,295[6]	
	Hectares	133	273		467	486	
Sugar cane	Mou		1,060[7]			1,760[6]	2,300[4]
	Hectares		71			117	153
Peanuts	Mou		2,340[7]			3,787[6]	
	Hectares		156			252	
Hemp	Mou					375[6]	
	Hectares					25	
Ramie	Mou					49[6]	
	Hectares					3	
Tobacco	Mou					374[6]	
	Hectares					25	
Mulberry	Mou	246[8]	240[7]			196[6]	
	Hectares	16	16			13	
Rapeseed	Mou		228[7]				
	Hectares		15				
Sesame	Mou		73[7]				
	Hectares		5				
Other crops	Mou	3,500[1]	4,060[1]			5,270[1]	3,160[9]
	Hectares	233	271			351	211
Fruits	Mou					1,000[9]	
	Hectares					67	
Citrus	Mou		100[7]				
	Hectares		7				
Bananas	Mou		98[7]				
	Hectares		7				
Pineapples	Mou		51[7]				
	Hectares		3				

312

TABLE 5.36 (Continued)

Crop	Unit, thousands	1949	1952	1954	1955	1957	1958
Tea	*Mou*					203[10]	
	Hectares					14	

[1] Sun Ching-chih, ed., *Hua-nan-ti-ch'u ching-chi ti-li (Economic Geography of South China)*, Peking: K'o-hsueh ch'u-pan-she, 1959, 147 pp.; translated in JPRS: 14,954, August 24, 1962, p. 63.
[2] *Ibid.*, p. 64.
[3] Liang Jen-ts'ai, *Kuang-tung ching-chi-ti-li (Economic Geography of Kwangtung)*, Peking: K'o-hsueh ch'u-pan-she, November, 1956, p. 25.
[4] Bureau of Agriculture, "Agricultural Production in Kwangtung," *TLCS*, No. 5 (May, 1959), pp. 205-7.
[5] Liang Jen-ts'ai, *op. cit.*, p. 97.
[6] Sun Ching-chih, ed., *op. cit.*, p. 71.
[7] Liang Jen-ts'ai, *op. cit.*, pp. 98-100.
[8] Sun Ching-chih, ed., *op. cit.*, p. 75.
[9] *Ibid.*, pp. 79-80.
[10] *Ibid.*, p. 78.

TABLE 5.37 Sown Area for Various Crops in Kwangsi Chuang Autonomous Region in 1957

Crops	In thousand *Mou*	In thousand Hectares
Food grains	56,152	3,743
Rice	33,909	2,261
Wheat	2,913	194
Corn	8,329	555
Potatoes	6,270	418
Others	4,731	315
Industrial crops	4,250	283
Cotton	114	7.6
Ramie	52	3.5
Jute	73	4.9
Tobacco	145	9.7
Sugar cane	562	37.5
Peanuts	2,357	157.1
Rapeseed	349	23.3
Sesame	405	27.0

Source: Sun Ching-chih, ed., *Hua-nan ti-ch'ü ching-chi ti-li (Economic Geography of South China)*, Peking: K'o-hsüeh ch'u-pan-she, 1959, 147 pp.; translated in JPRS: 14,954, August 24, 1962, pp. 252 and 258.

TABLE 5.38   Area Sown for Various Crops in Szechwan Province, 1949, 1952, and 1956-58

Crops	Unit, thousands	1949	1952	1956	1957	1958
All crops	Mou		161,655		195,880[1]	
	Hectares		10,777[2]		13,058	
Food grains	Mou		140,340		162,780[1]	
	Hectares		9,356[2]		10,852	
Rice	Mou		88,275		62,200[1]	
	Hectares		5,885[4]		4,147	
Wheat	Mou	15,030	15,690	18,900	20,400[1]	
	Hectares	1,002[3]	1,046[3]	1,260[3]	1,360[3]	
Corn	Mou		12,630		24,680[1]	
	Hectares		842[4]		1,645	
Barley	Mou				3,900[1]	
	Hectares				260	
Sweet potatoes	Mou				19,510[1]	
	Hectares				1,301	
Peas	Mou				11,660[1]	
	Hectares				777	
Beans	Mou				9,110[1]	
	Hectares				607	
Others	Mou				11,320[1]	
	Hectares				755	
Soybeans	Mou		3,690		5,030[1]	
	Hectares		246[2]		335	
Industrial crops	Mou		11,250		14,100[1]	
	Hectares		750[2]		940	
Cotton	Mou		3,645		5,020[1]	4,800
	Hectares		243[5]		334.7[5]	320[5]
Ramie	Mou				200[1]	
	Hectares				3,000	
Hemp	Mou				180[1]	
	Hectares				2,700	
Tobacco	Mou				730	
	Hectares				10,950	
Rapeseed	Mou	3,397.5	4,530		5,310[1]	
	Hectares	226.5[6]	302[6]		353.8[6]	
Peanuts	Mou	1,011.0	1,227		1,590[1]	
	Hectares	67.4[7]	81.8[7]		106.2[7]	
Sesame	Mou	247.5	255		270[1]	
	Hectares	16.5[7]	17[7]		17.7[7]	
Sugar cane	Mou	304.5	510		620[1]	
	Hectares	20.3[8]	34[8]		41.5[8]	
Others	Mou				180[1]	
	Hectares					

TABLE 5.38 (Continued)

Crops	Unit, thousands	1949	1952	1956	1957	1958
Other crops	Mou		6,375		13,970[1]	
	Hectares		425[2]		931	

[1] Sun Ching-chih, ed., *Hsi-nan ti-ch'u ching-chi ti-li (Economic Geography of Southwest China)*, K'o-hsueh ch'u-pan-she, 1960, 218 pp.; translated in JPRS: 15,069, August 31, 1962, pp. 100, 103, and 125.

[2] Ye A. Afanas'yeskiy, *Szechwan*, Moscow: Publishing House of Oriental Literature, 1960, 267 pp.; translated in JPRS: 15,306, September 17, 1962, p. 236.

[3] *Ibid.*, p. 249.

[4] *Ibid.*, p. 238.

[5] *Ibid.*, p. 257.

[6] *Ibid.*, p. 261.

[7] *Ibid.*, p. 262.

[8] *Ibid.*, p. 267.

TABLE 5.39 Sown Area for Various Crops in Kweichow Province, 1949, 1952, 1957, 1958

Crops	Unit, thousands	1949	1952	1957	1958
All crops	Mou	26,970	28,270	46,956	31,360
	Hectares	1,798	1,885	3,130	2,091
Food grains	Mou			36,910	
	Hectares			2,461	
Rice	Mou			13,420	
	Hectares			895	
Wheat	Mou			4,050	
	Hectares			270	
Corn	Mou			11,310	
	Hectares			754	
Barley	Mou			1,610	
	Hectares			107	
Sweet potatoes	Mou			1,130	
	Hectares			75	
Potatoes	Mou			1,080	
	Hectares			72	
Oats	Mou			820	
	Hectares			55	
Broad beans	Mou			520	
	Hectares			35	
Peas	Mou			660	
	Hectares			44	
Others	Mou			2,310	
	Hectares			154	
Soybeans	Mou			2,310	2,500
	Hectares			154	167

TABLE 5.39 (Continued)

Crops	Unit, thousands	1949	1952	1957	1958
Industrial crops	*Mou*	1,660	2,120	5,670	7,000
	Hectares	111	141	378	467
Cotton	*Mou*			370	
	Hectares			25	
Foreign	*Mou*			80	
	Hectares			5	
Native	*Mou*			290	
	Hectares			19	
Flax	*Mou*			110	
	Hectares			7	
Sugar cane	*Mou*			50	
	Hectares			3	
Rapeseed	*Mou*			3,780	
	Hectares			252	
Peanuts	*Mou*			130	
	Hectares			9	
Tobacco	*Mou*			920	
	Hectares			61	
Cured	*Mou*			720	
	Hectares			48	
Dried	*Mou*			200	
	Hectares			13	
Others	*Mou*			310	
	Hectares			21	
Other crops	*Mou*			2,066	
	Hectares			138	

Sources: Sun Ching-chih, ed., *Hsi-nan ti-ch'u ching-chi ti-li (Economic Geography of Southwest China)*, Peking: K'o-hsueh ch'u-pan-she, 1960, 218 pp.; translated in JPRS: 15,069, August 31, 1962, pp. 351, 361, 360, 372, and 375.

Crop	Unit, thousands	1949	1957
All crops	Mou		58,290
	Hectares		3,886
Food grains	Mou		49,550
	Hectares		3,303
Rice	Mou		15,930
	Hectares		1,062
Wheat	Mou		5,010
	Hectares		334
Corn	Mou		13,880
	Hectares		925
Barley	Mou		3,120
	Hectares		208
Yam	Mou		470
	Hectares		31
Potatoes	Mou		2,300
	Hectares		153
Horse beans	Mou		3,470
	Hectares		231
Peas	Mou		1,950
	Hectares		130
Others	Mou		3,420
	Hectares		228
Soybeans	Mou		2,100
	Hectares		140
Industrial crops	Mou	70	5,180
	Hectares	4.7	345
Cotton	Mou		380
	Hectares		25
Hemp	Mou		140
	Hectares		9
Sugar cane	Mou		300
	Hectares		20
Rapeseed	Mou		2,760
	Hectares		184
Peanuts	Mou		540
	Hectares		36
Tobacco	Mou		780
	Hectares		52
Native tobacco	Mou		130
	Hectares		9
Others	Mou		150
	Hectares		10
Other crops	Mou		1,460
	Hectares		97

Sources: Sun Ching-chih, ed., *Hsi-nan ti-ch'ü ching-chi
ti-li (Economic Geography of Southwest China)*, Peking:
K'o-hsüeh ch'u-pan-she, 1960, 218 pp.; translated in
JPRS: 15,069, August 31, 1962, pp. 521, 522, 531, and
536.

TABLE 5.41 Yield per Unit of Sown Area for Various Crops, 1949-59

Crop	Unit	1949[1]	1950[2]	1951[2]	1952[1]	1953[1]	1954[1]	1955[1]	1956[1]	1957[1]	1958[2]	1959[3]
Food grains	chin/mou	141.8	159.0	168	183.3	183.1	183.9	196.9	195.8	204.1	275	330
	kg/ha	1,063.5	1,192.5	1,260	1,374.8	1,373.3	1,379.3	1,476.8	1,468.5	1,530.8	2,062.5	2,475
Rice	chin/mou	252.3	281.0	300	321.5	335.5	328.9	356.6	330.1	358.9	463	
	kg/ha	1,892.3	2,107.5	2,250	2,411.3	2,516.3	2,466.8	2,674.5	2,475.8	2,691.8	3,472.5	
Wheat	chin/mou	85.6	85.0	100	97.5	95.1	115.4	114.5	121.3	114.4	145	
	kg/ha	642.0	562.5	750	731.3	713.3	865.5	858.8	909.8	858.0	1,088	
Coarse grains	chin/mou	100.7	118.0	118	136.2	131.8	129.1	139.7	135.0	138.8	181	
	kg/ha	755.3	885.0	885	1,021.5	988.5	968.3	1,047.8	1,012.5	1,041.0	1,357.5	
Corn	chin/mou				178.8	169.4	173.5	185.0	174.2	191.3		
	kg/ha				1,341.0	1,270.5	1,301.3	1,387.5	1,306.5	1,434.8		
Potatoes[a]	chin/mou	187.2	215.0	225	250.6	246.3	231.5	250.6	265.1	278.5		
	kg/ha	1,404	1,612.5	1,687.5	1,879.5	1,847.3	1,736.3	1,879.5	1,988.3	2,088.8		
Sweet	chin/mou				257.3	258.2	239.8	260.1	284.0	295.5		
	kg/ha				1,929.8	1,936.5	1,798.5	1,950.8	2,130.0	2,216.3		
Irish	chin/mou				232.8	200.5	199.3	219.7	206.2	218.0		
	kg/ha				1,746.0	1,503.8	1,494.8	1,647.8	1,546.5	1,635.0		
Soybeans	chin/mou	81.5			108.7	107.1	95.7	106.3	113.3	105.1		
	kg/ha	611.3			815.3	803.3	717.8	797.3	849.8	788.3		
Industrial Crops												
Cotton	chin/mou	21.6	24	25	31.2	30.2	26.0	35.1	30.8	37.9		
	kg/ha	162.0	180.0	187.5	234.0	226.5	195.0	263.3	231.0	284.3		
Jute	chin/mou	180.6			307.3	267.0	262.3	300.9	254.3	288.1		
	kg/ha	1,354.5			2,304.8	2,002.5	1,967.3	2,256.8	1,907.3	2,160.8		

TABLE 5.41 (Continued)

Crop	Unit	1949[1]	1950[2]	1951[2]	1952[1]	1953[1]	1954[1]	1955[1]	1956[1]	1957[1]	1958[2]	1959[3]
Flax	chin/mou				154.1	176.1	203.5	201.9	240.1	221.8		
	kg/ha				1,155.8	1,320.8	1,526.3	1,514.3	1,800.8	1,663.5		
Tobacco	chin/mou				135.9	137.8	131.2	141.8	131.3	102.9		
	kg/ha				1,019.3	1,033.5	984.0	1,063.5	984.8	771.8		
Cured	chin/mou	93.9			158.8	148.4	141.9	157.6	138.1	96.1		
	kg/ha	704.3			1,191.0	1,113.0	1,064.3	1,182.0	1,035.8	720.8		
Peanuts	chin/mou	134.8			171.1	159.8	176.0	172.0	172.3	134.9		
	kg/ha	1,011.0			1,283.3	1,198.5	1,320.0	1,290.0	1,292.3	1,011.8		
Rapeseed	chin/mou	64.6			66.7	70.3	68.6	55.3	56.8	51.3		
	kg/ha	484.5			500.3	527.3	514.5	414.8	426.0	384.8		
Sesame	chin/mou	52.5			60.6	63.8	29.2	53.9	47.5	44.2		
	kg/ha	393.8			454.5	478.5	219.0	404.3	356.3	331.5		
Sugar cane	chin/mou	3,255.4			5,200.4	4,988.1	5,237.4	5,294.9	5,220.2	5,197.5		
	kg/ha	24,415.5			39,003.0	37,410.8	39,280.5	39,711.8	39,151.5	38,981.3		
Sugar beets	chin/mou	1,593.8			1,819.4	1,383.7	1,805.8	1,852.6	1,468.7	1,256.1		
	kg/ha	11,953.5			13,645.5	10,377.8	13,543.5	13,894.5	11,015.3	9,420.8		

a Potatoes have been converted into grain equivalent by taking 4 chin of potatoes as 1 chin of grain.

1 Bureau of Planning, Ministry of Agriculture, A Collection of Statistical Data on Agricultural Production of China and Other Major Countries, Peking: Agricultural Publishing House, 1959, pp. 8, 12, 15, 18, 21, 24, 27, 30, 32, 35, 37, 39, 42, 45, 48, 51, 54, and 57.

2 TGY, p. 121.

3 Liu Jui-lung, "The Agricultural Front in 1960," Hung-ch'i, No. 2 (January 16, 1960), pp. 17-27, reference on p. 17.

TABLE 5.42 Output of Major Crops per Unit of Sown Area in Inner Mongolia Autonomous Region, 1947-58

Crop	Unit	1947	1948	1949	1950	1951	1952	1953	1954	1955	1956	1957	1958
Food grains	chin/mou	78	87	81	76	57	107	114	122	104	134	89	155
	kg/ha	585	653	683	570	428	803	855	915	780	1,005	668	1,163
Rice	chin/mou	202	202	191	163	178	227	274	272	319	300	139	274
	kg/ha	1,515	1,515	1,433	1,223	1,335	1,703	2,055	2,040	2,393	2,250	1,043	2,055
Wheat	chin/mou	57	64	65	55	49	80	98	127	112	128	112	101
	kg/ha	428	480	488	413	368	600	735	953	840	960	840	758
Coarse grains	chin/mou	77	84	78	75	53	101	110	117	97	129	79	145
	kg/ha	578	630	585	563	398	758	825	878	728	968	593	1,088
Potatoes	chin/mou	129	164	145	135	128	264	222	193	195	212	176	287
	kg/ha	968	1,230	1,088	1,013	960	1,980	1,665	1,448	1,463	1,590	1,320	2,153
Soybeans	chin/mou	57	67	65	74	56	103	103	111	78	100	73	126
	kg/ha	428	503	488	555	420	773	773	833	585	750	548	945

Source: NMKTC, p. 151.

TABLE 5.43 Output of Major Crops per Unit of Sown Area in Liaoning Province, 1949, 1952, and 1955-58

Crop	1949 *chin/mou*	1949 kg/ha	1952 *chin/mou*	1952 kg/ha	1955 *chin/mou*	1955 kg/ha	1956 *chin/mou*	1956 kg/ha	1957 *chin/mou*	1957 kg/ha	1958[1] *chin/mou*	1958[1] kg/ha
Food grains												
Rice									220[1]	1,650	289	2,168
Wheat									309[1]	2,318	362	2,715
Millet							56.7[2]	425	60[1]	450	73	548
Corn									161[1]	1,208	166	1,245
Kaoliang									330[1]	2,475	360	2,700
Potatoes									210[1]	1,575	252	1,890
Others									297[1]	2,228	311	2,333
									49[1]	368	111	833
Soybeans							178[3]	1,335	233[4]	1,748		
Cotton[5]	21.9	164	28.4	213	28.5	214	42.1	316				

[1] Derived from the data on output and sown acreage given in Wu Ch'uan-chun *et al.*, comp., *Tung-pei ti-ch'ü ching-chi ti-li (Economic Geography of Northeast China)* Peking: K'o-hsüeh ch'u-pan-she, 1959, 211 pp.; translated in JPRS: 15,388, September 21, 1962, pp. 86 and 90.

[2] Shen Yu-ching, "My Views on the Geographic Distribution of Wheat and the Prospects of Its Development in China," *TLCS*, pp. 339-45, reference on p. 344.

[3] Li Shu-yen, "A Survey of Agricultural Geography of Heilungkiang Province," *TLCS*, No. 11 (November, 1957), pp. 497-99, reference on p. 498.

[4] Wu Ch'uan-chun *et al.*, *op. cit.*, p. 95.

[5] Tsiang Yun-chi, "Cotton Production in China," *TLCS*, No. 10 (October, 1957), p. 467.

TABLE 5.44 Output of Major Crops Per Unit of Sown Area in Kirin Province, 1956-58

Crop	Unit	1956[1]	1957[2]	1958[3]
Food grains	chin/mou		168.2	237
	kg/ha		1,262.0	1,778
Rice	chin/mou		295.4	
	kg/ha		2,216.0	
Wheat	chin/mou	36.4	93.6	
	kg/ha	273.0	702.0	
Millet	chin/mou		137.0	
	kg/ha		1,028.0	
Corn	chin/mou		204.2	
	kg/ha		1,532.0	
Kaoliang	chin/mou		160.6	
	kg/ha		1,205.0	
Potatoes	chin/mou		212.8	
	kg/ha		1,596.0	
Others	chin/mou		99.6	
	kg/ha		747.0	
Industrial crops:				
Flax	chin/mou		192.0	
	kg/ha		1,440.0	
Amboric hemp	chin/mou		44.4	
	kg/ha		333.0	
Ramie	chin/mou		37.0	
	kg/ha		278.0	
Tobacco	chin/mou		123.6	
	kg/ha		927.0	
Sesame	chin/mou		16.4	
	kg/ha		123.0	
Sunflower	chin/mou		72.8	
	kg/ha		546.0	
Castor beans	chin/mou		30.2	
	kg/ha		227.0	
Beets	chin/mou		861.6	
	kg/ha		6,462.0	

[1] Shen Yu-ch'ing, "My Views on the Geographic Distribution of Wheat and the Prospect of Its Development in China," *TLCS*, No. 8 (August, 1957), pp. 339-45, reference on p. 344.

[2] Wu Ch'uan-chun *et al.*, comp., *Economic Geography of Northeast China (Tung-pei ti-ch'ü ching-chi ti-li)*, Peking: K'o-hsüeh ch'u-pan-she, 1959, 211 pp.; translated in JPRS: 15,388, September 21, 1962, p. 216.

[3] *Ibid.*, p. 221.

TABLE 5.45 Output of Major Crops Per Unit of Sown Area in Heilungkiang Province, 1943, 1949, and 1952-57, Kilograms per Hectare

Crop	1943[1]	1949[1]	1952[1]	1955[2]	1956	1957[1]	1953-57 average[1]
Food grains	1,130	1,200	1,379	1,437		1,242	1,282
Rice	2,270	1,822	2,689	3,160		1,910	2,312
Wheat	690	632	802		920[3]	993	837
Millet	1,150	880	1,292			1,186	1,108
Corn	1,415	1,309	1,749	1,698		1,468	1,356
Koaliang	1,310	1,152	1,509			1,150	1,303
Potatoes[a]	1,852	2,162	2,449	2,512		1,939	1,938
Others	713	716	850			764	762
Soybeans	1,105	939	1,173		1,050-1,125[4]	1,116	1,071
Industrial crops							
Flax	1,150	1,022	1,240			1,739	1,583
Sugar beets	8,600	13,350	12,664			9,490	11,381

[a] Potatoes are converted to grains at the ratio of 4 to 1.

[1] Wu Ch'uan *et al.*, comp., *Tung-pei ti-ch'u ching-chi ti-li (Economic Geography of Northeast China)*, Peking: K'o-hsueh ch'u-pan-she, 1959, 211 pp.; translation in JPRS: 15,388, September 21, 1962, p. 403.

[2] *Ibid.*, pp. 403-4.

[3] Shen Yu-ch'ing, "My Views on the Geographic Distribution of Wheat and the Prospect for Its Development in China," *TLCS*, No. 8 (August, 1957), pp. 339-45; reference on p. 344.

[4] Li Shu-yen, "A General Survey of the Agricultural Geography of Heilungkiang Province," *TLCS*, No. 11 (November, 1957), pp. 497-9; reference on p. 498.

TABLE 5.46 Output of Major Crops per Unit of Sown Area in Shensi Province, 1949-56

Crop	Unit	1949	1950	1951	1952	1953	1954	1955	1956
Wheat[1]	chin/mou		118.4	134.7	112.1	147.7	175.2	151.7	197.1
	kg/ha		888.0	1,010.3	840.8	1,107.8	1,314.0	1,137.8	1,478.8
Coarse grains[1]	chin/mou		92.8	101.2	99.4	112.9	107.5	100.3	119.3
	kg/ha		696.0	759.0	745.5	846.8	806.3	752.3	894.8
Cotton[2]	chin/mou	27.9	n.a.	n.a.	32.2	n.a.	n.a.	35.5	50.5
	kg/ha	209.3			241.5			266.3	378.8

[1] Shen Yu-ch'ing, "My Views on the Geographic Distribution of Wheat and the Prospect for Its Development in China," *TLCS*, No. 8 (August, 1957) pp. 339-45, references on p, 341.

[2] Tsiang Yun-chi, "Cotton Production in China," *TLCS*, No. 10 (October, 1957) p. 467.

TABLE 5.47   Output of Major Crops per Unit of Sown
Area in Kansu Province, 1956-57

Crops	Unit	1956[1]	1957[2]
Food grains	chin/mou		178. 3
	kg/ha		1, 337. 3
Wheat	chin/mou	171	
	kg/ha	1, 282. 5	
Coarse grains	chin/mou	161.9	
	kg/ha	1, 214. 3	
Cotton	chin/mou		46
	kg/ha		345

[1] Shen Yu-ching, "My Views on the Geographic Distribution of Wheat and the Prospect for Its Development in China," TLCS, No. 8 (August, 1957), pp. 339-45, reference on p. 345.

[2] Kansu Provincial Statistical Bureau, "Communique on the Results of the Implementation of the National Economic Plan for 1957 in Kansu Province," Kansu JP, Lanchow, June 12, 1958, p. 2.

TABLE 5.48   Output of Major Crops per Unit of Sown Area in Chinghai
Province, 1952, 1956, and 1957

Crop	Unit	1952	1956	1957
Food grains	chin/mou	149. 5[1,2]	235[1]	220. 5[2]
	kg/ha	1, 121. 3	1, 762. 5	1, 653. 8
Wheat	chin/mou		236. 2[3]	
	kg/ha		1, 771. 5	
Coarse grains	chin/mou		205. 2[3]	
	kg/ha		1,539	
Rapeseed	chin/mou	67. 6[2]		96[2]
	kg/ha	507		720

[1] Li Tsung-hai, "Great Achievements in Economic Construction in the National Minority Areas," Min-tzu tu'an-chieh (Unity of Nationalities), No. 10(October 6, 1959), pp. 36-39, reference on p. 36.

[2] Chinghai Provincial Statistical Bureau, "Communique on the Development of the National Economy of Chinghai Province and the Results of the Implementation of the First Five-Year Plan, 1953-1957," Chinghai JP, September 30, 1958, p. 2.

[3] Shen Yu-ch'ing, "My Views on the Geographic Distribution of Wheat and the Prospects for Its Development in China," TLCS, No. 8 (August, 1957), pp. 339-45, reference on p. 345.

TABLE 5.49 Output of Major Crops per Unit of Sown Area in Sinkiang-Uighur Autonomous Region, 1949-58

Crop	Unit	1949	1950	1951	1952	1953	1954	1955	1956	1958
Food grains	chin/mou	142.1[1]								263.5[1]
	kg/ha	1,065.8								1,976.3
Wheat	chin/mou								193[2]	
	kg/ha								1,447.5	
Coarse grains	chin/mou								242[2]	
	kg/ha								1,815.0	
Cotton	chin/mou	20.8[1,3]	22.1[3]	24.0[3]	27.9[3]	34.5[3]	38.1[3]	48.3[3]	58.7[4]	62.6[1]
	kg/ha	156.0	165.8	180.0	209.3	258.8	285.8	362.3	440.3	469.5

[1] Sai Fu-ting, "Great Achievements in Agriculture of Sinkiang in the Past Ten Years," *Chung-kuo nung-pao (Chinese Agricultural Bulletin)*, No. 19, 1959, pp. 19-23, reference on p. 21.

[2] Shen Yu-ch'ing, "My Views on the Geographic Distribution of Wheat and the Prospects of Its Development in China," *TLCS*, No. 8 (August, 1957), pp. 339-45, reference on p. 345.

[3] Teng Chin-chung, "Cotton Production in Sinkiang," *TLCS*, No. 5 (May, 1957), p. 207.

[4] Tsiang Yun-chi, "Cotton Production in China," *TLCS*, No. 10 (October, 1957), p. 467. This article gives slightly different figures on cotton yields per unit of sown area in Sinkiang: 20 *chin* for 1949, 29.1 *chin* for 1952 and 48.1 *chin* for 1955.

TABLE 5.50 Output of Major Crops per Unit of Sown Area in Shantung Province, 1949-56

Crop	Unit	1949	1950	1951	1952	1953	1954	1955	1956
Wheat[1]	chin/mou		82.2	86.3	109.6	90.1	111.3	101.7	122.9
	kg/ha		616.5	647.3	822.0	675.8	834.8	762.8	921.8
Coarse grains[1]	chin/mou		147.1	138.5	158.5	132.5	152.3	173.7	174.2
	kg/ha		1,103.3	1,038.8	1,188.8	993.8	1,142.3	1,302.8	1,306.5
Cotton[2]	chin/mou	25.0			32.7			36.7	40.9
	kg/ha	187.5			245.3			275.3	306.8

[1] Shen Yu-ch'ing, "My Views on the Geographic Distribution of Wheat and the Prospect for Its Development in China," *TLCS*, No. 8 (August, 1957), pp. 339-45, reference on p. 341.

[2] Tsiang Yun-chi, "Cotton Production in China," *TLCS*, No. 10 (October, 1957), p. 467.

TABLE 5.51 Output of Major Crops per Unit of Sown Area in Kiangsu Province, 1949-52 and 1955-58

Crop	Unit	1949	1951[1]	1952	1955	1956	1957[1]	1958[1]
Food grains:								
Rice	chin/mou		(323)		414[2]		(368)	676
	kg/ha		(2,423)		3,105		(2,763)	5,070
Wheat	chin/mou		(99)				(99)	98
	kg/ha		(741)				(743)	735
Millet	chin/mou							120
	kg/ha							900
Corn	chin/mou							456
	kg/ha							3,420
Soybeans	chin/mou		(94)				(99)	(179)
	kg/ha		(708)				(743)	(1,345)
Industrial crops								
Cotton	chin/mou	13.2[3]	(23)	28.6[3]	42.8[3]	25.2[3]	(38)	(70)
	kg/ha	99	(173)	215	321	189	(285)	(523)
Peanuts	chin/mou		(159)				(160)	(275)
	kg/ha		(1,194)				(1,198)	(2,066)

[1] Derived from the data on sown area and output given in Chin Chi-min, "Rapid Development of Agriculture in Kiangsu," *TLCS*, No. 6 (June, 1959), pp. 244-47, reference on p. 245.

[2] Wang Wei-p'ing, *Kiangsu, The Waterland*, Shanghai: Hsin-chi-shih ch'u-pan-she, December, 1956, p. 60.

[3] Tsiang Yun-chi, "Cotton Production in China," *TLCS*, No. 10 (October, 1957), p. 467.

TABLE 5.52 Output of Major Crops per Unit of Sown Area in Anhwei Province, 1949, 1955-57

Crop	Unit	1949	1952	1955	1956	1957
Food grains						
Rice	chin/mou					(362)[1]
	kg/ha					(2,711)
Early rice	chin/mou					364[2]
	kg/ha					2,730
Wheat	chin/mou					178[1]
	kg/ha					(1,337)
Coarse grains	chin/mou					(85)[1]
	kg/ha					(639)
Potatoes	chin/mou					(285)[1]
	kg/ha					(2,139)
Industrial crops						
Cotton	chin/mou	12.0[3]	19.1[3,4]	21.6[3]	20.8[3]	(32.4)[5]
	kg/ha	90.0	143.0	162.0	156.0	(243)
Cured tobacco	chin/mou	50.0[6]				
	kg/ha	375.0				

[1] Derived from data on output and sown acreage given in Sun Ching-chih, ed., *Hua-tung ti-ch'u ti-li (Economic Geography of East China)* Peking: Institute of Geography of the Chinese National Academy of Sciences, November, 1959, 153 pp.; translated in JPRS: 11,438, December 7, 1961, p. 141.

[2] Bureau of Agriculture, Anhwei Province, "Anhwei-The Province Produced 1,000 *chin* of Early Rince per *Mou*," *Chung-kuo nung-pao (Chinese Agricultural Bulletin)*, No. 22, 1958, pp. 8-13; reference on p. 8.

[3] Tsiang Yun-chi, "Cotton Production in China," *TLCS*, No. 10 (October, 1957), p. 467.

[4] Sun Ching-chih, ed., *op. cit.*, p. 145.

[5] Derived from data on the output and sown acreage of cotton in 1957 given in Tables 5.30 and 5.81.

[6] Sun Ching-chih, ed., *op. cit.*, p. 147.

327

TABLE 5.53 Output of Major Crops per Unit of Sown Area in Chekiang Province, 1949, 1952, and 1955-57

Crop	Unit	1949	1952	1955	1956	1957
Food grains[1]	*chin/mou*					381
	kg/ha					2,859
Rice	*chin/mou*					489
	kg/ha					3,667
Wheat	*chin/mou*					110
	kg/ha					824
Barley	*chin/mou*					124
	kg/ha					931
Maize	*chin/mou*					1,007
	kg/ha					1,616
Horse beans	*chin/mou*					107
	kg/ha					800
Sweet potatoes	*chin/mou*					621
	kg/ha					4,661
Others	*chin/mou*					202
	kg/ha					1,515
Industrial crops						
Cotton[2]	*chin/mou*	26.0	34.0	66.8	22.4	
	kg/ha	195.0	255.0	501.0	168.0	
Rapeseed[3]	*chin/mou*					54.5
	kg/ha					409.0

[1] Sun Ching-chih *et al.*, ed., *Hua-tung ti-ch'u ching-chi ti-li (Economic Geography of East China)* Peking: Institute of Geography of the Chinese National Academy of Sciences, November, 1959, 153 pp.; translated in JPRS: 11,438, December 7, 1961, pp. 215-16.

[2] Tsiang Yun-chi, "Cotton Production in China," *TLCS*, No. 10 (October, 1957), p. 465.

[3] Sun Ching-chin *et al.*, *po. cit.*, p. 221.

328

TABLE 5.54 Output of Major Crops per Unit of Sown Area in Fukien Province, 1949, 1955, and 1957-58

Crop	Unit	1949	1955	1957	1958
Food grains	chin/mou		391		1,000
	kg/ha		2,933		7,500
Sugar cane	chin/mou	2,292		6,647	10,000
	kg/ha	17,190		49,853	75,000
Tea	chin/mou		26		
	kg/ha		195		

Source: Sun Ching-chih, ed., *Hua-nan ti-ch'ü ching-chi ti-li (Economic Geography of South China)* Peking: K'o-hsüeh ch'u-pan-she, 1959, 147 pp,; translated from JPRS: 14,954, August 24, 1962, pp. 378, 386, and 391.

TABLE 5.55 Output of Food Grains and Cotton per Unit of Sown Area in Honan Province, 1949, 1952, and 1955-56

Crop	Unit	1949	1952	1955	1956
Food grains[1]	chin/mou				134.8
	kg/ha				1,011.0
Cotton[2]	chin/mou	23.9	24.7	27.8	25.6
	kg/ha	179.3	185.3	208.5	192.0

[1] Wang Kuang-wei, "Several Problems of Developing Agriculture," *HH*, No. 17 (September 3, 1957), pp. 25-26, reference on p. 26.
[2] Tsiang Yun-chi, "Cotton Production in China," *TLCS*, No. 10 (October, 1957), p. 467.

TABLE 5.56 Output of Major Corps per Unit of Sown Area in Hupeh Province, 1949, 1952, and 1955-57

Crop	Unit	1949[1]	1952[1]	1955[1]	1956[1]	1957[2]
Food grains	chin/mou					273
	kg/ha					2,048
Rice	chin/mou					465
	kg/ha					3,488
Wheat	chin/mou					141
	kg/ha					1,058
Barley	chin/mou					102
	kg/ha					765
Corn	chin/mou					173
	kg/ha					1,298
Millet	chin/mou					146
	kg/ha					1,095
Buckwheat	chin/mou					57
	kg/ha					428
Sweet potatoes	chin/mou					314
	kg/ha					2,355
Horse beans	chin/mou					102
	kg/ha					756
Garden peas	chin/mou					111
	kg/ha					833
Others	chin/mou					134
	kg/ha					1,005
Industrial crops:						
Cotton	chin/mou	17.4	31.9	32.2	44.6	52
	kg/ha	130.5	239.3	241.5	334.5	390
Ramie	chin/mou					108
	kg/ha					810
Sesame	chin/mou					68
	kg/ha					510
Peanuts	chin/mou					248
	kg/ha					1,860
Rapeseed	chin/mou					40
	kg/ha					300

[1] Tsiang Yun-chi, "Cotton Production in China," TLCS, No. 10 (October, 1957), p. 467.

[2] Sun Ching-chih, ed., Hua-chung ti-ch'u ching-chi ti-li (Economic Geography of Central China) Peking: K'o-hsueh ch'u-pan-she, December, 1958, 156 pp., tranlated in JPRS: 2227-N, February 10, 1960, pp. 77, 78, 86, and 89.

TABLE 5.57 Output of Major Crops per Unit of Sown Area in Hunan Province,
1949, 1952, and 1955-57

Crop	Unit	1949[1]	1952[1]	1955[1]	1956[1]	1957[2]
Food grains	chin/mou					227
	kg/ha					1,703
Rice	chin/mou					341
	kg/ha					2,558
Wheat	chin/mou					60
	kg/ha					450
Coarse grain:						
Barley	chin/mou					62
	kg/ha					465
Corn	chin/mou					230
	kg/ha					1,725
Kaoliang	chin/mou					244
	kg/ha					1,830
Millet	chin/mou					166
	kg/ha					1,245
Buckwheat	chin/mou					96
	kg/ha					720
Horse beans	chin/mou					36
	kg/ha					270
Garden peas	chin/mou					42
	kg/ha					315
Potatoes:						
Sweet	chin/mou					527
	kg/ha					3,953
Irish	chin/mou					307
	kg/ha					2,303
Industrial crops:						
Cotton	chin/mou	15.5	26.6	23.6	33.3	36
	kg/ha	116.0	200.0	177.0	250.0	270
Flax	chin/mou					74
	kg/ha					555
Peanuts	chin/mou					150
	kg/ha					1,125
Rapeseed	chin/mou					38
	kg/ha					285
Sesame	chin/mou					53
	kg/ha					398
Tobacco	chin/mou					245
	kg/ha					1,838

[1] Tsiang Yun-chi, "Cotton Production in China," *TLCS*, No. 10 (October, 1957), p. 467.

[2] Sun Ching-chih, ed., *Hua-chung ti-ch'ü ching-chi ti-li (Economic Geography of Central China)*, Peking: K'o-hsüeh ch'u-pan-she, December, 1958, 156 pp.; translated in JPRS: 2227-N, February 10, 1960, pp. 264, 265, and 279.

TABLE 5.58 Output of Major Crops per Unit of Sown Area in Kiangsi Province, 1949, 1952, and 1955-57

Crop	Unit	1949	1952	1955	1956	1957
Food grains	chin/mou					249.0[1]
	kg/ha					1,867.5
Rice	chin/mou					283.0[1]
	kg/ha					2,122.5
Wheat	chin/mou					51.0[1]
	kg/ha					382.5
Barley	chin/mou					67.0[1]
	kg/ha					502.5
Buckwheat	chin/mou					46.0[1]
	kg/ha					345.0
Millet	chin/mou					102.0[1]
	kg/ha					765.0
Corn	chin/mou					135.0[1]
	kg/ha					1,012.5
Horse beans	chin/mou					50.0[1]
	kg/ha					375.0
Garden peas	chin/mou					53.0[1]
	kg/ha					397.5
Potatoes	chin/mou					246.0[1]
	kg/ha					1,845.0
Others	chin/mou					57.0[1]
	kg/ha					427.5
Soybeans	chin/mou					(68.0)[2]
	kg/ha					(510.0)
Industrial crops:						
Cotton	chin/mou	15.0[3]	30.5[3]	21.5[3]	38.7[3]	47.0[4]
	kg/ha	112.5	228.8	161.3	290.3	352.5
Jute	chin/mou					263.0[4]
	kg/ha					1,972.5
Ramie	chin/mou					97.0[4]
	kg/ha					727.5
Peanuts	chin/mou					170.0[4]
	kg/ha					1,275.0
Sesame	chin/mou					44.0[4]
	kg/ha					330.0
Rapeseed	chin/mou					33.0[4]
	kg/ha					247.5
Sugar cane	chin/mou					4,794.0[4]
	kg/ha					35,955.0

[1] Sun Ching-chih, ed., *Hua-chung ti-ch'u ching-chi ti-li (Economic Geography of Central China)*, Peking; K'o-hsueh ch'u-pan-she, December, 1958, 1,956 pp.; translated in JPRS: 2227-N, February 10, 1960, p. 406.

[2] The sown acreage for soybeans in 1957 was 4,560,000 *mou* (see *ibid.*, p. 417), and the output of soybeans in 1957 was given as 310 million *chin* [see Liu Chun-hsin, "Speech Delivered at the Fifth Session of the First National People's Congress," *HHPYK*, No. 6 (March 25, 1958), pp. 27-30].

[3] Tsiang Yun-chi, "Cotton Production in China," *TLCS*, No. 10 (October, 1957), p. 467.

[4] Sun Ching-chih, *op. cit.*, p. 421.

TABLE 5.59   Output of Major Crops per Unit of Sown Area in Kwangtung Province, 1949, 1952, and 1957-58

Crop	1949 chin/mou	1949 kg/ha	1952 chin/mou	1952 kg/ha	1957 chin/mou	1957 kg/ha	1958 chin/mou	1958 kg/ha
Food grains					700[1]	5,250	723[1]	5,423
Industrial crops								
Sugar cane	3,063[2]	22,973	5,828[3]	43,710	7,300[4]	54,750	7,000[2]	52,500
Peanuts			138[3]	1,035				
Mulberry			1,660[3]	12,450				
Rapeseed			37[3]	278				
Sesame			45[3]	338				

[1] Kwangtung Provincial Statistcal Bureau, "Communique on the Development of the National Economy in Kwangtung Province in 1958 and the First Half of 1959," *Wen-hui-pao*, Hong Kong, October 5, 1959.

[2] Bureau of Agriculture, Kwangtung Province, "Agricultural Production in Kwangtung," *TLCS*, No. 5 (May, 1959), pp. 205-7.

[3] Liang Jen-ts'ai, *Kuang-tung ching-chi ti-li (Economic Geography of Kwangtung)*, Peking: K'o-hsueh ch'u-pan-she, November, 1956, pp, 98-100.

[4] *JMPJ*, November 26, 1958, p. 3.

TABLE 5.60   Output of Major Crops per Unit of Sown Area in Kwangsi Chuan Autonomous Region, 1957 and 1958

Crop	Unit	1957	1958
Food grains[1]	chin/mou		470.5
	kg/ha		3,529.0
Rice[2]	chin/mou	258.7	507.0
	kg/ha	1,940.0	3,803.0
Sweet potatoes[2]	chin/mou	180.9	
	kg/ha	1,357.0	
Industrial crops[2]			
Jute	chin/mou	173.7	
	kg/ha	1,303.0	
Sugar cane	chin/mou	2,968.7	
	kg/ha	22,265.0	

[1] Wei Kuo-ch'ing (Governor of Kwangsi), "Review the Achievements in the Past Ten Years and March Bravely Forward," *Min-tzu tu'an-chieh (Unity of Nationalities)*, No. 10 (October 6, 1959), pp. 9-12, reference on p. 11.

[2] Sun Ching-chih, ed., *Hsi-nan ti-ch'u ching-chi ti-li (Economic Geography of South China)*, Peking: K'o-hsueh ch'u-pan-she, 1959, 174 pp.; translated in JPRS: 14,954, August 24, 1962, p. 249.

TABLE 5.61 Output of Major Crops per Unit of Sown Area in Szechuan Province, 1949, 1952, and 1955-58

Crop	Unit	1949	1952	1955	1956	1957	1958
Food grains							
Rice	chin/mou					282[1]	
	kg/ha					2,115	
Wheat	chin/mou					440[1]	
	kg/ha					3,300	
Corn	chin/mou	132	101		165	161[1]	
	kg/ha	990[2]	760[2]		1,240[2]	1,200[2]	
Barley	chin/mou					173[1]	
	kg/ha					1,298	
Sweet potatoes	chin/mou					151[1]	
	kg/ha					1,133	
Pea	chin/mou					326[1]	
	kg/ha					2,445	
Horse beans	chin/mou					120[1]	
	kg/ha					900	
Others	chin/mou					116[1]	
	kg/ha					870	
Soybeans	chin/mou					144[1]	
	kg/ha					1,080	
Industrial crops	chin/mou					111[3]	
	kg/ha					833	
Cotton	chin/mou	17.9[4]	22.8[4]	26.5[4]	25.7[4]	28[5]	37[6]
	kg/ha	134	171	199	193	210	278

TABLE 5.61 (Continued)

Crop	Unit	1949	1952	1955	1956	1957	1958
Ramie	chin/mou					90[5]	
	kg/ha					675	
Hemp	chin/mou					106[5]	
	kg/ha					795	
Tobacco	chin/mou					143[5]	
	kg/ha					1,073	
Rapeseed	chin/mou	91[6]	84			104[5]	
	kg/ha	680	630			780[6]	
Peanuts	chin/mou	145	147			155[5]	
	kg/ha	1,090	1,100			1,160[6]	
Sesame	chin/mou	57	57			53[5]	
	kg/ha	430[8]	430[8]			400[6]	
Sugar cane	chin/mou	3,693	4,960			5,529[5]	
	kg/ha	27,700[9]	37,200[9]			41,500[9]	

[1] Sun Ching-chih, ed., *Hsi-na ti-ch'u ching-chi ti-li (Economic Geography of Southwest China)*, Peking: K'o-hsueh ch'u-pan-she, 1960, 218 pp; translated in JPRS: 15,069, August 31, 1962, p. 103.

[2] Ye A. Afanas'yeskiy, *Szechwan*, Moscow: Publishing House of Oriental Literature, 1960, 267 pp; translated in JPRS: 15,036, September 17, 1962, p. 123.

[3] Sun Ching-chih, *op. cit.*, p. 123.

[4] Tsiang Yun-chi, "Cotton Production in China," *TLCS*, No 10 (October, 1957), p. 467.

[5] Sun Ching-chih, *op. cit.*, p. 125.

[6] *Ibid.*, p. 126.

[7] Ye A. Afanas'yeskiy, *op. cit.*, p. 261.

[8] *Ibid.*, p. 262.

[9] *Ibid.*, p. 267.

TABLE 5.62   Output of Major Crops per Unit of Sown
Area in Kweichow Province in 1957

Crop	chin/mou	kg/ha
Food grains	285	2,137.5
Rice	501	3,757.5
Wheat	100	750.0
Corn	197	1,477.5
Barley	96	720.0
Sweet potatoes	366	2,745.0
Potatoes	206	1,545.0
Oats	71	532.5
Broad beans	79	592.5
Peas	76	570.0
Others	92	690.0
Soybeans	88	660.0
Industrial crops:		
Cotton	16	120.0
Foreign	21	157.5
Native	13	97.5
Flax	56	420.0
Sugar cane	3,801	28,507.5
Rapeseed	44	330.0
Peanuts	143	1,072.5
Tobacco	108	810.0
Cured	110	825.0
Dried	106	795.0

Sources: Sun Ching-chih, ed., *Hsi-nan ti-ch'u ching-chi ti-li (Economic Geography of Southwest China)*, Peking: K'o-hsueh ch'u-pan-she, 1960, 218 pp.; translated in JPRS: 15,069, August 31, 1962, pp. 361 and 375.

TABLE 5.63   Output of Major Crops per Unit of
Sown Area in Yunnan Province in
1957

Crop	*chin/mou*	kg/ha
Food grains	252	1,890
Rice	447	3,353
Wheat	123	923
Corn	193	1,448
Barley	92	690
Yam	247	1,853
Potatoes	243	1,823
Horse beans	143	1,073
Peas	82	615
Others	136	1,020
Industrial crops:		
Cotton	18	135
Hemp	62	465
Sugar cane	3,078	23,085
Rapeseed	54	405
Peanuts	113	848
Tobacco	79	593
Native tobacco	91	683

Sources: Sun Ching-chih, ed., *Hsi-nan ti-ch'ü
ching-chi ti-li (Economic Geography of
Southwest China)*, Peking: K'o-hsüeh ch'u-
pan-she, 1960, 218 pp.; translated in
JPRS: 15,069, August 31, 1962, pp. 522 and
531.

TABLE 5.64 Output of Major Crops, 1949-59, Thousand Tons

Crop	1949	1950	1951	1952	1953
Food grains:	108,100[1]	124,700[1]	135,050[1]	154,400[1]	156,900[1]
Rice[1]	48,650	55,100	60,550	68,450	71,250
Wheat[1]	13,800	14,500	17,250	18,100	18,300
Coarse grains[1]	35,800	42,700	43,250	51,500	50,700
Corn[3]				16,849	16,683
Potatoes[a, 1]	9,850	12,400	14,000	16,350	16,650
Sweet[4]				12,560	13,231
Irish[4]				3,096	2,598
Soybeans	5,086[5]			9,519[5]	9,931[5]
Industrial crops:					
Cotton[1]	444.5[1]	692.5[1]	1,303.5[1]	1,303.5[1]	1,174.5[1]
Jute[7]	32			191	120
Flax[7]				33	50
Tobacco[7]				435	407
Cured	43[8]			222[8]	213[8]
Peanuts	1,268[8]			2,316[8]	2,127[8]
Rapeseed	734			932	879
Sesame[9]	325.5			480.5	521
Sugar cane	2,642[8]			7,116[8]	7,209[8]
Sugar beets	191[8]			479[8]	505[8]
Other crops:					
Tea[10]	41	65	78.5	82.5	84.5
Fruits[11]				2,443	2,969
Apples				118	139
Citrus fruits				206.5	255
Bananas				110	115.5
Pears				393.5	530.5
Grapes				48.5	66.5

[a] Potatoes have been converted into grains equivalents by taking four kilograms of potatoes as one kilogram of grain.

[1] TGY, p. 119.

[2] JMJP, January 22, 1960.

[3] Bureau of Planning, Ministry of Agriculture, ed., A Collection of Statistical Data on Agricultural Production of China and Other Major Countries, Peking: Agricultural Publishing House, 1958, p. 22.

[4] Ibid., pp. 28, 31.

TABLE 5.64 (Continued)

1954	1955	1956	1957	1958	1959
160,450[1]	174,800[1]	182,500[1]	185,500[1]	250,000[1]	270,050[2]
70,850	78,000	82,450	86,800	113,700	
23,350	22,950	24,800	23,650	28,950	
49,250	54,950	53,400	52,650	61,950	
17,141	20,315	23,072	21,441		
17,000	18,900	21,850	21,900	45,400	
13,480	15,140	17,638	17,570		
2,690	3,060	3,284	3,375		
9,080[5]	9,121[5]	10,234[5]	10,045[5]	10,500[6]	11,500[2]
1,065[1]	1,518.5[1]	1,445[1]	1,640[1]	2,100[1]	2,410[2]
128	250	249	295		
75	88	72	58		
400	485	570	418		
232[8]	298[8]	399[8]	256[6]	380[6]	
2,767[8]	2,926[8]	3,336[8]	2,571[6]	2,800[6]	
878	969	920	888	1,100	
229	463.5	339	312		
8,592[8]	8,110[8]	8,678[8]	10,393[6]	13,525[6]	
989[8]	1,596[8]	1,654[8]	1,501[8]	2,900[6]	
92	108	120.5	111.5	140	
2,977.5	2,550	3,105	3,247.5	3,900	
173.5	202.5	220.5	221.5	297.5	
329	284.5	316	322	412	
144.5	96.5	98.5	73	158.5	
241	409.5	525.5	503.5	796.5	
76	64.5	80	85.5	111.5	

[5] *Ibid.*, p. 33.

[6] *TGY*, p. 124.

[7] Bureau of Planning, Ministry of Agriculture, ed., *op. cit.*, pp. 37, 40, 43.

[8] SSB, "Economic Statistical Abstract," *HHPYK*, No. 17 (September, 1957) pp. 30-50.

[9] Bureau of Planning, Ministry of Agriculture, ed., *op. cit.*, p. 52.

[10] *TGY*, p. 125.

[11] *Ibid.*, p. 127.

TABLE 5.65 Livestock on Farms and Ranches, 1949, 1952-59, Thousand Head

Animal	1949[1]	1952[1]	1953[1]	1954[1]	1955[1]	1956[1]	1957[1]	1958[2]	1959[3]
Large animals	59,775	76,173	80,455	84,980	87,388	87,370	83,457	85,060	85,360
Oxen	33,752	44,960	47,923	51,176	53,481	53,992	50,485		65,430
Buffaloes	10,184	11,640	12,160	12,447	12,470	12,609	13,127		
Horses	4,874	6,130	6,512	6,939	7,312	7,372	7,302		7,600
Asses	9,494	11,806	12,215	12,700	12,402	11,686	10,864		
Mules	1,471	1,637	1,645	1,718	1,723	1,711	1,679		
Camels	247	285	301	320	357	363	365		
Sheep and goats	42,347	61,778	72,023	81,297	84,218	91,654	98,582	108,860	112,530
Sheep	16,126	24,898	29,204	33,157	34,005	38,554	45,147		
Goats	26,221	36,880	42,819	48,147	50,213	53,100	53,435		
Pigs	57,752	89,765	96,131	101,718	87,920	84,026	145,895	160,000	180,000

[1] Bureau of Planning, Ministry of Agriculture, ed., A Collection of Statistical Data on Agricultural Production of China and Other Major Countries, Peking: Agricultural Publishing House, 1958, pp. 65-78.

[2] SSB, Communique on the Development of the National Economy in 1958, Peking: T'ung-chi ch'u-pan-she, 1959, p. 21.

[3] SSB, Communique on the Development of the National Economy in 1959, Peking: Jen-min jih-pao ch'u-pan-she, January, 1960, p. 4.

TABLE 5.66 Ownership of Livestock, July 1, 1956, Percent

Ownership	Oxen	Year-lings	Buff-aloes	Horses	Asses	Mules	Camels	Sheep	Goats	Pigs
Total	100.0	100.0	100.0	100.0	100.0	100.0	100.0	100.0	100.0	100.0
State-owned (state farms)	0.2	18.7	0.5	1.7	0.1	1.2	0.3	1.2	0.4	0.6
Collectively owned (agricultural producer cooperatives)	72.8	25.4	79.3	68.9	69.9	75.0	7.6	30.8	39.2	16.3
Privately owned	27.0	55.9	20.2	29.4	30.0	23.8	92.1	68.0	60.4	83.1
By members of cooperatives	12.8	9.7	9.8	11.2	24.8	10.6	14.9	41.5	43.4	73.1
By independent peasants and herders	14.2	46.2	10.4	18.2	5.2	13.2	77.2	26.5	17.0	10.0

Note: The total covers the whole country, except Chinghai, Sinkiang, and Hunan.
Sources: Data Office, *TCKTTH*, "A National Survey of Animals for 1956," *TCKTTH*, No. 23 (December, 1956), reprinted in *HHPYK*, No. 1 (January 10, 1957), pp. 88-90, reference on p. 89.

TABLE 5.67 Output of Silkworm Cocoons and Aquatic Products, 1949-58, Thousand Tons

Product	1949	1950	1951	1952	1953	1954	1955	1956	1957	1958
Silkworm cocoons[1]	43	58.5	73.5	123	72	90.5	131	134.5	112.5	141.5
Cocoons of cultivated silkworms	31	33.5	47	62	59.5	65	67	72.5	68	84.5
Tussah cocoons	12	25	26.5	61	12.5	25.5	64	62	44.5	57
Aquatic products[2]	448	912	1,332	1,666	1,900	2,293	2,518	2,648	3,120	4,060

[1] *TGY* p. 125. [2] *Ibid.*, p. 100.

TABLE 5.68   Output of Major Agricultural Products and Livestock in Inner Mongolia
Autonomous Region, 1936 and 1947-58

Product	1936	1947	1948	1949	1950	1951
Crops, thousand tons:						
Food grains	2,478.5	1,735	2,051	1,994.5	2,097	1,678.5
Rice	14.5	12	13	19.5	24	20.5
Wheat	114	93	115.5	126	114.5	113
Coarse grains	2,288	1,489	1,730.5	1,674.5	1,794.5	1,349
Potato crops	62	141	192	174.5	164	196
Soybeans	241	63	74.5	80	64.5	46.5
Industrial crops:						
Flax		2.8		3.5		
Sugar beets				0.3		
Oil-bearing crops		56.8		88.7		
Fruits						
Apples						
Pears						
Grapes						
Peaches						
Apricots						
Aquatic products, thousand tons		3.1				
Livestock, thousand head	9,376.1	8,281.8		9,408.2		
Large animals	2,470.2	2,680.8		3,103.7		
Cattle	1,320,0	1,721.0		2,057.0		
Horses	718.0	485.0		451.0		
Sheep	5,687.0	3,323.0		3,921.0		
Goats	1,219.0	2,278.0		2,383.0		
Small animals	6,905.9	5,601.0		6,304.5		
Hogs	875.2	887.8		1,008.6		

Source: NMKTC, pp. 146, 153, 155, 162, 172, 176, 177, 178, 179.

TABLE 5.68 (Continued)

1952	1953	1954	1955	1956	1957	1958
3,295.5	3,375	3,695	3,097.5	4,375.5	2.811	4,800
25	16	21	32	66	41.5	183
244.5	327	516	471	531.5	495	419
2,613	2,702	2,876.5	2,322	3,452.5	1,997	3,409
413	330	281.5	272.5	325.5	277.5	789
122	168.5	188.5	156.5	181.5	146	200
					5.6	9.2
					220.8	236.8
					123.8	136.6
					5.9	41.6
1.7					0.03	0.08
					0.21	8.5
					1.34	0.27
					0.14	0.67
					3.44	27.09
6.2						10.7
15,720.4					22,394.5	24,472.0
4,447.9					5,465.0	5,538.6
3,024.0					3,490.0	3,477.0
593.0					936.0	968.0
6,770.0					9,722.0	10.913.0
4,502.0					7,207.0	8,020.0
11,272.5					16,929.5	18,933.4
1,542.2					1,679.2	2,381.4

343

TABLE 5.69   Output of Major Crops and Livestock
in Hopei Province, 1949, 1952, and
1957

Product	1949	1952	1957
Crops, thousand tons:			
Food grains and soybeans	4,650[1]	9,439[1,2]	10,100[2]
Cotton		297[1,2]	315[2]
Livestock, thousand head:			
Hogs		5,619[2]	8,400[2]

[1] Chang Li "The Construction of Water Conservancy in Hopei
Province," *TLCS*, Vol. 10, No. 11 (November 6, 1959),
pp. 490-96, references on p. 491.
[2] Kao Shu-hsun, "Speech Delivered to the Fifth Session of the
First National People's Congress," *HHPYK*, No. 6 (March 25,
1958).

TABLE 5.70   Livestock in Shansi Province, 1952 and 1957,
Thousand Head

Animal	1952	1957
Cattle	1,913	2,037
Sheep and goats	4,581	6,269
Hogs	660	1,908

Source: Shansi Provincial Statistical
"Communique on the Results of the
Implementation of the First Five-
Year Plan for Shansi Province,"
Shansi JP, Taiyuan, May 12, 1958.

TABLE 5.71 Output of Major Agricultural Products and Livestock in Liaoning Province, 1949-58

Product	1949	1950	1951	1952	1953	1955	1956	1957	1958
Crops, thousand tons:									
Food grains								5,935[1]	7,515[1]
Rice	170[2]			300[2]				375[1]	260[1]
Wheat								652[7]	1,004[2]
Millet								30[1]	22[1]
Corn	852[2]			1,258[2]				765[1]	650[1]
Kaoliang	1,483[2]			1,932[2]				1,729[2]	4,152[2]
Tubers	150[2]			210[2]				1,997[2]	840[2]
Others								390[2]	558[2]
Soybeans	407[2]			553[2]				767[2]	985[2]
Industrial crops									
Cotton	41[2]		200[3]	275[2]			201[3]	112[2]	235[2]
Cured tobacco	1.5[2]			23[2]				19[2]	25[2]
Peanuts	22.2[4]								287[4]
Other Crops									
Apples	50[2]			85[2]	101.4[5]			167[2]	217[2]
Tussah silk	20[2]	49.8[5]		53[2]				33[2]	44[2]
Aquatic products, tons	62[a,6]	113[6]		145[6]	148[6]	185[6]		187[6]	201.5[7]
Marine aquatic products	61[a,6]	111[6]		142[6]	139[6]	180[6]		185[6]	
Freshwater aquatic products	1[a,6]	2[6]		3[6]	9[6]	5[6]		2[6]	
Livestock, thousand head:									
Pigs	2,110[8]								3,250[8]
Sheep	659[8]								1,910[8]

[a] 1948 figures.

[1] Wu Ch'uan-chun et al., comp., *Economic Geography of Northeast China (Tung-pei ti-ch'u ti-li)* Peking: K'o-hsüeh ch'u-pan-she, 1959, 211 pp.; translated in JPRS: 15,388, September 21, 1962, p. 90.

[2] *Ibid.*, p. 86.

[3] *Ibid.*, p. 95.

[4] Liaoning Provincial Statistical Bureau, "Tremendous Changes in Liaoning's Rural Outlook during the Past Decade," in *Liao-ning shih-nien*, Shenyang: Liaoning jen-min ch'u-pan-she, June, 1960, p. 149.

[5] Wu Ch'uan-chun, et al., *op. cit.*, p. 99.

[6] *Ibid.*, p. 105.

[7] Liaoning Provincial Statistical Bureau, *op. cit.*, p. 150.

[8] *Ibid.*, p. 151.

TABLE 5.72 Output of Major Agricultural Products and Livestock in Kirin Province, 1949, 1952, 1954, 1957, and 1958

Product	1949	1952	1954	1957	1958
Crops, thousand tons:					
Grains				4,280[1]	
Rice				630[1]	1,150[2]
Wheat				30[1]	70[2]
Millet				870[1]	
Corn				139[1]	
Kaoliang				860[1]	
Potatoes				170[1]	
Others				340[1]	
Economic crops, thousand tons:					
Flax		7.4[3]		10.3[3]	
Ambari hemp		5.0[3]		3.5[3]	
Kami		5.6[3]		5.7[3]	
Tobacco		13.5[3]		8.7[3]	
Sesame		5.6[3]		1.0[3]	
Sunflower		11.0[3]		15.3[3]	
Castor beans		14.2[3]		4.0[3]	
Beets		176.1[3]		217.1[3]	650[4]
Aquatic products, tons				16,343[5]	
Livestock, thousand head:					
Large animals	1,645[6]		2,315[6]	1,705[6]	1,728[7]
Horses				781[6]	
Cattle				669[6]	
Donkeys				121[6]	
Mules				134[6]	
Pigs	1,986[6]		2,260[6]		
Sheep and Goats	73[6]		337[6]		

[1] Wu Ch'uan-chun *et al.*, comp., *Economic Geography of Northeast China (Tung-pei ti-ch'u ching-chi ti-li)*, Peking: K'o-hsueh ch'u-pan-she, 1959, 211 pp.; translated in JPRS: 15,388, September 21, 1962, p. 216.

[2] Kirin Provincial Statistical Bureau, "Communique on the Fulfillment of the Economic Plan for 1958 in Kirin Province," *Kirin JP*, March 18, 1959, pp. 1-2.

[3] Wu Ch'uan-chun *et al.*, *op cit.*, p. 221.

[4] *Ibid.*, p. 220.

[5] *Ibid.*, p. 228.

[6] *Ibid.*, p. 226.

[7] Li Yu-wen, "Work Report of Kirin Provincial Government," *Kirin JP*, January 10, 1959.

TABLE 5.73 Output of Major Agricultural Products in Heilungkiang Province, 1949-58

Product	1949	1952	1953	1954	1955	1956	1957	1958
Crops, thousand tons [1]								
Grains and soybeans [2]		8,755	7,085	7,030	8,195	7,900	7,840	12,000
Sugar beets [3]							1,050	2,200
Livestock, thousand head: [4]								
Pigs	2,338	2,752					3,060	
Sheep	73	143					315	
Goats	7	10					16	
Cows		12					28	
Draft oxen	567	1,023					540	
Horses	1,001	1,358					1,442	
Mules	62	68					42	
Donkeys	47	67					33	
Fowls							9,000	

[1] Ou-yang ch'in, "Work Report of Heilungkiang Provincial People's Council for 1958," *Heilungkiang JP*, Harbin, January 25, 1959, pp. 1-3.

[2] Wang Kuang-wei, "Several Problems Concerning the Development of Agriculture," *HH*, No. 17 (September 3, 1957), pp. 25-28, reference on p. 25.

[3] Wu Ch'uan-chun *et al.*, comp., *Tung-pei ti-ch'u ching-chi ti-li (Economic Geography of Northeast China)*, Peking: K'o-hsueh ch'u-pan-she, 1959, 211 pp.; translated in JPRS: 15,388, September 21, 1962, p. 408.

[4] *Ibid.*, p. 416.

TABLE 5.74 Output of Food Grains
and Cotton in Shensi
Province, 1956 and
1957, Thousand Tons

Product	1956	1957
Food grains	5,400	4,500
Cotton	96	110.5

Source: Su Tzu-sheng, "Speech Delivered at the Fifth Session of
First National People's Congress,"
HHPYK, No. 6(March 25, 1958),
pp. 53-54.

TABLE 5.75 Output of Major Agricultural Products in Kansu Province, 1952
and 1957, Thousand Tons

Product	1952	1957
Food grains	2,679	4,250
Cotton	3.8	8.4
Oil-bearing crops	68	81

Source: Kansu Provincial Statistical Bureau,
"Communique on the Results of the Implementation of the National Economic Plan
for 1957 in Kansu Province," *Kansu JP*,
Lanchow, June 12, 1958.

TABLE 5.76 Output of Major Crops and Livestock in Chinghai Province, 1949, 1952,
and 1955-58

Product	1949	1952	1955	1956	1957	1958
Crops, thousand tons:						
Food grains	291[1,2]	371.5[1,2]	589.4[3]	610[3]	640[1,2]	(1,100)[4]
Rapeseed				11[2]	19.8[2]	
Livestock, thousand head	8,580[1]	9,700[1,2]			17,170[1,2]	
Cattle	7,152[3]		15,147[3]	15,950[3]		
Hogs		1,080[2]			2,160[2]	

[1] Yuan Jen-yuan (Governor of Chinghai) "Work Report of Chinghai Provincial People's Council," *Chinghai JP*, July 4, 1958, pp. 1-2.

[2] Chinghai Provincial Statistical Bureau, "Communique on the Development of the National Economy of Chinghai Province and the Results of the Implementation of the First Five-Year Plan, 1953-1957," *Chinghai JP*, September 30, 1958, p. 2.

[3] Sun Tso-pin, "Report to the Fifth Session of the First Chinahai Provincial People's Congress," *Chinghai JP*, August 13, 1957.

[4] The output of food grains in Chinghai Province in 1958 was reportedly 171.9 percent of the 1957 level. See Yuan Jen-yuan, "Work Report to Chinghai Provincial People's Council for 1958," *Chinghai JP*, May 21, 1959, pp. 1, 3.

TABLE 5.77 Output of Major Crops and Livestock in Sinkiang-Uihur Autonomous Region, 1949-58

Product	1949	1950	1951	1952	1953	1954	1955	1956	1957	1958
Crops, thousand tons										
Food grains	1,538[1]			1,606[2]					2,034[2,3]	3,200[2,3]
Cotton	4.9[4]	6[4]	9.5[4]	14.5[4]	15[4]	16[4]	26.7[4]		48.5[3]	57.5[1]
Oil-bearing crops									72.5[3]	75.5[1]
Livestock, thousand head	11,800[1]			14,000[2]					20,470[2,3]	22,230[1,2,3]

[1] Sai Fu-tng, "Great Achievements in Agriculture of Sinkiang in the Past Ten Years," *Chung-kuo nung-pao (Chinese Agricultural Bulletin)* No. 19, 1959, pp. 19-23, reference on p. 21.

[2] Sai Fu-ting, "Work Report of the Sinkiang-Uighur Autonomous Region People's Council on January 22, 1959, to the First Session of the Second People's Congress of Sinkiang-Uighur Autonomous Region," *Sunkiang JP*, January 30, 1959, pp. 2-3.

[3] Hsin Lan-t'ing, "Report on the 1959 Economic Plan for Sinkiang-Uighur Autonomous Region," *Sinkiang JP*, February 1, 1959, p. 2.

[4] Teng Chin-chung, "Cotton Production in Sinkiang," *TLCS*, No. 5 (May 1957), p. 207.

TABLE 5.78 Output of Major Agricultural Products and Livestock in Shangtung Province, 1955-58

Product	1955	1956	1957	1958
Crops, thousand tons:				
Food grains and soybeans	13,509[1]	14,675[1,2]	12,100[3]	19,000[3]
Food grains	11,978[1]	12,820[1]		
Rice	56.5[1]	76.5[1]		
Wheat	3,113[1]	3,698[1]		
Potatoes	2,967[1]	3,753[1]		
Soybeans	1,531[1]	1,855[1]		
Industrial crops				
Cotton		217[2,3]	181[3]	275[3]
Cured tobacco			67[3]	125[3]
Peanuts		1.3[2]	680[3]	1,075[3]
Aquatic products	286[1]	305[1]	300[4]	550[4]
Livestock				
Buffaloes		3,386[a,1]		
Horses	37[a,1]	48[a,1]		
Mules		86[a,1]		
Donkeys		1,513[a,1]		
Sheep	2,746[a]	3,587[a,1]		
Hogs	3,098[2]	5,239[2]		

[a] As of the end of June.

[1] Shantung Provincial Statistical Bureau, "Communique on the Results of the Implementation of the National Economic Plan for 1956 in Shantung Province," *Ta-chung JP*, August 9, 1957, p. 3.

[2] Wang Che-ju, "Report on the Draft of the 1957 Economic Plan and the Implementation of the 1956 Economic Plan for Shantung Provinces," *Ta-chung JP*, August 17, 1957, p. 2.

[3] Pai Ju-ping (Deputy Governor of Shantung), "Report on the Readjustment of Principal Targets of the 1959 National Economic Plan and the Further Development of the Production Increase and Economy Campaign in Shantung Province--Delivered to the Fifth Session of the Second Shangtung Provincial People's Congress on September 14, 1959," *Ta-chung JP*, September 16, 1959.

[4] NCNA, Tsinan, January 17, 1959.

TABLE 5.79   Output of Agricultural Products of
             Kiangsu and Shanguai Combined,
             1957 and 1958

Product	1957	1958
Grain crops, thousand tons	11,780	
Rice	6,711	
Wheat	1,574	
Barley	671	
Oats	730	
Maize	876	
Sorghum	175	
Sweet potatoes	517	
Others	528	
Aquatic products, thousand tons		500
Livestock, thousand head		
Large animals		1,900
Hogs	10,000	

Source: Sun Ching-chih, ed., *Hua-tung ti-ch'u ching-chi ti-li (Economic Geography of East China)* Peking: Research Institute of Geography of Chinese National Academy of Sciences, November, 1959, 153 pp.; translated in JPRS: 11,438, December 7, 1961, pp. 57, 68, 69.

TABLE 5.80 Output of Major Agricultural Products and Livestock in Kiangsu Province, 1950-52, 1955, and 1957-58

Product	1950	1951	1952	1955	1957	1958
Crops, thousand tons:						
Food grains		(9,940)[1]	15,120[2]	17,870[2]	12,230[3]	23,000[3,4]
Rice		4,992[5]		6,700[6]	6,589[5]	11,625[5]
Wheat		1,422[5]			1,546[5]	2,465[5]
Corn						1,769[7]
Potatoes						3,000[7]
Soybeans		663[5]			646[7]	733[7]
Industrial crops:						
Cotton		95[8]	137[9]	249[9]	191[1,8]	305[1,7]
Oil-bearing crops						330[7]
Peanuts		123[8]			200[8]	250[8]
Cured tobacco						19[7]
Sugar beets						4[7]
Silkworm cocoons, and bees:[10]						
Silkworm cocoons, thousand tons	7.7				10.1	11.5
Bees, thousand cases					27	
Aquatic products, thousand tons[10]					319	544
Livestock, thousand head:[10]						
Large domestic animals			1,790		2,020	
Pigs			6,000		9,890	10,190
Sheep			1,810		2,650	3,000
Rabbits					1,980	

[1] Chin Chi-min, "The Rapid Development of Agriculture in Kiangsu," *TLCS*, No. 6, (June, 1959), pp. 244-47, reference on p. 244. It was stated that the output of food grains in 1957 increased by 23 percent over the 1951 level.

[2] Wang Wei-p'ing, *Kiangsu, the Waterland*, Shanghai: Hsin-chih shih ch'u-pan-she, 1956, p. 58.

[3] Liu Shun-yuen, "Work Report to the Third Session of the Third Kiangsu Provincial Congress of the Chinese Communist Party on January 29, 1959," *HHPYK*, No. 7 (April 10, 1959), pp. 15-22, reference on p.15.

[4] *Ibid.*, p. 245.

[5] Chin Chi-min, *op. cit.*, p. 245.

[6] Wang Wei-p'ing, *op. cit.*, p. 59.

[7] Chin Chi-min, *op. cit.*, p. 246.

[8] *Ibid.*, p. 244.

[9] Wang Wei-p'ing, *op. cit.*, p. 64.

[10] Chin Chi-min, *op. cit.*, p. 247.

TABLE 5.81   Output of Major Agricultural Products and Livestock in Anhwei Province, 1949 and 1955-57

Product	1949	1955	1956	1957
Food grains and soybeans, thousand tons	4,550[1]	11,350[1]	10,900[2]	12,370[3]
Food grains				11,495[4]
Rice				6,095[4]
Wheat				2,005[4]
Coarse grains				1,760[4]
Potatoes				1,615[4]
Soybeans				(875)[5]
Other crops, thousand tons:				
Cotton			26[3]	49[3]
Tea	5[6]		19[3]	20[3]
Silkworm cocoons, thousand tons:	0.5[6]			1.8[6]
Aquatic products, thousand tons:		53[2]	87[2]	147[7]
Livestock, thousand head:				
Hogs		2,650[2]	3,410[2]	8,560[3]
Domestic animals		2,720[2]	2,840[2]	

[1] Hua Shu, "Is the Rate of Agricultural Growth in China High or Low?" *HHPYK*, No. 3 (February 10, 1957), pp. 59-62, reference on p. 62.

[2] Chang Kai-fan (Deputy Governor of Anhwei), "Government Work Report at the 4th Session of the First Provincial People's Congress of Anhwei, on September 21, 1957," *Anhwei JP*, September 23, 1957, pp. 2-3.

[3] Anhwei Provincial Statistical Bureau, "Communique on the Results of the Implementation of the National Economic Plan for 1957 in Anhwei Province," *Anhwei JP*, April 30, 1958.

[4] Sun Ching-chi, ed., *Hua-tung ti-ch'u ching-chi ti-li (Economic Geography of East China)*, Peking: Institute of Geography of the Chinese National Academy of Sciences, November, 1959, 153 pp.; translated in JPRS: 11,438, December 7, 1961, on p. 141.

[5] Derived as a residual.

[6] Sun Ching-chih, ed., *op. cit.*, p. 149.

[7] *Ibid.*, p. 153.

353

TABLE 5.82 Output of Major Agricultural Products and Livestock in Chekiang Province, 1950, 1952, and 1956-58

Product	1950	1952	1956	1957	1958
Crops thousand tons: [1]					
Grains crops[1]				7,793	
Rice				5,973	
Wheat				257	
Barley				189	
Maize				257	
Horsebeans				88	
Sweet potatoes				825	
Other				206	
Other crops:					
Cotton		20[2]		44[3]	
Hemp			117[3]	155[3]	
Rapeseed			65[3]	68[3]	
Citrus fruits				40[4]	
Tea	8[5]		22[3]	23[6]	
Silkworm cocoons, thousand tons:	8[7]		25[3]	25[7]	
Aquatic products, thousand tons: [8]					
Salt water aquatic products	86	165			
Freshwater aquatic products	10				
Algae	2				
Livestock, thousand head:					
Large animals[9]					1,080
Hogs		2,780[10]	3,734[3]	5,680[3]	

[1] Sun Ching-chi, ed., *Hua-tung ti-ch'u ching-chi ti-li (Economic Geography of East China)*, Peking: Institute of Geography of the Chinese National Academy of Sciences, November 1959, 153 pp.; translated in JPRS: 11,438, December 7, 1961, pp. 215-16.

[2] Wu Hsien, "Speech Delivered at the Fifth Session of the First National People's Congress," *HHPYK*, No. 6 (March 25, 1958) pp. 107-9, reference on p. 108.

[3] Wu Hsien, "Report on the Implementation of the Economic Plan for 1957 in Chekiang Province," *Chekiang kung-jen pao*, Hangchow, January 25, 1958.

[4] Sun Ching-chih, ed,. *op. cit.*, p. 225.

[5] *Ibid.*, p. 224.

[6] *Ibid.*, p. 223.

[7] *Ibid.*, pp. 221-22.

[8] *Ibid.*, pp. 228-30.

[9] *Ibid.*, p. 227.

TABLE 5.83 Output of Major Agricultural Products and Livestock in Fukien Province, 1950, 1952, 1955, 1957, and 1958

Product	1950	1952	1955	1957	1958
Crops, thousand tons:					
Food grains		3,663[1]		4,377[1,2]	
Rice				3,284[2]	
Industrial crops: [3]					
Sugar cane				1,236	
Jute				13.7	
Other crops:					
Tea				6.9[4,5]	9[4]
Fruits				118[6]	
Forest byproducts: [7]					
Dried bamboo shoots, tons	4,145		5,853		
Mushroom, tons	468		435		
Robin, tons	500		7,693		
Bamboo, thousand units	705		1,000		
Dried white fungus hing	16,000		70,000		
Aquatic products, thousand tons			82[8]	282[1]	
Marine aquatic products			70[8]		
Livestock, thousand head					
Hogs				4,138[4]	4,800[4]
Cattle				1,000[1]	

[1] Hou Tsen-ya, "Speech Delivered at the Fifth Session of the First National People's Congress," *Documents of the Fifth Session of the First National Republic of China*, Peking: People's Publishing House, 1958, pp. 622-30.

[2] Sun Ching-chih, ed., *Hua-nan ti-ch'u ching-chi ti-li (Economic Geography of South China)*, Peking: K'o-hsueh ch'u-pan-she, 1959, 147 pp.; translated in JPRS: 14,954, August 24, 1962, p. 378.

[3] *Ibid.*, pp. 385-86.

[4] Liang Ling-kuang (Governor of Fukien), "Fukien Provincial Plan for 1959," *Fukien JP*, Foochow, February 11, 1959, pp. 1-2.

[5] Sun Ching-chih, ed., *op. cit.*, p. 389.

[6] *Ibid.*, p. 392.

[7] *Ibid.*, p. 395.

[8] *Ibid.*, p. 398.

TABLE 5.84 Output of Major Crops and Livestock in Honan
Province, 1956, 1957, and 1959

Product	1956	1957	1959
Crops, thousand tons:			
Food grains		17,300[1]	
Wheat		3,720[1]	
Industrial crops:[2]			
Cotton		180	
Peanuts		234	
Sesame		0.1	
Livestock, thousand head:			
Hogs	3,590[1]	7,460[1]	15,060[3]

[1] Liu Min-pan, "Speech Delivered at the Fifth Session of the
First National Peoples' Congress," *Documents of the Fifth
Session of the First National People's Congress,*
Peking: People's Publishing House, 1958, pp. 655-58.

[2] Yang Wei-p'ing, "Work Report of the Honan Committee of the
Chinese Communist Party to the Third Session of the
First Honan Provincial Congress of the Chinese Communist
Party, on December 24, 1958," *Honan JP,* January 16, 1959,
pp. 1-3.

[3] Chao Wen-fu (Deputy Governor of Honan), "Address to the
Second Session of the Secion Honan Provincial People's
Congress on January 29, 1960," *Honan JP,* March 1, 1960,
pp. 3-4.

TABLE 5.85 Output of Major Crops and Livestock in Hupeh Province, 1949, 1952,
1955-57

Product	1949	1952	1955	1956	1957
Crops thousand tons:					
Food grains			9,400[1]	10,500[1]	10,966[2]
Rice	4,199[3]	5,316[3]			7,556[2]
Wheat	568.5[3]	807.5[3]			1,219[2]
Barley	407[3]	443[3]			477[2]
Corn					597[2]
Millet					116.5[2]
Buckwheat					41.5[2]
Sweet potatoes					447.5[2]
Horse beans					104.5[2]
Garden peas					97.5[2]
Others					340[2]
Industrial crops:					
Cotton	47.5[3]	134[3]	146[1]	200[1]	227[4]
Ramie	2.5[3]	9.5[3]			17.5[4]
Sesame	93.5[3]	117.5[3]			105[4]
Peanuts					138[4]
Rapeseed					53[4]
Other crops					
Tea	1.5[5]				
Livestock, thousand head					12,030[6]

[1] Hai Po, "The Remarkable Year
in the History of Hupeh,"
HHP YK, No. 3 (February 10,
1957), pp. 64-65.

[2] *Ibid.,* pp. 77-78.

[3] *Ibid.,* p. 67.
[4] *Ibid.,* p. 89.
[5] *Ibid.,* p. 99.
[6] *Ibid.,* p. 103.

356

TABLE 5.86 Output of Major Agricultural Products in Hunan Province, 1949, 1952, 1956, and 1957

Product	1949	1952	1956	1957
Crops, thousand tons:				
Food grains		10,258[1]		11,244[1]
Rice	5,671[2]	9,150[1]		9,667[1]
Wheat	252[2]	141[1]		150[1]
Coarse grains		296[1]		429[1]
Barley				68[3]
Corn				138[3]
Kaoliang				29[3]
Millet				10[3]
Buckwheat				26[3]
Horse beans				16[3]
Garden peas				17[3]
Potatoes		660[1]		989[1]
Sweet	203[2]			902[3]
Irish				34[3]
Soybeans		72[1]		90[1]
Industrial crops:				
Cotton	7[2]	27[1]		22[1]
Hemp		3[1]		31[1]
Flax	5[2]	8[1]		9[1]
Sugar cane		162[1]		58[1]
Peanuts		34[1]		38[1]
Rapeseed		90[1]		56[1]
Sesame		3[1]		6[1]
Tobacco				8[4]
Other crops:				
Tea		18[1]		18.3[1]
Forestry products, thousand tons:				
Tung oil		195[1]		22.5[1]
Tea oil		29[1]		47[1]
Aquatic products, thousand tons			41[1]	119[1]
Livestock, thousand head				
Cattle		2,690[1]		3,059[1,4]
Hogs		6,836[1]		10,900[1,4]

[1] Hunan Provincial Statistical Bureau, "Achievements of Huan Province in 1957 National Economic Work," *Hsin Hunan Pao*, Ch'ang-sha, May 4, 1958.

[2] Sun Ching-chih (ed), *Hua-chung ti-ch'u ching-chi ti-li (Economic Geography of Central China*, Peking: K'o-hsueh ch'u-pan-she, December, 1958, 156 pp.; translated in JPRS: 2227-N, Febuary 10, 1960, p. 231.

[3] *Ibid.*, pp. 264-65.

[4] *Ibid.*, p. 279.

[5] *Ibid.*, p. 298.

TABLE 5.87 Output of Major Crops and Livestock in Kiangsi Province, 1949, 1952, 1956, and 1957

Product	1949	1952	1956	1957
Crops, thousand tons:				
Food grains	3,875[1]	5,525[1]		6,832[2]
Rice	(3,626)[3]			6,237[2]
Wheat	(24)[3]			57[2]
Barley				35.5[2]
Buckwheat				52.5[2]
Millet				36.5[2]
Corn				17.5[2]
Horse beans				9[2]
Garden peas				12[2]
Potatoes	(111.8)[3]			364.5[2]
Others				10.5[2]
Soybeans	(47)[3]			155[1]
Industrial crops:				
Cotton	(1.6)[3]	13.6[1]	18.7[4]	26[5]
Jute	(4.4)[3]			29[5]
Ramie	(3.3)[3]			3.5[5]
Peanuts	(18.5)[3]			57.5[5]
Sesame	(25.7)[3]			29.5[5]
Rapeseed	(28)[3]			51.5[5]
Sugar cane				202[5]
Fruits				26[6]
Aquatic products, thousand tons				60[7]
Livestock, thousand head				
Cattle and buffaloes		1,800[1]		2,160[1]
Hogs		2,900[1]	3,100[4]	5,270[4,7]

[1] Liu Chun-hsiu, "Speech Delivered at the Fifth Session of the First National Peoples' Congress," HHPYK, No. 6 (March 25, 1958), pp. 27-30.

[2] Sun Ching-chih, ed., Hua-chung ti-ch'u ching-chi ti-hi, (Economic Geography of Central China) Peking: K'o-hsueh ch'u-pan-she, December, 1958, 156 pp.; translated in JPRS: 2227-N, February 10, 1960, p. 406.

[3] Derived from figures on percentage increase of the output of various crops in 1957 over 1949 (ibid., p. 396).

[4] Huang Hsien (Deputy Governor of Kiangsi), "Report to the First Session of the Second Kiangsi Provincial People's Congress on June 20, 1958," Kiangsi JP, Nanchang, July 4, 1958, p. 3.

[5] Sun Ching-chih, op. cit., p. 421.

[6] Ibid., p. 430.

[7] Ibid., pp. 433-35.

TABLE 5.88 Output of Major Agricultural Products and Livestock in Kwangtung Province, 1949-58

Product	1949	1950	1952	1953	1954	1955	1956	1957	1958
Crops, thousand tons:									
Food Grains	8,000[1]		9,500[2]		10,000[2]	10,900[3]	9,550[8]	12,200[4,5]	16,000[1,4]
Rice			7,000[6]	7,800[6]		9,000[7]			
Industrial crops:									
Jute								43[1,4]	60[1,4]
Peanuts			115[9]		191[10]	175[11]	200[8]	198[1,4]	274[1,4]
Rapeseeds			4[9]			3[12]	5[8]	4[1]	5[1]
Cured tobacco								5[1,4]	7[1,4]
Sugar cane			3,088[9]		3,500[3]	3,890[11]	3,889[8]	5,000[1,4]	6,720[1,4]
Other crops:									
Fruits								344[1]	447[1]
Citrus			40[9]						
Bananas			98[9]						
Pineapples			199[9]						
Silk cocoons, thousand tons							8[13]	9[4]	11[4]
Aquatic products			335[3]					677[14,15]	1,300[14]
Freshwater aquatic products								182[4]	
Livestock, thousand head									
Cattle and buffalo		3,198[16]		3,825[16]		4,590[16]			
Cattle								4,340[17]	
Sheep								2,500	
Hogs	4,140[1,4]	5,881[8]	6,550[3]	7,004[16]		7,270[16]		9,091[1,4,17]	10,764[1,4]

1 Chen Yu, "Report Delivered to the Second Session of the Second Kwangtung Provincial People's Congress," NFJP, Oct. 12, 1959.

2 Liang Jen-tsai, Kuang-tung ching-chi ti-li (Economic Geography of Kwangtung), Peking: K'o-hseh ch'u-pan-she, 1956, p. 25.

3 Ibid., p. 29.

4 Kwangtung Provincial Statistical Bureau, "Communique on the Development of the National Economy in Kwangtung Province in 1958 and the First Half of 1959," Wen-hui pao, Hong Kong, October 5, 1959.

5 Bureau of Agriculture, Kwangtung Province, "Agricultural Production in Kwangtung," TLCS, No. 5 (May, 1959), pp. 205-7, reference on p. 205.

6 NFJP, August 11, 1954.

7 NFJP, August 5, 1956.

8 NFJP, July 27, 1957.

9 Liang Jen-tsai, op. cit., pp. 98-100.

10 NFJP, December 3, 1955.

11 NFJP, December 28, 1955.

12 NFJP, June 16, 1956.

13 NFJP, November 16, 1957.

14 Sun Ching-chi, ed., Hua-nan ti-chu ching-chi ti-li (Economic Geography of South China) Peking: K'o-hsueh ch'u-pan-she, 1959, 147 pp.; translated in JPRS: 14,954, August 24, 1962, pp. 86-87.

15 Ibid. According to Chu Men Chuch, op. cit., the output of aquatic products in 1957 was only 620,000 tons.

16 Liang Jen-tsai, op. cit., p. 33.

17 Sun Ching-chi, ed., op. cit., p. 81.

TABLE 5.89   Output of Major Crops and Livestock in Kwangsi Chuang
Autonomous Region, 1949 and 1956-58

Product	1949	1956	1957	1958
Crops, thousand tons				
Food grains		5,250[1]	5,400[1,2]	7,100[3]
Sugar cane	4,135[4]		8,335[4]	
Oil-bearing crops	63[2]		140[2]	
Livestock, thousand head				
Buffaloes			4,290[5]	
Hogs		3,760[1]	5,560[5]	10,000[6]

[1] Tan Yin-chi (Secretary, CCP of Kwangsi Chuang Autonomous Region), "Speech
Delivered at the Fifth Session of the First National People's Congress,"
HHPYK, No. 6 (March 25, 1958), pp. 26-27.

[2] Sun Ching-chih (ed)., *Hua-nan ti-ch'u ching-chi ti-li (Economic Geography
of China)* Peking: K'o-hsueh ch'u-pan-she, 1959, 147 pp; translated in
JPRS: 14,954, August 24, 1962, p. 244.

[3] Wei Kuo-ch'ing (Governor of Kwangsi), "Government Work Report to the
Second Session of the First People's Congress of Kwangsi Chuang Auto-
onomous Region," *Kwangsi JP*, December 20, 1959.

[4] Sun Ching-chih, ed., *op. cit.*, p. 245.

[5] Wei Kuo-ch'ing, "Government Work Report to the First Session of the
First People's Congress of Kwangsi Chuang Autonomous Region," *Kwangsi
JP*, March 14, 1958, p. 3.

[6] Tan Yin-chi, "The Year of Great Leap Forward," *Min-tzu t'uan-chieh
(Unity of Nationalities)*, No. 1 (January 6, 1959), p. 2.

TABLE 5.90 Output of Major Crops and Livestock in Szechwan Province, 1949 and 1952-58

Product	1949	1952	1953	1954	1955	1956	1957	1958
Crops, thousand tons:								
Food grains								
Rice	9,232[3]	16,785[1]	18,165[1]	19,750[1]	20,230[1]	22,255[1]	22,979[2]	
Wheat	995[3]	10,503.5[3]					13,687[2]	
Corn	1,501.5[3]	897.5[3]				1,570[4]	1,638[2]	
Barley							2,134.5[2]	
Sweet potatoes	1,730[3]	2,029.5[3]					3,182.5[2]	
Peas							699[2]	
Beans							527[2]	
Others							817[2]	
Soybeans							269[5]	
Industrial crops:								
Cotton	15[3]	41.5[3]					70[6]	90[7]
Ramie							9[6]	
Hemp							9.5[6]	
Tobacco							52[6]	
Rapeseed	153.5[3]	189.5[3]					276.5[6]	
Peanuts	73.5[8]	90.3[8]					123.5[6]	
Sesame	7.03[8]	7.1[8]					7[6]	
Sugar cane	560.5[3]	1,259[3]					1,722.5[6]	
Livestock, thousand head:								
Oxen and cows[9]	3,923	4,706					4,858	
Buffaloes[9]	2,362	2,187					2,370	
Horses[9]	266	446					391	
Mules[9]	36	69					49	
Asses[9]	15	18					20	
Goats[9]	1,815	2,055					3,962	
Sheep[9]	1,484	1,654					1,864	
Hogs	10,190[3]	13,780[1,3]	17,130[1]	21,430[1]	19,000[1]	20,000[1]	25,000[3]	

1 Wang Kuang-wei, "Several Problems of Developing Agriculture," *HH*, No. 17 (September 3, 1957), pp. 25-28, reference on p. 25.

2 Sun Ching-chih, ed., *Hsi-nan ti-ch'u ching-chi ti-li (Economic Geography of Southwest China)*, Peking: K'o-hsueh ch'u-pan-she, 1960, 218 pp.; translated in JPRS: 15,069, August 31, 1962, p. 103.

3 *Ibid.*, p. 76.

4 Ye A. Afanas'yeskiy, *Szechwan*, Moscow: Publishing House of Oriental Literature, 1960, 267 pp.; translated in JPRS: 15,306, September 17, 1962, p. 249.

5 Sun Ching-chih, ed., *op. cit.*, p. 123

6 *Ibid.*, p. 125.

7 *Ibid.*, p. 126.

8 Afanas'yeskiy, *op. cit.*, p. 262.

9 *Ibid.*, p. 76.

TABLE 5.91   Output of Major Crops and Livestock in Kweichow Province, 1949, 1952, 1957, and 1958

Product	1949	1952	1957	1958
Crops, thousand tons:				
Food grains			5,255	
Rice	2,111	2,374	3,360	
Wheat	33	51	203	
Corn	601	740	1,116	
Barley			128	
Sweet potatoes			207	
Potatoes			112	
Oats			29	
Broad beans			21	
Peas			25	
Others			106	
Soybeans			115	
Industrial crops:				
Cotton	1.5	2.5	3	
Foriegn			1	
Native			2	
Flax			3	
Sugar cane			88	
Rapeseed	24.5	36.5	82.5	
Peanuts			10	
Tobacco	13	16	49.5	50.5
Cured	6		39	
Dried			11	
Livestock, thousand head:				
Buffaloes	700	760	920	
Cows	1,540	1,700	2,500	
Horses	210	240	310	
Hogs	2,880	3,600	6,150	

Source: Sun Ching-chih, ed, *Hsi-nan ti-ch'u ching-chi ti-li (Economic Geography of Southwest China)*, Peking: K'o-hsueh ch'u-pan-she, 1960, 218 pp.; translated in JPRS: 15,069, August 31, 1962, pp. 348, 361, 370, 372, and 377.

TABLE 5.92 Output of Major Crops and Livestock in Yunnan Province, 1949 and 1952-57

Product	1949	1952	1953	1954	1955	1956	1957
Crops, thousand tons:							
Food grains							
Rice	2,219.5[3]	4,150[1]	4,400[1]	4,900[1]	5,200[1]	6,250[1]	6,250[2]
Wheat	161.5[3]	2,566[3]					3,562[2]
Corn		196[3]					308.5[2]
Barley							1,336[2]
Yams							141.5[2]
Potatoes							58.5[2]
Horse beans							282.5[2]
Peas							203.5[2]
Others							79.5[2]
							233[2]
Industrial crops:							
Cotton	0.5[3]	2.5[3]					3.5[4]
Hemp							4.5[4]
Sugar cane	254[3]	304.5[3]					754.5[4]
Rapeseed	23[3]	21[3]					47[4]
Peanuts	6.5[3]	8.5[3]					30.5[4]
Tobacco	2[3]	5.5[3]					30.5[4]
Native tobacco							6[4]
Other crops							
Tea	2[5]						
Livestock, thousand head							
Large animals	1,850[3]	2,080[3]					5,340[6]
Oxen	950[3]	1,080[3]					3,030[6]
Buffaloes							1,390[6]
Small animals							11,230[6]
Hogs	2,730[3]	3,710[3]					6,520[6]

1 Editorial, *CHCC*, "The Necessity of Studying the Concrete Situation of Various Regions in Compiling Agricultural Plans," *CHCC*, No. 3 (March 9, 1957), pp. 2-3, reference on p. 2. It is not clear whether the output of soybeans was excluded from these estimates.

2 Sun Ching-chih, ed., *Hsi-nan ti-ch'u ching-chi ti-li* (*Economic Geography of Southwest China*), Peking: K'o-hsüeh ch'u-pan-she, 1960, 218 pp.; translated in JPRS: 15,069, August 31, 1962, p. 522.

3 *Ibid.*, p. 509.   5 *Ibid.*, p. 544.

4 *Ibid.*, p. 531.   6 *Ibid.*, pp. 558-59.

TABLE 5.93 Composition of the Gross Value of Agricultural Output at Constant Prices, 1949-59, Millions of Yuan

Sector	1949[1]	1950[1]	1951[1]	1952[2]	1953[2]	1954[2]	1955[2]	1956[3]	1957[1]	1958[1]	1959[4]
Gross value of agricultural output at 1952 prices	32,590	38,360	41,970	48,390	49,910	51,570	55,540	58,290	60,350		
Crop and animal raising				38,500	39,200	40,600	43,700	46,200			
Crops								39,800			
Animal raising								6,400			
Subsidiary work				9,900	10,700	10,900	11,800	12,100			
Processing for own use				7,600	8,300	8,400	8,800				
Work for others				2,300	2,400	2,500	3,000				
Gross value of agricultural output at 1957 prices									53,700	67,100	78,300

[1] *TGY*, p. 118.

[2] Chao Ch'ing-hsin, "Seasonal Variations of the Market after Agricultural Cooperativization," *CCYC*, No. 5, (October 17, 1956), pp. 19-38, reference on p. 25.

[3] Teng Shuang, "Introducing the National Agricultural Exhibition," *HHPYK*, No. 8 (April 25, 1957), pp. 91-98, and *1956 JMST*, p. 470.

[4] *Press Communique on the Development of the National Economy in 1959*, Peking: Jen-min jih-pao ch'u-pan-she, January, 1960, p. 1.

364

TABLE 5.94 Gross Value of Agricultural Output at Constant Prices of Various Provinces, 1949-59 Million of Yuan

Province	1949	1950	1951	1952	1953	1954	1955	1956	1957	1958	1959
Shansi[1]						1,400					
Inner Mongolia[2]	659	688	714	1,063	1,141	1,242	1,186	1,436	1,225	1,666	
Liaoning[3]	1,097			1,690			1,871	2,180	2,958	3,697	
Kirin						1,360[4]			2,501[5]	3,269[5]	3,831[6]
Heilungkiang				1,960[1]		1,789[8]			2,300[7]	3,750[9]	
Kansu[10]						857					
Chinghai[11]											
Sinkiang[12]				560					229		
Shantung[13]									901	1,290	
Kiangsu[14]									4,170	5,280	
Anhwei						1,581[15]			3,782	6,133	
Chekiang[17]				1,910	1,922	2,170				8,121[16]	
Fukien[18]						982					
Honan[19]						3,153					
Kiangsi	934[20]			1,542[21]					1,937[21]	2,800[25]	
Kwangtung				2,690[23]					3,400[24]	4,380[24]	
Szechuan						4,964[25]			5,680[26]	9,650[26]	
Kweichow[27]						789					
Yunnan[28]						1,339					

[a] Figures in this table are given in 1952 prices for 1949-57 and in 1957 prices for 1958 and 1959.

[1] Economic Research Institute, Chinese National Academy of Sciences, *Nation-wide Survey Data on Individual Handicrafts in 1954*, Peking: Sheng-huo, tu-shu, hsin chih san-lien shu-tien, 1957, p. 94

[2] *NMKTC*, p. 143

[3] Liaoning Provincial Statistical Bureau, 'Tremendous Changes in Liaoning's Rural Outlook during the Past Decade," in *Liaoning shih-nien* (*Liaoning in One Decade*), Shenyang: Liaoning jen-min ch'u-pan-she, 1960.

[4] Economic Research Institute, Chineses National Academy of Sciences, *op. cit.*, p. 47.

[5] Kirin Provincial Statistical Bureau, "Work Report of the Heilungkiang Provin-

Results of the Implementation of the National Economic Plan for 1958 in Kirin Province," *Kirin JP*, March 18, 1959, pp. 1-2

[6] Li Yu-wen (Governor of Kirin), "Work Report to the Third Session of the Second Kirin Provincial People's Congress on May 23, 1960," *Kirin JP*, May 25, 1960, pp. 2-3.

[7] Yang I-chen, "Report at the First Session of the Second Heilungkiang Provincial People's Congress on August 28, 1958, *Heilungkiang JP*, Harbin, September 19, 1958.

[8] Economic Research Institute, *op. cit.*, p. 52

[9] Ou-yang chin, "Work Report of the Heilungkiang Provin-

TABLE 5.94 (Continued)

cial People's Council for 1958," *Heilungkiang JP*, Harbin, January 25, 1959, pp. 1-3.

10 Economic Research Institute, Chinese National Academy of Sciences, *op. cit.*, p. 240.

11 Yuan Jen-yuan, "Work Report to the First Session of Second Chinghai Provincial People's Congress," *Chinghai JP*, July 4, 1958, pp. 1-2.

12 Sai Fu-ting, "Work Report to the First Session of the Second People's Congress in Sinkiang-Uigher Autonomous Region on January 22, 1959," *Sinkiang JP*, January 31, 1959, pp. 2-3.

13 Pai Ju-ping (Deputy Governor of Shantung), "Report on the Readjustment of Princpal Targets of the 1959 National Economic Plan and the Further Development of the Production Increase and Economy Campaign in Shantung—Delivered to the Fifth Session of the Second Shantung Provincial People's Congress on September 14, 1959," *Ta-chung JP*, September 16, 1959.

14 Liu Shun-yuen, "Work Report of the Kiangsu Provincial Committee of the Chinese Communist Party to the Third Session of the Third Provincial Congress on January 29, 1959," *HHPYK*, No. 7 (April 10, 1959), pp. 15-22, reference on p. 15.

15 Economic Research Institue, Chinese National Academy of Sciences, *op. cit.*, p. 118.

16 Tseng Hsi-sheng (Governor of Anhwei), "Continue to Advance under the Banner of the General Line," *Anhwei JP*, Hofei, February 12, 1959, pp. 1-3.

17 Economic Research Institue, Chinese National Academy of

Sciences, *op. cit.*, p. 106.

18 *Ibid.*, p. 130.

19 *Ibid.*, pp. 157-58.

20 Liu Chun-hsin, "Speech Delivered to the Fifth Session of the First National People's Congress," *HHPYK*, No. 6 (March 25, 1958), pp. 27-32.

21 Huang Hsien (Deputy Governor of Kiangsi), "Report on the Draft of the Second Five-Year Plan of Kiangsi Province for the Development of the National Economy," *Kiangsi JP*, Nanchang, July 3, 1958, p. 2

22 Yang Shang-kuei, "Report to the Third Session of the Fifth Provincial Congress of the Chinese Communist Party on the 1958 Great Leap Forward in Kiangsi, on January 7, 1959," *Kiangsi JP*, Nanchang, January 26, 1959.

23 Ho Hsian-yi, "Speech Delivered to the Fifth Session of the First National People's Congress," *HHPYK*, No. 5 (March 10, 1958), pp. 63-64.

24 Kwangtung Provincial Statistical Bureau, "Communique on the Development of the National Economy in Kwangtung Province in 1958 and the First Half of 1959," *Wen-hui-pao*, Hong Kong, October 5, 1959.

25 Economic Research Institute, Chinese National Academy of Sciences, *op. cit.*, p. 205.

26 Li Ping (Deputy Governor of Szechuan), "Report on the Drafts of the 1959 Economic Plan for Szechuan Province," *Szechuan JP*, Chengtu, June 25, 1959, p. 2

27 Economic Research Institute, Chinese National Academy of Sciences, *op. cit.*, p. 222

28 *Ibid.*, pp. 214-15.

TABLE 5.95 Development of State Farms, 1950-55

Size	1950	1952	1953	1954	1955
Number of farms	1,215	2,336	2,376	2,415	2,242
Area cultivated, thousand hectares	155	247	251	295	395
Employees and workers, thousand persons	43	97	111	137	134
Employees	19	28	33	34	29
Workers	24	69	78	103	105
Number of tractors	1,106	1,532	1,627	2,235	2,839
Number of harvesting combines	155	275	352	430	657
Draft animals, thousand head	19	42	50	52	58

Note: The state farms in this table include both mechanized and nonmechanized farms operated by central and local governments. The decrease in the number of state farms in 1955 was due to amalgamation of some farms and to conversion of some others into experiment stations and ranches.

Sources: SSB, Communique on the Results of the Implementation of the National Economic Plan for 1955 (with Economic Statistical Abstract), Peking: T'ung-chi ch'u-pan-she, 1956, p. 35.

TABLE 5.96 Development of State Mechanized Farms, 1950-55

Size	1950	1952	1953	1954	1955
Number of farm	36	50	59	97	106
Area cultivated, thousand hectares	89.3	135.8	141.3	185.5	269.3
Number of employees and workers, thousand persons	11.2	24.9	28.8	56.6	57.2
Employees	4.5	5.9	7.5	13.7	12.7
Workers	7.7	19.0	21.3	42.9	44.5
Number of tractors, standard units	1,160	1,532	1,627	2,235	2,839
Number of harvesting combines	155	275	352	430	657
Draft animals, thousand head	4.1	8.3	7.9	13.3	13.1

Note: The state mechanized farms in this table are those operated by central and local governments.

Source: SSB, Communique on the Results of the Implementation of the National Economic Plan for 1955 (with Economic Statistical Abstract), Peking: T'ung chi ch'u-pan-she, 1956, p. 36.

TABLE 5.97 Development of State Farms and Ranches under the Ministry of State Farms and Reclamation, 1949-58

Size	Unit	1949	1952	1957	1958
Number of farms		18	404	710	1,442
Area cultivated:	Thousand Mou	460	3,820	15,380	34,080
	Thousand hectares	31	255	1,025	2,272
Area reclaimed:	Thousand Mou	--	2,240	4,060	12,430
	Thousand hectares	--	149	271	829
Area used for production,	Thousand Mou	460	8,480	17,990	39,820
Number of workers and and employees	Thousand persons	4	390	500	990
Number of tractors	Standard units	401	1,792	10,177	16,955
Number of harvesting combines		13	283	1,537	1,982
Number of trucks		28	229	3,444	4,284

Source: TGY, p. 134.

TABLE 5.98 Development of State Farms in the Inner Mongolia Autonomous Region, 1949, 1952, 1957, and 1958

Size	1949	1952	1957	1958
Number of farms	2	8	19	21
Number of tractors, standard tractors	--	18.3	122.0	180.0
Number of grain combines	--	2	17	27
Number of heavy trucks	--	2	5	9
Productive area, thousand *mou*	12.5	48.2	1,054.2	2,490.6
Area Cultivated, thousand *mou*	12.5	36.1	199.7	375.8
Area reclaimed, thousand *mou*	--	--	18.2	105.4
Number of workers	80	409	2,047	3,301

Note: Figures for tractors are calculated at 15 horsepower for a standard tractor.

Source: *NMKTC*, p. 158.

TABLE 5.99 Development of State Livestock Farms in the Inner Mongolia Autonomous Region, 1949, 1952, 1957, 1958

Size	1949	1952	1957	1958
Number of farms	3	16	38	55
Area, thousand *mou*	2,842	8,047	22,604	27,817
Grazing area, thousand *mou*	--	8,022	17,373	20,885
Number of livestock, head	2,533	22,645	114,711	169,312
Number of workers	107	582	4,019	8,150

Source: *MNKTC*, p. 185.

TABLE 5.100 Development of State Farms in Shantung Province, 1955-56

Type of farm	Unit	1955	1956
State farms			
Number of state farms			137
Cultivated area:	Thousand *mou*	328	486
	Thousand hectares	21.8	32.4
Number of tractors,	Standard units	82.7	154.3
Number of grain harvesting machines		11	13
Mechanized state farms:			
Number			6
Cultivated area:	Thousand *mou*		65
	Thousand hectares		4.3
Number of tractors,	Standard units		60.6
Number of grain harvesting machines			10

Source: Shantung Provincial Statistical Bureau, "Communique on the Results of the Implementation of the National Economic Plan for 1956 in Shantung Province," *Ta-chung JP*, August 9, 1957, p. 3.

TABLE 5.101 Agricultural and Meteorological Services 1949–58

Service	1949	1950	1951	1952	1953	1954	1955	1956	1957	1958
Agricultural:										
Agricultural technical stations		10	43	232	3,632	4,549	7,997	14,230	13,669	
Livestock breeding stations		148	274	389	578	308	454	545	821	
Veterinary stations		251	576	1,005	1,734	1,343	1,266	2,257	2,930	
Steppe development stations		--	--	1	7	5	4	9	23	
Meteorological:										
Meteorological observations	101	158	191	317	357	511	715	1,377	1,647	2,755
Meteorological stations and weather forecasting stations	5	18	19	34	43	55	67	99	110	230
	96	140	172	283	314	456	648	1,278	1,537	2,525

Source: *TGY*, pp. 136 and 137.

TABLE 5.102 Meteorological Services in Inner Mongolia Autonomous Region, 1949–58

Service	1949	1950	1951	1952	1953	1954	1955	1956	1957	1958
Total	4	4	4	14	16	28	36	87	97	247
Meteorological stations	--	--	--	1	1	3	4	5	5	10
Meterological and weather stations	4	4	4	13	15	25	32	82	92	237

Source: *NMKTC*, p. 161.

TABLE 5.103 Number of Tractors Used for Farming 1949-59, Standard Units[a]

Area	1949	1950	1951	1952	1953	1954	1955	1956	1957	1958	1959
National total	401[1]	1,286[1]	1,410[1]	2,006[1]	2,719[1]	5,061[1]	8,094[1]	19,367[1]	24,629[1]	45,330[1]	59,000[2]
Inner Mongolia Autonomous Region[3]		30.6	30.6	74.2	89.0	227.6	259.6	608.0	814.8	1,292.6	

[a] A standard tractor is one with 15 horsepower.

[1] TGY, p. 135.

[2] Chen Cheng-jen, "Speeding Up Technical Transformation of Agriculture," Hung-ch'i, No. 4 (February 16, 1960).

[3] NMKTC, p. 159.

TABLE 5.104 Cooperativization of Agriculture by Farming Households, 1950-56 Thousand Households[a]

Farming household	1950[1]	1951[1]	1952[1]	1953[1]	1954[1]	1955[1]	1956[2]
National total	105,536		113,683	116,325	117,331	119,201	120,000
Those joining agricultural producer cooperatives		b	59	275	2,297	16,921	117,829
Advanced type		b	1.8	2.1	12	40	107,422
Elementary type		b	57	273	2,285	16,881	10,407
Those joining mutual-aid teams	11,313		45,364	45,637	68,478	60,389	--
Full year			11,448	13,329	30,713	32,843	--
Seasonal			33,916	32,308	37,765	27,546	--
Those joining cooperatives and teams	11,313	21,002	45,423	45,912	70,775	77,310	107,829

[a] The households joining cooperatives and teams refer to only those that have participated in production during the year and in the sharing of the autumn harvest product.

[b] In 1950, 32 households join advanced agricultural producer cooperatives and 187 joined preliminary ones, and in 1951 the corresponding figures are 30 and 1,588 households.

[1] SSB, Communique on the Results of the Implementation of the National Economic Plan for 1955, (with Economic Statistical Abstract), Peking: T'ung chi ch'u-pan-she, 1956, p. 37.

[2] SSB, "Communique on the Results of the Implementation of the National Economic Plan for 1956," JMJP, August 2, 1957, and TGY, p. 37.

TABLE 5.105 Number of Agricultural Producer Cooperatives, 1950-56

Agricultural producer cooperatives	1950[1]	1952[1]	1953[1]	1954[1]	1955[1]	1956[2]
Total	19	3,644	15,068	114,366	633,742	760,000
Advanced type	1	10	15	201	529	746,000
Elementary type	18	3,634	15,053	114,165	633,213	14,000

Note: Except for 1956, the number of agricultural producer cooperatives pertains to the end of autumn harvest. For 1956, the number pertains to the end of the year.

[1] SSB, *Communique on the Results of the Implementation of the National Economic for 1955 (with Economic Statistical Abstract)*, Peking: T'ung-chi ch'u-pan-she, 1956, p. 38.

[2] "Teng Tzu-hui's Report at the National Conference of Model Agricultural Workers," *JMJP*, February 22, 1957, and Chen Cheng-jen, "The Problems of Agricultural Cooperation and Production," *HHPYK*, No. 7 (April 1957), pp. 20-26.

TABLE 5.106 Development of the People's Communes in 1958

Size	End of August	Early September	Mid September	Late September	End of December
Number of people's communes	8,730	12,824	16,989	26,425	26,578
Number of peasant households joining people's communes, thousands	37,780	59,790	81,220	121,940	123,250
Percentage of peasant households joining people's communes to total number of peasant household	30.4	48.1	65.3	98.0	99.1
Average number of households in each commune	4,328	4,662	4,781	4,614	4,637

Source: *TGY*, p. 43.

TABLE 6.1 Length of Railway, Highway, Water, and Air Traffic Lines, 1949-59, Kilometers

Route	1949[1]	1950[1]	1951[1]	1952[1]	1953[1]	1954[1]	1955[1]	1956[1]	1957[1]	1958[1]	1959[2]
Railways	21,989	22,512	23,352	24,512	25,072	25,873	27,171	29,237	29,862	31,193	
Highways	80,768	99,600	114,428	126,675	137,103	146,138	167,282	226,318	254,624	400,000	480,000
Inland waterways	73,615	n.a.	n.a.	95,025	n.a.	n.a.	99,938	103,619	144,101	150,000	160,000
Routes navigable by steamboats	24,182	n.a.	n.a.	30,508	n.a.	n.a.	31,685	38,304	39,194	40,000	
Civil air routes	--	11,387	10,497	13,123	13,971	15,243	15,511	19,082	26,445	32,995	

[1] TGY, pp. 144-45.   [2] NCNA release, February 19, 1960.

TABLE 6.2 Length of Railway and Highway Traffic Lines in National Minority Areas, 1949, 1952, 1957, and 1958, Kilometers

Route	1949	1952	1957	1958
Railways	3,511	3,787	5,486	6,353
Highways	11,430	25,648	65,408	94,879

Source: TGY, p. 160.

TABLE 6.3 Length of Railway, Highway, Water, and Air Traffic Lines in Inner Mongolia Autonomous Region, 1947-57, Kilometers

Route	1947	1949	1950	1951	1952	1953	1954	1955	1956	1957	1958
Railways	1,839	1,839	1,839	1,839	1,856	1,927	2,315	2,377	2,571	3,134	3,508
Highways	1,974	2,394	3,259	4,037	4,821	5,495	6,253	8,325	11,036	13,020	18,020
Inland waterways	879	879	879	879	879	879	879	879	879	829	829
Routes navigable by steamboats								480	480	522	575
Civil air routes											1,248

Note: Railway mileage does not include forest lines. During 1958, 510 km of narrow-gauge tracks for forest railways were laid in the region.

Source: NMKTC, p. 197

372

TABLE 6.4 Freight and Passenger Transport, 1949-59

Type of transport	1949[1]	1950[1]	1951[1]	1952[1]	1953[1]	1954[1]	1955[1]	1956[1]	1957[1]	1958[1]	1959[2]
Freight transport:											
Volume of goods carried, thousand tons	67,130	115,690	135,060	168,590	212,270	264,670	278,430	372,150	411,710	633,760	542,000
By railways	55,890	99,830	110,830	132,170	161,310	192,880	193,760	246,050	274,200	381,090	
By motor vehicles	5,790	9,210	14,120	22,100	30,940	43,030	48,960	79,130	83,730	176,300	
By ships and barges	5,430	6,650	10,110	14,320	20,010	28,750	35,700	46,960	53,770	76,360	
Freight turnover million ton-km	22,980	42,690	59,340	71,540	93,010	113,830	125,120	152,060	172,930	236,400	
By railways	18,400	39,410	51,560	60,160	78,140	93,240	98,150	120,350	134,590	185,520	
By motor vehicles	250	380	570	770	1,300	1,940	2,520	3,490	3,940	6,960	
By ships and barges	4,310	2,900	7,210	10,610	13,570	18,640	24,440	28,210	34,390	43,910	
By airplanes		0.82	n.a.	2.43	n.a.	n.a.	n.a.	n.a.	8.25	13.31	
Passenger transport:											
Passengers carried, thousands	134,940	200,990	219,860	240,350	350,010	367,350	361,250	495,860	622,710	735,620	
By railways	102,970	156,910	160,370	163,520	228,610	232,860	208,010	252,110	312,620	345,690	
Passenger turnover, million passenger-km	15,410	23,900	26,850	24,670	34,820	36,900	35,190	46,380	49,490	57,060	
By railways	13,000	21,240	23,050	20,060	28,170	29,470	26,740	34,380	36,130	40,920	
By airplane		9.78	n.a.	24.09	n.a.	n.a.	n.a.	n.a.	79.87	108.99	

Note: Transport by human and animal power is not included.

1 Compiled from *TGY*, pp. 146, 148, 150, and 152.
2 NCNA release, January 23, 1960.

373

TABLE 6.5 Development of Railway Transportation, 1949-59

Transport	1949[1]	1950[1]	1951[1]	1952[1]	1953[1]	1954[1]	1955[1]	1956[1]	1957[1]	1958[1]	1959[2]
Length of railway lines, km	21,989	22,512	23,352	24,518	25,072	25,873	27,171	29,237	29,862	31,193	
Freight carried: By railways Volume of goods, thousand tons	55,890	99,830	110,830	132,170	161,310	192,880	193,760	246,050	274,200	381,090	542,000
Freight turnover, million ton-km	18,400	39,410	51,560	60,160	78,140	93,240	98,150	120,350	134,590	185,520	
Passengers carried: Number of passengers, thousands	102,970	156,910	160,370	163,520	228,610	232,860	208,010	252,110	312,620	345,690	
Passenger turnover, million passenger-km	13,000	21,240	23,050	20,060	28,170	29,470	26,740	34,380	36,130	40,920	

[1] Compiled from TGY, pp. 144, 146, 148, and 150.
[2] NCNA release, January 23, 1960.

TABLE 6.6 Development of Highway Transportation, 1949-59

Transport	1949[1]	1950[1]	1951[1]	1952[1]	1953[1]	1954[1]	1955[1]	1956[1]	1957[1]	1958[1]	1959[2]
Length of highway lines, km	80,768	99,600	114,428	126,675	137,103	146,138	167,282	226,318	254,624	400,000	480,000
Freight carried: By motor vehicles Volume of goods, thousand tons	5,790	9,210	14,120	22,100	30,940	43,030	48,960	79,130	83,730	176,300	
Freight turnover, million ton-km	250	380	570	770	1,300	1,940	2,520	3,490	3,940	6,960	

[1] Compiled from *TGY*, pp. 144, 146, and 148.
[2] NCNA release, February 19, 1960.

TABLE 6.7 Development of Highway Transport in Inner Mongolia Autonomous Region, 1952-58

Transport	1952	1953	1954	1955	1956	1957	1958
Highway mileage, km	4,821	5,495	6,253	8,325	11,036	13,020	18,020
Freight carried: Volume of goods, thousand tons	278.3	2,262.3	4,704.7	9,283.0	14,636.5	14,794.8	23,424.3
Freight turnover, thousand ton-km	22,136	67,775	121,194	168,093	162,050	202,706	296,375
Passengers carried: Number of persons, thousand persons	153.9	380.9	569.1	849.6	1,282.5	1,859.5	1,775.9
Passenger turnover, thousand passenger-km	18,627	43,451	61,846	84,880	116,800	148,886	137,377

Sources: Compiled from *NMKTC*, pp. 197, 204, and 206.

TABLE 6.8 Development of Water Transportation, 1949-59 [a]

Type of transport	1949	1950	1951	1952	1953	1954	1955	1956	1957	1958	1959
TGY data: [1]											
Length of inland waterways, km:	73,615	n.a.	n.a.	95,025	n.a.	n.a.	99,938	103,619	144,101	150,000	160,000
Routes navigable by steamboats	24,182	n.a.	n.a.	30,508	n.a.	n, a.	31,685	38,304	39,194	40,000	
Freight carried by ships and barges:											
Volume of goods, thousand tons	5,430	6,650	10,110	14,320	20,010	28,750	35,700	46,960	53,770	76,360	
Freight turnover, million ton-km	4,310	2,900	7,210	10,610	13,570	18,640	24,440	28,210	34,390	43,910	
Data from SSB annual communiques: [2]											
Volume of goods carried by ships and barges, thousand tons											
Coast	828	n.a.	n.a.	5,765	5,925	9,907	10,450				
Inland waterways	4,504	n.a.	n.a.	9,407	15,338	20,476	26,322				
Yangtze and Sungari	2,176	n.a.	n.a.	4,883	6,551	8,634					
Other rivers	2,328	n.a.	n.a.	4,524	8,787	11,842					

TABLE 6.8 (Continued)

Type of transport	1949	1950	1951	1952	1953	1954	1955	1956	1957	1958	1959
Freight turn-over carried by ships and barges, million ton-km											
Coast[b]	1,677	n.a.	n.a.	3,628	5,631	7,891	10,425				
Inland waterways											
Yangtze and Sungari	1,129	n.a.	n.a.	2,678	3,968	5,505					
Other rivers	548	n.a.	n.a.	950	1,663	2,386					

[a] Freight carried by junks is not included.

[b] Data on coastal freight turnover were originally given in ton-nautical miles, and have been converted into ton-kilometers at the rate of 1.853 km per international nautical mile.

1 *TGY* data: 1949-58: Compiled from *TGY*, pp. 144, 146, and 148; 1959: NCNA release, February 19, 1960.

2 Data from SSB annual communiques: SSB, *Communique on the Development of the National Economy and the Results of the Implementation of the State Plan for 1954*, Peking: T'ung-chi ch'u-pan-she, 1955, p. 30; and SSB, *Communique on the Results of the Implementation of the National Economic Plan for 1955*, Peking: T'ung-chi ch'u-pan-she, 1956, p. 39.

TABLE 6.9 Development of Water Transportation in Inner Mongolia Autonomous Region, 1952-58

Type of transport	1952	1953	1954	1955	1956	1957	1958
Inner waterway mileage, km	879	879	879	879	879	879	829
Routes navigable by steamboats				480	480	522	575
Freight carried:							
Volume of goods, thousand tons	56.2	56.6	86.1	119.0	140.5	116.7	79.7
Freight turnover, thousand ton-km	21,241	21,169	26,565	36,760	40,426	34,359	14,395

Sources: Compiled from *NMKTC*, pp. 197, 204, and 206.

TABLE 6.10 Development of Civil Aviation, 1950-58

Type of transport	1950	1951	1952	1953	1954	1955	1956	1957	1958
Length of civil air routes, km[1]	11,387	10,497	13,123	13,971	15,243	15,511	19,082	26,445	32,995
Freight[a]									
Volume of goods, tons	767[2]	n.a.	2,047[3]	3,607[3]	4,734[3]	4,711[3]	n.a.		
Freight turnover, thousand ton-km	820[4]	n.a.	2,430[4]	4,466[5]	5,602[5]	5,143[5]	n.a.	8,250[4]	13,310[4]
Passenger turnover, thousand passenger-km[4]	9,780	n.a.	24,090	n.a.	n.a.	n.a.	n.a.	79,870	108,990
Total flight hours for industrial and agricultural purposes, hours[4]			959	n.a.	n.a.	n.a.	n.a.	9,168	17,845

[a] Including mails.

1 *TGY*, pp. 144.

2 SSB, *Communique on the Development of the National Economy and the Results of the Implementation of the State Plan for 1954*. Peking: T'ung-chi ch'u-pan-she, 1955, p. 31.

3 *Ibid.*, and SSB, *Communique on the Results of the Implementation of the National Economic Plan for 1955*. Peking: T'ung-chi ch'u-pan-she, 1956, p. 40.

4 *TGY*, p. 152.

5 SSB, *1955 Communique*, *op. cit.*

TABLE 6.11 Distribution of Freight Turnover by Ownership of Transport Enterprises, 1949-57

		Percentage distribution, percent[1]			Absolute amount, million ton-km			
Year	Total	State enterprises	State-private joint enterprises	Private enterprises	Total[2]	State enterprises[3]	State-private joint enterprises[3]	Private enterprises[3]
	(1)	(2)	(3)	(4)	(5)	(6)	(7)	(8)
1949	100.0	88.5	--	11.5	22,980	(20,337)	--	(2,643)
1950	100.0	95.3	--	4.7	42,690	(40,684)	--	(2,006)
1951	100.0	94.7	--	5.3	59,340	(56,195)	--	(3,145)
1952	100.0	95.8	0.7	3.5	71,540	(68,535)	(501)	(2,504)
1953	100.0	95.8	1.3	2.9	93,010	(89,104)	(1,209)	(2,697)
1954	100.0	95.3	3.1	1.6	113,830	(108,480)	(3,529)	(1,821)
1955	100.0	94.8	4.6	0.6	125,120	(118,614)	(5,756)	(750)
1956	100.0	99.3	0.7	--	152,060	(150,996)	(1,064)	--
1957	100.0	99.7	0.3	--	172,930	(172,411)	(518)	--

Note: Figures in this table do not include the freight turnover of wooden junks, animal-drawn carts, wheelbarrows, and other vehicles that are not mechanically operated.

[1] TGY, p. 41.
[2] TGY, p. 148.
[3] Derived from multiplying total amount by corresponding percentages.

TABLE 6.12   Distribution of Freight Turnover Carried by Barges, Ships, and
Motor Vehicles, by Ownership of Transport Enterprise, 1952-56,
Million Ton-km

Ownership	1952[1]	1953[1]	1954[1]	1955[1]	1956[2]
Coastal and inland-waterway steam barges and ships	8,642	10,286	15,936	18,823	21,500
State enterprises (central and local)	5,392	6,636	10,991	12,730	n. a.
State-private joint enterprises	555	1,261	3,540	5,765	n. a.
Private enterprises	2,695	2,389	1,405	328	n. a.
Highway motor vehicles	678	1,182	1,867	2,517	3,500
Local state enterprises	339	647	1,307	1,958	n. a.
State-private joint enterprises	4	11	37	101	n. a.
Transportation cooperatives	--	--	--	6	n. a.
Private enterprises	335	524	523	452	n. a.
Total	9,320	11,468	17,803	21,340	25,000
State and joint enterprises	6,290	8,555	15,875	20,554	19,500
Transportation cooperatives	--	--	--	6	4,250
Private enterprises	3,030	2,913	1,928	780	1,250

[1] SSB, *Communique on the Results of the Implementation of the National Economic Plan for 1955, (with Economic Statistical Abstract)*, Peking: T'ung-chi ch'u-pan-she, p. 41.

[2] SSB, ''Communique on the Results of the Implementation of the National Economic Plan for 1956,'' *JMJP*, August 2, 1957.

TABLE 6.13   Percentage Distribution of the Total Freight Turnover in Inner
Mongolia Autonomous Region, by Ownership of Transport
Enterprises, 1952-57

Year	Total (1)	State enterprises (2)	Transportation cooperatives (3)	Private enterprises (4)
1952	100.0	20.7		79.3
1953	100.0	20.3		79.7
1954	100.0	20.5		79.5
1955	100.0	30.2		68.8
1956	100.0	42.1	30.5	27.4
1957	100.0	44.9	49.4	5.7

Source: *NMKTC*, p. 51.

TABLE 6.14 Major Indicators of Railway Freight Transportation, 1949-58

Indicator	1949[1]	1950[2]	1952[1]	1956[2]	1957[1]	1958[1]
Average daily run per freight locomotive, km	308.7		396.8	363.2	366.0	391.0
Average gross weight hauled per freight locomotive, tons	1,011.2	1,015.7	1,245.3	1,513.1	1,520.2	1,704.0
Average daily efficiency per freight locomotive, thousand ton-km	295.0		434.0		477.0	600.0
Coal consumption per freight locomotive per thousand ton-km, kg	25.2		19.5		14.6	14.8
Average turnaround time per freight car, days	4.39		2.90		2.84	2.75
Average turnaround distance per freight car, km	668.7		676.1		709.2	703.6
Average daily run per freight car, km	154.9		233.1	243.1	249.9	255.6
Average stopping time per freight car per run, hours			11.4		10.7	10.4
Average speed per freight train including stops, km/hr	19.9		25.5		25.2	25.7
Average load per freight car, tons	26.6	26.6	28.9	33.8	34.7	37.6
Average daily efficiency per freight car, ton/km	2,509.0		4,557.6		5,999.0	6,596.0

[1] *TGY*, p. 153.
[2] Teng Tai-yuen (Minister of Railways), "Railway Construction in China during the Past Five Years," in *Eight Glorious Years*, Hong Kong: New Democratic Press, 1958, pp. 36, 43.

TABLE 6.15 Major Indicators of Highway Freight Transportation, 1950, 1952, 1957, and 1958

Indicator	1950	1952	1957	1958
Percentage of trucks in serviceable condition	63.7	71.0	71.7	82.5
Percentage of trucks in actual use	30.1	39.5	66.3	77.9
Average daily run per truck, km	79.8	109.2	162.2	174.3
Average daily efficiency per ton of capacity of trucks, ton-km	18	32	78	113

Source: *TGY*, p. 154.

TABLE 6.16   Index of Labor Productivity in Transport, 1957 and 1958,
Percent (1952 = 100)

Indicator	1957	1958
Average amount of freight transported per person employed in railways	176.0	213.3
Average amount of freight transported per person employed in inland waterways	250.6	328.3
Average amount of freight transported per person employed in coastal shipping	133.6	235.3

Source: *TGY*, p. 155.

TABLE 6.17   Unit Cost in State-Operated Transportation Enterprises, 1950-58

	1950	1952	1956	1957	1958
Index (1952 = 100):[1]					
Railways		100.0		88.1	74.5
Inland waterways		100.0		60.5	48.7
Coastal shipping		100.0		69.7	52.9
Amount, yuan per thousand ton-km:					
Railways	9.84[2]	8.58[2]	7.51[2]	(7.56)[3]	(6.39)[3]

[1] *TGY*, p. 156.
[2] Teng Tai-yuan (Minister of Railways), "Railway Construction in China during the Past Five Years," in *Eight Glorious Years*, Hong Kong: New Democratic Press, 1958, pp. 36-43.
[3] Derived from the indices given above for railways for 1957 and 1958 and the average cost per thousand ton-km given for 1952.

TABLE 6.18   Cost of Transportation by Railways and the Yangtze River in 1956,
Yuan per Thousand Converted Ton-Kilometers

	Railways (1)	Yangtze River (2)
Total	7.67	10.97
Wages and subsidiary wages	2.19	3.11
Fuel and power	0.92	2.27
Material	0.73	0.74
Repairs	0.64	1.51
Depreciation charges	2.74	2.20
Other	0.45	1.14

Source: Hsu Feng and Li Yuen, "Why Is the Cost of Transportation of the Yangtze River Higher than That of
Railways?" *CHCC*, No. 3 (March 9, 1958), pp. 20-23.

TABLE 6.19 Development of Post and Tele-Communications, 1949-58

Indicator	1949	1950	1951	1952	1953	1954	1955	1956	1957	1958
Total length of postal postal routes, thousand km	706	863	1,107	1,290	1,515	1,640	1,739	1,811	2,223	3,012
Length of tele-communication wires, thousand km	576	653	768	882	1,029	1,138	1,272	1,856	2,094	3,202
Long-distance telephones	292	308	338	365	456	487	512	564	611	719
Intra-city telephones	75	80	95	111	130	152	174	216	231	301
Intra-county telephones	209	265	335	406	443	499	586	1,076	1,252	2,182
Total volume of business, million yuan[a]		166.4	226.3	243.5	299.9	327.8	364.5	431.4	420.3	553.9

[a] Data on the total volume of business transacted in post and tele-communications were given in 1952 prices for 1949 through 1957, and in 1957 prices for 1958.

Source: *TGY*, p. 157.

TABLE 6.20   Development of Post and Tele-Communications in the Inner Mongolia
Autonomous Region, 1952-58

	1952	1953	1954	1955	1956	1957	1958
Total length of postal routes, km	32,621	43,068	51,370	55,450	61,595	76,595	91,818
Length of tele-communication wires, kilometers	20,315	24,047	26,236	30,532	41,214	46,300	66,032
Long-distance telephones	14,716	17,263	18,566	20,027	22,900	25,697	31,513
Intra-city telephones	2,020	2,469	3,189	4,823	5,104	6,616	8,390
Intra-county telephones	3,579	4,315	4,481	5,682	13,210	13,987	26,129
Total volume of business, thousand yuan	2,638					7,119	9,926

Source: *NMK TC*, p. 208.

TABLE 6.21   Development of Post and Tele-Communications in Rural Areas, 1952-58

Indicator	1952	1953	1954	1955	1956	1957	1958
Postal routes in rural areas, thousand km	1,044	1,237	1,324	1,424	1,414	1,795	2,574
Percentage of total number of towns and townships having postal service	59.0	65.1	75.2	78.2	96.1	99.0	100.0[a]
Percentage of total number of towns and townships having telephones	9.4	13.0	14.9	19.3	62.0	69.3	97.7[a]

[a] Referring to the percentage of people's communes having postal (or telephone) service
in relation to the total number of people's communes.

Source: *TGY*, p. 159.

384

TABLE 7.1 Development of State, Cooperative, and Private Trade, by Number of Agencies, Operating Personnel, Capital Funds, and Trade Volume, 1950-55

Type of trade	1950	1951	1952	1953	1954	1955
State trade: [1]						
Number of agencies	8,000	n.a.	31,444	37,587	50,228	97,405
Number of operating personnel, thousands	216	n.a.	535	n.a.	n.a.	1,122
Trade volume, million yuan						33,410
Cooperative trade:						
Number of agencies, thousands: [1]	44	n.a.	113	n.a.	n.a.	236
Rural	39	n.a.	99	n.a.	n.a.	n.a.
Urban	5	n.a.	14	n.a.	n.a.	n.a.
Number of operating personnel, thousands: [1]	166	n.a.	711	n.a.	n.a.	1,101
Capital funds, thousand yuan: [2]	32,890	n.a.	243,677	286,328	341,466	
Trade volume, million yuan: [1]						15,090
Private trade: [3]						
Number of agencies, thousands	4,020	4,500	4,300	4,140	3,140	2,954
Number of operating personnel, thousands	6,620	7,400	6,768	6,079	4,464	3,901
Number of workers and employees, thousands	967	1,167	917	766	437	315
Capital funds, million yuan	1,990	2,200	2,020	1,920	1,420	1,010
Trade volume, million yuan	18,140	24,220	19,170	22,300	13,380	12,010

[1] Data Office, *TCKTTH*, "Development of China's Trade Network and Its Basic Situation in 1955," *TCKTTH*, No. 18 (September 29, 1956), pp. 7-10. A different set of data on the number of agencies, operating personnel and trade volume of state trade were given by Wang Che and Liu Shou-chun, and appear to be inconsistent with the series shown in the table. Such inconsistencies cannot be explained with available information. The Wang-Liu data, which were given in percentages, are given in Table 7.1A.

TABLE 7.1A Development of State Trade, 1950-56, Percent

	1951	1952	1953	1954	1955	1956
Number of agencies, preceding year=100	156.12	127.7	114.23	139.96	135.8	131.61
Number of operating personnel preceding year=100		924.66	112.0	128.4	179.11	258.06
Trade volume, 1950=100	146	330	520	707	810	

Source: Wang Che and Liu Shou-Chun, *The Function of State-Operated Trade in Chin* *during the Transition Period*, Peking: People's Press, 1957.

[2] SSB, *Communique on the Results of the Implementation of the National Economic Plan for 1954 (with Economic Statistical Abstract)*, Peking: T'ung-chi ch'u-pan-she, 1955, p. 35.

[3] Ch'ien Hua *et al.*, *Changes in Private Industry and Trade in China during the Past Seven Years (1949-56)*, Peking: Ts'ai-cheng ching-chi ch'u'pan-she, 1957, p. 9.

TABLE 7.2 Distribution of Domestic Trade between Urban and Rural Areas, 1955

Area	Commercial agencies, thousands	Operating personnel, thousands	Retail volume, million yuan [a]
	(1)	(2)	(3)
Total	3,287	6,132	31,540
Urban areas	1,860	3,708	14,800
Eight large cities [b]	482	920	4,810
Rural areas	1,427	2,424	16,740

[a] According to the original source, figures on the total retail volume were compiled from materials supplied by various business-affairs departments. These figures differ somewhat from the data released by the State Statistical Bureau.

[b] The eight large cities are Peking, Shanghai, Tientsin, Shenyang, Canton, Chungking, Sian, and Wuhan.

Source: Data Office, *TCKTTH*, "Development of China's Trade Network and Its Basic Situation in 1955," *TCKTTH*, No. 18 (September 29, 1956), pp. 7-10.

TABLE 7.3 Wholesale and Retail Trade, by Number of Agencies and Trade Volume and by Forms of Ownership, 1955

Type of trade	Total	State	Cooperative	Private
	(1)	(2)	(3)	(4)
Wholesale:				
Number of agencies, thousands	269	72	72	125
Wholesale volume, million yuan	28,970	24,090	3,440	1,160
Retail:				
Number of agencies, thousands	3,082	71	183	2,646
Retail volume, million yuan	31,540	9,320	11,650	9,770

Note: According to the original source, figures on the wholesale and retail volume in this table were compiled from materials supplied by various business-affairs departments. These figures differ somewhat from the data released by the State Statistical Bureau.

Source: Data Office, *TCKTTH*, "Development of China's Trade Network and Its Basic Situation in 1955," *TCKTTH*, No. 18 (September 29, 1956), pp. 7-10.

TABLE 7.4 Distribution of Retail Trade Network in Urban and Rural Areas, by Density and by Labor Productivity, 1955

Area	Coastal areas	Inland areas
	(1)	(2)
National average:		
Average size of population served by each retail outlet	165	269
Average size of population served by each retail trade employee	105	183
Average amount of retail volume per employee	5,933	7,432
Urban areas:		
Average size of population served by each retail outlet	47	50
Average size of population served by each retail trade employee	30	36
Rural areas:		
Average size of population served by each retail outlet	297	566
Average size of population served by each retail trade employee	189	362

Source: Data Office, *TCKTTH*, "Development of China's Trade Network and Its Basic Situation in 1955," *TCKTTH*, No. 18 (September 29, 1956), pp. 7-10.

TABLE 7.5 Distribution of Retail Trade Network in Urban and Rural Areas,
by Commodity, 1955

Area	Food	Clothing	Groceries	Drugs
	(1)	(2)	(3)	(4)
Number of commercial agencies, thousands	o0	185	364	211
Urban areas	18	52	139	44
Rural areas	42	133	225	167
Average size of urban population served by each agency	4,938	1,694	628	1,998
Average number of villages served by each agency	5	1.5	1	more than one

Source: Data Office, *TCKTTH*, "Development of China's Trade Network and Its
Basic Situation in 1955," *TCKTTH*, No. 18 (September 29, 1956), pp. 7-10.

TABLE 7.6 Number of Agencies of State Trade, by Commodity
Groups, 1952-55

Commodity group	1952	1953	1954	1955
Total	31,444	37,587	50,228	97,405
Food	13,177	16,000	22,352	53,839
Oil and Fats	302	286	931	3,326
Textile products	815	790	1,855	2,648

Source: Data Office, *TCKTTH*, "Development of China's Trade
Network and Its Basic Situation in 1955," *TCKTTH*, No. 18
(September 29, 1956), pp. 7-10.

TABLE 7.7 Development of Cooperative Trade, 1949-55

Indicator	1949[1]	1950[2]	1952[2]	1953[2]	1954[2]	1955[3]
Number of cooperatives	20,133	43,501	35,096	32,313	32,062	
Rural supply and marketing cooperatives		39,436	32,788	30,445	30,576	
Urban consumer cooperatives		4,065	2,308	1,868	1,486	
Number of members, thousands	10,640	30,470	14,796	15,775	17,048	
Rural supply and marketing cooperatives		25,690	13,821	14,698	16,110	138,207
Urban consumers' cooperatives		4,780	975	1,077	938	
Capital funds, thousand yuan	11,580	32,890	243,677	286,328	341,466	
Rural supply and marketing cooperatives		27,360	224,331	261,170	371,235	
Urban consumers' cooperatives		5,530	19,346	25,158	24,231	
Trade volume, million yuan		(868)	(5,515)	(9,140)	(15,972)	(15,069)
Wholesale		58	516	772	1,528	3,521
Retail		810	4,999	8,368	14,444	11,548

[1] Ch'u Ch'ing, Chu Chung-chien, and Wang Chi-min, *The Reorganization of Rural Markets in China*, Peking: Ts'ai-cheng ching-chi ch'u-pan-she, 1957, p. 18.

[2] SSB, *Communique on the Results of the Implementation of the National Economic Plan for 1954 (with Economic Statistical Abstract)*, Peking: T'ung-chi ch'u-pan-she, 1955, p. 35.

[3] Data Office, *TCKTTH*, "Development of China's Trade Network and Its Basic Situation in 1955," *TCKTTH*, No. 18 (September 29, 1965), pp. 7-10, reference on p. 8.

TABLE 7.8 Development of Private Trade, by Type of Merchant, 1950-55

Type of merchant	1950	1951	1952	1953	1954	1955
Resident merchants:						
Number of trading units, thousands	1,850	2,220	1,820	1,500	1,130	856
Number of operating personnel, thousands	4,237	4,842	4,012	3,161	2,261	1,635
Capital funds, million yuan	1,850	2,030	1,860	1,750	1,300	880
Trade volume, million yuan			15,360	17,830	10,340	8,280
Itinerant merchants:						
Number of trading units, thousands	200	220	300	270	130	66
Number of operating personnel, thousands	220	241	329	292	144	75
Capital funds, million yuan	50	70	80	70	40	20
Trade volume, million yuan			870	810	360	190
Number of trading units, thousands	1,970	2,060	2,180	2,370	1,880	2,032
Number of operating personnel, thousands	2,163	2,317	2,427	2,626	2,059	2,191
Capital funds, million yuan	90	100	80	100	80	110
Trade volume, million yuan			2,940	3,660	2,680	3,540

Source: Ch'ien Hua *et al.*, *Changes in Private Industry and Trade in China during the Past Seven Years (1949-1956)*, Peking: Ts'ai-cheng ching-chi ch'u-pan-she, 1957, pp. 53 and 123.

TABLE 7.9 Private Wholesale Trade, August 31, 1955

Indicator	Total	Resident wholesalers	Itinerant wholesalers	Peddling wholesalers
	(1)	(2)	(3)	(4)
Number of trading units, thousands	125	42	66	17
Number of operating personnel, thousands	236	140	75	21
Workers and employees, thousands	53.3	52	1	0.3
Capital funds, million yuan	180	150	20	10
Trade volume, million yuan [a]	1,270	990	190	90

[a] The original source did not indicate whether the trade volume pertained to the whole year or to the first eight months of 1955.

Source: Ch'ien Hua *et al.*, *Changes in Private Industry and Trade in China during the Past Seven Years (1949-1956)*, Peking: Ts'ai-cheng ching-chi ch'u-pan-she, 1957, p. 132.

TABLE 7.10 Changes in Volume of Private Trade of Eight Large Cities by Branch of Trade, 1953-55, Percent (1953=100)

Branch	1954			1955		
	Total	Private wholesale	Private retail	Total	Private wholesale	Private retail
	(1)	(2)	(3)	(4)	(5)	(6)
Total	45.97	29.32	62.59	36.70	13.71	59.66
Food grains	43.04	3.68	53.11	76.72	9.38	93.95
Other food products	65.24	32.69	92.74	61.33	21.60	94.89
Fuels	74.31	35.24	87.36	67.44	23.43	82.15
Textile products	37.18	17.59	54.41	31.67	4.29	55.74
Cultural, educational, and art supplies	45.67	39.49	51.49	25.67	13.37	37.27
Daily necessities	45.92	34.14	51.85	38.06	20.90	46.70
Construction equipment and material	68.99	48.10	80.28	37.11	12.99	53.22
Industrial and transportation equipment and material	38.40	39.62	37.41	19.91	18.78	20.82
Drugs	42.44	31.23	62.66	26.44	11.36	53.65
Import trade	20.66	19.36	106.81	3.65	3.38	3.31
Sale agents	17.63	9.82	145.52	5.80	3.69	40.33
Miscellaneous	69.67	68.09	70.82	61.96	50.96	69.97

Note: The eight large cities are Peking, Tientsin, Shanghai, Wuhan, Canton, Chungking, Sian, and Shenyang.

Source: Ch'ien Hua et al., *Changes in Private Industry and Trade in China during the Past Seven Years (1949-1956)*, Peking: Ts'ai-chang ching-chi ch'u-pan-she, 1957, p. 124.

TABLE 7.11 Trade Volume of Free Market, 1953-56

Volume	1953	1954	1955	1956
Estimate according to Method I: [a]				
Retail volume of free market, million yuan	14,720	10,890	9,160	9,860
Retail volume of free market as percentage of social commodity retail volume	42.0	28.0	22.9	21.2
Estimate according to Method II: [b]				
Trade volume of the free market, million yuan	17,020	12,000	10,340	11,520
Trade volume of free market as percentage of total commodity value [c]	35.8	24.9	21.0	18.4

[a] The trade volume of the free market estimated according to Method I is derived by deducting from the social commodity retail volume, the retail volume of state and cooperative trade and that part of the retail volume of joint and private trade for which commodities are supplied by state and cooperative stores. The trade volume of the free market thus estimated is composed of that part of the retail volume of joint and private trade and restaurants for which commoditiee are supplied by joint and private sectors, and the volume of commodities which producers sell directly to consumers.

[b] The trade volume of the free market estimated according to Method II is derived by deducting from the total commodity value the value of commodities which state and cooperative trade purchases from joint enterprises and private producers. The remainder consists of the following elements: (1) the value of commodities which producers sell directly to consumers; (2) the value of commodities which producers sell to other producers; (3) the value of commodities which producers sell to joint and private commercial agencies and restaurants.

[c] The total commodity value refers to the value of both industrial and agricultural commodity production. Included is also the value of producer goods purchased by peasants. For the meaning of industrial and agricultural commodity production, see the sections on industry and agriculture.

Source: Wang P'ing, "The Scope of the Free Market and Its Changes in China," TCKC, No. 11 (June 14, 1957), pp. 28-29.

TABLE 7.12 Trade Volume of Free Market, by Type of Buyer, 1953-56, Million Yuan

Volume	1953	1954	1955	1956
Total	17,020	12,000	10,340	11,520
Volume of commodities sold directly to consumers	5,550	5,700	5,760	6,120
Volume of commodities sold to other producers	2,300	1,110	1,180	1,660
Volume of commodities sold to joint and private commercial agencies and restaurants	9,170	5,190	3,400	3,740

Note: The total volume of the free market in this table was estimated by deducting from the total commodity value the value of commodities which state and cooperative trade purchased from joint enterprises and private producers. For the methods of estimating the trade volume of the free market and the concept of the total commodity value, see notes to Table 7.11.

Source: Wang P'ing, "The Scope of the Free Market and Its Changes in China," TCKT, No. 11 (June 14, 1957), pp. 28-29.

TABLE 7.13   Trade Volume of Free Market, by Type of Product, 1953-56

Type of product	1953	1954	1955	1956
Percentage distribution [1]				
Total	100.0	100.0	100.0	100.0
Free market for industrial products	25.0	19.8	15.4	15.1
Free market for agricultural products	58.6	58.5	65.8	65.1
Free market for handicraft products	16.4	21.7	18.8	19.8
Amount, million yuan				
Total [1]	17,020	12,000	10,340	11,520
Free market for industrial products [2]	(4,255)	(2,376)	(1,592)	(1,740)
Free market for agricultural products [2]	(9,974)	(7,020)	(6,804)	(7,500)
Free market for handicraft products [2]	(2,791)	(2,604)	(1,944)	(2,280)

Note: The total trade volume of the free market in this table was estimated by
deducting from the total commodity value the value of commodities which state
and cooperative trade purchased from joint enterprises and private producers.
For the methods of estimating the trade volume of the free market and the
concept of the total commodity value, see notes to Table 7.11.
[1] Wang P'ing, "The Scope of the Free Market and Its Changes in China," *TCKT*,
    No. 11 (June 14, 1957), pp. 28-29.
[2] Derived from multiplying total amount by index for each type of product.

TABLE 7.14   Wholesale Volume of Regular Commercial Organizations, 1950-55,
             Millions of Yuan

	1950 [1]	1951 [2]	1952 [1]	1953 [1]	1954 [1]	1955 [1]
Total	10,544	(16,420)	18,969	26,449	27,842	27,847
State-operated stores	2,448		11,469	17,543	23,347	22,884
Cooperatives	58	(5,650)	516	772	1,528	3,521
State-private and cooperative shops	12		102	119	134	226
Private shops	8,026	10,770	6,882	8,015	2,833	1,216

[1] SSB, *Communique on the Results of the Implementation of the National Economic
    Plan for 1955 (with Economic Statistical Abstract)*, Peking: Statistical
    Publishing House, 1956, p. 44.
[2] Derived from indices given by Yang Po, "A Preliminary Analysis of the Process
    of Socialist Transformation of Private Trade in China," *TCKTTH*, No. 15
    (August, 1956), pp. 7-10.

TABLE 7.15 Retail Volume, by Ownership of Commercial Establishment, 1950-59, Millions of Yuan

Volume	1950	1951	1952	1953
Social-commodity retail volume:				
TGY Data:				
Total volume	17,060[1]	23,430[1]	27,680[1]	34,800[1]
Data from annual communiques:				
Total	16,794[3]	n.a.	27,665[3]	35,041[3]
State stores	1,311[3]	n.a.	4,384[3]	5,941[3]
Cooperatives	819[3]	n.a.	5,051[3]	8,519[3]
State-private and cooper-ative shops	31[3]	n.a.	77[3]	152[3]
Private shops, including peasant trade	14,613[3]	n.a.	18,153[3]	20,429[3]
Retail volume of commercial organizations:				
TGY data:				
Total[5]	(11,946)	(17,008)	(21,127)	(27,746)
State stores and cooperatives[6]	1,780	4,150	9,000	13,790
State-private and cooper-ative shops[5]	(12)	(17)	(42)	(111)
Private shops[5]	(10,154)	(12,841)	(12,085)	(13,845)
Data from annual communiques:				
Total	12,083[7]	(17,750)[8]	21,027[7]	27,981[7]
State stores	1,172[7]		3,841[7]	5,452[7]
Cooperatives	810[7]	(4,490)[8]	4,999[7]	8,368[7]
State-private and cooper-ative shops	12[7]		38[7]	79[7]
Private shops	10,089[7]	(13,260)[8]	12,149[7]	14,081[7]

[1] *TGY*, p. 166.

[2] *JMJP*, March 31, 1960.

[3] SSB, *Communique on the Results of the Implementation of the National Economic Plan for 1955, (with Economic Statistical Abstract)*, Peking: Statistical Publishing House, 1956, p. 42.

[4] Computed from indices given by Hsu Chung-yi, "In Retrosprect of Domestic Trade in the Past Five Years," in *Eight Glorious Years*, Hong Kong: New Democratic Press, 1958, pp. 59-65.

TABLE 7.16 Retail Volume in Urban and Rural Areas, 1953-58

Area	1953	1954	1955	1956	1957	1958
Social commodity retail volume, million yuan[a]				(46,870)[1]	48,050[2]	(56,090)[1]
Urban areas				(22,300)[3]	23,240[2]	(24,560)[4]
Rural areas				(24,570)[3]	24,810[2]	(31,530)[4]
Index of social commodity retail volume in rural areas, percent (1952=100)[5]	118.4	135.7	149.6	166		

[a] The figures for the social commodity retail volume derived in this table do not correspond to the *TGY* data shown in Table 7.15. The discrepancies probably resulted from a revision made later for the *TGY* series.

TABLE 7.15 (Continued)

1954	1955	1956	1957	1958	1959
38,110[1]	39,220[1]	46,100[1]	47,420[1]	54,800[1]	63,800[2]
38,962[3]	40,002[3]	(47,113)[4]			
7,611[3]	10,785[3]				
14,901[3]	12,211[3]				
1,827[3]	5,065[3]				
14,623[3]	11,941[3]				
(31,521)	(32,307)	(38,448)	(39,909)		
21,750	21,840	26,260	26,220		
(1,702)	(4,717)	(10,573)	(12,611)		
(8,069)	(5,750)	(1,615)	(1,078)		
31,586[7]	32,321[7]	38,550[9]			
7,017[7]	10,204[9]	} 26,180[9]			
14,444[7]	11,548[7]				
1,770[7]	4,919[7]	11,165[9]			
8,355[7]	5,650[7]	1,155[9]			

[5] Computed from percentages given in TGY, p. 40.

[6] *TGY*, p. 39.

[7] SSB, *1955 Communique, op. cit.*, p. 44.

[8] Computed from indices given by Yang Po, "Preliminary Analysis of the Process of Socialist Transformation of Private Trade in China," *TCKTTH*, No. 15 (August, 1956), pp. 7-10.

[9] SSB, "Communique on the Results of the Implementation of the National Economic Plan for 1956," *JMJP*, August 2, 1957.

TABLE 7.16 (Continued)

[1] Derived as a sum of items in lines for urban and rural areas.

[2] Data Office, *TCYC*, "A General Survey of the Commodity Circulation in the Domestic Market in 1957," *TCYC*, No. 4 (April 23, 1958), pp. 24-25.

[3] *Ibid.* Reportedly, in 1957, the annual rate of increase of the urban retail volume was 4.2 percent and that of rural retail volume was 1 percent.

[4] Chao I-wen, "Changes in the Retail Market since the Great Leap Forward," *CYHTTH*, No. 5 (May 11, 1959), pp. 30-31. According to Chao, in 1958, the increase in the retail volume in urban areas was 27.1 percent.

[5] Ch'u Ch'ing, Chu Chung-chien, and Wang Chi-min, *Reorganization of the Rural Market in China*, Peking: Tsai-cheng ching-chi ch'u-pan-she, 1957, p. 27. These figures were preliminary estamates made by the National Federation of Supply and Marketing Cooperatives.

TABLE 7.17 Retail Volume of National Minority Areas in Selected Provinces, 1949-58, Million Yuan

Area	1949	1950	1951	1952	1953	1954	1955	1956	1957	1958
National minority areas:[1]										
Social commodity retail volume				1,790						4,690
Retail volume of state stores and cooperatives				770						4,400
Inner Mongolia:[2]										
Social commodity retail volume	10.5	15.1	22.0	34.7	45.8	63.8	64.6	80.7	85.5	102.5
Retail volume of state stores	2.0	5.2	7.9	16.7	26.5	43.9	46.7	58.3	59.6	78.0
Chinghai Province:[3]										
Social commodity retail volume									267.7	
Retail volume of state stores									143.4	
Kansu Province:[4]										
Social commodity retail volume								884.0	980.0	
Hunan Province:[5]										
Social commodity retail volume								1,607.5	1,695.1	
Shantung Province:[6]										
Social commodity retail volume							2,588.5	3,046.7		
Kiangsu Province:[7]										
Social commodity retail volume									3,523	4,383
Producer goods									811	1,340
Consumer goods									2,712	3,043

1 *TGY*, p. 174.
2 *NMKTC*, pp. 49 and 213.
3 Chinghai Provincial Statistical Bureau, "Communique on the Development of the National Economy in Chinghai Province and the Results of the Implementation of the First Five-Year Plan, 1953-1957," *Chinghai JP*, Hsi-ning, September 30, 1958, p. 2.
4 Kansu Provincial Statistical Bureau, "Communique on the Results of the Implementation of the National Economic Plan for 1957 in Kansu Province, *Kansu JP*, Lanchow, June 12, 1958, p. 2.
5 Hunan Provincial Statistical Bureau, "Achievements of Hunan Province in 1957 National Economic Work," *Hsin Hunan Pao*, Changsha, May 4, 1958.
6 Wang Che-ju, "Report on the Implementation of the 1956 Economic Plan in Shantung Province," *Ta-chung JP*, Tsinan, August 17, 1957, p. 2.
7 Liu Shun-yuen, "Work Report to the Third Session of the Third Provincial Congress of the Chinese Communist Party," *HHPYK*, No. 7 (April 10, 1959), pp. 15-22.

TABLE 7.18   Retail Sales of Major Consumer Goods, 1950-58

Commodity	1950[1]	1952[2]	1953[3]	1954[3]	1955[3]	1956[3]	1957[4]	1958[1]
Grain, million *chin*	55,510	(63,043)					(77,543)	89,950
Edible vegetable oil, million *chin*	1,080							2,130
Table salt, thousand tons	2,061							4,000
Sugar, thousand tons	243							981
Pork, thousand tons	1,400							1,764
Aquatic products, thousand tons	721							2,470
Cotton cloth, million meters	2,170	(3,491)	(4,734)	(4,639)	(4,634)	(6,210)	(4,154)	4,860
Rubber shoes, thousand pairs	41,927	(64,412)	(76,972)	(83,361)	(68,023)	(103,395)	(117,230)	178,190
Matches, million boxes	6,500							11,914
Machine-made paper, tons	140,000	(217,428)					(334,839)	519,000

[1] *TGY*, p. 167

[2] Computed from percentages given in SSB, *Communique on the Results of the Implementation of the First Five-Year Plan for the Development of the National Economy (1953-1957)*, Peking: Statistical Publishing House, 1959, p. 11.

[3] Computed from data on percentage increase of retail sales over preceding years given by Hsu Chung-yi, "In Retrospect of Domestic Trade in the Past Five Years," in *Eight Glorious Years*, Hong Kong: New Democratic Press, 1958, pp. 59-65.

[4] Computed from percentage given in SSB, *Communique on the Development of the National Economy in 1958*, Peking: Statistical Publishing House, 1959, p. 22.

TABLE 7.19   Retail Sales of Major Consumer Goods in Inner
              Mongolia Autonomous Region 1949 and 1958

Commodity	1949	1958
Food, 10,000 *chin*	77,443	151,491
Edible vegetable oil, 10,000 *chin*	125	2,536
Table salt, *shih tan*	479,346	1,401,120
Sugar, *shih tan*	15,978	167,720
Meat, tons	2,722	20,676
Wine, *shih tan*	23,640	318,360
Tea, *shih tan*	11,836	62,114
Cigarette, cases	3,029	105,505
Cotton cloth, 10,000 meters	2,959	9,309
Rubber shoes, pairs	71,000	2,028,259
Towels, dozens	53,261	418,621
Soap, cases	8,374	177,739
Knitted goods, dozens	91,730	1,304,133
Matches, pieces	59,179	199,742
Kerosene, tons	503	9,697

Source: *NMKTC*, p. 217

TABLE 7.20   Retail Sales of Major Commodities in Kansu
              Province, 1950 and 1956

Commodity	1950	1956
Food grains, million tons	681	1,423
Edible vegetable oil, thousand tons	13	19
Cotton cloth, thousand bolts	1,840	4,380
Coal, thousand tons	233	626

Source: Ma Yi-chao (Director of Kansu Provincial Statistical Bureau), "The Living Standards of the People in
Kansu Province," *TCKT*, No. 14 (July 29, 1957), pp. 21,32.

TABLE 7.21 Production and Sales of Cotton Textile Products, 1950-56

Commodity	1950	1951	1952	1953	1954	1955	1956
Output:							
Cotton cloth, million meters[a]	2,522	3,058	3,829	4,685	5,230	4,361	5,803
Knitted cotton textile products, thousand bales[b]	245.3	281.5	303.9	468.7	563.8	624.6	711.8
Social retail volume:							
Cotton cloth, million meters[a]	1,709	2,310	2,881	3,999	3,888	3,936	5,281
Knitted cotton textile products, thousand bales[b]			371.4	425.3	490.2	491.3	663.9

[a] Not including native cloth.
[b] Converted to yarn and measured in terms of bales.
Source: *CH*, p. 182.

TABLE 7.22 Production and Sales of Machine-Made Paper, 1952-57, Tons

Commodity	1952	1953	1954	1955	1956	1957
Inventory at beginning of year	162,375	305,854	397,020	406,451	311,145	141,886
Output	371,760	427,138	518,273	574,621	729,319	912,989
Import	140,100	100,990	33,506	29,025	41,266	44,670
Social consumption	367,971	434,464	532,118	656,206	884,441	848,000
Export	410	2,498	10,230	42,746	55,403	47,000
Year-end inventory	350,854	397,020	406,451	311,145	141,886	204,545

Source: *CH*, p. 216.

TABLE 7.23 Production and Sales of Resin, 1950-57, Percent

Index	1950	1951	1952	1953	1954	1955	1956	1957
Output index (1936=100)	79	141	262	134	279	495	687	744
Index of sales volume (1950=100)	100	151	308	353	393	476	1,000	1,113

Source: The Second Department of the Bureau of Native Products and Rejected Objects, the Ministry of Commerce, "The Ways of Resolving the Problem of Supply and Demand of Resin," *CYHTTH*, No. 3 (March 11, 1959), pp. 28-29.

TABLE 7.24 Production and Sales of Gamier, 1954-58, Tons

Quantity	1954	1955	1956	1957	1958
Output	156	568	1,275	2,000	5,193
Sales volume	12,475	9,940	13,511	17,493	28,104

Source: The Second Department of the Bureau of Native Products and Rejected Objects, Ministry of Commerce, "A Brief Survey of Production and Sales of Gamier," *CYHTTH*, No. 5 (May 11, 1959), p. 32.

TABLE 7.25 Retail Sales of Major Subsidiary Food Products of Supply and Marketing Cooperatives, 1952-55, Thousand Tons

Commodity	1952	1953	1954	1955
Table salt	1,106	1,724	2,606	2,663
Sugar	63	n.a.	n.a.	359
Edible vegetable oils	273	n.a.	n.a.	669

Source: Ch'u Ching, Chu Chung-chien, and Wang Chi-min, *The Reorganization of Rural Markets in China*, Peking: Ts'ai-cheng ching-chi ch'u-pan-she, 1957, p. 44.

TABLE 7.26 Percentage Distribution of Retail Volume
of Producer Goods Supplied to Agri-
culture, by Commodity, 1953-56

Commodity	1953	1954	1955	1956
Total	100.0	100.0	100.0	100.0
Fertilizer	38.0	33.9	35.7	33.2
Insecticide sprayers	0.8	1.8	2.1	3.9
Irrigation implements	--	0.5	1.0	3.7
New-style farm implements	0.4	0.6	3.1	8.4
Old-style farm implements	23.0	20.5	17.1	12.8
Building materials	--	7.3	11.8	11.0
Others	37.8	35.4	29.2	17.0

Source: Ch'u Ch'ing, Chu Chung-chien, and Wang Chi-min, *The
Reorganization of Rural Markets in China*, Peking: Ts'ai-cheng
ching-chi ch'u-pan-she, 1957, p. 41.

TABLE 7.27 Supply of Major Producer Goods to Agriculture, 1951-58

Commodity	1951	1952	1953	1954	1955	1956	1957	1958
Chemical fertilizer, thousand tons[1]		318	592	802	1,255	1,608	1,944	2,708
Supplied by supply and marketing cooperatives[2]	130	295	555	792	1,144	1,295		
Insecticides, thousand tons[1]		15	19	41	67	159	149	478
Insecticide sprayers, thousand units[1]		251	198	315	429	1,308	647	3,351
Two-wheeled share plows, thousands		1	15	23	426	1,086	95	628
Power machines, thousand hp[1]		13	14	22	45	189	265	1,083

[1] *TGY*, p. 17.
[2] Ch'u Ch'ing, Chu Chung-chien, and Wang Chi-min, *The Reorganization of Rural
Markets in China*, Peking: Ts'ai- cheng ching-chi ch'u-pan-she, 1957, p. 42.

TABLE 7.28 Supply of Major Producer Goods to Agriculture in Inner Mongolia
Autonomous Region, 1952-58

Commodity	1952	1953	1954	1955	1956	1957	1958
Chemical fertilizer, tons	--	14	856	699	745	696	2,617
Insecticides, tons	--	268	294	494	1,128	1,546	2,224
Insecticide sprayers	--	483	696	1,245	7,015	7,357	9,649
Two-wheeled share plows	69	146	326	6,538	60,853	1,480	5,862
Power machines	--	--	--	--	7	38	1,058

Source: *NMKTC*, p. 216.

TABLE 7.29 Government Purchase of Agricultural Products and Products of Agricultural Side Occupations, 1949-58, Million Yuan

Area	1949	1950	1951	1952	1953	1954	1955	1956	1957	1958
National total [1]		8,000	10,500	12,970	15,320	17,360	17,800	18,400	20,280	22,760
National minority areas [2]				750						2,020
Purchased by state trading companies and cooperatives				480						2,930
Inner Mongolia Autonomous Region [3]	1.60	4.66	6.34	8.96	14.89	29.93	24.55	26.58	27.28	31.18
Hunan Province [4]				490.90				732.70	806.56	
Purchased by state trading companies and cooperatives								564.60	656.44	

[1] *TGY*, p. 168.
[2] *TGY*, p. 174.
[3] *NMKTC*, p. 214.
[4] Hunan Provincial Statistical Bureau, "Achievements of Hunan Province in 1957 National Economic Work," *Hsin Hunan Pao*, Changsha, May 4, 1958.

TABLE 7.30 Government Purchase of Principal Agricultural Products and Products of Agricultural Side Occupations, 1950-58, thousand Tons

Product	1950	1953	1954	1955	1956	1957	1958
Grain, thousand tons[a],[1]	33,425						52,960
Edible vegetable oils, thousand tons[a],[b],[1]	565						880
Hogs, thousand head	35,843[1]	9,637[2]	26,162[2]	27,686[2]	32,225[2]	37,249[2]	46,732[1]
Eggs, thousand tons[1]	164						405
Tea, thousand tons	60[1]				107[3]	96[3]	120[1]
Cotton, thousand tons[a]	411[1]			1,241[4]			1,530[1]
Cured tobacco, thousand tons[1]	51						277
Hemp, thousand tons[3]					60	66	
Ramie, thousand tons[3]					32	34	
Jute, thousand tons[2]					217	254	

[a] Including taxes in kind.
[b] Including oil-yielding plants in terms of amount of oil extracted.
[1] TGY, p. 169.
[2] CYHHTTH, , No. 3 (March 11, 1959), p. 31.
[3] Data Office, TCYC, "A General Survey of the Commodity Circulation in the Domestic Market in 1957," TCYC, No. 4 (April 23, 1958), pp. 24-25.
[4] CH, p. 189.

TABLE 7.31 Production and Government Purchase of Food Grains,[a] 1953-57, Thousand Tons

Amount	1953-54	1954-55	1955-56	1956-57
Output	142,530	145,420	158,360	165,890
Government purchase	41,500	45,135	42,995	41,715
Sold by the government to rural areas[b]	17,115	23,180	18,175	23,000
Sold by the government to urban areas and armed forces	17,705	18,555	17,925	19,550
Retained by peasants[c]	118,145	123,465	133,540	147,175

[a] Food grains include soybeans.
[b] Including the amount of food grains sold by the state to the food industry for processing, which is in turn sold to the peasants in rural areas.
[c] Including the amount of food grains sold by the state to rural areas.
Source: Data Office, TCKT, "The Basic Situation of the Unified Purchase and Unified Sales of Food Grains in China," TCKT, No. 19, (October 14, 1957), pp. 31-32, 28.

TABLE 7.32 Production and Government Purchase of Live Hogs, 1953-57

Indicator	1953	1954	1955	1956	1957
Number of live hogs on July 1, thousnad head	96,131.3	101.718.2	87,919.6	84,472.4	115,297.0
Number of peasants per hog reared	5.3	5.1	6.0	6.4	4.8
Number of hogs in fattening process, thousand head	76,270	81,340	69,890	66,780	93,210
Number of hogs purchased, thousand head	9,637	26,162	27,686.4	32,225.4	37,249.3

Source: *CYHTTH*, No. 3 (March 11, 1959), p. 31.

TABLE 7.33 Government Purchase of Cotton, by Region 1955, Thousand Tons

Region	Cotton
Total	1,240.9
Coastal areas	780.8
Inland areas	460.1
Northeast China	23.7
North China	646.8
East China	308.0
Shanghai	8.5
Central China	131.0
South China	0.05
Southwest China	58.7
Northwest China	72.6

Source: *CH*, p. 189.

TABLE 7.34 Government Purchase of Principal Agricultural Products and Products of Agricultural Side Occupations in the Inner Mongolia Autonomous Region, 1949 and 1958

Product	1949	1958	Product	1949	1958
Grain, tons	57,390	897,150	Soybeans, tons	17,125	61,140
Edible vegetable oil, tons	5,335	38,245	Sugar, tons	--	233,599
			Herbs, tons	678	7,846
Hogs, head	353	454,517			
Eggs, tons	130	1,101			

Source: *NMKTC*, p. 215.

TABLE 7.35 Rate of Marketable Output in Total Output
of Major Agricultural Products,
1952-55, Percent

Commodity	1952	1953	1954	1955
Food grains	23.4	25.2	30.8	26.7
Cotton	78.3	76.1	79.1	82.5
Cured tobacco	93.9	99.0	94.0	99.0

Source: Ch'u Ching, Chu Chung-chien, and Wang Chi-
min, *The Reorganization of Rural Markets in
China*, Peking: Tsai-cheng ching-chi ch'u-pan-
she, 1957, p. 28.

TABLE 7.36 Indices of Foreign Trade, 1950-55

Year	Index(1950=100)			Percentage of import in total trade	Percentage of export in total trade
	Total trade	Total import	Total export		
	(1)	(2)	(3)	(4)	(5)
1950	100	100	100	51	49
1951	143	165	120	59	41
1952	156	176	135	58	42
1953	195	216	173	57	43
1954	204	209	199	52	48
1955	265	286	242	55	45

Source: Figures in this table were released at the Chinese Export-
Commodity Fair held in Canton in 1956 and reproduced in *Asia
Keizai Jumpo*, Tokyo, Japan, No. 316 (March, 1957), pp. 6-13.

TABLE 7.37 Volume of Import and Export Trade,
1950-58, Million Yuan

Year	Total volume of import and export trade[1]	Volume of import trade[2]	Volume of export trade[2]
	(1)	(2)	(3)
1950	4,150	(2,120)	(2,030)
1951	5,950	(3,510)	(2,440)
1952	6,460	(3,750)	(2,710)
1953	8,090	(4,570)	(3,520)
1954	8,470	(4,420)	(4,050)
1955	10,980	(6,070)	(4,910)
1956	10,870		
1957	10,450		
1958	12,870		

[1] *TGY*, p. 175.
[2] Derived from multiplying total by respective
indices of Table 7.36.

TABLE 7.38 Distribution of Volume of Export Trade, by Category of Commodity, 1950-58

Product	1950	1951	1952	1953	1954	1955	1956	1957	1958
Percentage distribution[1]									
Industrial and mining products	9.3	14.0	17.9	18.4	24.0	25.5	26.1	28.4	27.5
Processed products of agriculture and side occupations	33.2	31.4	22.8	25.9	27.7	28.4	31.3	31.5	37.0
Products of agriculture and side occupations	57.5	54.6	59.3	55.7	48.3	46.1	42.6	40.1	35.5
Total	100.0	100.0	100.0	100.0	100.0	100.0	100.0	100.0	100.0
Amount, Million yuan:									
Industrial and mining products[2]	(189)	(342)	(485)	(648)	(972)	(1,252)			
Processed products of agriculture and side occupation[2]	(674)	(766)	(618)	(912)	(1,122)	(1,394)			
Products of agriculture and subsidiary occupations[2]	(1,167)	(1,332)	(1,607)	(1,960)	(1,956)	(2,264)			
Total[3]	(2,030)	(2,440)	(2,710)	(3,520)	(4,050)	(4,910)			

1 TGY, p. 176.
2 Derived from multiplying total volume by corresponding percentages.
3 Table 7.37.

TABLE 7.39 Distribution of Volume of Import Trade between Producer and Comsumer Goods, 1950-58

Goods	1950	1951	1952	1953	1954	1955	1956	1957	1958
Percentage distribution: [1]									
Producer goods	87.2	83.1	90.6	93.0	92.8	94.5	92.4	92.7	93.7
Consumer goods	12.8	16.9	9.4	7.0	7.2	5.5	7.6	7.3	6.3
Total	100.0	100.0	100.0	100.0	100.0	100.0	100.0	100.0	100.0
Amount, million yuan:									
Producer goods [2]	(1,850)	(2,920)	(3,400)	(4,250)	(4,100)	(5,740)			
Consumer goods [2]	(270)	(590)	(350)	(320)	(320)	(330)			
Total [3]	(2,120)	(3,510)	(3,750)	(4,570)	(4,420)	(6,070)			

[1] *TGY*, p. 176.
[2] Derived from multiplying total volume by corresponding percentages.
[3] Table 7.37.

407

TABLE 7.40 Percentage Distribution of Volume of Foreign Trade, by Customs House, 1952-54

Customs house	1952 Total	Export	Import	1953 Total	Export	Import	1954 Total	Export	Import
Total	100.0	100.0	100.0	100.0	100.0	100.0	100.0	100.0	100.0
Man-chou-li	27.7	19.1	36.7	38.8	39.4	38.1	46.5	44.6	48.8
Shui-feng-ho	2.3	4.2	0.3	2.3	3.8	0.5	3.2	5.6	0.5
An-tung	0.9	1.8	--	1.6	3.0	--	2.6	4.8	--
Dairen	4.6	6.7	3.0	3.9	5.5	1.9	3.1	5.2	0.7
Tientsin	16.3	17.7	14.9	14.6	12.7	16.8	9.0	7.6	10.6
Chin-huang-tao	6.0	2.9	9.4	3.5	1.2	6.3	1.0	0.7	1.3
Tsingtao	5.1	8.8	1.2	5.6	6.5	4.5	3.5	4.7	2.2
Shanghai	8.7	14.6	2.5	6.2	8.4	3.7	8.1	9.6	6.0
Canton	13.5	6.9	20.5	12.1	7.8	17.3	2.7	2.4	2.9
Huangpu	--	--	--	--	--	--	11.3	3.3	20.6
Kowloon	2.8	1.9	3.7	2.9	1.6	4.4	1.4	2.1	0.5
Urumchi	2.2	2.3	2.2	2.3	1.4	3.4	0.9	1.2	0.6
Others	9.9	13.1	5.6	6.2	8.7	3.1	6.7	8.2	5.3

Source: Ch'en Chi-shih and Liu Po-wu, *Foreign Trade Statistics*, Peking: Finance and Economics Press, 1958, p. 144.

TABLE 7.41 Export of Food Grains and Soybeans, 1953-57

Indicator	1953-54	1954-55	1955-56	1956-57
Percentage exported of output of food grains[1]	1.1	1.4	1.4	1.4
Output of food grains, thousand tons[1]	142,530	145,420	158,360	165,890
Export of food grains, thousand tons[2]	(1,568)	(2,159)	(2,217)	(2,322)
Percentage of exported soybeans in export of food grains, percent[1]	56.1	56.2	51.7	55.8
Export of soybeans thousand tons[3]	(879)	(1,212)	(1,148)	(1,296)

Note: Food grains include soybeans.

[1] Data Office, *TCKT*, "The Basic situation of the Unified Purchase and Unified Sales of Food Grains in China," *TCKT*, No. 19 (October 14, 1957), pp. 31-32, 28.
[2] Derived from multiplying total output by percentage exported.
[3] Derived from total export of food grains by percentage of soybeans exported.

TABLE 7.42 Production and Import of Cotton, 1949-56, Thousand Tons

Type of trade	1949	1950	1951	1952	1953	1954	1955	1956
Output	444.4	692.5	1,030.6	1,303.7	1,174.8	1,064.9	1,518.4	1,445.2
Import	51.7	133.9	61.3	76.8	11.0	42.0	86.4	44.1

Source: *CH*, p. 182.

TABLE 8.1 Price Indices, 1950–58

Index	1950	1951	1952	1953	1954	1955	1956	1957	1958
Wholesale price:[a]									
1950=100[1]	100.0	117.9	118.1	116.6	117.1	117.8	117.2		
March, 1950=100[1,2]		92.4	92.6	91.3	91.8	92.4	91.9	92.7	92.7
1952=100[3,4]	84.7	99.8	100.0	98.7	99.1	99.7	99.2	100.1	100.1
Retail price:									
Nationwide average (1952=100)[3]			100.0	103.2	105.5	106.3	106.3	108.6	108.3
Eight big cities[b]									
1950=100[1]	100.0	111.9	112.9	117.1	117.5	119.1	119.5		
March, 1950=100:									
TGY data[2]		94.6	93.7	98.3	100.2	101.1	101.1	102.2	101.4
TCKT data[1]		88.0	88.8	92.1	92.4	93.7	94.0		
1952=100:									
Hsu Chung-yi data[5]	88.6	99.1	100.0	103.7	104.1	105.5	105.8		
Wen-hui pao data[6]		101.0	100.0	104.9	106.9	107.9	107.8		
Rural areas (1952=100)[5]			100.0	100.9	104.5	105.7	105.3	107.7	
Industrial products sold in rural areas:									
1930-36=100[7]						283.2	280.4	283.8	
1950=100[7,8]	100.0	110.2	109.7	108.2	110.3	111.9	110.8	112.1	
1952=100[3]			100.0	98.5	100.2	101.4	100.4	101.6	101.0
Government purchases of agricultural products:									
1930-36=100[7]						254.4	262.0	275.1	
1950=100[7,8]	100.0	119.6	121.6	132.5	136.7	135.1	139.2	146.2	
1952=100[3]			100.0	110.1	113.8	113.2	116.6	122.4	125.1
Cost-of-living for workers and employees in 12 cities (1952=100)[9]				105.6	106.9	107.3	107.1	109.2[c]	

[a] The number of cities covered was 15 in 1950, 25 in 1951, 47 in 1952, 44 in 1953, 42 in 1954, and 37 in 1955. The number for 1956 through 1958 are not known.

[b] The eight big cities are Peking, Shanghai, Tientsin, Shenyang, Canton, Sian, Wuhan, and Chungking.

[c] Preliminary estimate.

[1] TCKT, No. 11 (June 14, 1957), p. 25.

[2] TGY, p. 174.

[3] TGY, p. 173.

[4] SSB, Communique on the Results of the Implementation of the National Economic Plan for 1955 (with Economic Statistical Abstract), Peking: T'ung'chi ch'u-pan-she, 1956, p. 46.

[5] Hsu Chung-yi, "Domestic trade during the past Five Years, in Eight Glorious Years, Hong Kong: New Democratic Press, 1958, pp. 59-65.

[6] Wen-hui pao, Hong Kong, June 1, 1958.

[7] Chang Yi-fei, 'Problems Concerning Relative Prices of Industrial and Agricultural Products," No. 11, 1958, p. 25.

[8] Data Office, TCKT, "A Survey of Changes in the Price Differentials between Industrial and Agricultural Products since Liberation,' ' TCKT, No. 17 (September 14, 1957), pp. 4-7.

[9] Data Office, TCYC, ' 'Changes in Market Prices in 1957 and Their Effects on People's Living Conditions,'·' TCYC, No. 4 (April 23, 1958), pp. 25-26.

TABLE 8.2 Price Indices of Selected Commodities, 1951-57

Index	1951	1952	1953	1954	1955	1956	1957	1958
Wholesale price:								
Coal (December 31, 1953=100)[1]				102.05	100.46	100.04	100.04	100.04
Retail price:								
Ammonium sulfhate (1950=100)[2]	93.0	n.a.	78.0	69.0	69.0	69.0	69.0	69.0
Insecticide "666" (1952=100)[2]		100.0	n.a.	46.0	n.a.	28.0	n.a.	21.0
Insecticide sprayers (1952=100)[2]		100.0	n.a.	n.a.	n.a.	71.0	71.0	71.0
Medium-sized doublewheel plows (1954=100)[2]				100.0	62.0	62.0	62.0	62.0
Drugs (1950=100)[3]	116.51	96.15	84.48	81.71	81.67	81.40	80.0	76.0

[1] Keng Chuan-san, "Current Prices of Coal," *ccyc*, No. 3 (March 17, 1959), p. 29. Figures given in this line were officially announced wholesale prices (*p'i-fa p'ai-chia*) in 31 large and medium cities.

[2] Chiao Yu-po, "A Survey of the Prices of Several Major Agricultural Producer Goods," *ccyc*, No. 3 (Masch 17, 1959) pp. 31-32. It may be noted that the prices of major agricultural producer goods were under the unified control of the central government and that there was only one single retail price for each of these goods throughout the country at a given time.

[3] Wang Hua-min, "Measures for lowering the Prices of Drugs in the Past Several Years," *ccyc*, No. (March 17, 1959), p. 35.

TABLE 8.3 Price Indices in Eight Large Cities, 1956

Index	Peking	Tientsin	Shanghai	Wuhan	Canton	Chungking	Sian	Shenyang
1956 prices (1955=100):								
Retail	100.3	99.8	100.9	100.1	99.4	103.6	97.5	99.7
Cost-of-living	100.1	99.3	100.4	99.5	99.5	104.0	94.4	97.9
December, 1956 prices (December, 1955=100):								
Wholesale		100.06	100.1	98.65	100.3	102.2	98.91	99.53
Retail	101.4	101.5	99.8	101.5	102.1	104.1	98.2	102.9
Cost-of-living	101.3	101.5	99.5	102.4	101.7	105.2	91.5	102.1

Source: Data Office, *TCKT*, "A Survey of Domestic Market Prices in 1956," *TCKT*, No. 7 (April 14, 1957), pp. 31–32.

TABLE 8.4 Wholesale Price Index, by
Commodity Group, 1956
(1955=100)

Commodity group	Index
Food grains	100.5
Subsidiary food	100.5
Texile products	99.2
Fuel	100.2
Building materials	97.5
Industrial supplies	97.9
Miscellaneous	96.8
Special indigenous products	102.2

Source: Data Office, *TCKT*, "A Survey of
Domestic Market Prices in 1956,"
TCKT, No. 7 (April 14, 1957), pp.
31–32.

TABLE 8.5 Monthly Wholesale Price Index, 1950-56 (December of preceding year=100)

Month	1950[1]	1951[1]	1952[1]	1953[1]	1954[1]	1955[1]	1956[2]
January	126.6	102.0	99.3	101.2	100.0	100.4	99.9
February	203.3	102.2	98.7	101.3	100.0	100.5	99.9
March	226.3	102.9	97.8	100.9	100.0	100.2	99.7
April	169.9	104.4	96.8	100.6	100.0	100.1	99.6
May	156.7	105.1	96.3	100.4	100.0	100.0	99.6
June	155.8	106.6	95.6	100.6	100.0	100.0	99.6
July	166.8	107.3	95.1	100.8	100.0	100.0	99.6
August	173.6	111.9	94.8	100.8	100.1	99.9	99.6
September	177.8	114.7	94.3	101.1	100.2	99.8	99.7
October	185.8	115.1	93.5	101.1	100.4	99.8	99.6
November	193.3	114.3	93.7	101.2	100.5	99.9	99.7
December	193.2	113.2	93.7	101.2	100.7	99.9	99.7

Note: The number of cities covered: 15 in 1950; 25 in 1951; 47 in 1952; 44 in 1953; 42 in 1954; 37 in 1955. The number of cities covered in 1956 is not known.

[1] SSB, *Communique on the Results of the Implementation of the National Economic Plan for 1955 (with Economic Statistical Abstract)*, Peking: T'ung-chi ch'u-pan-she, 1956, p. 46.

[2] SSB, *Communique on the Results of the Implementation of the National Economic Plan for 1956 (with Economic Statistical Abstract)*, Peking: T'ung-chi ch'u-pan-she, 1957, p. 60.

TABLE 8.6 Monthly Wholesale Price Index, 1950-54 (March, 1950=100)

	1950	1951	1952	1953	1954
January		87.1	96.0	91.7	91.7
February		87.3	95.4	91.8	91.7
March	100.0	87.8	94.5	91.4	91.7
April	75.1	89.1	93.5	91.1	91.7
May	69.2	89.7	93.1	91.0	91.7
June	68.8	91.0	92.4	91.1	91.7
July	73.7	91.6	91.9	91.3	91.7
August	76.7	95.5	91.6	91.3	91.8
September	78.6	97.9	91.1	91.6	91.9
October	82.1	98.3	90.4	91.6	92.1
November	85.4	97.6	90.6	91.7	92.1
December	85.4	96.6	90.6	91.7	92.3

Note: The number of cities covered: 15 in 1950; 25 in 1951; 47 in 1952; 44 in 1953; 42 in 1954.

Source: SSB, *Communique on the Results of the Implementation of the National Economic Plan for 1954 (with Economic Statistical Abstract)*, Peking: T'ung-chi ch'u-pan-she, 1955, p. 36.

TABLE 8.7 Monthly Wholesale Price Index in Shanghai, July, 1949-December, 1957 (1952=100). Weighted Arithmetic Mean

Date	Total (1)	Food (2)	Subsidiary Food (3)	Textile Products (4)	Fuel (5)	Building Material (6)	Industrial Supply (7)	Miscellaneous (8)	Special Indigenous Products (9)
1949									
July	18.22	24.57	23.62	20.46	32.05	19.08	13.46	17.30	21.66
August	7.05	15.67	11.55	8.35	16.65	7.01	3.22	5.87	10.08
September	7.96	16.23	11.73	9.20	17.30	8.70	3.97	7.60	10.00
October	9.31	13.59	12.13	11.00	17.78	9.00	5.73	9.26	10.79
November	13.21	14.56	14.83	14.07	24.44	15.95	11.94	11.83	14.02
December	30.73	34.59	37.24	34.09	47.24	32.91	25.15	29.28	37.78
1950									
January	41.06	52.78	54.26	46.03	68.93	40.88	30.72	39.95	47.27
February	75.06	103.46	108.98	81.11	105.97	62.25	57.91	78.69	73.00
March	49.41	86.25	72.76	56.23	91.17	45.76	30.71	48.59	52.76
April	72.25	122.58	111.87	90.44	115.61	53.24	34.73	78.81	64.24
May	77.24	125.62	112.59	93.40	127.01	61.45	36.61	91.57	72.19
June	64.44	115.77	86.62	78.20	126.11	48.91	31.69	71.29	55.53
July	62.22	110.87	82.10	78.81	103.00	46.68	32.35	63.81	57.22
August	64.40	105.58	85.75	78.77	92.41	58.36	50.59	72.46	69.15
September	75.99	101.62	108.92	82.34	89.15	63.64	61.17	79.30	74.96
October	78.99	98.52	126.06	81.78	89.99	68.69	68.60	80.52	76.85
November	82.11	94.31	132.26	82.87	91.20	79.82	75.76	82.01	79.36
December	86.88	97.36	131.59	84.21	101.32	75.17	82.97	90.25	87.45
1951									
January	91.45	93.15	132.20	84.12	118.90	76.97	94.68	93.47	92.77
February	90.29	89.83	125.08	82.14	125.83	68.29	95.05	92.26	93.54
March	99.30	95.99	106.85	97.55	125.02	82.74	98.76	104.08	118.02
April	91.87	95.56	110.16	89.49	127.76	58.74	92.13	95.42	92.59
May	91.17	93.69	106.35	89.36	127.79	61.07	88.56	96.69	100.85
June	91.33	95.87	101.25	89.02	132.29	61.81	85.82	98.56	117.25
July	95.19	94.75	98.40	97.45	135.21	66.54	86.59	102.73	120.31
August	96.78	95.18	99.28	97.45	134.57	70.59	90.96	103.79	120.88

413

TABLE 8.7 (Continued, 1)

Date	Total (1)	Food (2)	Subsidiary Food (3)	Textile Products (4)	Fuel (5)	Building Material (6)	Industrial Supply (7)	Miscellaneous (8)	Special Indigenous Products (9)
June	99.32	97.65	102.05	97.45	134.01	74.64	97.64	104.90	123.73
July	101.53	99.62	101.81	97.45	132.26	89.53	102.55	105.32	134.13
August	103.24	95.19	105.19	102.31	120.55	95.63	103.31	106.55	133.97
September	104.64	96.12	112.11	103.15	121.81	96.24	104.46	108.85	132.61
October	104.65	94.87	114.35	103.15	112.78	103.27	105.50	108.93	127.68
November	106.02	95.16	117.07	103.08	112.36	107.39	112.52	108.76	108.08
December	105.83	98.19	114.17	101.21	108.82	107.43	115.10	108.41	104.14
1952	100.00	100.00	100.00	100.00	100.00	100.00	100.00	100.00	100.00
January	104.46	99.73	110.92	101.21	107.86	109.04	107.94	107.90	102.96
February	102.46	102.27	104.93	99.96	103.88	107.50	103.23	106.35	102.24
March	100.02	104.45	99.23	99.34	101.89	106.38	95.49	102.47	101.88
April	98.60	103.63	98.52	99.34	101.89	103.74	92.18	98.32	99.99
May	98.76	102.17	97.52	99.34	101.89	100.26	95.50	97.54	100.12
June	99.19	101.11	97.06	99.34	101.89	99.91	99.07	97.44	100.16
July	99.27	101.11	96.59	99.34	101.62	98.09	99.77	97.79	100.16
August	99.66	98.71	98.31	100.11	100.68	98.09	100.82	97.98	100.15
September	99.76	96.40	101.36	100.50	97.81	96.51	101.60	98.46	98.36
October	99.58	96.17	101.56	100.50	93.53	95.02	102.46	98.32	98.35
November	99.39	97.09	101.08	100.50	93.53	92.74	100.99	98.70	97.95
December	98.85	97.16	92.93	100.50	93.53	92.74	100.94	98.73	97.67
1953	98.48	103.46	93.05	98.18	93.33	96.45	100.96	99.08	96.90
January	99.46	100.03	88.51	100.50	93.53	93.66	101.51	102.35	98.52
February	99.33	100.02	87.42	100.50	93.53	93.80	101.68	102.15	97.70
March	99.12	99.78	87.82	100.50	93.53	93.83	100.73	101.77	97.54
April	97.98	104.98	88.00	97.55	93.53	94.53	99.88	100.21	97.64
May	97.59	104.98	88.98	97.55	93.53	93.80	99.52	97.90	97.52
June	97.57	104.43	89.62	97.55	93.53	93.73	99.60	97.71	97.32

414

TABLE 8.7 (Continued, 2)

Date	Total	Food	Subsidiary Food	Textile Products	Fuel	Building Material	Industrial Supply	Miscellaneous	Special Indigenous Products
	(1)	(2)	(3)	(4)	(5)	(6)	(7)	(8)	(9)
July	97.82	104.61	90.44	97.55	93.53	96.00	100.47	97.54	97.32
August	98.16	104.77	93.76	97.55	93.53	96.83	101.08	97.39	97.04
September	98.48	104.62	98.33	97.55	93.33	97.04	101.66	97.44	95.01
October	98.38	104.41	99.52	97.20	92.86	97.04	101.79	97.33	94.82
November	98.92	104.43	102.06	97.13	92.79	100.48	102.17	98.60	95.59
December	98.99	104.43	102.13	97.13	92.79	106.61	101.52	98.48	96.79
1954									
January	98.88	104.37	107.52	97.13	93.18	106.78	97.40	98.40	100.01
Febrary	98.74	104.43	102.13	97.13	92.79	106.17	99.64	98.26	98.97
March	98.54	104.43	102.13	97.13	92.79	106.17	98.50	98.21	98.97
April	98.49	104.43	102.89	97.13	92.79	106.17	97.62	98.17	99.90
May	98.57	104.43	103.97	97.13	92.80	106.03	97.44	98.10	100.74
June	98.74	104.43	106.48	97.13	93.18	105.77	97.31	98.01	100.74
July	98.85	104.34	108.04	97.13	93.18	105.83	97.19	98.13	100.74
August	98.94	104.32	108.39	97.13	93.18	107.73	97.19	98.23	100.85
September	99.05	104.32	109.72	97.13	93.18	107.52	97.19	98.31	100.86
October	99.02	104.32	110.22	97.13	93.18	107.48	97.19	98.31	99.56
November	99.07	104.32	110.73	97.13	93.18	107.48	97.19	98.39	99.55
December	99.03	104.32	111.26	97.13	93.83	107.48	96.42	98.45	99.51
1955									
January	99.48	104.32	114.21	97.13	94.11	107.48	95.90	100.27	99.74
Febrary	99.22	104.32	114.83	97.13	94.11	108.07	92.59	101.66	100.02
March	99.81	104.32	115.39	97.13	94.11	107.04	95.90	101.76	99.85
April	99.81	104.32	115.44	97.13	94.11	106.84	95.90	101.76	99.99
May	99.26	104.32	114.94	97.13	94.11	106.84	92.82	101.76	99.99
June	99.19	104.32	114.34	97.13	94.11	106.84	92.69	101.76	99.99
July	99.16	104.32	113.96	97.13	94.11	106.84	92.69	101.76	99.99
August	99.23	104.32	113.96	97.13	94.11	110.20	92.69	101.76	99.99

TABLE 8.7 (Continued, 3)

Date	Total (1)	Food (2)	Subsidiary Food (3)	Textile Products (4)	Fuel (5)	Building Material (6)	Industrial Supply (7)	Miscellaneous (8)	Special Indigenous Products (9)
July	99.23	104.32	113,96	97.13	94.11	110.20	92.69	101.76	99.99
August	99.19	104.32	114.10	97.13	94.11	110.11	92.35	101.76	100.00
September	98.98	104.32	114.77	97.13	94.11	108.83	91.03	101.63	100.14
October	98.91	104.32	115.23	97.13	94.11	107.70	90.77	101.41	100.14
November	98.96	104.32	115.71	97.13	94.11	107.70	90.77	101.41	100.28
December	98.97	104.32	116.19	97.13	94.11	107.70	90.77	101.41	99.87
1956									
January	98.96	104.32	116.22	97.13	94.11	107.48	90.77	101.74	98.65
February	98.97	104.32	117.14	97.13	94.11	107.70	90.77	101.41	98.65
March	98.97	104.32	117.14	97.13	94.11	107.50	90.77	101.41	98.65
April	98.96	104.32	116.51	97.13	94.11	107.55	90.77	101.57	98.65
May	98.92	104.32	115.23	97.13	94.11	107.55	90.77	101.84	98.65
June	98.91	104.32	115.07	97.13	94.11	107.55	90.77	101.84	98.65
July	98.91	104.32	115.07	97.13	94.11	106.53	90.77	101.84	98.65
August	98.89	104.32	115.07	97.13	94.11	106.60	90.77	101.84	98.65
September	98.89	104.32	116.29	97.13	94.11	106.60	90.77	101.84	98.65
October	98.96	104.32	117.04	97.13	94.11	108.23	90.77	101.84	98.65
November	99.04	104.32	117.53	97.13	94.11	108.23	90.77	101.84	98.65
December	99.07	104.32	117.53	97.13	94.11	108.23	90.77	101.84	98.65
1957	99.40	104.32	121.57	97.13	94.11	108.54	90.77	101.60	99.57

Source: Shanghai Economic Research Institute of the Chinese Academy of Sciences and Economic Research Institute of the Shanghai Academy of Social Sciences, *A Collection of Shanghai Price Data Before and After the Liberation (1921-1957)*, Shanghai: Shanghai People's Press, 1958. pp. 454-59.

416

TABLE 8.8 Wholesale Prices of Major Commodities in Shanghai, 1949-57, Yuan

Commodity	1949	1950	1951	1952	1953	1954	1955	1956	1957
Flour (first-grade *hung-hu-ch'iang*), per 22 kg	1.36[a]	7.15[a]	7.81[a]	7.28[a]	8.05	8.10	8.70[b]	8.70[b]	8.70[b]
Wheat (medium grade), per 50 kg	2.01	10.13	10.92	10.55	10.56	10.43	10.30[c]	9.97[c]	9.50[c]
Nonglutinous rice (medium white), per 50 kg	3.20[a]	14.78[a]	12.88[a]	14.21[a]	13.81	14.00	15.15[b]	15.15[b]	15.15
Nonglutinous rice (grade B), per 50 kg	2.84[a]	12.89[a]	10.88[a]	11.97[a]	11.27	11.20	12.10[b]	12.10[b]	12.10
Beans (medium-grade yellow beans), per 50 kg	2.82[a]	12.69[a]	11.61[a]	10.43[a]	9.70	9.80	10.75[b]	10.75[b]	10.75
Edible oil (raw oil), per 50 kg	11.26[a]	50.38[a]	50.46[a]	45.96[a]	45.70	49.39	61.00[b]	61.00[b]	61.00
Table salt (Huai salt), per 50 kg	2.48[a]	17.13[a]	12.38[a]	11.32[a]	10.93	10.54	10.65	10.65	12.30
Sugar (Soviet manufactured), per 50 kg	11.39	62.67	61.43	65.60	49.00	55.97	62.69	62.70	62.70
Pork (upper grade), per 50 kg	11.42[a]	61.25[a]	61.44[a]	50.81[a]	55.08	64.14	65.05	67.00	73.11
Eggs (fresh chicken eggs), per 50 kg	11.45[a]	38.19[a]	41.71[a]	38.72[a]	43.10	49.64	51.68	52.20	55.39
Cotton yarn (20-count "lan-fan", per bale	118.23	546.48	717.25	746.67	733.56	737.00	737.00	737.00	737.00
White cotton cloth (12 pound dragon head), per bolt	5.16	24.09	27.51	28.29	28.10	27.80	27.80	27.80	27.80
Printed cotton cloth, (*ho-hua-lu* serge), per bolt	5.95[a]	24.03[a]	27.95[a]	28.37[a]	20.60	27.10	27.10	27.10	27.10
Dyed cotton cloth (worker-peasant blue cloth), per bolt	7.83[a]	36.11[a]	42.06[a]	42.60[a]	41.86	41.00	41.00	41.00	41.00
Bituminous coal (Kai-luan No. 1 splinters), per metric ton	12.08	38.01	35.68	33.86	33.31	33.00	33.00	33.00	33.00
Anthracite coal (unified splinters), per metric ton	13.16	26.64	28.16	30.80	30.80	31.67	32.10	32.10	32.10

TABLE 8.8 (Continued, 1)

Commodity	1949	1950	1951	1952	1953	1954	1955	1956	1957
Kerosene (Soviet manufactured, No. 2), per 164 kg	40.03	126.69	192.86	153.20	131.91	131.46	137.10	137.10	137.10
Gasoline (Soviet manufactured, No. 2), per 145 kg	45.28	252.54	255.70	148.74	120.64	120.64	120.64	120.64	120.64
Diesel (Soviet manufactured, No. 2), per metric ton	141.25	557.93	743.12	495.27	462.00	462.00	462.00	462.00	462.00
Lumber (3"x6"x14"), per cum	23.24[a]	87.83[a]	126.62[a]	149.45[a]	146.31	175.11	182.89	186.60	186.00
Cement (Taishan), per metric ton	22.00	80.80	80.62	89.41	82.62	83.00	80.06	73.00	73.00
Glass plate (2 mm, 16"x24"), per 100 sq m	6.72	18.39	17.82	18.00	16.46	16.10	16.10	15.25	14.30
Gray brick (1¾"x8½"), per ten thousand pieces	51.27[a]	194.38[a]	239.77[a]	306.14[a]	308.03	291.77	266.28	278.58	324.00
Wrought iron (19m/mx18), per metric ton	199.00[a]	770.33[a]	988.41[a]	785.63[a]	735.92	660.83	660.00	660.00	660.00
Steel plate (1/8"x4"x8"), per metric ton	219.66[a]	855.21[a]	1,559.88[a]	1,867.66[a]	1,463.91	1,407.44	1,163.27	1,140.00	1,140.00
Iron pipe (2", A Grade), per metric ton	386.78[a]	1,787.64[a]	2,881.86[a]	2,847.37[a]	1,818.20	1,756.54	1,467.53	1,290.00	1,290.00
Copper wire (No. 8), per metric ton	1,225.29[a]	5,748.55[a]	6,836.23[a]	7,007.73[a]	8,170.00	8,170.00	8,170.00	8,170.00	8,170.00
Pig iron (No. 2), per metric ton	67.67[a]	204.07[a]	238.46[a]	258.24[a]	229.58	246.00	227.70	220.00	220.00
Rubber (No. 3 Singapore red), per metric ton	325.56[a]	3,103.26[a]	5,483.86[a]	5,975.97[a]	6,000.00	6,000.00	6,000.00	6,000.00	6,000.00
Caustic soda (Yung-li), per kg	0.17	0.47	0.98	1.01	1.01	0.99	0.98	0.96	0.96
Soda ash (Nanking-hua 246°), per kg	0.59	2.21	4.24	3.80	3.75	3.75	3.75	3.75	3.75
Matches (Mei-li, short stalk), per 100 cases	4.18[a]	16.32[a]	17.24[a]	17.85[a]	17.58	17.00	17.00	17.00	17.00
Soap (Worker-peasant), per 120 pieces	4.12[a]	15.83[a]	16.76[a]	17.54[a]	16.48	16.25	16.25	17.38	17.37

TABLE 8.8 (Continued. 2)

Commodity	1949	1950	1951	1952	1953	1954	1955	1956	1957
Alkali (Yung-li pure), per 80 kg	6.46	19.15	26.01	32.47	32.50	32.00	32.00	32.00	32.00
Sulfur dyestuffs (Soviet made), per 50 kg	19.52[a]	105.58[a]	147.10[a]	150.24[a]	152.13	142.03	138.91	131.50	131.50
Newsprint (Soviet Union 30"x42"), yuan per ling	4.59[a]	23.34[a]	38.40[a]	37.14[a]	30.16	29.50	29.50	29.50	29.50
Cigarettes ("Flying Horse"), per 200 pieces	0.27[a]	1.52[a]	1.93[a]	1.82[a]	1.91	1.94	2.10	2.10	2.10
Towel (Bell 414), per dozen	1.48[a]	7.77[a]	9.40[a]	8.78[a]	8.75	8.71	8.71	8.71	8.71
Cotton socks (Dog 303), per dozen	1.25[a]	5.58[a]	7.40[a]	7.36[a]	7.33	7.33	7.33	7.33	7.33
Penicillin (France 200.000 units, U.P.R.), per bottle	0.19[a]	0.78[a]	1.15[a]	0.78[a]	0.71	0.68	0.71	0.71	0.71
Gunny sacks (29"x43", 2.5 pounds), per sack	0.48	2.33	3.21	2.72	2.18	2.05	2.10	2.10	2.10
Tung oil (full degree), per 50 kg	11.75[a]	62.37[a]	59.83[a]	52.12[a]	39.99	42.36	48.07	54.50	63.80
Bean cake (No. 4), per 50 kg	1.61[a]	7.42[a]	6.62[a]	7.00[a]	7.10	7.86	8.28	8.40	8.40
Tobacco (medium-and low-grade No. 5), per 50 kg	16.04[a]	56.73[a]	121.80[a]	91.40[a]	101.76	106.22	106.75	106.75	106.75
Hemp bast (ta-chu, ramie-green grade No. 1), per 50 kg	12.04[a]	59.67[a]	72.28[a]	72.42[a]	71.12	74.62	76.50	76.50	76.50
Raw cotton (7/8" medium-grade fine staple cotton), per 50 kg	23.52[a]	85.55[a]	94.10[a]	94.28[a]	91.29	92.21	90.00[c]	90.00[c]	90.00
Cowhide, per 50 kg	18.58	88.70	165.87	128.36	159.00	159.00	158.09	116.00	131.17

Note: Figures with the letter a refer to market prices; those with the letter b refer to unfied sale prices (t'ung-hsiao-chia); and those with the letter c refer to procurement prices (shou-ko-chia). Figures without any letter indicate announced prices (p'ai-chia).

Source: Compiled from Shanghai Economic Research Institute of the Chinese Academy of Sciences and Economic Research Institute of Shanghai Academy of Social Sciences, A Collection of Price Data Before and After the Liberation (1921-1957). Shanghai: Shanghai People's Press, 1958, pp. 470-563.

419

TABLE 8.9   Retail Index, by Commodity Group, 1956 (1955=100)

Commodity Group	Index
Food	100.0
Subsidiary food	100.9
Tobacco, liquor, and tea	98.2
Other food products	101.6
Clothing	100.0
Fuel	100.0
Daily necessities	101.8
Drugs	100.0
Household utensils	96.3
Cultural and educational supplies	101.4

Source: Data Office, *TCKT*, "A Survey of Domestic Market Prices in 1956," *TCKT*, No. 7 (April 14, 1957), pp. 31-32.

TABLE 8.10   Quarterly Retail Price Index in Urban and Rural Areas in 1957 (Same Quarter of 1956=100)

Area	First quarter	Second quarter	Third quarter	Fourth quarter
Urban	102.4	104.0	102.3	100.9
Rural	101.8	102.7	102.1	102.2

Source: Data Office, *TCYC*, "Changes in Market Prices in 1957 and Their Effects on People's Livelihood," *TCYC*, No. 4 (April 23, 1958), pp. 25-26.

TABLE 8.11   Price Indices in the Inner Mongolia Autonomous Region, 1951-58

Year	Retail price of industrial products		Government purchase price of agricultural products	
	1950=100	1952=100	1950=100	1952=100
	(1)	(2)	(3)	(4)
1951	112.66		142.49	
1952	123.13	100.00	150.29	100.00
1953	128.45	113.31	162.98	103.17
1954	132.59	121.38	172.77	105.66
1955	136.86	120.64	171.48	109.80
1956	141.37	119.50	171.00	113.11
1957	138.91	124.87	177.83	112.32
1958	140.19	127.60	185.65	110.32

Source: *NMKTC*, pp. 119-220.

TABLE 8.12   Index of Retail Prices of Major Cities during First Quarter of 1957 (First Quarter of 1956=100)

City	Retail price index	City	Retail price index
Hsinin	95.9	Canton	102.9
Lanchow	97.0	Wuhan	105.1
Sian	98.7	Changsha	106.4
Urumchi	99.7	Chengtu	106.5
Shanghai	100.4	Chungking	106.9
Peking	100.6	Harbin	107.6
Tientsin	101.0	Chang-	
Shenyang	101.3	chun	109.7

Source: Data Office, *TCKT*, "A General Survey of Market Prices during the First Quarter of 1957," *TCKT*, No. 11 (June 14, 1957), pp. 26-27.

TABLE 8.13 Retail Price Indices of Major Commodity Groups in
Eight Large Cities, 1953-56 (1952=100)

Commodity group	1953	1954	1955	1956
Food grains	104.7	105.1	105.2	105.4
Subsidiary food products	112.9	116.2	118.7	119.0
Cigarettes, wine, and tea	99.8	106.0	110.3	108.3
Clothing	100.0	99.8	101.5	102.0
Fuels	103.0	104.8	106.2	105.6
Daily necessities	100.7	99.7	100.5	100.6
Drugs	67.4	68.5	68.9	68.5
Cultural and educational supplies	90.4	84.4	84.2	85.4

Note: The eight cities are: Peking, Shanghai, Tientsin, Shenyang,
Canton, Chungking, Sian, and Wuhan.

Source: Hsu Chung-yi, "In Retrospect of Domestic Trade during the
Past Five-Years," in *Eight Glorious Years*, Hong Kong: New Democratic Press, 1958, 59-65.

TABLE 8.14 Index of Retail Prices of Main Commodity Groups
in Major Cities, during First Quarter of 1957
(First Quarter of 1956=100)

Category	Twenty-nine cities	Of which: eight large cities
	(1)	(2)
Food	100.1	100.5
Subsidiary food	108.2	104.7
Seasonal vegetables	127.7	112.8
Nonseasonal vegetables	98.6	97.2
Meat, eggs, and fish	105.1	104.7
Seasoning	101.3	100.8
Clothing	99.6	99.8
Fuel	100.6	100.1
Daily necessities	101.5	101.9
Drugs	99.7	99.6
Utensils	102.4	103.3

Source: Data Office, *TCKT*, "A General Survey of Market
Prices during the First Quarter of 1957," *TCKT*, No.
11 (June 14, 1957), pp. 26-27.

TABLE 8.15   Retail Prices Index in Shanghai, 1953-57 (1952=100).
Weighted Arithmetic Mean

Category	1953	1954	1955	1956	1957
Total	105. 28	107. 15	108. 14	109. 12	110. 5
Food	103. 13	103. 62	103. 62	103. 62	103. 6
Subsidiary food	114. 27	116. 70	118. 80	120. 49	122. 9
Seasonal vegetables	135. 69	117. 35	124. 61	117. 36	113. 7
Nonseasonal vegetables	132. 73	107. 90	107. 10	107. 66	105. 7
Meat, eggs, chicken, and fish	110. 08	123. 43	120. 37	125. 74	130. 3
Seasoning	94. 09	104. 54	116. 24	115. 18	116. 2
Cigarettes, liquor, and tea	105. 43	113. 25	117. 23	115. 57	114. 7
Cigarettes	99. 31	100. 38	108. 82	107. 59	107. 5
Liquor	120. 65	145. 96	134. 52	129. 41	128. 9
Tea	100. 00	98. 88	102. 95	112. 07	114. 0
Other food products:	103. 68	103. 15	100. 72	102. 36	108. 5
Refreshments	100. 00	98. 89	98. 77	98. 77	98. 8
Candy	94. 78	96. 65	100. 67	91. 83	91. 0
Fruits	128. 72	127. 23	102. 06	113. 10	135. 9
Clothing	102. 51	103. 20	105. 45	106. 82	107. 8
Cloth	100. 94	102. 26	104. 98	107. 32	109. 0
Readymade clothes	97. 18	96. 69	99. 22	99. 93	99. 9
Other clothes	109. 07	108. 77	109. 60	108. 53	108. 5
Fuel	96. 74	96. 71	98. 71	98. 07	98. 0
Daily necessities	98. 45	98. 63	99. 52	104. 42	105. 7
Drugs	88. 34	99. 13	93. 15	91. 70	83. 0
New drugs	76. 45	62. 92	63. 14	61. 83	60. 3
Traditional drugs	113. 69	176. 28	141. 66	141. 66	141. 1
Household utensils	112. 53	121. 65	125. 12	121. 10	127. 5
Cultural and educational supplies	92. 75	88. 51	87. 23	90. 30	88. 0

Source: Shanghai Economic Research Institute of the Chinese Academy of
Sciences and Economic Research Institute of the Shanghai Academy of Social
Sciences, *A Collection of Shanghai Price Data Before and After the Libera-
tion (1921-1957)*, Shanghai: Shanghai People's Press, 1958, p. 460.

TABLE 8.16   Cost-of-Living Index for Workers in Shanghai, 1950-52
(June 10-20, 1949=100)

Year	Total	Food	Housing	Clothing	Miscellaneous
1950	1, 675. 53	1, 713. 83	1, 342. 37	1, 472. 17	2, 212. 69
1951	1, 639. 82	1, 577. 24	1, 429. 81	1, 817. 25	2, 336. 63
1952	1, 617. 86	1, 536. 99	1, 460. 79	1, 853. 14	2, 256. 41

Source: Shanghai Economic Research Institute of the Chinese Academy
of Sciences and Economic Research Institute of the Shanghai Academy of Social Sciences, *A Collection of Shanghai Price Data Before and After the Liberation (1921-1957)* Shanghai: Shanghai
People's Press, 1958, pp. 461-462.

TABLE 8.17 Cost-of-Living Index for Workers and Employers in Shanghai, 1953-57 (1952=100), Weighted Arithmetic Mean

Category	1953	1954	1955	1956	1957
Total	105.76	106.62	107.76	108.15	109.0
Food	110.18	110.85	112.07	113.08	113.9
Staple food	103.90	104.98	104.98	104.98	105.0
Subsidiary food	115.78	115.03	117.32	119.37	120.7
Meat, eggs, and fish	109.79	119.64	117.40	123.20	
Vegetables	135.55	115.53	117.69	114.57	
Seasoning products	94.85	105.39	116.55	115.24	
Cigarettes, liquor, and tea	108.15	116.26	119.14	118.15	119.3
Other food products	102.24	101.76	98.07	99.49	102.4
Nonfood products	100.81	101.02	102.44	103.17	103.3
Clothing	102.34	102.51	104.26	105.38	106.4
Fuel	101.40	101.82	105.12	104.48	104.3
Household utensils	112.53	121.64	124.72	120.98	130.1
Daily necessities	98.02	98.89	99.32	104.46	105.5
Cultural and educational supplies	96.62	90.49	92.94	90.54	85.1
Drugs	79.50	75.66	63.28	63.01	61.4
Service expenditures	99.61	101.85	102.37	100.76	100.8
Rent, water, and electricity	99.93	100.23	100.74	100.74	100.7
Other service expenditures	99.10	104.49	105.04	101.21	101.2

Source: Shanghai Economic Research Institute of the Chinese Academy of Sciences and Economic Research Institute of the Shanghai Academy of Social Sciences, *A Collection of Shanghai Price Data Before and After the Liberation (1921-1957)*, Shanghai: Shanghai People's Press, 1958, p. 463.

TABLE 8.18 Agricultural Purchase-Price Indices, by Category of Products, 1956 and 1958

| Category | 1956[1] | | | 1958[2] |
	1930-36=100	1950=100	1952=100	(1957=100)
Total	262.0	139.2	116.6	102.2
Food grains	230.4	139.9	115.7	102.6
Industrial crops	257.1	122.6	109.8	101.2
Animal products	294.0	127.3	121.9	103.3
Special indigenous products	309.5	194.6	127.9	102.8

[1] Data Office, *TCKT*, "A Survey of Changes in Price Differential between Industrial and Agricultural Products since Liberation," *TCKT*, No. 17 (September 14, 1957), pp. 4-7; and Chang Yi-fei, "Problems Concerning Price Ratios between Industrial and Agricultural Products," *HCS*, No. 11, 1958, p. 25.

[2] "Agricultural Purchase Price Indices and Price Ratios between Industrial and Agricultural Products in 1958," *CYHTTH*, No. 4 (April 11, 1959), p. 13.

TABLE 8.19   Ratio between Purchase-Price Indices for In-
             dustrial Crops and Food Grains, 1950-58

Year	1930-36= 100[1]	1950=100[1]	1952=100[1]	1957=100[2]
	(1)	(2)	(3)	(4)
1950	125.4	100.0		
1951	124.7	100.1		
1952	116.4	93.1	100.0	
1953	104.2	82.4	88.9	
1954	110.0	87.0	94.1	
1955	111.3	87.4	94.6	
1956	111.6	87.6	99.5	
1957				100.0
1958				(99.0)

Note: Figures are derived from dividing the purchase-
      price index for industrial crops by that for food grains.

[1] Data Office, *TCKT*, "A Survey of Changes in Price
     Differentials between Industrial and Agricultural
     Products since Liberation," *TCKT*, No. 17 (Sept-
     ember 14, 1957), pp. 4-7.
[2] Derived from data given in "Agricultural Purchase
     Price Indices and Price Ratios between Industrial
     and Agricultural Products in 1958," *CYHTTH*, No. 4
     (April 11, 1959), p. 13.

TABLE 8.20   Ratios of Index of Industrial Retail Prices
             in Rural Areas to Agricultural Purchase-
             Price Index, 1950-58

Year	1936=100[1]	1930-36=100[2]	1950=100[2]	1952=100[3]
1950	145.3	131.8	100.0	
1951		124.4	92.2	
1952		121.8	90.3	(100.0)
1953		109.6	81.7	(89.5)
1954		109.2	80.7	(88.0)
1955		111.3	82.8	(89.6)
1956		107.0	79.6	(86.1)
1957		103.2	76.7	(83.0)
1958				(80.7)

Note: Figures are derived from dividing the index of retail
      prices of industrial products in rural areas by the index
      for agricultural products.
[1] Data Office, *TCKT*, "A Survey of Changes in Price Dif-
     ferentials between Industrial and Agricultural Products
     since Liberation," *TCKT*, No. 17 (September 14, 1957),
     pp. 4-7.
[2] *Ibid.*, and Chang Yi-fei, "Problems Concerning Price Ratios
     between Industrial and Agricultural Products," *HCS*, No.
     11, 1958, p. 25.
[3] Derived from data given in *TGY*, p. 173.

TABLE 8.21   Ratios of Index of Industrial Retail Prices in Rural Areas to
Agricultural Purchase-Price Index, by Area, 1956

Index	National average	Coastal areas	Inland areas	National minority areas	Han nationlity areas
1930-36=100:					
Agricultural purchase price	262.0	259.5	255.4	297.8	255.1
Industrial retail price	280.4	296.0	263.1	259.1	280.9
Ratio	107.0	114.1	103.0	87.0	110.1
1950=100:					
Agricultural purchase price	139.2	131.2	147.9	160.4	137.8
Industrial retail price	110.8	110.1	110.3	109.6	110.2
Ratio	79.6	83.9	74.6	68.3	78.0
1952=100:					
Agricultural purchase price	116.6	116.4	118.4	116.4	117.4
Industrial retail price	100.4	101.0	98.5	99.4	99.8
Ratio	86.1	86.8	83.2	85.3	85.0

Note: In 1956, as compared with the prewar years (1930-36), the price differential between industrial and agricultural products increased by 20.1
percent or more in Liaoning, Kirin, Chekiang, and Fukien; by 10.1 to 20
percent in Hopei, Heilungkiang, Shangtung, Kiangsu, Hunan, Kwangsi, and
Shensi; by 10 percent or less in Anhwei, Honan, Kwangtung, Szechuan, and
Kweichow; the price differentials decreased in Shansi, Hupeh, Inner Mongolia
and Kansu. Compared with 1950 levels, the price differentials between industrial and agricultural products in 1956 decreased by less than 10 percent
in Hopei; by 30.1 to 50 percent in Szechuan, Kansu, and Sinkiang; by 10.1
to 30 percent in other provinces. Compared with 1952 levels, the price dif-
ferentials in 1956 decreased by less than 10 percent in Hopei, Shansi,
Shensi, Inner Mongolia, Kiangsu, and Kiangsi; by 10.1 to 20 percent in
Liaoning, Kirin, Heilungkiang, Kansu, Shantung, Anhwei, Chekiang, Honan,
Hupeh, Kwangsi, and Kweichow; and by 20.1 to 30 percent in Sinkiang,
Fukien, Kwangtung, and Szechuan.
Sources: Data Office, *TCKT*, "A Survey of Changes in Price Differentials
between Industrial and Agricultural Products since Liberation," *TCKT*,
No. 17 (September 14, 1957), pp. 4-7; and Chang Yi-fei, "Problems Con-
cerning Price Ratios between Industrial and Agricultural Products,"
HCS, No. 11, 1958, p. 25.

TABLE 8.22 Ratios of Index of Industrial Retail Prices in Rural Areas to Agricultural Purchase-Price Index in Seven Province;, 1956

Province	1930-36=100	1950=100	1952=100
	(1)	(2)	(3)
Liaoning[1]	134.5	86.0	
Kirin[1]	121.6	80.1	
Sinkiang[1]			61.1
Fukien[1]	122.9	86.9	76.4
Chekiang[1]	120.4	74.4	
Szechuan[1]			77.5
Kansu[2]			87.3

[1] Data Office, *TCKT*, "A Survey of Changes in Price Differentials between Industrial and Agricultural Products since Liberation," *TCKT*, No. 17 (September 14, 1957), pp. 4-7, reference on p. 7.

[2] Ma Yi-chao (Director of Kansu Provincial Statistical Bureau), "The Living Standards of the People in Kansu Province," *TCKT*, No, 14 (July 29, 1957), pp. 21 and 32.

TABLE 8.23 Ratio of Index of Industrial Retail Prices in Rural Areas to Index of Agricultural Purchase Prices in National Minority Areas, 1952 and 1957

Year	1930-36=100	1950=100
1952	73.89	83.34
1957	64.32	68.70

Source: Li Tsung-hai, "The Great Achievements in Economic Construction in the National Minority Areas, *Min-tsu t'uan-chieh (Unity of Nationalities)*, No. 10 (October 6, 1959), pp. 36-39.

TABLE 8.24 Ratios of Price Index for Food to Price Index for Cloth, 1951-56 (1950=100)

Area	1951	1952	1953	1954	1955	1956
National average	91.6	89.9	77.4	75.7	75.8	74.2
Inner Mongolia						67.4
Sinkiang						60.6
Kiangsu						83.6
Anhwei						91.1
Chekiang						94.3
Szechuan						54.4
Kwichow						56.7

Note: The original source did not explain what types of price index were used in computing the ratios.

Source: Data Office, *TCKT*, "A Survey of Changes in Price Differentials between Industrial and Agricultural Products since Liberation," *TCKT*, No. 17 (September 14, 1957), pp. 4-7, reference on p. 7.

TABLE 8.25 Exchange Rate between Wheat and White Fine Cloth in Seven Provinces, 1950, 1952, and 1956, Number of Feet of White Fine Cloth per Hundred *chin* of Wheat

Province	1950	1952	1956	Province	1950	1952	1956
Hopei	32.15	32.13	37.46	Kansu	16.72	28.62	31.22
Shansi	25.09	31.94	37.22	Sinkiang	24.77	28.17	35.48
Shantung	39.29	30.27	35.40	Hunan	18.69	21.50	25.36
Honan	25.97	25.22	32.97				

Source: Data Office, *TCKT*, "A Survey of Changes in Price Differentials between Industrial and Agricultural Products since Liberation," *TCKT*, No. 17 (September 14, 1957), pp. 4-7.

TABLE 8.26 Rate of Exchange between Industrial Products and Agricultural and Animal Products in the Inner Mongolia Autonomous Region, 1950 and 1953

Agricultural and animal products	Per foot of cloth		Per piece of brick tea	
	1950	1958	1950	1958
Wheat, 100 *shih chin*	25. 83	33. 10	2. 66	3. 18
Kaoliang, 100 *shih chin*	9. 75	17. 24	1. 11	1. 69
Maize, 100 *shih chin*	9. 22	17. 24	1. 05	1. 69
Flax, 100 *shih chin*	30. 70	48. 67	3. 04	4. 61
Rapeseed, 100 *shih chin*	23. 21	42. 42	2. 34	4. 02
Hogs, head	107. 86	177. 76	11. 25	17. 08
Eggs, 100 *shih chin*	58. 85	157. 78	6. 25	15. 15
Horses, head	427. 63	821. 67	50. 21	77. 88
Cattle, head	303. 88	459. 19	33. 92	43. 52
Sheep, head	27. 46	55. 75	3. 10	5. 29
Sheepskins, pieces	8. 41	14. 96	0. 96	1. 42
Wool, 100 *shih chin*	213. 88	303. 34	24. 24	28. 76

Source: *NMKTC*, p. 221.

TABLE 8.27 Rate of Exchange between Selected Products in Kansu Province, 1930- 36 and 1955

Product	1930- 36	1955
Meters of white fine cloth per 50 kg of wheat	10. 22	10. 98
Meters of white fine cloth per 50 kg of sheep wool	58. 99	131. 76
Kilograms of wheat per 50 kg of hemp	195. 47	227. 32

Source: Ma Yi-chao (Director of Kansu Provincial Statistical Bureau), "The Living Standards of the People in Kansu Province," *TCKT*, No. 14 (July 29, 1957), pp. 21, 32.

TABLE 9.1 Social Purchasing Power, 1950-58

Purchasing power	1950	1951	1952	1953	1954	1955	1956	1957	1958
Social:									
Index:									
1950=100 (Wang Che and Liu Shou-chun data)[1]	100.0	125.0	156.25	187.5	213.4				
1952=100:									
Wang Che and Liu Shou-chun data[1]			100.0	126.0	139.5	145.3	166.3	173.0	
Hsu Ti-hsin data[2]			100.0	126.7	140.8	144.6	170.3	171.1	
Ts'ai Ching data[3]			100.0						
Hsu Chung-yi data[4]			100.0	127.5	138.0	145.4	168.1	171.1	
Amount, million yuan:									
Po I-po's report[5]			27,660			40,200	46,500	47,320	
Ts'ai Ching data[3]								47,320	
Residents, million yuan:									
Rural[6]	10,380						24,500		30,000
Urban:									
Within state plan[5]							12,910		
Collective units, million yuan[7]							(7,440)		

TABLE 9.1 (Continued)

1 Wang Che and Liu Shou-chun, *The Function of State-Operated Trade in China during the Transition Period*, Peking: People's Press, 1957, p. 23.

2 Hsu Ti-hsin, *An Analysis of the National Economy of China during the Transition Period*, rev. ed, Peking: Science Press, 1959, p. 201.

3 Tsai Ching, "The Increasing Living Standards of the 600 Million People," in *Eight Glorious Years*, Hong Kong: New Democratic Press, 1958, pp. 180-84.

4 Hsu Chung-yi, "Domestic Trade in the Past Five Years," in *Eight Glorious Years*, Hong Kong: New Democratic Press, 1958, pp. 59-65.

5 Po I-po, "Report on the Results of the 1956 Plan for 1957," *JMJP*, July 2, 1957.

6 T'an Chen-lin, "A Study of the Income and the Living Standards of the Chinese Peasants," *HHPYK*, No. 11 (June, 1957), pp. 105-111; "Great Changes in the Peasant Livelihood in the Past Ten Years," *Chung-kuo nung-pao (Chinese Agricultural Bulletin)*, No. 19, 1959, pp. 33-35.

7 Derived from the information that the purchasing power of the collective units accounted for approximately 16 percent of the social purchasing power. The 16 percent was given by Wu Ting-ch'eng, "Explanation of Certain Problems Concerning the Proposal for Computing the Social Purchasing Power," *CHCC*, No. 9 (September 9, 1957), pp. 27-29, but Wu did not specify the time period to which the percentage be applied. The percentage was used by Choh-ming Li to derive the purchasing power of the collective units for 1956 on the ground that the ratio was reportedly rather stable during the First Five-Year Period. (See Choh-ming Li, *Economic Development of Communist China*, University of California Press, 1959, p. 158.) The same figure (7,440 million yuan) for 1956 was also derived by Dwight H. Perkins, "Price Stability and Development in Mainland China (1951-1963)," *Journal of Political Economy*, August, 1964, pp. 360-75.

TABLE 9.2 Per Capita Income and Expenditure of Workers and
Employees and of Peasants for the National Average
and Selected Provinces, 1955, Current Yuan

Province	Excluding noncommodity expenditures		Including noncommodity expenditures	
	Income	Expenditure	Income	Expenditure
	(1)	(2)	(3)	(4)
National average:	148	138	183	173
Workers and employees	98	93	102	97
Peasants	90[a]	85[a]	94[a]	89[a]
Liaoning:	170	157	207	194
Workers and employees	128	111	133	166
Peasants	122[a]	105[a]	127[a]	110[a]
Hopei:				
Workers and employees:	138	132	166	160
Not including Tientsin	149	136	176	163
Including Tientsin	109	97	114	102
Peasants	98[a]	86[a]	103[a]	91[a]
Kiangsu:				
Workers and employees:	144	133	189	178
Not including Shanghai	189	173	243	227
Including Shanghai	129	115	136	122
Peasants	123[a]	109[a]	130[a]	116[a]
Hupeh:	128	120	154	146
Workers and employees	88	75	90	77
Peasants	84[a]	71[a]	86[a]	73[a]
Szechuan:	123	116	157	150
Workers and employees	74	70	76	72
Peasants	68[a]	64[a]	70[a]	66[a]
Shensi:	172	136	213	177
Workers and employees	100	98	105	103
Peasants	94[a]	92[a]	99[a]	97[a]

[a] Excluding the consumption of handicraft products made by peasants for
own use.
Source: Data Office, TCKT, "Problems Concerning the Living Standards of
Peasants and Workers," TCKT, No. 13 (July 14, 1957), pp. 4-5, 24.

TABLE 9.3 Survey Data on the Income and Expenditure of Peasant Households
in 1955[a]

Indicator	Total	Members of agricultural producer cooperatives	Poor peasants	Middle peasants	Rich peasants	Previous landlords
	(1)	(2)	(3)	(4)	(5)	(6)
Labor and cultivated area:						
Average number of persons per household	4.8	5.1	4.2	5.0	6,0	4.2
Average number of laborers per household	2.4	2.6	2.0	2.5	3.0	2.2
Average size of cultivated area per household, mou	15.80	16.17	11.24	17.72	31.16	12.81

TABLE 9.3 (Continued)

Indicator	Total	Members of agricultural producer cooperatives	Poor peasants	Middle peasants	Rich peasants	Previous landlords
	(1)	(2)	(3)	(4)	(5)	(6)
Average cultivated area per person, *mou*	3.29	3.17	2.68	3.54	5.03	3.05
Income, yuan:						
Average per household						
Total	692.9	704.6	488.7	774.4	1,297.0	497.2
Agricultural	420.6	466.4	272.6	479.7	860.6	286.0
From subsidiary occupations	172.8	160.5	138.5	187.0	254.0	133.3
Other	99.5	77.7	77.6	107.7	182.4	77.9
Average income per *mou* of cultivated land		28.8	24.3	27.1	27.7	22.3
Expenditure per household, yuan	667.7	702.3[b]	473.6	743.2	1,272.2	497.1
By use:						
Consumption	454.0		334.8	499.6	821.9	
Production	156.2					
Taxes	35.4					
Other	22.0					
By means of payment:						
Cash	225.0					
In kind	442.7					
Money expenditure per household, yuan:[c]						
Consumer goods			105.2	128.6	232.0	
Producer goods			30.3	79.8	127.2	
Per capita consumption of major consumer goods:						
Food grains, *chin* per person	373	391	353	378	413	361
Meat, *chin* per person	9.2	9.3	7.4	9.8	11.4	7.1
Edible oil, *chin* per person	2.5	2.3	2.3	2.6	3.0	2.2
Cotton cloth, meters per person	5.1	6.8	3.9	5.4	10.0	3.0
Commodity rate of food production, percent	25.7	30.0[d]	22.1	25.2	43.1	28.1

[a] Data in this table were obtained by the State Statistical Bureau from a sample survey covering more than 16,000 peasant households in 25 provinces.
[b] Not including public expenditures of the agricultural producer cooperatives.
[c] Money expenditure refers to the amount of money spent on the purchase of commodities.
[d] Not including the amount of food grains sold by agricultural producer cooperatives.
Source: Data Office, *TCKT*, "A Brief Summary of Data on the Income and Expenditure of Peasant Households in 1954," *TCKT*, No. 10 (May 29, 1957), pp. 31-33.

431

TABLE 9.4　Per Capita Income and Expenditure of Peasants in Kirin Province, 1941, 1952, 1955, and 1956, in 1952 yuan[a]

Indicator	1941	1952	1955	1956
Income per capita:				
Including production for own use[b]	65	101	99	95
Not including production for own use	51.0	82.0	77.0	76.0
Consumption expenditure per capita:				
Including production for own use[b]	68	95	98	95
Not including production for own use	53.44	74.91	76.30	75.08
Food expenditure	36.98	45.45	46.86	46.00
Food grains	20.21	21.58	21.63	24.52
Subsidiary food	16.03	22.05	22.40	18.47
Other food products	--	0.68	0.94	0.74
Cigarettes, liquor, and tea	0.74	1.14	1.42	1.77
Payments to restaurants	--	--	0.47	0.50
Expenditure on nonfood products	12.71	26.90	26.01	25.28
Fuel	7.17	6.83	7.20	7.77
Daily necessities	0.85	1.83	3.19	2.46
Clothing	4.69	14.62	12.17	11.78
Drugs	--	1.57	2.17	1.53
Others	--	2.05	1.28	1.74
Noncommodity expenditure	3.74	2.56	3.43	3.80
Rent, water, and electricity	1.86	--	0.04	--
Service payments	0.55	0.56	1.12	1.31
Culture and recreation	0.34	0.55	0.45	0.73
Others	0.99	1.45	1.82	1.76

[a] Figures for 1941 were estimated by the Kirin Provincial Statistical Bureau on the basis of the survey data compiled by the Ministry of Industry of the Manchukuo. Figures for 1952, 1955, and 1956 were derived by the bureau from the peasant household budget studies and purchasing power surveys and from data on the social retail volume.

[b] Production for own use was valued at the average sale prices in urban areas.

Source: Kirin Provincial Statistical Bureau, "A Comparison of the Living Standards of Workers and Peasants in Kirin Province Before and After the Liberation," *TCKT*, No. 14 (July 29, 1957), pp. 14-18.

TABLE 9.5 Per Capita Income and Consumption of Peasants in
Hunan Province, 1936, 1952, and 1956

Indicator	1936	1952	1956
Income, 1952 yuan			
Per household	69.71	70.44	83.2
Per capita			
Poor peasants	59.2		83.5
Middle peasants	78.8		86.2
Rich peasants	118.8		102.6
Landlords	127.3		75.3
Consumption per capita:			
Food grains, kilograms	238	254	278
Edible oil, kilograms	1.5	1.6	2.2
Meat, kilograms	4.4	4.2	4.7
Salt, kilograms	4.3	6.6	6.6
Cotton cloth, meters	3.1	3.3	5.5

Note: Figures in this table were computed by Hunan Provincial Statistical Bureau from data on income and expenditure of peasant households.

Source: Hunan Provincial Statistical Bureau, "We Have Be-
gun the Work of Using and Analyzing Survey Data on the
Income and Expenditure of Peasant Households," *TCKT*,
No. 1 (January 14, 1958), pp. 13-14.

TABLE 9.6 Per Capita Income and Expenditure of Workers and Employees in
Kirin Province, 1941, 1952, 1955, and 1956 in 1952 Yuan

Indicator	1941	1952	1955	1956
Income per capita	105.0	146.0	158.0	173.0
Consumption expenditure per capita:	104.04	144.77	156.72	167.72
Food expenditure	62.76	64.82	71.55	74.08
Food grains	25.82	36.56	35.31	35.57
Subsidiary food	26.10	21.87	25.75	25.84
Other food products	3.00	1.76	4.29	4.28
Cigarettes, liquor, and tea	5.85	4.63	4.25	5.11
Payments to restaurants	1.99	--	1.95	3.28
Expenditure on nonfood products	26.98	59.46	61.83	68.07
Fuel	12.95	10.44	13.40	12.49
Daily necessities	2.61	6.73	5.59	5.93
Clothing	9.19	34.96	26.13	30.26
Drugs	0.72	2.17	11.64	11.04
Others	1.51	5.16	5.07	8.35
Noncommodity expenditure	14.30	20.49	23.34	25.57
Rent, water, and electri-city	6.16	8.14	8.47	6.84
Service payments	4.14	3.95	7.56	8.46
Culture and recreation	0.52	1.84	1.45	1.59
Others	3.48	6.56	5.86	8.68

Note: Figures for 1941 were estimated by Kirin Provincial Statistical Bureau on the basis of the survey reports of the Southern Manchurian Railway Company. Figures for 1952, 1955, and 1956 were derived by the bureau
from wage data, family buget studies, purchasing power surveys, and data
on social retail volume.

Source: Kirin Provincial Statistical Bureau, "A Comparison of the Living
Standards of Workers and Peasants in Kirin Province Before and After the
Liberation," *TCKT*, No. 14 (July 29, 1957), pp. 14-18.

TABLE 9.7 Increase in Peasant Due to Changes in Prices, 1953-57, Millions of 1952 Yuan

Increase	1953	1954	1955	1956	1957[a]
Increase in peasant income due to increase in government purchase prices for agricultural products.	1,570	2,190	2,200	2,780	4,020
Increase in peasant expenditure on industrial products due to increase in industrial prices	-210	30	230	70	210
Increase in peasant expenditure on agricultural products due to increase in agricultural prices	480	770	850	1,010	1,270
Increase in peasant income due to decrease in differential between industrial and agricultural prices	1,780	2,160	1,970	2,710	3,810
Net increase in peasant income due to all price changes.	1,300	1,390	1,120	1,700	2,540

[a] 1957 figures are anticipated estimates.

Source: Data Office, *TCYC*. "Changes in Market Prices in 1957 and Their Effects on the People's Livelihood," *TCYC*, No. 4 (April 23, 1958), pp. 25-26.

TABLE 9.8 Per Capita Consumption Expenditure of Workers and Employees and of Peasants, 1936, 1952-56, Yuan

Expenditure	1936	1952	1953	1954	1955	1956
Per capita consumption expenditure of workers and employees, SSB data[1]		167.7	176.6	177.9	179.9	199.8
Per capita consumption expenditure of peasants: SSB data[1]		72.8	74.7	76.8	82.5	84.2
Survey data of the Chinese Academy of Sciences[2]	61.2	72.0				81.0

Note: The SSB data were given in 1952 prices, but the original source did not indicate whether the survey data of the Chinese Academy of Sciences were given in current or in 1952 prices.

[1] Research Office, SSB, "A Preliminary Analysis of the Production and Distribution in China's National Income," *TCYC*, No. 1 (January 23, 1958), pp. 11-15.

[2] Ts'ai Ching, "The Increasing Living Standards of the 600 Million People during the Past Five Years," in *Eight Glorious Years*, Hong Kong: New Democratic Press, 1958, pp. 180-184.

TABLE 9.9   Percentage Distribution of the Per Capita Consumption Expenditures of Workers and Employees and of Peasants among Various Categories, 1955

Category of Expenditure	Workers and Employees	Peasants	Category of Expenditure	Workers and Employees	Peasants
Total	100	100	Daily		
Food	55	58	necessities	13	22
Clothing	12	15	Services	20	5

Note: Figures in this table were based on survey data on family budgets of workers and employees and of peasants.

Source: Data Office, *TCKT*, "The Problem Concerning the Living Standards of Workers and Peasants," *TCKT*, No. 13 (July 14, 1957), pp. 4-5, 24.

TABLE 9.10   Consumption Expenditures of Peasant Households with Different Levels of Income in 1955, Yuan

	600 and above	500 to 599	400 to 499	300 to 399	250 to 299	200 to 249	150 to 199	100 to 149	99 to below
Annual average income net of expenditures on food and producer goods	101.75	73.70	58.60	49.40	41.21	35.70	29.15	22.70	15.90
Consumption expenditure:									
Subsidiary food	10.55	9.10	8.70	7.60	6.80	6.70	5.80	5.09	3.90
Clothing	18.95	14.62	13.02	11.57	9.93	8.87	7.27	6.00	4.14
Culture and recreation	0.74	0.74	0.62	0.59	0.50	0.48	0.31	0.27	0.16
Drugs	4.40	3.60	2.50	1.90	1.86	1.34	1.19	0.91	0.59
Miscellaneous	3.70	3.30	2.97	2.48	2.26	2.18	1.80	1.60	1.20

Source: *CYHTTH*, No. 2 (February 11, 1959), p. 33.

435

TABLE 9.11 Composition of Consumption Expenditure
of Workers in Shanghai, 1929-30 and
1956, Percent

Category of expenditures	1929-30	1956
Total	100.00	100.00
Food Products	58.52	52.53
Staple food	28,91	15.59
Subsidiary food	24.10	23.76
Meat, fish, and eggs	8.94	12.09
Vegetables	9.45	6.78
Tobacco, wine, and tea	4.28	4.07
Nonfood products	17.44	24.44
Clothing	7.62	11.88
Fuel	6.06	3.05
Services	24.22	23.03
Rent	8.48	1.94
Recreation	0.28	0.98
Medical care	1.36	0.45
Transportation	1.20	2.56

Source: Data Office, TCKT, "Changes in the
Living Standards of Workers in Shanghai during
the Past 27 Years," TCKT, No. 13 (July 14,
1957), pp. 6-7.

TABLE 9.12 Consumption per Capita of Major Consumer Goods, 1949-58

Product	1949	1950	1951	1952	1953	1954	1955	1956	1957	1958
Cotton cloth, meters per person[1]		3.82	4.98	6.07	7.82	7.21	7.06	8.83		
Machine-made cloth:										
CYHTTH data[2]	2.55			5.19				8.36	6.15	6.87
CH data[1]		3.06	4.06	4.96	6.72	6.39	6.34	8.23		
Native cloth[1]		0.76	0.92	1.11	1.10	0.82	0.71	0.60		
Rubber footwear, pairs per hundred person[3]	5.1			11.4					18.5	25.3
Urban areas	40			60					69	63
Rural areas	1.05			4.7					9.6	18
Paper, per person:										
Machine-made and handicraft paper[4]								1.79		
Machine-made paper[4]				0.64	0.74	0.88	1.07	1.47		
Paper for daily household consumption[5]				0.36					0.62	
Urban areas				1.18					1.54	
Rural areas				0.25					0.46	

[1] CH, p. 186.

[2] Wang Min-teh, "The Development of Production and Sales of Cotton Textile Products," CYHTTH, (February 11, 1959), pp. 30-31.

[3] Department of Long-Term Planning, Bureau of Economic Planning, Minister of Commerce, "A Survey of the Demand and Supply of Shoes," CYHTTH, No. 4 (April 11, 1959), pp. 27-28.

[4] CH, p. 219.

[5] Shih Wei-cheng, "The Problems Concerning the Supply and Demand of Paper," CYHTTH, No. 1 (January 11, 1959), pp. 31-32.

TABLE 9.13 Total and Per Capita Consumption of Food Grains in Urban and Rural Areas, 1953-57

Area	1953-54	1954-55	1955-56	1956-57
National:				
Total consumption, thousand tons	130,570	137,990	147,270	161,305
Per capita consumption, kilograms	227.0	234.30	249.65	262.25
Urban areas:				
Total consumption, thousand tons	21,660	22,305	22,610	24,715
Per capita consumption, kilograms	289.8	279.05	278.35	282.35
Rural areas:				
Total consumption, thousand tons	108,910	115,685	124,660	136,590
Per capita consumption, kilograms	218.2	227.25	239.40	258.90

Note: Food grains include soybeans.

Source: Data Office, *TCKT*, "The Basic Situation of Unified Purchase and Sales of Food Grains in China," *TCKT*, No. 19 (October 14, 1957), pp. 31-32, 28.

TABLE 9.14 Per Capita Annual Consumption of Pork and Vegetables in Peking, 1949-58, Kilograms

Year	Pork	Vegetables	Year	Pork	Vegetables
	(1)	(2)		(1)	(2)
1949	3.35	25.89	1954	10.10	98.19
1950	4.75	43.96	1955	7.89	107.38
1951	6.08	76.20	1956	8.50	127.88
1952	6.76	87.26	1957	9.12	139.27
1953	8,20	93.30	1958	10.40	139.27

Source: Chou Ch'ung-kuang, "On the Establishment of Bases for Subsidiary Food Production," *CYHTTH*, No. 3 (March 11, 1959), pp. 14-15.

TABLE 9.15 Amount of Major Consumer Goods Consumed by Workers and Employees and by Peasants in 1955

Commodity	Workers and employees	Peasants
Food grains, kg per person	158.45	188.8
Pork, kg per person	5.90	3.3
Vegetables, kg per person	81.25	88.6
Edible vegetable oil, kg per person	4.55	1.2
Sugar, kg per person	1.30	0.4
Cotton cloth, meters per person	11.37	8.8

Note: Figures in this table were based on survey data on family budgets of workers and employees and of peasants.

Source: Data Office, TCKT, "The Problem Concerning the Living Standards of Workers and Peasants," TCKT, No. 13, (July 14, 1957), pp. 4-5, 24.

TABLE 9.16 Amount of Major Consumer Goods Consumed Annually by Peasants, 1952 and 1956

Commodity	1952	1956
Food grains (excluding soybeans), kg per person	221.75	243.75
Pork, kg per person	4.95	3.85
Edible vegetable oil, kg per person	1.60	1.90
Sugar, kg per person	0.50	0.85
Cotton cloth (including native cloth), meters per person	4.67	6.67
Knitted goods, kg per person	0.07	0.15
Pongee and satin, meters per ten thousand persons	2.23	5.25
Thermos, units per ten thousand persons	36.09	142.25
Soap, pieces per thousand persons	67.0	123.0
Bicycles, units per ten thousand persons	0.36	2.99

Source: Ts'ai Ching, "The Increasing Living Standards of the 600 Million People during the Past Five Years," in *Eight Glorious Years*, Hong Kong: New Democratic Press, 1958, pp. 180-184.

TABLE 9.17 Amount of Meat, Poultry, and Fishery Products
and Cotton Consumed by Workers and Employees
with Different Income Levels in 1956

Income per capita	Meat, poultry, and fishery products, kgrams per person	Cotton cloth, meters per person[a]
(1)	(2)	(3)
Above 300 yuan	26.95	22.17
230-350 yuan	18.95	15.05
170-230 yuan	14.75	13.38
110-170 yuan	11.30	8.97
80-110 yuan	8.50	7.12
Below 80 yuan	5.80	6.53

[a] Including ready-made clothes.
Source: CYHTTH, No. 2 (February 11, 1959), p. 33.

TABLE 9.18 Amount of Major Consumer Goods Consumed Annually per Peasant in
Kansu Province, 1954 and 1956

Commodity	1954	1956
Food grains kilograms	223.8	238.6
Fine grains, kilograms	83.6	90.9
Fine cloth, meters	3.32	5.48
Meat, kilograms	1.76	2.62
Edible oil, kilograms	0.62	0.98

Note: Figures in this table were computed from
the survey data on income and expenditure of
780 peasant households.

Source: Ma Yi-chao (Director of Kansu Provincial
Statistical Bureau), "The Living Standards of
the People in Kansu Province," TCKT, No. 14
(July 29, 1957), pp. 21, 32.

TABLE 9.19 Amount of Major Consumer Goods Consumed per Capita
by Rich, Middle, and Poor Peasants in Hunan Province in 1956

Commodity	Rich peasants	Middle peasants	Poor peasants
Food grains, kilograms	236.5	275.0	234.0
Edible oil, kilograms	2.3	1.7	1.5
Meat, kilograms	6.5	4.7	3.0
Cotton cloth, meters	5.9	5.5	4.9

Note: Figures in this table were computed by Hunan Provincial
Statistical Bureau from survey data on the income and expenditure of 510 peasant households. The percentage distribution of these households among various peasant classes
was as follows: 24.8 percent for rich peasant households;
62 percent for middle peasant households; and 13.2 percent
for poor peasant households.

Source: Hunan Provincial Statistical Bureau, "We Have Begun
the Work of Utilizing and Analyzing Survey Data on the Income and expenditure of Peasant Households," TCKT, No. 1
(January 14, 1958), pp, 13-14.

TABLE 9.20 Amount of Major Consumer Goods Consumed Annually per Worker in Shanghai, 1929-30 and 1956

Commodity	1929-30	1956
Rice, kilograms	120.04	135.37
Pork, kilograms	4.89	8.10
Poulty, kilograms	0.38	1.35
Fishery products, kilograms	5.08	13.70
Eggs, units	22.20	84.23
Vegetables, kilograms	79.78	96.75
Sugar, kilograms	1.20	2.08
Edible vegetables oil, kilograms	6.29	5.10
Edible animal oil, kilograms	0.23	0.35
Cotton cloth, meters	6.43	14.00
Rubber footwear, pairs	0.10	0.51
Leather footwear, pairs	0.17	0.27
Socks, pairs	1,26	2.08

Source: Niu Chung-huang, "The Development of Socialist Construction in China and the Improvement of the Living Standards of the Chinese People," *HH*, No. 15 (August 3, 1957), pp. 15-17.

TABLE 9.21 Housing Conditions of Workers in Shanghai, 1929-30 and 1956, Square Meters

Average living space	1929-30	1956
Per family	14.89	22.59
Per person	3.22	4.78

Source: Data Office, *TCKT*, "Changes in the Living Standards of Workers in Shanghai during the Past 27 Years," *TCKT*, No. 13 (July 14, 1957) pp. 6-7.

TABLE 10.1   State Revenue, 1950-59 (Millions of Current Yuan)

Revenue	1950	1951	1952	1953	1954	1955	1956	1957	1958	1959
Total Revenue	6,520[1]	12,960[1]	17,560[1]	21,760[1]	26,230[1]	27,200[1]	28,740[1]	31,020[1]	41,860[1]	54,160[2]
Tax Revenue	4,900[1]	8,110[1]	9,770[1]	11,970[1]	13,220[1]	12,750[1]	14,090[1,3]	15,490[1]	18,730[1]	20,470[2]
Industrial and Commercial taxes	2,263[4]	4,745[4]	6,147[4]	8,250[4,5]	8,972[4,5]	8,725[4,5]	10,098[3,5]			
Private business[6]	1,910	3,312	3,458	3,422	2,872	1,671				
Cooperatives[6]			190	534	925	1,128				
State-private joint enterprises[6]			184	265	422	556				
State enterprises[7]			(2,315)	(4,029)	(4,753)	(5,370)				
Agricultural taxes	1,910[4]	2,169[4]	2,704[4,5]	2,711[4,5]	3,278[4,5]	3,054[4,5]	2,965[3,5]	2,970[8]	3,260[8]	
Salt taxes	269[4]	339[4]	405[4,5]	461[4,5]	521[4,5]	481[4,5]	483[5]			
Custom duties	356[4]	694[4]	481[4,5]	505[4,5]	412[4,5]	466[4,5]	542[5]			
Revenue from state enterprises	870[1]	3,050[1]	5,730[1]	7,670[1]	9,960[1]	11,190[1]	13,430[1,3]	14,420[1]	22,020[1]	33,360[2]
Revenue from credit and insurance operations	330[1]	570[1]	190[1]	490[1]	1,790[1]	2,360[1]	724[1,3]	700[1]	800[1]	
Domestic bonds	260[6]	--	--	--	836[6]	619[6]	607[3]	650[9]	790[8]	
Foreign loans		2,174[6]	--	438[6]	877[6]	1,654[6]	117[6]	23[3,9]	--	
Insurance operations				(52)[7]	(77)[7]	(87)[7]	--	27[9]	10[8]	
Other revenue	420[1]	1,230[1]	1,870[1]	1,630[1]	1,260[1]	900[1]	500[1]	410[1]	310[1]	330[2]

Note: Figures in this table do not include carryover from the preceding year.

1 TGY. pp. 21-22.
2 Li Hsien-nien, "Report on the 1959 State Final Accounts and a Draft of the 1960 State Budget," 1960 JMST, pp. 182-87.
3 Li Hsien-nien, *Report on the 1956 State Final Accounts and the 1957 State Budget*, Peking: Finance Publishing House, 1957, pp. 9-48; also in *1958 JMST*, pp. 214-24.
4 Ko Chih-ta, *China's Budget during the Transition Period*, Peking: Finance Publishing House, 1957, p. 58.
5 "State Budgetary Revenue and Expenditure during the First Five-Year Period," *Ts'ai-cheng (Public Finance)*, No. 8 (August 5, 1957), pp. 32-33.
6 Feng Chi-hsi, "The Growth of China's National Economy as Seen through the State Budget," *TCKT*, No. 12 (June 29, 1957), pp. 28-33
7 Derived as a residual.
8 Li Hsien-nien, *Report on the 1958 State Final Accounts and the 1959 State Budget*, Peking: Finance Publishing House, 1959, pp. 7-20.
9 Li Hsien-nien, "Report on the Implementation of the 1957 State Budget and a Draft of the 1958 State Budget," *1959 JMST*, pp. 226-34.

441

TABLE 10.2 Sources of State Revenue, by Ownership of Establishment, 1950-56, Ten Thousand Yuan

Sector	1950[a,1]	1951[a,1]	1952[1]	1953[1]	1954[b,1]	1955[b,1]	1956[b,c,1]	1958[2]
Total revenue	651,912	1,269,919	1,755,968	2,176,236	2,535,258	2,554,604	2,958,949	4,186,000
State enterprises	222,179	626,775	1,018,074	1,369,638	1,653,963	1,815,713	2,199,609	3,512,000
Cooperatives[d]	--	--	18,950	53,437	92,539	112,751	156,200	--
State-private joint enterprises	--	--	18,418	26,521	42,183	55,553	157,537	--
Peasants[e]	193,165	230,708	280,891	292,655	360,710	337,479	331,549	573,000
Private enterprises	214,574	363,924	372,242	367,516	338,224	195,756	76,634	--
Others	21,994	48,512	47,393	66,469	47,639	37,352	37,420	101,000

[a] Figures for 1950 and 1951 do not include bank overdraft.

[b] Figures for 1954 through 1956 do not include foreign loans.

[c] Figures for 1956 are preliminary estimates. For this reason the figure for total revenue in 1956 does not correspond with the revised figure given in the preceding tables.

[d] Revenue from cooperatives refer to the amount of industrial and commercial taxes paid by various cooperative organizations.

[e] Revenue from peasants refer to agricultural taxes paid by agricultural producer cooperatives and individual peasants, and to bonds subscribed by them.

[1] Feng Chi-hsi, "The Growth of the National Economy of China as Seen through the State Budget, *TCKT*, No. 12 (June 29, 1957), pp. 28, 33.
[2] Li Hsien-nien, *Report on the 1958 Final Accounts and the 1959 State Budget*, Peking: Finance Publishing House, 1959, pp. 7-20

TABLE 10.3 Agricultural Taxes as Percentages of Agricultural Output, 1936 and 1949-56

Agricultural taxes	1936	1949	1950	1951	1952	1953	1954	1955	1956
Percentages of agricultural output:									
Nationwide		13.89	12.63	11.99	13.2[1]	12.1[1]	12.9[1]	11.5[1]	11.4[2,3]
Kansu province[4]					10.08	9.04	9.33	8.14	6.93
Percentages of the gross value of agricultural output and of the output of sideline occupations[3]	15.89				7.5				6.04

Note: Agricultural taxes in this table include the taxes levied by *hsiang* and village governments.

[1] Feng Chi-hsi, "The Growth of the National Economy of China as Seen Through the State Budget," *TCKT*, No. 12 (June 29, 1957), pp. 28-33.

[2] Chang Hao-jan, "Is the Burden of the Peasants Too Heavy?" *HH*, No. 16 (August 3, 1957), pp. 16-17.

[3] Nan Pin, "Break the Two Poisonous Arrows of the Rightist Elements to Undermine the Worker-Peasant Alliance," *HH*, No. 19 (October 3, 1957), pp. 18-19.

[4] Ma Yi-chao (Director of Kansu Provincial Statistical Bureau), "The Living Standards of the People in Kansu Province," *TCKT*, No. 14 (July 27, 1957), pp. 21, 32.

TABLE 10.4 Source of Revenue from State Enterprises, 1955 and 1956,
(Millions of Current Yuan)

Enterprise	1955[1]	1956[2]
Total	11,194	13,426
Industry	5,073	5,447
Transportation and posts and tele-communications		2,132
Trade, food, foreign trade, etc.	3,319[a]	4,414

[a] For domestic trade only.

[1] Li Hsien-nien, "Report on the 1955 State Final Accounts and the 1956 State Budget," *1957 JMST*, pp. 159-166.

[2] Li Hsien-nien, "Report on the 1956 State Final Accounts and a Draft of the 1957 State Budget," *1958 JMST*, pp. 214-224.

TABLE 10.5 Sales and Terms of Domestic Bonds, 1949-58

Name of issue	Planned sales — Million commodity units	Planned sales — Million yuan	Actual sales, million yuan	Years of maturity	Annual rate of interest, percent
	(1)	(2)	(3)	(4)	(5)
1949 Production Development Bond for the Northeast	20		33		
1950 Production Development Bond for the Northeast	30		42	5	5
1950 People's Victory Bond	100		260.12	5	4
1954 Economic Construction Bond		600	844.066	8	4
1955 Economic Construction Bond		600	621.745	10	4
1956 Economic Construction Bond		600	606.54	10	4
1957 Economic Construction Bond		600	672.68	10	4
1958 Economic Construction Bond		630	790	10	4

Sources: Ko Chih-ta, *China's Budget during the Transition Period*, Peking: Finance Publishing House, 1957, p. 84; *1951 JMST*, p. "shen" 15; *1955 JMST*, pp. 435-37; *1956 JMST*, p. 541; *1957 JMST*, 537; *1958 JMST*, p. 570; and *1959 JMST*, p. 372.

TABLE 10.6 Distribution of Domestic Bonds, 1950 and 1954-58, Thousand Yuan

Year	Total	Workers and employees	Peasants	Private industry and commerce	All others
	(1)	(2)	(3)	(4)	(5)
1950[1]	260,120	30,170	17,950	183,650	28,350
1954[1]	836,130	273,190	140,460	394,020	28,460
1955[1]	619,310	217,080	135,170	244,420	22,640
1956[2]	606,535				
1957[3]	650,000		290,000		
1958[3]	790,000		320,000		

[1] Feng Chi-hsi, "The Growth of the National Economy as Seen through the State Budget," *TCKT*, No. 12 (June 29, 1957), p. 30

[2] Li Hsien-nien, *Report on the 1956 State Final Accounts and the 1957 State Budget*, Peking: Finance Publishing House, 1957, pp. 9-48.

[3] Li Hsien-nien, *Report on the 1958 State Final Accounts and the 1959 State Budget*, Peking: Finance Publishing House, 1959, pp. 7-20.

TABLE 10.7   State Expenditure, 1950-59, Millions of Current Yuan

Expenditure	1950	1951	1952	1953	1954	1955	1956	1957	1958	1959
Total expenditure	6,810[1]	11,900[1]	16,790[1]	21,490[1]	24,630[1]	26,920[1]	30,580[1]	29,020[1]	40,960[1]	52,770[2]
Economic construction	1,740[1]	3,510[1]	7,630[1]	8,650[1]	12,360[1]	13,760[1]	15,910[1]	14,910[1]	26,270[1]	32,170[2]
Industry	666[3]	1,418[3]	2,731[3]	4,286[3]	5,738[3]	5,960[3]	8,828[4]			
Heavy[3]	386	820	2,026	3,693	4,846	5,489				
Light[3]	280	599	705	594	893	471				
Agriculture, forestry, water conservancy, and metereological service	199[3]	435[3]	914[3]	1,191[3]	1,375[3]	1,498[3]	2,284[4]			
Transportation and post and tele-communications	352[3]	675[3]	1,037[3]	1,227[3]	1,760[3]	1,925[3]	2,782[4]			
Food supply, domestic and foreign trade, and banking	383[3]	564[3]	1,468[3]	1,027[3]	1,761[3]	3,359[3]	940[4]			
Urban public utilities	50[3]	174[3]	380[3]	355[3]	328[3]	329[3]	400[4]			
Social services, culture and education, and health	750[1]	1,340[1]	2,280[1]	3,360[1]	3,460[1]	3,190[1]	4,600[1]	4,640[1]	4,350[1]	5,860[2]
Culture, education, and health	624[3]	1,187[3]	1,828[3]	2,876[3]	2,843[3]	2,678[3]	4,021[4]			
Culture and broadcasting	61[3]	94[3]	126[3]	181[3]	190[3]	185[3]	263[4]			
Education and training	491[3]	921[3]	1,313[3]	2,082[3]	2,105[3]	2,016[3]	2,955[4]			
Science	--	8[3]	11[3]	32[3]	34[3]	38[3]	244[4]			
Health	71[3]	163[3]	374[3]	565[3]	490[3]	406[3]	489[4]			

TABLE 10.7 (Continued)

Expenditure	1950	1951	1952	1953	1954	1955	1956	1957	1958	1959
Social relief and pensions	132[3]	157[3]	451[3]	485[3]	618[3]	511[3]	575[4]			
Pensions and awards[3]	n.a.	63	208	278	198	214	n.a.			
Social relief and welfare[3]	n.a.	94	243	207	420	297	n.a.			
National defense	2,830[1]	5,060[1]	4,370[1]	5,680[1]	5,810[1]	6,500[1]	6,120[1]	5,510[1]	5,000[1]	5,800[2]
Administration	1,310[1]	1,750[1]	1,730[1]	2,120[1]	2,160[1]	2,150[1]	2,660[1]	2,270[1]	2,270[1]	2,900[2]
Repayment of loans	3[5]	42[5]	392[5]	91[5]	210[5]	666[5]	721[5]			970[2]
Aid to foreign countries[a]							404[6]			350[2]
Credit funds to state banks								953[7]	1,650[8]	4,430[2]
Other[a]							161[6]		240[8]	290[2]

[a] For 1950-55, aid to foreign countries was included in the category "Other."

[1] TGY, pp. 23-24.

[2] Li Hsien-nien, "Report on the 1959 State Final Accounts and a Draft of the 1960 State Budget," 1960 JMST, pp. 182-87.

[3] Feng Chi-hsi, "The Growth of China's National Economy as Seen through the State Budget," TCKT, No. 12 (June 29, 1957), pp. 28-33.

[4] "State Budgetary Revenue and Expenditure during the First Five-Year Plan Period," Ts'ai-cheng (Public Finance), No. 8 (August 5, 1957), pp. 32-33.

[5] Ko Chih-ta, China's Budget during the Transition Period, Peking: Finance Publishing House, 1957, p. 135.

[6] Li Hsien-nien, Report on the 1956 State Final Accounts and the 1957 State Budget, Peking: Finance Publishing House, 1957, pp. 9-48; also in 1958 JMST, pp. 214-24.

[7] Li Hsien-nien, "Report on the Implementation of the 1957 State Budget and a Draft of the 1958 State Budget," 1959 JMST, pp. 226-34.

[8] Li Hsien-nien, Report on the 1958 State Final Accounts and the 1959 State Budget, Peking: Finance Publishing House, 1959, pp. 7-20.

TABLE 10.8 Expenditure of Central and Local Governments, 1951-56, Million Yuan

Year	Total (1)	Central government (2)	Local governments (3)
1951	11,910	8,890	3,020
1952	16,790	11,930	4,860
1953	21,490	16,300	5,190
1954	24,630	18,590	6,040
1955	29,340	22,910	6,430
1856	30,570	21,720	8,850

Source: Ko Chih-ta, *China's Budget during the Transition Period*, Peking: Finance Publishing House, 1957, p. 37; and "State Budgetary Revenue and Expenditure during the First Five Year Plan Period," *Ts'ai-cheng (Public Finance)*, No. 8 (August 5, 1957), pp. 32-33.

TABLE 10.9 State Expenditures on Culture, Education, Health, and Relief, 1951-56, Ten Thousand Yuan

Expenditure	1951	1952	1953	1954	1955	1956
Culture:						
Motion pictures, theatrical troupes, and arts	1,481	1,999	4,319	3,766	3,284	3,860
Museums, libraries, and cultural centers	647	2,312	3,562	3,475	2,779	4,114
Education:						
Higher education	11,351	20,512	42,582	46,752	39,909	55,880
Intermediate education	13,976	39,438	72,206	74,346	69,104	104,269
Elementary education	56,029	49,951	63,343	64,923	64,905	43,198
Industrial and agricultural spare-time cultural schools and elimination of illiteracy	--	2,413	5,053	2,308	2,177	4,215
Public health:						
Construction of medical clinics and subsidies	6,093	16,368	33,292	28,299	21,253	21,857
Maternity and infant health services and creches	483	1,517	2,448	1,822	1,066	1,043
Free medical services	--	--	10,468	9,866	9,999	10,020
Social relief:						
Urban relief	2,083	3,714	5,418	3,678	3,915	7,100
Rural relief	7,138	14,426	12,762	37,395	22,663	11,547

Note: Figures for 1956 are preliminary estimates. The figure for the expenditure on elementary education in 1956 was the amount of budgetary appropriations and the preliminary estimate of the actual amount of expenditure was 700,470 000 yuan. The amount of actual expenditure in excess of budgetary appropriations (268,490,000 yuan) was financed by *hsiang* and villages.

Source: Feng Chi-hsi, "The Growth of the National Economy of China as Seen through the State Budget," *TCKT*, No. 12 (June 29, 1957), pp. 28-33.

TABLE 10.10 Revenue and Expenditure of Peking, 1954-58, Thousand Yuan

Item	1954[1]	1955[1]	1956[1]	1957[2]	1958[2]
Revenue:					
Revenue retained by the Municipal Government		148,456	n.a.	198,450	247,212
Industrial and commercial taxes		62,569	44,000	} 79,004	} 38,000
Agricultural taxes		1,238	--		
Income of local state enterprises		72,976	83,549	101,851	206,212
Public bonds		--		8,782	
Others		11,673		8,813	3,000
Previous year's surplus		45,744			
Subsidy from the Central Government		19,842		8,326	283,403
Total revenue of the Municipal Government		214,042	224,414	219,027	493,173
Expenditure:		205,119	224,414	206,469	474,558
Economic construction	86,845	98,379	117,972	96,446	360,576
Local state industry		17,531	30,177		203,028
State-private joint enterprises		3,233	--		--
Construction		3,058	9,150		n.a.
Agriculture, forestry, and water conservancy		6,434	9,642		42,133
Transportation		3,340	3,920		n.a.
Urban construction		64,783	65,083		99,500
Social services, culture, and education		66,190	73,745	76,899	81,080
Culture and education		52,550	53,329		56,637
Public health		11,118	13,002		19,056
Pensions and relief		2,522	7,414		3,024
Others		--	--		2,363
Administration		28,219	29,162	28,142	26,060
Miscellaneous		3,408	3,535	4,962	4,342
General reserve					2,500
Surplus		8,923	--	5,985	18,615

Note: Data for 1954, 1955, and 1957 are actual figures, and those for 1956 and 1958 are budgetary figures.

[1] Chang Yu-yu (Vice Major of Peking), "Report on the 1955 Final Accounts and the 1956 Budget for Peking," *Peking JP*, August 9, 1956.

[2] Chang Yu-yu, "Report on the 1957 Final Accounts and the 1958 Budget for Peking," *Peking JP*, August 23, 1958.

TABLE 10.11   Revenue and Expenditure of Shanghai, 1955-59, Thousand Yuan

Item	1955[1]	1956[2]	1957[2]	1958[3]	1959[3]
Revenue:					
Revenue retained by the Municipal Government	238,580	288,080	350,370	1,372,000	7,219,000
Taxes	81,700	76,500	61,600	63,000	2,350,000
Income of local state enterprises and undertakings	107.230	163,820	244,450	1,234,000	4,859,000
Others	49,650	47,760	44,320	75,000	10,000
Other incomes of the Municpal Government	15,870	17,630	18,000	37,000	107,000
Previous year's surplus	50,840	44,890	1,130	83,000	132,000
Total revenue of the Municpal Government	305,290	350,600	369,500	1,492,000	7,458,000
Expenditure	260,400	349,470	369,500	1,362,000	7,458,000
Economic construction	41,230	102,930	160,450	1,019,000	652,000
Industry	8,040	n.a.	87,900	n.a.	n.a.
Agriculture and water conservancy	4,470	n.a.	6,950	n.a.	n.a.
Transportation and communications	2,880	n.a.	22,690	n.a.	n.a.
Urban public utilities	25,840	n.a.	38,410	n.a.	n.a.
Others			4,500		
Social services, culture, and education	67,590	104.650	133,200	171,00	242,000
Education and labor training	40,000	n.a.	78,800	n.a.	n.a.
Culture, publications, broadcasting, and athetics	6,660	n.a.	13,730	n.a.	n.a.
Public health	12,240	n.a.	27,910	n.a.	n.a.
Pensions and relief	8,690	n.a.	12,760	n.a.	n.a.
Administration	69,250	73,030	67,170	60,000	87,000
Miscellanous	10,160	3,950	3,270	5,000	5,000
Delivery to the Central Government	72,170	64,910	90	107,000	5,940,000
General reserve	--	--	5,320	--	92,000
Bank credit funds	--	--	--	--	440,000
Surplus	44,890	1,130	--	130,000	--

Note: Data for 1955, 1956, and 1958 are actual figures on revenue and expenditure, and those for 1957 and 1959 are budgetary figures.

[1] Tsao Ti-chiu, (Vice Mayor of Shanghai), "Report on the 1955 Final Accounts and the 1956 Budget for Shanghai," *Hsin-wen JP*, August 9, 1956.

[2] Tsao Ti-chiu, "Report on the 1956 Final Accounts and the 1957 Draft Budget for Shanghai," *Wen-hui-pao*, August 28, 1957.

[3] Ma I-hsin (Director of the Bureau of Finance of Shanghai Municipal Government), "Report on the 1958 Final Accounts and the 1959 Draft Budget for Shanghai," *Wen-hui-pao*, June 14, 1959.

TABLE 10.12 Revenue and Expenditure of Shansi Provinces, 1955 and 1957, Thousand Yuan

Item	1955[1]	1956[2]	1957[2]
Revenue:			
Total revenue	302,817	322,170	340,800
Industry and commercial taxes	n.a.	177,197	188,000
Agricultural taxes	n.a.	77,377	80,658
Income of local state enterprises and undertakings	n.a.	48,909	52,116
Public bonds	n.a.	13,417	14,674
Others	n.a.	5,270	5,352
Revenue delivered to the Central Government	n.a.	119,391	n.a.
Revenue retained by the Provincial Government	n.a.	202,779	n.a.
Previous year's surplus	3,751	25,343	n.a.
Subsidy from the Central Government	n.a.	81,035	n.a.
Total revenue of the Provincial Government	221,228	309,157	n.a.
Expenditure	195,885	302,173	290,413
Economic construction	67,816	131,049	124,059
Industry and construction	28,495	52,905	44,100
Agriculture, forestry, water conservancy and metereological services	17,716	33,175	31,129
Transportation and communications	6,094	15,425	15,484
Urban public utilities	15,511	29,544	30,578
Others	--	--	2,768
Social services, culture, and education	62,191	103,199	102,709
Culture, education, and health	n.a.	82,230	83,386
Pensions and relief	13,740	20,969	19,129
Science	n.a.	n.a.	194
Administration	50,749	66,211	59,824
Miscellaneous	14,129	1,714	1,067
General reserve	--	--	2,754
Surplus	25,343	6,984	n.a.

Note: Data for 1955 and 1956 are actual figures, and those for 1957 are budgetary figures.

[1] Wu Kuang-t'ang, "Report on the 1955 Final Accounts and the 1956 Budget of Shansi Province," *Shansi JP,* December 9, 1956.

[2] Wu Kuang-t'ang, "Report on the 1956 Final Accounts and the 1957 Budget of Shansi Province," *Shansi JP,* August 27, 1957.

TABLE 10.13 Revenue and Expenditure of Inner Mongolia Autonomous Region, 1947-58, Thousand Yuan

	1947	1948	1949	1950	1951	1952	1953	1954	1955	1956	1957	1958
Revenue	404	2,649	7,390	56,121	72,226	160,814	110,870	195,023	210,902	283,736	321,981	766,080
Taxes	34	694	4,314	35,879	28,705	65,443	49,808	123,724	142,493	178,339	215,794	253,309
Income from local state enterprises and under-takings	10	200	1,961	15,682	13,058	50,494	25,500	52,596	63,240	93,280	94,093	210,651
Other	360	1,755	1,115	4,560	30,463	44,877	35,562	18,703	5,169	12,117	12,094	302,120
Expenditure	391	2,617	7,856	47,776	63,717	116,133	141,595	184,452	214,807	291,368	303,985	706,867
Economic con-struction	258	541	1,289	15,851	8,858	32,450	51,867	78,549	82,547	145,931	121,631	545,907
Social service, culture, and educa-tion	1	48	315	4,519	12,922	26,836	47,414	41,988	40,253	74,351	81,565	86,776
Administration	81	743	3,276	15,198	25,601	33,293	39,544	57,247	51,235	68,641	63,313	69,515
Miscellaneous	51	1,285	2,976	12,208	16,336	23,554	2,770	6,668	40,772	2,445	37,476	4,669

Note: In this table, revenue does not include surplus from the previous year and miscellaneous expenditures include funds delivered to the Central Government.

Source: *NMKTC*, pp. 28, 30.

TABLE 10.14 Revenue and Expenditure of Liaoning Province, 1955-57, Thousand Yuan

Item	1955	1956	1957
Revenue:			
Revenue retained by the Provincial Government		363,050	n.a.
Local taxes		65,060	67,000
Agricultural taxes		18,880	18,460
Agricultural sur-taxes		5,000	n.a.
Income of local state enterprises		242,890	306,210
Public bonds		15,020	16,410
Others		16,200	12,000
Previous year's surplus		66,480	11,500
Subsidy from the Central Government		27,720	n.a.
Total revenue of the Provincial Government	363,620	457,260	463,670
Expenditure		445,760	402,840
Economic construction		163,240	127,150
Industry		53,890	37,810
Agriculture, forestry, and water conservancy		61,830	35,790
Transportation and communications		17,370	9,040
Urban public utilities		27,230	32,980
Construction		2,570	1,660
Others		350	9,870
Social services, culture, and education		175,570	171,610
Education		110,670	113,760
Culture		7,270	5,310
Public health		24,180	24,840
Pensions and relief		16,380	15,420
Labor training		7,180	6,670
Athletics		5,030	2,030
Broadcasting		1,120	1,540
Agricultural scientific research		3,740	2,040
Administration	84,060	104,950	98,420
Miscellaneous		2,000	1,700
Surplus		11,500	59,830

Note: Data for 1955 and 1956 are actual figures, and those for 1957 are budgetary figures.

Source: Huang Ta, "Report of Liaoning Provincial People's Council on the 1956 Final Accounts and the 1957 Budget," *Liaoning jih-pao,* May 15, 1957.

453

TABLE 10.15   Revenue and Expenditure of Kirin Province, 1955-57,
Thousand Yuan[a]

Item	1955[1]	1956[2]	1957[2]
Revenue:			
Revenue retained by the Provincial Government	155,850	193,860	232,300
Taxes[b]	102,170	121,060	150,430
Income of local state enterprises and undertakings	36,640	59,390	67,470
Public bonds	--	5,190	5,800
Others	17,040	8,220	8,600
Previous year's surplus	20,310	7,190	13,120
Subsidy from the Central Government	17,360	96,390	4,250
Total revenue of the Provincial Government	193,520	297,440	249,670
Expenditures	180,640[c]	273,230	249,670
Economic construction	57,250	109,880	84,300
Industry	20,570	32,500	18,420
Agriculture, forestry, water conservancy, and meterological services	21,450	57,430	45,100
Transportation and communications	n.a.	8,170	8,020
Urban construction	13,470	11,780	9,690
Others	n.a.	--	3,070
Social services, culture, and education	72,460	98,590	106,620
Education, culture, and labor training	} 63,480	69,970	56,480
Public health		13,480	11,550
Pensions	} 8,980	4,460	5,360
Relief		8,850	11,650
Others	--	1,830	21,580
Administration	48,450	62,250	53,840
Miscellaneous	2,480	2,510	2,680
General reserve	--	--	2,220
Surplus	12,880[d]	24,210[e]	--

[a] Data for 1955 and 1956 are actual figures, and those for 1957 are budgetary.

[b] Not including tax revenue delivered to the Central Government.

[c] Components do not add up to the total, and the reason for the discrepancy is not known.

[d] Including 5,690,000 yuan of revolving funds.

[e] The surplus for 1956 was 13,120,000 yuan. Thus, this figure must include either revolving funds, or reserve, or both.

[1] Wang Fan-ju (Deputy Governor and Director of the Bureau of Finance, Kirin Province), "The Report of the Kirin Provincial People's Council on the 1955 Final Accounts and the 1956 Budget," *Kirin JP*, December 7, 1956.

[2] Wang Fan-ju, "Report on the 1956 Final Accounts and A Draft of the 1957 Budget," *Kirin JP*, July 29, 1957.

TABLE 10.16 Revenue and Expenditure of Heilungkiang Province, 1955, Thousand Yuan

Item	Amount
Revenue	284,280
Taxes	126,490
Income of local state enterprises and undertakings	71,900
Other revenue	12,920
Previous year's surplus	28,940
Subsidy from the Central Government	44,040
Expenditure	252,380
Economic construction	90,610
Industry	22,530
Agriculture	45,250
Forestry	4,780
Water conservancy	4,010
Transportation and communications	2,830
Urban construction	9,550
Social services, culture, and education	79,370
Relief	9,600
Administration	81,310
Others	1,090
Surplus	31,900

Source: Ch'en Chien-fei, "Report on the Final
Accounts for 1955 and the Implementation of the
Budget for 1956 in Heilungkiang Province,"
Heilungkiang JP, January 13, 1957.

Table 10.17 Revenue and Expenditure of Shensi Province, 1955-57,
Thousand Yuan[a]

Item	1955	1956	1957
Revenue:			
Total revenue	45,610	571,410	586,790
Industry and commercial taxes		366,110	349,500
Agricultural taxes		124,780	126,280
Total revenue of the Provincial Government		370,370	n.a.
Expenditure	355,640	367,480	348,090[b]
Economic construction		135,350	138,190
Social services, culture, and education		127,840	133,240
Administration		100,260	87,420
Miscellaneous		4,030	--
Surplus		2,890	n.a.

[a] Data for 1955 and 1956 are actual figures, and those for 1957
are budgetary figures.
[b] The components do not add up to the total shown. The reason for
the discrepancy is not known.
Source: *Ch'ang-chiang jih-pao*, August 27, 1957.

TABLE 10.18   Revenue and Expenditure of Chinghai Province, 1955-57,
Thousand Yuan

Item	1955	1956	1957
Revenue:			
Total revenue	39,150	58,544	69,980
Industrial and Commercial taxes		27,777	35,000
Agricultural taxes		6,244	9,721
Pastoral taxes		1,387	3,000
Income of local state enterprises and undertakings		11,244	17,745
Local industry		1,925	3,108
Construction		710	920
Agriculture and pasture		199	220
Forestry		605	260
Transportation		3,894	6,840
Urban public utilities		2,227	24
Culture, education, and health		145	210
Various undertakings		3,766	6,163
Public bonds		636	2,273
Others		2,687	2,241
Revenue delivered to the Central Government	--	8,569	--
Revenue retained by the Provincial Government	39,150	49,975	69,980
Previous year's surplus		6,744	322
Subsidy from the Central Government	34,470	112,564	97,497
Total revenue of the Provincial Government		169,283	167,799
Expenditure	77,110	168,961	167,799
Economic construction	21,190	94,040	95,237
Construction		10,272	2,773
Industry		12,985	18,746
Agriculture (including land reclamation)		8,783	6,744
Pastoral		5,588	5,637
Forestry (including lumber industry)		2,003	2,056
Water conservancy		4,711	10,382
Meteorological services		1,244	2,417
Transportation		34,271	28,418
Post and tele-communications		1,143	360

TABLE 10.18 (Continued)

Item	1955	1956	1957
Urban public utilities		2,227	3,208
Culture, education and health		90	60
Investment in joint enterprises		179	--
Others		544	14,436
Social services, culture, and education	14,530	28,577	27,504
Culture		2,563	3,031
Education		12,732	12,840
Labor training		3,072	2,412
Athletic		327	194
Science		542	644
Communications and broadcasting		338	846
Public health		5,296	4,928
Pensions		206	} 2,609
Social relief and welfare		2,606	
Administration	41,175	42,476	40,341
Others		3,868	3,116
General reserve			1,601
Surplus		322	--

Note: Data for 1955 and 1956 are actual figures, and those for 1957 are budgetary figures.

Source: Sun Chun-i (Deputy Governor of Chinghai), "Report on the 1956 Final Accounts and the 1957 Budget for Chinghai Province," *Chinghai JP*, August 14, 1957.

TABLE 10.19 Revenue and Expenditure of Sinkiang-Uighur Autonomous
Region, 1954-56, Thousand Yuan

Item	1954	1955	1956
Revenue:			
Total revenue of the Regional Government	148,917	173,057	203,326
Industrial and commercial taxes	86,781	101,291	119,000
Agricultural taxes	34,498	35,788	32,666
Income of local state enterprises and undertakings	15,128	28,140	39,170
Public bonds	--	--	6,990
Others	n.a.	7,838	6,000
Expenditure	142,863	173,050	232,376
Economic construction	33,839	48,048	84,514
Industry		9,868	22,557
Agriculture, forestry, water conservancy, ect.	8,510	15,345	32,761
Transportation and communications		18,073	18,351
Others		81,716	10,845
Social services, culture, and education	45,742	53,376	65,425
Culture and education			34,506
Public health			22,336
Administration		65,258	71,568
Others		6,368	1,869
General reserve			9,000
Surplus or deficit	6,054	7	-28,550

Note: Data for 1954 and 1955 are actual figures, and those for
1956 are budgetary figures.
Source: Liu Tzu-mo (Director of the Bureau of Finance, Sinkiang-
Uighur Autonomous Region), "Report on the 1955 Final Accounts
and the 1956 Budget of Sinkiang-Uighur Autonomous Region,"
Sinkiang JP, August 3, 1956.

TABLE 10.20 Revenue and Expenditure of Shantung Province, 1955-57, Thousand Yuan

Item	1955	1956	1957
Revenue:			
Total revenue	932,510	1,030,978	1,093,014
Industrial and commercial taxes	562,670	641,336	685,000
Agricultural taxes	245,650	247,490	249,754
Income of local state and joint enterprises and undertakings	75,610	96,857	106,031
Public bonds	32,880	32,018	38,931
Others	16,700	13,277	13,298
Revenue delivered to the Central Government		708,006	673,211
Revenue retained by the Provincial Governments		322,972	419,803
Previous year's surplus		45,796	--
Subsidy from the Central Government		97,978	47,884
Total revenue of the Provincial Government		466,746	467,687
Expenditure	306,490	471,550	467,687
Economic construction	67,510	146,172	123,138
Industry, construction, and urban public utilities		22,955	36,193
Agriculture, forestry, water conservancy, and meteorological services		102,275	75,879
Transportation and communications		20,942	11,066
Social services, culture, and education	137,190	185,304	207,933
Culture, education, athletics, labor training, science publications, and broadcasting		121,048	147,497
Public health		27,593	24,934
Pensions and relief		36,660	35,502
Administration	101,120	137,178	126,002
Miscellaneous	670	2,899	5,577
General reserve			4,537
Surplus or deficit		-4,804	--

Note: Data for 1955 and 1956 are actural figures, and those for 1957 are budgetary figures.

Source: Yuan Tzu-yang (Deputy Governor of Shantung), "Report on the 1956 Final Accounts and the 1957 Draft Budget for Shantung Province," *Ta-chung JP*, August 17, 1957.

TABLE 10.21 Revenue and Expenditure of Anhwei Province, 1956-58,
Thousand Yuan

Item	1956[1]	1957[2]	1958[2]
Revenue:			
Total revenue	343,310	438,875	647,622
Industrial and commercial taxes	193,850	236,911	291,460
Agricultural taxes	103,350	136,025	146,170
Income of local state enterprises and undertakings	27,470	39,554	187,444
Public bonds	11,710	17,372	18,048
Others	6,930	9,013	4,500
Revenue delivered to the Central Government	35,890	124,010	n.a.
Revenue retained by the Provincial Government	307,420	314,865	n.a.
Previous year's surplus	49,640	13,609	n.a.
Other income of the Provincial Government	38,250	16,430	n.a.
Subsidy from the Central Government	--	46,671	n.a.
Total revenue of the Provincial Government[3]	395,310	391,575	n.a.
Expenditure	381,700	356,471	941,460
Economic construction	139,350	132,855	720,562
Industry	25,590	n.a.	332,658
Agriculture, forestry, water conservancy, and metereological services	82,750	n.a.	251,624
Transportation and communication	15,100	n.a.	28,274
Others	15,910	n.a.	108,006
Social services, culture, and education	157,860	151,064	144,693
Education	68,770	n.a.	n.a.
Public health	25,970	n.a.	n.a.
Culture	5,370	n.a.	n.a.
Relief	31,800	29,163	n.a.
Others	25,950	n.a.	n.a.
Administration	82,520	68,943	64,604
Miscellaneous	1,970	3,629	4,847
Reserve	--		6,754
Surplus[4]	13,610	35,104	n.a.

Note: Data for 1956 and 1957 are actual figures, and those for 1958 are budgetary figures.

[1] Chang Hao (Deputy Director of the Bureau of Finance, Anhwei Province), "Report on the Final Accounts for 1956 and the Preliminary Budget for 1957 in Anhwei Province," *Anhwei JP*, September 24, 1957.

[2] Chang Hao, "Report on the Final Accounts for 1957 and the Preliminary Budget for 1958 in Anhwei Province," *Anhwei JP*, November 10, 1958.

[3] Derived as sum of four previous lines.

[4] Derived as total revenue of the Provincial Government minus expenditure.

TABLE 10.22   Revenue and Expenditure of Kiangsi Province, 1955-57,
Thousand Yuan[a]

Item	1955[1]	1956[2]	1957[2]
Revenue:			
Total revenue	272,971	317,626	320,258
Industrial and commercial taxes	144,127	165,692	167,500
Agricultural taxes	98,337	99,117	93,982
Income of local state enterprises and undertakings	24,737	34,691	41,692
Public bonds	--	11,831	13,584
Others	5,770	6,295	3,500
Revenue delivered to the Central Government	121,316	108,036	102,621
Revenue retained by the Provincial Government	151,655	209,590	217,637
Previous year's surplus	41,061	26,399	9,095
Total revenue of the Provincial Government	192,716	235,989	226,732
Expenditure	163,287	226,894	220,677
Economic construction	39,818	70,388	66,801
Industry	4,988	14,667	17,809
Agriculture, forestry, water conservancy and meterological services	21,727	31,624	26,719
Transportation and communications	7,581	15,781	10,174
Urban public utilities	5,106	6,441	1,998
Investment in state-private jointly operated enterprises	416	1,875	2,654
Others	--	--	6,447
Social services, culture, and education	71,564	86,112	90,616
Education	35,322	44,668	51,314
Public health	9,483	13,522	12,814
Pensions and relief	22,772	18,893	18,845
Culture, labor training broadcasting, and athletics	3,986	9,029	7,643
Administration	51,492	67,728	58,123
Miscellaneous	413	2,666	2,974
Reserve			2,163
Surplus	29,429[b]	9,095	6,055

[a] Data for 1955 and 1956 are actual figures, and those for 1957 are budgetary figures.

[b] Including 303,000 yuan of supplementary revolving funds.

[1] Liang Ta-shan (Director of the Bureau of Finance, Kiangsi Province), "Report on the 1955 Final Accounts and the 1956 Budget for Kiangsi Province," *Kiangsi JP*, November 2, 1956.

[2] Hsu Kuang-yuan (Director of the Bureau of Finance, Kiangsi Province), "Report on the 1956 Final Accounts and the 1957 Budget for Kiangsi Province," *Kiangsi JP*, April 1, 1957.

461

TABLE 10.23   Revenue and Expenditure of Szechwan Province, 1955-57, Thousand Yuan

Item	1955	1956	1957
Revenue:			
Total revenue	984,460	1,022,756	1,065,544
Industrial and commercial taxes	538,930	558,763	572,200
Agricultural taxes	273,620	273,349	289,075
Income of local state enterprises and undertakings	97,640	115,152	136,019
Public bonds	50,530	54,294	47,696
Others	23,740	21,202	20,554
Revenue delivered to the Central Government		663,719	541,928
Revenue retained by the Provincial Government		359,037	523,616
Previous year's surplus		142,211	14,392
Subsidy from the Central Government		24,458	--
Total revenue of the Provincial Government		525,806	538,008
Expenditure		511,414	540,693
Economic construction	77,060	134,731	119,930
Industry		53,547	32,267
Agriculture, forestry, water conservancy, and metereological services		35,446	34,248
Transportation and communications		31,667	32,391
Urban public utilities and construction		13,946	19,379
Others		125	1,645
Social services, culture, and education		198,231	240,797
Education		116,334	157,174
Culture		6,992	6,770
Public health		24,259	25,184
Pensions and relief		35,702	35,066
Labor training, athletics, science, broadcasting, ect.		14,944	16,603
Administration		162,094	157,296
Others		16,358	16,068
General reserve			6,602
Surplus or deficit		14,392	-2,685

Note: Data for 1955 and 1956 are actual figures, and those for 1957 are budgetary figures.

Source: Chang Fu-cheng (Director of the Bureau of Finance, Szechwan Province), "Report on the 1956 Final Accounts and a Draft of the 1957 Budget for Szechwan Province," *Szechwan JP*, August 24, 1957.

TABLE 10.24 Revenue and Expenditure of Yunnan Province,
1955-57, Thousand Yuan

Item	1955	1956	1957
Revenue:			
Total revenue	245,320	261,220	275,510
Industrial and commercial taxes	142,880	158,730	170,500
Agriculture taxes	56,900	55,170	51,130
Income of local state enterprises and undertakings	27,230	31,720	37,460
Local industry	8,280	8,700	8,710
Transportation	11,700	14,210	16,240
Others	7,250	8,810	12,510
Public bonds	9,760	10,220	11,950
Others	8,550	5,380	4,470
Revenue delivered to the Central Government	n.a.	108,100	39,290
Revenue retained by the Provincial Government	n.a.	153,120	236,220
Previous year's surplus	n.a.	27,640	2,470
Subsidy from the Central Government	n.a.	59,130	--
Total revenue of the Provincial Government	178,870	239,890	238,690
Expenditure	152,230	237,420	238,690
Economic construction	40,920	81,180	78,380
Local industry	10,940	18,470	12,510
Agriculture, forestry, water conservancy, and Meterological services	12,330	28,090	24,950
Transportation and communications	15,390	31,950	33,010
Others	2,260	2,670	7,910
Social services, culture and education	48,680	67,550	77,840
Culture, education, and health	41,200	58,400	69,580
Pensions and relief	7,480	9,150	8,260
Administration	n.a.	80,140	75,410
Miscellaneous	n.a.	8,550	3,920
General reserve	--	--	3,140
Surplus	27,640	2,470	--

Note: Data for 1955 and 1956 are actual figures, and those for
1957 are budgetary figures.
Source: Wu Tso-min (Deputy Governor of Yunnan), "Report on the
1956 Final Accounts and the 1957 Budget for Yunnan Province,"
Yunnan jih-pao, August 17, 1957.

TABLE 10.25 Revenue and Expenditure of Honan Province, 1955-57, Thousand Yuan

Item	1955[1]	1956[2]	1957[2]
Revenue:			
Total revenue	663,802	693,630	711,450
Industrial and commercial taxes	351,056	370,760	373,000
Agricultural taxes	238,876	219,520	233,420
Income of local state enterprises and undertakings	49,672	66,630	71,368
Public bonds		22,500	23,960
Others	24,198	14,220	9,710
Revenue delivered to the Central Government	324,280	n.a.	n.a.
Revenue retained by the Provincial Government	269,522	n.a.	n.a.
Previous year's surplus	60,333	n.a.	n.a.
Subsidy from the Central Government	12,476	n.a.	n.a.
Total revenue of the Provincial Government[3]	342,331	458,760	450,750
Expenditure	298,117	431,540	n.a.
Economic construction	78,007	153,680	119,550
Industry			27,750
Agriculture			20,690
Forestry			4,610
Water conservancy			40,570
Meteorological services			610
Transportation and communications			12,070
Urban public utilities			11,160
Social services, culture, and education	132,146	172,890	212,480
Education			126,690
Public health			184,500
Culture			4,670
Pensions			11,850
Relief			41,660
Labor training			7,190
Broadcasting, athletics, and others			1,970
Administration	82,408	104,790	100,940
Reserve			6,630
Miscellaneous	5,556	180	n.a.
Surplus[4]	44,214	27,230	n.a.

Note: Data for 1955 are actual figures, and those for 1957 are budgetary figures.

[1] Li Yu-shan (Deputy Chief of the Office of Finance, Grain, and Trade of the People's Council of Honan Province), "Report on the Final Accounts for 1955 and the Implementation of the Budget for 1956 in Honan Province," *Honan JP*, November 29. 1956.

[2] Chi Wen-chien (Deputy Governor of Honan Province,) "Report on the Final Accounts for 1956 and A Draft of the Budget for 1957 in Honan Province," *Honan JP*, August 25, 1957.

[3] Derived as sum of three previous lines.

[4] Derived as Total Revenue of the Provincial Government minus Expenditure.

TABLE 10.26 Revenue and Expenditure of Kwangsi Province, 1955-57, Thousand Yuan

Item	1955	1956	1957
Revenue:			
Total revenue	n.a.	267,557	245,248
Industrial and commercial taxes	131,820	135,655	132,000
Agricultural taxes	n.a.	83,762	66,769
Income of local state enterprises and undertakings	22,550	33,360	34,349
Public bonds	7,350	6,471	8,910
Others	10,260	8,309	3,220
Revenue delivered to the Central Government	n.a.	106,404	--
Revenue retained by the Provincial Government	n.a.	161,153	245,248
Previous year's surplus	n.a.	13,445	--
Subsidy from the Central Government	n.a.	56,860	10,940
Total revenue of the Provincial Government	n.a.	231,358	256,188
Expenditure	152,740	238,508	256,188
Economic construction	45,920	78,532	73,750
Industry and construction	22,450	20,626	17,496
Agriculture	7,770	11,198	
Land reclamation	n.a.	8,972	31,070
Forestry	2,130	4,764	
Water conservancy	6,170	14,846	
Transportation and communications	3,630	11,431	11,136
Urban public utilities	n.a.	1,747	1,607
Others	n.a.	4,678	12,441
Social services, culture, and education	57,270	92,984	107,876
Education	37,420	55,186	67,130
Culture	2,080	4,324	4,192
Public health	7,590	10,225	10,645
Broadcasts	170	519	1,250
Science	n.a.	1,333	1,160
Relief	3,380	10,347	18,105
Others	n.a.	10,960	5,394
Administration	47,240	65,682	61,347
Miscellaneous	2,310	1,310	2,137
General reserve	--	--	3,750
Revolving funds	--	--	7,238
Surplus	n.a.	- 7,150	--

Note: Data for 1955 and 1956 are actual figures, and those for 1957 budgetary figures.

Source: Tung Chin-chai (Acting Director of the Bureau of Finance, Kwangsi Province), "Report on the 1956 Final Accounts and A Draft of the 1957 Budget for Kwangsi Province," *Kwangsi jih-pao,* August 25, 1957.

TABLE 10.27   Revenue and Expenditure of Kwangtung Province, 1953-58, Thousand Yuan[a]

Item	1953[1]	1954[2]	1955[3]	1956[4]	1957[5]	1958[5]
Revenue:						
Total revenue	359,720	1,005,081	978,217	1,013,649	1,189,094	1,843,830
Industrial and commercial taxes		598,400	602,135	661,590		
Agricultural taxes			210,844	189,939		
Income of local state enterprises and undertakings		69,490	81,266	86,021		
Public bonds			41,961	34,539		
Others		61,810	42,011	22,595		
Revenue delivered to the Central Government			690,691	722,781		
Revenue retained by the Provincial Government			277,526	290,868		
Previous year's surplus		87,330	99,507	55,658		
Other incomes of the Provincial Government		19,260	32,038	18,965		
Subsidy from the Central Government		29,750	40,606	99,177		
Total revenue of the Provincial Government[6]	307,880	479,410	459,677	464,668	572,460	1,054,400
Expenditure	235,410	353,510	393,261	482,779	527,890	1,054,400
Economic construction		91,950	115,847	144,965		
Industry		20,260	34,367	41,762		

TABLE 10.27 (Continued)

Item	1953[1]	1954[2]	1955[3]	1956[4]	1957[5]	1958[5]
Agriculture, forestry, water conservancy, and meterological services		33,210	54,627	60,984		
Transportation and communications		n.a.	7,508	29,471		
Other			19,345	12,748		
Social services, culture, and education		142,350	142,269	192,523		
Administration		109,100	108,528	137,155		
Miscellaneous[b]		10,110	16,617	8,136		
Surplus or deficit[7]	72,470	125,900[c]	66,416[c]	-18,111	44,570	--

[a] Data for 1953–57 are actual figures, and those for 1958 are budgetary figures.

[b] Including "funds for supporting the Central Government."

[c] Including "revolving funds."

[1] Ho Hsi-ming (Deputy Governor of Kwangtung Province), "Report on the 1954 Budget of Kwangtung Province," NFJP, August 17, 1954.

[2] Chang Yung-li (Chief of the Office of Finance, Grain, and Trade of the People's Council of Kwangtung Province), "Report on the 1954 Final Accounts and the 1955 Budget for Kwangtung Province," NFJP, December 3, 1955.

[3] Chi Chin-chang (Director of the Bureau of Finance,

Kwangtung Province), "Report on the 1955 Final Accounts and the 1956 Budget for Kwangtung Province," NFJP, August 5, 1956.

[4] Chi Chin-chang, "Report on the 1956 Final Account and A Draft of the 1957 Budget for Kwangtung Province," NFJP, July 27, 1957.

[5] "The Report on the Final Accounts and Budget by Deputy Governor Wei Chin-fei at the Kwangtung Provincial Congress," Chung-kuo hsin-wen, September 2, 1958.

[6] Derived as sum of four previous lines.

[7] Derived as Total revenue of the Provincial Government minus Expenditure.

TABLE 10.28   Bank Deposits of the Public, 1949-59

End of year	Total, thousand yuan		All cities[a], million yuan[3]	Rural areas million yuan[4]
	TKP[1]	Chung-kuo chin-jung[2]		
	(1)	(2)	(3)	(4)
1949	10,070	10,070		
1950	131,700	131,700		
1951	543,370			
1952	860,880	840,070		121
1953	1,319,180		1,060	
1954	1,639,790		1,278	
1955	1,560,000			
1956	2,235,380			779
1957	2,790,000	2,740,070		
1959		4,720,000		

[a] *Ten Great Years* (p. 219) gives the following data on the index of urban savings deposits for 1950 through 1957, with 1950 being the base year:

1950	1951	1952	1953	1954	1955	1956	1957
100	416.5	655.0	925.4	1,082.4	1,286.7	1,697.0	2,119.4

[1] *TKP*, March 19, 1958.

[2] *Chung-kuo chin-jung*, September 25, 1959, and February 19, 1960.

[3] *JMJP*, February 27, 1955.

[4] T'an Chen-lin, "A Study of the Income and the Living Standards of the Chinese Peasants," *HHPYK*, No. 11 (June, 1957), pp. 105-11.

TABLE 10.29   Index of Bank Deposits of Urban
Residents in Inner Mongolia
Autonomous Region, 1950-58
(1950=100)

End of Year	Index	End of Year	Index
1951	184.4	1955	946.5
1952	271.0	1956	2,040.3
1953	408.0	1957	2,906.8
1954	697.6	1958	4,519.6

Source: *NMKTC*, p. 289.

TABLE 10.30 Agricultural Loans Issued by State Banks, 1950-58, Thousand Yuan

Year	Amount of Loans during year		Year-end loan balance		Loan balance at the end of June[3]
	Chung-kuo chin jung data[1]	Nung-ts'un chin jung data[2]	Nung-ts'un chin-jung data[2]	Tseng Lin data[3]	
	(1)	(2)	(3)	(4)	(5)
1950	212,410	212,410	94,900	80,400	
1951	399,540	401,470	204,820	205,940	
1952	966,180	1,076,270	481,550	437,980	165,510
1953	1,051,410	1,263,980	666,180	569,550	463,630
1954	788,280	840,590	782,670	758,660	833,920
1955	1,004,150	1,004,130	1,000,670		932,780
1956	3,408,440	3,387,070	3,029,470		1,168,430
1957	2,257,420				
1958	3,837,420				

[1] Department of Agricultural Finance of the People's Bank of China, "Great Achievements in the Work on Agricultural Finance since 1949," Chung-kuo chin-jung (China's Finance), September 25, 1959, p. 2.

[2] Nung-ts'un chin-jung (Agricultural Finance), No. 19, 1957, p. 10; reproduced in Yang Pei-hsin, "Ways of Collecting Agricultural Development Funds in China," CCYC, No. 1 (January 17, 1958), p. 22.

[3] Tsen Lin, "Rural Markets at the Height of Agricultural Cooperation," CCYC, No. 2 (April 17, 1956), p. 7.

TABLE 10.31 Development of Rural Credit Cooperatives, 1953-58

Year	Number of cooperatives[a]	Capital funds, thousand yuan	Deposit balance, thousand yuan	Loan balance, thousand yuan[b]
	(1)	(2)	(3)	(4)
1953	9,418	12,010	11,000	8,430
1954	124,068	128,770	158,900	97,690
1955	159,363	204,520	606,700	281,540
1956	102,558	280,080	1,078,690	500,520
1957	88,368	310,180	2,065,810	565,820
1958	--	415,540	4,026,080	1,698,370

[a] In 1956 and 1957, the number of credit cooperatives declined because of the merger of villages. In 1958, the credit cooperatives were merged into local branched of the People's Bank.

[b] The loan balance for a given year was the amount of loans lent to the peasants net of the amount of loan borrowed from state banks.

Source: Department of Agricultural Finance of the People's Bank of China, "Great Achievements in the Work on Agricultural Finance since 1949," Chung-kuo chin-jung (China's Finance), September 25, 1959, p. 2.

TABLE 10.32 Monthly Rate of Interest Charged by State Banks on Loans, by Types of Borrower, August, 1053-May, 1961, Percent

Type of borrower	August, 1953[1]	October, 1955[1]	January, 1958[2]	January, 1959[3]	May, 1961[4]
State industry	0.45-0.48	0.48	0.60	0.60	0.60
State trade	0.69	0.60	0.60	0.60	0.60
Supply and marketing cooperatives		0.60	0.60		
Northeast China	0.51				
Other regions	0.63				
Handicraft producer cooperatives	0.42	0.48	0.60	0.60	0.60
Handicraft supply and marketing cooperatives and production teams		0.60	0.60	0.60	0.60
Individual handicrafts	0.90-1.35	0.90	0.72		
Individual traders	0.90-1.35	0.90	0.72		
State-private joint industry	0.48-1.40	0.69	0.72	0.60	0.60
State-private joint trade		0.81	0.72	0.60	0.60
Private industry	0.90-1.65	0.99	0.72		
Private trade	1.35-1.95	1.35	0.72		
State farms			0.48	0.60	0.48
Agricultural producer cooperatives (or people's communes)	0.75	0.60	0.48	0.60	0.48
Individual peasants	0.75	0.75	0.72	0.60	0.48
Poor peasant cooperative funds		0.40	0.40		
Agricultural mutual-aid teams	0.75	0.75			
Rural credit cooperatives			0.51		

[1] People's Bank of China, ed., *A Collection of Financial Laws and Regulations, 1955*, Peking: Finance Publishing House, 1956, p. 40.

[2] People's Bank of China, ed., *A Collection of Financial Laws and Regulations, 1957*, Peking: Finance Publishing House, 1958, p. 57.

[3] *TKP*, December 31, 1958.

[4] *TKP*, April 30, 1961.

TABLE 10.33 Nontrade Exchange Rates between Chinese People's Currency and the Currencies of Other Communist Countries as of February, 1965

Currency, 100 units	Equivalent in people's currency, yuan	Currency, 100 units	Equivalent in people's currency, yuan
Soviet ruble	129.00	North Korean won	89.58
Hungarian forint	9.84	Rumanian leu	15.54
Polish zloty	8.43	Albanian lek	1.54
East German mark	40.31	North Vietnam dollar	67.19
Bulgarian lev	165.38	Mongolian tugrik	30.86
Czechoslovak koruna	13.37		

Source: Administrative Bureau for Business with Foreign Countries, People's Bank of China, "Conversion Rates of People's Currency against Foreign Currencies," *Shih-shih shou-Ts'e (Handbook on Current Events)*, No. 3 (February, 1965), pp. 37-38.

TABLE 10.34 Exchange Rates between Chinese People's Currency and Currencies of Twenty Non-Communist Countries, as of February, 1965

Currency	Equivalent in people's currency, yuan	
	Buying	Selling
Rupee of Ceylon, 100	51.60	52.20
Swedish krona, 100	47.40	47.80
Danish krone, 100	35.40	35.80
Burmese dollar, 100	51.60	52.20
Norwegian kroner, 100	34.40	34.64
Moroccan dirham, 100	48.40	48.80
Iraqi dinar, 100	685.90	692.70
Guinea franc, 10,000	99.20	100.20
Mali franc, 10,000	99.20	100.20
Ghana pound, 100	685.90	692.70
Algerian dinar, 100	49.70	50.10
Franc of the African Money Community, 10,000[a]	99.20	100.20
Burundi franc, 100	4.90	4.94
Pound sterling, 100	685.90	692.70
Swiss franc, 100	57.00	57.60
Malayan dollar, 100	80.60	81.40
Indian rupee, 100	51.69	52.20
Pakistan rupee, 100	51.60	52.20
Canadian dollar, 100	227.20	229.40
French franc, 100	49.70	50.10

[a] In May, 1962, The African countries Dahomey, Ivory Coast, Mauritania, Niger, Senegal, and Upper Volta, which have newly gained their independence, formed the "West African Money League" and issued on November 1 a common currency known as "franc of the African Money Community"; 100 AMC francs are equal to two French francs.

Source: Administrative Bureau for Business with Foreign Countries, People's Bank of China, "Conversion Rates of People's Currency against Foreign Currencies," *Shih-shih-sho-ts'e (Handbook on Current Events)*, No. 3 (February, 1965), pp. 37-38.

TABLE 11.1 Year-End Number of Workers and Employees, 1949-60, Thousand Persons

Sector	1949	1950	1951	1952	1953
National total:					
TGY data	8,004[1]	10,239[1]	12,815[1]	15,804[1]	18,256[1]
Chung-kuo kung-jen data				15,804	18,165
TCKT data	8,000			15,800	
By sex: [4]					
Female	600	n.a.	n.a.	1,848	2,132
Male	7,404	n.a.	n.a.	13.956	16,124
By nature of work: [5]					
In productive branches	(5,023)	(6,236)	(8,176)	(10,446)	(12,359)
In nonproductive branches	(2,801)	(4,003)	(4,639)	(5,358)	(5,897)
By type of work:					
Production workers[6]	3,004	n.a.	n.a.	4,939	6,188
Engineering and technical personnel[6]	n.a.	n.a.	n.a.	164	210
Others[7]	n.a.	n.a.	n.a.	(10,701)	(11,858)
Within the state plan				10,124[8]	n.a.
By coverage of labor insurance:					
Covered by labor insurance[11]	600	1,400	2,600	3,300	4,830
Not covered by labor insurance[7]	(7,404)	(8,839)	(10,215)	(12,504)	(13,426)
By coverage of free medical care:					
Covered by free medical care				4,000[12]	5,496[12]
Not covered by free medical care[7]				(11,804)	(12,760)

[a] The number of workers and employees for 1958 includes those employed in newly opened industrial establishments at the hsien (county) level and below and the workers and employees in those industrial and commercial enterprises, grain agencies, and cultural and educational organizations which the state transferred to the communes.

[b] Planned figure.

[c] Originally reported as 24,190,000 and revised to 24,170,000 in TCKT, No. 18 (September 29, 1957), p. 23.

[1] TGY, p. 180.

[2] Hsu Hsin-hsueh, "Accelerated and Proportional Development of the National Economy," Hung-ch'i, No. 3 (February 3, 1960), pp. 6-9.

[3] Li Fu-chun, "Report on A Draft of the National Economic Plan for 1960," CHYTC, No. 4, 1960, p. 3.

[4] TGY, p. 182.

TABLE 11.1   (Continued)

1954	1955	1956	1957	1958[a]	1959	1960
18,809[1]	19,076[1]	24,230[1]	24,506[1]	45,323[1]	44,156[2]	45,960[b,3]
18,840	19,031	24,179	24,327			
			24,170[c]			
2,435	2,473	3,266	3,286	7,000		
16,374	16,603	20,964	21,220	38,323		
(12,922)	(13,067)	(17,494)	(17,865)	(42,570)		
(5,887)	(6,009)	(6,736)	(6,641)	(2,753)		
6,408	6,477	8,626	9,008	25,623		
262	344	449	496	618		
(12,139)	(12,255)	(15,155)	(15,002)	(19,082)		
n.a.	19,610[9]	22,400[10]	n.a.	45,323[1]	44,156[2]	
5,380	5,710	7,417	11,500	13,779		
(13,429)	(13,366)	(16,813)	(13,006)	(31,544)		
5,666[12]	5,937[12]	6,613[12]	6,572[13]	6,877[13]		
(13,143)	(13,139)	(17,617)	(17,934)	(38,446)		

[5] Derived from data on percentages of workers and employees in productive branches given in *TGY*, p. 185.

[6] *TGY*, pp. 183-84.

[7] Derived as a residual.

[8] *First Five-Year Plan for Development of the National Economy of the People's Republic of China in 1953-1957*, Peking: Foreign Languages Press, 1956, p. 190.

[9] Data Office, *CHCC*, "A Survey of Labor and Wages in 1956," *CHCC*, No. 3 (March 9, 1957), pp. 14-15.

[10] SSB, "Communique on the Results of the Implementation of the National Economic Plan for 1956," *1958 JMST*, p. 458.

[11] *TGY*, p. 218.

[12] SSB, *Communique on the Results of the Implementation of the National Economic Plan for 1956*, Peking: Statistics Publishing House, p. 68.

[13] *TGY*, p. 219.

TABLE 11.2 Year-End Number of Workers and Employees, by Branch, 1949-58, Thousand Persons

Branch	1949	1950	1951
Total[1]	8,004	10,239	12,815
Industry	3,060[2]		
Within state plan[6]	(1,416)		
State and cooperative enterprises[7]	(1,311)		
State-private joint enterprises[8]	105	131	166
Private enterprises (outside state plan)	1,644[9]	1,816[9]	2,023[9]
Basic construction	200[2]		
Within state plan	130[13]		
State and joint enterprises			
State enterprises			
Private enterprises	70[13]		
Agriculture, water conservancy, forestry, and meteorological services (state enterprises only)	640[2]		
Transportation and communication	634[16]		
Within state plan			
State enterprises			
State-private joint enterprises			
Private enterprises			
Trade and restaurants	1,222[17]		
Trade			
Within state plan			
State enterprises		216[19]	
Cooperative enterprises		166[19]	
State-private joint enterprises			
Private enterprises[21]		967	1,167
Restaurants[21]		72	126
Finance, banking, and insurance within state plan			
State enterprises			
State-private joint enterprises			
Social services, culture, and education			
Public health[22]		780	
Government administration			
Urban public utilities			

[1] TGY, p. 180.

[2] Data Office, TCKT, "Statistical Data on the Improved Conditions of Living of the Workers and Employees," TCKT, No. 14, (July 29, 1957), pp. 13-14.

[3] Sum of components.

[4] Data Office, TCYC, "The Rapid Development of Industrial Construction in China," TCYC, No. 9 (September 23, 1958), pp. 4-5.

[5] Chao Er-lu, "The Machine Industry in the Past Ten Years," Ten Glorious Years, Peking: People's Daily Press, December 1959, pp. 139-156.

[6] Derived by subtracting Private enterprises from Industry.

[7] Derived by subtracting items in State-private joint enterprises from Industry, Within state plan.

[8] Chao I-wen, Industry in New China, Peking: Statistics Publishing House, p.75.

[9] Ch'ien Hua, et al., Changes in Private Industry and Trade during the Past Seven Years (1949-1956), Peking: Finance and Economics Publishing House, 1957, p. 8.

[10] V. Gel'bras, "Dastizheniya Kitayaskoy Narodnoy Respubliki v oblasti truda in zarabotnoy platy za desyat' let" ("Achievements of the Chinese People's Republic in the Area of Labor and Wages in the Last Ten Years"), Sotsialisticheskiy (Socialist Labor), No. 9, 1959, p. 30.

[11] Data Office, TCYC, "The Great Leap Forward in Basic Construction," TCYC, No. 9 (September 23, 1958), p. 10.

[12] SSB, The Great Ten Years - Statistics on Economic and Cultural Achievements in the People's Republic of China, Peking: 1959, p. 44.

[13] Data Office, TCKT, "Great Achievements in Basic Construction in China During the Past Seven Years," TCKT, No. 17 (September 14, 1957), pp. 1-3.

[14] First Five-Year Plan for Development of the National Economy of the People's Republic of China in 1953-1957, Peking: Foreign Languages Press, 1956, p. 190.

TABLE 11.2 (Continued)

1952	1953	1954	1955	1956	1957	1958
15,804	18,256	18,809	19,076	24,230	24,506	45,323
5,260[2]	(6,122)[3]	(6,282)[3]	(5,981)[3]	7,710[2]	7,907[4]	25,600[5]
(3,203)	(3,891)	(4,486)	(4,671)	(7,696)		
(2,955)	(3,621)	(3,953)	(3,886)	(5,310)		
248	270	533	785	2,386		
2,057[9]	2,231[9]	1,796[9]	1,310[9]	14[10]		
1,050[2]				2,950[2]	1,910[11]	5,336[12]
1,021[14]						
	2,170[15]				1,540[11]	
239[14]				1,560[2]		2,955[16]
1,130[2]						
716[14]	776[15]					
707[14]						
9[14]				4,799[17]		
(414)[18]						
2,724[17]						
(2,599)[18]						
(1,682)[18]						
535[19]	660[15]		1,122[19]			
711[19]	840[15]		1,101[19]		2,300[20]	
(436)[18]					1,400[20]	
917	766	437	315			
125	167	209	222			
305[14]	377[15]					
298[14]						
8[14]						
2,280[14]						
1,040					1,908	2,160
1,523[14]				(2,885)[23]		
41[14]						

[15] SSB, *Communique on the Development of the National Economy and the Results of the Implementation of the State Plan for 1953*, Peking: Statistical Publishing House, 1954, pp. 15-16.

[16] Chang Pang-ying, "Rapid Development of Transportation and Communication in China," *Cheng-hsieh hui-k'an (Chinese People's Political Consultative Conference Bulletin)*, No. 6 (December 31, 1959), pp. 1-13.

[17] P. Shelekasov, "Naseleniye i trudovyye resursy v KNR" (Population and Labor Resources in the Chinese People's Republic"), *Byulleten' nauchnoy informatsu. Trudi zarabatnaya plata (Bulletin of Scientific Information, Labor and Wages)*, No. 6, 1958, pp. 55-59.

[18] Residual.

[19] Data Office, *TCKTTH*, "The Development of the Chinese Trade Network and Its Basic Conditions in 1955," *TCKTTH*, No. 18 (September 29, 1956), pp. 7-10.

[20] Ye. A. Konovalov, "Razvitiye vnutrenney targovli Kitayskoy Narodnoy Respubliki" ("The Development of the Domestic Trade of the Chinese People's Republic") in Akademiya nauk SSSR (Academy of Sciences of the U.S.S.R.), *Kratiye soobshcheniya Institute naradoy Azii (Brief Communications of the Institute of the Asian Peoples)*, No. 49, 1961, p. 110.

[21] Ch'ien Hua, et al., *Changes in Private Industry and Trade in China in the Past Seven Years (1949-1956)*, Peking: Finance and Economics Publishing House, 1957, pp. 9 and 52.

[22] *TGY*, p. 222.

[23] The number of workers and employees in government administration in 1956 was equal to 24.7 percent of that in industry, basic construction, transportation, and communication. See Hsu Kang, "Labor and Wage Work Should be in Conformity with the Policy of Overall Arrangements and Building Our Nation Industrially and Economically." *ccyc*, No. 2 (February 17, 1958), pp. 21-30.

475

TABLE 11.3 Year-End Number of Workers and Employees, by Type of Work, 1949-58, Thousand Persons

Branch	1949	1950	1951
National total:			
Workers and employees[1]	8,004	10,239	12,815
Production workers[2]	3,004		
Engineering and technical personnel[2]			
Industry:			
Workers and employees	3,060[3]		
Production workers	753[7]		
Engineering and technical personnel			
Basic construction:			
Workers and employees	200[3]		
Building and installation			
Survey and design			
Geological prospecting			
Transportation and communication:			
Workers and employees	640[3]		
Workers and employees in posts and tele-communications	103[17]		
Public health:			
Total personnel[19]		780	
Doctors and pharmacists		41[20]	
Practioners of Chinese medicine			
Feldshers		53[19]	
Nurses		38[19]	
Midwives[24]		61	
Within the state system		16[19]	
Outside the state system		45[25]	

[1] *TGY*, p. 180.

[2] *TGY*, pp. 183-84.

[3] Data Office, *TCKT*, "Statistical Data on the Improved Conditions of Living of the Workers and Employees," *TCKT*, No. 14 (July 29, 1957), pp. 13-14.

[4] Table 11.2.

[5] Data Office, *TCYC*, "The Rapid Development of Industrial Construction in China," *TCYC*, No. 9 (September 23, 1958), pp. 4-5.

[6] Chao Er-lu, "The Machine Industry in the Past Ten Years," *Ten Glorious Years*, Peking: People's Daily Press, December, 1959, pp. 139-56.

[7] Chao I-wen, *Industry in New China*, Peking: Statistics Publishing House, 1957, p. 35.

[8] Chou En-lai, "Government Work Report Delivered to the First Session of the Second National People's Congress on April 18, 1959," *JMJP*, April 19, 1959, and SSB, *Communique on the Results of the Implementation of the First Five-Year Plan for developing the National Economy (1953-1957)*, Peking: Statistics Publishing House, 1959, p. 8.

[9] Data Office, *TCYC*, "The Great Leap Forward in Basic Construction," *TCYC*, No. 9 (September 23, 1958), p. 10.

[10] SSB, *The Great Ten Years - Statistics on Economic and Cultural Achievements of the People's Republic of China*, Peking, 1959, p. 44.

[11] SSB, "Communique on National Economic Development and Fulfillment of the State Plan in 1953," September 12, 1954; *People's China*, No. 22 (November 16, 1954), Supplement, pp. 1-9, reference on p. 7.

[12] Data Office, *TCKTTH*, "The Basic Conditions of the Building Trade in China," *TCKTTH*, No. 24 (December 29, 1956), pp. 31-33.

[13] "Kung Hsiang-cheng Talks on National Construction to Architects in Conference," NCNA, February 12, 1957, translated in U.S. Consulate General in Hong Kong, *Survey of China Mainland Press*, No. 1477, February 26, 1957, p. 7.

TABLE 11.3 (Continued)

1952	1953	1954	1955	1956	1957	1958
15,804	18,256	18,809	19,076	24,230	24,506	45,323
4,939	6,188	6,408	6,477	8,626	9,008	25,623
164	210	262	344	449	496	618
5,260[3]	(6,122)[4]	(6,282)[4]	(5,981)[4]	7,710[3]	7,907[5]	25,600[6]
58[8]					175[8]	
1,050[3]				2,950[3]	1,910[9]	5,336[10]
	1,540[11]					
			90[12]	110[13]		200[14]
30[10]				240[15]		420[10]
1,130[3]				1,560[3]		2,955[16]
135[17]				221[17]		290[18]
1,040					1,908	2,160
52[20]	56[20]	63[20]	70[20]	75[21]	74[19]	75[19]
			487[20]	500[19]	550[22]	
67[19]		86[23]			136[19]	131[19]
61[19]		94[23]			128[19]	138[19]
291					715	810
22[19]		32[23]			36[19]	35[19]
269[26]			312[27]	570[28]	679[25]	775[23]

[14] Ch'en Yun, "Some Immediate Problems Concerning Basic Construction Operations," *Hung-ch'i*, No. 5 (March 1, 1959).

[15] Data Office, *TCKT*, "Great Achievements in China's Basic Construction in the Past Seven Years," *TCKT*, No. 17 (September 14, 1957), p. 3.

[16] Chang Pang-ying, "Rapid Development of Transportation and Communication in China," *Cheng-hsieh hui-kan (Chinese People's Political Consulative Conference Bulletin)*, No. 6 (December 31, 1959), pp. 1-13.

[17] *Jen-min yu-tien (People's Posts and Telecommunications)*, No. 13 (July 7, 1957), p. 1.

[18] *Jen-min yu-tien*, No. 10 (May 22, 1959), p. 5.

[19] *TGY*, p. 222.

[20] SSB, *Communuque on the Results of the Implementation of the National Economic Plan for 1955 (with Economic Statistical Abstract)*, Peking: Statistics Publishing House, 1956, p. 56.

[21] *1958 JMST*, p. 636.

[22] SSB, *Communique on the Results of the Implementation of the First Five-Year Plan*, op. cit. p. 9.

[23] Chin Hsin-chung and I. G. Kachergin, *Zdravookhraneniye i meditsina v Kitayskoy Narodnoy Respublike* (Public Health and Medicine in the Chinese People's Republic), Moscow, 1959, p. 63.

[24] The sum of components.

[25] Data Office, *TCYC*, "A Brief Survey of the Development of Health Work in China," *TCYC*, No. 5 (May 23, 1958), pp 33-35.

[26] Soong Ching-ling, "We Build for the Children and Peace," *People's China*, No. 11 (June 1, 1953), p. 6.

[27] "Maternity and Child Health Service Improved in Rural Areas," *NCNA*, March, 1957; translated in U.S. Consulate General in Hong Kong, *Survey of China Mainland Press*, No. 1487, March 12, 1957, p. 14.

[28] Speech of Li Te-ch'uan, Minister of Public Health, delivered at the Third National Congress of Chinese Women and broadcast on the Chinese Home Service, Peking, September 11, 1957.

TABLE 11.4 Year-End Number of Workers and Employees in Metal-Processing, Building Materials, Food-Processing, and Textile Industries, 1949 and 1952-58

Industry	1949	1952	1953	1954	1955	1956	1957	1958
Metal processing	376,886[1]	846,140[1]			960,477[1]	1,337,912[1]	1,403,000[2]	4,204,000[2]
Production workers		(562,340)[3]	(617,810)[3]	(650,190)[3]	(632,710)[3]	(744,200)[3]		
Building materials	150,000[4]							1,320,000[4]
Food processing					1,200,000[5]			
Textile							1,282,000[6]	

[1] *CH*, p. 129.

[2] "Important Indicators of Growth in the Machinery Industry in the Past Ten Years," *Chi-hsieh kung-yeh chou-pao (Machinery Industry Weekly)*, No. 40 (October 1, 1959), p. 4.

[3] These figures are the quotients of the value of the total industrial fixed assets and the value of industrial fixed assets per production worker in the metal-processing industry. These data are given in *CH*, p. 119.

[4] Lai Chi-fa, "Splendid Achievements and Glorious Duties," *Chien-chu Ts'ai-liao kung-yeh (Building Materials Industry)*, No. 18 (September 22, 1959), p. 4.

[5] Cheng Ko-huan, "The Significance and Function of the Food Processing industry in the National Economy," *Shih-p'in kung-yeh (Food Processing Industry)*, No. 1 (January 13, 1957), p. 7.

[6] *Kung-jen jih-pao (Workers' Daily)*, December 21, 1957, p. 2.

TABLE 11.5 Average Annual Number of Workers and Employees, 1952-58, Thousands

Coverage	1952	1953	1954	1955	1956	1957	1958
National total	15,110[1]	(17,680)[2]	(18,630)[2]	18,730[1]	22,310[1]	24,000[3]	32,000[3]
Within the state plan				15,822[4]	21,179[4]	(23,940)[5]	32,000[3]

[1] Data Office, *TCKT*, "Statistical Data on Improved Conditions of Living of Workers and Employees," *TCKT*, No. 14 (July 29, 1957), pp. 13-14.

[2] Computed from data on the total wage funds given in *Chin-jun yen-chiu (Financial Research)*, No. 2, 1958, p. 6, and on the annual wage of workers and employees (given in *TGY*, p. 216).

[3] *TGY*, p. 180.

[4] Po I-po, "Report on the Results of the Implementation of the National Economic Plan for 1956 and a Draft Plan for 1957," *HHPYK*, No. 14, (July, 1957) p. 30; and SSB, "Communique on the Results of the Implementation of the National Economic Plan for 1956," *1958 JMST*, pp. 456-459.

[5] Computed from data on the total wage funds and on the annual average wage within the state plan, given, respectively, in *Peking Review*, April 29, 1958, p. 14, and *TGY*, p. 216.

479

TABLE 11.6 Average Annual Number of Workers and Employees, by Branch of Industry and by Class of Worker, 1949-56

Branch of industry	1949	1950
Iron and steel: [1]		
Workers and employees (nationwide)		
Production workers (nationwide)		
Coal: [2]		
Workers and employees (nationeide)		
Industrial production personnel (nationwide, including handicrafts)		385,057
Production workers (nationwide, including handicrafts)		326,886
Production workers (nationwide, not including handicrafts)		
Engineering and technical personnel (nationwide, including handicrafts)		11,871
Engineering and technical personnel (nationwide, not including handicrafts)		
Electric power: [3]		
Workers and employees (nationwide)		
Workers and employees (within the state plan)	42,658	
Industrial production personnel (nationwide)		
Industrial production personnel (within the state plan)	41,232	
Production workers (nationwide)		
Production workers (within the state plan)	23,872	
Engineering and technical personnel (nationwide)		
Engineering and technical personnel (within the state plan)	3,137	
Metal-processing, production workers (nationwide) [4]		
Chemicals, production workers (nationwide) [4]		
Building materials, production workers (nationwide) [4]		
Textiles: [5]		
Workers and employees (nationwide)	745,105	794,267
State enterprises		
Cooperative enterprises		
State-private joint enterprises		
Private enterprises		
Production workers (nationwide)	583,259	622,032
Engineering and technical personnel	7,989	9,532
Paper:		
Workers and employees (nationwide)		
Production workers (nationwide)	(32,300) [6]	(39,200) [6]
Engineering and technical personnel (within the state plan)		

[1] *CH*, p. 27.

[2] *CH*, pp. 90 and 99.

[3] *CH*, pp. 48 and 67.

[4] Derived as quotients of the total amount of electricity consumed and the consumption of electricity per production worker in metal-processing, chemical, and building materials industries. These data appear in *CH*, pp. 72-73.

TABLE 11.6   (Continued)

1951	1952	1953	1954	1955	1956
	211,587	254,109	261,521	276,902	304,269
	134,415	153,605	177,327	185,647	209,153
	481,000	506,000	527,000	549,000	576,000
395,830	422,861				
335,139	355,140				
	318,000	324,000	366,000	373,000	404,000
11,805	13,260				
	12,000	15,000	19,000	24,000	30,000
	60,923				114,088
	57,165				
	57,953				100,633
	54,485				
	29,700				
	27,595				59,538
	4,237				10,793
	3,971				
	(510,000)				(743,800)
	(72,600)				(109,900)
	(271,400)				(381,800)
864,448	971,723	1,075,003	1,085,592	1,105,668	1,219,693
	298,813	342,173	364,115	382,042	465,420
	22,650	28,703	33,017	54,398	17,207
	87,500	113,837	255,130	364,896	736,332
	562,760	590,290	433,330	304,332	734
686,193	777,528	846,945	863,054	866,901	942,006
11,257	16,068	21,306	25,710	30,317	37,592
	77,094[7]	90,549[7]	89,774[7]	84,309[7]	85,839[7]
(50,200)[6]	53,808[7]	61,162[7]	62,178[7]	57,386[7]	56,941[7]
	1,616[7]	2,208[7]	2,858[7]	3,616[7]	4,069[7]

[5] CH, pp. 156, 174, and 176.
[6] Derived from the data on the gross value of output of the paper industry and
  the gross value of output per production worker in the same industry given
  in CH, p. 203.
[7] CH, p. 211.

TABLE 11.7 Distribution of Workers and Employees in Selected Branches, by Sex, September 30, 1955

Branch	Percentage distribution			Number		
	Total	Male	Female	Total	Male	Female
	(1)	(2)	(3)	(4)	(5)	(6)
Total	100.0	86.9	13.1	15,355,168	(13,342,832)	2,012,336
Industry	100.0	81.6	18.4	4,152,000	(3,388,000)	(764,000)
Basic construction	100.0	96.7	3.3			
Banking and insurance	100.0	83.3	16.7			
Culture, education, and health	100.0	78.46	21.53			

Source: Data Office, *TCKTTH*, "The Size, Composition and Distribution of Workers and Employees in China in 1955," *TCKTTH*, No. 23 (December, 1956); reprinted in *HHPYK*, No. 2 (January 25, 1957), pp. 87–89.

TABLE 11.8   Number of Workers and Employees, by Branch and by Area, September 30, 1955, Thousands

Area	Total (1)	Industry (2)	Trade (3)	Transportation and communication (4)	Education (5)
Total	15,355	4,152	2,572	1,120	2,168
Coastal areas	7,300	2,322	1,144	647	979
Peking	623	129	49	31	54
Tientsin	353	157	50	28	26
Shanghai	788	430	72	57	42
Liaoning	1,584	754	179	89	127
Inland areas	8,055	1,830	1,428	473	1,189

Source: Data Office, *TCKTH*, "The Size, Composition and Distribution of Workers and Employees in China in 1955," *TCKTH*, No. 23 (December, 1956); reprinted in *HHPYK*, No. 2 (January 25, 1957), pp. 87-89.

TABLE 11.9 Percentage Distribution of Workers and Employees in Industry and Basic Construction, by Age, September 30, 1955

Age	Total	Industry	Basic construction
	(1)	(2)	(3)
Total	100.0	100.0	100.0
Below 18 years	1.0	1.1	0.6
18-25 years	38.3	38.4	37.9
26-35 years	35.9	35.4	37.9
36-45 years	17.1	17.0	17.1
46-50 years	4.3	4.4	3.9
51-55 years	2.2	2.3	1.8
56-60 years	0.9	1.0	0.6
61 years and over	0.3	0.4	0.2

Source: Data Office, *TCKTTH*, "The Size, Composition, and Distribution of Workers and Employees in China in 1955," *TCKTTH*, No. 23 (December, 1956); reprinted in *HHPYK*, No. 2 (January 25, 1957), pp. 87-89.

TABLE 11.10 Number of Specialists, by Type of Work, September, 1955

Category of specialists	Number
Engineering-technical personnel	608,613
Engineers	31,940
Technicians	321,928
Others	254,745
Scientists	11,438
Teachers	1,631,607
College teachers	17,955
Medical personnel	369,984
Cultural and art personnel	88,496

Source: Data Office, *TCKTTH*, "The Size, Composition and Distribution of Workers and Employees in China in 1955," *TCKTTH*, No. 23 (December, 1956); reprinted in *HHPYK*, No. 2 (January 25, 1957), pp. 87-89.

TABLE 11.11 Gross Value of Social Output per Worker and Gross Value of Output per Worker in Industry and Handicraft, 1949-56, in 1952 Yuan

Branch	1949	1950	1951	1952	1953	1954	1955	1956
All branches, nationwide, per worker or employee[1]					(4,872)			6,222
Industry, per production worker:								
Nationwide[2]				7,506	8,546	9,288	10,274	12,172
Within the state plan[3]					9,016	10,372	11,387	12,200
State, joint, and private enterprises[4]							11,500	
State and joint enterprises[5]	4,839	6,037	7,087	8,049				
Joint enterprises[6]		4,257	6,553	9,297	10,880	13,401	13,358	
Private enterprises[6]		4,357	5,928	6,801	7,848	7,222	6,879	
Handicrafts								
Individual handicraftsmen, per man						920[7]	1,060[8]	
Handicraft cooperatives and handicraft teams, per member							1,357[8]	
Handicraft cooperatives, per member							1,970[8]	
Mechanized and semimechanized handicraft cooperatives per member							5,444[9]	

[1] Niu Chung-huang, *Accumulation and Consumption in China's National Income*, Peking: Chinese Youth Publishing House, 1957, p. 93. The figure for 1953 is a derived estimate. According to Niu, the annual rate of growth of labor productivity, calculated on the basis of the gross value of social output and the number of workers and employees, was 8.5 percent during the period 1953-56. The gross value of social output used in the computation covers industry, basic construction, transportation and communication, and trade but excludes agriculture and individual economic units.

[2] *Chung-kuo kung-jen (Chinese Workers)*, No. 4 (February 27, 1958), pp. 7-8.

[3] Chao I-wen, *Industry in New China*, Peking: Statistics Publishing House, 1957, p. 24.

[4] Data Office, *TCKTTH*, "Several Problems concerning Socialist Industrialization in China," *TCKTTH*, No. 21 (November 14, 1956); reprinted in *HHPYK*, No. 1 (January 10, 1957), pp. 69-71, reference on p. 70.

[5] Chao I-wen, *op. cit.*, p. 22.

[6] Data Office, *TCKTTH*, "A Survey of the Development of State Capitalism in Industry in China," *TCKTTH*, No. 20 (October 29, 1956); reprinted in *HHPYK*, No. 2 (January 25, 1957), pp. 66-70, reference on p. 67.

[7] Teng Chieh, "Socialist Transformation of Handicraft Industry," in *Lectures on Political Economy*, Peking: Chinese Youth Publishing House, 1957, p.7.

[8] *Ibid.*, p. 11.

[9] *Ibid.*, p. 12.

485

TABLE 11.12 Level of Labor Productivity, in Selected Industries, 1949-56, in 1952 Yuan, Calculated as Gross Value of Output per Production Worker

Industry	1949	1950	1951	1952	1953	1954	1955	1956
Iron and steel, nationwide	3,069[1]	7,049[1]	8,547[1]	10,239[2]	11,235[2]	13,287[2]	15,582[2]	19,625[2]
Electric power:								
State, joint, and private enterprises[3]								14,219
State and joint enterprises[3]	7,356			12,065	13,085	14,327	14,212	
Enterprises under the Ministry of Electric Power Industry[4]		9,349		14,787				
Metal processing, with the state plan[5]	2,962			6,767			10,814	12,569
Fuel, nationwide[6]							4,119	
Textiles, nationwide	6,812[7]	7,463[7]	8,680[7]	10,309[7]	11,578[8]	12,790[8]	12,276[8]	13,693[8]
Paper, nationwide	4,235[9]	6,417[9]	9,157[9]	10,928[9]	16,486[10]	19,464[10]	21,605[10]	23,147[10]
Food processing, nationwide[6]							27,295	

1 CH, p. 10.
2 CH, p. 27.
3 CH, p. 67.
4 CH, p. 50.
5 CH, p. 129.
6 Wang Szu-hua, "On the Gross Value of Industrial Output," TCKT, No. 13, (July 14, 1957), pp. 14-17.
7 CH, p. 157.
8 CH, p. 170.
9 CH, p. 203.
10 CH, p. 212.

TABLE 11.13 Net Value of Social Output per Worker and Net Value of Output per Worker in Industry, Construction, Transportation, and Trade, Nationwide, 1953, 1955, and 1956, in 1952 Yuan

Branch	1953	1955	1956
All branches, per worker or employee	2,228[1]		2,766[1]
Industry:			
Per worker or employee	(2,211)[2]	(2,734)[3]	3,140[2,3]
Per production worker	(3,062)[2]		4,382[2]
Fuel production, per production worker[4]		1,884	
Food processing, per production worker[4]		9,863	
Construction, per worker or employee[3]		(838)	936
Transportation and communication, per worker or employee[3]		(1,528)	1,950
Trade, per worker or employee[3]		(2,492)	2,499

[1] Niu Chung-huang, *Accumulation and Consumption in China's National Income*, Peking: Chinese Youth Publishing House, 1957, p. 93. The figure for 1953 is a derived estimate. According to Niu, the annual rate of growth of labor productivity, calculated on the basis of the net value of social output and the number of workers and employees, was 7.5 percent during the period 1953-56. The net value of social output used in the computation includes industry, construction, transportation and communication, and trade but excludes agriculture and individual economic units.

[2] *Ibid.*, p. 102. The figures for 1953 were derived estimates. Reportedly, the annual rate of growth of labor productivity was 12.4 percent during the period 1953-1956, while the measure was computed on the basis of the net value of industrial output and the number of workers and employees in industry, but the rate became 12.7 percent while the number of production workers, instead of workers and employees, was used in the computation.

[3] *Ibid.*, p. 104. Figures for 1955 were derived from relative numbers given by Niu.

[4] Wang Szu-hua, "On the Gross Value of Industrial Output," *TCKT*, no. 13 (July 14, 1957), pp. 14-17.

TABLE 11.14   Index of Labor Productivity, by Branch, 1950-59

Branch	1950	1951
All branches, nationwide, net value of social output per production worker (1952=100)[1]		
Industry,		
Nationwide		
Gross value of output per worker or employee (1957=100)		
Gross value of output per production worker		
1949=100[2]		
1950=100[3]	100.0	
1952=100[2]		
1958=100[4]		
Within the state plan, gross value of output per production worker		
1949=100[5]		
1950=100[6]	100.0	
1952=100[7]		
State and cooperative enterprises,, gross value of output per production worker		
1952=100[8]		
1953=100[6]		
State and cooperative enterprises (large-scale), gross value of output per production worker (1952=100)[6]		
State enterprises		
Gross value of output per worker or employee (1950=100)[9]	100.0	
Gross value of output per production worker		
1949=100[10]	126.0	144.0
1952=100		
State-private joint enterprises, gross value of output per production worker (1950=100)[12]	100.0	154.0
Private enterprises, gross value of output per production worker (1950=100)[12]	100.0	136.0
Construction		
Nationwide, gross value of output per worker or employee (1952=100)[13]		
Building and installation enterprises (nationwide), gross value of output per production worker (1955=100)[14]		
Building and installation enterprises (within the state plan), gross value of output per production worker (1952=100)[13]		
Transportation and communication		
Within the state plan, gross value of output per production worker (1953=100)		
Railway transport within the state plan, gross value of output per transport worker (1955=100)		

[1] Hsu Ti-hsin, *An Analysis of China's National Economy during the Transition Period*, rev. ed., Peking: Science Press, 1959, p. 158.

[2] Ma Wen-jui (Minister of Labor), "Ten Years of Struggling for Promoting the Rapid Development of Labor Productivity and the Improvement of the Living Standards of Workers and Employees," in *Ten Glorious Years*, Peking: People's Daily Press, 1959, pp. 256-68.

[3] Chao I-wen, *Industry in New China*, Peking: Statistics Publishing House, 1957, p. 33.

[4] *Press Communique on the Development of the National Economy in 1959*, Peking: People's Daily Press, February, 1960, p. 7.

[5] Chao I-wen, *op. cit.*, pp. 22-23.

[6] Su Shao-chih and Hu Chien-mei, *The National Income of a Socialist Society*, Shanghai: People's Press, 1956, p. 63.

[7] Chung Chao-hsiu, "Raise the Wage Level Properly on the Basis of Developing Productio and Increasing Labor Productivity," *TCKTTH*, No. 16 (August 29, 1956), pp. 10-12.

[8] Data Office, *TCKTTH*, "A Survey of Socialist Industrialization in China," *TCKTTH*, No. 22 (November 29, 1956); reprinted in *HHPYK*, No. 2 (January 25, 1957), p. 58.

TABLE 11.14   (Continued)

1952	1953	1954	1955	1956	1957	1958	1959
100.0	112.0	116.7	122.5	137.6	160.5		
					100.0	108.0	
142.7							
				189.0			
100.0					161.0		
						100.0	155.5
166.3							
			189.0				
100.0	112.0	128.8	141.8				
100.0	111.7	127.7	140.0				
	100.0	115.0					
100.0	113.0						
			189.1				
161.0							
100.0				170.4[11]			
218.0	255.0	315.0	314.0				
156.0	180.0	166.0	158.0				
100.0	111.7	127.2	139.0	159.9			
			100.0	106.0			
100.0	122.7	156.1	176.7	182.5			
	100.0[15]	112.0[15]					
			100.0[14]	120.0[14]			

[9] Liu Tzu-chiu, "The Situation and Problems of the Wage Reform," *HHPYK*, No. 21 (November 6, 1956), pp. 208-10.

[10] Data Office, *TCKTTH*, *op. cit.*, p. 55.

[11] Chiang Po, "Labor Productivity," *Cheng-chi huseh-hsi (Political Study)*, No. 7 (April 12, 1959), pp. 37-38.

[12] Data Office, *TCKTTH*, "A Survey of the Development of State Capitalism in Industry in China," *TCKTTH*, No. 20 (October 29, 1956); reprinted in *HHPYK*, No. 2 (January 25, 1957), p. 67.

[13] Data Office, *TCKT*, "The Basic Situation of the Production Activities of Construction Enterprises in China during the Past Four Years," *TCKT*, No. 18 (September 29, 1957), pp. 31-32.

[14] SSB, "Communique on the Results of the Implementation of the National Economic Plan for 1956," *TCKT*, No. 15 (August 14, 1957), p. 6.

[15] SSB, *Communique on the Development of the National Economy and the Results of the Implementation of the State Plan in 1954*, Peking: Statistics Publishing House, 1955, p. 15.

TABLE 11.15 Index of Labor Productivity in Selected Industries, 1952-55

Industry	1952	1953	1954	1955
Iron and steel				
Within the state plan (1954=100)[1]			100.0	116.1
State and joint enterprises, large-scale (1952=100)[2]	100.0	116.0		
Enterprises under the Ministry of Metallurgical Industry (1951=100)[3]	137.0			
Nonferrous metals				
Within the state plan (1954=100)[1]			100.0	115.7
State and joint enterprises, large-scale (1952=100)[2]	100.0	116.0		
Enterprises under the Ministry of Metallurgical Industry (1951=100)[3]	107.0			
Coal, state and joint enterprises, large-scale (1952=100)[2]	100.0	116.0		
Electric power				
State and joint enterprises, large-scale (1952=100)[2]	100.0	112.0		
Enterprises under the Ministry of Electric Power Industry (1951=100)[3]	112.0			
Machine-building				
Within the state plan (1954=100)[1]			100.0	112.9
State and joint enterprises, large-scale (1952=100)[2]	100.0	121.0		
Chemicals				
Within the state plan (1954=100)[1]			100.0	115.2
State and joint enterprises, large-scale (1952=100)[2]	100.0	126.0		
Enterprises under the Ministry of Chemical Industry (1951=100)[3]	142.0			
Petroleum				
State and joint enterprises, large-scale (1952=100)[2]	100.0	117.0		
Enterprises under the Ministry of Petroleum Industry (1951=100)[3]	135.0			
Rubber				
State and joint enterprises, large-scale (1952=100)[2]	100.0	113.0		
Enterprises under the Ministry of Chemical Industry (1951=100)[3]	118.0			
Textiles				
State and joint enterprises, large-scale (1952=100)[2]	100.0	110.0		
Enterprises under the Ministry of Textile Industry (1951=100)[3]	132.0			
Paper, central state enterprises				
1951=100[3]	123.0			
1954=100[4]			100.0	121.0

[1] SSB, *Communique on the Results of the Implaementation of the National Economic Plan for 1955*, Peking: Statistics Publishing House, 1956, p. 10.

[2] SSB, *Communique on the Economic Development and the Implementation of the State Plan in 1953, and Communique on the Recovery and Developement of the National Economy, Culture and Education in 1952* (rev.), Peking: Finance and Economics Publishing House, 1954, p. 16.

[3] *Ibid.*, p. 35.

[4] Wang Szu-hua, 'On the Gross Value of Industrial Output," ' *TCKT*, No. 13 (July 13, 1957), pp. 14-1

TABLE 11.16   Total Amount of Wages of Workers and Employees, 1952-58

Coverage	1952	1953	1954	1955	1956	1957	1958
National total							
SSB data, million yuan	6,740[1]	8,770	9,670	10,000[1]	13,610[1]	15,250[2]	(21,000)[3]
Hui Ling data, million yuan[4]				10,570	12,990	14,150	
Within the state plan, million yuan					(12,910)[5]	15,250[2]	
Government agencies and state enterprises, million yuan[6]		6,500	7,400	8,300	10,700		
State and joint industrial enterprises, (1953=100), percent[7]		100	119				

[1] Data Office, *TCKT*, "Statistical Data on the Improved Conditions of Living of Workers and Employees," *TCTK*, No. 14 (July 29, 1957) p. 13.

[2] *Peking Review*, April 29, 1958, p. 14.

[3] Derived from data on the average number of workers and employees and on the average wage for 1958 given in *TGY*, pp. 180 and 216.

[4] Hui Ling, "Energetically Develop People's Savings to Support the Demand for Capital Funds under Socialism," *Chin-jung yen-chiu (Financial Research)*, No. 2, 1958, p. 6.

[5] Po I-po, "Report on the Results of the Implementation of the National Economic Plan for 1956 and a Draft Plan for 1957," *HHPYK*, No. 14 (July, 1957), p. 36. According to Po I-po, the total amount of wages within the state plan for 1957 would be 14,120 million yuan, representing an increase of 121 million yuan over the 1956 level.

[6] Wang Mao, *National Construction and People's Living*, Peking: Popular Reading Material Publishing House, 1957, p. 25.

[7] SSB, *Communique on the Development of the National Economy and the Results of the Implementation of the State Plan in 1954*, Peking: Statistics Publishing House, 1955, p. 16.

TABLE 11.17 Average Annual Wages per Worker, 1950-60, in Current Yuan

Branch	1950	1951	1952	1953	1954	1955	1956	1957	1958[a]	1959	1960[b]
National average, workers and employees											
Nationwide	(350)		446[1]	496[1]	519[1]	534[1]	610[1]	637[1]	656[1]	(689)[2]	(730)[3]
Within the state plan	355							637[1]	656[1]	(689)[2]	(730)[3]
Industry, Workers and employees											
Nationwide[4]			(525)				664				
Within the state plan[5]											
Central state enterprises[6]								765			
Production workers, nationwide[7]							650				
Construction, workers and employees, within the state plan[8]						613	701				
Transportation and communication, workers and employees, within the state plan[8]						645	746				
Agriculture, forestry, and meteorological services, workers and employees, within the state plan[8]						461	498				
Trade, workers and employees, within the state plan[8]						443	490				
Finance, workers and employees, within the state plan[8]						532	586				

TABLE 11.17 (Continued)

Branch	1950	1951	1952	1953	1954	1955	1956	1957	1958[a]	1959	1960[b]
Health, culture, and education, workers and employees, within the state plan[8]						448	548				

[a] The figure for 1958 average wage is calculated on the basis of the number of workers and employees employed in 1957. It does not include those newly employed in 1958.

[b] Planned figure.

1 *TGY*, p. 216.

2 *Press Communique on the Development of the National Economy in 1959*, Peking: People's Daily Press, February, 1960, p. 7. It was indicated that the average wages of the workers and employees (not including the newly increased workers and employees) rose by approximately 5 percent from 1958 to 1959.

3 Li Fu-chun, "Report on a Draft of the National Economic Plan for 1960," *CHYTC*, No. 4, 1960, p. 3. It was stated that the planned percentage increase of the average wage from 1958 to 1959 would be 6 percent.

4 Chao I-wen, *Industry in New China*, Peking: Statistics Publishing House, 1957, pp. 32-33. The Figures for 1950 and 1952 are derived estimates. According to Chao, the average wage of workers and employees in industry rose by 49.9 percent from 1950 to 1952, and by 89.6 percent from 1950 to 1956.

5 *Ibid.*, p. 32.

6 *JMJP*, December 11, 1957.

7 Szu Ying, "It Is Wrong to Say That the Nation is Rich While the People Are Poor," *Chung-kuo kung-jen (Chinese Worker)*, No. 21 (November 12, 1957), pp. 3-5.

8 These figures were reported in a Soviet periodical, *Trud i Zarabatnaya Plata (Labor and Wages)*, No. 10, 1959, p. 62.

TABLE 11.18 Average Annual Wage of Selected Industries, 1950-58, in Current Yuan

Industry	1950	1951	1952	1953	1954	1955	1956	1957	1958
Iron and steel									
Workers and employees, nationwide									
Within the state plan			587.4[1]	679.2[1]	686.2[1]	691.3[1]	797.8[1]		
Production workers, nationwide									
Within the state plan			597.7[1]	685.5[1]	691.5[1]	674.5[1]	797.1[1]		
Coal, production workers, enterprises under the Ministry of Coal Industry			604.8[2]						932.2[2]
Electric power									
Workers and employees, enterprises under the Ministry of Electric Power Industry	455.0[3]	551.0[3]	800.0[3]						
Industrial production personnel, enterprises under the Ministry of Electric Power Industry	456.0[3]	554.0[3]	781.0[3]						
Production workers, nationwide							793.0[4]		
Enterprises under the Ministry of Electric Power Industry	468.0[3]	572.0[3]	810.0[3]						
Engineering and technical personnel, enterprises under the Ministry of Electric Power Industry	603.0[3]	798.0[3]	1,494.0[3]						
Metal processing									
Workers and employees, within the state plan		477.0[5]	586.0[5]			665.0[5]	751.0[5]		

494

TABLE 11.18 (Continued)

Industry	1950	1951	1952	1953	1954	1955	1956	1957	1958
Timber									
Workers and employees, nationwide								887.0[a,6]	
Production workers, enterprises under the Ministry of Forestry			525.0[6]				810.0[4]		
Textiles									
Workers and employees, state and joint enterprises	455.0[7]		560.0[7]	595.0[8]	640.0[8]	649.0[8]	654.0[8]		
Production workers, state and joint enterprises	442.0[7]		553.0[7]	591.0[8]	626.0[8]	599.0[8]	627.0[8]		
Paper									
Workers and employees, nationwide			496.0[9]	590.2[9]	609.2[9]	624.3[9]	638.4[9]		
Production workers, nationwide			503.3[9]	573.9[9]	582.7[9]	588.5[9]	596.1[9]		
Printing, production workers, nationwide							600.0[4]		

[a] Planned figure.

1 CH., p. 32.

2 Chao Fu-hsiang, "New Situation of the Material and Cultural Living of the Workers and Employees in the Coal Industry," Mei-t'an kung-yeh (Coal Industry), Nos. 20-21 (September 30, 1959), p. 23.

3 CH., p. 52.

4 Su Hsin, "Comments on an Erroneous View Concerning Distribution According to Work Done," Hsueh-hsi (Study), No. 7 (April 3, 1958), pp. 25-26.

5 CH., p. 129.

6 Kung Chu-hua and Li Yuan, "An Account for the Timber Industry," TCKT, No. 14 (July 29, 1957), pp. 29-30.

7 CH., p. 156.

8 CH., p. 175.

9 CH., p. 212.

495

TABLE 11.19 Index of Average Money Wage, by Branch, 1952-59 (In percent)

Branch	1952	1953	1954	1955	1956	1957	1958	1959
National average, workers and employees								
Nationwide (1949=100)[1]	170.0[1]							
(1952=100)[2]	100.0[2]	111.2[2]	116.3[2]	119.8[2]	136.9[2]	142.7[1]		
(1958=100).							100.0[3]	105.0[3]
Within the state plan (1952=100)[4]	100.0[4]	(110.1)[4]	(114.9)[4]	(119.4)[4]				
State and joint enterprises (1952=100)[5]	100.0[5]	111.4[5]	116.3[5]	119.8[5]	136.9[5]	142.8[5]		
Industry, workers and employees								
Nationwide (1949=100)[6]	170.0[6]							
(1950=100)[7]	149.9[7]				189.6[7]			
Within the state plan (1950=100)[8]	157.7[8]							
(1952=100)	100.0[4]	111.4[4]	114.0[4]	114.7[4]				
(1955=100)				100.0[7]	113.5[7]			
State and joint enterprises (1953=100)[9]		100.0[9]	102.6[9]					
State enterprises (1950=100)[10]				171.9[10]				
Enterprises under various central industrial ministries (1951=100)[11]	110.0[11]							
Coal, workers and employees, nationwide (1952=100)[12]	100.0[12]					148.2[12]		
Building materials, workers and employees								
Within the state plan (1952=100)[13]	100.0[13]							140.0[13]
Cement, workers and employee								
Within the state plan (1952=100)[14]	100.0[14]						140.0[14]	
Construction								
Workers and employees, within the state plan (1952=100)[15]	100.0[15]	103.1[15]	105.9[15]	107.6[15]	122.6[15]			
Building and installation workers, within the state plan (1952=100)[15]	100.0[15]	102.2[15]	104.8[15]	103.2[15]	118.2[15]			
Railway transport, workers and employees								
Within the state plan (1952=100)[16]	100.0[16]				129.0[16]			

TABLE 11.19 (Continued)

Branch	1952	1953	1954	1955	1956	1957	1958	1959
Government administration, workers and employees								
Within the state plan (1951=100)[11] (1955=100)	115.0[11]							

[1] Ma Wen-jui (Minister of Labor), "Ten Years of Struggle for Promoting the Rapid Development of Labor Productivity and Improvement of the Living Conditions of Workers and Employees," in *Ten Glorious Years*, Peking: People's Daily Press, December, 1959, p.261. It was stated that the average wage of workers and employees in the country rose by approximately 70 percent during the rehabilitation period.

[2] Data Office, *TCYC*, "Changes in the Market Prices during 1957 and Their Effects on People's Living," *TCYC*, No. 4 (April 23, 1958), p. 26.

[3] *Press Communique on the Development of the National Economy in 1959*, Peking: People's Daily Press, February 1960, p. 7. It was reported that the average wage of workers and employees (not including the newly hired workers and employees) rose by approximately 5 percent from 1958 to 1959.

[4] Derived from relative numbers given in Chung Chao-hsiao, "Raise the Wage Level Properly on the Basis of Developing Production and Increasing Labor Productivity," *TCKTTH*, No. 16 (August 29, 1956), pp. 10-12.

[5] Hsu Ti-hsin, *An Analysis of China's National Economy during the Transition Period*, rev. ed., Peking: Science Press, 1959, p. 159.

[6] Lu Hsian-hsien, "Marching along the Road to Happy Life," *Chung-kuo kung-jen (Chinese Worker)*, No. 17 (September 12, 1959), pp. 15-17.

[7] Chao I-wen, *Industry in New China*, Peking: Statistics Publishing House, 1957, p. 33.

[8] Wang Yung, "Correctly Understand the Relationship between Wages and Production," *Chung-kuo kung-jen (Chinese Worker)*, No. 22 (November 27, 1957), pp. 19-20.

[9] SSB, *Communique on the Development of the National Economy and the Results of the Implementation of the State Plan in 1954*, Peking; Statistics Publishing House, 1955, p.16.

[10] Liu Tzu-chiu, "The Situation and Problems of the Wage Reform" *HHPYK*, No. 21 (November 6, 1956), pp.208-10.

[11] SSB, *Communique on the Development of the National Economy and the Results of the Implementation of the State Plan in 1953, and Communique on the Recovery and Development of the National Economy, Culture and Education in 1952*, Peking: Finance and Economics Publishing House, 1954, p. 85.

[12] Mei Hsin, "The Glorious Achievements of the Coal Industry during the Past Five Years," in *Eight Glorious Years*, Hong Kong: New Democracy Press, 1958, p. 23.

[13] Lai Chih-fa, "Glorious Achievements and Splendid Duties," *Chien-chu tsai-liao kung-yeh, (Building Materials Industry)*, No. 18 (September 22, 1959), pp. 3-7.

[14] Peng Wan-yueh, "The Past and Present of the Cement Industry," *Chien-chu ts'ai-liao kung-yeh*, pp. 22-24.

[15] Data Office, *TCKT*, "The Basic Situation of the Production Activities of Construction Enterprises in China during the Past Four Years," *TCKT*, No. 18 (September 29, 1957), pp. 31-32.

[16] Teng Tai-yuan (Minister of Railways), "The Railway Construction in China during the Past Five Years," in *Eight Glorious Years, op. cit.*, p. 14.

TABLE 11.20 Index of Average Real Wages, 1952-56

Branch	1953	1954	1955	1956
National average, workers and employees				
Nationwide (1952=100) [1]	105.4	108.8	111.7	127.8
Within the state plan (1952=100) [2]	(104.3)	(107.5)	(111.3)	
Industry, workers and employees				
Within the state plan (1952=100) [2]	105.5	106.7	106.7	
State and joint enterprises (1952=100) [3]	105.0			
Construction, building and installation workers, within the state plan (1953=100) [2]	100.0	101.5		

[1] Data Office, *TCYC*, "Changes in the Market Prices during 1957 and Their Effects on People's Living," *TCYC*, No. 4 (April 23, 1958), pp. 25-26.

[2] Derived from the relative numbers given in Chung Chao-hsiu, "Raise the Wage Level Properly on the Basis of Developing Production and Increasing Labor Productivity," *TCKTTH*, No. 16 (August 29, 1956), pp. 10-12.

[3] SSB, *Communique on the National Economic Development and the Results of the Impementation of the State Plan in 1953*, Peking: Finance and Economics Publishing House, 1954, p. 16.

498

BIBLIOGRAPHY (Text and Tables)

The following list is limited to the publications cited in the text and the statistical tables:

COMMUNIST CHINESE PUBLICATIONS

IN CHINESE

Laws and Regulations

ISSUED BY THE GOVERNMENT ADMINISTRATIVE COUNCIL

Central Office of Population Census and Registration. "How to Distinguish between Permanent Residents and Absentees," *1955 JMST*, pp. 28–29.

Economic and Financial Commission of Government Administrative Council. "A Notice Concerning Certain Revisions of the Tax System (dated December 31, 1952)," *1953 JMST*, pp. 290–91.

"A Directive on Clarifying Current Statistical Schedules and Forbidding Improper Issuance of Statistical Schedules (Promulgated on September 5, 1953)," *Chung-hua jen-min kung-ho-kuo fa-kuei hui-pien (Collection of Laws of the Central People's Government)*. Peking: Law Publishing House, 1955, pp. 71–76.

"A Decision on Enforcing Compulsory Insurance on the Properties of Government Agencies, State Enterprises and Cooperatives and on Passengers, Issued on February 3, 1951," in Commission on Financial and Economic Affairs of the Government Administrative Council, ed., *Chung-yang ts'ai-ching cheng-ts'e fa-ling hui-pien (Collection of Fiscal and Economic Laws and Regulations of the Central Government)*, IV (Peking, March, 1952), 285–86.

"A Decision on the Strengthening of Statistical Organizations and Statistical Work (Promulgated on January 8, 1953)," in *Chung-hua jen-min kung-ho-kuo fa-kuei hui-pien (Collection of Laws of the Central People's Government)*. Peking: Law Publishing House, 1955, pp. 69–70.

"A Decision on Unifying the State Financial and Economic Work, Approved at the 22nd Meeting on March 3, 1950," in Commission on Financial and Economic Affairs of the Government Administrative Council, ed., *Chung-yang ts' ai-ching cheng-ts'e fa-ling hui-pien (Collection of Fiscal and Economic Policy Statements, Laws, and Regulations of the Central Government)*, I, (Peking, August, 1950), 26–31.

"Directive on the Agricultural Tax Work in 1951," *JMJP*, June 23, 1951.

"Provisional Regulations Concerning State-Private Jointly Operated Industrial Enterprises (Promulgated on September 5, 1956)," in *Chung-hua jen-min-kung-ho-kuo fa-kuei hui-pien (Collection of the Laws and Regulations of the People's Republic of China)*, edited by the Ministry of Justice and the Editorial Committee of Laws and Regulations. Peking: Law Publishing House, 1956, pp. 246–52.

"Provisional Regulations of Taxes on Industry and Commerce (Approved on January 27, 1950 at the 17th meeting of the Government Administrative Council and Promulgated on January 30, 1950)," in *Chung-yang shui-wu fa-kuei huei-pien (Collection of Laws and Regulations Concerning the Tax Affairs of the Central Government)*. Peking: Central Bureau of Tax Affairs of the Ministry of Finance of the Central People's Government, October, 1952, pp. 115–31.

"Provisional Regulations on the Commodity Tax (Approved on January 27, 1950 at the 17th meeting of the Government Administrative Council and Promulgated on January 30, 1950)," in *Chung-yang shui-wu fa-kuei hui-pien (Collection of Laws and Regulations Concerning the Tax Affairs of the Central Government)*. Peking: Central Bureau of Tax Affairs of the Ministry of Finance of the Central People's Government, October, 1952, pp. 23–31.

"Provisional Regulations on the Agricultural Tax in Newly Liberated Areas, Approved on September 5, 1950," in Commission on Financial and Economic Affairs of the Government Administrative Council ed., *Chung-yang ts'ai-ching cheng ts'e fa-ling hui-pien (Collection of Fiscal and Economic Policy Statements, Laws, and Regulations of the Central Government)*, II (Peking, June, 1951), 301–11.

"Provisional Regulations on the Interest-Income Tax (Approved at the 63rd meeting of the Government Administrative Council on December 15,

499

1950, and Promulgated on December 29, 1950),"
in *Chung-yang shui-wu fa-kuei hui-pien* (*Collection of Laws and Regulations Concerning the Tax Affairs of the Central Government*). Peking: Central Bureau of Tax Affairs of the Ministry of Finance of the Central People's Government, October, 1952, pp. 233–35.

"Provisional Regulations on the Stamp Tax (Approved at the 63rd meeting of the Government Administrative Council on December 15, 1950, and Promulgated on December 19, 1950)," in *Chung-yang shui-wu fa-kuei hui-pien* (*Collection of Laws and Regulations Concerning he Tax Affairs of the Central Government*), Peking Central Bureau of Tax Affairs of the Ministry of Finance of the Central People's Government, October, 1952, pp. 239–47.

"Provisional Regulations on Special Consumption Behavior Tax, Promulgated on January 16, 1951," in *Chung-yang shui-wu fa-kuei hui-pien* (*Collection of Laws and Regulations Concerning the Tax Affairs of the Central Government*). Peking: Central Bureau of Tax Affairs of the Ministry of Finance of the Central People's Government, October, 1952, pp. 281–83.

"Provisional Regulations on the Urban Real Estate Tax, Promulgated on August 8, 1951," in *Chung-yang shui-wu fa-kuei hui-pien* (*Collection of Laws and Regulations Concerning the Tax Affairs of the Central Government*). Peking: Central Bureau of Tax Affairs of the Ministry of Finance of the Central People's Government, October, 1952, pp. 271–74.

"Provisional Regulations on the Operation of Vehicles and Vessels, Approved and Promulgated on September 13, 1951," in *Chung-yang shui-wu fa-kuei hui-pien* (*Collection of Laws and Regulations on the Tax Affairs of the Central Government*). Peking: Central Bureau of Tax Affairs of the Ministry of Finance of the Central People's Government, October, 1952, pp. 291–95.

"Measures for National Census and Registration of Population," *1955 JMST*, pp. 25–27.

"Notice Concerning the Exemption of the Income Tax on Interest from the First People's Victory Bonds, January 27, 1951," in *Chung-yang shui-wu fa-kuei hui-pien* (*Collection of Laws and Regulations Concerning the Tax Affairs of the Central Government*), Peking: Central Bureau of Tax Affairs of the Ministry of Finance of the Central People's Government, October, 1952, p. 235.

Ministry of Finance. "Regulations on the Standards of Determining Land Area and Normal Annual Yield for Agricultural Taxation," in Commission on Financial and Economic Affairs of the Government Administrative Council, ed., *Chung-yang ts'ai-ching cheng-ts'e fa-ling hui-pien* (*Collection of Fiscal and Economic Policy Statements, Laws, and Regulations of the Central Government*), II (Peking, June, 1951), 314–15.

"Ministry of Public Security Promulgates Regulations Governing Urban Population," *NCNA*, Peking, July 16, 1951.

"Provisional Regulations Concerning Liquidation and Evaluation of the Assets of State Enterprises," *JMJP*, August 3, 1951.

"Regulations on the Composition of the Total Amount of Wages, promulgated on March 7, 1951," in Commission on Financial and Economic Affairs of the Government Administrative Council, ed., *Chung-yang ts'ai-ching cheng-ts'ai fa-ling hui-pien* (*Collection of Fiscal and Economic Policy Statements, Laws, and Regulations of the Central Government*), III (Peking, March, 1952), 1060–62.

ISSUED BY THE STATE COUNCIL

Bureau of Customs of the Ministry of Foreign Trade, ed. *Regulations on the Customs Duties of the People's Republic of China*. Peking: Law Publishing House, 1961.

"Detailed Explanations Regarding the Enforcement of the Regulations on the Consolidated Industrial and Commercial Tax (Draft), Issued by the Ministry of Finance on September 13, 1958," in *Jen-min shui-wu* (*People's Tax Affairs*), No. 18 (September 19, 1958), pp. 8–10.

Ministry of Finance. "A Notice Concerning the Abolition of the Income Tax on the Joint Enterprises under the Fixed-Interest System," *Jen-min shui-wu* (*People's Tax Affairs*), No. 14 (July 19, 1958).

Ministry of Finance and the People's Bank. "Joint Notice on Resolution of Current Problems Concerning Working Capital of the State Farms," in Ministry of Finance, ed., *Chung-yang ts'ai-cheng fa-kuei hui-pien* (*Collections of Financial Laws and Regulations of the Central Government, January–June, 1959*). Peking: Financial Publishing House, 1960, pp. 99–100.

"Provisional Regulations Concerning the Problems of Classifying Certain Expenditures in the Financial Plans of the State Enterprises in 1956 (Promulgated on October 6, 1955)," in Ministry of Finance, ed., *Chung-yang ts'ai-cheng fa-kuei hui-pien* (*Collections of the Financial Laws and Regulations of the Central Government, 1955*). Peking: Financial Publishing House, 1957, pp. 365–70.

"Regulations on the Consolidated Industrial and Commercial Tax (Draft), Approved by the 101st meeting of the Standing Committee of the National People's Congress on September 11, 1958, and Promulgated by the State Council on September 3, 1958," in *Jen-min shui-wu* (*People's Tax Affairs*), No. 18 (September 19, 1958), pp. 3–7.

"A Decision on Improving the System of Tax Management (Approved by the 75th Meeting of the State Council on April 11, 1958, and Promulgated on June 9, 1958)," *HHPYK*, no. 12 (June 25, 1958)," pp. 88–89.

"Directive Concerning Establishment of a Permanent System of Population Registration," *1956 JMST*, pp. 329–30.

"Notice on Transferring the Work of Registration and Statistics of Rural Households and the Nationality Work to the Ministry of Public Security," *Chung-hua jen-min kung-huo-kuo fa-kuei juipien* (*Collections of Laws and Regulations of the People's Republic of China*), January–June, 1956, pp. 173–75.

"Resolution on the Criteria for Demarcation of Urban and Rural Areas (Adopted on November 7, 1955)," *TCKTTH*, No. 12 (December 17, 1955), p. 4.

"Supplementary Regulations Concerning the Transfer of the Unified Control of Working Capital of the State Enterprises to the People's Bank," in Ministry of Finance, ed., *Chung-yang ts'ai-cheng fa-kuei hui-pien (Collections of Financial Laws and Regulations of the Central Government, January–June, 1959)*. Peking: Financial Publishing House, 1960, pp. 82–85.

"State Council's Approval on the Abolition of the Income Tax on Interest from Bank Deposits Beginning in 1959 (January 6, 1959)," in Ministry of Finance, ed., *Chung-yang ts'ai-cheng fa-kuei hui-pien (Collections of Financial Laws and Regulations of the Central Government, January–June, 1959)*. Peking: Financial Publishing House, October, 1959, p. 115.

"The State Council's Decision on Improving the System of Fiscal Administration," *1958 JMST*, p. 568.

State Planning Commission and Ministry of Finance. "Regulations Concerning the Agents of Production, Cost Items, and the Cost Accounting of State Industrial Enterprises," *Chi-yeh kuai-chi (Enterprise Accounting)*, No. 17 (September 7, 1959), pp. 5–7.

SSB. "Provisional Regulations on the Composition of the Total Amount of Wages (Approved by the State Council on May 21, 1955)," *TCKTTH*, No. 1 (January 14, 1956), pp. 7–8.

"Unified Accounting Items and Accounting Reporting Forms of State Enterprises," in Ministry of Finance, ed., *Chung-yang ts'ai-cheng fa-kuei hui-pien (Collections of the Financial Laws and Regulations of the Central Government)*. Peking: Financial Publishing House, 1955, p. 23.

APPROVED BY THE STANDING COMMITTEE OF THE NATIONAL PEOPLE'S CONGRESS

"Regulations for Household Registration (Adopted on January 9, 1958, by the Standing Committee of the National People's Congress at its 91st Meeting," *1959 JMST*, pp. 288–89.

"Regulations on the Agricultural Tax of the People's Republic of China, Approved by the 96th Meeting of the Standing Committee of the National People's Congress on June 3, 1958," *HHPYK*, No. 12 (June 25, 1958), pp. 82–83.

"Regulations on Local Economic Construction Bonds (Approved by the 97th Meeting of the Standing Committee of the National People's Congress on June 5, 1958)," *HHPYK*, No. 12 (June 25, 1958), p. 91.

Official Reports and Statements and Other Governmental Documents

THE CENTRAL GOVERNMENT

Administrative Bureau for Business with Foreign Countries, People's Bank of China. "Conversion Rates of People's Currency against Foreign Currencies," *Shih-shih shou-ts'e (Handbook on Current Events)*, No. 3 (February, 1965), pp. 37–38.

Brief Explanation of the Terminologies Used in the Draft of the Second Five-Year Plan," *CHCC*, No. 10 (October 9, 1956).

Bureau of Planning, Ministry of Agriculture, ed. *Chung-kuo yu shih-chieh chu-yao kuo-chia nung-yeh shen-ch'an t'ung-chi tzu-liao hui-pien (Collection of Statistical Data on Agricultural Production of China and Other Major Countries)*. Peking: Agricultural Publishing House, 1958, 99 pp.

Chang Lin-chih (Minister of Coal Industry). "Struggle for the Rapid Development of the Coal Industry," in *Hui-huang ti shih-nien (Ten Glorious Years)*. Peking: People's Daily Press, December, 1959, pp. 128–138.

Chang Pang-ying. "Rapid Development of Transportation and Communications in China," *Cheng-hsieh hui-k'an (Chinese People's Political Consultative Conference Bulletin)*, No. 6 (December 31, 1959), pp. 1–13.

Chao Er-lu. "The Machine Industry in the Past Ten Years," in *Hui-huang ti shih-nien (Ten Glorious Years)*. Peking: People's Daily Press, December, 1959, pp. 139–56.

Ch'en Yun. "Some Immediate Problems Concerning Basic Construction Operations," *Hung-ch'i*, No. 5 (March 1, 1959).

Chung-hua-jen-min-kung-ho-kuo fa-chan kuo-min ching-chi ti-i wu-nien-chi-hua (The First Five-Year Plan for the Development of the National Economy of the People's Republic of China, 1953–1957). Peking: People's Publishing House, August, 1955, 238 pp.

Department of Agricultural Finance of the People's Bank of China. "Great Achievements in the Work on Agricultural Finance since 1959," *Chung-kuo-chin-jung (China's Finance)*, September 25, 1959, p. 2.

Department of Financial Affairs, Ministry of Water Conservancy and Electric Power. "A Review of the Financial Accounting Work of the Electric Power Industry during the Past Ten Years," *Chi-yeh kuai-chi (Enterprise Accounting)*, No. 18 (September 22, 1959), p. 13.

Department of Long-Term Planning, Bureau of Economic Planning, Ministry of Commerce. "A Survey of the Demand and Supply of Shoes," *CYHTTH*, No. 4 (April 11, 1959), pp. 27–28.

Department of Methodology, Bureau of Consolidated Economic Planning, State Economic Commission. "Major Changes in the Tabulation Forms for National Economic Planning for 1958," *CHCC*, No. 8 (August, 1957), pp. 24–27.

Documents of the Fifth Session of the First National People's Congress. Peking: People's Publishing House, 1958.

Fu Tso-yi (Minister of Water Conservancy and Electric Power). "The Great Leap Forward of Water Conservancy and Electric Power Construction," in *Hui-huang ti shih-nien (Ten Glorious Years)*. Peking: People's Daily Press, December, 1959, pp. 157–71.

"Government Work Report of Premier Chou En-lai to the First Session of the Third National People's Congress," *Hung-ch'i*, No. 1 (January 6, 1965), pp. 4–19.

Jui Mu. "The Development of Civil Legislation since 1949," in *1956 JMST*, pp. 334–39.

Jung Tzu-ho. "The Question of Balance for State

Budget, for State Credit Plan, and for Supply and Demand of Commodities," *Ts'ai-cheng (Public Finance)*, No. 6 (June 5, 1957), pp. 1–4.

Lai Chi-fa. "Splendid Achievements and Glorious Duties," *Chien-chu ts'ai-liao kung-yeh (Building Materials Industry)*, No. 18 (September 22, 1959).

Li Chu-chen (Minister of Light Industry). "The Leap Forward of Light Industry," *Chung-kuo ching-kung-yeh* (Chinese Light Industry), No. 18 (September 28, 1959), pp. 3–7.

Li Fu-chun. "On the Big Leap Forward in China's Socialist Construction," *Hung-ch'i*, No. 19 (October, 1959).

———— "Report on a Draft of the National Economic Plan for 1960," *CHYTC*, No. 4, 1960.

Li Hsien-nien. "Report on the 1955 Final Accounts and the 1956 State Budget," *HHPYK*, No. 14 (July 21, 1956), pp. 1–9.

———— "Report on the 1956 State Final Accounts and the 1957 State Budget," *1958 JMST*, pp. 214–24.

———— "Report on the Implementation of the 1957 State Budget and a Draft of the 1958 State Budget," *1959 JMST*, pp. 226–34.

———— "Report on the 1958 State Final Accounts and the 1959 State Budget." Peking: Financial Publishing House, 1959, 20 pp.

———— "Report on the 1959 State Final Accounts and a Draft of the 1960 State Budget," *1960 JMST*, pp. 182–87.

Liu Hsian-san (Vice Minister of Coal Industry). "Strengthen Business Management Work and March Bravely Forward to Increase Accumulation," *Mei-t'an Kung-yeh* (*Coal Industry*), No. 9 (May 4, 1959), pp. 5–6.

Liu Jui-lung. "The Agricultural Front in 1960," *Hung-ch'i*, No. 2 (January 16, 1960), pp. 17–27.

Ma Wen-jui (Minister of Labor). "Ten Years of Struggling for Promoting the Rapid Development of Labor Productivity and the Improvement of the Living Standards of Workers and Employees," in *Hui-huang ti shih-nien (Ten Glorious Years)*. Peking: People's Daily Press, 1960, pp. 256–68.

Ma Yi-chao (Director of Kansu Provincial Statistical Bureau). "The Living Standards of the People in Kansu Province," *TCKT*, No. 14 (July 29, 1957), pp. 21, 32.

Ministry of Interior ed. *Chung-hua jen-min kung-ho-kuo hsing-cheng chü-hua chien-tse (Simplified Handbook of the Administrative Divisions of the People's Republic of China)*. Peking: Law Publishing House, May, 1957.

Po I-po. "On the Correct Handling of the Problem of the Relationship between Accumulation and Consumption," *HHPYK*, No. 20 (October, 1956), pp. 72–76.

———— "Report on the Results of the Implementation of the National Economic Plan for 1956 and a Draft of the National Economic Plan for 1957," *HHPYK*, No. 14 (July, 1957), p. 30.

———— "Report on the Draft 1958 National Economic Plan," *HHPYK*, No. 5 (March, 1958), pp. 12–13.

———— "Struggle for the New Victory of Industrial Production and Construction in China," *Hung-ch'i*, Nos. 3–4 (February 1, 1961), pp. 19–25.

The Second Department of the Bureau of Native Products and Rejected Objects, the Ministry of Commerce, "The Ways of Resolving the Problem of Supply and Demand of Resin," *CYHTTH*, No. 3 (March 11, 1959), pp. 28–29.

Soong Ch'ing-ling. "We Build for the Children and Peace," *People's China*, No. 11 (June 1, 1953).

State Planning Commission, ed. *Chung-hua-jen-min-kung-ho kuo fa-chan kuo-min-ching-chi ti ti-i-ko wu-nien-chi-hua ti min-tzu chien-hsi (Brief Explanations of the Terminologies in the First Five-Year Plan for the Development of the National Economy of the People's Republic of China)*. Peking: People's Publishing House, 1955, 50 pp.

T'an Chen-lin. "A Study of the Income and the Living Standards of the Chinese Peasants," *HHPYK*, No. 11 (June, 1957), pp. 105–11.

Teng Chieh. "Socialist Transformation of Handicraft Industry," in *Cheng-chi ching-chi-hsueh chiang-hua (Lectures on Political Economy)*. Peking: Chinese Youth Publishing House, 1957.

Teng Hsiao-p'ing. "Census and General Election Completed in China: Population of China over 600 Million," *NCNA*, Peking, June 19, 1954.

Teng Tai-yuen (Minister of Railways). "Railway Construction in China during the Past Five Years," in *Kuang-hui ti pa-nien (Eight Glorious Years)*. Hong Kong: New Democratic Press, 1958, pp. 36, 43.

Tin Yuan (Director, Bureau of Glass and Ceramics Industry of the Ministry of Construction Engineering). "Ten Years of Rapid Development of the Glass Industry," *Ch-ien-chu tsai-hao kung-yeh (Building Materials Industry)*, No. 19 (September 22, 1959), pp. 16–17.

Tsiang Kuang-nai (Minister of Textile Industry). "Ten Glorious Years of the Textile Industry," in *Hui-huang ti shih-nien (Ten Glorious Years)*, Peking: People's Daily Press, December, 1959, pp. 236–44.

Wang Ho-shou (Minister of Metallurgical Industry). "Rapid Development of the Iron and Steel Industry in China," in *Hui-huang ti shih-nien (Ten Glorious Years)*. Peking: People's Daily Press, December, 1959, pp. 113–27.

Yao Yi-lin. "Commerce in the Past Ten Years," in *Hui-huang ti shih-nien (Ten Glorious Years)*. Peking: People's Daily Press, 1959, pp. 359–76.

THE PROVINCIAL GOVERNMENTS

Bureau of Agriculture, Anhwei Province. "Anhwei—The Province Produces 1,000 *Chin* of Early Rice per *Mou*," *Chung-kuo nung-pao* (*Chinese Agricultural Bulletin*), No. 22, 1958, pp. 8–13.

Bureau of Agriculture, Kwangtung Province. "Agricultural Production in Kwangtung," *TLCS*, No. 5 (May, 1959), pp. 205–7.

Bureau of Electric Power Industry of Sinkiang–Uighur Autonomous Region. "The Ten Years of the Electric Power Industry in Sinkiang–Uighur Autonomous Region," *Shui-li yü tien-li (Water Conservation and Electric Power)*, No. 18 (September 20, 1959), pp. 31–33.

Chang K'ai-fan (Deputy Governor of Anhwei Province). "Government Work Report at the Fourth Session of the First Provincial People's Congress of Anhwei on September 21, 1957," *Anhwei JP*, September 23, 1957, p. 203.

Chao Wen-fu (Deputy Governor of Honan). "Address to the Second Session of the Second Honan Provincial People's Congress on January 29, 1960," *Honan JP,* March 1, 1960, pp. 3–4.

Ch'en Cheng-jen. "Speeding Up Technical Transformation of Agriculture," *Hung-ch'i,* No. 4 (February 16, 1960).

Ch'en Yu. "Report Delivered to the Second Session of the Second Kwangtung Provincial People's Congress," *NFJP,* October 12, 1959.

"Deputy Mayor Wan Li's Report to the Second Session of the Third People's Congress of Peking," *JMJP,* September 11, 1959.

Ho Hsian-yi. "Speech Delivered to the Fifth Session of the First National People's Congress," *HHPYK,* No. 5 (March 10, 1958), pp. 63–64.

Hou Tsen-ya. "Speech Delivered at the Fifth Session of the First National People's Congress," *Documents of the Fifth Session of the First National People's Republic of China,* Peking: People's Publishing House, 1958, pp. 622–630.

Hsin Lan-t'ing. "Report on the 1959 Economic Plan for Sinkiang-Uighur Autonomous Region," *Sinkiang JP,* February 1, 1959, p. 2.

Huang Hsien (Deputy Governor of Kiangsi Province). "Report on Draft Summary of the Second Five-Year Plan for the Development of the National Economy in Kiangsi Province," *Kiangsi JP,* July 3, 1958, p. 2.

——— "Report to the First Session of the Second Kiangsi Provincial People's Congress on June 20, 1958," *Kiangsi JP,* July 4, 1958, p. 3.

Kao Shu-hsün. "Speech Delivered to the Fifth Session of the First National People's Congress," *HHPYK,* No. 6 (March 25, 1958).

Li Pin (Deputy Governor of Szechuan Province). "Draft of 1959 Economic Plan for Szechuan Province," *Szechuan JP,* June 25, 1959, p. 2.

Li Yu-wen (Governor of Kirin Province). "Work Report to the Third Session of the Second Kirin Provincial People's Congress on May 23, 1960," *Kirin JP,* May 25, 1960, pp. 2–3.

Liang Ling-kuang (Governor of Fukien Province). "Fukien Provincial Plan for 1959," *Fukien JP,* February 11, 1959, pp. 1–2.

Liu Chun-hsiu. "Speech Delivered at the Fifth Session of the First National People's Congress," *HHPYK,* No. 6 (March 25, 1958), pp. 27–30.

Liu Shun-yuan. "Work Report to the Third Session of the Third Kiangsu Provincial Congress of the Chinese Communist Party," *HHPYK,* No. 7 (April 10, 1959), pp. 15–22.

Ou-yang Ch'in. "Heilungkiang 1958 Work Report," *Heilungkiang JP,* January 25, 1959, pp. 1–3.

Pai Ju-ping (Deputy Governor of Shantung Province). "Report on the Draft Plan for the Economic Development of Shantung in 1959." *Tsingtao jih-pao,* May 25, 1959, p. 2.

——— "Report on the Readjustment of Principal Targets of the 1959 National Economic Plan and the Further Development of the Production Increase and Economy Campaign in Shantung Province – Delivered to the Fifth Session of the Second Shantung Provincial People's Congress on September 14, 1959," *Ta-chung JP,* September 16, 1959.

Price Department, Bureau of Commerce, Kwangtung Province. "The Method of Estimating Agricultural Costs in the People's Communes, *CYHTTH,* No. 2 (February 11, 1959), pp. 20–21.

Sai Fu-ting (First Secretary of the Sinkiang–Uighur Autonomous Region Committee of the Chinese Communist Party). "Great Achievements in Agriculture of Sinkiang in the Past Ten Years," *Chung-kuo nung-pao (Chinese Agricultural Bulletin),* No. 19, 1959, pp. 19–23.

——— "Report to the First Session of the Second People's Congress of the Sinkiang–Uighur Autonomous Region on January 22, 1959," *Sinkiang JP,* January 30, 1959, pp. 2–3.

Su Tzu-sheng. "Speech Delivered at the Fifth Session of the First National People's Congress," *HHPYK,* No. 6 (March 25, 1958), pp. 53–54.

Sun Tso-pin. "Report to the Fifth Session of the First Chinghai Provincial People's Congress," *Chinghai JP,* August 13, 1957.

Tan Ying-chi (Secretary of the CCP of Kwangsi Chuang Autonomous Region). "Speech Delivered at the Fifth Session of the First National People's Congress," *HHPYK,* No. 6 (March 25, 1958), pp. 26–27.

"Teng Tzu-hui's Report at the National Conference of Model Agricultural Workers," *JMJP,* February 22, 1957.

Tsao Ti-ch'iu (Deputy Mayor of Shanghai), "Work Report of Shanghai's Municipal People's Council," *Wen-hui-pao,* Shanghai, June 14, 1959.

——— "Shanghai's 1960 Economic Plan," *Chieh-fan jih-pao (Liberation Daily),* May 18, 1960, pp. 2–3.

Tseng Hsi-sheng (Governor of Anhwei Province). "Continue to Advance under the Banner of the General Line – 1958 Work Report on Anhewi Province," *Anhwei JP,* February 12, 1959, pp. 103.

Wang Che-ju (Deputy Governor of Shantung Province). "Report on the 1957 Economic Plan and the Implementation of the 1956 Economic Plan for Shantung," *Ta-chung JP,* August 17, 1957, p. 2.

Wei Kuo-ch'ing (Governor of Kwangsi Chuang Autonomous Region). "Government Work Report to the First Session of the First People's Congress of Kwangsi Chuang Autonomous Region," *Kwangsi jih-pao,* March 14, 1958, p. 3.

——— "Reviewing the Achievements in the Past Ten Years and Marching Bravely Forward," *Min-tzu t'uan-chieh (Unity of Nationalities),* No. 10 (October 6, 1959), pp. 9–12.

——— "Government Work Report to the Second Session of the First People's Congress of Kwangsi Chuang Autonomous Region," *Kwangsi jih-pao,* December 20, 1959.

Wu Hsien. "Report on the Implementation of Chekiang's Economic Plan for 1957," *Chekiang kung-jen pao,* Hangchow, January 25, 1958.

——— "Speech Delivered at the Fifth Session of the First National People's Congress," *HHPYK,* No. 6 (March 25, 1958), pp. 107–109.

Yang I-chen. "Report at the First Session of the Second Heilungkiang Provincial People's Congress on August 28, 1958," *Heilungkiang JP,* September 19, 1958.

Yang Shang-kuei. "Report to the Third Session of the Fifth Provincial Congress of the Chinese Communist Party on the 1958 Great Leap Forward in Kiangsi, on January 7, 1959," *Kiangsi JP,*

January 26, 1959.

Yang Wei-p'ing. "Work Report of the Honan Committee of the Chinese Communist Party to the Third Session of the First Honan Provincial Congress of the Chinese Communist Party, on December 24, 1958," *Honan JP*, January 16, 1959, pp. 1–3.

Yuan Jen-yuan (Governor of Chinghai Province). "Work Report of Chinghai Provincial People's Council," *Chinghai JP*, July 4, 1958, pp. 1–2.

—— "Chinghai 1958 Work Report and 1959 Work Plans," *Chinghai JP*, May 21, 1959, pp. 1, 3.

PROVINCIAL BUDGETARY REPORTS

Chang Fu-cheng (Director of the Bureau of Finance of Szechuan Province). "Report on the 1956 Final Accounts for Szechuan Province," *Szechuan JP*, August 24, 1957.

Chang Hao (Deputy Director of the Bureau of Finance of Anhwei Province). "Report on the Final Accounts for 1956 and the Preliminary Budget for 1957 in Anhwei Province," *Anhwei JP*, September 24, 1957.

—— "Report on the Final Accounts for 1957 and the Preliminary Budget for 1958 in Anhwei Province," *Anhwei JP*, November 10, 1958.

Chang Yu-yü (Vice-Mayor Of Peking). "Report on the 1955 Final Accounts and the 1956 Budget for Peking," *Peking jih-pao*, August 9, 1956.

—— "Report on the 1957 Final Accounts and the 1958 Budget for Peking," *Peking jih-pao*, August 23, 1958.

Chang Yung-li (Chief of the Office of Finance, Grain, and Trade of the People's Council of Kwangtung Province). "Report on the 1954 Final Accounts and the 1955 Budget for Kwangtung Province," *NFJP*, December 3, 1955.

Ch'en Chien-fei. "Report on the Final Accounts for 1955 and the Implementation of the Budget for 1956 in Heilungkiang Province," *Heilungkiang JP*, January 13, 1957.

Chi Chin-chang (Director of the Bureau of Finance of Kwangtung Province). "Report on the 1955 Final Accounts and the 1956 Budget for Kwangtung Province," *NFJP*, August 5, 1956.

—— "Report on the 1956 Final Accounts and A Draft of the 1957 Budget for Kwangtung Province," *NFJP*, July 27, 1957.

Chi Wei-chien (Deputy Governor of Honan Province). "Report on the Final Accounts for 1956 and a Draft of the Budget for 1957 in Honan Province," *Honan JP*, August 25, 1957.

Ho Hsi-ming (Deputy Governor of Kwangtung Province). "Report on the 1954 Budget of Kwangtung Province," *NFJP*, August 17, 1954.

Hsu Kuang-yuan (Director of the Bureau of Finance of Kiangsi Province). "Report on the 1956 Final Accounts and the 1957 Budget for Kiangsi Province," *Kiangsi JP*, April 1, 1957.

Huang Ta. "Report of Liaoning Provincial People's Council on the 1956 Final Accounts and the 1957 Budget," *Liaoning jih-pao*, May 15, 1957.

Li Yu-shan (Deputy Chief of the Offiice of Finance, Grain, and Trade of the People's Council of Honan

Province). "Report on the Final Accounts for 1955 and the Implementation of the Budget for 1956 in Honan Province," *Honan JP*, November 29, 1956.

Liang Ta-shan (Director of the Bureau of Finance of Kiangsi Province). "Report on the 1955 Final Accounts and the 1956 Budget for Kiangsi Province," *Kiangsi JP*, November 2, 1956.

Liu Tzu-mo (Director of the Bureau of Finance of the Sinkiang-Uighur Autonomous Region). "Report on the 1955 Final Accounts and the 1956 Budget of the Sinkiang-Uighur Autonomous Region," *Sinkiang JP*, August 3, 1956.

Ma I-hsin (Director of the Bureau of Finance of Shanghai Municipal Government). "Report on the 1958 Final Accounts and the 1959 Draft Budget for Shaighai *Wen-hui-pao*, June 14, 1959.

"The Report on the Final Accounts and Budget by Deputy Governor Wei Chin-fei at the Kwangtung Provincial Congress," *Chung-kuo hsin-wen*, September 2, 1958.

Sun Chun-i (Deputy Governor of Chinghai Province). "Report on the 1956 Final Accounts and the 1957 Budget for Chinghai Province," *Chinghai JP*, August 14, 1957.

Tsao Ti-chiu (Vice-Mayor of Shanghai). "Report on the 1955 Final Accounts and the 1956 Budget for Shanghai," *Hsin-wen jih-pao*, August 9, 1956.

—— "Report on the 1956 Final Accounts and the 1957 Draft Budget for Shanghai," *Wen-hui-pao*, August 28, 1957.

Tung Chin-chai (Acting Director of the Bureau of Finance of Kwangsi Province). "Report on the 1956 Final Accounts and A Draft of the 1957 Budget for Kwangsi Province," *Kwangsi jih-pao*, August 25, 1957.

Wang Fan-ju (Deputy Governor and Director of the Bureau of Finance of Kirin Province). "The Report of the Kirin Provincial People's Council on the 1955 Final Accounts and the 1956 Budget," *Kirin JP*, December 7, 1956.

—— "Report on the 1956 Final Accounts and A Draft of the 1957 Budget," *Kirin JP*, July 29, 1957.

Wu Kuang-t'ang. "Report on the 1955 Final Accounts and the 1956 Budget of Shansi Province," *Shansi JP*, December 9, 1956.

—— "Report on the 1956 Final Accounts and the 1957 Budget of Shansi Province," *Shansi JP*, August 27, 1957.

Wu Tso-min (Deputy Governor of Yunnan). "Report on the 1956 Final Accounts and the 1957 Budget for Yunnan Province," *Yunnan jih-pao*, August 17, 1957.

Yuan Tzu-yang (Deputy Governor of Shantung Province). "Report on the 1956 Final Accounts and the 1957 Draft Budget for Shantung Province," *Ta-chung JP*, August 17, 1957.

State and Provincial Statistical Bureaus' Publications

STATE STATISTICAL BUREAU

Annual Communiqués

Kuan-yü 1953 nien-tu kuo-min-ching-chi-fa-chan

ho kuo-chia-chi-hua chi-hsing che-ko ti kung-pao
(*Communiqué on the National Economic Development and the Results of the Implementation of the State Plan in 1953*), with an appendix of "Communiqué on the Recovery and Development of the National Economy, Culture, and Education in 1952." Peking: Financial and Economic Publishing House, 1954, 39 pp.

Kuan-yü 1954 nine-tu kuo-min-ching-chi-fa-chan ho kuo-chia-chi-hua chi-hsing che-ko ti kung pao (*Communiqué on the National Economic Development and the Results of the Implementation of the State Plan in 1954*), with an appendix of statistical abstract for 1949–54. Peking: Statistical Publishing House, October, 1955, 42 pp.

Kuan-yü 1955 nien-tu kuo-min ching-chi chi-hua chi-hsing che-huo ti kung-pao (*Communiqué on the Results of the Implementation of the National Economic Plan for 1956*), with an appendix of statistical abstract for 1949–55. Peking: Statistical Publishing House, 1956.

Kuan-yü 1956 nien-tu kuo-min ching-chi chi-hua chi-hsing che-kuo ti kung-pao (*Communiqué on The Results of the Implementation of the National Economic Plan for 1956*), with an appendix of statistical abstract for 1949–56. Peking: Statistical Publishing House, 1957.

Kuan-yü fa-chan kuo-min-ching-chi ti ti-i-ko-wu-nien (1953–1957) chi-hua chi-hsing-che-ko ti kung-pao (*Communiqué on the Results of the Implementation of the First Five-Year Plan for the National Economic Development (1953–1957)*, and *Kuan-yü 1958 nien kuo-min ching-chi fa-chan ch'in-k'uang ti kung-pao* (*Communiqué on the National Economic Development in 1958*). Peking: Statistical Publishing House, 1959, 29 pp.

Kuang-yü 1959 nien kuo-min ching-chi fa-chan ch'in-k uang ti hsin-wen kung-pao (*Press Communiqué on the National Economic Development in 1959*). Peking: People's Daily Press, 20 pp.

Official Reports and Statements

Chia Chi-yun. "Several Problems in the Present Reform Movement of Statistical Services," *TCKT*, No. 15 (August, 1958), pp. 5–10.

Department of Agricultural Statistics, SSB. "Basic Experience from the Income and Expenditure Survey of Peasant Households for 1954," *TCKTTH*, No. 10 (May 29, 1956), pp. 20, 25–27.

——— "Several Views on the Statistics Concerning the Living Conditions of Rural Residents," *CYHTTH*, No. 3 (March 11, 1959), pp. 16–18.

Department of Comprehensive Statistics, SSB. "On the Gross and the Net Value of Output," *TCYC*, No. 2 (February 23, 1958), pp. 27–30.

Department of Industrial Statistics, SSB. "Attention Should Be Paid to Several Problems Concerning the 1957 Annual Report on Industry," *TCKT*, No. 23 (December 14, 1957), p. 16.

Department of Trade Statistics, SSB. "Explanations of Some Problems Concerning the Unified Catalogue of Commodities in Domestic Trade," *TCKTTH*, No. 9 (December, 1954), pp. 38–41.

——— "An Explanation Concerning the Revision of the Statistical System of Supply and Marketing Cooperatives for 1956," *TCKTTH*, No. 12 (December 17, 1955), pp. 19–21.

——— "Carefully Set Up the Balance Sheet for Monetary Income and Outlay of Residents, and Compile the Social Purchasing Power," *TCKT*, No. 17 (September 14, 1957), pp. 30–33.

"Director Hsüeh Mu-ch'iao's Report at the Sixth National Statistical Conference," *TCKT*, No. 21 (November, 1957), pp. 1–21.

Hsüeh Mu-ch'iao. "Report at the Sixth National Statistical Conference," *TCKT*, No. 21 (November 14, 1957), pp. 1–21.

——— "Exert Efforts to Improve Agricultural Statistical Work," *TCKT*, No. 22 (November 29, 1957), pp. 7–11.

——— "How Does Statistical Work Make a Great Leap?" *TCKT*, No. 5 (March, 1958), pp. 1–5.

SSB. "A Directive Concerning the Strengthening of Industrial Statistical Work," *TCKTTH*, No. 6 (September, 1954), pp. 1–3.

——— "Explanation of Several Major Questions Concerning the Criteria for Demarcation of Urban and Rural Areas," *TCKTTH*, No. 12 (December 17, 1955), pp. 5–6.

Sun Yeh-fan. "Several Problems Concerning the Income and Expenditure Survey of Peasant Households," *TCKT*, No. 6 (March 29, 1957), pp. 11–17.

T'ao Jan. "Report at the Wuhan Meeting of Statistical Workers," *TCYC*, No. 5 (May 23, 1958), pp. 4–9.

Special Releases and Statistical Surveys

Data Office, *CHCC*. "A Survey of Labor and Wages in 1956," *CHCC*, No. 3 (March 9, 1957), pp. 14–15.

Data Office, *TCKT*. "A Brief Summary of Data on the Income and Expenditure of Peasant Households in 1954," *TCKT*, No. 10 (May 29, 1957), pp. 31–33.

——— "A General Survey of Industrial Capital in China," *TCKT*, No. 1 (January 14, 1957), pp. 31–33.

——— "A Survey of Changes in the Price Differentials between Industrial and Agricultural Products since Liberation," *TCKT*, No. 17 (September 14, 1957), pp. 4–7.

——— "A Survey of Domestic Market Prices in 1956," *TCKT*, No. 7 (April 14, 1957), pp. 31–32.

——— "A Survey of Market Prices during the First Quarter of 1957," *TCKT*, No. 11 (June 14, 1957), pp. 26–27.

——— "The Basic Situation of the Production Activities of the Construction Industry in China in the Past Four Years," *TCKT*, No. 18 (September 29, 1957), pp. 31–32.

——— "The Basic Situation of the Unified Purchase and Unified Sales of Food Grains in China," *TCKT*, No. 19 (October 14, 1957), pp. 28, 31–32.

——— "Changes in the Living Standards of Workers in Shanghai during the Past 27 years," *TCKT*, No. 13 (July 14, 1957), pp. 6–7.

——— "Changes in Market Prices in 1957 and Their

Effects on People's Living Conditions," *TCYC*, No. 4 (April 23, 1958), pp. 25–26.

——— "The Great Achievements of Basic Construction in China in the Past Seven Years," *TCKT*, No. 17 (September 14, 1957), pp. 1–3.

——— "Problems Concerning the Living Standards of Peasants and Workers," *TCKT*, No. 13 (July 14, 1957), pp. 4–5, 24.

——— "Statistical Data on the Actual Amount of Several Major Materials Consumed Per Unit of Output in China during 1953–1956," *TCKT*, No. 18 (September 29, 1957), p. 18.

——— "Statistical Data on the Improved Living Conditions of the Workers and Employees," *TCKT*, No. 14 (July 29, 1957), pp. 13–14.

——— "Statistical Data on the Population of China, 1949–1956," *TCKT*, No. 11 (June 14, 1957), pp. 24–25.

——— "The Technological Level of Industrial Production in China," *TCKT*, No. 8 (April 29, 1957), pp. 30–33.

Data Office, *TCKTTH*. "A General Survey of the Size, Composition, and Distribution of Workers and Employees in 1955," *TCKTTH*, No. 23 (December 14, 1956), pp. 28–30, 33.

——— "A General Survey of Socialist Industrialization in China," *TCKTTH*, No. 22 (November 29, 1956), pp. 25–33.

——— "A National Survey of Animals for 1956," *TCKTTH*, No. 23 (December, 1956); reprinted in *HHPYK*, No. 1 (January 10, 1957), pp. 88–90.

——— "A Survey of the Development of State Capitalism in Industry in China," *TCKTTH*, No. 20 (October 29, 1956); reprinted in *HHPYK*, No. 1 (January 10, 1957), pp. 69–71.

——— "The Basic Situation of the Construction Industry in China," *TCKTTH*, No. 24 (December 29, 1956), pp. 31–33.

——— "Development of China's Trade Network and Its Basic Situation in 1955," *TCKTTH*, No. 18 (September 29, 1956), pp. 7–10.

——— "The Scope and Development of Basic Construction in China," *TCKTTH*, No. 18 (September 29, 1956), pp. 4–6.

——— "Several Problems Concerning Socialist Industrialization in China," *TCKTTH*, No. 21 November, 1956); reprinted in *HHPYK*, No. 1 (January 10, 1957), pp. 67–71.

Data Office, *TCYC*. "A Brief Survey of the Development of Health Work in China," *TCYC*, No. 5 (May 23, 1958), pp. 33–35.

——— "A Survey of the Commodity Circulation in the Domestic Market in 1957," *TCYC*, No. 4 (April 23, 1958), pp. 24–25.

——— "A Survey of the Implementation of the Norms for the Consumption of Raw Materials in Major Products of Light Industry in the Past Several Years," *TCYC*, No. 2 (February 23, 1958), pp. 16–20.

——— "A Survey of Production Increase and Cost Reduction in the Light Industry in China," *TCYC*, No. 2 (February 23, 1958), pp. 12–15.

——— "The Great Achievements of China's National Economic Construction in the Past Nine Years," *TCYC*, No. 9 (September 23, 1958), pp. 1–3.

——— "The Great Leap Forward in Basic Construction," *TCYC*, No. 9 (September 23, 1958), pp. 10–12.

——— "The Rapid Development of Industrial Construction in China," *TCYC*, No. 9 (September 23, 1958), pp. 4–5.

SSB. "Communiqué on the Results of the Population Census of the Whole Country," *TCKTTH*, No. 8 (November, 1954), pp. 1–2.

——— "The Great Changes in the Production of Private Industry during the Past Several Years," *TCKTTH*, No. 7 (April 14, 1957).

———, comp. *Ten Great Years, Statistics of the Economic and Cultural Achievements of the People's Republic of China*. Peking: Foreign Language Press, 1960, 223 pp.

SSB, Department of Industrial Statistics, ed., *Wo-kuo kang-t'ieh tien-li mei-t'an chi-h'sieh fan-chih tsao-chih kung-yeh ti chin-hsi (The Past and Present of the Iron and Steel, Electric Power, Coal, Machinery, Textile, and Paper Industries in China)*. Peking: Statistical Publishing House, 1958.

SSB, Research Office. "A Preliminary Analysis of the Production and Distribution of China's National Income," *TCYC*, No. 1 (January 23, 1958), pp. 11–15.

Work Papers

"Diverse Opinions on the Methods of Computing the Gross Value of Industrial Output," *TCKTTH*, No. 24 (December 29, 1956), pp. 5–10.

"Materials on Methods of Computing the Gross Value of Industrial Output," *TCKTTH*, No. 17 (September 14, 1956), pp. 2–5.

"Several Problems of Computing the Gross Value of Industrial Output," *TCKTTH*, No. 17 (September 14, 1956), pp. 1–2.

Several Problems Concerning the Adoption of Constant Budgetary Prices in Basic Construction," *TCKT*, No. 1 (January 14, 1957), pp. 10–15.

"Several Problems Concerning the Methods of Measuring the Completed Amount of Basic Construction Investment," *TCKT*, No. 10 (May 29, 1957), pp. 4–8.

Statistical Handbooks

Department of Industrial Statistics, SSB, *Kung-yeh t'ung-chi-hsüeh chiang-yi (Notes on Industrial Statistics)*. Peking: Statistical Publishing House, 1956.

Editorial Committee for Statistical Work Handbook. *Nung-yeh t'ung-chi kung-tso shou-tse (Handbook for Agricultural Statistical Work)*. Peking: Statistical Publishing House, 1956.

——— *Kung-yeh t'ung-chi kung-tso shou-tse (Handbook for Industrial Statistical Work)*. Peking: Statistical Publishing House, 1956.

——— *Lao-tung t'ung-chi shou-tse (Handbook for Labor Statistical Work)*. Peking: Statistical Publishing House, 1958.

——— *Shang-yeh t'ung-chi shou-tse (Handbook for*

Trade Statistical Work). Peking: Statistical Publishing House, 1957.

———— *Yung-shu yu-tien t'ung-chi kung-tso shou-tse (Statistical Work Handbook for Transportation and Post and Tele-Communications)*. Peking: Statistical Publishing House, 1956.

PROVINCIAL STATISTICAL BUREAUS

Anhwei Provincial Statistical Bureau. "Communiqué on the Results of the Implementation of the National Economic Plan for 1956 in Anhwei Province," *Anhwei JP*, September 25, 1957, p. 2.

———— "Communiqué on the Results of the Implementation of the National Economic Plan for 1957 in Anhwei Province," *Anhwei JP*, April 30, 1958.

Chinghai Provincial Statistical Bureau. "Communiqué on the Results of the Implementation of the First Five-Year Plan for the Development of the National Economy in Chinghai Province, 1953–1957," *Chinghai JP*, September 30, 1958, p. 2.

Department of Trade, Statistical Bureau of Heilungkiang Province. "Some Understanding from the Processing and Compilation of Trade Statistical Data," *TCKT*, No. 22 (November 29, 1957), pp. 21–23.

Hunan Provincial Statistical Bureau. "Achievements of Hunan Province in Economic Work in 1957," *Hsin Hunan Pao*, May 4, 1958.

———— "We Have Begun the Work of Using and Analyzing Survey Data on the Income and Expenditure of Peasant Households," *TCKT*, No. 1 (January 14, 1957), pp. 13–14.

Kansu Provincial Statistical Bureau. "Communiqué on the Results of the Implementation of the National Economic Plan for 1957 in Kansu Province," *Kansu JP*, June 12, 1958, p. 2.

Kirin Provincial Statistical Bureau. "A Comparison of the Living Standards of Workers and Employees in Kirin Province Before and After the Liberation," *TCKT*, No. 14 (July 29, 1957), pp. 14–18.

———— "Communiqué on the Fulfillment of the Economic Plan for 1958 in Kirin Province," *Kirin JP*, March 18, 1959, pp. 1–2.

Kwangtung Provincial Statistical Bureau. "Communiqué on the Development of the National Economy in Kwangtung Province in 1958 and the First Half of 1959," *Wen-hui-pao*, Hong Kong, October 5, 1959.

Liaoning Provincial Statistical Bureau. "Tremendous Changes in Liaoning's Rural Outlook during the Past Decade," in *Liao-ning shih-nien (Liaoning in Ten Years)*. Shenyang: Liaoning People's Publishing House, June, 1960.

Nei-meng-ku tzu-chih-ch'ü ching-chi ho wen-hua chien-she ch'eng-chiu ti t'ung-chi (Statistics on Achievements of the Inner Mongolian Autonomous Region in Economic and Cultural Construction). Peking, 1960, 252 pp.; translated in *JPRS:* 16,962, January 3, 1953, 294 pp.

Shansi Provincial Statistical Bureau. "Communiqué on the Results of the Implementation of the First Five-Year Plan for Shansi Province," *Shansi JP*, May 12, 1958.

Shantung Provincial Statistical Bureau. "Communiqué

on the Results of the Implementation of the National Economic Plan for 1956 in Shantung Province," *Ta-ching JP*, August 9, 1957, p. 3.

Books

Chao I-wen. *Hsin-chung-kuo ti kung-yeh (Industry in New China)*. Peking: Statistical Publishing House, 1957, 121 pp.

Ch'en Chi-shih and Liu Po-wu. *Tuei-wai mo-yi t'ung-chi-hsüeh (Foreign Trade Statistics)*. Peking: Financial and Economic Publishing House, 1958.

Ch'en Yi. *Kuo-yin shang-yeh chi-yeh ti shang-p'in liu-chuang chi-hua (The Commodity Turnover Planning of State Commercial Enterprises)*. Shanghai: People's Publishing House, 1956.

Ch'ien Hua *et al. Ch'i-nien-lai wo-kuo shih-yiu kung-shang-yeh ti pien-hua (1959–1956) (Changes in Private Industry and Trade in China during the Past Seven Years, (1959–1956))*. Peking: Financial and Economic Publishing House, 1957, 184 pp.

Ch'u Ch'ing, Chu Chung-chien, and Wang Chi-min. *Wo-kuo nung-ts'un shih-ch'ang ti kai-tsu (The Reorganization of Rural Markets in China)*. Peking: Financial and Economic Publishing House, 1957, 94 pp.

Chung-hua jen-min kung-ho-kuo fen-sheng ching-t'u (Detailed Provincial Atlas of the Chinese People's Republic). Shanghai: Map Publishing House, 1955.

Chung-kuo fen-sheng ti-t'u shuo-ming (An Explanation of Provincial Atlas of China). Third edition, Shanghai: Map Publishing House, 1957.

Department of Planning and Statistics Hupeh University. *Kung-yeh t'ung-chi hsüeh (Industrial Statistics)*. Wuhan: People's Publishing House, 1960.

Institute of Geography of the Chinese Academy of Sciences, ed. *Hua-pei ching-chi ti-li (Economic Geography of North China)*, Peking, July 1957; translated in *JPRS:* 140-DC, May 23, 1958.

Feng Ta-lin. *Ti-yi wu-nien chi-hua chi-chien kung-yeh ho yung-shu yeh ti chi-pen chien-she (Basic Construction in Industry and Transportation during the First Five-Year Plan)*. Shanghai: New Knowledge Press, 1956.

Handicraft Section of the Institute of Economic Research, Chinese National Academy of Sciences, ed. *1954 nien chuang-kuo ko-ti shou-kung-yeh tiao-cha tzu-liao (Nationwide Survey Data on Individual Handicrafts in 1954.)* Peking: San-lien Book Store, 1957, 252 pp.

Hsü Ch'ien, Tai Shih-kuang, Yu Tao, *et al.*, eds. *Ching-chi t'ung-chi-hsüeh chiang-hua (Lectures on Economic Statistics)*. Peking: Statistical Publishing House, 1957.

Hsü Ti-hsin. *Wo-kuo kuo-tu shih-chih kuo-min ching-chi ti feng-hsi (An Analysis of China's National Economy in the Transition Period)*. Revised edition, Peking: Science Press, 1959, 331 pp.

Ko Chi-ta. *Kuo-tu shih-chi ti chung-kuo yü-shüan (China's Budget during the Transition Period)*. Peking: Financial Publishing House, 1957, 170 pp.

Liang Jen-tsai. *Kuang-tung ching-chi ti-li (Economic Geography of Kwangtung)*. Peking: Science Press, November, 1956, 102 pp.

Lo Ken-mo. *She-hui chu-yi chih-tu hsia ti shang-p'in ho chia-ko wen-ti (Problems of Commodity and Value under Socialism).* Peking: Science Press, September, 1957, 181 pp.

Niu Chung-huang. *Wo-kuo kuo-min shou-ju ti chi-jui ho hsiao-fei (Accumulation and Consumption in China's National Income).* Peking: Chinese Youth Press, November, 1957, 144 pp.

———— *Wo-kuo ti-i-ko wu-nien-chi-hua-shih-chi ti sheng-ch'ang ho hsiao-fei kuang-hsi (The Relation between Production and Consumption in China during the First Five-Year Plan Period).* Peking: Financial and Economic Publishing House, February, 1959, 148 pp.

Shanghai Economic Research Institute of the Chinese National Academy of Sciences and Economic Research Institute of the Shanghai Academy of Social Sciences. *Shang-hai Chieh-fang chien-hou wu-chia tzu-liao hui-pien, 1921–1957 (A Collection of Shanghai Price Data Before and After the Liberation, 1921–1957).* Shanghai: Shanghai People's Publishing House, 1958, 600 pp.

Sheng Mu-chieh. *She-hui tsu-yi kung-yeh ti liu-tung tzu-ching (Working Capital of Socialist Industrial Enterprises),* Shanghai: People's Publishing House, 1956, 121 pp.

Su Shao-chih and Hu Chien-mei, *She-hui-chu-yi-she-hui ti kuo-min shou-ju (The National Income of a Socialist Society).* Shanghai: Shanghai People's Publishing House, February, 1960.

Su Yang-nei, ed. *Kuo-min ching-chi shih-yung ts'u-tien (Practical Dictionary of the National Economy).* Shanghai: Chu-min Publishing House, 1953.

Sun Ching-chih, ed. *Hsi-nan ti ch'ü ching-chi ti-li (Economic Geography of Southwest China).* Peking: Science Press, 1960, 218 pp; translated in *JPRS:* 15,069, August 31, 1962, 737 pp.

————, ed. *Hua-chung ti-ch'ü ching-chi ti-li (Economic Geography of Central China).* Peking: Science Press, December, 1958, 156 pp.; translated in *JPRS:* 2227-N, February 10, 1960, 514 pp.

————, ed. *Hua-nan ti-ch'ü ching-chi ti-li (Economic Geography of South China),* Peking: Science Press, 1959, 147 pp; translated in *JPRS:* 14,954, August 24, 1962, 514 pp.

————, *et al. Nei-meng-ku tzu-chih-ch'ü ching-chi ti-li (Economic Geography of the Inner Mongolian Autonomous Region),* Peking: Science Press, March 1946.

————, *et al.,* ed. *Hua-tung ti-ch'ü ching-chi ti-li (Economic Geography of East China).* Peking: Science Press, 1959, 1953 pp.; translated in *JPRS:* 11,438, December 7, 1961, 338 pp.

Teng Chieh. *Chung-kuo shou-kung-yeh ko-tsao ti chu-pu tsung-chieh (Preliminary Results of the Socialist Transformation of the Handicraft Industry in China).* Peking: People's Publishing House, 1958, 116 pp.

Wang Che and Liu Shou-chün. *Kuo yin shang-yeh tsai wo-kuo kuo-tu-shih-chi ti tso-yung (The Function of State-Operated Trade in China during the Transition Period).* Peking: People's Publishing House, 1957, 78 pp.

Wang Mao. *Kuo-chia-chien-she ho jen-min-sheng-huo (National Construction and People's Living).* Peking: Popular Reading Material Publishing House, 1957.

Wang Wei-p'ing. *Shui-hsiang chiang-su (Kiangsu, The Waterland).* Shanghai: New Knowledge Publishing House, December, 1956, 92 pp.

Wu Ch'uan-chun *et al. Tung-pei ti-ch'ü ching-chi ti-li (Economic Geography of Northeast China).* Peking: Science Press, 1959, 211 pp.; translated in *JPRS:* 15,388, September 21, 1962, 571 pp.

Yung Chung. *Wo-kuo ti chi-pen chien-she (Basic Construction in China).* Peking: Workers' Publishing House, 1956, 74 pp.

Articles

Chai Mou-chou. "Our Method of Predicting the Results of an Investment Plan," *TCKT,* No. 4 (February 28, 1957), pp. 15–16.

Chang Ching-eng. "The Utilization of Productive Potentials," *CHCC,* No. 4 (April 9, 1958), p. 25.

Chang Hao-jan. "Is the Burden of the Peasants Too Heavy?" *HH,* No. 16 (August 3, 1957), pp. 16–17.

Chang Li. "The Construction of Water Conservancy in Hopei Province," *TLCS,* Vol. 10, No. 11 (November 6, 1959), pp. 490–96.

Chang Shen and Wang En-yung. "A Brief Discussion on the Fixed Assets of Industrial Enterprises and Their Depreciation," *CCYC,* No. 5 (October 17, 1956), pp. 69–78.

Chang Shu-shan. "Attention Should be Given to the Coordinated Development of the Production of the Iron and Steel Industry," *CHCC,* No. 4 (April 9, 1957), pp. 14–15.

Chang Tsi-shen and Yang Teh-jun. "Several Views on the Method of Computing Social Purchasing Power," *CYHTTH,* No. 2 (February 11, 1959), pp. 16–18.

Chang Wei-ta. "The Methods of Calculating the Depreciation Rate of Fixed Assets Used in Production," *CCYC,* No. 3 (June 17, 1956), pp. 99–112.

Chang Wen and Chao Li-kuang. "An Analysis of Factors Forming Commodity Prices under Socialism" *HCS,* No. 12 (December 20, 1963), pp. 28–35.

Chang Yi-fei. "Problems Concerning Relative Prices of Industrial and Agricultural Products," *HCS,* No. 11, 1958.

Chao Ch'ing-hsin. "Seasonal Variations of the Market after Agricultural Cooperatization," *CCYC,* No. 5 (October 17, 1956), pp. 19–38.

Chao Fu-hsiang. "New Situation of the Material and Cultural Living of the Workers and Employees in in the Coal Industry," *Mei-t'an kung-yeh (Coal Industry),* Nos. 20–21 (September 30, 1959), p. 23.

Chao I-wen. "Changes in the Retail Market since the Great Leap Forward," *CYHTTH,* No. 5 (May 11, 1959), pp. 30–31.

———— "My Recognition of Dogmatism in Statistical Services," *TCYC,* No. 5 May 23, 1958), pp. 9–11.

———— "Socialist Transformation of the Capitalist Industry in China," *TCKTTH,* No. 22 (November 29, 1956), pp. 25–33.

Chao Li-kuang and Hsiang Ching-chuan. "Objective Criteria for Commodity Price Differentials and Bases for Determining These Differentials under Socialism," *CCYC*, No. 2 (February 17, 1964), pp. 52–61.

Ch'en Chin-ching. "The Great Achievements of Socialist Construction in China during the Past Ten Years," *CCYC*, No. 10 (October 17, 1959), pp. 1–10.

Ch'en Kang-lin and Hsia Wu. "Tabular Forms for Labor and Wage Planning," *CHCC*, No. 10 (October 9, 1957), pp. 29–33.

Ch'en Cheng-jen. "The Problems of Agricultural Cooperation and Production," *HHPYK*, No. 7 (April, 1957), pp. 20–26.

Ch'en Chien-fei. "Blooming, All the Places, Towns and Villages Together Have Carried Out a Great Leap Forward in Statistical Work throughout the Province," *TCKT*, No. 14 (July 29, 1958), pp. 8–12.

Ch'en Chih-ho. "Problems Concerning the Subject of the Statistical Enumeration of the Labor Force," *CHYTC*, No. 11 (August 23, 1959), pp. 27–30.

——— "Several Views on Improving Labor and Wage Statistical Work" *TCYC*, No. 5 (May 23, 1958), pp. 12–15.

Ch'en Han-chang. "Total Sown Area Should Include Acreage for Stubbled Crops and Secondary Interplanted Crops," *TCKT*, No. 3 (February, 1957), pp. 15–16.

Ch'en Hsi-jun. "Price Planning," *CHCC*, No. 6 (January 23, 1956), pp. 30–33.

Ch'en Tieh-cheng. "Tabular Forms for Transport Planning," *CHCC*, No. 3 (March 9, 1957), pp. 29–33.

Ch'en Tsen-yu. "On the Methods of Classifying Producer Goods and Consumer Goods," *TCYC*, No. 18 (September 29, 1957), pp. 16–18.

Ch'en Wu-ying. "The Need of a Unified Commodity Catalogue for Regular Statistical Schedules of Trade," *TCKT*, No. 22 (November 29, 1957), pp. 14–15.

Cheng Kuo-huan. "The Significance and Function of the Food Processing Industry in the National Economy," *Shih-p'in kung-yeh (Food Processing Industry)*, No. 1 (January 13, 1957).

Ch'eng Po. "Raising Quality and Lowering Price Are the Keys to the Development of the Canned Food Industry," *CHCC*, No. 7 (July 9, 1958), pp. 17–19.

Chi Ts'ung-wei. "On the Balanced Growth of Industry in China," *CHCC*, No. 7 (July 9, 1957), pp. 4–8.

Chiang Po. "Labor Productivity," *Chen-chi hsueh-hsi (Political Study)*, No. 7 (April 12, 1959), pp. 37–38.

Chiao Yu-po. "A Survey of the Prices of Several Major Agricultural Producer Goods" *CCYC*, No. 3 (March 17, 1959), pp. 31–32.

Chin Chi-min. "Rapid Development of Agriculture in Kiangsu," *TLCS*, No. 6 (June, 1959), pp. 244–47.

Chou Ch'ung-kung. "On the Establishment of Bases for Subsidiary Food Production," *CYHTTH*, No. 3 (March 11, 1959), pp. 14–15.

Chu Chao-chin. "Looking at the Relationships among Agriculture, Light Industry and Heavy Industry from the Relationships between the Two Major Divisions of Social Products," *KMJP*, August 13, 1962.

Chu Yuan-ch'ien. "The Problem of Agricultural Surplus Labor in China at Present," *Chiao-hsueh yü yen-chiu (Teaching and Research)*, No. 2 (February 4, 1957), pp. 17–20.

Chung Chao-hsiu. "Raise the Wage Level Properly on the Basis of Developing Production and Increasing Labor Productivity," *TCKTTH*, No. 16 (August 29, 1956), pp. 10–12.

Chung Chi-sheng. "Several Problems Concerning the Compilation of Retail Price Indices at the Present time," *Hsia-men ta-hsüeh hsüeh-pao (Amoy University Journal)*, social science edition. No. 2, December, 1957, pp. 95–110.

Chung Lin and Hsiao Lu. "The 1953 National Census of Population," *TCKTTH*, No. 10 (October 17, 1955), pp. 19–22.

Du Bois, Wm. B. "Excerpts of Du Bois Speech," NCNA, Peking, February 24, 1959.

Fan Jo-i. "A Brief Discussion of Agricultural Price Policy," *CCYC*, No. 2 (February 17, 1959), pp. 26–30.

——— "On the Rate of Profit of Capital Funds and the Policy of Construction," *CHCC*, No. 8 (August 9, 1958), pp. 21–23.

——— "The Pricing Policy of Products of Heavy Industry," *CCYC*, No. 3 (June, 1957), pp. 54–67.

Fang Pin-chu. "Views on Improving the Sampling Methods Used in the Family Budget Survey of Workers and Employees," *TCKT*, No. 4 (February 28, 1957), pp. 11–14.

Feng Chi-hsi. "The Growth of China's National Economy as View from the State Budget," *TCKT*, No. 12 (June 29, 1957), pp. 28–33.

Hai Po. "The Remarkable Year in the History of Hupeh," *HHPYK*, No. 3 (February 10, 1957), pp. 64–65.

Han Po. "On the Economization of Agricultural Operating Expenses," *CHCC*, No. 2 (February 9, 1958), pp. 17–21.

Ho Kan. "An Introduction of the Program for the Income and Expenditure Survey of Peasant Households for 1955," *TCKTTH*, No. 6 (March 29, 1956), pp. 19–21.

——— "My Views on the Tendency of a Single Survey of Income and Expenditure of Peasant Households to Deviate from Reality," *TCKTTH*, No. 18 (September 29, 1956), pp. 28–30.

Ho Wei. "The Significance and Methods of Comparing Current Agricultural Prices with Pre-War Levels," *HH*, No. 7 (April 18, 1957), pp. 15–17, 21.

Ho Wen-ho. "Oppose Dogmatism and Develop the Spirit of Independent Creation," *TCKT*, No. 12 (July, 1958), pp. 9–12.

Hsiang Ou and Li Lai. "Sugar Manufacturing Industry in China," *TLCS*, September, 1957, pp. 392–96.

Hsieh Tseng-hung. "Average Coefficients of Utilization of Blast Furnaces of the Ministry of Metallurgical Industry," *CHCC*, No. 4 (April 9, 1958), p. 23.

Hsieh Ying *et al.* "How Can It Be Said That Trade Statistics Cannot reflect Market Changes?"

TCKT, No. 17 (September 14, 1957), pp. 23–25.

Hsü Chung-yi. "In Retrospect of Domestic Trade in the Past Five Years," in *Kuang-hui ti pa-nien* (*Eight Glorious Years*). Hong Kong: New Democratic Press, 1958, pp. 59–65.

Hsü Feng and Li Yuen. "Why Is the Cost of Transportation of the Yangtze River Higher than That of Railways?" *CHCC*, No. 3 (March 9, 1958), pp. 20–23.

Hsü Hsin-hsüeh. "Accelerated and Proportional Development of the National Economy," *Hung-ch'i*, No. 3 (February 3, 1960), pp. 6–9.

Hsü Kang. "Labor and Wage Work Should Be in Conformity with the Policy of Overall Arrangements and Building Our Nation Industrially and Economically," *CCYC*, No. 2 (February 17, 1958, pp. 21–30.

———— "Make a Success of Wage Statistical Work in 1959," *CHYTC*, No. 4 (February 23, 1959).

———— "Several Problems Concerning the Contents of the National Wage Survey for Workers and Employees," *TCKTTH*, No. 16 (August 29, 1956), pp. 13–14.

———— "Several Views on the Methods of Computing Labor Productivity," *TCKT*, No. 2 (February 29, 1957), p. 12.

Hsü Ping-wen. "The Relationship between the Classification of the Two Major Divisions of Social Products and the Classifications of Agriculture, Light Industry, and Heavy Industry," *TKP*, March 30, 1962.

Hu Ch'ing-lai, Li Ming, and Ts'ung Ch'un-ch'uan. "The Marine Products Industry in China," *TLCS*, Vol. 7, no. 1 (January, 1956), pp. 6–8.

Hu I-min. "Liaoning's Rapid Industrial Growth Is the Victory of the Party General Line," in *Liaoning shih-nien* (*Lianong in Ten Years*). Shenyang: Liaoning People's Publishing House, June, 1960; translated in JPRS: 17, 182, January 17, 1963.

Hu Huan-yung. "An Index Chart of Area and Population of China by Province and Region," *TLCS*, Vol. 8, No. 9 (September, 1957), pp. 390–391.

Hua Shu. "Is the Rate of Agricultural Growth in China High or Low?" *HHPYK*, No. 3 (February 10, 1959), pp. 59–62.

Huang Chien-t'o. "Agricultural Statistical Work Must Cope with the New Situation Arising from the Universal Establishment of Rural People's Communes," *CHYTC*, No. 2 (January 23, 1959), pp. 15–17.

———— "Carefully Improve the Work of Income and Expenditure Survey of Peasant Households in Our Country," *TCYC*, No. 2 (February 23, 1958), pp. 4–11.

———— "Major Tasks in the Agricultural Statistical Work Program for 1960," *CHYTC*, No. 2 (February, 1960), pp. 18–22.

———— "Sum Up Work Experiences and Make Effort to Improve Agricultural Statistical Work," *TCKT*, No. 8 (April 29, 1957), pp. 5–8.

Huang Meng-fan. "Agricultural Production Statistics," *TCKTTH*, No. 12 (June, 1956), pp. 30–33.

Hui Ling. "Energetically Develop People's Savings to Support the Demand for Capital Funds under Socialism," *Chin-jung yen-chiu* (*Financial Research*), No. 2, 1958.

Keng Chuan-san. "Current Prices of Coal," *CCYC*, No. 3 (March 17, 1959), p. 29.

K'o Po. "Industrial Output Statistics," *TCKTTH*, No. 11 (June 14, 1956), pp. 30–33.

Ku Tieh-liu. "Energetically Develop Local Non-ferrous Metals Industry," *CHCC*, No. 3 (March 9, 1958), pp. 10–13.

Kung Chien-yao. "A Discussion of Statistical Methods of Investigating the Volume of Agricultural Harvests," *TCKTTH*, No. 10 (October 17, 1955), pp. 33–36.

Kung Ching-yao. "The Method of Computing the Rate of Harvest," *TCKTTH*, No. 6 (March, 1956), pp. 16–18.

Kung Chun-hua and Li Yuan. "An Account for the Timber Industry," *TCKT*, No. 14 (July 29, 1957), pp. 29–30.

Kuo Keng-chih "Some Views on the Selection of Research Topics on Basic Construction Statistics," *TCKT*, No. 4 (February 28, 1957), pp. 9–11.

Li Ch'eng-jui. "The Agricultural Tax System and the Peasants' Burdens in Several People's Revolutionary Bases during the Anti-Japanese War," *CCYC*, No. 2 (April 17, 1956), pp. 100–15.

Li Hsiung. "The Development of Metallurgical Science and Technology in China during the Past Ten Years," *Ching-shu hsüeh-pao* (*Metallurgical Journal*), IV, No. 3 (September, 1959), 1–8.

Li Hui-hung, Sun Chi-jen, and Wang Hua-hsin. "Views on the Problem of Classifying Light and Heavy Industry," *TCYC*, No. 18 (September 29, 1957), pp. 13–15.

Li Lin-ku. "The Structure of Socialism and the Population Problem," *HCS*, No. 4 (April, 1960).

Li Shu-yen. "A General Survey of the Agricultural Geography of Heilungkiang Province." *TLCS*, No. 11 (November, 1957), pp. 497–99.

Li Tsung-hai. "Great Achievements in Economic Construction in the National Minority Areas," *Min-tzu tu'an-chieh* (*Unity of Nationalities*), No. 10 (October 6, 1959), pp. 36–39.

Liao Hsien-hao. "Tabular Forms for Agricultural Production Planning," *CHCC*, No. 4 (May 9, 1957), pp. 30–33.

Liu Hung-ju and Tai Ch'ien-tin. "The Stability of the People's Currency Is an Indication of the Supreme Superiority of the New Chinese Socialism," *Kuang-ming jih-pao*, February 8, 1965, p. 4.

Liu Kai-mo. "The Work of the Norm for Material Consumption Should Be Strengthened in the Midst of the Anti-Waste Movement," *CHCC*, No. 3 (March 9, 1958), pp. 24–25.

Liu Ke-p'ing. "Great Leap Forward in Production, Great Unity of Nationalities," *JMJP*, April 10, 1959.

Liu Te-ling. "Why Are the Statistics of July 1 Taken as the Annual Figures for the Basic Conditions of Agricultural Producer Co-operatives, Cultivated Acreage, and Livestock?" *TCKTTH*, No. 4 (February 29, 1956), pp. 14 and 24.

Liu Tzu-chiu. "The Situation and Problems of the Wage Reform," *HHPYK*, No. 21 (November 6, 1956), pp. 208–10.

Liu You-chin. "On the Problems of Classifying Light and Heavy Industry," *TCYC*, No. 7 (July 23,

1958), pp. 18–21.

Lou Chi-cheng. "Major Technical-Economic Norms of the Cement Industry," *CHCC*, No. 7 (July 9, 1957), pp. 29–30.

Lu Ch-ang-fu. "Several Methods of Estimating the Trade Volume of Subsidiary Food Products in the Free Market," *TCKT*, No. 22 (November 29, 1959), p. 25.

Lu Hsian-hsien. "Marching Along the Road to Happy Life," *Chung-kuo kung-jen (Chinese Worker)*, No. 17 (September 12, 1959), pp. 15–17.

Lu Ko. "Basic Construction Statistics," *TCKTTH*, No. 13 (July 14, 1956), pp. 30–33.

Lung Hua-yung, Chi Hsi-yung, and Ch'en Min-kai. "Several Problems Concerning the Measurement of the Value Output of Construction," *TCKT*, No. 8 (April, 1957), pp. 14–16.

Ma Hsin. "Building Industry of Ningsia Hui Autonomous Region around Coal Production," *JMJP*, August 16, 1959.

Ma Yin-chu. "A New Theory of Population," *JMJP*, July 5, 1957.

Mei Hsin. "The Glorious Achievements of the Coal Industry during the Past Five Years," in *Kuang-hui ti pa-nien (Eight Glorious Years)*. Hong Kong: New Democratic Press, 1958.

Nan Pin. "Break the Two Poisonous Arrows of the Rightist Elements to Undermine the Worker-Peasant Alliance," *HH*, No. 19 (October 3, 1957), pp. 18–19.

Niu Chung-huang. "The Development of Socialist Construction in China and the Improvement of the Living Standards of the Chinese People," *HH*, No. 15 (August 3, 1957), pp. 15–17.

Pai Chien-hua. "600 Million People – A Great Strength for Socialist Construction of Our Country," *TCKTTH*, No. 8 (November 12, 1954), pp. 9–10.

Pan Hsueh-ming. "Industrial Development in Shanghai," *TLCS*, No. 7 (July 6, 1957), pp. 302–305.

Peng Jung-chuan. "The Tabular Forms for Basic Construction Planning," *CHCC*, No. 5 (May 9, 1957), pp. 29–33.

Peng Wan-yeh. "The Past and Present of the Cement Industry," *Chien-chu ts'ai-liao kung-yeh (Building Materials Industry)*, No. 18 (September 22, 1959), pp. 22–24.

Shen Yu-ch'ing. "My Views on the Geographic Distribution of Wheat and the Prospect for Its Development in China," *TLCS*, No. 8 (August, 1957), pp. 339–345.

Shih Wei-cheng. "The Problems Concerning the Supply and Demand of Paper," *CYHTTH*, No. 1 (January 11, 1959), pp. 31–32.

Su Hsin. "Comment on an Erroneous Point of View Concerning Distribution According to Labor," *HH*, No. 7 (April 3, 1958), pp. 25–26.

Sun Chih-fang. "Tabular Forms for Commercial Planning," *CHCC*, No. 2 (February 9, 1957), pp. 27–31.

Szu Ying. "It Is Wrong to Say That the Nation Is Rich While the People Are Poor," *Chung-kuo kung-jen (Chinese Worker)*, No. 21 (November 12, 1957), pp. 3–5.

Tan Yin-chi. "The Year of Great Leap Forward," *Min-tzu t'uan-chieh (Unity of Nationalities)*,

No. 1 (January 6, 1959), p. 2.

Tai Shih-kuang. "Population Statistics," *TCKTTH*, No. 3 (February 14, 1956) and No. 4 (February 29, 1956).

Teng Chin-chung. "Cotton Production in Sinkiang," *TLCS*, No. 8 (August, 1957).

T'ien Feng-t'iao "The Problem of Planned Birth and Population Increase in Our Country," *Jen-min pao-chien (People's Health)*, Vol. I, No. 5 (May, 1959).

Ts'ai Ching. "The Increasing Living Standards of the 600 Million People," in *Kuang-hui ti pa-nien (Eight Glorious Years)*. Hong Kong: New Democratic Press, 1958, pp. 180–184.

Tsen Lin. "Rural Markets at the Height of Agricultural Cooperation," *CCYC*, No. 2 (April 17, 1956).

Tsing Yun-chi. "Cotton Production in China," *TLCS*, No. 10 (October, 1957).

Tzu Ssu. "Producer Goods and Products of Heavy Industry Are Conceptually Different," *HH*, No. 3 (February 3, 1957), p. 23.

Wang Chien-chen. "Evaluation of People's Living Conditions through Price Indices," *TKP*, September 24, 1957.

Wang Hu-sheng. "Some Problems Concerning the Clarification between Heavy and Light Industry," *CCYC*, No. 4 (April 17, 1963), pp. 16–26.

Wang Hua-min. "Measures for Lowering the Prices of Drugs in the Past Several Years," *CCYC*, No. 3 (March 17, 1959), p. 35.

Wang Keng-chin. "My Views on Methods of Calculating the Value of Gross Agricultural Output," *TCKT*, No. 4 (February 28, 1957), pp. 3–4.

Wang Kuang-shen. "The Concept of the Indicator 'Annual Average Output of Food Grains per *Mou*,' and A Preliminary Enquiry into the Methods of Computing It," *TCYC*, No. 1 (January 23, 1958), pp. 33–38.

Wang Kuang-wei. "Several Problems of Developing Agriculture," *HH*, No. 17 (September 3, 1957), pp. 25–26.

———— "Views on Allocating Agricultural Labor Force," *CHCC*, No. 8 (August 9, 1957), pp. 6–9.

Wang Min-teh. "The Development of Production and Sales of Cotton Textile Products," *CYHTTH*, No. 2 (February 11, 1959), pp. 30–31.

Wang Mai-pu. "Our Views on Computing Labor Productivity According to All Personnel," *TCKTTH*, No. 18 (September 29, 1956), pp. 19–20.

Wang Pei-hsun. "Several Problems Concering Present Trade Statistical Work Need to Be Studied and Discussed," *TCKT*, No. 8 (April 29, 1957), pp. 17–19.

Wang P'ing. "The Scope of the Free Market and Its Changes in China," *TCKT*, No. 11 (June 14, 1957), pp. 28–29.

Wang Sheng-ming. "On Fluctuations in the Growth of a Socialist Economy," *CCYC*, No. 1 (January 17, 1960).

Wang Shu-pen. "Review of 'Preliminary Analysis of the Accumulation in the Lien-pan Agricultural Producer Cooperative' by Fukien Province," *TCYC*, No. 7 (July 23, 1958), pp. 13–17.

Wang Szu-hua. "On the Gross Value of Industrial Output," *TCKT*, No. 13 (July 14, 1957), pp. 14–17.

Wang Yung. "Correctly Understand the Relationship between Wages and Production," *Chung-kuo kung-jen* (*Chinese Worker*), No. 22 (November 27, 1957), pp. 19–20.

Wu Ting-ch'eng. "Explanation of Certain Problems Concerning the Proposal for Computing Social Purchasing Power," *CHCC*, No. 9 (September 9, 1957), pp. 27–29.

Wu Yuan-hung. "How to Establish Survey and Accounting Networks of Agricultural Costs in the People's Communes," *CCYC*, No. 8 (August 17, 1959), pp. 63–64.

Yang Chien-pai. "On the Great Significance of the Production, Distribution and Expenditure of the National Income in a Socialist Economy," *HCS*, No. 3, 1960.

Yang Ch'ing-wen. "Two Problems of Industrial Location," *CHCC*, No. 8 (August 9, 1957), pp. 13–15.

Yang Hung-tao. "Several Problems Concerning Profits in the Formation of Industrial Prices," *CCYC*, No. 8 (August 17, 1963), pp. 43–49, 66.

Yang Pan-chieh. "A Proposal for the Adoption of Constant Prices in the Preparation of Basic Construction Planning and Budget," *CHCC*, No. 2 (February 9, 1958), pp. 30–31.

Yang Pei-hsin. "Ways of Collecting Agricultural Development Funds in China," *CCYC*, No. 1 (January 17, 1958).

Yang Pen-chuang. "The Family Budget Survey of Workers and Employees," *TCKTTH*, No. 10 (October 17, 1955), pp. 46–47.

Yang Po. "A Discussion of the Problems Concerning the Compilation of the Index of the Cost of Living of Workers and Employees," *TCKTTH*, No. 11 (June 14, 1956), pp. 4–5, 25.

——— "A Preliminary Analysis of the Process of Socialist Transformation of Private Trade in China," *TCKTTH*, No. 15 (August, 1956), pp. 7–10.

——— "An Understanding of the Proportion between Consumption and Accumulation in the National Expenditure of China," *HH*, No. 20 (October 18, 1957), pp. 24–26.

——— "On the Distribution of China's National Income," *CCYC*, No. 6 (December 17, 1957).

Yen Chen-chung. "Dynamic Equilibrium? Or Static Equilibrium?" *CHCC*, No. 4 (April 9, 1958), p. 22.

Yen I-shen. "Some Views on the Production of Means of Production and Materials for Consumption in Relation to Government Revenue and Expenditure," *CCYC*, No. 7 (July 17, 1959).

Yi I-chu. "Notes on the 'Wall Map of the Population Density of China,'" *TLCS*, Vol. 7, No. 11 (November 14, 1956), pp. 502–504.

Yin Shan-shou and Chu Feng-shu. "Our Views on the Methods of Computing the Annual Output of Food Grains per *mou*," *TCKTTH*, No. 13 (July 14, 1956), pp. 15–17.

Yu Tao and Wang Wen-sheng. "Statistics of National Wealth and Fixed Assets," *TCKTTH*, No. 5 (March 14, 1956), pp. 36–40.

Yueh Wei. "The Method of Computing National Income," *CCYC*, No. 3 (June 17, 1956), pp. 48–66.

——— "On the Principles and Methods of Studying the Problem of Accumulation," *TCYC*, No. 5 (May 23, 1958), pp. 16–21.

——— "Problems of Computing National Product," *TCKTTH*, No. 1 (January, 1956), pp. 15–17.

——— "Some Understanding from the Use of the Method of Estimation," *TCKTTH*, No. 18 (September 29, 1956), pp. 25–27.

Editorials, News Reports, and Unsigned Articles

"A Brief Summary of the Development of Handicraft Production of Paper in 1958," *Tsao-chi kung-yeh* (*Paper-making Industry*), No. 2 (February 7, 1959), p. 47

"A List of Tax Items and Tax Rates for the Consolidated Industrial and Commercial Tax," *Jen-min shu-wu* (*People's Tax Affairs*), No. 18 (September 19, 1958), pp. 4–7.

"Agricultural Purchase Price Indices and Price Ratios between Industrial and Agricultural Products in 1958," *CYHTTH*, No. 4 (April 11, 1959), p. 13.

"Census and Registration Work Compiled in Areas with 60 Per Cent of Population in China," *JMJP*, March 11, 1954.

CHCC editorial. "Important Problems in the Implementation of the 1958 Basic Construction Plan," *CHCC*, No. 2 (February 9, 1958), pp. 4–6.

——— "The Necessity of Studying the Concrete Situation of Various Regions in Compiling Agricultural Plans," *CHCC*, No. 3 (March 9, 1957), pp. 2–3.

"Classified Commodity Catalogue," *TKP*, April 4, 1959; reprinted in *1959 JMST*, p. 383.

"Conversion Rates Between People's Currency and Certain Foreign Currencies," *CHCC*, No. 12 (December 9, 1957), p. 29.

"Data on the Electric Power Industry of Certain Countries in Early 1958," *Shui-li yü shui-tien chien-she* (*Water Conservation and Hydro-electric Construction*), No. 9, 1959, pp. 58–59.

"Give Priority to the Elimination of Floods in Agricultural Construction," *CHCC*, No. 1 (January 9, 1958), pp. 15–19.

"Great Changes in the Peasant Livelihood in the Past Ten Years," *Chung-kuo nung-pao* (*Chinese Agricultural Bulletin*), No. 19, 1959, pp. 33–35.

"Important Indicators of Growth in the Machinery Industry in the Past Ten Years," *Chi-hsieh kung-yeh chou-pao* (*Machinery Industry Weekly*), No. 40 (October 1, 1959) p. 4.

JMJP editorial. "The Operation of Statistical Services by the Whole Party and All the People," *JMJP*, August 13, 1958.

"Lectures on Fundamentals of Industrial Management," *Chung-kuo ch'ing-kung-yeh* (*Light Industry in China*), No. 18 (September 28, 1959), pp. 33–34.

"Maternity and Child Health Service Improved in Rural Areas," NCNA, March, 1957; translated in U.S. Consulate General in Hong Kong, *Survey of China Mainland Press*, No. 1487, March 12, 1957, p. 14.

"The National Trade Statistical Work Conference

Has Been Satisfactorily Concluded," *TCKT*, No. 23 (December 14, 1957), p. 33.

Shui-li yü tien-li editorial. "March Bravely Forward to Develop Rapidly the Electric Power Industry," *Shui-li yü tien-li* (*Water Conservancy and Electric Power*), No. 18 (September 20, 1959), pp. 6–9.

"Socialist Educational Materials for the Workers," *Chung-kuo kung-jen* (*Chinese Workers*), No. 4 (February 27, 1958).

"Statistical Services in the Rural People's Communes Are Being Inaugurated," *CHYTC*, No. 2 (January 23, 1959), p. 20.

"State Budgetary Revenues and Expenditures during the First Five-Year Plan Period," *Ts'ai-cheng* (*Public Finance*), No. 8 (August 5, 1957), pp. 32–33.

IN ENGLISH

Ch'en Ta. *New China's Population Census of 1953 and Its Relation to National Reconstruction and Demographic Research*. Stockholm: International Statistical Institute, August, 1957.

Du Bois, Wm. B. "I Sing to China," *China Reconstructs*, Vol. 8, No. 6 (June, 1959), p. 24.

"Great Victories in China's Economic Construction in 1960," *China Pictorial*, No 2 (February, 1961), pp. 2–3.

Lu Kuang "China's National Income," *Peking Review*, Vol I, No. 6 (April 8, 1958), 7–9.

Tai Shih-kuang, *1953 Population Census of China*. Calcutta: Indian Statistical Institute, December, 1956.

NONCOMMUNIST CHINESE PUBLICATIONS

IN CHINESE

Directorate General of Budget, Accounts and Statistics, Republic of China, *Chung-hua-min-kuo t'ung-chi nien-chien* (*Statistical Yearbook of the Republic of China*). Nanking: Bureau of Statistics, 1948.

IN ENGLISH

Buck, John Lossing. *Land Utilization in China*. New York: Council on Economic and Cultural Affairs, Inc., 1956, 494 pp.

Chandrasekhar, S. *China's Population: Census and Vital Statistics*. Hong Kong University Press, 1959, 69 pp.

Chao, Kuo-chün. *Agrarian Policies of Mainland China: A Documentary Study (1949–1956)*. Cambridge, Mass.: Harvard University Press, 1957.

Ecklund, George N. *Taxation in Communist China*. Washington, D.C.: U.S. Central Intelligence Agency, 1961.

Galenson, Walter. *Labor Productivity in Soviet and American Industry*. New York: Columbia University Press, 1955.

Gerschenkron, Alexander. *A Dollar Index of Soviet Machinery Output 1927/1928 to 1937*. Santa Monica, Calif.: The RAND Corporation, 1951.

Government of India, Ministry of Food and Agriculture. *Report of the Indian Delegation to China on Agricultural Planning and Techniques*. New Delhi, July–August, 1956.

Grossman, Gregory. *Soviet Statistics of Physical Output of Industrial Commodities*. Princeton, N.J.: Princeton University Press, 1960.

Kwang, Ching-wen. "The Budgetary System of the People's Republic of China: A Preliminary Survey," *Public Finance*, XVIII, No. 304 (1963), 253–86.

Li, Choh-Ming. *Economic Development of Communist China*, Berkeley: University of California Press, 1959, 284 pp.

——— *The Statistical System of Communist China*, Berkeley: University of California Press, 1962, 171 pp.

Liu, Ta-Chung, and Kung-Chia Yeh. *Economy of the Chinese Mainland: National Income and Economic Development, 1933–1959*. Princeton, N.J.: Princeton University Press, 1965.

U.S. Bureau of the Census. *Cities of Mainland China: 1953 and 1958*, by Morris B. Ullman. International Population Reports, Series P-95, No. 59. Washington, D.C.: U.S. Government Printing Office, August, 1961, 46 pp.

——— *Nonagricultural Employment in Mainland China: 1949–1958*, by John Philip Emerson. Washington, D.C.: U.S. Government Printing Office, August, 1961, 240 pp.

——— *The Size, Composition, and Growth of the Population of Mainland China*, by John S. Aird. International Population Statistics Report, Series P-90, No. 15. Washington, D.C.: U.S. Government Printing Office, 1961, 100 pp.

IN RUSSIAN

Afanas'yeskiy, Ye. A. *Szechuan*. Moscow: Publishing House of Oriental Literature, 1961, 267 pp.; translated in JPRS: 15,306, September 17, 1962, 272 pp.

Bol'shaya Sovetskaya entsiklopediya (*Great Soviet Encyclopedia*), second edition, Moscow.

Bruk, S. I. "Etnicheskiy sostav i razmeshcheniye Naseleniya v Sinkiangskom ingurskom avtonomnom rayone Kitayskoy narodnoy rspublik (Ethnic Composition and Distribution of the Population in Sinkiang Uighur Autonomous Region, Chinese People's Republic)," *Sovetskaya etnograiya* (*Soviet Ethnography*), No. 2, 1956, pp. 89–94.

Chin Hsin-chung and I. G. Kachergin, *Zdrayookhraneniye i medikina v Kitayskoy Narodnoy Respublike* (*Public Health and Medicine in the Chinese People's Republic*). Moscow, 1959.

Gel'bras, V. "Dastizheniya Katayaskoy Narodnoy Respubliki v oblasti truda in zarabotnoy platz za desyot'let (Achievements of the Chinese People's Republic in the Area of Labor and Wages in the Last Ten Years)," *Sotsialisticheskiy* (*Socialist Labor*), No. 9, 1959.

Kalmykova, V. G., and I. Kh. Ovdiyenko. *Severozapadnyy Kitay* (*Northest China*). Moscow, 1957.

Konovalov, Ye. A. "Razvitiye vnutrenney targovli Kitayskoy Narodnoy Respubliki (The Development of the Domestic Trade of the Chinese People's Republic)," in Akademiya nau SSSR (Academy of Sciences of the U.S.S.R.), *Kratiye soobshcheniya Institute Narodoy Azii (Brief Communications of the Institute of the Asian Peoples)*, No. 49, 1961.

Krotevich, S. K. "Veskitayskaya perepis'naseleniya 1953 g" (The All-China Population Census of 1953)", *Vestnik statistiki (Statistical Herald)*, No. 5, September, 1955.

———— Veskitayskay perepis'naseleniya 1953 g (The All-China Population Census of 1953)," *Paslevoyenniye perepisi'naseleniya (Postwar Population Census)*. Moscow: Gasstatizdat, 1957.

Shelekasov, P. "Naseleniye i trudovyye resursy v KNR (Population and Labor Resources in the Chinese People's Republic)," *Byulleton'nauchnoy informatsu, Trudizarabatnaya plata (Bulletin of Scientific Information, Labor and Wages)*, No. 6, 1958, pp. 55–59.

Shiger, A. G. *Administrativno-territorial'noye deleniye zarubezhaykh stran (Adminstrative-territorial Division of Foreign Countries)*. Second edition, Moscow, 1957.

Zaychikov, V. T., ed. *Vastochnyy Kitay (Eastern China)*. Moscow: Institut Geograpii, 1955.

IN FRENCH

Pressat, Roland. "La Population de la Chine et son Economie," *Population,* Vol. 13, No. 4, October – December, 1958.

IN JAPANESE

Asia Keizai Jumpo, Tokyo, Japan, No. 316 (March, 1957).

LIST OF ABBREVIATIONS
(Text and Tables)

COMMUNIST CHINESE PUBLICATIONS FREQUENTLY CITED

NEWSPAPERS

National

JMJP Jen-min jih-pao (*People's Daily*), Peking.
TKP Ta-kung-pao (*Impartial Daily*), Peking.

PROVINCIAL

Anhwei JP An-hui jih-pao (*Anhwei Daily*), Hofei, Anhwei.
Chekiang JP Che-chiang jih-pao (*Chekiang Daily*), Hanchow, Chekiang.
Chinghai JP Ching-hai jih-pao (*Tsinghai Daily*), Sining, Tsinghai.
Fukien JP, Fu-chien jih-pao (*Fukien Daily*), Foochow, Fukien.
Heilungkiang JP, Hei-lung-chiang jih-pao (*Heilung-kiang Daily*), Harbin, Heilungkiang.
Honan JP, Ho-nan jih-pao (*Honan Daily*), Kaifen, Honan.
Kansu JP, Kan-su jih-pao (*Kansu Daily*), Lanchow, Kansu.
Kiangsi JP, Chiang-hsi jih-pao (*Kiangsi Daily*), Nan-chang, Kiangsi.
Kirin JP, Chi-lin jih-pao (*Kirin Daily*), Changchun, Kirin.
NFJP, Nan-fang jih-pao (*Southern Daily*), Canton, Kwangtung.
Shansi JP, Shan-hsi jih-pao (*Shansi Daily*), Taiyuan, Shansi.
Sinkiang JP, Hsin-chiang jih-pao (*Sinkiang Daily*), Tihua, Sinkiang.
Szechuan JP, Ssu-ch'uan jih-pao (*Szechuan Daily*), Chengtu, Szechuan.
Ta-chung JP, Ta-chung jih-pao (*The Public Daily*), Tsinan, Shantung.

PERIODICALS

CCYC, Ching-chi yen-chiu (*Economic Research*).
CHCC, Chi-hua ching-chi (*Planned Economy*).
CHYTC, Chi-hua yü t'ung-chi (*Planning and Statistics*).

CYHTTH, Chung-yang ho-tso t'ung-hsun (*Central Cooperative Bulletin*).
HCS, Hsin-chien-she (*New Construction*).
HH, Hsueh-hsi (*Study*).
HHPYK, Hsin-hua pan-yueh-k'an (*New China Semi-Monthly*).
TCKT, T'ung-chi kung-tso (*Statistical Work*).
TCKTTH, T'ung-chi kung-tso t'ung-hsün (*Statistical Work Bulletin*).
TCYC, T'ung-chi yen-chiu (*Statistical Research*).
TLCS, Ti-li chih-shih (*Geographical Knowledge*).

PEOPLE'S HANDBOOKS

1950 JMST, 1950 Jen-min shou-tse (*People's Handbook of 1950*), Shanghai: Ta-kung-pao she, January, 1950.
1951 JMST, 1951 Jen-min shou-t'se (*People's Handbook of 1951*), Shanghai: Ta-kung-pao she, January, 1951.
1952 JMST, 1952 Jen-min shou-t'se (*People's Handbook of 1952*), Shanghai: Ta-kung-pao she, August, 1952.
1953 JMST, 1953 Jen-min-shou-t'se (*People's Handbook of 1953*), edited by Chang Feng-chou, *et al.*, Tientsin. Ta-kung-pao she, 1953.
1955 JMST, 1955 Jen-min-shou-t'se (*People's Handbook of 1955*), Tientsin: Ta-kung-pao she, January, 1955.
1956 JMST, 1956 Jen-min-shou-t'se (*People's Handbook of 1956*), Tientsin: Ta-kung-pao she, May, 1956.
1957 JMST, 1957 Jen-min shou-t'se (*People's Handbook of 1957*), Peking: Ta-kung-pao she, April, 1957.
1958 JMST, 1958 Jen-min shou-t'se (*People's Handbook of 1958*), Peking: Ta-kung-pao she, May, 1958.
1959 JMST, 1959 Jen-min shou-t'se (*People's Handbook of 1959*), Peking: Ta-kung-pao she, September, 1959.

BOOKS

CH, Department of Industrial Statistics, ed., *Wo-kuo kang-t'ieh tien-li mei-t'an chi-hsieh fan-chih tsao-*

chih kung-yeh ti chin-hsi (*The Past and Present of the Iron-and-Steel, Electric Power, Coal, Machinery, Textile, and Paper Industries in China*), Peking: Statistical Publishing House, 1958.

NMKTC, Nei-meng-ku tzu-chih-ch'ü ching-chi ho wen-hua chien-she ch'eng-chiu ti t'ung-chi (*Statistics on Achievements of the Inner Mongolian Autonomous Region in Economic and Cultural Construction*), Peking, 1960, 252 pp.; translated in JPRS: 16,962, January 3, 1963, 294 pp.

TGY, State Statistical Bureau, comp., *Ten Great Years, Statistics of the Economic and Cultural Achievements of the People's Republic of China,* Peking: Foreign Language Press, 1960, 223 pp.

ENGLISH TRANSLATIONS OF CHINESE PUBLICATIONS

JPRS, U.S. Joint Publications Research Service.

COMMUNIST CHINESE GOVERNMENT AGENCIES

NCNA, New China News Agency.
SSB, State Statistical Bureau.

Indexes

INDEX TO THE TEXT

INDEX TO THE TABLES

For Product Safety Concerns and Information please contact our
EU representative GPSR@taylorandfrancis.com Taylor & Francis
Verlag GmbH, Kaufingerstraße 24, 80331 München, Germany